ENGLAND EXPECTS

ENGLAND EXPECTS

A History of the England Football Team

JAMES CORBETT

For my grandfather, Charles Mills

First published 2006 by
Aurum Press Limited
25 Bedford Avenue
London WC1B 3AT
www.aurumpress.co.uk

A catalogue record for this book is available from the British
Library.

ISBN 1 84513 147 9

10 9 8 7 6 5 4 3 2 1
2010 2009 2008 2007 2006

Designed and typeset in Minion and Helvetica Neue by
SX Composing DTP, Rayleigh, Essex

Printed and bound in Great Britain by MPG Books, Bodmin

CONTENTS

ACKNOWLEDGEMENTS

ONE OF THE questions I'm often asked about my work, is where, exactly, have I been able to get access to footage of matches that I describe. While researching and writing *England Expects* I had available a number of websites that hosted goals and action dating back almost 50 years. These were non-profit sites, put up by enthusiasts who merely wished to share their love of this great game and proved an invaluable source, until – literally overnight – FIFA in all of their wisdom oversaw the closure of almost all of them. I'm sure they had sound commercial reasons for doing so, but two years on there is still no officially sanctioned alternative and the release of material on VHS and DVD remains patchy.

Where action was beyond my own memory or not readily available on archive film, I found the National Newspaper Library in Colindale an invaluable resource. The sixties is often heralded as the golden era of football, but the same was true of football writing. If you picked up the *Observer*, you were treated to Hugh McIlvanney and Arthur Hopcraft, the *Sunday Times* and it was Brian Glanville, *The Times* and Geoffrey Green, while the *Daily Mirror* boasted Ken Jones. Of course McIlvanney, Glanville and Jones still write today, but it was a joy reading the reports of these men from the last five decades, more so the books they have written. I've listed a lengthy bibliography, but I should draw attention to Jones's *Jules Rimet Still Gleaming?* – a history of England at the World Cup. I found writing about Alf Ramsey – a deeply introverted and obsessively private man – a challenging task, but Jones knew the England manager better than most and I found his account of England in the sixties and early seventies particularly illuminating when it came to Sir Alf.

The staff at the library of the Royal Society were generous in their time when guiding me through the papers of Sir Harold Thompson; and students of the game should visit the National Archives at Kew for a few surprising discoveries.

The Football Association wished me well with my 'school project' when I asked to use their library. When I pointed out that I was actually writing a book and that they hadn't bothered to properly consider my request, they sent me the same email again – at which point I gave up.

A couple of websites not yet closed down by FIFA are worth looking at. Roger Elliot has painstakingly compiled a list of every international line-up and result since 1872 (http://members. fortunecity.co.uk/rogerelliott/mainpage.htm) and England Football Online (http://www.englandfootballonline.com/New.html) is a historian's dreamland with all manner of fascinating takes on the national team.

At Aurum, I would like to thank Graham Coster and Bill McCreadie for taking a chance on this labour of love. Rob Bagchi and Phoebe Clapham transformed the manuscript into the book you're reading today, while Sarah Whale expertly dealt with the PR. My thanks to all. Nor, of course, would this book have been written without my agent, Toby Eady, a consummate professional, friend and mentor. Thanks also to his colleague, William Fisher, who unfailingly responds to my moans and groans with good cheer and encouragement.

Writing is a singular passion and probably brings out the worst in me. To my many friends, family and various colleagues I owe a debt of gratitude for – alternately – forbearance, hospitality, inspiration, patience, or simply their good company. In no particular order: Bill and Ben Corbett, Claire and Patrick Cogan, Laura Cameron-Lewis, Aline Conus, Jason Cowley, Mukul Devichand, Randy Hatfield, Daniel Lewis, James Macintyre, the Millers of Vicarstown, my uncles Charles and Peter Mills, Cath Mills, George Orr, Freyan Panthaki, David Pearson, Dick White, Anne and Joe Wright and Vicky Willan. My parents and my brothers David, Andrew and Michael were always there for me, as was my sister Anna, who was also an immense help checking and double checking various facts, figures and dates.

In particular, my wife Catherine has lived with infinite patience while this obsession has progressed from inception to completion. How she's managed without uttering a word of complaint is astonishing; the fact that she knows nothing and cares less about football, yet has uncomplainingly seen her husband consumed by the game in every waking and sleeping moment I find even more staggering. One day, I promise, I'll write something she might enjoy.

This book is dedicated to my grandfather, Charles Mills, a man of warmth, wit, humour, and, above all else, respect for others. Short of watching Everton or England win, I can't think of any better place in the world to spend an evening than his front room, sipping malt whisky and discussing football long into the night.

'England expects that every man will do his duty.'

Admiral Lord Nelson, 21 October 1805

'Football is like the dilemma of a love affair. If you don't take it seriously, you get no pleasure from it. If you do take it seriously, and as a player you have to, somewhere along the line, it will break your heart.'

Eddie Hapgood, England captain, 1939

Introduction

'THE LAND OF HOPE AND GLORY'

THE COMING BATTLE had been expected for weeks; but the scheming, the relentless plotting, the attention to detail went on until just minutes before first blood was finally drawn. Surveying his fleet from the poop deck of HMS *Victory*, Admiral Lord Nelson contemplated his final plans before going into battle in this foreign place many miles from home. His men needed a message, he decided, a rallying call, a few words of inspiration before they faced death or glory. And so the most famous battle cry in history went out to his fleet of twenty-seven ships waiting in the Bay of Trafalgar: 'England expects that every man will do his duty'.

Like Hastings and Agincourt, Trafalgar would become a defining moment in our nation's history, and even two centuries on Nelson's order still carries huge resonance. The admiral had no need to expand his few words as each of his men had an intuitive grasp of what England expected: that no matter how insurmountable the odds, they were to win – or at least die trying. They understood too what their 'duty' encompassed, not just as combatants, but as Englishmen as well: honour, loyalty, respect, obedience, bloody-mindedness, pride, dignity and a sense of fair play. Nelson's call was also a reminder of what was at stake on the eve of battle, as if it were these unspoken values that were being defended. Indeed the words have hummed in England's consciousness ever since.

Now that massive conflagrations on which the very future of our nation depends seem – mercifully – to be part of our past, we look to our sportsmen to bring these same qualities onto the field of play. It is common and even clichéd to use battlefield analogies for sport, but in looking at what Trafalgar meant and means I think that it is unusually apposite. Like so much of this country's history it was about pluck and punching above the nation's weight, and the effects of the victory also left a huge psychological imprint on our national consciousness. Trafalgar marked the onset of a century of unchallenged naval hegemony and another fifty years of empire. At one stage England ruled one-third of the planet's land mass and throughout the nineteenth century was the world's cultural and scientific heartbeat. The British empire is now part of our past, but in many ways we have struggled to get over no longer leading the world. Today this heritage manifests itself in a number of outwardly eccentric ways, but never is it more apparent than in the way in which we vest colossal – and colossally unfair – hopes in our sportsmen and women. If England could dominate the globe politically and culturally back then, why not in sport – and more particularly, football – today?

Perhaps more than any other nation on earth, the England football team shoulders the insatiable hopes, dreams and delusions of its people. Whether we have Michael Owen or Michael Ricketts leading the attack and regardless of whether we're playing Argentina or Andorra, deep down we still believe that it is our right to come out on top. As well as having an entire national mood hinging on their every success or failure, our footballers also have to contend with a country of self-appointed experts, their every touch, positional nuance and decision scrutinised by dozens of TV camera angles and millions of eyes. Football is our passion and our lifeblood. Our obsession with it merely heightens the pressure, the inexorable sense of expectation. 'The point about football in Britain,' declared Arthur Hopcraft in the introduction to his 1968 exposition of the domestic game, *The Football Man*, 'is that it is not just a sport people take to, like cricket or tennis . . . It is built into the urban psyche, as much a common experience to our children as are uncles and school. It is not a phenomenon; it is an everyday matter.' Arguably the fervour of the 1960s has been surpassed in the twenty-first century's media era: had Hopcraft been alive today he might have mused that we now know our football better than we do our families.

Of course, the fate of the nation does not rest with England's footballers, but governments have stood and fallen on the back of the national team's showing and men have been made and broken by its success and failure. When, almost with a degree of inevitability, England fall at international tournaments, it is seen as symbolic of a pervading amateurishness, and national weakness and decline. No wonder the frustration and intolerable pressure facing a succession of England managers have led them to dub their job the 'impossible' one.

Fair play, decency and respect are purportedly the hallmarks of Englishness, an Englishman's 'duty' if you like, and this is also reflected in the expectations we hold for our footballers, another layer of impossibility with which they have to deal. Most obviously it is the 'duty' of England's footballers to win, but we also expect them to do so in a manner that is stylish and fair, which can afford dignity to us as a nation. England expects more than the cynicism and cheating that have characterised successive Italian or Argentine teams, or even the shabby personal affairs of its recent manager, Sven-Göran Eriksson. Perhaps more than losing, not fulfilling this lofty sense of duty is the worst crime a footballer can commit against Queen and country. From the belief that professionals were a corrupting influence in the game's early days, via the 1938 Nazi salute in Berlin, the Revie affair and David Beckham's sending-off in St Etienne, the hysterical reaction that has met those who have failed in this onerous responsibility illustrates the depth and character of England's expectation.

Yet we have much to be proud of. We are football's founding nation (which may itself be part of the problem), and the game probably represents this country's greatest cultural export. English football is, and has always has been, revered the world over – even in countries who we feel have surpassed us. We have given birth to and been represented by great players in almost every generation, from Steve Bloomer to David Beckham and Tommy Lawton to Frank Lampard. We have won the World Cup, once, a feat only bettered in the modern era by Germany, Brazil and Argentina, equal to the achievements of Italy and France, and more than other footballing powers, such as Spain and the Netherlands have achieved. England has been led by some genuinely great men, individuals like Alf Ramsey and Bobby Robson whose names are inscribed in the game's lore. We have partaken in some of the most glorious examples of football at its most wondrous and dramatic: as losers, true – against Hungary in the 1950s, Brazil in 1970 and West Germany in 1970 and 1990; but also as winners: against the great Italy sides of the 1930s and 1940s, against Brazil in 1956, and Portugal and West Germany in 1966, against the Argentina of Maradona, and the Holland of Bergkamp, Overmars and Kluivert. Most unforgettably in my lifetime we beat Germany 5–1 in Germany. But in amongst the hysteria and breast-beating that follows defeat this all tends to be pushed to the back, forgotten. It is perhaps symptomatic of this perpetual state of national angst and unwillingness to celebrate our greatness that it has taken 134 years of England internationals for this book to be written.

While the dreams of fans will always be of victory, in the cold light of day many in this country are actually content to see their heroes give it their all. Maybe that's what sets English football apart. In Italy, for example, stars returning home after World Cup failure are ritually showered with rotten fruit, and sometimes more overt violence. In England we celebrate defeat so long as it has been achieved in a gutsy enough manner. Witness the heroes' welcome received by Bobby Robson's England side after Italia '90, 'celebrations' more prominent than those that greeted Ramsey's World Cup winners twenty-four years earlier. Maybe, expectation is the wrong word to use after all. True, we're disappointed year after year by the relative failure of our national side, but is it the initial sense of expectation that drives this emotion? Personally I don't think so. Like football fans for clubs and countries across the planet we are driven not by expectation, but by that one thing that inspires amongst all of us our passion and unrequited love for this great game: hope.

James Corbett
London
March 2006

• 1 •

MEN OF DESTINY

FULHAM BROADWAY hums with the noise of expectation. As people race to their homes or seek sanctuary in the pubs and bars of this cosmopolitan bit of London, the common chatter in the air is of diamond formations, Wayne Rooney and Michael Owen, combinations of results that will ensure English qualification for the following summer's European Championships in Portugal, and Turkish fans with murder on their minds. I'm late, but I'm not the only one. Dodging a path through tourists, non-believers and those simply oblivious to the rising exodus, I hear the slightly desperate voice of a small boy, bedecked in a baseball cap with a St George's Cross on its front.

'Come on Mum,' he implores of his all too carefree parent. 'We're going to miss the start.'

Finally, I reach the Jolly Maltster, a pub whose crapness, for this evening at least, is shrouded in the magnificence of the largest television screen in SW6. Barely have I muscled through to the bar, passed drinks over heads and put my pound in the correct score sweep (I plump for a 0–0 draw, disloyally my Belgian friend goes for a Turkey victory, everyone else goes for an England win) than the teams are coming out. A cacophony of Istanbul noise is beamed by satellite all over England, temporarily overcoming the voices of the commentators and bringing home to millions the size of the task facing our nation's footballers. This won't be a night for the faint at heart.

The players line up, the national anthems are played, England's first. In Istanbul a chorus of boos drowns out every note of music, although some of the players still mouth the words; in Fulham, the pub briefly quietens to a hush, around me faces contorted with hope, fear, pride, anticipation. This is England in the early twenty-first century; this is how many of us watch our country. No national stadium, often no hope of getting tickets, not even allowed to visit 'dangerous' Turkey, the pub with its big screen, standing area and clientele of the fanatical and hopeful has become a latter day theatre of dreams. What makes us indistinct from previous generations is the light in our hearts that never goes out. England expects.

Football has come a long way, but in many ways it has come no distance at all. It was in another pub – the Freemasons' Tavern, near Lincolns Inn, two-and-a-half miles down the road – almost exactly 140 years earlier, on 26 October 1863, where it all began. This was the London of Charles Dickens and Wilkie Collins, of Victorian civility and middle-class prosperity, and street urchins and dire poverty. It was the centre of a globe on which Britain was the predominant power, the heart of modern society, the birthplace of a new world order based on principles of democracy, civility and muscular Christianity. Leading the charge were what we would today recognise as 'mid-Victorians': reformers, liberals, men of education, or sometimes just organisation. It was the decade when Dr Barnardo was opening his first children's home and Florence Nightingale creating the modern hospital; railways were being burrowed underneath London for the first time and across the nation, wherever there was a cause, be it religion, science, education or even sport, the reformers would dabble, creating many of the great institutions we know today.

Imbued with this sort of reformist zeal, twenty or so men had assembled that autumn night in the Freemasons' Tavern. The meeting had been convened by Ebenezer Cobb Morley (1831–1924), a Temple-based solicitor and renaissance man. His interests were many, but most notably orientated towards sport: he was a rower of some note (later participating in the Grand Challenge Cup at Henley); heavily involved in the organisation of athletics; the founder of a gymnasium near his home in Barnes; and with a keen interest in hunting. But his great love was football. He had been born in Hull, but lived in Barnes from 1858, and after playing football on its green had formed the Barnes club in 1862.

Football in England had a long history; and beyond its waters longer still. Homer describes in the *Odyssey* how when Odysseus gets shipwrecked he is washed up on a beach where a 'princess and her retinues threw their veils to the wind, struck up a game of ball'. The Chinese of the Han Dynasty (202BC–AD220) called it 'tsu chu', the Romans 'harpastum' and the Greeks 'episkyros'. In England the first recorded reference came in 1174 when William Fitz Stephen wrote: 'After dinner all the youth of the City goes out into the fields for the very popular game of ball, the elders and the men of wealth coming on horseback to view the contests of their juniors, arousing in them a stirring of natural heat by viewing so much activity and by participation in the joys of unrestrained youth.'[1] Variations of the game were played throughout the Middle Ages – often tied to feast days and religious ceremonies – which differed in their methods, rules and attendant levels of violence. It was usually regarded as the sport of the common man, and its participants frequently brushed with the stern face of authority. In 1314, Edward II, preparing to fight the Scots, ordered his men to concentrate on archery practice, not football; a century later, in 1457, James II of Scotland banned football (and golf) altogether; and a further century down the line Elizabeth I proclaimed 'no foteball play to be used or suffered within the city of London'.* Even as recently as 1801 Joseph Strutt had written in *Sports and Pastimes of the People of England*: 'When the exercise becomes exceedingly violent, the players kick each other without the least ceremony. The game was formerly much in vogue among the common people, though of late years it seems to have fallen into disrepute and is all but little practiced.'[2] The conclusions drawn then and before were inescapable: football was rough, tough, unruly and frequently disreputable. It was the sport of the mob, and, in an increasingly civilised society, was seemingly dying.

From its early nineteenth-century deathbed the sport made a remarkable recovery. The revival began on the playing fields of England's public schools three decades after the publication of Strutt's tome. Like football, public schools of this era were distinctly removed from the institutions we know today. Conditions were frequently abysmal, education second rate, brutality rife. Charles Dickens was just one who was contemptuous of the whole shebang, satirising their squalid state in his 1839 novel *Nicholas Nickleby*. Teachers, he wrote, were 'ignorant, sordid, brutal men, to whom few considerate persons would have entrusted the board and lodging of a horse or a dog; they formed the worthy cornerstone of a structure, which, for absurdity and a magnificent high-minded *laissez aller*

---

*Nevertheless, recent research has since uncovered evidence that her father, Henry VIII, himself played football.

neglect, has rarely been exceeded in the world'. Little wonder then that Charterhouse was down to just ninety-nine pupils in 1835 and Harrow sixty-nine nine years later. Taking their cue – in part at least – from the moral furore whipped up by Dickens, the public schools undertook a hasty fight back. Visionary headmasters revolutionised the institutions, chastening pupils, improving their standards, instigating greater academic rigour, ensuring religious principles underpinned every boy's education and encouraging sport as a means of instilling discipline and order in their charges. Despite its reputation as the sport of the commoner, the game had long been played in the schools (in Eton, for example, since 1747) albeit without formalised rules. Instead, the game had evolved year by year, with each institution employing its own loose code.* As part of their reformist drive headmasters began to formalise the laws – on a school-by-school basis – as football became all but part of the curriculum. By the 1850s, graduates of these institutions were moving on to university and professional life but struggling to agree on a uniform code when playing old boys of rival institutions. A 250-word set of rules was agreed on at Cambridge University in 1862, but beyond its environs there was no uniformity, no central body to govern the game and provide an organisational structure, until Ebenezer Morley stepped into the void.

Morley himself had not been a public-school man, so was not inherently favourable to one variation of football or another. Yet at Barnes, the debates and disputes about the way in which the game should be played were persistent and Morley sought to bring an end to the squabbling. He led the way with an exchange of letters in the leading sports journal of the day, *Bell's Life,* suggesting that football should have a single set of rules following in the tradition of Cambridge. The correspondence eventually led to the meeting at the Freemasons' Tavern, which had been convened 'for the purpose of forming an association with the object of establishing a definite code of rules for the regulation of the game'. Present were representatives from eleven clubs (Barnes, the War Office Club, Crusaders, Forest of Leytonstone, Kilburn No Names, Crystal Palace, Blackheath, Kensington School, Percival House, Surbiton and Blackheath

---

* Rugby had perhaps the most famous tradition, after one of its pupils, William Webb-Ellis, picked up the ball and ran in 1823.

School), but just one public school (Charterhouse), the rest skulking suspiciously on the sidelines. Together they formed the Football Association and, in three further meetings over the following six weeks, formulated rules for the new organisation and drafted – finally – a unitary set of laws for the game. Only on the latter was there major disagreement, over the issue of 'hacking' ('I think if you do away with it,' argued Mr Campbell of Blackheath School, 'you will do away with all the courage and pluck of the game, and I will be bound to bring over a lot of Frenchmen who would beat you with a week's practice . . .'), which was outlawed by a vote of thirteen to four at the Football Association's sixth meeting in December. Sullenly, its key proponent Blackheath withdrew its membership (eight years later, in 1871, they would be one of the main forces behind the creation of the Rugby Football Union). That same month, John Lillywhite of Seymour Street in Euston was given the sole rights to issue and sell the FA law book, which appeared in a pocket-sized version costing a shilling, and in a larger 'roller' form for clubrooms, priced 1s 6d. Then, on Saturday, 19 December 1863, came the first representative match between Morley's Barnes and Richmond, on Barnes Green. 'Very little difficulty was experienced on either side in playing the new rules,' reported *The Field*, 'and the game was characterised by great good temper, the rules being so simple and easy of observance that it was difficult for disputes to arise.' The first proper match under association rules ended 0–0, yet from such humble, even dull, origins the first breath of the game as we recognise it had been drawn.

The early years of the FA were spent refining the laws of the game (any player could handle the ball until 1866; goalkeepers were interchangeable until 1871, and so on) and spreading the gospel of conformity. Consisting as they did of a few committed followers who merely preached to other enthusiasts, the missionary zeal with which they pursued their cause was hardly relentless. Charles Alcock, who had founded the Forest Club near Epping Forest (from 1864 known as Wanderers), later wrote: 'The work was necessarily slow, and for several years the history of the association was singularly uneventful.' Yet he, and other disciples, could see that their quest was not wholly fruitless: 'By degrees, though, the progress of absorption took effect,' he wrote, 'and as year by year the influence of the association extended, there was a corresponding willingness among those who had before adhered to their own particular variation of the game to recognise the importance, if not necessity, of a uniform set of rules.'[3]

Alcock was to be the key influence in elevating association football from the pursuit of the few to the obsession of the masses. 'Like a thread of gold his career runs through the weaving of the story of "Soccer",' eulogised one early football historian. 'And his tall and dignified form strides the river of the game from its source.'[4] Born in Sunderland in 1842 and educated at Harrow, after helping found Wanderers he served as their captain and was asked to join the FA's committee in 1866. Four years later he was appointed Honorary Secretary, also finding time to hold down a similar position at Surrey County Cricket Club. From the outset Alcock sought to make his mark, introducing an agenda that even in these early days was to revolutionise the game and have an impact far beyond his own life-time. As the legendary *Times* correspondent Geoffrey Green would write: 'It was he above all others who gave football the first real impetus that sent it rolling over hill and dale, through town and country and finally across seven seas.'[5] At Harrow, Alcock had played in inter-house 'sudden death' competitions and remembered vividly the thrill of these schoolboy encounters. Among his colleagues at the FA and *The Sportsman* newspaper (for which Alcock was a regular contributor), he floated the idea of initiating a knock-out com-petition along similar lines and found it met with enthusiastic approval. The FA swiftly agreed to his proposal and on 20 July 1871 put out the announcement: 'That it is desirable that a Challenge Cup should be established in connection with the Association for which all clubs belonging to the Association should be invited to compete.' Thus, in a single short sentence, the FA Cup was born.

Standing just eighteen inches high in its original form, the FA Cup dominates the early history of football.* In its first year only fifteen of the FA's fifty members entered, almost all London-based, and Alcock himself captained Wanderers to a 1–0 victory over Royal Engineers in the final. Although the first seven finals would each see either Alcock's men or Royal Engineers emerge with their name inscribed across its

---

* It was stolen in 1895 and never recovered. The second trophy was presented to Lord Kinnaird to commemorate his twenty-first year as FA President in 1911; the third trophy was replaced with an exact replica in 1992 – the cup that we know today.

base, with every passing year the competition – the *only* competition – increased in strength: its number of entrants (some of whom had initially been put off through fear of it leading to an 'unhealthy rivalry' or worse still 'bitterness') rose exponentially, the level of interest it attracted – while not quite that of a national obsession – certainly moved football on from being the leisure pursuit of a few former public schoolboys to become a sport which attracted national attention and participation.

For most men, creating the FA Cup then captaining your side to victory in the inaugural final would be the achievements of a lifetime, but Alcock was no ordinary mortal. Already his mind had been filled with ideas of international football between England and Scotland or, in the absence of a Scottish equivalent of the FA (Queen's Park were the one team of any repute north of Hadrian's Wall), a representative match between the players of the two countries. On 3 November 1870 he had written to the *Glasgow Herald* announcing that a game between England and Scotland – 'the best elevens at their disposal' – would take place in London in sixteen days' time, adding: 'In Scotland, once essentially the land of football, there still should be a spark left of the old fire . . .' Scottish players were invited to send applications to Alcock's friend and fellow FA Committee member, Lord Kinnaird. But when the game was played at Kennington Oval – Alcock in the England line-up, Kinnaird in Scotland's – it turned out to be a humdrum affair, with the English winning 1–0. Subsequent matches the following February (1–1), November (2–1) and in February 1872 (1–0) failed to arouse widespread enthusiasm. Alcock concluded that matters as they existed simply would not do. The problem, as he saw it, was that there were no Scottish players prepared to make the onerous journey south and a lack of ready recruits in the capital. As he later put it: 'The eleven which represented Scotland was, in great measure, composed of players merely of Scottish extraction and, in some cases, perhaps of even less substantial qualifications.'[6] To counter such difficulties he turned his missionary zeal northwards.

These were football's pioneer days. The preoccupation still lay with spreading the word, reaching the masses and attaining uniformity. If something was absent – like the FA Cup – you invented it; if you sought to internationalise the code, you sent away a delegation and hoped that they could wow the locals. On 3 October 1872 the FA put out another missive: 'In order to further the interests of the Association in Scotland, it has been decided that during the current season, a team should be sent to Glasgow to play a match v Scotland.' The aims of the English were twofold: to 'teach' the Scots how to play the association game and to broaden its Caledonian appeal. Nevertheless, their plans were not without controversy; indeed those who followed rugby rules – the dominant strain of football in Scotland – were furious at the notion of the English challenging their hegemony. 'The very suggestion of such a contest under association rules was quite enough to rouse the ire of the rugby union players north of the Tweed,' Alcock remembered. 'The captains of the Scotch rugby clubs were determined to not have their rights usurped.'[7] A furious volley of correspondence was fired off to the *Scotsman*, but to little avail. On Saturday, 30 November 1872 at the West of Scotland Cricket Ground in Partick, players from Scotland and England lined up for the first ever international match.

After three days of heavy rain and a morning of light drizzle, the clouds had opened up to let in bursts of late autumnal sunshine to beam down delicately on west Glasgow. The pitch was a little greasy but otherwise considered to be in 'good order'; the admission fee, as it had been for the first FA Cup final, was a shilling – a steep price given the average industrial wage was just 20s per week. Still, it didn't put people off and estimates put the attendance at between 2000 and 4000 (though reported receipts of £109 suggest a figure somewhere in between). Whatever the precise figure, it was universally acknowledged that the game was played, in the words of the *North Daily Mail* correspondent, 'in the presence of the largest assemblage seen at any football match in Scotland . . . including a good number of ladies'.

The England team was drawn from eight different clubs, including four from the ranks of Oxford University, but Alcock himself was absent from his country's line-up. Despite playing on home soil, Scotland's old problem of getting players of sufficient quality resurfaced. Lord Kinnaird and Lt. Renny-Tailyour, the Scots' two most prominent English-based players, had each been unable to make the journey and the hosts were also apparently blighted by a lack of preparation, having had 'the greatest difficulty in performing at practice before the event'. But, in selecting six men from Queen's Park, they stumbled upon the secret of success that was for some years to elude their English counterparts – teamwork.

England reverted to the tactical norms of the day, lining up with a goalkeeper (only formally introduced a year earlier), a back, two half-backs and seven forwards. The Scots were slightly more conservative, playing with one fewer forward and an additional back. Fears that the visitors would not knit together effectively, coming as they did from so many different clubs, were soon dispelled, although this may have owed more to the effectiveness of their inherent individualism, born from England's solitary tactic, dribbling. 'The magnificent dribbling of the England captain Kirke-Smith and Brockbank, seconded as it was by the fine back play of Welch Greenhalgh and Chappell, was greatly admired by the immense concourse of spectators, who kept the utmost order,' reported *Bell's Life*. England's forwards were more dangerous on the break, but lacked the potency to overcome a resolute Scottish defence. 'The only thing which saved the Scottish team from defeat,' noted one observer, 'considering the powerful forward play of England, was the magnificent defensive play and tactics shown by their backs, which was also taken advantage of by the forwards.' In the end, the match ended – like the first representative game a decade earlier – in a goalless draw but everyone seemed to leave with a smile on their face. *Bell's Life* concluded: 'A splendid display of football in the really scientific sense of the word, and a most determined effort on the part of representatives of two nationalities to overcome each other.' Alcock too was able to reflect on a positive day's work: 'The Football Association could hardly have had a better advertisement, and the enterprise of those who had been mainly responsible for the ratification of the match was fully rewarded by the great impetus it gave to the diffusion of Association rules throughout the west of Scotland.'[8]

The belief that the match would serve as a prelude for the expansion of the game in Scotland was soon proven. In the months that followed, more than a dozen Scottish clubs were formed to join the ten that existed and within months the Scottish Football Association had been formed. By then, England and Scotland had met for a second time, on 8 March 1873 at Kennington Oval. London's first international match attracted a crowd of similar magnitude to the one in Partick, including – and certainly not for the last time – a sizeable detachment of boisterous, noisy Scots. Besides this contingent the bulk of the attendance consisted of the fanatical and the devoted, the very 'gentlemen' who had helped pioneer football's rise

– with the shilling entrance fee again proving beyond the means of many ordinary folk. Still, some did gain entry, if only through foul means rather than fair. 'While the janitor was employed in admitting carriages at the larger gate,' reported one witness, 'some hundreds took it upon themselves to enter with the carriages without the necessity of reaching to their pockets to pay the absurd fee of 1s for admission.'[9]

England's selectors had staged a series of trial matches in the run-up to the game and retained just three of the men who had been held in Partick. Leading the English attack was the dashing figure of Captain Kenyon-Slaney of the Household Brigade, who was 'of the greatest service' to his side, scoring twice – including the decisive goal – as the hosts marched to a 4–2 victory. England's performance generated much excitement and 'occasionally the boundary lines were disregarded' as the crowd let the occasion overcome them and spilled onto the pitch, several times holding up play as the two umpires cleared the playing area. 'If any proof were necessary to evince the growing victory of the winter game over the wielders of willow,' recorded *Bell's Life*, 'there was sufficient evidence on this occasion to convince the most sceptical that football, if only aided by fine weather, is a game that could take its place among the leading pastimes of the day.' The superiority of England's footballers was only tentative though. A year later Scotland defeated England 2–1 at Hamilton Crescent, Glasgow, a win that marked the onset of a run which would see just one defeat over the following fourteen years.

Football in general continued to evolve into an increasingly sophisticated sport. The laws were constantly revised – 1871 had seen goalkeepers first mentioned; 1873 marked the introduction of corners; 1882 the two-handed throw-in – and the tactics developed. In 1863, when Barnes had played the first representative match, they deployed two behinds and nine forwards; by 1870 most teams were deploying a goalkeeper, back, two half-backs and seven forwards; and by the turn of the decade, a goalkeeper, two backs, three half-backs and five forwards, in what became known as the 'WM' formation. Incredibly, this tactic prevailed, almost unmodified, until the early 1960s, or from the first performance of Tchaikovsky's 1812 Overture to the days when the Beatles were 'twisting and shouting' their way to the top of the British and American pop charts.

The WM formation created a happy medium between the English

dribbling game and the passing of the Scots, which had respectively bestowed little success on the English and much on their neighbours. Today it is difficult to picture just how England played but all accounts point at something akin to a playground scramble, with everybody chasing desperately after every loose ball and, when in possession, doing everything they possibly could to retain it before making a George Best-like solo run on goal. When Alfred Gibson and William Pickford compiled football's first great history *Association Football and the Men who Made It* in 1906 they wrote that when 'dribbling was the great game, one only passed the ball when one was completely hemmed in, and not always then'.[10] From such chaos came several drubbings at the hands of the Scots: 1–3 at Kennington Oval in 1877; 2–7 at Hampden Park a year later and, worst of all, 1–6 at Kennington in 1881. After the 1878 match, *Bell's Life* had published a letter signed by 'A Disgusted Englishman'. Although he hardly lambasted his compatriots, he struck at the heart of the problem: 'The England players we had down this time were a splendid lot of players individually, but to my idea they played very selfishly, each one of them appearing to play for himself and not for the success of the side.'

Still, England did occasionally prove that individual genius could overcome team ethic. In the land of dribblers, the king of the left wing was Sheffield's William Mosforth. A tough, quick individual with supreme close control and an eye for goal, Mosforth was an early star and hero of northern England's most influential club. When England met Scotland at Kennington on 5 April 1879, they did so on the back of three straight defeats. Mosforth's early goal looked to have brought a change in fortune, but when Scotland streaked into a 4–1 half-time lead such hopes seemed not just confounded, but utterly extinguished. This England team, however, was imbued with greater grit and resolve than some of its predecessors. E.C. Bambridge of Swifts led the way with a dash that spanned half the length of the pitch and ended with an unstoppable shot past Scotland's goalkeeper, Robert Parlane. Then, improbably, Arthur Goodyer and Norman Bailey pulled the scoreline back to 4–4 and England pushed strongly for the most unlikely of winners. With just five minutes remaining, the Scots appeared to have added a fifth and the game, according to Mosforth, descended into chaos. He recalled:

The Scottish umpire said 'goal', the English one was just as confident that it was 'offside'. And so the hapless referee, Lord Kinnaird, was called upon. He was surrounded by the Scottish players, and Mr C.W. Alcock came running from the pavilion to render him apparently necessary succour. But the Scotsmen chased him back again, and Lord Kinnaird stated that he thought the goal was 'offside'. The consequence was that the Scotsmen were unable to settle down any more, and, before the close, either Bambridge or Mosforth put on a fifth goal for England. 'I don't know which of us it was,' he said. 'But I know that they carried me off the field afterwards, so I must have played pretty well.'

That victory in 1879 was but a rare one and, as such, was celebrated long and hard into the night. Charles Alcock, on the other hand, took more simple pleasures: from spreading his gospel, in doing what hadn't previously been done, and taking the game he loved on to the next level. 'They were glorious days in the way of enjoyment, those of the late 1860s and throughout the 1870s,' he would write.

> Then it was at least the game pure and unadulterated. No gates to speak of – down our way, at least. Those were the days primeval. To go to Glasgow – a railway journey of over 800 miles there and back – for an hour and a half's football at one's own expense was not in a way grateful and comforting. How we did it is not easy to say. But it was done, and plenty of fun it brought with it, even if one had to travel through the night in draughty carriages with hard seats – a severely economical style.

The inroads made by football were increasingly tangible too. In 1876, the Welsh had followed the lead of the English and Scots in forming their own Football Association and the Irish followed suit four years later. On 18 November 1879 England played their first international against Wales, winning 2–1 at Kennington; while the Irish, whom England first met in February 1882, provided an ample source of goals for English forwards usually unable to whet their appetites against the formidable Scots: England won the first encounter 13–0 and in their first ten meetings hit an aggregate of seventy-one goals to Ireland's five.

Still, Scottish hegemony was deemed a serious problem. For N.L. Jackson, an early follower of the national side, it was an unpalatable state of affairs. He had become an FA Committee member in 1879 and

Honorary Assistant Secretary to Alcock in 1881. Like his boss, Jackson sought to leave his mark on the game. He believed that England had been beaten with such frequency because of the superior teamwork of their opponents and conceived the idea of the leading amateurs regularly playing together to foster greater understanding when the national side played. To such ends he helped set up Corinthians football club in 1882. Essentially an old boys' club, with forty of its fifty members elected each year, it was underpinned by unwritten rules that only former public school and university men be asked to play and that they entered no competitions. Their ethos was to teach 'young England the general education that befits a gentlemen and also the particular education that develops future international players'.[11] Jackson's own belief that with 'plenty of practice together they would acquire a certain amount of combination' certainly reaped dividends. Although a run of victories over the Scots was not immediate, the thrashings ceased, the over-reliance on dribbling ended and England began to pass the ball and work as a team. Corinthians' influence on the make-up of the national team was enormous: of the eighty-eight caps gained by Englishmen against Scotland over the next seven years, fifty-two went to the club's players.[12]

Jackson's enterprise, however, went against prevailing trends. By the early 1880s association football had successfully invaded popular consciousness. Regional football associations had begun to form across England in the late 1870s, providing, on a local level, cup competitions and the same sort of organisational structure that the Football Association sought to implement nationally. Their work complemented the FA and provided the springboard for fledgling clubs like Sheffield Wednesday, Stoke City, Aston Villa, Middlesbrough and Everton to expand from mere offshoots of church or cricket clubs to become major players in their own right. Soon attendances for some exhibition games or cup matches were outnumbering crowds at international matches, although they could still be measured in the low thousands. Yet football was, for many, an obsession. One of the tasks of William Pickford, in his days on the staff of a Lancashire newspaper, was to visit the office on a Saturday evening when the football results were telegraphed through, copy them onto large sheets of paper and stick them in windows for the inspection of large crowds. It was becoming a genuinely national game too. The first ten FA Cup finals had involved just six clubs: Wanderers, Royal

Engineers, Old Etonians, Oxford University, Old Carthusians and Clapham Rovers; but in 1882, a team from the north threatened to break this southern dominance. Blackburn Rovers, from a pool of seventy-three entrants – the largest yet – progressed to the final and journeyed to the Oval with a large contingent of fans in an effort to try and usurp Old Etonians, runners-up a year earlier. High on confidence, one Lancastrian poet boldly lauded victory prior to kick-off:

> The English Cup, by brilliant play
> From Cockney land they brought away;
> Let's hope in Blackburn it will stay
> To cheer the Blackburn Rovers.[13]

His prediction of impending victory was premature: Old Etonians prevailed as 1–0 winners and Lord Kinnaird, who captained the winners, celebrated with a handstand on the Oval pavilion. A year later Rovers' townsmen, Blackburn Olympic, returned to South London and went one better, coming away with a 2–1 extra-time victory over Kinnaird's men. The game had taken yet another path: never again would the old boys or university men reap FA Cup glory and it would be another eighteen years before a southern club took the trophy again.

In the midst of this football frenzy, Alcock initially seemed unsure whether he was entirely in favour of the trail football was blazing into the public's hearts and minds. In the *Football Annual* of 1882, he had written:

> What was 10 or 15 years ago the recreation of a few has now become the pursuit of thousands, an athletic exercise carried on under a strict system, and in many cases, by an enforced team of training almost magnified into a profession. Whether the introduction of so serious and almost businesslike an element into the sport is a healthy one or not, this is not the place to enquire, but there are many old football fogies who recall with no small satisfaction the days when football had not grown to be so important as to make umpires necessary, and the 'gate' the first subject for conversation.

Alcock could see that the expansion of football from a contest between public schoolboys and university men to a game involving crowds often numbering thousands, meant that its progression to professionalism was never far away. The emergence of the sport as a genuinely classless one pushed its case even further. Leading clubs with working-class players did not want to see their better players using up all their physical strength in manual or semi-skilled work during a working week that could include five twelve-hour days and a half-day on Saturday. With such rigorous hours the norm even clerical jobs were exhausting. Although payment beyond compensation for lost wages and expenses had been specifically outlawed by the FA in 1882, many clubs circumvented the ruling: players' wives or a nominee often received payment instead; alternatively a footballer was sometimes engaged by a sympathetic fan in a 'job' that did not really exist. Towards the mid-1880s a number of leading Scottish players had left their homeland and 'discovered' jobs, conveniently located near such football hotbeds as Preston, Blackburn or Liverpool, where they would invariably find roles in the leading local teams. The suspicion that they were 'sham amateurs' was never far away. When Major Suddell, Preston North End's manager, came out in 1884 and unashamedly stated that he sought to create the strongest possible team at Deepdale, and if that meant remunerating its players then so be it, he earned his club a Football Association ban. Burnley and Great Lever of Bolton earned similar rebukes after FA investigations uncovered payments to their players, but they were understood to be the mere tip of the iceberg. Across the country genuine amateurs were struggling against men whose exclusive occupation was practising, training and playing the game.

Despite happy memories of football's pioneer days, Alcock realised that the game had moved on and banning clubs rested uneasily with him. Equally, he disliked the argument of those opposed to professionalism who claimed that it would be 'degrading' for 'respectable' men to play with or against professionals. For him, there was something inherently wrong with such elitism creeping into the sport. True, football as he had known it had been the leisure pursuit of the few, but he came to see no reason why it should not take its course and become the love of millions. Slowly he began to press for professionalism to be legalised. His efforts met with opposition from the Scottish and Midlands associations and within the FA's own headquarters at Holborn, but the Honorary Secretary stood firm. 'Professionals are a necessity to the growth of the game,' he argued, 'and I object to the idea that they are the utter outcasts some people represent them to be. Furthermore, I object to the argument that it is immoral to work for a living, and I cannot see why men should not, without object, labour at football as at cricket.' Eventually, once the FA was faced with the threat of disintegration in 1885 after the northern clubs had threatened to break away into a renegade 'British Association', the opponents relented in July of that year and professionalism was legalised.

On the international stage, Corinthian spirit still dominated. Despite their amateur status, footballers began to be recognised as heroes in a way that would have been inconceivable to their forbears. Of course, William Mosforth had been greatly admired in his time but even he could not match some of the eulogies being meted out to his international heirs of the mid-1880s. The pick of them were the brothers Arthur and Percy Walters, two Charterhouse old boys, who had formed a defensive pairing for Corinthians, turned out for their respective universities and, a year after playing against each other in the 1884 Varsity match, their country. Gibson and Pickford recorded that they 'were unique as a pair of backs. England never had a finer pair; I doubt if they ever had a couple equal to them. They may never get a better pair.'[14] For five years they maintained the England defensive line with fraternal distinction, but their time was to come to an untimely and tragic end when a younger brother took ill during a match and died. Devastated, their parents asked the surviving siblings to give up the sport, to which they mournfully agreed. Not for the last time, England had been deprived of some of its finest young talents.

The real star of the national team, however, was the forward, W.N. Cobbold. In many ways he was the first modern footballer, a man who actually considered where he was running, and who he was playing to, rather than putting his head down and simply charging blindly onwards. 'The first idea of any forward,' he believed, 'should be that he is only a connecting link in a chain which should, as a rule, be kept in line, and that the whole secret of good play lies in combination.'[15] He provided, noted Alcock, 'the first application of any real method in the attack, in the south at least . . . [He was] one of the most skilful forwards of the modern school, he was the first, as far as my knowledge goes, to evolve the mechanical precision which has been continued by his successors in office.'[16] The Cambridge University alumnus made his international debut against the Scots in 1883 and marked the occasion with a goal. In total he played on nine occasions for his country, scoring seven times; but it was his team-work and skill rather than the longevity of his career that saw his name engrained in early football legend. 'If one were to ask who were the three greatest footballers of all time?' mused Gibson and Pickford in 1906, 'no matter what other two were named, W.N. Cobbold would perhaps come first to the lips.'[17] He was, they added, 'power-fully built, strong on his legs, and with determination written all over him. It was probably this latter quality that exalted him above his fellows.'[18]

Yet, in 1888, Cobbold was to miss English football's first great triumph. During the decade two key developments impacted on the national team. The latter was minor enough – the introduction of international caps. N.L. Jackson had mooted the idea at an FA Committee meeting in January 1886 when he proposed: 'That all players taking part for England in future international matches be presented with a white silk cap with red rose embroidered on the front. These to be termed "International Caps".'* The former held greater sway. With both Wales and Ireland entering the international fray it was decided from 1884 to increase the competitiveness of international matches by inaugurating a competition – the Home Championship. It took the form of a mini-league, which Scotland topped in the first two years. After tying at the top in 1885–86, when England drew the deciding match 1–1 at Hampden, the Scots regained the title a year later. Yet as the 1887–88 contest got under way, there was a growing sense that England could end Scottish dominance. Few, however, could have anticipated the way in which it was smashed to pieces.

On 17 March 1888 the England party travelled north of the border with a side mixed almost equally between amateurs and professionals. Together they had been 'trained to their work as never a team sent out by the English association', but finally it seemed that the elusive balance between individuality and teamwork, attacking verve and defensive nous, had been struck. England clicked together as never before. 'The great fault, one cannot help designating it defect, in all previous international elevens, was lack of combination and want of staying power among the forwards,' wrote the *North Daily Mail*, 'but

* The motion carried, although the design was modified to blue velvet and later the rose was substituted for the three lions and a silver tassel added.

this could not be laid to their charge on Saturday, for their dribbling, passing and general play were splendid, and much admired by all who saw the contest, and we can scarcely single out individual worth.' England strode into a 4–0 half-time lead through Lindley, Hodgetts, Dewhurst and Goodall, then Dewhurst made it five without reply in the second half. Years of hurt, in one wondrous sweep, had been avenged. Later that month England recorded successive 5–1 victories over Wales and Ireland to take the Home Championship outright for the first time.

Yet before they had the opportunity to defend their title, the development of English football had taken another dramatic twist. At Birmingham's largest club, Aston Villa, was a committee man full of the same sort of laudatory ambitions for the game as Alcock had been in the 1870s. William McGregor was a forty-one-year-old Scot, a draper by trade, with a tidy sideline in the manufacture of football jerseys. But by conviction he was a staunch Methodist and prominent Liberal in Birmingham's political circles at a time when Joseph Chamberlain was president of the local association. Taking inspiration from his political and religious faith as well as Birmingham's reputation as the thriving centre of Victorian reform, McGregor was one of the first men to realise the sociological importance of football: it kept men off the streets, enhanced civic prestige and inspired loyalty in the municipality. But he was also aware of the limitations of domestic football's organisational structure: the system was ad hoc and open to petty rivalries; games were frequently prone to cancellation when one or other opponent was lured into a fixture that promised a higher gate and greater receipts and the frequent chaos of the fixture list was often exacerbated by the interruption of unscheduled cup matches. McGregor's counterpart, Thomas Keates, at Merseyside's premier club, Everton, was all too aware of the problem: 'The contrast in the attendances at cup ties and ordinary matches, the trifling interest taken in the latter by the public and the insignificance had long vexed the souls of club managers. How can we vitalise the torpid? That was the question.'[19]

William McGregor had the answer: a regular, competitive system of fixtures involving only the top clubs, along the lines of the County Cricket Championship. The season would still allow for local cup competitions, the FA Cup and internationals, but interest would be maintained after a team had been knocked out in the early stages.

During the 1886–87 season, McGregor toured the country, seeking the support of his colleagues at other clubs. Perhaps surprisingly, the response he got was not always favourable and concerns were voiced about upsetting the FA and the cost of regularised fixtures. After various expeditions, McGregor made his first formal move on 2 March 1888, writing to five clubs – Blackburn Rovers, Bolton Wanderers, Preston North End, West Bromwich Albion and Aston Villa – laying out his ideas: a division of ten or twelve clubs who would play each other in home and away matches played under FA rules, and a formal association to be managed by representatives from each member. He also asked for suggestions for additional members. Further meetings were scheduled in London in late March, then in Manchester's Royal Hotel in mid-April. Here the Football League was formally created. The credo, according to McGregor, was:

> The League should never aspire to be a legislating body . . . by the very nature of things the League must be a selfish body. Its interests are wholly bound up in the welfare of its affiliated clubs, and what happens outside is, in a sense, of secondary importance . . . The League has work to do; the Association has its work to do and there need be no clashing.[20]

McGregor had no interest in the amateurs, and the amateurs little interest in mixing it with the professionals. Instead, the league's founder members (Accrington, Aston Villa, Blackburn Rovers, Bolton Wanderers, Burnley, Derby County, Everton, Notts County, Preston North End, Stoke City, West Bromwich Albion and Wolverhampton Wanderers) consisted of representatives from major towns across the Midlands and north of England; the southern clubs, who were still fully to embrace professionalism, were left to wait and follow later. Less than five months on from the meeting the Football League kicked off – at Pikes Lane, Bolton; Anfield Road, Everton; the Victoria Ground, Stoke; Deepdale and Dudley Road, Wolverhampton.[21] Derby County recorded the biggest victory of the day, defeating Bolton 6–3 on their own turf; Everton, the biggest crowd, with 10,000 turning out to see their 2–1 win over Accrington.

In less than a quarter of a century, the game had evolved from the nascent pastime of the middle classes into a widespread, mass spectator sport. The expectation that football would merely serve to tire and discipline the unruly youth of the dwindling public schools had been surpassed a hundred times over. It had become the passion not just of its thousand score of players, but tens of thousands more who now flocked to watch these young athletes at play. Competitive football, which had burst into stride with the inaugural internationals and birth of the FA Cup, had reached a merry canter with the first Home International Championships, then hit a sprint with the onset of professionalism and the conception of the Football League. The game would never be the same again.

2

GENTLEMAN FOOTBALLERS, SOCCER SUPERSTARS

FOOTBALL'S INCREDIBLE TRANSFORMATION from the game of the mob to the sport of the elite, and then into Britain's national pastime, had come at a cost only to the Football Association's founding fathers. Never again would eager old boys like Charles Alcock or Lord Kinnaird dominate the ranks of their respective national teams or lay claim to FA Cup glory. Their role now was almost wholly concerned with the administration of football and ensuring that the extraordinary inroads it had made into the public's consciousness was not just maintained, but extended. Football, as far as they were concerned, would not just be some Victorian fad: it would endure.

The game was being reclaimed by the masses and the advent of the Football League and its subsequent expansion (from twelve to twenty-eight clubs in 1892; thirty-six in 1898; and forty teams on the eve of the 1905–06 season) cemented that standing. Almost every town north of Birmingham could boast a professional league team by the turn of the nineteenth century and many of those south (Woolwich Arsenal were the only southern-based league member) could claim non-league or amateur teams of considerable repute. Football newspapers and specials began to be published all over the country; coaching manuals; memoirs; even histories of the game were produced and other paraphernalia, like cigarette cards, would become highly popular. In 1892, the periodical *Nineteenth Century* published an article entitled 'The New Football Mania' which described the fever that was taking over the land: 'In all our large towns, and most of the small ones, north of Birmingham to the Tweed, from September to April, Saturday is consecrated to football. Saturday evenings are devoted to football symposia, and the newspapers issue special editions.' Local teams were 'better known than the local members of Parliament', and support had spread across divides of age and sex:

> Many old people and women are so caught by it that they would not, on any ordinary account, miss a local match . . . The multitude flock to the field in their workaday dirt and with their workaday adjectives very loose on their tongues. In Lancashire and the Black Country it is really surprising what a number of emphatic and even mysterious expletives may be heard on these Saturday afternoons. Some of them are, however, remarkably unpleasant and not fit for a lady's ears, even to the remotest echo!

'It is,' the article concluded, 'ludicrous to see how boys of a very tender age get possessed of a frenzy at some of these matches.'[1]

This brave new world was ripe for heroes and the England team's first recognisable superstar, ironically, spoke with a Scottish accent. John Goodall was born of Scottish parents in London in 1863, but brought up in Kilmarnock, Ayrshire. His brother Archie, via the same qualification, would himself later play for Ireland. John started his career with Kilmarnock Athletic after learning the game as a bare-footed boy before becoming an iron-turner (lathe operator) and moving south to join Great Lever. He signed for Preston North End as a professional in 1885. Goodall was essentially a centre-forward, but was also one of football's great thinkers, a skilful player who would never resort to the standard cut and thrust of centre-forward play. 'He was the inspirer, the initiator, the key, the mainspring of the whole team,' wrote Alfred Gibson and William Pickford.[2] He could score with abandon too and throughout his career ws a prolific marksman. 'His methods as a forward represent the triumph of mind over matter,' Gibson and Pickford noted. 'Let others play the game of human skittles if they please, Goodall would always try the effects of strategy.'[3] A good-humoured man, a peculiar player, renowned for his exemplary sportsmanship, he was 'a prince of good fellows and a prince of players . . . if his name were not already Goodall he might be truly named John All Good.'[4] He had made his international debut in the 5–0 romp over the Scots at Hampden in March 1888 and would shine for England in fourteen appearances spanning a decade which would witness a dozen goals from his boots.

To keep up with the game's rapid expansion in the north of England, the Football Association had altered its selection procedures to keep a watchful eye on the development of young hopefuls. Seven members of the FA Council were appointed as a sub-committee to select the international team, each representing various districts so as to map the whole country. J.J. Bentley, the President of the Football League, later explained the procedure:

> Up to December each season not much notice was taken of the players but, from that time forward, the selector worth his place will rarely miss a match somewhere or other and occasionally the whole of the committee arrange to visit one particular game, having special seats reserved. Views are exchanged and at the end of the game we generally have an idea as to which men have a chance of a cap. I know at least one club that used to be simply delighted when informed of the committee's visit, as one of their players always seemed to score more goals than usual.[5]

The changes had come after Scotland wrested back the Home Championship in 1889 after a 3–2 win at Kennington Oval. The next year, both countries shared it in the wake of a draw at Hampden after each had earlier handed out their annual thrashing to the Irish and defeated the Welsh, but England would regain it in 1892 and retain it for the following three years.

South of the border prejudice against professionals was still rife a full decade after the Football Association had legalised players' remuneration. Derided for being money-hungry, accused of lacking grace and flair, criticised for lacking in sportsmanship, in many minds the professionals stood in contempt. Corinthians, hailed as the saviours of English football, had much to do with this schism, consciously or not. Applauded for their strong moral fibre, their grace on the field and fair-minded attacking play, every time the character of the professional was called into question – which was often – they would be held up as an example that should be followed. The comparisons were unfair and frequently ridiculous. True, Corinthians could claim to be the epitome of gentlemanly conduct and fair play at all times, but then they never participated in any sort of competitive matches. As for the suggestion that there was something vulgar in accepting money to play top-class football, the majority of its members had the education and employment opportunities to pursue a career that would allow them time to train and partake in their pastime of choice. Confronted with the cut and thrust of the Football

League, or placed on a factory floor and forced to work a sixty-hour week (as many professionals otherwise would have been), would such principles have been so rigorously adhered to?

The body of contemporary literature, where it contains insights into a footballer's life, is almost completely dominated by these so-called gentlemen. Grumbles about the gamesmanship and corrupting influence of professionals are frequent. *Ethical World* said much about prevalent attitudes when it suggested that, under commercial pressure, football 'degenerates more and more into organised brutality and breeds brutality in spectators'. Others were still more contemptuous. The wonderfully named Elphinstone Jackson wrote in 1898: 'The aggressiveness of the professional element asserted itself in many ways. Not content with almost filling the international teams with professionals, *it did all in its powers to reduce one or two amateurs who did play to the level of the professionals*. All were taken to the same hotel, all were expected to travel and to feed together.' Not until that same year did the amateurs deign to eat with their professional team-mates, when 'rather than appear to be exclusive or run the chance of making themselves unpopular with the "pros" [the amateurs] consented to lunch with them on the day of the match'.[6] Such a sea change was too much for some. S.S. (Stanley) Harris of Cambridge University and Corinthians had his international career cut short because he refused to pass to professionals. 'Harris has not taken kindly to the rather stereotyped methods of the paid player,' noted Pickford and Gibson. 'He finds it difficult to sink his individuality, with the result that he does not part with the ball so readily or so often as the professional alongside him.'[7]

That Harris should have feared subduing his individuality said much about the notion that the amateur and professional games were somehow wholly different. Gibson and Pickford, writing in 1906, seemed imbued with this idea:

The professional is as a rule more mechanical and less individual in his methods. He has learned his football in a school where experiments are frowned upon. The paid player, as a class, has learned that certain methods are regarded with favour, and that these methods frequently meet with success. He therefore cultivates this manner until he arrives at a state of mechanical perfection. In theory at least, he is master of the conventional style. It is obviously the business of his opponents to upset his theories and the forward who has no native ingenuity – no resource of his own – is a pitiable object. An amateur forward of the highest class has usually all the knowledge of the orthodox game and also the ability to play it; but if he be a football genius he also possess a style of his own, with brains enough to improvise on the moment a new mode of attack or an original method of defence. Speaking in broad and general terms one may say that the professional forward is the exponent of certain well known methods of attack which have become mechanical, while the amateur adopts methods which include the professional theory and adds an individual style of his own creation.[8]

Although some amateurs were contemptuous of the professionals and not above taking private dressing rooms if they could, in football there was not the same sort of distinction between the two breeds as in cricket or rugby. Until the Second World War there were often separate changing rooms and travel arrangements for amateur and professional cricketers, and the notion of addressing an amateur by anything other than 'Mr' was deemed the height of bad manners. Rugby went even further and divorced into two separate codes altogether.

That football's schism wasn't all pervasive had much to do with men like Corinthians' great forward, G.O. Smith. A Charterhouse and Oxford alumnus, and later a joint headmaster in Barnet (with his international colleague W.J. Oakley), Smith made his international debut against the Irish in February 1893 and established himself in the England team a year later. Though nominally a centre-forward, he was also a tremendous passer of the ball and, like W.N. Cobbold, a decade earlier, a team player *par excellence*. Gibson and Pickford would record that Smith was:

Great in all the qualities which go to make up the man who is the keystone of the arch of a team, it was in the making and receiving passes that he excelled all others. And it was in making the pass that he was most deadly. No defender, however experienced, could anticipate what he was going to do. He had an instinct for throwing the enemy off his guard, and at the same time of doing the right thing in the right way at the right moment.[9]

But it was his personality that set him apart: Smith was a man in the midst of a love affair with the game, who played for fun and claimed (disingenuously) that if he were a millionaire he would still play every week. Though he believed – as a purist – in the inherent superiority of the amateur game, there were few of the airs and graces that went with the likes of S.S. Harris. If a man was good enough on the field, he was good enough off it. As one contemporary described him, Smith 'was the finest type of amateur, one who would always shake hands with us professionals in a manner which said plainly that he was pleased to meet them. In those far off days professional footballers were looked upon with something bordering on contempt and would not mix with us. But "G.O." was a true sportsman and brilliant centre forward and was beloved for it.'[10]

Smith's progress to the unlikely status of headmaster-footballer-superstar was, of course, aided by his professional colleagues. For Corinthians he could shine, but without the competitiveness that came with FA Cup or League football, he could never be a soccer hero in the true sense. International football, however, was a different proposition. Alongside him and Goodall in the England forward line were other individuals whose names have been added to football's lore. West Bromwich Albion's winger, Billy Bassett, was one such individual, first earning an international call-up as early as 1888. Standing just 5ft 5in tall he possessed great acceleration and agility (one of his strengths was stepping off, then back onto the field of play to avoid the attentions of the opposing full-back) but it was for his deadly crossing that he was most famous. Bassett was a big game player, although some fans accused him of being a prima donna (doubtless also in the knowledge of his astronomical wages – at a reported £43 per week, ten times the average), saying that if he met a tough centre-half in the rigours of the League he was not up for the challenge. 'But the fact remains that Bassett never played an indifferent game on any occasion when the reputation of his club or his country was at stake,' wrote Gibson and Pickford, 'and in estimating his worth one has to remember that throughout his football career he was the most marked man the game knew.'[11]

Bassett's later days as an England international were aided in no small part by the rise of Derby County's extraordinary inside-right, Steve Bloomer. Born in the nail-making town of Cradley in 1874, Bloomer was brought up in Derby and, when his exceptional talents were spotted by The Rams, was lucky to fall under the tutelage of no less a figure than John Goodall, who had joined from Preston in 1889.

'He talked to me and passed on his learnings . . . straight to the point he told you what to do and expected it to be done,' Bloomer would later say of his mentor. 'I always maintain that no player has ever known so much about football and its methods and policies than this old friend of mine.'[12] Like many of his contemporaries, he was a great all rounder, also playing cricket at district level, but it was his great pace that set him apart. Bloomer could run 100 yards in 11.5 seconds (at a time when the world record stood around the ten-second mark) and his speed and directness caused opposing defenders untold nightmares. 'Embroidery and fancy work he leaves to the artists that like that sort of thing. He is possessed with the one grand idea – to get goals and to get them with the least possible expenditure of time and energy.'[13] Word soon spread of Bloomer's prowess to the extent that stories became embellished with elements of fantasy. Known to cartwheel in celebration – sometimes before the ball had even struck the back of the net – he would recall how: 'Word got around that I did this to put the goalkeeper off. Nothing of the sort was in my mind. It was simply that I knew intuitively that I had sent a shot which the goalie would never save, and on impulse my cartwheel was turned out of delight before I realised I was playing on a crowded football field.'[14]

Paying heed to all the talk about the prodigy, England's selectors gave Bloomer a run out on his home turf at Derby against Ireland in March 1895. More and more, those in the 'promising' category were ventured against the Irish and Welsh ahead of the one match that really mattered – Scotland. Bloomer did not disappoint. Against what one newspaper described as a 'woefully weak' Irish side, Bloomer, Goodall and Bassett tore them apart. The Derby men each claimed a brace, the winger one, as England romped to a 9–0 victory. A month later, when England met Scotland in front of a record 42,500 crowd at the recently built Goodison Park, Bloomer scored one and pressured a Scottish defender into putting into his own net, as England romped home 3–0 victors. 'In the dressing room after the match my good friend John Goodall shook hands with me and congratulated me on playing so well,' recalled Bloomer. '"But Steve," he added, shaking his head wisely, "don't let this get any bigger." And he tapped my head! It was an excellent piece of advice from an old and experienced player to an almost raw recruit and I believe I took the advice to heart.' Not too much though – Bloomer was always insistent he scored twice that day.

Goodison's 42,500-strong crowd represented a landmark attendance for an international in England. A year later, on 4 April 1896,
Scotland – who had already surpassed the 40,000 mark – went one
better, when 56,500 turned out at Parkhead. Those present witnessed
the hosts wreak long-awaited revenge on their neighbours with a 2–1
win that brought the Home Championship back north again. Off the
pitch, however, events had failed to pass without incident. Already,
two years earlier, there had been ugly scenes when ticketless fans had
stormed a barricade and in the ensuing confusion some had been
injured; while others, including many pressmen, had been displaced
from their allocated seats. The whole incident had said much about
the rising intensity of supporters' passions, but also, rather more
worryingly, the inability of the authorities to successfully manage
large crowds. The prevalent attitude seemed to be: pile 'em high
and hope for the best. Two years on at Parkhead, interest was greater
than ever before. 'The rush eastwards from the centre of the city
began as early as 11 o'clock forenoon; and during all the intervening
hours kept going with ever-increasing intensity,' reported the *Daily
Mail*.

> Ordinary and special trains running in that direction were crowded, and must
> have greatly relieved the street traffic, yet the Gallowgate and London Road,
> the main avenues leading towards the ground for several hours presented
> something like the appearance of Clapham Road, London on Derby Day.
> There was a continuous rush of cars, omnibuses, brakes (four in hand as well
> as pairs), hansoms, four-wheelers, tradesmen's vans and the picturesque
> costers' barrows. The spectacle was decidedly interesting, whilst the deafening
> clatter could only be duly appreciated by householders on either route. Not
> that the residents as a whole felt any grievance at the unwonted bustle.
> Windows of houses were kept open most of the time, and the housewives
> with their children manifested interest in the passing show.

Inside the ground the crowd was so tightly packed that those at the
front were eventually forced through the crash barriers and onto the
side of the pitch. Irked that the pitch-side spectators had a superior
vista, those crammed into the back of the terrace began to rain down
a volley of stones, cinders, oranges and empty bottles on their fellow
spectators. 'For a time the attacked party withstood the fusillade,'
reported the *Mail*, 'but ultimately could bear it no longer and the

police and soldiers aiding in front with their arms the assault of missiles from the rear the raiders were driven back across the cycle track.' It was an ugly scene, almost a riot, and not until 3.15 p.m. did play get under way. Still, the Scottish Football Association could rest easily: nobody had been fatally imperilled; and they could count record receipts of £3640. Nevertheless, it was to prove a worrying portent.

Scotland retained the Home Championship in 1897 after recording another 2–1 win, at Crystal Palace. A year later though, England were filled with greater urgency and were in a greater position than ever before to seize the trophy back. The emergence of a half-back partnership of formidable standing aided the rearguard and provided a strong basis of support for the England attack. Sheffield United's Ernest Needham had already provided a steely presence to his country since 1894, but for the 1898 Home Internationals he was partnered by Frank Forman of Nottingham Forest (for whom his brother Fred, himself a sometime international, also turned out) and suddenly England were imbued with greater solidity. Standing at 5ft 11½in, Forman, wrote Gibson and Pickford, 'was a sore thorn in the sides of the "nippiest" and like the Roman warrior of old, he often held the bridge in the face of the most determined assaults'. He was also a consummate passer, and he would spray long raking balls across the field to willing forwards. Yet 'his look of disgust when an unlucky vanguardsman failed to take advantage of one of these chances was most amusing to see'. He also possessed one of the 'deadliest and hardest shots at goal amongst his contemporaries'. Sometimes he could be difficult, sulky and idiosyncratic, but he was a good man and admired and respected by his friends, who used the refrain of a contemporary song: 'He's all right when you know him, but you've got to know him first.'[15] Needham was a different sort of footballer: a clever player, never one to go diving into tackles, with the pace and presence of mind to follow his opponents around and make sure they ran into the proverbial brick wall. He 'could dribble like a forward', seldom lost possession when doing so, and his passing and crossing were supremely accurate.[16] In many ways his football philosophy was indicative of the priorities of the day. 'Keep an eye on your wing man,' he would say, 'and lend what help you can to the centre-half now and then. But it is the outside man who must be your first priority.' He meant his own outside man of course, and supplementing his own side's attacks rather than hovering around an opponent defending.

England's half-backs weren't the only ones instilled with a great will to succeed. The captain, Charles Wreford-Brown (invariably of Corinthians) briefed the players beforehand and, with a glint in his eye, told them that he would be the 'happiest man alive' if England recorded victory. Just three minutes of the match had passed when his countrymen were on their way to fulfilling his ambition. 'Spikesley made a zigzag run well down on the Scotch goal,' reported the *Daily Mail*.

> And both Drummond and Doyle, seeing the danger, rushed out to meet the intruder. Unfortunately, Drummond got the ball at a bad angle and kicked it right in front of his own goal. It went up in the air and came bounding down in front of Anderson, and before any of the Scotch defenders had time to rectify the blunder Athersmith tipped the leather to Wheldon, and that player, posing only for a moment, sent it spinning into the net.

Wreford-Brown 'jumped for joy' and summoned Wheldon over. Dipping his hand into his pocket the England captain produced a gold sovereign and slipped it into the goalscorer's hand! When Bloomer put England 2–0 ahead in the twenty-third minute 'another sovereign came out of these mysterious pockets' and was slipped into the inside-forward's hands, which he handed to the referee Tom Robertson for safekeeping.

England dominated proceedings, while the Scots 'lacked cohesion and speed, and her representatives' play was, perhaps the poorest shown by an international team for years'. In particular, Needham's combination with Fred Spikesley and Fred Wheldon on the left stood out. 'Nothing in international football has been finer than that,' recorded Gibson and Pickford. 'The three men filled into one another's methods like hands into their proper gloves, and all the brilliance of the Scottish defence was dumbfounded and beaten.'[17] On seventy-two minutes Bloomer sealed a 3–1 win, with a side-footed shot that he hit beyond the grasp of the Scottish goalkeeper, Athersmith. Once more a gold sovereign was produced, which Bloomer again handed to Robertson, who joked: 'If you keep this up Steve, I shall have to go for my handbag!' Afterwards, Wreford-Brown invited all the England players to his rooms, where they celebrated victory with several bottles of champagne.

The turn of the nineteenth century brought rising anxieties about Britain's place in the world. Britannia still ruled the seas, vast swathes of Africa, the Indian sub-continent and could lay claim to being the dominant influence in Canada, Australasia and much else in between, but no longer was her hegemony unchallenged. Economic recession had seen Germany and the United States emerge as greater industrial and agricultural powers and the scientific and cultural heartbeat Britain had long given to world affairs began to develop symptoms of arrhythmia. The mood of uncertainty was heightened by several challenges to imperial and domestic rule: the Boers' invasion of Natal and Cape Provinces had escalated into war in autumn 1899; growing discontent was emerging on the streets of Ireland after Home Rule had been fudged a decade earlier; and disenfranchised women were preparing to wage a militant assault on government as they fought for the vote. Then, in January 1901, after sixty-four years on the throne, Queen Victoria died. The great certainties of the nineteenth century all seemed to be slipping away at once. Would Britain ever be great again?

While the nation's economic and cultural influence was diminishing, football, by contrast, was spreading quickly and expansively. Expatriates, sailors, visitors to British shores, and even, occasionally, visiting teams, were disseminating word of the game over land and sea, hill and field. Many of the European football associations and today's great continental teams owe their origins to this period. Milan was founded by an émigré Englishman in 1899; Juventus the same year; Real Madrid and Bayern Munich in 1900. Some clubs began touring the continent at the end of the domestic season, but on the international stage the FA refused to send over a full England team to face one of the emergent nations. The Home Championship was the centrepiece of international football – indeed it *was* international football: no second-rate continentals were going to imperil its sanctity.

In any case England had enough worries with the challenges thrown up by the other home nations. Despite retaining the Home

Championship in 1899 (when England's victories included a 13–2 victory over Ireland at Roker Park), winning it again in 1901, 1904 and 1905, and sharing it in 1903; intermingled in the glories of those tournaments were rather more traumatic days, both on and off the field. In April 1900 Scotland handed down a 4–1 thrashing in front of 63,000 fans at Parkhead; and on several other occasions England made hard work of the Welsh and Irish, sometimes failing to secure the win that was expected as a matter of routine. Off the field, events sometimes took on an even more epicedian complexion.

On Saturday, 5 April 1902, England met Scotland in the Home Championship decider at Ibrox. Predictably the stadium was full to capacity and probably beyond it. Play got under way under a typical sea of noise, and then, disaster struck. 'One minute the game was proceeding calmly and being keenly followed by the vast concourse,' recalled Steve Bloomer, who was lining up at inside-right.

> The next minute there was a terrible crash like the many peals of thunder in a great storm joining together in unison. The players stood as though rooted to the spot and there before our eyes we saw part of a huge stand, packed with people, crashing to the ground. The memory of that awful picture is still with me, with people crashing through iron railings as if they were matchwood. The groans, cries of fear and the uproar which followed beggars description.[18]

A wooden stand had collapsed plunging spectators forty feet through broken boards, killing twenty-six and injuring 500. Play continued, with the rest of the crowd and players largely unaware of the scale of what had happened. When, at half-time, the enormity of events struck home, J.C. Clegg, the FA chairman, was insistent the game was played lest its abandonment create more panic. Bloomer described it as the 'hardest moment' of his life when he learned that he would have to play on. He probably wasn't the only one. The second half was played out in a desultory manner and the result was subsequently scrubbed from the records. Nevertheless, it did little to wake up football's legislators to the necessity of sound crowd management.

Two years later, in March 1904, the England squad were reminded of English unpopularity in Ireland. Already the squad had tasted a portent of Irish hostility in 1902 when the England party had been invited to the Empire Music Hall after the match. It was a time when the Boer War was drawing to its conclusion and 'everything in the garden was lovely,' remembered Bloomer. 'Until photographs of British and Boer generals came on screen.' The British were booed relentlessly, the Boers cheered like heroes. Then from the 'gods' a hail of 'Irish confetti' showered the visitors. 'When a very high English official stopped an orange on his bald head [it was] the signal for us to depart.'[19] When Bloomer returned to Belfast, little had changed. After Ireland had taken a surprise early lead, as the England players were preparing to kick off Bloomer noticed two spectators jump over the railings. 'A few seconds later I nearly jumped out of the ground altogether when bang, bang, bang went revolver shots from behind me. There were two excited spectators firing shots into the air, a revolver in each hand and a merry dance on either leg.' Policemen returned them to their places in the stands and play recommenced. At the end of the game, as the players were getting into cabs to take them back to their hotel 'a perfect storm of grass sods, bottles and stones was rained in on us and there we were, officials and players, ducking and diving out of the line of fire. It was a pretty hot fusillade while it lasted but the driver, encouraged by our yells, put on speed and soon left the laughing crowd behind.'[20]

By the mid-1900s the England team was in something of a state of transition. G.O. Smith had left the international fray in 1901, after twenty caps and twelve goals. 'G.O. was a genius in football and like all geniuses he rose on stepping stones of his real self by taking infinite pains in terms of his natural gifts,' remembered C.B. Fry the Repton- and Oxford-educated scholar, Corinthian, Southampton and (on one occasion) England full-back. 'He swung a marvellously heavy foot in shooting, always along the turf and terrifically swift . . . in fact he was as straight and hard a shot as I have ever met . . . except perhaps only Steve Bloomer of Derby County, on one of Steve's special days.'[21] Bloomer himself would complete a big money transfer to Middlesbrough in 1905, but, already past his thirtieth birthday, was now something of a lesser light.

Other men, as ever, came in their place and some were to fill the England shirt illustriously. Blackburn Rovers' reluctant hero, Bob Crompton, a right-back, stepped up to international football in 1902 against Wales and would go on to make forty-one appearances for his country spanning twelve years. Born in Blackburn in 1879, the defender had been spotted playing for a Sunday league team by Rovers, but as an apprentice plumber, top-class swimmer and water polo player, didn't want to give up any of his interests by sacrificing his amateur status. As a compromise he joined Blackburn initially as an unpaid amateur. Although his distribution was not said to be the best, his defensive attributes more than compensated. 'He studies his opponents' tactics closely and develops an anticipation of their moves, which almost amounts to intuition,' noted one contemporary. He was, of course, a very different type of amateur to the likes of Smith, but the fact that he combined football (for which he was later paid) with a profession enabled him to be one of the first professional footballers to own a car.

One man who carried on the tradition famously set by Smith and others was Vivian Woodward, a forward with Tottenham Hotspur and later Chelsea, who clung on proudly to his amateur status despite never turning out for Corinthians. He was, reckoned the ubiquitous Gibson and Pickford, 'essentially a brainy player. He has no set style . . . Because Woodward has acted in a given manner once is a fairly good reason to think that he will not repeat himself.'[22] One facet of his play that was continually repeated was his scoring: no fewer than twenty-nine goals in twenty-three international appearances, a record that would neither be matched nor beaten until the 1950s.

Despite Woodward's prominence and eventual legendary status, amateur and professional football were still deemed to belong to different worlds. Certainly a rough and ready professional was no fit man to lead England. A captain, believed W.J. Oakley of Oxford University and Corinthians (and himself an England captain in the late 1890s), must possess three key attributes: 'a thorough knowledge of the men that form his eleven'; 'he must be able to form a quick judgement as regards altering the position of his men on the field'; 'thirdly, and above all else, he must remember to set a good example to play an absolutely fair game himself'.[23] Indeed the very future of football lay in the hands of captains and their maintenance of fair play. 'If he does this he will be doing very good work for football and will have earned the thanks of everyone who has the true interests of the game at heart.' Given the low regard in which professionals were held, mercifully there were amateurs to show them the way.

Yet it wasn't just differing standards of gentility that separated paid from unpaid. There was also, apparently, a different method of play between amateurs and professionals. G.O. Smith described it in 1899 when he wrote:

> That which we have called the amateur style is the faster of the two; every man on the side makes the best use of his pace, passes forward, not backwards, the object being to outrun the opposing backs and to reach the goal as quickly and with as little deviation as possible . . . In the second, or professional, style, the principle followed is quite different; the object is to reach goal, not by a straight or go-ahead course, but by degrees; the pass is made quite as often to a full-back or to a half-back or to a forward lying back as in the direction of goal.[24]

The aim, then, of the professional game was seemingly attrition – to gradually wear down the defence of the opposing 'back division' and hope that chances came along. The amateur game was, by contrast, all about attacking verve and speed and skill. 'There can indeed be no more pleasant a sight in the eyes of the appreciative onlooker,' believed Smith, 'than a line of forwards going straight down the field without swerving aside or turning back, but making direct for goal.' Maybe not, but to a contemporary eye there does seem to be some tactical naivety about the amateurs, and the professionals – were they really all that dour? Despite his apparent egalitarianism off the pitch, Smith was in no doubt that the Corinthians' game was inherently superior. The professional game, he believed, 'compares very unfavourably with what we have called the amateur system; the ball is passed and re-passed again and again with but little advantage to the side, and sometimes after a long period of manoeuvring no ground has been covered and the position of the game remains just as it was'.[25]

When England met Scotland at Hampden Park in April 1906, Smith's belief in the coarseness of the professional game seemed to carry some credence. By keeping one man at the back and pushing the rest of their defence within twenty yards of the Scottish goal line, with no rule about offside being restricted to the defender's half and the law insistent on three players being between the attacker and the goal at the moment of the pass forward, the Scots were trapped. Inside the rules of the game, but certainly outside its spirit, England caused consternation, but didn't reap success – Scotland won 2–1.[26] Nevertheless, the belief of S.S. Harris – present in the side that afternoon – that the amateurs were somehow being 'corrupted' seemed to be borne out: the visitors' tactics had infuriated the 100,000-strong Scottish crowd and would lead to months of debate about notions of fair play. The creation of an England amateur team in 1906 helped to address the dilemma of the amateurs' innocence and the FA's obsession with its protection. Amateurs still mixed with the professionals in the full international team, but henceforth their role became even less prominent, and claims about the merits of playing for fun and the vulgarity of playing for a living, equally, became less prevalent.

Still, there was a growing belief that international football was becoming dull and possibly irrelevant. The Home Championship, despite Wales's first success in 1907, was deemed a two-horse race between the English and the Scots. 'Internationals have lost their significance,' opined the *Daily Mail*. 'When we oppose Scotland, Wales or Ireland, we are not facing these countries, we are facing English football.' International crowds, in England at least, were frequently dwarfed by run-of-the-mill league fixtures; fans' passions and interest centred on the League Championship race or the FA Cup, where a mix and variety of opponents were present and anything could, and indeed did, happen.

Part of the problem came within the FA. So outward-looking and receptive to new developments in its first quarter century, it turned inwards thereafter and blithely ignored the game's rapid ascent across the rest of the world. Although they had sent a representative team to tour Germany in 1899, notions of international football within its headquarters at Holborn seemingly did not extend beyond the British Isles. A letter from the Dutch association in 1902 suggesting European unity, an international championship and uniformity of laws in all countries was met with indifference – perhaps surprisingly given the high priority usually given to the latter issue. A year later the French suggested a European federation, but again came up against the isolationist resolve of the English. 'The Council of the Football Association cannot see the advantages of such a Federation,' came the reply from the FA, 'but on all matters upon which joint action is preferable they would prefer to confer.'[27]

The two central figures pushing for an international federation, the Dutch banker Carl Hirshman and the Frenchman Robert Guérin, viewed England – the birthplace of the organised game – as the natural head of the sport. Yet even without the inventor's backing they boldly pushed forward with such plans. In May 1904 representatives from Belgium, Denmark, France, Holland, Spain and Switzerland met in Paris and founded the Fédération Internationale de Football Association (FIFA). At Holborn there was some surprise that the continentals had moved so swiftly and without English support, but a committee under Lord Kinnaird was appointed to review the situation. Despite nagging doubts about FIFA's definition of amateurism and its policy towards the game's laws there were some regrets about their earlier insularity. At an international conference in early 1905, the FA formally approved FIFA's existence, and eighteen months later at a FIFA conference in Berne, the home associations were invested into the new body. Guérin stood aside as the organisation's president and the FA Treasurer D.B. Woolfall took his place.

Despite embracing and even taking control of this fledgling organisation there was no radical change in attitudes within the Football Association. As far as internationals went, British football was still the patently superior brand: why waste time running rings around second-rate continentals? No FIFA member outside Britain would be invited to England until Belgium's visit in 1923, but perhaps imbued with the same sort of zeal that had prompted the very first international four decades earlier, the FA accepted an invitation for the England team to tour central Europe in June 1908. In front of crowds as tiny as the eventual scorelines were emphatic, England gave several shows of mastery: Austria were crushed 6–1 and 11–1, Hungary 7–0 and Bohemia 4–0. That same summer the England amateur team, with Vivian Woodward at the helm, strolled to victory at the London Olympics, a feat they were to repeat in Gothenburg in 1912. The full England team repeated their tour of the Habsburg domains in 1909, but again prevailed with rampant ease, which bordered on embarrassing. Hungary were defeated 4–2 and 8–2, Austria 8–1. Given the standard of opposition the FA took the decision, perhaps wisely, that the England amateur team would in future provide a more equal contest. Even their superiority was rarely threatened, with twenty-one wins in twenty-six matches and just three defeats.[28]

Domestically, football continued to thrive. The promotion of three London clubs – Chelsea, Tottenham Hotspur and Woolwich Arsenal

– to the top flight of the Football League ensured that at the very highest level the game prevailed as the national sport, and maintained interest south of Watford throughout the whole season. Attendances continued to rise and rise, so too did the very stature of the game. When King George V became the first monarch to attend the FA Cup final in 1914, *The Times* wrote of the occasion:

> In the last two or three years League matches at Stamford Bridge and elsewhere have been attended by persons to whom the dangerous epithet 'fashionable' might be applied. Professional football of the best kind is no longer regarded as a spectacle suitable only for the proletariat. The King's presence at the Cup final, let us hope, will put an end to the old snobbish notion that true-blue sportsmen ought to ignore games played by those who cannot afford to play without being paid for their services.

Internationally, the Home Championship continued largely as an epic struggle between England and Scotland, though that same year Ireland upset everybody (particularly England, whom they defeated 3–0 at Ayresome Park, Middlesbrough) and took the crown for the first time. Little did anyone know then that the trophy was to remain in the Emerald Isle for an inordinately long period.

The twentieth century's first decade and a half of international relations had seen a marked growth in rivalry between Britain and Germany. For most men familial rivalry would begin and end with competitions over the shiniest car or largest house; King George V's cousin Kaiser Wilhelm II upped the stakes by seizing (mostly worthless) chunks of Africa to try and compete with Britain's imperial holdings, and by lifting the size of the German naval fleet to rival that of the Royal Navy. True, it was ostensibly petty, but the peoples and governments of both countries whipped themselves into a state of high anxiety. Fatally, at the same time each nation embroiled itself in a web of alliances with neighbours near and far. In the summer of 1914, relations were not good, but neither were they explicitly martial. But then, on 28 June Archduke Franz Ferdinand, heir to the Austro-Hungarian throne, was assassinated by the Serbian student, Gavrilo Princip. In the weeks that followed, the stand-off between Austria-Hungary and Serbia became war, then, because of the disastrous tangle of alliances and mess of military planning, exploded into a continent-wide conflagration. When Germany invaded

Belgium on the morning of 4 August it placed a 'moral obligation' on Britain to rush to their Belgian ally's defence. Later that day, Britain declared war on Germany.

The outbreak of war brought an immediate dilemma: was it appropriate to begin the Football League programme less than a month later? Rugby union and cricket sharply concluded their programmes in a pique of patriotism but football's administrators gave the prospect greater consideration. As the Everton director, Thomas Keates, put it:

> The situation was bristling with perplexities for everybody. The directors decided to be guided by public opinion, in conjunction with the League and Football Association. To the impulsive, panic-stricken section of the community, the idea of any entertainments, or sporting games being tolerated, was unthinkable. The experienced governing bodies of the country were soon convinced that the wise and sound policy was to carry on, as far as it was possible, as usual. Every suspension would create additional unemployment, undermine the courage of the population, and be commercially and economically disastrous. Diversion and cheering entertainment was found to be the most essential tonic and sustainer for the men at the front as well as for those by the home fires.

The 'over by Christmas' mentality also prevailed. Yet the decision to continue with the Football League programme was the source of intense controversy. Clubs were accused of 'helping the enemy' and the Dean of Lincoln spoke for many dissenters when he wrote to the Football Association of 'onlookers who, while so many of their fellow men are giving themselves in their country's peril, still go gazing at football'. *The Times* published a letter on 8 September from the temperance leader N.F. Charrington to the King saying that the continuation of the game was a disgrace. Football, sullied unfairly by the furore over professionalism, now faced the charge of being unpatriotic and a distraction to the war effort. Newspaper campaigns castigated the sport, comparing it unfavourably to rugby and cricket; crowds dropped; and in the wave of jingoism that swept England, ill-feeling towards the game permeated.

By spring 1915 and with no end in sight to the fighting, thoughts of the Home Championship were waylaid and when the 1914–15 domestic campaign ended, so too did competitive football. Few then could have imagined that it would be another four years before a ball was again kicked in anger.

War changed football along with everything else, but few of the changes were more fundamental than the death of the gentleman footballer. After fighting ended the feeling still lingered that other sports, particularly rugby, had been more patriotic in 1914, as if the association game had fundamentally failed in its 'duty' to obey the sentiment of the day: putting everything down and throwing all its energy behind king and country. The number of rugby clubs increased post war, but more significant was the switch in codes by many public schools – irked by the idea that soccer had 'helped the enemy' – to the oval ball. Association football, the child of the public schoolboys and university men, became, more than ever, the preserve of the working class. As with so much of working-class culture, it subsequently became an object of thinly veiled disdain and was somehow seen as being a lesser game than those of Webb-Ellis and the willow. Sometimes it would be shunned or ignored; for a period it would actively be persecuted by government – as it had been when football was the game of the mob. Though in hearts and minds and sheer weight of numbers it remained the national sport, not until the 1990s, when football became gentrified, would it again be regarded as the staple of all social classes.

3

THE BIRTH OF WEMBLEY AND
INTER-WAR FOOTBALL

'PEACE,' THE FRENCH Prime Minister, Georges Clemenceau, once reflected, 'is harder to make than war.' After four and a half years of bitter, bloody fighting he, and the leaders of thirty-one other states, converged on Paris to agree a just settlement for its victors, and rather more onerous terms for its losers. It was January 1919, two months after an armistice had brought a conclusion to what Clemenceau's British counterpart, David Lloyd George, termed 'the war to end all wars'. The world had been turned on its head. Kaiser Wilhelm of Germany had abdicated; three of the planet's four great empires – those of the Ottomans, Habsburgs and Romanovs – had disintegrated virtually overnight; Marxist Bolsheviks had seized power in Russia, which had crumbled into the bloody chaos of civil war; Ireland had descended into outright rebellion, which would itself lead to civil conflict, brutal severance into two sectors and eventually independence for its southern rump; while the rest of Britain was only standing intact because of the self-serving generosity of American finance, to which it would seemingly remain indebted until almost the end of the century. More than 900,000 Britons lost their lives out of a total of more than 8.5 million dead on all sides.

When peace came, retribution was swift. It took just two months for the Paris Peace Conference to be convened, a year for the squabbling over punishment and divvying of spoils. Hopes of what any fair-minded individual would consider a 'just peace' were soon eroded. Clemenceau sought to send Germany back to the dark ages by imposing reparations worth a total of $23,000,000,000,000, a sum far in excess of what the defeated Germans could possibly afford – or anybody else for that matter. Lloyd George, who initially had no thought of exacting impossible amounts of reparation from Germany, had his hand forced by a British people perhaps understandably in the thrall of bitterness and jingoism. Parts of Germany were shaved off and handed to newly constituted rivals; the remainder was cast into international isolation and hit with the bill to end all bills. 'There is no subtler, no surer means of overturning the existing basis of society than to debauch the currency,' wrote the economist John Maynard Keynes in his great polemic, *The Economic Consequences of Peace*. 'One who, though an Englishman, feels himself a European also, . . . cannot disinterest himself from the further unfolding of the great historic drama of these days which will destroy great institutions, but may also create a new world.' Many blithely dismissed him as unpatriotic or a mere controversialist, yet it would be just two decades before the apocalyptic vision sinisterly hinted by Keynes would come to fruition, and Europe would again stand on the edge of the abyss.

Imbued with the spirit of the day, the Football Association announced that its national side would not play against any of the defeated powers, or, for good measure, any other nation who dared do so. FIFA's view that sport should transcend political differences held little sway: in April 1920 the home associations withdrew from the organisation. Although they briefly returned four years later, neither Wales nor Northern Ireland played a single match against non-British opposition in the 1920s, nor did Scotland until a brief European tour in 1929.[1] The Football Association would whinge from the fringes for much of this period but were not so wholly isolationist. Not infrequently during the 1920s they would engage the national team in friendlies with France, Sweden and Belgium (and once, Luxembourg), but it would be 1929 before they extended the hand of football friendship beyond this triumvirate.

Home internationals recommenced in the 1919–20 season. Four Victory Internationals with Scotland and Wales had preceded England's visit to troubled Ireland in 25 October 1919, but the visitors started their campaign unimpressively with a 1–1 draw. More dismal still was a 1–2 defeat by Wales at Highbury the following March. It was only Wales's second win on English soil and served as the prompt for England's selectors to ring changes for the crucial showdown of the international calendar – the meeting with Scotland.

The two great rivals met at Hillsborough on 10 April 1920. In a slumber against Wales and Ireland, England finally came to life, although it was to take seventy minutes for them to wake up. Days of spring showers had created a mud heap of a pitch, but rising above the mire, Chelsea's centre-forward, Jack Cock, had given England a tenth-minute lead. Three minutes later Tom Miller equalised for Scotland, but within ninety seconds Derby County's outside-left, Alfred Quantrill, had restored the advantage. 'Contrary to speculation,' reported Alfred Davis in the *Daily Mail*, 'England proved better in attack than defence. There was no failure in the forward line in which [Fred] Morris and [Bob] Kelly were the outstanding figures. Playing in an international match for the first time they showed the cool skill and resource of veterans combined with pace, dash and fine shooting power.' But the defence was porous and, aided by the fine finishing of Andrew Wilson, Alex Donaldson and Miller as well as the heroics of Kenneth Campbell between their goalposts, Scotland not only went in at half-time level, but two goals to the good.

Faced by a 2–4 deficit in pitiless driving rain, another defeat was imminent for England. Yet few of its forbears had possessed the extraordinary cut, thrust and spirit of this team's forward line. On sixty-seven minutes Kelly had pulled a goal back; within a minute Morris had made it 4–4; and five minutes later Kelly completed the comeback with England's winning goal. It had been 'a wonderful display of football of the very best class', recorded Davis; for England's left-back, Jesse Pennington, for whom it marked the last of twenty-five international appearances, it was 'the greatest match I ever played in'. 'It rained throughout the game,' he recalled,

> We hardly kept our feet, especially in the first half when we faced the wind and the rain . . . I felt at half-time we might still win and I told the team this. I have never seen such great football from two teams in such internationals. This was to be my last international, but it left a lasting impression not for that fact, but because of the craftsmanship of both sets of forwards.[2]

England's dramatic victory would be a rare ray of light in what was a bleak international era. It would be fully seven years before victory would again be recorded over the Scots, and ten until the Home Championship next came to rest outright on English soil. Part of the problem lay with the selection of teams by committee and the lack of continuity that this bred. Votes after trial matches between 'hopefuls' and 'likelys' or representative games between English and Scottish league XIs provided line-ups of men who were elevated to the

England team on the basis of a good showing, rather than the conviction that they would successfully fit into the side. If they failed to produce a sound performance on their international debut, matters would be compounded by their subsequent exile. Virtually every match England played saw evidence of failed experiments, trial by error, short-sighted planning. 'The English selectors of these days were not particularly intelligent in their methods,' recalled one of their latter charges, Cliff Bastin. 'With them, the emphasis always seemed to be laid on the individual performance of a player, rather than with the team as a whole. It was a queer and unsatisfactory system.'[3] Throughout the next ten years, the meetings with the Scots alone would see England use eight goalkeepers, eleven different full-backs, twenty-three half-backs (ten men shared the number six shirt alone), fourteen wingers, and seven centre-forwards.[4]

Still, meetings with the continentals helped sustain the myth of superiority. Victories such as the 6–1 win over Belgium in March 1923, 4–1 against France two months later and 4–0 and 9–1 against the Belgians in 1924 and 1928 showed, unequivocally, that the English were still masters. Moreover, if the Europeans had made progress, it hadn't been by much.

The FA, meanwhile, had made one rather more tangible contribution to the English game. The idea of holding a British Empire Exhibition had been talked of prior to the outbreak of war, and plans, long put on ice, had, by early 1921, with governmental and royal support, moved on apace. London's north-west suburb Wembley had been designated as the site and its centrepiece would be a 'great national sports ground' built on the ruins of Sir Edward Watkin's infamous tower, a folly that had been designed to rival the Eiffel Tower. (After structural and financial problems saw his project abandoned, Watkin's monument had been left like an incomplete Tower of Babel.) The FA were given an option on the stadium, and in May 1921 signed an agreement to host the FA Cup final there for the following twenty-one years. Work began twelve months later, and in just 300 days it was finished, with two domed towers dramatically adding to the north London vista.

Days after its completion, on 28 April 1923, Bolton Wanderers and West Ham United met in the new stadium for its first ever match – the FA Cup final. Two years earlier, when the FA had committed to Wembley, no one could have envisaged the extraordinary enthusiasm it would generate: now, everybody wanted to see the new stadium. Fans of both finalists turned out; supporters of fallen rivals; the curious; the fanatical; and those who simply sought to partake in a little bit of history. By 1 p.m. Wembley was full to its 127,000-strong capacity; by 1.45 p.m., when the gates were finally shut, an estimated 200,000 had filled every inch of the ground with tens of thousands stuck outside.[5] The game kicked off nearly an hour late, Bolton emerged 2–0 victors, and, miraculously, no one was killed or seriously injured. English football's new home had been born. A year later, on 12 April 1924, it would see its first international: a 1–1 draw with Scotland.

In Europe, the great folly of the Paris peace settlements had cruelly been brought to bear. When Germany was unable to meet its commitments, it printed more paper money as a short-term measure and hyperinflation and economic collapse set in. The French responded by invading the Ruhr Valley to try and expropriate what they were owed, but their aggression merely heightened the malaise. Elsewhere, nations unhappy with the injustices of lands and resources taken, or the perceived inequality of how they were redistributed, bristled with indignation. Some saw it as a cause for war; others, like Italy, took recourse in the politics of extremes. Everywhere, it seemed, fascist and communist political parties were growing in prominence, and standing on the fringes of the mainstream. Some rapprochement came with the Dawes Plan and the Locarno Treaty (December 1925), which respectively restructured German finances and obligations and guaranteed the frontiers of most European powers with a series of intertwined agreements. Goodwill was the order of the day at last, but the peace was as tentative as the stability of many of the continent's governments and economies.

In the midst of these slowly warming relations, in 1924, the British associations were persuaded to rejoin FIFA. Not that much changed: Sweden, Belgium, France and Luxembourg were still the only countries England deigned to play against, and disagreements over issues as diverse as 'charging' goalkeepers, substitutes and the status of amateurs were frequent. On the latter, where the principal point of contention was over 'broken-time' payments (a rule that authorised amateurs to be paid for time lost at work: in short, FIFA recognised the law; the British didn't) the British associations and FIFA were to fall out in spectacular fashion. At a conference between the Executive Committee of FIFA and the Executive of the International Olympic

Committee in August 1927, broken-time payments were authorised for the following year's Olympics in Amsterdam. The Football Association was furious. 'It is against all our standards, and I cannot think that England will ever accept it,' wailed H.J. Huband, one of the FA's main champions of amateurism. 'Such a ruling, in my opinion, will prevent us entering the Olympic Games, which were formed in the interests of pure amateur sport. If we did enter a team it would mean that our players would go straight.' Such a notion was, of course, utterly unacceptable to the home associations, who again withdrew their membership and returned to a state of splendid isolation.

Still, the mediocrity of the national side continued. A 3–3 draw against Northern Ireland in October 1926 handed the initiative in the Home Championship to the Scots once more, but more worrisome were the state of the team and the trail of results that they had left in their wake since the war's end. The meeting with Northern Ireland had been England's thirty-second post-war international, of which they had won just fourteen. Take away the nine wins from ten meetings with various whipping boys from the continent, and one is left with a truer reflection of the state of the malaise. As for the team itself – Albert McInroy, Warney Cresswell, Samuel Wadsworth, Willis Edwards, John Hill, George Green, Joseph Spence, George Brown, Norman Bullock, William Walker and James Ruffell – beyond fans of their respective clubs, the names of such figures evoke scant, if any, recognition now, or even in the more distant past. In short, there were no heroes, no legends, no individuals on the verge of steeping their name into the rich lore of the game; just a vacuum, in which the good, but not great, thrived, and sometimes not even that. Into the void, however, stepped an immortal figure.

On Merseyside, a twenty-year-old centre-forward with a rocket shot and bullet header, boasting the physique, strength and positional sense more commonly associated with men older and more experienced than his tender years, had been causing a sensation. Hailing from the 'third side of the Mersey' at Tranmere, his fantastic goalscoring exploits had soon attracted a nationwide flood of attention from leading clubs. For the prodigy there was, however, only one club, and in March 1925, William Ralph 'Dixie' Dean signed for his boyhood heroes, Everton. Dean was to be the dominant figure in football at club and international level in the late 1920s and early

1930s. Later his goalscoring feats were to become part of football folk-lore and his famous smile adorned postage stamps, Madame Tussaud's waxworks and the walls of the National Portrait Gallery amongst others. English football was his fiefdom and he ruled over it as master and king, ruthlessly punishing his opponents with countless goals.

Dean could shoot with either foot, hold up play, set up his fellow forwards and mix it with the best, but it was his phenomenal aerial ability for which he was most famed. 'The secret of heading is to catch it on your forehead,' he once explained. 'If you get it on top of your head it will knock you dead in no time. I was not as tall as many of the centre-halves I have played against, but I never had any difficulty beating them in the air. It wasn't a matter of leaping higher than they could. It was just a matter of going up at the right time.'[6]

Yet Dean's career, indeed his whole life, had nearly struck an abrupt halt before his twentieth birthday had been reached. Out with a girlfriend on a summer afternoon ride in North Wales in June 1926, a motorcycle combination, dodging in and out of traffic, crashed head on into his motorbike. The girl walked away almost unhurt but Dean suffered a horrifying catalogue of injuries that included a fractured skull, broken jaw, eye injuries, multiple bruising and con-cussion. He was unconscious for thirty-six hours and although fears that he might lose his life quickly receded, Everton's club doctor gloomily predicted that Dean would 'never play again'.

The footballer surprised everybody. His recovery was longwinded by his own impatient standards but from a medical perspective incredibly quick, and three months after the crash, in October 1926, he was playing for Everton again. By February of the following year, he was lining up for England against Wales in Wrexham, and marked his debut with a brace of goals in a 3–2 win. Seven weeks later, England travelled up to Hampden to face Scotland: could Dean replicate his magic?

England were without a win in Scotland since April 1904, when Steve Bloomer had scored the only goal of the game at Parkhead. It was a miserable run that everybody south of Hadrian's Wall was desperate to bring to an end. Tim Paton, the Yorkshire cotton millionaire, had offered £10 a man bonus if England could overcome the Scots, plus £10 per goal scored. For the England players, who received a measly £6 or a medal for each international appearance (despite the huge attendances), it was a significant amount. England, nevertheless, got off to a nervous start. ('While the English team were being photographed before the match I noticed that the knees of some of the players were chattering,' noted 'Broadcaster' in the *Daily Express*. 'It may have been due to the cold, but I *hae* my *doots*.') They fell behind to an Alan Morton strike. Dean, however, was never a man to pass up the opportunity of a goal – or a bonus. When Sidney Bishop sent him free in the sixty-fifth minute, he took little hesitation in hitting an equaliser past Harkness. As the minutes passed, a draw seemed the most likely conclusion, until Dean once more intervened. 'One defender came for him,' wrote 'Broadcaster', 'and then another, and then another. They all seemed around him, but although he did not seem to be travelling much faster than they were, he stuck to the ball like a leech, kept them off somehow, and, as the goalkeeper came out, slipped the ball neatly past him for the winner.' The Scottish crowd were dumbstruck. 'You've heard all about the Hampden roar,' recalled Dean. 'Well, when our first one went in you could have heard a pin drop. And when I got the second in the old onion bag I thought I was playing in a cemetery.'[7]

On England's summer tour, Dean hit hat-tricks against Belgium and Luxembourg and a brace against France. Not yet twenty-one, he had struck twelve goals in his first five games. 'We knew that we had a legend,' one Evertonian who grew up watching the striker remembered. 'Everybody was talking about him, his name was on every man's lips, even Liverpudlians. I can remember, I used to go and watch a local team and they had a centre-forward who had shaped himself on the great man, even to the point of his hairstyle – I don't know how he did it – but they used to call him "Dixie". That was just the way it was. He dominated the scene . . .'[8]

Dean's astonishing rise had coincided with a change to the offside law at the end of the 1924–25 season. The amendment reduced the number of opponents allowed between the attacker and goal line from three to two, which ostensibly seemed a minor alteration but the impact on the goals-for columns in league tables was immediate and dramatic. In the Football League the annual figure rose from 4700 in 1924–25 to a staggering 6373 the following campaign and, as defences struggled to get to grips with the new rule, it was boom time for strikers. George Camsell was the first major beneficiary, scoring fifty-nine goals for Middlesbrough in the Second Division during the 1926–27 season. Dean was to go one better than the Boro man, scoring an incredible sixty First Division goals in 1927–28. 'People ask me if that sixty-goal record will ever be beaten,' Dean later reflected. 'I think it will. But there's only one man who'll do it. That's the fella who walks on water. I think he's about the only one.'

However Dean's amazing form in the blue of Everton that season was not replicated in the white of his country. Defeats to Northern Ireland (0–2) and Wales (1–2) in autumn 1927 left England with the spectre of going through the Home Championships without a point to their name should they lose to Scotland in their final match, on 31 March 1928. Still, they had home advantage and, buoyed by Dean's form at Goodison, were confident of victory. Indeed, the Scottish team were dismissed by one English correspondent as being 'under-nourished'. That was probably a reference to their diminutive forward line, none of whom was taller than 5ft 7in: but on the vast terrain of the Wembley turf, Scotland were to stand apart as veritable giants. Despite having a let off in the opening minute when Nelson slipped and William Smith shot against a Scottish post, within two minutes the Scots had taken the lead, setting the tone for a rampant performance that would see the visitors lauded as 'Wembley Wizards'. 'In all the annals of international football I do not think there is a parallel to this match,' wrote J.H. Freeman in the *Daily Mail*. 'The inferiority of the England side was so marked that the confusion and bewilderment of individual players against the science and skill and pace of Scotland's dazzling team became positively ludicrous.' In total the Scots plundered five goals; England one, a last-minute free-kick from the boot of Robert Kelly offering scant consolation on a day when they had been played off the park. 'The success of the Scots,' added the *Glasgow Herald*, 'was primarily another demonstration that Scottish skill, science and trickery will prevail against the less attractive and simpler methods of the English style.' That opinion held as true then as it had for many of their meetings down the years: in fifty-two matches the Scots now had twenty-three victories; England just fifteen.

Though some confidence may have been restored by the customary thrashings handed out on that summer's tour of Europe, further blows were to come. Scotland again took the Home Championship in April 1929 after winning 1–0 in the decider with England, after Cheyne had scored directly from a corner kick two minutes from the end. Though France and Belgium were seen off 4–1 and 5–1 a month later, England came unstuck against continental opposition for the first time. In Madrid, on 15 May 1929, after journeying by train across Europe from Belgium, England took on Spain. Managed by the one time Middlesbrough and England winger Fred Pentland, the Spanish were an emerging football power. Domestically the country's two great teams, Real Madrid and Barcelona, were clubs of enormous wealth and support and Spain's national side was packed with superstars from each. Under a searing sun, England's pale-skinned players huffed and puffed until their faces were red with exertion, but still seemed to be heading for a 3–2 win after goals by Joseph Bradford and a brace by Joseph Carter. Then, with just minutes left, disaster struck. First, Jaime Lazcano pulled the scores level, and, with the 30,000-strong crowd screaming encouragement, Severino Goiburo grabbed a dramatic winner. After fifty-seven years of internationals, twenty-one of which had been contested against continental opposition, England had finally been beaten by a non-British team. The world was catching up.

England's decision to play Spain may have suggested a tempering of relations with FIFA, but this was certainly not the case. Over the obscure issue of 'broken-time' payments, football's codifiers and its world governing body remained utterly at loggerheads, leaving the British associations to sulk in the cold. To do so was to exclude them from international football's next big development.

FIFA had long discussed the idea of a football world cup and the French – as with the creation of so many of the game's great institutions – led the way. Football, of course, already had the Olympic Games, but the tediously intractable problem of amateurism prevented it from being representative of the game's best talent, even if not all its entrants followed the Corinthian ethos with the same obtuse diligence as the British. At FIFA's congress in 1926, the Fédération Française de Football (FFF) Secretary Henri Delaunay proclaimed: 'Today international football can no longer be held within the confines of the Olympics; and many countries where professionalism is now recognised and organised cannot any longer be represented there by their best players.' An inaugural competition, hosted by Uruguay (who had generously offered to pay all the accommodation and transport costs of the entrants), was staged in 1930. Inevitably, the British associations declined to enter, though they were not alone. Just four European nations – Belgium, France,

Romania and Yugoslavia – made the trip to South America, where they were joined by nine others. Of the Europeans only Yugoslavia made it past the qualifying round, but were crushed 6–1 by Uruguay, and the hosts went on to defeat Argentina 4–2 in the first World Cup final.

After years of war, recession and reconstruction, the late 1920s had, for much of the world, been boom years. Culturally, commercially, technologically, 'The Roaring Twenties' were good times, with living standards rising and people richer, healthier and, if not happier, certainly more comfortable than ever before. Radio, 'talkie' films, cars, even package holidays added new dimensions to the ordinary working man's existence. The General Strike of 1926 was a salutory reminder that many still trod a fine line between mild prosperity and dire poverty but, in general, they were more contented times than most had ever known. This came to an abrupt halt. On 29 October 1929, after a month of dramatic decline, the Wall Street stock exchange crashed, taking with it nearly half of its earlier market value. It shattered business confidence, dried up American investment abroad, stopped the flow of trade and plunged the world into economic depression. In Britain, unemployment rose dramatically, though less so than in Germany or the United States, or other parts of Europe. A coalition government was formed with the avowed intention of economic reconstruction in September 1931; but elsewhere in Europe, extremists on the left and right, who had lingered long on the political fringes, suddenly came to the fore. The continent stood on the epoch of another age of extremes.

Dixie Dean had experienced differing fortunes since his famous sixty-goal haul in 1928. Everton had stormed to the league title that season, but injuries had subdued his prowess in the subsequent campaign (although he had still managed twenty-six goals in thirty League and FA Cup appearances) and the 1929–30 season (when he scored twenty-five in twenty-seven starts) when Everton were relegated. Yet his fame and reputation preceded him wherever he went. In an age without European club football, when even international football was seldom played beyond the confines of home internationals, it was difficult for a player to make a name for himself outside his home country, and sometimes even county. English football – though regarded by its own public as the best in the world – was isolated by technological handicaps and the reluctance of the Football Association to engage in more ties with 'foreign' nations. Television was still confined to Logie-Baird's laboratory, cinema footage limited to the occasional Pathe news clip and radio broadcasts were in their infancy. Even friendlies against other European nations were a rarity: of Dean's sixteen England caps only six came against countries from outside Britain. Given all these factors, the chance of a player being well known, much less as a legend, outside his own league was difficult, if not near impossible.

Dean was different. His sixty-goal haul and feats for Everton and England had brought him not only immortality on Merseyside, but worldwide fame. In John Keith's excellent biography of the player, he recalls an anecdote from the late actor Patrick Connolly.* During the Second World War, Connolly was based in the western desert when he had to take an Italian prisoner. Furious at being captured, the Italian spat into the sand and cursed 'Fuck a ya Weenston Churchill and fuck a ya Deexie Dean!' Even the American baseball legend Babe Ruth insisted on meeting Dean when visiting London in the late thirties.†

Nevertheless, Dean's chances to prove himself beyond the domestic stage were limited to his intermittent overseas tours with Everton and a handful of 'foreign' internationals. The last of these came in December 1931 against Spain at Highbury. Spain's star was their goalkeeper Ricardo Zamora, like Dean, one of the few players of the time whose fame transcended his nation's borders. Zamora had been signed by Real Madrid from Barcelona a year earlier for a world record fee (for a goalkeeper) of £6000. He had just received a £3000

---

* Best known by his stage name 'Bill Dean' – taken in honour of his hero – or as *Brookside*'s Harry Cross.
† Ruth's request to meet him was unconnected to Dean's minor fame on the baseball field. In the summer of 1934 Dean joined a local baseball club, the Caledonians. Baseball was at the time highly popular in the north-west and Dean immediately took to the sport, even representing England.

bonus from Real, who paid him £40 per week – five times as much as Dean. To much excitement, the game was billed as the world's greatest goalkeeper against its best striker; moreover it provided an opportunity for England to avenge their 1929 meeting, when Spain had been the first 'foreign' team to beat them. Zamora, however, was a prima donna. He insisted on playing in ridiculous rubber knee-caps and prefaced his appearance with a catalogue of overly theatrical dives. When hostilities opened on the pitch, Dean was to upstage him, setting up England's first and scoring the last in a 7–1 thrashing.

Dean's last England appearance came ten months later, against Northern Ireland in Blackpool. He failed to add to his total of eighteen international goals (England won 1–0, with Barclay scoring the winner) and bowed out with sixteen caps to his name at the age of twenty-five, a tally he would surely have bettered were it not for the often baffling whims of the selectors. In one game, out the next, back two matches later, this constant state of flux was the order of the day. Little wonder then that Dean was limited to sixteen caps, little surprise that other great players of the day won fewer still. More meddlesome than ever before, the selectors had been damned in a 1930 article in *Athletic News*, which coloured the picture of indecision and tinkering with hard facts. 'In the eleven seasons before the Great War,' wrote 'Rover', 'England used ninety-nine different players, forty-seven in defence and forty-two in attack. In the eleven seasons of full internationals since, however, England have picked no less than 145 players (eighty-one in defence and sixty-four in attack) for the same number (thirty-three) of matches. *And sixty-six of them have still to gain a second cap.*'[9]

Yet bestriding English football in the 1920s and early 1930s was a revolutionary figure, whose influence would eventually change the fundamental nature of the way in which clubs and eventually the national team were run. If Dixie Dean was the star of the era, Huddersfield Town and Arsenal were its great teams, and leading them to unprecedented runs of success was their inspirational manager, Herbert Chapman. Born in Kiveton Park, Yorkshire, in January 1878, Chapman had played out the indistinct career of a journeyman, before turning his hand to management with Northampton Town, Leeds City and, crucially, in 1920, Huddersfield Town. Most clubs then only employed a 'secretary manager' – part administrator, part selector. He was expected to function as a middleman between the coach, captain and team, and members of the board, who retained the last word on selection. The role of captain was more like that of a modern international cricket captain. He had a say in team selection and tactics (if there were any – most players had a notorious aversion to such matters) and to an extent was responsible for the daily running of the team in partnership with the coach. Yet they were, wrote Chapman's biographer Stephen Studd, 'days when teams took to the field without an overall plan of how they were to set about winning, when the only initiative that came from management was to encourage friendships in the team so that players were more ready to discuss tactics among themselves.'[10] Chapman himself was contemptuous of the state of affairs, recalling of his own playing days that 'no attempt was made to organise victory. The most that I remember was the occasional chat between, say two men playing on the same wing.' He developed a tactical framework around which his teams played and developed revolutionary new tactics, such as the centre-half 'stopper'. The board of directors were confined to the administrative running of the club, the manager, largely to the team, although, in Chapman's case, his position was all pervasive and he involved himself in everything from the renaming of the local tube station to the pioneering of floodlights.

He reaped enormous success in West Yorkshire and north London. At Huddersfield he won the FA Cup in 1922 and the Division One Championship in 1924 and 1925, and the Terriers side he had built won it for a third consecutive year after he abdicated the Leeds Road hot-seat to go to Highbury. Arsenal, much like Huddersfield when he had arrived in 1920 – having led a largely nomadic existence in their formative years – were a side without any great record of success. Chapman took five years to bring a trophy to Highbury – the 1930 FA Cup – but by then had created a side capable of more: a team that would win five League Championships in the decade that followed.

Impressed by his incredible record, the Football Association made him the first professional manager to travel with the England team when they journeyed to Rome, to face Italy in May 1933. He gave a team talk beforehand, lost the dressing-room key at half-time and was pleased enough with a credible 1–1 draw. But it was not, however, his team. The regal responsibility of actually picking it had fallen – as ever – to the fourteen-man International Selection Committee. Although it may have been appropriate for the committed enthusiasts of

Charles Alcock's generation to pick fellow amateurs, by the 1930s the board of selectors was an anachronism and Chapman knew it. 'The idea might be startling,' he wrote soon afterwards,

> but I would like the English selectors to choose twenty of the most promising young players in the game and arrange for them to be brought together once a week under a selector, a coach and a trainer. The object of it would be to enable them to go out and practice with definite schemes planned . . . If this proposal were carried out, I think the result would be astonishing . . . I must say I have no hope of this international building policy being adopted . . . But it is on these new lines that some of the continental countries are working.[11]

Whether his lack of confidence was misplaced or justified remains to be seen. Certainly Chapman's mantra that the impossible was achievable could have eventually carried the day and seen him installed as England manager, but fate, in this instance, turned against him. Seven months later he was dead. His insistence on watching Arsenal's third team in the chill winds of January 1934 brought him a dose of pneumonia that proved fatal. His apostle, George Allison, carried on the good work initiated by him at Arsenal, but not until Arsène Wenger's arrival sixty-two years later would a man with such charisma and vision rule over Highbury's marble halls; for England, it would be just thirty years, but only then because the hegemony of the International Selection Committee had become a complete embarrassment. With a man of Chapman's force and conviction lurking in the shadows, maybe, just maybe, they may not have clung on for so long.

The team that Herbert built nevertheless dominated the ranks of the England side. When England played a return with Italy – freshly crowned world champions – in November 1934 there were seven Arsenal men in the line-up (appropriately the game was played at Highbury). In goal was Frank Moss, who had emerged to vie for the number one jersey with its long-term custodian, Henry Hibbs; Edris (Eddie) Hapgood filled the left-back berth and took the captain's armband; on the opposite side of defence was the tall elegant figure of George Male; Wilf Copping, a rough tough left-half who brought to the team the sort of gritty elegance one would expect from a man who not only hailed from the Yorkshire coalmining belt but had served down the pit too; and the inside-right, Edwin Bowden, came in for his second cap. But the two golden boys of the Arsenal and England team were Ted Drake and Cliff Bastin.

The shy, imperceptible figure of Bastin – dubbed 'Boy' by his Highbury colleagues – was every bit the prodigy Dean had once been. He had made his debut for Exeter City at fifteen, Arsenal at seventeen, England at nineteen, and by his twenty-first birthday, a year prior to the Italy match, had won every major honour in the game. A winger and inside-right of skill and swerve, Bastin often dropped deep and took up play from there; a thunderous shooting ability aided a stunning strike rate that had seen totals as magnificent as the thirty-three league goals, largely from the right wing, in the 1931–32 season. 'Though neither fast nor exceptionally clever, Bastin was one of the greatest footballers of his generation,' Charles Buchan – one of his Highbury forbears – would write of him. 'He had an ice-cool brain and always seemed to be in the right place at the right time.'

Bastin's forward partner, Ted Drake, was an individual blessed with a similarly prolific goalscoring record. The twenty-three-year-old had joined Arsenal from Southampton only the previous March in a huge £6000 deal and would be central to the club's continued success after Chapman's untimely death. Tough, abrasive and direct, 'there was no finesse about Drake,' his Highbury colleague, Bernard Joy, reported. 'He went for the ball in a blunt, uncompromising way. A human dynamo, big-hearted and well-built, he had great speed and a powerful shot.'

There was one other prodigy lining up for England that December afternoon in north London. Stanley Matthews may have played for unglamorous Stoke City, but the nineteen-year-old winger's fantastic exploits had already earned him nationwide renown. A dribbler, feinter and swerver, Matthews' dashing football typified an era when, for most players, the emphasis rested on entertainment and victory often came a close second in the scheme of priorities. Yet Matthews himself was imbued with the dedicated mindset of a winner, undertaking a relentless and diligent training routine that began every morning at dawn – this in addition to the exercise schedule at the club – and saw him follow a fastidious diet, abstaining from cigarettes and alcohol. A maverick, Matthews was a man destined for a place among the football gods. He had made his international debut six weeks earlier in the 4–0 win over Wales, marking the occasion with a goal;

the challenge now was to add to his burgeoning fame against the world champions.

'Once in the dressing room,' Matthews recalled, 'the importance of the game got to me. The butterflies fluttered about in my stomach and having changed first, yet again, I walked around the dressing room attempting to chat to my team-mates in an effort to ease my tension.'[12] The referee called the players and, studs clanking on concrete, they made their way onto the Highbury turf to a roar from a crowd of 56,000 (that included many of the local expatriate Italian community). Pleasantries were exchanged, play got under way and the realisation soon struck the young winger that this would not be an afternoon for the faint of heart. 'From the very first tackles,' he remembered, 'I was left in no doubt that this was going to be a rough house of a game.' Just two minutes had passed when Monti crunched the colossus Drake and came off unquestionably worse, leaving the pitch with a broken foot. His injury merely raised the ire of the World Cup-holders, and tackles fair and foul continued to fly.

Rising above the maelstrom was Stanley Matthews. Receiving a pass from Copping he took off down the wing, heading straight for the opposing defender Luigi Allemandi. Matthews swerved one way, the Italian the other, and suddenly the Stoke man was free. Looking up, he saw Eric Brook charging towards the far post from the opposite wing. Matthews spun a cross in, and Brook met the ball at full pelt, sending it soaring past Ceresoli and into the back of the Italian net. Highbury exploded into a deafening cheer.

Five minutes later England's lead was doubled. Bastin was cynically hacked down by Ferraris just outside the Italian penalty area. Brook was entrusted with the free-kick, but while the Italians expected a cross to the head of Drake, the left-winger hit an unstoppable strike that, in the words of Matthews 'nigh on ripped the net from the stanchions'.[13] The Italian goalkeeper Carlo Ceresoli stood crestfallen as Highbury once more erupted.

The Italians' response was robust – in attacking both the England goal, and its players. Bertolini smashed Eddie Hapgood in the face with his elbow, flattening the captain's nose, and he left the field with blood pouring from the wound; tackles flew in thunderously from both sides; the Italians rained down shots on Moss, testing the resolve of him and his defence to the limit. But just as the visitors seemed to be clawing a way back into the game, Drake latched onto a long ball and tore away, hitting a fearsome shot past Ceresoli to make it 3–0 to England. The world champions were reeling.

Drake soon paid the price for his effort, receiving a high, hard tackle that left a gaping wound in his calf. Bloodied and in tears, he was stretchered off. More tackles, kicks and even punches came, but England began to fight back in what was becoming the 'Battle of Highbury'. Leading the charge was Wilf Copping. 'It was dirty trick after dirty trick until me and Jack Barker [the Derby centre-half] showed them what tackling was all about,' he wrote with relish. The left-half was a hardman of renown, a player who wouldn't shave in the days leading up to a match because he felt it added to his intimidating visage (although he was never once sent off or even cautioned); who, it was joked, had not been signed by George Allison, but had been 'quarried'. He stood 'about 5ft 9in and sturdily built, the vast expanse of his forehead sat above a brutalised nose and a bristling square jaw,' the esteemed *Daily Mirror* correspondent, Ken Jones (who was later to come under Copping's supervision while a novice professional), would write of him. 'Utterly contemptuous of cowardice, his hardness was legendary. He taught tackling from the top down, "forehead in first", and stressed the importance of numerical superiority. In the days before substitutes, "It's easier to play against ten men than eleven, even easier against nine" was one of his favourite expressions. No wonder the Italians flinched from him.'[14]

Some of the visitors might have shuddered at Copping's antics, but it was the home dressing room at half-time that resembled a casualty ward. 'The language and comments coming from my England team mates made my hair stand on end,' recalled Matthews. 'I was still only nineteen, but came to the conclusion that I'd led a sheltered life.' Hapgood returned for the second half to a chorus of approval from the Highbury faithful, his shirt resplendent with the crimson stains of his earlier wound; but after conceding three first-half goals, it was the Italians who dictated the second period. Giuseppe Meazza struck goals two minutes either side of the hour-mark to bring Italy right back into the game, but England defended staunchly and heroically and clung on for a famous 3–2 victory.

Defeating the world champions boosted English pride and prestige at a time when it was still recovering from the dismal twenties, and amongst its fans helped restore the faltering expectation that football's mother nation could lead the world, even if the idea that they *should* do so never quite died. England had won the Home Championship in 1930 and 1932 and would share it in 1931 and 1935, while the Scots, for the first time, had been overtaken as England's great rivals for the crown by Wales. Of course every man who represented his country – whomever it may be – played for pride and victory, but for some nations football, and sport in general, had become more than just a game. Leaders extolling the superiority of their people would increasingly, in the absence of war, use football as a battlefield, an arena in which the greatness of their nation could be brought to bear over another. Benito Mussolini was the first to seriously pursue this line, and suggestions of a fix had hung darkly over Italy's 1934 World Cup victory. Even against England, rumours pervaded about fantastic inducements – offered directly from Il Duce himself – for an Italian victory, which included Alfa Romeo cars and much-coveted exemption from military service. Little wonder, perhaps, that the Italians had fought so relentlessly and been imbued with such brutality.

Mussolini was not the only European leader aggressively extolling the legend of his nation's greatness. In Germany, its people troubled since the end of the war by debts, hyperinflation, unstable democracy, unemployment and yet more economic collapse in the wake of the Wall Street crash, had taken the radical option in January 1933, and plumped for Mussolini's fascist ally, Adolf Hitler. With swift brutality, the Nazi leader had swept away the apparatus of German democracy, plunged into the country's economic and domestic problems head on, and set about re-establishing Germany's place on the world stage. For Europe, German revanchism had by the mid-1930s become a niggling worry; for political, religious and ethnic minorities within the Reich, Hitler's intolerance and inherent belief in Aryan superiority offered rather more pressing concerns.

England met Hitler's Germany at White Hart Lane on 4 December 1935. Five years earlier in Berlin the two countries had played out a 3–3 draw in a game that for many had symbolised an end to the bitterness which had pervaded in the wake of the Great War. Though England had met Fascist Italy on home and foreign soil, the visit of the fledgling German dictatorship's footballers threw up a different proposition. Only a week before the game the General Secretary of the Trade Union Congress (TUC) had written to the Home Secretary, John Simon, asking him to ban the match because they feared a German motorcade with displays of swastikas riding through the centre of London. 'There will be a grave risk, in view of public opinion in this country of serious disturbances of the peace, if an attempt is made to carry out the game.' Simon was dismissive in his response: 'Wednesday's match has no political significance whatsoever and does not imply any view of either government as to the policy or institutions of the other. It is a game of football, which nobody need attend unless he wishes, and I hope that all who take an interest in it from any side will do their utmost to discourage the idea that a sporting fixture in this country has any political implications.'[15] Simon was right to an extent, and TUC fears were grossly exaggerated although fourteen anti-fascist protesters were arrested before the game.

Yet at the same time there was a kind of expectation within the British government that as representatives of the country, it was the duty of the football authorities and the footballers too to do the government's bidding for it. Obedience is, of course, one of the central tenets of Englishness. In this case it meant pandering to far from benign regimes as part of its infamous policy of appeasement. For instance, the Football Association approved the flying of the swastika flag – a symbol of anti-semitism fluttering high above the home of one of Europe's few great Jewish clubs. This ill-conceived gesture was just one of several during this era designed to sustain the approval of Europe's resurgent far right. Football, it seemed, had achieved such primacy that it had become an instrument of diplomacy. The expectation that every man would 'do his duty' meant toeing the line of Baldwin and Chamberlain's governments.

Amidst all this controversy a football match was played that was an otherwise peaceful affair. England won 3–0 and the German goalkeeper, Hans Jakob, would recall in his 1949 memoirs: 'After the game we received ovations and cheers as seldom before abroad. This was London, this was the people of the motherland of football.'[16]

If there were any doubts about Nazi Germany's intentions, Hitler soon made them abundantly clear. Three months after the match at Tottenham German troops reoccupied the Rhineland (which had been demilitarised after the Paris Peace Conference) and in the summer of 1936, at the Berlin Olympics, a display of Nazi and German strength in propaganda, if not sporting achievement, was shown to the world. Later that year both Italy and Germany began supplying Franco's fascists in the Spanish Civil War. Britain, ham-strung by a financial straightjacket, purportedly turned a blind eye and Winston Churchill's 'All Party Group Opposed to Nazism' accused the Prime Minister, Stanley Baldwin, of 'appeasement'. By early 1938 it is doubtful that even Churchill could have summoned a masterplan to check Hitler's advances. On 11 March 1938, Germany forcibly incorporated Austria into the Reich. Weeks later, German nationals living in Czechoslovakia began to make noises about their treatment under a 'foreign' government and Hitler himself began to publicly question Czechoslovakia's validity. Was this Germany's next target? In the midst of all this, on 14 May 1938, the football teams of England and Germany met in Berlin's Olympic Stadium. That day politics and football would become tangled as never before.

'I've kicked a football into Mussolini's lap in Rome, and experienced the worst refereeing of my life in Milan,' England's captain Eddie Hapgood recalled.

> I've been to Switzerland, Rumania, Hungary, Czechoslovakia, Holland, Austria, Belgium, Finland, France, Norway, Denmark, Sweden and Yugoslavia. I've eaten garlic until I've never wanted to eat another thing in my life . . . I've seen the oil wells of Poletsi, the gondolas of Venice, beautiful Vienna, and all the other great cities of Europe. I've been V-bombed in Brussels before the Rhine crossing, bombed and 'rocketed' in London, I've been in a shipwreck, a train crash, and inches short of a plane accident . . . but the worst moment of my life, and one I would not willingly go through again, was giving the Nazi salute in Berlin.[17]

No one incident in the history of British sport has caused such consternation and controversy; no single event has come to symbolise five years of British appeasement of Nazi Germany more than the moment England's footballers gave the 'Heil Hitler' salute one May afternoon in 1938.

The common thread of events tells of supplicant FA officials being ordered by Britain's arch-appeaser, its ambassador Sir Neville Henderson ('Our Nazi in Berlin'), to give the salute for the betterment of Anglo-German relations and to keep the baying mob of a Nazi crowd quiet. The England players argued vociferously against the idea, but, against their will gave the salute, before ultimately winning the day, thrashing a team of 'Aryan supermen' 6–3. The myth perpetuated and grew over six decades, starting with Eddie Hapgood's account (published in 1944) and carried on over decades until it was memorably addressed by Stanley Matthews in his 2001 autobiography, *The Way It Was*.

Though the recollections of Hapgood and Matthews sometimes contradict each other, their essence remains the same. Hapgood claimed that uproar had been caused at the Berlin Olympics two years earlier when British athletes gave neither the Nazi salute, nor, as most countries had done, the Olympic salute (right arm flung sideways, not forward and upward like the Nazi salute). Seeking to avoid a repeat of the controversy, Charles Wreford-Brown (himself an England captain in the 1890s) and the new FA Secretary Stanley Rous visited Sir Neville Henderson some days prior to the match. He apparently told the FA men that it was not only an act of courtesy, but, moreover, necessary 'in order to get the crowd in good temper'. According to Matthews' version the players were then not told until just minutes before the match, when an unnamed FA official came into the dressing room and told the players the sorry news.

'The dressing room erupted,' recorded Matthews. 'There was bedlam. All the England players were livid and totally opposed to this, myself included. Everyone was shouting at once. Eddie Hapgood, normally a respectful and devoted captain, wagged his finger at the official and told him what he could do with the Nazi salute, which involved putting it where the sun doesn't shine.'*

The official left the room, only to return several minutes later, saying that it had been a direct order from Sir Neville Henderson himself and it had been rubber stamped by Rous. The players were

---

* Hapgood, by contrast had earlier claimed that Rous and Wreford-Brown had summoned him and given him instructions to which the captain responded: 'We are of the British Empire and I do not see any reason why we should give the Nazi salute.' He then went to give the squad the unhappy news, and Wreford-Brown and Rous later repeated the order. 'Privately he told us that he and Mr Rous felt as sick as we did,' added Hapgood, 'but that, under the circumstances, it was the correct thing to do.'

told that the political situation in Europe was so grave that only the slightest spark would light the fuse of war.

Furious, the players trotted down four flights of stairs from the changing rooms (they were situated high in the stands) and made their way out onto a pitch surrounded by swastikas and watched over by such Nazi luminaries as Hermann Goering, Rudolf Hess and Joseph Goebbels. The players, believed Hapgood, 'sensed that this was not merely a football match, but something deeper, a challenge from Germany which England had to answer, and not only answer, but to defeat.'[18]

On the pitch the players lined up, readying themselves for what was to happen. In footage shown a million times, Hapgood looked down the line – and this is incontrovertible – seems to visibly wince as he and his team-mates raise their arm for the playing of the German national anthem, and then drop them again, less than a minute later.

Hapgood won the toss and elected to play with the setting sun behind him. Looking over at the Germans he thought: 'This, then, was the mighty German team, which had been chosen with as much thoroughness as if it was destined to be Hitler's personal bodyguard. For months past, the Nazi soccer chiefs had been holding trials, had searched and tapped the football resources of the Reich, had discarded this player and that, and had even gone into over-run Austria for the pick of their talent, in an endeavour to discover a combination capable of taking on England's best.'[19]

During the pre-match kick in, Matthews went to retrieve a loose ball, when something incredible happened. Two lone voices, from 'the sea' of Nazi flags called out: 'Let them have it Stan. Come on England!'

Sixty years later, in his autobiography *The Way it Was*, Matthews would recall:

> I scanned the sea of faces and the hundreds of swastikas before I saw the most uplifting sight I have ever seen at a football ground. There, right at the front of the terracing were two Englishmen who had draped a small Union Jack over the perimeter fencing in front of them. Whether they were civil servants from the British Embassy, on holiday or what I don't know, but the brave and uplifting words of those two solitary English supporters among 110,000 Nazis had a profound effect on me and the rest of the England team that day.[20]

Matthews pointed out the two men with the union jack to his team-mates, who were immediately 'galvanised, determined and uplifted' by the supporters' show. Later, Matthews would admit: 'Up to that point, I had never given much thought to our national flag. That afternoon however, small as that particular version was, it took on the greatest symbolism for me and my England team-mates. It seemed to stand for everything we believed in, everything we had left behind in England and wanted to preserve. Above all, it reminded me that we were not after all alone.'[21]

England played well from the start. In the first minute Frank Broome forced Hans Jakob into the first of many saves, setting the tone for an opening quarter-hour which saw England largely camped in the hosts' half. Willingham's free-kick went narrowly over; Bastin shot inches wide and Broome, who normally played on the wing with Aston Villa but was employed against Germany as a roving centre-forward, caused the opposition defence endless problems with his pace, skill and mobility, likewise Matthews. Two and a half years previously, when the countries had last met, he had been almost wholly subdued by Reinhold Münzenberg, a beast of a left-back ('built like a Coca-Cola machine,' according to Matthews, 'and with a neck that looked like it could dent an axe') whose exemplary defensive performance that day had even caused the young winger to call his own extraordinary talents into question. Thirty months on, Matthews was tormenting him with abandon, flying past him again and again. On one such occasion the Stoke man set up Len Goulden, whose thunderous shot was only palmed away by Jakob as far as Bastin, who volleyed the loose ball home. 1–0 England, the crowd were silent. Four minutes later Germany were level when Gellesch scrambled home a corner, and though the hosts had a goal disallowed soon after, for the rest of the half it was all England. Debutant Jackie Robinson headed home Bastin's cross to make it 2–1 and three minutes later, Broome reacted fastest to Goulden's long ball, took it past Goldbrunner ('like a trout slipping round a rock' wrote the *Sunday Dispatch* correspondent) and slammed a shot past Jakob. Then, on forty-one minutes, the arch-tormentor Matthews took off on a dribble just inside his own half. Weaving a path through the German defence he caught a clear sight of goal, and slipped the ball past Jakob to make the score 4–1. Germany pulled a goal back from another corner on the stroke of half-time, but it was the visitors who were in buoyant mood as they made the long march up to the dressing room at the interval. 'We took to that walk,' recalled Matthews, 'as if we were a group of high-spirited lads making our way to the local pub for a night out.'[22]

The best was still to come. Jackie Robinson added a fifth, and though Pesser pulled another goal back for the Germans, Matthews was still to make one more divine intervention. Fifteen minutes from time a series of one-touch passes found the winger wide on the right and he took off on another march forward. Running directly at the hapless Münzenberg Matthews criss-crossed his legs over the ball, swept it with the outside of the right boot around the full-back and followed it. 'I glanced across and saw Len Goulden steaming in just left of the centre of midfield, some thirty-five yards from goal,' he remembered.

I arced around the ball in order to get some power behind the cross and picked my spot just ahead of Len. He met the ball at around knee-height. My initial thought was that he'd control it and take it on to get nearer the German goal, but he didn't. Len met the ball on the run; without surrendering any pace, his left leg cocked back like the trigger of a gun, snapped forward and he met the ball full face on the volley . . . from twenty-five yards the ball screamed into the roof of the net with such power that the netting was ripped from the two pegs by which it was tied to the crossbar.

It was, reckoned Matthews more than sixty years later, 'the greatest goal I ever saw in football'.

'Let them salute that one,' yelled Goulden as he carried on running arms aloft.[23]

The game was beyond Germany, victory had been secured. 'We had won 6–3, perhaps one of the greatest wins of all time by an English soccer side,' recalled Hapgood, 'certainly the most satisfactory.'[24]

Events on the pitch are beyond dispute, even if some of Matthews' details do seem like the embellishments of an old man; off it, those recounted make convincing and convenient reading given the benefit of hindsight. Yet at the time, the furore stoked by the salute was less intense than it seems now. In the days that followed *The Times* noted that giving it had 'made a good impression', and L.V. Manning in the *Sunday Graphic* thought that the match had been 'set off on the right note'. Several other newspapers mentioned the gesture with approval, but some were critical. 'The FA have blundered badly,' wrote Paul Irwin in the following week's *Reynolds News*; things were 'getting to a sorry pitch when the game's rulers can begin to tamper with a man's political feelings, professional hoofer of the wee ba' though he may be.'

If journalists and commentators of the day were not fully attuned to the odiousness of the Nazi regime or able to recognise the significance of the Nazi salute, were the players? Even Matthews, whose own account in places reads along the lines of *Escape to Victory*, admitted: 'I don't think any of the England players knew what Nazi Fascism meant.'[25] Indeed the fascist salute had been offered in 1933 when England had met Italy without any eyebrows being raised; and if the swastika could fly over White Hart Lane two years later, why would saluting the German national anthem in Berlin be so controversial? Was it merely the timing; or simply that it was so visible?

Brushing away the sands of time, what seems an even more extraordinary and contentious incident was the visit by a full complement of the England squad five years earlier to the home of Benito Mussolini. The Italian dictator met the team, posed for photographs and even signed autographs. Far from being appalled by the visit, some of the players even seemed to be in awe of their host. Writing in 1950, Cliff Bastin recalled:

> We were ushered into the beautiful palace where the dictator lived – a palace which, ironically, was dedicated to peace. Mussolini had evidently decided to keep us waiting. At last, his bodyguards came into the room, and, eventually the dictator himself entered, resplendent in morning dress. Never have I known such an astonishing personality. I have always considered Herbert Chapman to have been outstanding in this respect, but compared with Mussolini on this occasion he was an utter nonentity.[26]

(Eddie Hapgood's main memory, by contrast, was of being taller than the dictator.)

In Berlin, far from being an overt statement of affinity with the Nazis, the infamous salute was rather more a matter of routine. According to Rous's account, he and Wreford-Brown had been told on their arrival in Berlin that the Germans would stand to the British national anthem, and were asked if the England team would return the compliment by giving the Hitler salute during the playing of theirs. Aware of the potential sensitivity of doing so, the two visited Sir Neville Henderson and asked for his advice. 'When I go in to see Herr Hitler I give him the Nazi salute because that is the normal courtesy expected,' explained the ambassador. 'It carries no hint of approval of anything Hitler or his regime may do. And if I do it,' he concluded, 'why should you or your team object?'[27] Rous spoke with the rest of the squad, saying that compliance with the German request would affect whether the game was played in a friendly or hostile atmosphere; he recalled: 'All agreed they had no objection, and no doubt saw it as a bit of fun rather than of any political significance.'[28]

Whether they really regarded it as 'a bit of fun' is another matter, but certainly the England party, rather than running against a phalanx of Nazi hatred, had been impressed by what they had already seen and experienced of Berlin. 'I had been led to believe that the city was a purgatory of militarisation and uniforms, and, with memories of Rome in 1933, I had vivid pictures of what I would see,' recalled Bastin. 'To my surprise, I hardly saw one uniform throughout the time I was there. Perhaps the Germans had taken them off for the occasion of our visit . . . or perhaps the reason was that Hitler, who was out of the city at the time, had taken the bulk of the uniformed goose-steppers with him.'[29] German hospitality was, according to the Arsenal man, 'excellent'. He added: 'There must have been a large amount of anti-British feeling, whipped up by the Nazis, in Berlin at that time, but if there was, I, for one, did not notice any.'[30] In fact, far from being a Nazi stronghold, Berlin was probably the major German city *least* in thrall of Hitler's grubby ideology.

As for the idea that the German team was transfixed by a fanatical desire to prove German mastery at all costs; well, quite frankly, it is nonsense. The Germans were in awe of the English. (It was the Italians who were desperate to clinch victory over the 'masters' but not because of the dictates of racial nationalism but simply to qualify their World Cup success, which they would replicate that summer in France.) German fans loved and respected British football. Why else would they come to London in their droves in 1935 (and again in the 1950s)? Why else would Aston Villa draw a crowd of 100,000 on the *same* ground *the very next day*? As Simon Kuper records in *Ajax, The Dutch, The War*: 'Odes to the British game were *de rigueur* in German football books of the time. Introducing [Paul] Janes [German full-back and captain throughout the 1930s], the journalist Richard Kirn actually refers to English footballers of the early years of the century as "a sort of *übermenschen* [supermen]". [Otto] Nerz, the German manager until 1937, was an Anglophile who often travelled to Britain to study the game, but even humble fans knew their English football.' *Fußball* magazine carried a regular page from England headlined 'At the source of the World's Game' with detailed reports of all manner of matches – not just the big ones. Even the week after England's victory *Fußball Woche*, the German FA's official magazine, judged in an eighteen-page special 'The English showed how football should be played . . . It was perfect football.'[31] Nor was this a team of ideologically brainwashed Aryan goons, hand picked or groomed over months. Indeed they were made up largely of the team that had performed ingloriously at the 1936 Olympic Games: nine of them had faced Norway a year earlier, and seven had played Scotland in October 1936.[32] The reality was that the Germans were simply not that good a team, certainly not a patch on the Austrian side they had wiped away with the *Anschluss*. Indeed, they would be knocked out at the first stage of that summer's World Cup finals in France. Bastin confirmed their mediocre pedigree: 'The much vaunted German team proved to be a moderately good side, but I thought their standard considerably below that of other continental teams which I have met.'[33]

Who was telling the truth? Football-wise the facts are plain to see: England came, saw and conquered a rather ordinary team. As to the reception they received in Germany, there was nothing to suggest that the squad ran a gauntlet of anything other than German hospitality. Regarding the infamous salute, the sharply contradictory accounts suggest that time and the course of history have seen certain players exaggerate the pressures applied, and the righteousness of their opposition to the Nazi regime. What is certain is that the salute was far less significant then than later. Bastin stated in 1950:

> Personally, I didn't feel very strongly about the incident. We had been requested to give the salute by the British ambassador, in accordance with the insipid policy of appeasement . . . We gave our own salute immediately afterwards, and it seemed to me that this palliated any indignity there might have been in stretching out our arms in the Nazi fashion. If we had been requested to give the Nazi sign alone, then I would have been angry.[34]

In short, the players may not have liked it; they may not have fully known what they were doing, or its significance then or later; indeed they may well have hated fascism and Hitler; but rightly or wrongly they had made the salute because of the wishes of those in authority and in the name of national interest. They had fulfilled the expectations of their masters, but for most, the gesture held no great meaning. As the Leeds full-back, Bert Sproston put it to Stanley Matthews: 'I'm just a working class lad from Leeds and I've not 'ad much of an education and I know nowt 'bout politics and t'like. All I know is football. But t'way I see it, yon 'Itler fella is an evil little twat.'[35]

Sproston's observation was brought sharply into focus that summer. Throughout July and August 1938 Hitler had been making hostile statements about what he styled as 'Czech persecutions' of the increasingly militant German minority in the Sudetenland. The implication was clear: after the completion of the *Anschluss* with Austria in March, Czechoslovakia was Germany's next target. Prime Minister Neville Chamberlain desperately searched for a way to maintain peace, even if it meant the bestowal of the Czech borderlands to Germany. As Czechoslovakia had a military alliance with France, war would result if the Czechs resisted the Germans and called upon French aid. In one last burst of shuttle diplomacy between 15 and 30 September Chamberlain travelled to Germany three times to meet Hitler. From the last meeting, held at Munich on 30 September, he took back what he believed to be an agreement that the German-speaking portions of Czechoslovakia constituted Hitler's last territorial claim in Europe and that Germany, as well as Britain, would renounce war as a means of settling international claims. He had, he claimed with some pride, brought 'peace for our time'.

In Britain, life and football carried on. England's selectors continued to invest the hopes of the nation in new talent and were blessed with the emergence of some genuinely great players. At Everton, injuries and creeping years had, by the mid-1930s, started to reduce Dixie Dean's effectiveness. Mindful of the club's utter reliance on his goalscoring genius, the club's directors began to cast their net in search of a replacement. At Burnley they found him. Born in Farnworth, near Bolton, in October 1919, Tommy Lawton had been an outstanding schoolboy footballer, breaking all manner of regional scoring records, before signing on at Turf Moor. He made his league bow while still a sixteen-year-old amateur, signing professional forms in October 1936 on his seventeenth birthday. Four days later, Burnley came up against Tottenham who even in the Second Division boasted an array of international stars, including the England centre-back Arthur Rowe. Lawton hit a hat-trick. Two months later he was at Goodison.

Dean immediately took the youngster under his wing. 'I know you're here to take my place,' he told Lawton on his arrival. 'Anything I can do to help you I will. I promise, anything at all.' 'He impressed me right away,' Dean later said. 'He was quiet and listened.'

The apprentice's progress was swift. Though he made just ten appearances in the 1936–37 season, the following year he supplanted Dean in the Everton side and topped the First Division scoring charts with twenty-eight goals. Barely a week past his nineteenth birthday, in October 1938, the youngster received an England call-up, to face Wales at Ninian Park. He marked that occasion with a goal (in a 2–4 defeat), as indeed he did against a Rest of Europe side (3–0), Norway (4–0) and Northern Ireland (7–0) over the course of the month that followed.

Lining up alongside Lawton when England had met Northern Ireland at Old Trafford that autumn afternoon had been two old school friends in the half-back line. Joe Mercer was a Goodison Park colleague of Lawton, and came from football stock. Born in Ellesmere Port in 1914, he had a father, Joe senior, who had been a professional with Nottingham Forest, and Joe junior had been picked up by Everton at the age of fifteen, and eventually blooded a week before the 1933 FA Cup final. Teased for his skinny bandy legs and famous for his broad smile, he had been a fixture in the first team from the mid-1930s and was a mainstay of the side that would go on to win the League Championship in the 1938–39 season. Stan Cullis, two years Mercer's junior, may well have joined his school friend at Goodison, but for his father's staunch Black Country roots. He wrote to Wolves' famously flamboyant manager, Major Frank Buckley, who signed him up in 1934 after a trial. At Molineux his ascendancy was quick: captain of the A team at seventeen, the reserves at eighteen, and the first team by the time he was nineteen. He would win his international spurs a year later. An attack-minded player, despite his defensive position, Cullis was strong in the tackle and able in the air, but also skilful and composed on the ball. Not surprisingly, given Buckley's faith in him, he led well on and off the field – despite his young years – and was an articulate, intelligent man, frequently teased by his fellow players for his study of foreign languages (he was fluent in both French and Esperanto) at night school. Later, Eddie Hapgood would pick him in his greatest-ever team, calling him 'an intelligent, defensive centre-half who varied his play by attacking when the situation warranted this method. Stanley has mannerisms which sometimes annoy onlookers, but nothing ruffles him. He goes his own way, thoughtfully, always looking for the opportunity of a crack down the middle.'

Mercer's finest hour in an England shirt was to come in April 1939, when England met Scotland at Hampden Park. Without a win there since Dean's famous double in 1927, England were looking to salvage some pride after the earlier defeat to Wales. Under rain so heavy that, utterly drenched at half-time and without a spare kit, the England men had to play in the unfamiliar colours of Queen's Park in the second half. In a virtual repeat of what had happened with Dean leading the line twelve years earlier, Lawton scored two minutes from time to give England a 2–1 victory. Yet for once it was not the teenager who grabbed the plaudits, but Mercer, who won the man of the match award. 'Mercer was ever in the thick of the throbbing battle,' eulogised the *Daily Express*, 'which, with the wind and pitiless, ceaseless rain, provided the severest of all tests of skill, stamina, and heart. Mercer had them all.'

Politically the situation in Europe continued to blacken. On 15 March, the German army had, virtually without warning, occupied the rest of Czechoslovakia, despite it not being inhabited by Germans. In the weeks that followed, Britain offered a guarantee to Polish territory (whither Hitler would obviously be looking next); signed a military alliance with Poland; and undertook serious preparation for conflict, including the first peacetime military conscription.

In the midst of this obvious path to war, Stanley Rous visited Robert Vansittart, the Permanent Under-Secretary at the Foreign Office to seek advice about England's forthcoming summer tour of the continent. Given Europe's troubled state, asked the FA Secretary, would it be wise to undertake the tour at all? The civil servant asked him when it would be. 'The end of May,' replied Rous. 'In that case it will be all right,' responded Vansittart, 'It is August which will be the danger month.'[36]

Two months later, with more trepidation than a year earlier, the England squad journeyed by Orient Express to Milan, from where they would travel on to Belgrade and Bucharest. But it was Italy, after the 'Battle of Highbury' and with the worsening political situation, where most concerns were focused. Just a day before the party's arrival Mussolini had told the world that 'we will march with Germany to give Europe peace and justice'. The dictator's position and allegiance were seemingly beyond question: would England's footballers meet the first volley of fire in the seemingly impending battle?

As the Orient Express pulled into Milan's beautiful marble-walled station, the players could see a crowd of hundreds awaiting them. Who were they, the players wondered. Partisan locals? Fascist goons? Or maybe just fans, ready to intimidate the arriving team? As the train drew to a halt and the doors opened, the first cry went out: 'Viva Inglesi!' and the crowd burst into a spontaneous round of applause. 'Milan overwhelmed us,' recalled Hapgood. 'Thousands of excited youths and girls mobbed us for autographs, and it was some time before we could get away to our hotel; where things became just as hectic.'[37] Indeed, the two-minute walk to the hotel took more than thirty as the players were met by streets packed with thousands of cheering well-wishers. Were these two nations really on the precipice of war?

If the players were briefly deluded by the friendliness of the Italian people, they need not have been about its government's political ambitions. A number of the squad were deeply struck by a delegation of Maltese fans who had travelled all the way from Valletta to support England. (They 'had made the trip just as Arsenal supporters would go by excursion to Sheffield or some such place,' remembered Hapgood.[38]) One who got talking to Matthews spoke of the concerns of the Maltese people and their vulnerability in the face of a German-Italian axis. Matthews promised he would do his utmost to win. 'At the very least,' pleaded the man, 'do not let them beat you.'[39]

Matthews kept his word, but England were unable to record more than a 2–2 draw against the twice-crowned world champions. From Milan the England party journeyed to Venice and from there they took the overnight train to Belgrade, where again they were greeted by large crowds, even though this time they alighted their train at 6.30 a.m.! 'Your visit cements the friendship between our two countries,' announced the local dignitary who had met the party. 'For the England football team to visit our country is indeed a proud day for our country.' He then made a presentation to Eddie Hapgood, who he asked to 'give his opinion on football'.

Hapgood, a lion on the field, was somewhat bashful off it and was momentarily confounded by the task. After an awkward silence and some embarrassed smiles from his colleagues he composed himself. 'Sir, the England players thank you and your fellow countrymen for this marvellous reception,' he said, 'We feel honoured and humbled by its warmth and feel it is testimony to the friendship between our two nations. As for my opinion on football, to me it's like the dilemma of a love affair. If you don't take it seriously, you get no pleasure from it. If you do take it seriously, and as a player you have to, somewhere along the line, it will break your heart.'[40] The crowd and England players erupted into applause.

Yugoslavia won 2–1 and from there the England party travelled to Romania, where they recorded a 2–0 victory, before making the long journey home. Yet with every revolution of the Orient Express's mighty wheels, the spectre of war seemed to come closer.

In August, stunned Europeans stood agape as Germany signed a non-aggression pact with its great ideological foes, the USSR. A green light had seemingly been given for the invasion of Poland. On 25 August, the day before the Football League season started, Neville Chamberlain reiterated Britain's guarantee to Poland, not, it seemed that anyone in Germany was listening any more. Football went ahead the following day, with aggregate crowds of 600,000 turning out to see league fixtures. After a round of midweek games, at 6.30 a.m. on Friday 1 September, the German invasion of Poland began. Later on that day children began to be evacuated from London, but it was announced that the following day's fixtures would go ahead as planned.

On Saturday, 2 September, Britain issued an ultimatum to Germany stating that it must withdraw from Poland immediately. The whole world awaited Hitler's response. Raich Carter who was travelling south with his Sunderland team-mates for a game with Arsenal remembered seeing reservists on the train. 'I have little recollection of the game itself,' he would say of the match. 'Were there any thrills? Was there a large crowd, or a handful of spectators? I remember only the consciousness that something was going to happen at any moment. For the first time in my life, football seemed unimportant.'[41]

No word had come from Germany at the end of the day. War was now inevitable. At eleven o'clock the following morning the ultimatum expired and Neville Chamberlain's grave voice spoke from wireless sets across the nation:

> This morning, the British Ambassador in Berlin handed the German government a final note stating that, unless we heard from them by eleven o'clock that they were prepared at once to withdraw their troops from Poland, a state of war would exist between us. I have to tell you now that no such undertaking has been received, and that consequently this country is at war with Germany.

The seeds of antipathy planted in Paris two decades earlier had finally, horribly, burst into life. The world was at war again.

4

FOOTBALL AT WAR

War had been expected for more than a year, but when its angry knocking finally came, it immediately threw those who had long anticipated it. 'We speculated on what we should do,' remembered Raich Carter, who had listened to Chamberlain's broadcast with his Sunderland team-mates in London's Russell Hotel the morning after his side met Arsenal. 'Football would finish, but how soon? And what of the more immediate problem of getting back to Sunderland? We were a long way from home. What would the train services be like? Trains would be running, we supposed.'[1] Minutes later air-raid sirens wailed. Several of Carter's team-mates went outside to see what was happening, but were chased back inside by an ARP warden and directed away from the windows. 'We sat on the floor waiting in suspense and not knowing what was happening until the "All clear" sounded. A false alarm.'

Carter and his Sunderland team-mates made it back to Wearside without incident. But the following day, when he went to Roker Park to collect his pay, there was no training. 'Nobody knew what was going to happen. The manager could tell us nothing. There was little doubt though, that Sunderland FC would soon be finished.'[2] On Tuesday the players went back to the ground, but did nothing and went back home. Wednesday was the same. 'Nobody had even the heart to kick a ball about,' recalled Carter. 'The inactivity added to the feeling of unrest and gloom.' The following Saturday's fixtures were cancelled and when the players went to collect their pay on the Monday they were given half a week's wages and told that they 'were finished'.[3]

Lambasted in 1914 for blithely carrying on, this time football's authorities were ready for the arrival of war. In 1938 a consultative committee of the FA had decided 'That in the event of war, a meeting be convened comprising the officers of the FA and the management committee of the Football League for the purpose of deciding the course of action to be taken with regard to the game.' Rous convened a meeting on 8 September 1939 and with fifteen members decided that all football, except for the forces, would be suspended until further notice to the contrary. At the same time, the Football League announced that players' contracts would be torn up, though in keeping with their semi-feudal existences, their playing registrations would be retained by their clubs lest they retain some value when fighting stopped. Like thousands of others, players were suddenly unemployed, their 'benefit' in most cases forgotten about, most left without any idea of what they were going to do.*

Footballers took work as and when they could. Joe Mercer went to work at Cammell Laird shipyard; Dixie Dean retired, after spells in Ireland and with Notts County, to an abattoir; Raich Carter became a fireman. His wages of £3 a week represented a substantial drop from the £8 he had earned at Sunderland, but he was lucky. The same men expected to do its nation's bidding barely a year earlier were effectively left on the scrapheap. Players had no unemployment protection under national insurance and unless they could find jobs were either left to rely on the goodwill of others or forced into virtual penury until conscription came. They were not the only ones left rueing their losses. A Bolton fan took his club to court, trying to get a refund for his season ticket, but his claim was dismissed by the judge.[4]

Within days of football's suspension friendly matches had been permitted. The move came after Stanley Rous had been invited to a meeting at the Home Office where Ernest Bevin made it clear that it was preferable for the national sport to be officially organised. Nevertheless, fears of German bombing raids and the rationalising of key resources, such as fuel, saw heavy restrictions imposed on the game. Crowds were restricted to 15,000 all ticket affairs in larger grounds; 8000 or half the capacity, whichever was smaller, elsewhere. As conscription began to take hold FA wartime regulations which allowed for guesting became more prevalent. Players played for their clubs when they could, but it invariably depended upon where they were stationed and when they could get leave. With strangers turning

---

* There were some exceptions. Lawton and Mercer, for instance, accepted their share.

out for some clubs and others fielding teams of hitherto unknowns the competitive nature of football was fundamentally altered. More and more fans realised that what they were seeing was often a mere sop.

At the same time though, without the pressures that came with being paid professionals chasing championships or dodging the drop, a more attacking, entertaining brand of football ensued. Players showed off, unveiling repertoires of tricks previously left behind on the training ground or even the schoolyard, defenders seemingly forgot about defending and the average number of goals per game doubled from three in the 1938–39 season to six in the first months of the war. As the *Manchester Guardian* put it on New Year's Day 1940, goalkeepers 'must be questioning the wisdom of Dr Johnson's preference for being attacked rather than ignored'.[5] Sometimes games just descended into farce. Brighton turned up for a match with Norwich with only half a team, managed to obtain some local reserves, but still lost 18–0. Charlton Athletic played their milkman, thinking he was the expected guest. There was a mercenary element too. The match fee did much to help players after the ending of formal contracts and was a welcome boost to meagre service salaries. One player boasted of having played for eight different clubs in nine weeks.[6] For others, the war years simply represented good times football-wise. Arsenal's Denis Compton believed the war years to be 'the best time of my life as far as football was concerned'. Joe Mercer would recall: 'For seven years I probably played twice, sometimes three times a week . . . It was a funny kind of thing in the war . . . sometimes I didn't know who I was playing for: the army, the command, the unit, England or the club. I know once the CO said when I wanted a pass to play, "Mercer, I don't know whether you want a pass to come into the camp, or to stay out."'[7]

The crowd restrictions – obviously – affected attendances, along with everything else. The forty-one league matches played on 4 November 1939 produced an aggregate attendance of 101,000, as against 685,000 who watched forty-four matches a year earlier.[8] When bombing raids commenced in 1940, they plunged even further. Some clubs, like Charlton or Millwall, which were situated near dockyards (prime Luftwaffe targets) on occasion experienced crowds of just 300.

Stanley Rous urged players to sign up for the army's Physical Training Corps with the promise that they would become Sergeant

Instructors (though it subsequently emerged that they were only made 'Temporary Sergeant Instructors'). Joe Mercer was amongst the first to be recruited, Lawton, in January 1940, the last. Welcomed at first as 'celebrity soldiers', their frequent leaves of absence to play football came to be regarded by some fellow combatants as unfair privileges and, after Dunkirk, some players and other stars of track and field were sarcastically derided 'PT Commandos' and later 'D-Day Dodgers'. The suggestions clearly rankled, and after the war Tommy Lawton spoke out vigorously in defence of his and other colleagues' war records:

> I was one of the fortunates who, by reason of my retention in this country on Army service, was able to get in my weekly game throughout the period of hostilities. And incidentally there was periodical hostility from people who thought it wrong that fit, able-bodied young fellows like myself should be playing football in England while their husbands, sons and sweethearts were fighting in the sun-baked deserts of Libya and the Middle East, were flying out over Europe or were dying in the dangerous seas. I am not going to defend myself, I have done nothing to defend myself against. The War Moguls ordered that I stayed in England to do my war job. Football was incidental, but in its way it too played a part. I appeared in hundreds of charity matches for England, the Army, combined services and unit sides. Let me make it clear. I didn't ask to stay in England.

Most footballers were lucky in their postings though. Those that were not tended to come under the command of a pettifogger or jobsworth superior. Eddie Hapgood was stationed under one such officious moron at the RAF Cardington base in Bedfordshire.

On his first day at the roll-call the corporal came to Hapgood's name.

'Any relation to the Arsenal player?'

'The same sir,' replied Hapgood.

'Oh-ho,' leered the corporal. 'Well sonny boy, you played for a classy team, so I'm going to give you some classy jobs round here.' He threw a tin of floor polish at Hapgood, which the England player controlled with his thigh, caught with his right foot and flicked back to the corporal. The corporal was not amused and had Hapgood spend the next month polishing the barrack room floor and cleaning out toilets. For 'doing his bit' Hapgood spent two and a half months in and out of the infirmary with multiple septic whitlows on both hands. Later in the war he was placed on a charge for alleged insolence when he had politely gesticulated when explaining he was needed for a match. His real crime, as a conscript, was not knowing RAF protocol, and he was eventually allowed to turn out for Arsenal that afternoon, albeit still under charge and with a two-man escort.[9]

Football's stature rose as the fighting escalated. It became an important fundraiser for the war effort, with gate receipts, collections and donations of equipment going the way of the armed forces and other causes such as Mrs Churchill's fund for Russia. The FA invested more than £30,000 in war stocks and transformed its headquarters in Lancaster Gate into a kind of bazaar where all manner of remaindered and surplus stock was put on sale in aid of war-related charities. The unlikely sight of Stanley Rous negotiating with owners of bombed-out department stores for parts of their inventory was not an infrequent one, and goods which might have otherwise fallen into the hands of spivs and looters were resold, with the proceeds going to charity. King George VI, Queen Elizabeth, Winston Churchill, King Haakon of Norway (in exile in London) and General Montgomery all made appearances at football grounds at various stages of the war. Indeed, Montgomery, who was something of a regular at his local club, Portsmouth, was made club president in 1944 – a position he would hold for years.

Football's return to notions of 'respectability' in the early forties seemed half a world away from the 'unpatriotic' game of 'traitors' so sneered at and castigated three decades earlier. Yet football during the Great War had also played an important part in the war effort, even if it wasn't always readily appreciated or even apparent. The Seventeenth Service Battalion of the Middlesex Regiment was nominally designated 'the footballer's battalion'. Initially MPs, clergymen and civic dignitaries' exhortations for professional footballers to enlist met with little success and *The Times* harangued clubs for even employing professionals, accusing them of 'bribing a needed recruit to refrain from enlistment'. The Colonel of the Footballers' Battalion regarded the failure of players to enlist as a 'public scandal', complaining that only 122 professionals out of 1800 had signed up.[10] Yet when the League and FA Cup programme came to a close in 1915 many – including the Clapton Orient team *en masse* – signed up for his regiment and others.

Some players didn't get the chance. Steve Bloomer, retired from playing, was a coach based in Berlin when war broke out. 'I was one of the happy throng of Britishers assembled on the boulevards of Berlin at the start of August 1914,' he would recall. 'I remember one night we went home, aliens in a strange land, and there was rumour of war in the air. Ah well, what did it matter? It hadn't been declared and there was plenty of time to do something about it when it was an accomplished fact. So we went home perfectly happy and not a bit worried.'[11] When there was a mass internment in November 1914 Bloomer was one of 600 men rounded up and placed in an internment camp. He spent the war in Ruhleben camp organising camp leagues and suchlike, in what must have been difficult circumstances.

Football also played an important part on the Great War battlefield. Frequently a ball would be kicked over the top of a trench and soldiers would chase after it when advancing on enemy lines. The practice was almost suicidally dangerous in a conflict when men frequently served as mere fodder for the patter of enemy guns. Reporting in July 1916 on the advance of a battalion of the East Surrey Regiment on enemy trenches at Contalmaison, a Reuters correspondent captured the essence of one of these 'death dribbles'.

> The captain of one of the companies had provided four footballs, one for each platoon, urging them to keep up a dribbling competition all the way over the mile and a quarter of ground they had to traverse. As the company formed on emerging from the trench, the platoon commanders kicked off and the match against Death commenced. The gallant captain himself fell early in the charge, and men began to drop rapidly under the hail of machine gun bullets. But still the footballs were booted onwards, with hoarse cries of encouragement or defiance, until they disappeared in the dense smother behind which the Germans were shooting. Then when the bombs and bayonets had done their work, and the enemy had cleared out, the Surrey men looked for their footballs and recovered two of them in the captured traverses. They will be sent to the Regimental depot at Kingston as trophies worth preserving.[12]

Often, as the reporter pointed out, these footballs would be recovered and preserved in a glass case or kept on a silver stand as a treasured memento of glorious and tragic days. 'Touchstone', the Daily Mail's laureate, immortalised the charge of the Surreys in verse:

On through the hail of slaughter,
Where gallant comrades fall,
Where blood is poured like water,
They drive the trickling ball.
The fear of death before them,
Is but an empty name,
True to the land that bore them,
The Surreys play the game.

But just as football could divide, so it could unite. One of the most extraordinary incidents in more than four years of fighting came in Christmas 1914 when an informal truce broke out on the Flanders front between British and German forces, culminating in football matches played across the blood-strewn mud of no man's land. The movement came from lower ranks, and largely, it seems, initially from the German side. In the days leading up to Christmas, bouts of carol singing broke out, Christmas trees were produced and, eventually, choruses of '*Stille Nacht*' were matched by verses of 'Silent Night'. In trenches, sometimes just metres apart, men from both sides got talking and cessations were organised, initially so that corpses of fallen comrades could be recovered. Soon, brave individuals clambered out of their warrens and met in the middle as they went about their sad duties. From that moment – to the horror of those running the war – fraternisation of a sort was in progress. Gifts of cigarettes, cakes, chocolates and other provisions were exchanged. Germany, like Italy in later years, was a nation of waiters and many of their soldiers spoke good English having worked in London or elsewhere. Some were even keen to know how their teams were performing back in England. Lance Corporal Hines of the Westminsters reported in the *Chester Chronicle* on 9 January 1915 that a German he encountered greeted him, 'Good morning, sir; I [used to] live at Alexander Road, Hornsey. And I would see Woolwich Arsenal play Tottenham tomorrow.'[13]

From such promptings, games of football came to be organised across the front. Unit histories and personal testimonies of combatants are replete with stories and references to these matches. W.V. Matthews of the Queen's Westminsters recalled, 'we got out of our trenches in the morning and played football, and then we went out in front [of the line] and walked over to meet [the Germans]. We then shook hands and exchanged souvenirs . . . they could talk English, and it gave me an opportunity of exercising my little German.' G.A. Farmer of the Westminsters 'found our men playing football at the back of the[ir] trench, and the enemy walking about the top of their trench [and watching]. It was hard to think we were at war with one another.'[14] The Westminsters, however, were unsuccessful in their attempts to persuade their enemies to join in. Yet others actually engaged in matches with the Germans. On 15 January 1915, *The Times* published a letter from a major in the medical corps reporting that in his sector the Saxons serenaded their enemies with verses of 'God Save the King', presented the British with a bottle of wine with which to 'drink the King's health', following which his regiment 'actually had a football match with the Saxons'. The account is backed up by the regiment's official history, which described the 'droll scene' of *'Tommy und Fritz'* first chasing hares, then kicking about a football. 'This developed into a regulation football match with caps casually laid out as goals. The frozen ground was no great matter. Then we organised each side into teams, lining up in motley rows, the football in the centre.' The end result: *'Das Spiel endete 3:2 für Fritz'* (a Saxon win . . .).[15]

Participants in these matches, however, took their chances and there were breaches of the mutual understanding that had under-pinned the truce. Uncontrollable snipers, zealous officers, drunkenness and bouts of misunderstanding or mistrust at various stages saw the peace broken, and newly made friends reminded of the tentativeness of their fraternity. Indeed, just as quickly as peace broke out, it ended. The truce was all but over by New Year, the killing resumed and, as Stanley Weintraub observes in *Silent Night*, the definitive account of these extraordinary events: 'On both sides in 1915, there would be more dead on any single day than yards gained in the entire year.'

Although regional football leagues had continued throughout the Great War's duration, there had been no international football until the four victory internationals of 1919. By contrast, when fighting resumed in September 1939 international matches resumed as early as 11 November, when England met Wales at Ninian Park, Cardiff and played out a 1–1 draw. In total thirty-six wartime and victory internationals were played over nearly seven years of war and the transitional period that followed. Of these England won twenty-two, drew six and lost eight, called upon seventy-eight different players and wowed crowds with some of the best football the nation's footballers had ever played. None of these games was afforded 'official' status, though this should not detract from the fact that they were second class in billing only.

Certainly the line-ups were more reminiscent of pre-war offerings than those that many clubs could muster. Matthews, Mercer, Cullis, Lawton and Hapgood all featured regularly for England in matches, which more than anything else on offer during the war represented 'real' football. Less hampered by attendance restrictions than other wartime matches, crowds sometimes bordered on their peace-time figures – 40,000 saw England play Wales at Wembley in April 1940; 75,000 watched Scotland against England at Hampden Park a month later; and by 1943 more than 100,000 were regularly filling Hampden's vast stands. By then, of course, the worst of the bombing raids were over. At their peak in 1940, just two internationals had been played and at the meeting between Scotland and England 6000 ticket holders had stayed away after a Lord Haw-Haw propaganda broadcast had promised listeners that the Luftwaffe would flatten Hampden by half-time (it didn't, of course . . .). 1941, by contrast, saw England play six internationals; 1942 five; and 1943 five again.

That year would see arguably England's greatest ever side in some seventy years of international football. They were, remembered Mercer, 'a wonderful bunch to play with . . . I never played with a team so eager to do well. In those matches everybody fancied himself a bit, everybody wanted the ball. Every time you gave a pass, you made nine enemies. The spirit was as keen as that.' Undoubtedly aided by the fact that the FA Wartime Committee's control over selection was only nominal and Stanley Rous was able to serve effectively as its manager, continuity bred success. 'The attitude was entirely different,' Mercer recalled.

> Throughout the war, players played for the team, not to please the selection committee. We often knew immediately after one game which of us would be playing in the next. Mr Rous would talk to whoever was captain, usually Stan Cullis or myself, and then say who he wanted for the next game. It may sound a bit casual, but it gave us all the feeling we were being dealt with by someone who knew us, not by a committee of people we might never see.[16]

England took first blood in the year's internationals, defeating the Scots 4–0 at Hampden on 17 April with Raich Carter (2), Dennis Westcott and Denis Compton grabbing the goals. Though England could only manage a 1–1 draw with Wales on 8 May, they would put eight past the Welsh in September, in front of 80,000 at Wembley. England's finest hour, however, was still to come.

On 16 October 1943, Scotland visited Maine Road, Manchester. Having been played off the park on home soil earlier on in the year, the visitors knew that they were on a hiding to nothing. Bill Shankly, who had played in the April match, remembered: 'When I heard the team I said two prayers. One of thanks for the Scots for leaving me out, and one on behalf of Adam Little who had taken my place. I knew then we'd do well to get away with less than five goals against.'[17] Indeed by half-time five goals had come the hosts' way – four from Lawton alone – and by the game's conclusion they had struck eight without reply, Hagan (2), Carter and Matthews claiming England's others. 'I doubt if an English crowd will enjoy a football exhibition as much again,' reported Frank Butler in the *Daily Express.* 'Stanley Matthews, at the top of his form, provided the best entertainment with his uncanny footwork and body swerve, which gave Scotland's defence ninety minutes of nervous strain.' Mercer would describe it as the 'greatest' game he could remember; his school friend Cullis 'the finest football' he had ever seen; even Shankly, never normally known for his magnanimity towards England, shared their opinion. 'This was a great England team,' he would say. 'They had wonderful players in the side and just as many waiting to get a game . . . If I had been picking a team at the time from the best players [in Scotland], I would have picked that same side. But the thing is, I wouldn't have picked myself to play against them . . . Scotland had no chance!'[18]

VE Day in May 1945 would bring with it 'Victory Internationals' against the Home Nations, plus France, Belgium and Switzerland. Pilloried after fighting had ended in 1918, the FA in 1945, having satisfied the expectation that they worked in the national interest this time, were able to publish a self-congratulatory pamphlet, entitled 'Victory was the Goal'. In the foreword the FA President, the Earl of Athlone, paid tribute to 'the many ways in which football and the Football Association contributed to the war effort and . . . that great army of footballers whose valiant service in many fields held so materially to bring us victory and peace'.[19]

Fans, however, hankered for a return to normality. The fifteen-month interval from peace to the Football League's resumption seemed, for many, as long as the wait for peace itself had been. Victory internationals offered a tantalising prospect of what was to follow, so too did the FA Cup, which returned a season ahead of league and full international football. On 27 April 1946, 98,000 watched Derby County beat Charlton in the first post-war FA Cup final and *The Times'* correspondent was able to record: 'Here at last . . . after seven years is the real thing.' Football would never look back.

5

WAKING UP TO THE WORLD

War had changed everything, but peace brought few comforts. Families mourned their dead, servicemen tried to make sense of civvy street, children became acquainted with unknown fathers. Thousands were still without homes, some communities had been destroyed in their entirety. Life would never be the same again. Rationing and austerity made for a hard, monotonous slog, depriving all but the rich and well connected of material extras. There was room for some optimism though. An ambitious post-war reconstruction programme was under way, Clement Attlee's Labour government had begun to establish a welfare state that promised to look after its citizens from 'the cradle to the grave', and the country was in the midst of a 'baby boom'. But just as vestiges of normality seemed to be returning, a harsh, bitter winter in the early months of 1947 saw a flu epidemic sweep Europe killing thousands and, with fuel supplies low, made for a cold, miserable season for millions more. Life remained hard and for the most part dull.

To escape the rigours of the real world, for most there were just two avenues – cinema, which thirty million people were attending every week; and football. Like cinema, English football was enjoying a peak of attendances unparalleled in its history. For ninety minutes the problems and routine of the rest of the week could be laid to rest with every thought, utterance and emotion invested in the fortunes of the team. Victory would put you on top of the world; a draw leave you contemplating what might have been; and defeat? – well, there was always next week. Soccer superstars had breathed with the gods since the 1880s, but with every passing year seemed to assume greater importance in people's hearts and minds. Bestriding the First Division week in week out, immortalised in comic books, Pathe newsreels and cigarette cards, to millions these were the men that mattered, these were the figures who made even the most humdrum existence worth living. In 1947 there seemed to be more of them than ever before.

But when a dozen of these giants embarked on a training camp in the Scottish village of Aberfoyle in May of that year, for the children of the local primary school it was all too much. It started with some excited whispers at the back of the classroom, followed by a couple of peeks out of its window. Then, one of the bolder students ran over to the window to get a better look; soon a crowd stood watching with him. Finally, their teacher saw sense, abandoned the lesson and took the children outside. There, she approached George Hardwick, defensive lynchpin of Middlesbrough, captain of England, and, for the following Saturday at least, Great Britain. Would he mind if the children watched the training session? Looking down at the excited, expectant faces, he smiled. No, he said, that wouldn't be a problem. So, for the next two hours, the pupils of this small Scottish school watched an event almost unique in the history of British football: a team consisting of members of all four parts of the union, training ahead of a game with the Rest of Europe – the 'Match of the Century' no less.

It was two years after VE Day and at the end of the first full campaign of Football League and international fixtures since war had broken out. Football's first season back had seen Liverpool crowned First Division champions and Charlton Athletic FA Cup winners. For England, full internationals had returned the previous September with two games in three days, against Northern Ireland in Belfast, then, for the first time, against the Republic of Ireland. For the players – so used to the meagreness and monotony of rationing – the visit to Ireland was remembered as much for an eight-course lunch at Dublin's Gresham Hotel (including steaks of a size equivalent to a week's meat ration back home) than any great football or political significance, but the occasion marked in earnest the beginning of the end of England's international isolation. Already the Football Association had rejoined FIFA after a delegation from football's governing body, financially bankrupt after the war, had sent a delegation to London cap in hand and offered a vice-presidency, and retention of representation on the International Board (the game's law-making council). Each of the home nations rejoined, agreeing that FIFA would take the proceeds of a celebratory match between Great Britain and the Rest of Europe at Hampden Park in May 1947, which is why – instead of studying – the children of Aberfoyle Primary School were watching Stanley Matthews, Billy Liddell and others being put through their paces on that sunny spring afternoon.

The following day 135,000 filled Hampden Park to see what the *Daily Herald* dubbed 'the ultimate showdown of soccer styles'. England could lay claim to five of the players in the line-up: Hardwick, Matthews, Lawton, Manchester City's inspirational goalkeeper Frank Swift and Middlesbrough's sublimely gifted inside-forward and playmaker, Wilf Mannion; Scotland three men; Wales two and Northern Ireland just one representative.* Johnny Carey, Manchester United's captain, was named skipper of the Rest of Europe side (he was also bilingual in a team that boasted nine nationalities and seven languages); there were no Germans – still a nation of pariahs; and, on account of several withdrawals, fewer Italians than had originally been selected. It was still a formidable side and boasted several individuals whose names have gone into the game's Valhalla, most notably the two Swedes – Gunnar Gren and Gunnar Nordahl – who were dominant influences in Torino's magnificent, all-conquering team; Willie Steffen, the Swiss defender, who had once turned out for Chelsea; and the fantastically gifted Czechoslovak left-half, Josef Ludl. 'The question before us,' mused *The Times* correspondent, 'can all this individual brilliance be blended into a show of teamwork?' His question was addressed as much to the British side as to the Europeans.

He need not have worried. The Europeans were only really in the contest for the first half-hour. Gunnar Nordahl uncharacteristically fluffed two early chances with the scoreline goalless after Europe had begun at a furious pace, but it was Mannion who opened the scoring when he latched onto a mis-hit shot by Billy Steel and poked the ball past the visitors' French goalkeeper, Julien Darui. Then Praest, the Danish winger, sold George Hardwick a dummy once, twice, and sent Nordahl free to equalise. Europe pushed hard for the lead, repeatedly making Britain's backs look ordinary and wowing Hampden with an array of individual trickery and skills, but seemingly falling down on

* If the game was played today it is difficult to imagine any representatives from Scotland or Northern Ireland there on merit, and maybe only Ryan Giggs making the cut from Wales.

team ethic. Then, on thirty-three minutes, Ludl handled Matthews' cross inside his own area, the referee pointed to the spot and Mannion converted the penalty. Two minutes later Steel set off on a fast, direct dribble and with Europe's defence retreating, shot from twenty-five yards, beating the surprised Darui. A minute later, Mannion rolled Lawton's pass past the Frenchman and the centre-forward tapped home to make doubly sure it reached its destination. Four rampant minutes had turned the game on its head: Great Britain had a seemingly unassailable 4–1 lead.

Shell shocked at half-time, the Europeans changed their tactics, trying to hit the British on the counter-attack. The switch merely served to encourage their opponents whose forwards, despite the sterling efforts of Carey, were in irresistible form. Mannion, so often at the heart of play, prompted desperate yells of 'Man-e-yan, Man-e-yan' from the Italian defender Parola each time he gained possession and, after hitting a post, he pressured the hapless Parola into putting the ball into his own net for Great Britain's fifth. Yet it was Matthews who elevated the game to a flight of fantasy. 'To me,' wrote Stanley Russell in the following day's *Sunday Pictorial*, 'the memories will always be of Matthews' great – really great – start in what many people believe will be his last big match in this country.' With seven minutes remaining, the thirty-two-year-old lifted a pinpoint cross into Europe's penalty area, which Lawton rose to power home and complete the scoring. 'But for Darui in goal,' remarked *The Times*, 'Britain's score might well have reached double figures.'

Great Britain had taught Europe a football lesson, fully living up to expectations of superiority and allowing the game's homelands to bask in the glow of self-satisfaction. The 'continentals' were still, in the words of one reporter, 'the pupils'. Victory in such comprehensive terms had shown that there was little or nothing to be learned from them: the architects of the game were still the masters. Others were even more dismissive of the defeated visitors. The '"Match of the Century" lacks glamour, so far as the English enthusiasts are concerned,' noted *Football Update and Tom Stenner's Magazine*, 'because it is rather remote; and there is nothing familiar about the European team apart from Willie Steffen, whom we have admired playing for Chelsea. From the pools point of view it is just one more match, and one, I fancy, that most people will want to avoid. There are just too many unknown quantities about it.'[1] The rest of the world, in football terms, was therefore distant, inferior, and worst of all 'different'. They were irrelevant and, as proved by this outcome, British football, if not its dominant English strain, was still indisputably the greatest.

If the outlook of English supporters was still arrogant, nay chauvinistic, much else had changed. The FA Secretary, Stanley Rous, had set about fundamentally altering the structure of training and coaching in England with a fervent zeal. He had reached the conclusion that most coaching in the English game was at best rudimentary and, more often, simply non-existent. Training usually consisted of little more than endless 'lapping' of the cinder track which encircled most pitches (hardly any clubs could lay claim to proper training facilities); while the George Allisons and Herbert Chapmans remained a rarity in dressing rooms where the very word 'tactics' was considered a dirty one.

Rous sought to overhaul this haphazard, amateurish state of affairs. The first step in his revolution was the creation of a system of education spreading down to the grassroots of the game. He created the position of Director of Coaching, giving the new man a blank canvas on which to paint a structure in England to allow former players and laymen to learn how to bring the best out of their men technically, tactically and physically. He was also expected to collate his principles in a series of manuals, where routines of best practice would be available for all to see. The other responsibility was as 'Chief Coach' of the English national team, where such experience could regularly be brought to bear on the country's finest footballers. Not that the 'Chief Coach' would be able to pick them – that job was still the International Selection Committee's staunchly defended orbit.

Still, it was progress of a sort. For this multi-faceted job Rous appointed Walter Winterbottom, a thirty-three-year-old former Manchester United defender with academic experience – then a rarity – in physical training. Born in Oldham in 1913, Winterbottom had been an outstanding schoolboy footballer at Oldham Grammar School but had initially chosen study over starting out as a pro-fessional. Several twists saw him return to the game. Firstly, at college Winterbottom became a close friend of Eddie Lever, a professional at Portsmouth, who opened his mind to the theory and tactics of the sport; then, while working as a schoolmaster in Oldham and playing centre-half for Royston Amateurs and Mossley, he had been spotted by Manchester United but only agreed to go to Old Trafford on the condition that he could incorporate playing for United with study at the Carnegie College of Physical Training. He made his league debut against Leeds United in 1936, but a spinal injury ruined his career after just twenty-six games and he joined the Carnegie staff as a sports lecturer. Later, Winterbottom was to have the proverbial 'good war'. He became a wing commander in the RAF but was seconded to the Air Ministry where he was appointed Head of Physical Training. He also guested for Chelsea and was twice called up as a reserve for war-time internationals, but it was his experience with the air force that alerted Rous to his abilities.

As Director of Coaching Winterbottom had to start from scratch. He formed a nationwide network of coaches reaching from professional clubs down into primary schools and created a training centre at Lilleshall, which provided courses for everybody from schoolboys to club secretaries. Later he would establish a programme of youth and 'B' internationals, plus inter-league games, which provided a theoretical system of promotion to England's first XI. Yet it was as chief coach to the national team where, with narrower responsibilities, Winterbottom faced the greatest pressure. At the outset the Football Association hierarchy, seemingly so enlightened in heeding Rous's advice, had not wanted a chief coach, and had only agreed to the role after considerable persuasion from the Secretary. Thereafter they made a difficult job virtually impossible by retaining team selection. 'Most of the FA councillors did not want a national team manager, but I persuaded them to rather reluctantly appoint one,' Rous later recalled. 'They gave Walter the responsibility, but saw to it that they retained the power. Anybody assessing what Walter achieved for English football must think of him first and foremost as a coach and an organiser extraordinaire.'[2] Indeed Winterbottom's time as England Chief Coach was notable, in large part, for the brick walls he was to repeatedly run up against. Yet conversely in the 1940s – and even for much of the next decade – there was little public or player disquiet about the absurd state of affairs and it was only later, after several sharp shocks, that the selection of England teams came under closer scrutiny and criticism. English football superiority, it seemed, was regarded as a *fait accompli* not just by the FA's blazer brigade, but by the fans too. Winterbottom would be seen as incidental to the national team's successes and failures, not central to them.

The players themselves had given a cautious welcome to the appointment. Lawton sullenly referred to him as 'that PT instructor and Man Utd reserve' ('You're going to tell Stan Matthews how to play outside-right? And me how to score goals? You've another thing coming.'[3]) while others voiced disapproval at his attempts to impose a gameplan or incredulity at some of his theories. One of his later charges described him, not unkindly, as 'a distinguished, quietly spoken man who talked as if he had swallowed a dictionary and often sounded more like a university lecturer than a football coach'.[4] Of course, he had once been a lecturer, but to players with just an elementary schooling behind them, such verbosity was sometimes baffling. Moreover, the players came from an era that preceded coaching and tactical team talks. On another occasion Winterbottom explained how he wanted Lawton and Shackleton to concentrate on moving through the middle and scoring after an interchange of wall passes. 'Excuse me,' piped up Shackleton. 'Which side of the net do you want me to put the ball?' The majority of players simply did not want to know about tactics, they just wanted to play.

Towards the end of his managerial career Bob Ferrier wrote an illuminating account – *Soccer Partnership: Billy Wright and Walter Winterbottom* – with the England manager's cooperation. In it, he told of how the bulk of his squad were against the fundamental principle of Winterbottom's management:

> There was simple, basic opposition to the fact of having an England manager, any manager. England international players were selected for their high ability to play the game, and out of simple experience of playing together they ought to be able to knit quickly and effectively on the field without the need for long sessions of training or preparation. Such was the argument. But it was a fallacious argument, based on false premises. Given the differences in playing techniques and temperaments found in any group of international players, it was clearly necessary to have a third party to bring some unison and directed purpose to the work.

Even if his own importance wasn't always recognised, Winterbottom's England still carried an overwhelming burden of expectation. Although he couldn't always pick the players he wanted, in his first days as national coach, at least, Winterbottom had at his disposal a glut of talent unparalleled in the history of the English game.

Some of it predated the war. The scheming inside-forward Raich Carter had made his international bow as early as 1934. Now with Derby County, this stylish quick-witted football genius was seemingly set on proving his heyday was not past. Also making his England debut in 1934 had been Stanley Matthews. Thirty-one when competitive internationals returned, this wizard of the wing had been back to his pre-war best in the Football League's first season back. Most thought an Indian summer was beyond him but they failed to reckon with Matthews' relentlessly diligent training routine (which began every morning at 6 a.m.) and fastidious dietary requirements. Stoke City's management was so sure that he was imminently destined for the scrapheap of old pros that they cashed in on him, selling him to Blackpool the week after Great Britain's thrashing of Europe.

Tommy Lawton, boy wonder of the pre-war years and hero of so many wartime and victory internationals, was still there but had made the first of several catastrophic moves which would send his career into an irreversible decline. He had fled Merseyside and his beloved Everton in November 1945 after his marriage to a local girl had broken down, joining Chelsea for £11,500. It was a move he always regretted ('on reflection,' he later admitted, 'I should have stayed and transferred the wife') and arguments with the Chelsea management limited his stay at Stamford Bridge to just two years. Then, lured by the promise of financial inducements beyond the statutory maximum wage, he agreed to join Notts County, who paid a record fee of £20,000 to take him to the Third Division (South). Taking such a radical step was a staggering choice for England's finest centre-forward and another move he came to mourn. In the short term it didn't hamper his selection prospects for England, but after ten months and five caps at Meadow Lane, the FA selectors could no longer justify the inclusion of a player who was plying his trade at such a low level and called time on his international career. His last game for England came in September 1948 against Denmark – Lawton was just twenty-eight.

Many of the wartime stars never got to experience the post-1946 international era. Some simply drifted into obscurity, others went back to their clubs but never got the call once more able players emerged from the shadows or returned from the fighting. Others took advantage of the new fad for clubs to appoint managers: Stan Cullis found great success as Wolves boss; Cliff Britton less, when in charge of Burnley, Everton, Preston and Hull; Joe Mercer eventually turned his hand to club management too, with Sheffield United, Aston Villa and Manchester City. Some, like the cricket-playing Comptons, pursued other paths to international glory. Several other stars of England's wartime and victory teams did replicate early successes in their country's colours. George Hardwick and Frank Swift were central figures in the England team of the immediate post-war years, while Neil Franklin was an exquisite unruffled presence at the back of the England team, adding to his tally of sixteen consecutive wartime and victory caps with a run of twenty-seven full ones that extended up to 1950. A non-smoking teetotaller and devoted family man, Stanley Matthews wrote of him:

> Neil won everything in the air, tackled with superb timing and when the ball was at his feet possessed the nous to pass it with all the guile and intelligence of the most cerebral of inside-forwards . . . [He] oozed class and self-control in equal measures. When his legs were kicked from under him he would rise to his feet, look pityingly at the perpetrator of the shabby assault and with a gentle, disapproving shake of his head, turn and trot away to take up his position.[5]

Stan Mortensen, an inside- and centre-forward who, like several of his contemporaries, was blessed with the courage (or foolhardiness) to put his head where others would think twice about putting their feet, had already won several wartime caps when, virtually at the war's end, he had been dragged almost dead from a crashed bomber in which he had been the gunner. So severe had been the crash that two of his crewmates were killed and a third lost his legs. Mortensen, who had been lucky to survive his head injuries, let alone play professional football again, completed his recovery with a full England debut against Portugal in May 1947.

Along with this complement of stars stood several other names about whom little was known nationally beyond excited whispers. The Wolves half-back, Billy Wright, a stylish, calming presence blessed with a bite in the tackle and precision in the pass, was one of those rare figures who emerge but once every generation. He had the intuition to anticipate where every ball he needed to intercept was coming from before it had been played, and where every pass he made was directed prior to receiving it. Born in Ironbridge, Shropshire in

February 1924, he had had much of his early career wiped out by the war, but he almost hadn't got that far. As a teenage apprentice he had nearly been rejected by Wolves' eccentric manager, Major Buckley, on account of his size. The half-back burst into tears as he changed out of his kit, but was then summoned back to Buckley's office. He had a reprieve – Buckley had changed his mind because he thought Wright was a 'nice lad'. If the Major's belief in Wright's personal qualities redeemed him, the mentoring of a master of the half-back line – Stan Cullis – as a player, coach, and eventually manager, helped transform Wright from a steady teenager into one of the finest players to ever turn out for England.

Much had been heard by 1946 of a right-winger for Preston North End, a plumber by trade who had electrified the northern section of the Wartime League, helping his club emerge as champions and FA Cup winners, before heading off to join the fighting. Little, however, had since been seen of Tom Finney. Would he successfully make the step up to the harsh realities of real First Division and international football? Damn right he would. Born in April 1922 under the shadow of Deepdale, as a fourteen-year-old plumber's apprentice the prodigy had been offered a job on the Preston ground staff (the usual progression to the first team offered to exceptional youngsters) but his father had made him stick to his apprenticeship and learn a trade while playing for the Lilywhites' 'B' and youth teams. He never played for the first team before the war, but during it made the step up to wartime games where, along with Bill Shankly and others, he was part of one of the most exceptional wartime sides. In September 1946, just one month after his belated Football League debut for Preston, Finney made the first of seventy-six England appearances, serving as understudy for the injured Matthews and putting in a bright debut performance. Two months later, *Picture Post* paid him the following tribute:

> Finney has the power possessed only by the very few football geniuses who are unforgettable – the power to take over the whole game, the power to dictate the run of play, the power to stop the match, almost, until everybody is in the position he wants, and then to dispose of the ball in a manner entirely original, entirely unexpected, entirely correct, to the unmarked man from nowhere. Alex James had such a power. One hardly expects to see it twice in a decade.[6]

Later, it would become a perennial debate amongst football fans of the era as to who exactly was best: Matthews, the grand old master; or his 'apprentice' Finney, the 'Preston Plumber'. Almost always, for more than a decade following the war, one or the other would play on the England right; sometimes both appeared in the same line-up: Finney on the left, Matthews on the right. Despite their shared position their styles were very different: Finney was a close dribbler, who twisted and turned before accelerating off; Matthews, a feinter, would swerve and check his way through a defence, pause and then beat them all again. Both were virtuosos, certainly geniuses with the ball, yet between them – extraordinarily – they were to win just one major trophy. Despite suggestions to the contrary, there was no animosity between the two men, no real rivalry. Indeed, Finney got to know the normally reserved Matthews better than most, rooming with him, and sharing train journeys down to London for internationals.

The other great virtuoso who found his name on the England team sheet for the first official international that late September afternoon in Belfast was Middlesbrough's Wilf Mannion. The blond 'Golden Boy' of Ayresome Park would glide around the field, an almost aristocratic presence in a game usually full of yeomen. A creator of goals and frequent scorer himself, his range of passing was as unique as his close control and array of individual trickery. 'Mannion is Mozartian in his exquisite workmanship,' Donny Davies once mused in the *Manchester Guardian*. 'His style is so graceful and so courtly that he wouldn't be out of place if he played in a lace ruffle and the perruque.'

With Mannion providing the 'Mozartian' creative heartbeat to the team (and a debut hat-trick) England waltzed past Northern Ireland – emerging 7–2 victors – and south to Dublin, where Finney's goal was enough to gain victory. Emphatic wins over Wales (3–0) and Holland (8–2) gave England a 100 per cent record for 1946. Plaudits came thick and fast, eulogising England's thrilling new forward line with some quarters even laying high praise at the door of its new coach. Following the win in Northern Ireland John Macadam of *News Chronicle* gave praise to both:

> When you have finished handing bouquets to the classic England side, reach
> down to the bottom of the basket and grasp one for Walter Winterbottom,
> team manager, OC tactics, and one of the few intellectuals of the game of

association football . . . He is primarily a believer in the team principle in the co-ordination of eleven brilliant individuals into a cohesive machine. Certainly his first effort – the Belfast match – justifies all his theories. The team bristles with individuality and yet remains a team. Lawton, the only inveterate scorer, played a beautiful game and scored only one goal. No longer do we believe in one glory-getter standing out there in front to receive all the custom.[7]

Certainly Macadam's eulogy was not unjustified, but for how long would this happy state of affairs last?

A rising trend in the inter-war years had been the end of season tour of the continent which had increasingly become the norm, and a week after Great Britain's trouncing of the Rest of Europe in May 1947, England's footballers travelled to Switzerland (from where they would go on to Portugal) in an effort to underline English football's superiority. It was the first time the national side had flown to an international, but despite the relative comfort of the journey and the sense of confidence that came, frankly, simply from being English, they were strangely subdued against the Swiss. In the twenty-seventh minute a pass by Amado found Fatton completely unmarked and he slipped the ball past Swift for the game's only goal. A freak result or wake-up call?

Events a week later in Lisbon suggested it was a fluke. Mortensen made his full international debut in place of Carter and Finney came in for Langton on the left. England were transformed. Playing in the splendour of Lisbon's brand new Estadio Nacional, which had cost £350,000 to build – an unheard of amount in austerity-riddled Europe – England's finest tore their hosts apart. Within two minutes they led 2–0 through goals by Mortensen and Lawton; and when Lawton made it 3–0 shortly after, the Portuguese switched balls to a smaller, lighter version. It made not the slightest difference. Finney scored England's fourth with a virtuoso goal: picking the ball up on the halfway line, he had beaten his marker, darted into the Portuguese half, feinted past another, reached the byline, checked, taken the ball past a third defender as if he were invisible, before rifling a shot past the goalkeeper Azvedo from an oblique angle. To a chorus of whistles and boos the hapless, hopeless 'keeper was substituted illegally and was made to run a gauntlet of abuse and missiles as he walked tearfully around the pitch to the dressing room. Winterbottom protested to the referee, but the players weren't too bothered. 'Well you'll just have to go and get another four past him,' mused Frank Swift. And they did precisely that, set on their way by Lawton, who made it five to complete his hat-trick before the French referee blew for half-time.

The interval offered brief respite for the Portuguese. In the second half Lawton added his fourth, a feat matched by Mortensen who scored three more times to take England's tally to nine. By that time the Portuguese spectators realised that they were witnessing a performance of rare vintage and stood applauding their opponents' every move. Then, with just minutes left, Billy Wright sent Matthews running down the right. Having already seen his friend and rival Finney score after working his way through the Portuguese defence with all the directness of a visitor to Hampton Court maze, he too decided to go it alone. Cutting inside, he approached the defence, seemingly disappearing like an illusionist on one side and re-emerging in the clear on the other and, with just Capela ahead of him, tapped the ball beyond his reach and into the net to make it 10–0. The rout was complete. 'This was the closest thing I ever saw to perfection on the football field,' recalled Wright. 'Everything we tried came off, and Portugal just didn't know what had hit them.'[8]

If these forays onto foreign soil provided interesting and exotic diversions from the routine of domestic football and colourful insights for Pathe newsreels, as far as the majority of fans and players were concerned the Home Championship was still the predominant version of international football. England had won the 1946–47 competition and got off to a winning start in the next season's campaign, winning 3–0 against Wales at Ninian Park in October 1947, but had only managed a 2–2 draw against Northern Ireland at Goodison Park a month later. It meant that much rested on England's meeting with Scotland, due to be staged at Hampden the following April. If England avoided defeat, they would retain their crown; only victory would win the competition for the Scots.

At Blackpool Matthews and Mortensen had forged an almost subliminal understanding: the wing wizard and the powerful, prolific centre-forward. Their method was perfectly simple: Matthews would weave towards the byline and send in a testing cross which the lurking 'Morty' would invariably be on hand to meet. Their results together were often simply perfect: for Blackpool it took them to the 1948 FA Cup final after Mortensen had scored in every round and Matthews picked up the inaugural Player of the Year Award. For England, where the presence of Mannion, Lawton and Finney only added to their prowess, the partnership was equally devastating. Mortensen came into the game against Scotland having scored nine in his first five appearances for his country (including a hat-trick in his previous match), but the Scots' strategy meant that he would have to be patient in waiting for his chances to come. Scotland were set on quick tackling and getting to the ball first, forcing England to defend deeply and in numbers, leaving them heavily reliant on counter-attacks. After two early let-offs Finney broke down the left a minute before half-time. First he lost the ball to the Scots right-back, John Govan, but the defender dallied on his clearance, allowing Finney to nip in, reclaiming possession before striking a precise shot past Ian Black to give England a 1–0 lead.

The competitive nature of the game had already seen several injuries, but these were days when men were men and inferior individuals had no place on a football pitch. England's left-back and captain George Hardwick picked up a knee injury (which would actually end his international career) but with no substitutes to replace him was forced to spend most of the match as a passenger out on the wing. Frank Swift played on, despite two broken ribs after he was knocked out by Billy Liddell who had tried to bundle him and the ball into the net, but with Hardwick already hobbling uselessly on the flank, he fought on valiantly to the point of collapse by the game's conclusion. Grey faced, he would be led away in a police-escorted ambulance. 'I knew Hardwick was hobbling but I could not pack up and leave the old country in the cart,' he explained. Later still, at Manchester station he collapsed as a result of his injuries.[9] His counterpart Ian Black was weak in the face of some rumbustious challenges; McCauley hounded Mortensen – his 'tackling for a player with a reputation for polish was pretty robust at times' noted one observer; while Scotland's centre-back, George Young clashed heads horribly with Lawton, leaving the Scot with a nasty cut to his head that 'bled like a battered pugilist'. Bruised and buffeted, both teams fought on and England secured victory with twenty-five minutes remaining. McCauley was caught dawdling and Lawton stole in, played Mortensen through and the Blackpool man scored with ease. 'Sure foot, sure shot, sure goal,' noted one reporter.

Yet again England had been impressive in victory, with the two wide men – Finney and Matthews – both attracting much praise. Once themselves masters of wing play, the Scots were generous in their congratulations and one fan even submitted a commendatory ode to a local newspaper:

> At Bannockburn, all Scotsmen know
> We really laid the English low.
> The reason for this victory sublime?
> I think I've tumbled to the cause.
> We won because the battle was
> 600 years before Tom Finney's time!

Less impressed were the denizens at Lancaster Gate. After the game Finney, Lawton and Matthews were each called to the FA's headquarters to answer questions about their expense claims. For internationals they were allowed a £14 match fee, second-class rail travel, plus 'reasonable expenses'. According to the FA, Matthews' claim for sixpence for refreshments on the journey north failed to fall into the latter category.

At the disciplinary hearing he was greeted by the FA's Treasurer, Mr Ewbank ('a man with the mind of an accounting ledger' according to Matthews), complete with a wing-collared shirt (a complete anachronism even in 1948), and an unknown official with a face that 'looked as if he had been weaned on a lemon'. Asked to explain himself, Matthews told him that the sixpence was for the cup of tea and scone he had bought at Carlisle station en route to join the England squad.

'The emoluments which accrue when a player has the honour of being chosen to represent England are not inconsiderable,' thundered Ewbank, 'Fourteen pounds I consider a substantial sum for ninety minutes' work and recompense enough to cover any personal expenses you see fit to incur.' (Later, Matthews would joke: 'Emoluments which accrue? I felt as if I was playing a forgotten scene out of David Copperfield!') Without looking up, Ewbank drew a line through the expense and gesticulated towards the door to indicate that Matthews was no longer needed. Without saying goodbye, he merely nodded and 'the look of disdain on the face of his sidekick was such you'd have thought I'd tried to fiddle them out of a million pounds and fifty caps'.[10]

Obviously, the meanness of the FA grated, not least given that receipts for the match had stood at nearly £30,000, of which just £154 would find its way to the players of each team (plus, of course, 'reasonable expenses'). Yet also at stake at the time was the wider issue of players' weekly wages. In England the maximum annual salary a player could earn was £600 plus cup bonuses. Clubs could also contribute (though not all did) up to £150 per year towards a benefit, payable after five years. It was still two to three times the average salary, but there was little or no security. Players had to insure themselves in case their career ended through injury (by contrast, the clubs would cover *themselves* for any potential loss of transfer fee or similar). Pegged to a maximum wage, tied to their clubs, left to the whims of their chairmen, footballers were, almost literally, slaves to soccer.

In the late 1940s the Professional Footballers Association (PFA) pushed for a pay increase, longer contracts, abolition of the maximum wage and freedom of movement on completion of the existing contract. Jimmy Guthrie, the PFA Chairman, recorded in his autobiography, *Soccer Rebel*: 'We made some progress, but not enough. The maximum went up to £15 but there was no give to the other issues. The player was bound to his club for life whilst the employers could, if they so wished, kick out the injured or unsatisfactory man with only fourteen days' notice.' Tom Finney was later offered £120 per week, a £10,000 signing-on fee and a luxury villa to sign for an Italian club, but when the idea was put to his chairman he had snorted: 'What's £10,000 to thee lad?' Any hope of a transfer ended there and then. Although Finney's was an extreme case and football made few players rich, it wasn't a bad life. 'In comparison with the average working man you were doing well,' Lawton later said. 'There was a lot of unemployment and even for those in work the average wage was about £1.50 a week. What we earned was a fortune compared to the man on the street, but you had to live up to it. You had to dress correctly, be seen in the right clothes, and not let the club down like that, which cost money. And you knew you wouldn't be doing it forever.'[11]

That summer, appalled by the prevailing status quo and frustrated by Middlesbrough's refusal to grant him a transfer, Wilf Mannion decided to take matters into his own hands. He went on strike. His club held obstinately firm and refused to back down, and so for more than six months their golden boy kicked his heels on the sidelines. 'Personal liberty is a precious thing. It is one of the things we went to war about,' wrote the elegant hand of the *Sunday People*'s Alan Hoby:

> David Jack, giving the club's side told me recently: 'If Mannion won't play for us, he will never play in League football again.' Frankly this seems to me to savour of dictatorship. Security: the roving, restless search for security. That is what the Mannion mess typifies. There is no security in soccer. That is why he is sticking it out even though he is leading a life of misery. Saturday afternoons are torture to him. 'I love football,' he says, 'and feel lost without it.' Security. Liberty. Fraternity. I wonder when the FA and the Football League are going to understand the true meaning of those three words.

Fraternity, however, was seemingly as rare a commodity in football as liberty and security. Nobody joined Mannion's protest. When the matter was brought up in parliament by the Labour MP Ellis Smith, Harry French, Middlesbrough's vice-chairman hit back: 'Mannion's attitude to his transfer, if he maintains it, will mean that he will be out of football forever. Under such circumstances we will not transfer him.' He was speaking from a position of strength: unless the FA changed its attitude – which was highly unlikely since its ruling council was made up of men just like him. French knew full well that no MP could touch him, no matter how vindictive his stance seemed. Sometimes it even seemed self-defeating. When Celtic offered Middlesbrough an enormous £30,000 fee plus any two internationals from their star-studded line-up, it was turned down. Eventually the club got their way, and Mannion, almost forced to penury, called off his strike and re-signed for them – at the statutory maximum wage.

The eventual abolition of such constraints would come too late for Mannion and others of his era. Later, in retirement, he would be reduced to working as a tea boy in a Middlesbrough chemicals factory. Yet partly in response to his stance, the financial incentives for playing for England moved up a level – to £30 per match in 1950 when the maximum wage was £12 during the season and £10 during the summer. 'Take off the tax and one game would pay off the mortgage (£6 per month) for three months,' recalled Nat Lofthouse. 'I never had a lot of a brain but it didn't take me long to work out that if I stayed in the England team I'd be all right.'[12]

Before Mannion took his principled but ultimately futile sabbatical he was able to make a rather more telling impact for his country. On 16 May 1948 England travelled to Turin to face the world champions on their own turf. If some had dismissed 'The Game of the Century' between Britain and Europe a year earlier as something of a football circus ('The teams of Babel,' sniggered one commentator) nobody doubted the importance of this test to England's football 'superiority' – either in England or in Italy.

Turin was full, hotels booked out, shops, cinemas and cafes open through the night to entertain the deluge of visitors who had travelled from all over Italy for the match. For the Italian team the stakes were high: its manager, Vittorio Pozzo, had arranged for a 100,000 lire per man win bonus. Walter Winterbottom had no pecuniary incentives to offer but had relentlessly put his own men through their paces. Mortensen later wrote: 'We trained as never before. I put in two or three days of the hardest work of my football life and when we finally moved off to Turin we were all in the peak of physical condition, more like men in August than in May.' England's coach had already seen Italy beat France 3–0 away and been deeply impressed. 'They were toying with the French in the second half,' he said. 'They were lobbing the ball to each other, keeping it off the ground all the time and still passing to each other, trapping it on their chests or their knees and then forcing it through to someone else . . . It was incredible . . . they were a great, great side.'[13]

Come the big day, the temperature was touching 100ºC and the huge, white-shirted crowd shaded from the blazing sun under black umbrellas. Italy included seven of the legendary Torino team (who would be tragically wiped out *en masse* a year later in the Superga air disaster), with Valentino Mazzola, the hero of Italian football, at centre-forward and captain. From the outset he tormented the English defence, even under the watchful eye of the impeccable Billy Wright. Nonetheless England took the lead after only four minutes when Matthews played in Mortensen, who cut in from the left before hammering home a shot from the narrowest of angles, which flew past Bacigalupo. (After the match the *Times* football correspondent, Geoffrey Green, asked Mortensen whether the goal had been intentional. The forward gave Green a wry smile and responded, 'No, Bacigalupo got a fingertip to it and I meant to avoid his fingers by an inch or so!')

Italy fought back strongly. Twice Menti had goals disallowed for offside and several times England's captain and goalkeeper, Frank Swift, was tested to the limit of his ability, punching, palming, parrying the ball away. His methods weren't always pretty, but his was an indomitable presence. Even when he was beaten, Laurie Scott was on hand to clear the ball off the line causing the forlorn Guglielmo Gabetto to punch the turf in a mixture of disbelief and frustration. In the face of this onslaught and completely against the run of play, England doubled their lead on twenty-four minutes. This time Franklin's pass found Matthews, who again played in his Blackpool team-mate Mortensen. Under the close attention of Grezar and Parola, he changed pace, leaving both men for dead, before hooking a cross back for Lawton, who rifled a thunderous shot into the back of the net.

Still the Italians kept attacking, and still the English defence held them at bay. At half-time the heat had become so oppressive that the Italians were sprayed down with soda siphons and Henry Cockburn claimed he was so exhausted that he couldn't continue. 'Stop it,' ordered Winterbottom. 'I've seen the Italians, and they're worse than you.'

It was kidology, of course, and as the second half got under way the Italians maintained their onslaught seemingly impervious to the blistering intensity of the sun. Mazzola raced clean through but shot straight at Swift; then Gabetto hit the crossbar and Swift dived full length to block the rebound before again denying Mazzola. Yet with nineteen minutes remaining, England put the game beyond the Italians' reach. First, Mannion smartly lobbed the ball to Finney, who volleyed home first time; then, minutes later Finney made it 4–0 when Mortensen turned provider. Italy would go on to emerge as masters of what came to be known as *catenaccio* but England had given them an early lesson in defensive mastery and speed and skill on the counter-attack.

England's win sent Italy into a period of national mourning. Match reports were enclosed by black borders and Italy's football association president was dismissed. The victors could, by contrast, justifiably claim to be the best team in the world. Eighteen months later, on 30 November 1949 at White Hart Lane, they would prove it was no fluke. By then Lawton and Swift had each faded from the international scene and Winterbottom had appointed Billy Wright as captain, thus beginning in earnest one of football's most enduring 'Sergeant-Lieutenant' relationships. England had also lost their unbeaten home record to overseas opposition, losing 0–2 at Goodison to the Republic of Ireland (although – doubtless to Irish chagrin – their country was still not universally recognised as existing 'overseas') but the Italy side had changed beyond recognition after the Superga crash.

England too could lay claim to a number of new faces, perhaps most notably a full-back by the name of Alf Ramsey. Born in Dagenham in 1920 (although throughout his playing days and well into his managerial career he claimed to be two years younger) he had served his football apprenticeship in Southampton's wartime team, later playing as a peacetime professional with Southampton. But it was not until a £21,000 move took him to Tottenham Hotspur, when he came under the astute management of Arthur Rowe, that his career really took off. Lacking the natural gifts of many of his colleagues, Ramsey was a diligent, intelligent player who worked on being the best at what he was good at. A positional master, his football brain put him in places where he would intercept before the ball got to the winger; and if it did ever reach the attacker, he was a man who would jockey a defender, never diving in – always a great reader of the game, a thinker, never one to be rushed into over-hasty action. Later, as a manager, he would describe Martin Peters as being ten years ahead of his time, yet in many ways Ramsey the player was too: working on his defects, playing to his strengths, and not blithely hoping – as many of his contemporaries did – that natural talent alone would carry him through. Under Rowe's tutelage – one of the few English managers of the late 1940s with genuinely original ideas – Ramsey would obsess about the tactical side of the game. 'Alf was never a great one for small talk when he was with England parties,' recalled his international colleague Jackie Milburn. 'Football was his one subject of conversation. He was always a pepper and salt man, working out moves and analysing formations with the cruet on the table.'

Playing on home turf, Ramsey took his place against Italy at right-back and, as in Turin, England weathered a storm of opposition attacks. Bert Williams, Swift's replacement in England's goal, saved superbly at point-blank range from Carapellese; before nonchalantly repeating the feat against Martino and then outdoing himself with a fabulous reflex save that saw him parry away Lorenzo's shot. England offered little in attack but with fourteen minutes remaining went in front when Jack Rowley rocketed a left-footed shot past Moro. If that represented some good fortune for England, it was nothing compared to the stroke of luck that followed. With just minutes left on the clock, Billy Wright picked the ball up just inside the Italy half and sent a high hopeful hoof, which Moro misjudged appallingly. The ball flew over the goalkeeper's head and trickled into the Italian net to make it 2–0.

England's fans were able to leave north London safe in the knowledge that their country's footballers – unimpressive though they had been in victory – had again beaten purportedly the best team in the world (although their World Cup triumph had been twelve years previously). Others, however, sensed that England's peak had passed and that mere luck had carried them through: defeat against the Republic of Ireland should have been a wake-up call and some of the inadequacies displayed against Italy should have heightened that sense. As the journalist Ralph Finn wrote of the Italy win: 'In everything but the final score they were our superiors. Their football was yards faster than ours. They were supreme individualists yet they allied this self-conscious artistry to a teamwork which made ours look paltry by comparison.'[14]

Victory over Italy marked England's final encounter in a hateful, hurtful decade of world affairs. The détente and optimism which had accompanied the end of war in Europe and the Far East had been all too brief. An iron curtain had fallen with a hollow clunk, cutting off from the west not just the USSR, but Soviet-dominated Eastern Europe and parts of Asia too. Some countries were even dissected into Soviet- and American-dominated zones: East and West Germany; North and South Korea. In the latter, war was to break out in rival sectors in 1950. Football-wise, in the short term anyway, it meant that just as England was waking up to the world, a large part of it was suddenly put out of reach by feuding governments.

Yet, though the international outlook was gloomy, domestically it was a time of rising affluence. Little by little austerity, wage controls, unemployment and rationing were becoming things of the past after a decade of war and reconstruction and before that, economic depression. Perversely this was bad news for football. Although 1948–49 had been the pinnacle year for football crowds with 41,259,414 watching Football League games (seventeen million in the First Division alone), as the hard times of the late 1940s gave way to rising material prosperity in the early 1950s, less people attended matches. Between 1952 and 1954 football attendances were to drop by six million and, with people now diverted by a host of new leisure pursuits, by the end of the decade they had slipped below the thirty million mark, a figure that was never again reached apart from a fleeting resurgence after the 1966 World Cup finals. Television played a part in this decline, although the initial effect of this new medium as a way of watching football was negligible. When the BBC televised its first international match between England and Wales in November 1948 (commentated on by the ubiquitous Kenneth Wolstenholme), a crowd of 68,750 had still turned out at Villa Park despite its taking place on a Wednesday afternoon.

With attendances at their apogee it is surprising to note the degree to which parochialism still flourished. Public interest in the fourth World Cup finals to be staged in Brazil in the summer of 1950 was largely negligible even though it was England's first and they were favourites. The great unknowns of Europe were still of secondary interest to the Scots, Welsh or Irish, and the South Americans might as well have existed across the seas of space rather than the Atlantic Ocean. (England, of course, were still to face a non-European country at football.) Few fans were to make the gruelling and expensive journey to South America and none at home, even those few people in possession of TV sets, were able to receive any sort of live transmission in the absence of satellite technology.

On their return to FIFA, the four British associations had been indulgently rewarded with two qualifying spots from the best-placed countries of the Home Championship tournament preceding the finals. Scotland had pigheadedly announced that if they did not *win* the Home Championship, they had no wish to go to Brazil. When both countries emphatically beat the Irish (England won 9–2, Scotland 8–2) and recorded victories over the Welsh, it meant that everything, for Scotland anyway, rested on their meeting on 15 April 1950 at Hampden Park. As ever there seemed something preordained by recent tradition about the day: a massive crowd (133,250); a hotly contested match; a Scotland team so utterly desperate to win that their best chances were snatched and England riding their luck before grabbing a late winner. And so it came to pass: Billy Steel shot straight at Bert Williams when it seemed easier to score; Liddell missed an open goal and then, with England under intense Scots pressure, Mannion dummied Dickinson's pass, Bobby Langton picked up the ball, ran and released Roy Bentley, who fired England into the lead. Six minutes from the end, Bauld shot against Williams's crossbar, the ball bounced safely away and with it, Scottish World Cup dreams. The SFA obstinately refused to change its mind. Billy Wright pleaded with George Young, the Scots captain, to appeal, arguing that their presence in Brazil would make a great difference to England but it was all to no avail.

Even if the Scots had deigned to turn up, it was not a fully subscribed competition anyway. The Argentinians had pulled out as a result of a longstanding squabble with the Brazilian federation; the French had initially failed to qualify but were invited to the finals after Turkey's refusal to come, accepted, then, after a disappointing run-up to the competition, sullenly withdrew; Germany were still excluded from FIFA after the war; Hungary and the USSR hid behind the Iron Curtain; Austria withdrew on account of having 'too young' a side; and when Portugal refused to take Scotland's place, the fourth World Cup finals was left with just thirteen teams.

Despite the omissions, FIFA took the absurd decision to go ahead as planned with four pools of countries, even if that meant two groups of four, one of three and a fourth consisting of just Uruguay and lowly Bolivia. The winners would qualify to a final pool of four teams and there would be no final as such, with the world champion being the one at the top of the final mini-league pool. England were drawn with the United States, Chile and Spain – which seemed to offer an easy passage to the final pool.

Yet England's build-up had been anything but smooth. First, on 14 May, they had journeyed to Lisbon, scene of the 10–0 massacre three years earlier. Portugal were now managed by Ted Smith, the one time

Millwall centre-half, but little heed had apparently been paid to his defensive coaching as Finney tore them apart at will. At half-time the scoreline stood at 3–0 in England's favour and even when Portugal pulled a goal back just after the interval, a fabulous solo effort from Finney restored England's advantage. This time, however, the Portuguese fans stayed loyal to their countrymen. 'A British crowd yells. A Scots crowd yells still more loudly. But these Continental crowds literally scream as though each fan present were being done to death,' remembered Finney. 'Such blood-curdling horrifying falsetto encouragement I have never heard. We were the bulls and the matadors were making a kill.'[15] Spurred on, Portugal dominated the second half and ultimately deserved more than the 5–3 final scoreline. Finney had 'had one of those days of which a player dreams', noted one observer, but of the team as a whole the assessment was damning. Charles Buchan, reporting in the *News Chronicle*, was blunt in his opinion: 'This England team will not do for Rio.' Three days later in Brussels, England had to overcome a 0–1 half-time deficit to emerge 4–1 victors over Belgium. But again, the nature of their win, emphatic though it ultimately was, had been unimpressive. On the other hand, England had still won seventeen of their previous twenty-one matches; and in the twenty-nine games since the end of the war, they had recorded victory in twenty-three, scoring more than 100 goals (an average of 3.5 per match).

A bigger blow was to come. England's imperious centre-half, Neil Franklin, had been granted permission by the FA to miss the matches against Portugal and Belgium, ostensibly on account of his wife's difficult pregnancy. In reality it was cover for clandestine negotiations with two former internationals, Jock Dodds of Scotland and England's George Eastham, who were acting for teams in Colombia. Because Colombia had left FIFA its clubs were essentially free to poach players from wherever they liked without the need to pay a transfer fee. It was a practice that had previously been confined to Argentina, where a number of famous players had been lured from their homelands by enormous wages, and temptation was now thrust the way of British stars bound by such appalling restrictions at home. As one of Franklin's contemporaries also contemplating the switch put it:

We are the only entertainers in the world who cannot negotiate for higher wages. We are burdened with a maximum wage. We have contracts which last only a year; and we are not free to move freely when they run out. If there are other countries besides Colombia not bound by the rules of the International Football Association we will go to them when they offer us extra freedom and more money.[16]

Compared to what England paid, the sums involved were huge. Franklin was offered a £2000 signing on fee and wages of £120 per week to join Santa Fe – ten times what he was paid at Stoke. Along with several others – including his Stoke City team-mate George Mountford and Manchester United's Charlie Mitten – he accepted. Inevitably the FA took a dim view of the affair, banning Franklin for a year, which ended any possibility of his presence at the World Cup.

The move turned out to be a disaster for the defender. In a team dominated by Argentinians, the newcomers were hated. 'You hit a man over the head with a bottle with the same sort of nonchalance as you would say "don't talk rubbish" at home,' he later said. 'The players are just as bad. Their tempers are always at exploding point and it only needs a tiny spark to turn a football game into a brawl.'[17] Most of the 'Bogotá Bandits', including Franklin, returned within months, having failed to make any serious money. He returned to action in 1951 with Hull City but was a pale imitation of the player who had so graced the England and Stoke back lines in the immediate post-war years, and his career fizzled out without distinction. Football's administrators could reflect on his demise with a degree of *schadenfreude*: the status quo had prevailed; here was a warning to those who might dare to challenge it.

But for England, on the eve of the finals, it was a devastating blow. Nobody else in Franklin's position came even remotely close to matching his pedigree as a footballer, much less his experience. 'Franklin is a phenomenon,' *Picture Post* had written in a fulsome tribute in February 1949. 'Off the field he is a nice, quiet boy, with good manners and no airs, and no remarkable style. On the field he is transfigured. He is a master; and such an easy master, to whom nothing seems any trouble at all.'[18] Having played in twenty-seven consecutive post-war internationals, there was simply no ready replacement for him. In the days before two regular centre-halves, the position was in many ways as important as that of the goalkeeper. His absence was crucially to undermine England then, and over following years.

Much can be derived from the level of preparations the FA undertook ahead of the World Cup finals about how seriously they regarded the tournament. At very best the arrangements made could be described as half-hearted. Not until 14 June 1950, eleven days ahead of the opening match in Rio de Janeiro, did the England squad begin training, at Dulwich Hamlet's ground, where they didn't even have the use of the first team pitch. A few days later they made the exhausting thirty-one hour journey to Brazil. With them was just one selector – the Grimsby fish merchant, Arthur Drewry – whose presence was more a reflection on how seriously the minions at Lancaster Gate took the tournament than faith in Winterbottom's abilities as a manager: quite simply, nobody could be bothered making the journey. At the same time, though, the FA had arranged a 'goodwill tour' of Canada, and Manchester United a tour of the United States. Accordingly, United had requested that none of their players be selected for England duty. Stanley Matthews was sent to Canada as a 'football ambassador' and was not due to arrive in Brazil until after England's first match. Still, in North America he was testing himself against such steely opposition as the Swedish amateurs of Jonkopings (whom the FA side beat 7–1).

England were based at the Luxor Hotel on Copacabana Beach, 'a paradise of millionaires', according to Jackie Milburn, but ill-suited to the squad's needs. Rather than sending their own men out the FA had taken the advice of Arsenal's manager Tom Whittaker, who had travelled to Brazil for an end of season tour a year earlier, but the circumstances were – obviously – very different and the hotel inappropriate for the World Cup hopefuls. The food, for instance, was so bad that according to Stan Mortensen 'even the dustbins had ulcers'. The first meal the players had was cold ham and fried eggs swimming in black oil and it steadily got worse, with a number of the squad taken ill and others existing solely on bananas. 'Were bananas the best food in preparation for a match?' asked one journalist. 'Probably not,' responded Mortensen, 'but you should see us climb the trees!' In the end Winterbottom decided that the only way around the problem was to go to the hotel kitchen and supervise the cooking himself.

Of course there were cultural differences too. In a pre-globalised world, Brazil was merely a name on a map. Hardly any of the England party knew anything about the country, its footballers or even what a

Brazilian looked like. Eddy Baily later recalled that the only Brazilian he had ever seen was the Hollywood actress Carmen Miranda – and she was best known for leaping around film sets with fruit piled up on her head. More crucially perhaps, nobody had seen them play, not even Winterbottom.

England opened the tournament against Chile at the still incomplete Maracana Stadium, under rain that poured relentlessly down on a 29,703-strong crowd, who filled a mere eighth of the stadium's vast environs. Liverpool's Lawrie Hughes made his debut in place of the departed Franklin; Chile, England's first ever non-European opponents, were not an entirely unknown quantity: their centre-forward and captain, George Robledo, who had been born in Chile of a local man and a Yorkshirewoman, had been brought up in England and starred for Barnsley and Newcastle. It turned out to be a poor game (the players later complained that the smoggy Rio air impaired their efforts) with England taking the lead in the thirty-eighth minute, when Mortensen headed home Jimmy Mullen's centre. Twice they survived scares: when Robledo's free-kick hit the post, then when Carvalho hit the bar; before scoring a second, decisive goal midway through the second half. Mortensen sent Finney racing down the right, and his cross was met by Mannion, whose glancing shot nestled neatly inside the near post. It concluded a satisfactory start to World Cup football and Charles Buchan, who had previously dismissed England's chances, reported: 'On their display in the second half at any rate, England can win this trophy. I have no doubt now that they will beat Spain and the US and win the Group Championship. This was as good an England team as I've seen for a very long time.'

Next up, four days later, were the United States, purportedly the group's whipping boys. For the match, England moved to Belo Horizonte and found the mountain air rather more invigorating than Rio. Staying as guests of the Morro Velho gold mine – English owned and the employer of 2000 expatriate British workers – Winterbottom's men began training there with a cricket match against the press. Nobody, not even their own manager, gave the Americans a chance. Eight of the United States' players were American born and three were immigrants: Joe Marca (Belgium); Ed McIlvenney (Scotland), who had recently been given a free transfer by Wrexham; and Larry Gaetjens (Haiti). In goal they boasted a former baseball player, Frank Borghi, and their centre-half, Charles Colombo, inexplicably played in leather gloves. In the British press much ribaldry was printed in the run-up to the tie, with the *Daily Express* generously proclaiming: 'It would be fair to give them [the US] three goals of a start'.

From the incomplete magnificence of the Maracana, Belo Horizonte's Mineiro Stadium represented a sea change in standards. The players were forced to change in small wooden huts and the pitch was little better than scrubland, surrounded by a high wall that gave the impression of a bullring rather than a football ground. Winterbottom was not happy: 'They were so awful I ordered the team to change at a nearby athletic club. The rest of the ground, you wouldn't really recognise it as such. There was also a fourteen-foot high wall around the pitch – it was like playing football in a bull ring – and the grass on the pitch was very rough and lumpy.'[19] England boasted an unchanged side, despite the late arrival of Matthews whom Winterbottom had wished to include. Stanley Rous argued the case for him, but the sole selector, Arthur Drewry, flatly dismissed his pleas. 'My policy is to never change a winning team,' he sniffed. Naturally the glorified fishmonger knew best, but everyone knew that it was an absurd state of affairs.

Drewry's side nevertheless laid siege to the United States goal, peppering it with shots from near and far, hitting posts, crossbars, stray legs and anything else the American defence could throw in the way. Yet the excellence of Borghi in goal and the efforts in defence of McIlvenny and Colombo kept England out, while the intelligent passing of John Souza gave the England defence no rest. The pitch was cramped and narrow, meaning that the English were unable to make full use of the flanks and, as the game progressed without the deadlock being broken, they became increasingly unsettled. Then, on thirty-eight minutes, the impossible happened. McIlvenney's throw found Walter Bahr, who shot from twenty-five yards; the ball hit the back of Gaetjens' head and deflected over the sprawling, forlorn figure of Bert Williams to give the US a 1–0 lead. It was a fluke but it made the half-time scoreline a freak.

After the interval England continued to pile pressure on the American goal. Mortensen shot over; Bentley's over-elaboration undid a clear chance; Mannion's shot cleared the bar when he was unmarked; Ramsey forced a fine save from Borghi, and so it went on. The Americans, meanwhile, mixed their play with some gamesmanship: one of their favoured tactics was kicking the ball into the stands where a sympathetic crowd would pass it around to kill time; another, to stroll ponderously into position when awarded a set piece. Time ran down, chances wore thin and finally, the Italian referee's whistle confirmed that a miracle had occurred: the United States had beaten England.

The result was telexed through by the Reuters correspondent, who was the only journalist of the eight present with a telephone link to Rio and the outside world. When it reached the office of one London newspaper, a sub-editor assumed a transmission error and corrected it – England 10 United States 1.

It had been a bad day for English sport in general. In cricket England had lost their first-ever Test match at home to the West Indies, while British hopes at Wimbledon had been extinguished for another year with the defeat of Tony Mottram by the Australian Geoff Brown. It was a rude awakening. 'England,' wrote Geoffrey Green, 'it was thought, could win wearing bowler hats, carrying umbrellas, without raising perspiration.'[20] It had been as clear an indication as they had ever had that the expectation that England's status as the game's inventors was no guarantee of success, that merely *being* England was not enough.

The Americans' win briefly catapulted their motley assortment of foreign ringers and local amateurs out of the pit of obscurity, but they soon plummeted back into it. It would take almost fifty years, an expensive – and ultimately abortive – league, plus a World Cup on American soil for football in the US to begin to take off. Even then they failed to dent the dominance of the *ancien regime* of the soccer world, its European and South American heartlands.

For England, all was not entirely lost after the defeat, but it would be an uphill struggle to progress to the final round. In short, they had to beat Spain by three goals to face them again in a play-off, by four or more to go through on superior goal average. Drewry, the fishmonger, finally acceded to Winterbottom's wishes and included Matthews, also handing debuts to Eddy Bailey and Bill Eckersley, but it was all to no avail. The Spanish defence held as firm as the Americans and with five minutes remaining Zarraonandia hit England on the break to win the match 1–0. A crestfallen squad flew straight home (nearly crashing en route), and nobody from the party stayed to see if anything could be gleaned from the second half of the competition. The deciding match was a final of sorts between Brazil and Uruguay, with the hosts needing just a draw to win. Refereed by the Englishman George Reader (later chairman of Southampton) in front of a world record crowd of 199,854, Uruguay upset the odds and emerged 2–1 winners and world champions for the second time.

Some soul searching was inevitable after England's exit. The *Daily Mirror* carried a comment piece by Tom Phillips, written before the Spain match ('I don't intend to change a word,' he promised) about the tendency of Englishmen to complain and look for excuses whenever the national team lost abroad. At home, there was a 'sense of proportion', but on the continent 'foreign air and customs affect the English peculiarity'. He continued:

> If we are beaten in Italy, members of the English colony there will write to us moaning of the terrible blow England's prestige has suffered. What has happened is this. The Italians (or whatever nation it is), who have never had much to cheer about anyhow, any time, have in their excitable way pulled the legs of every Englishman they could find. And the English, instead of remembering their ability to hit back as they do in real emergencies, in domestic political crises or in the war, take, as they say in my part of the country, 'the water in'. They weep in the corner.[21]

Others were more considered in their response, but asked questions not of the hare-brained notion that Drewry rather than Winterbottom had picked the team, but of England's captain, Billy Wright.

At Lancaster Gate, in an effort to improve the standard of the England team, Stanley Rous formed a 'Technical Sub-Committee' charged with the task of examining 'by what means the work of the International Committee and its Selection Sub-Committee could be made more effective'. It included the chairmen of each selection committee (senior, intermediate, amateur and youth) and was given the authority to consult with players, managers and directors. Yet nothing was agreed on and no progress was made. There was nothing to be learned from the South Americans because they had suspended their league programme and therefore gained an unfair advantage; nobody could decide on the best way to prepare for matches. Should players be given tactics, or merely go out and play their best? Some thought they should resort to a tactical orthodoxy; others that their minds ought not be confused with blackboards and dossiers. The Tottenham manager, Arthur Rowe, left the second of these meetings disheartened. 'As much as anyone I wanted the England team to be on top, but I was left with the impression that nothing had really changed,' he said. 'When my World Cup players [Baily, Ditchburn, Nicholson and Ramsey] came back from Brazil they told me that despite the difficulties England should have done much better. As I suspected, England suffered most from poor organisation. My view was that the bulk of preparation for future foreign tours and World Cups should be done at home.'[22] In fact it was not until the 1951–52 season that a proper period of pre-match practice was obtained. Before then, players quite frequently met their international team-mates on the morning of the match, sometimes not until they had reached the dressing room because of the reluctance of club chairmen to release players.

Confidence was invariably shaken by the Brazilian fiasco but the squad of players England could rely on was still packed full of outstanding individuals whose names have been immortalised in their club's histories, if, alas, not always their country's. Billy Wright, Alf Ramsey, Wilf Mannion and Tom Finney were each as fine a figure in their respective positions as England had ever known. Likewise, the irrepressible Stanley Matthews, thirty-five years old and repeatedly written off on account of his age. His form was so perpetually out-standing that even the most obtuse England selector could not ignore his claims. When the goals started to dry up for his Blackpool team-mate Stan Mortensen, his fellow Lancastrian, Nat Lofthouse of Bolton Wanderers, took the England number nine shirt and seized his opportunity with gusto. A son of the town where he would see out his entire career, he had made his debut in a wartime match as a fifteen-year-old and took full league football in his stride. A big, powerful centre-forward, a physically imposing challenge for any defender, Lofthouse was as good a centre-forward as had ever played for England. Most importantly, he scored goals in the air and from scorching shots with abandon.

England, however, had their shortcomings. The selectors could choose from many fine goalkeepers – Bert Williams was one; his successor, Gil Merrick of Birmingham City another – but there was no great individual like Frank Swift or Henry Hibbs. Likewise, after Neil Franklin's demise, no suitable replacement had emerged at centre-half. Indeed, so short was the supply of top-class number fives that the *Daily Mirror* came to cruelly dub one of Franklin's successors, Malcolm Barrass, 'Malcolm *Em*Barrass'.

No serious decline set in after the World Cup but little really changed in its aftermath. The selectors still ruled the roost, Winterbottom began to spend a little more time with his players, and there was no widespread questioning of the status quo so long as results remained generally impressive and that famous unbeaten home run remained intact. Complacency took root and life went on as normal. True, Yugoslavia nearly won at Highbury in November 1950 (it ended 2–2), likewise France the following October (again it finished 2–2), but these were overshadowed by other victories. Argentina were beaten in impressive fashion at Wembley (2–1 in May 1951), the good run against Italy continued with a 1–1 draw in Turin in May 1952, and a week later Lofthouse's name entered folklore as 'The Lion of Vienna' after his virtuoso display in the famous 3–2 victory over Austria. When England hammered Belgium 5–0 at Wembley in November 1952, one newspaper headline boasted: 'Recovery complete: England on top again'.

That same week it was announced that Hungary – crowned Olympic champions in Helsinki that summer – would play England at Wembley the following November. Stanley Rous had brokered the arrangement – a far from easy task given the prevailing political situation and the Hungarian government's hold over sports. Rous had also arranged a friendly match against the Rest of Europe to celebrate the Football Association's ninetieth anniversary a month prior to the Hungary game, but first England had to embark on an ambitious tour of South America in May and June 1953.

Two weeks before the squad flew out, Matthews and Mortensen had combined to win Blackpool the FA Cup for the first time in one of the most dramatic finals in the competition's history. Mortensen, who had scored a hat-trick that day, was not included in the party; Matthews, who had the tie named after him (erroneously in his own modest opinion) but had not appeared for his country in two years, was picked following a public clamour, but sat the tour out to rest a persistent injury. While Britain braced itself for the impending coronation of Queen Elizabeth II, England's footballers were kicking off their summer tour in Buenos Aires in a match that all but started a fifty-year-long feud with the Argentinian national side.

'Conditions were in our favour and they didn't like it,' recalled Billy Wright. 'They began elbowing and tripping, shirt-pulling whenever one of our players looked like breaking clear.'[23] Mercifully, perhaps, torrential rain brought a halt to proceedings after twenty-five minutes; the AFA officials claimed that the pitch would not be ready for a rematch for 'five days' and the England party flew on to Santiago without fulfilling the fixture. England followed their 2–0 win over Chile in the World Cup with a 2–1 win on Chilean soil. Manchester United's forward, Tommy Taylor, the most expensive player in English football at £29,999 (his manager, Matt Busby, had not wanted to burden him with the pressure of being the first £30,000 player), scored the first on his debut, Lofthouse the deciding goal. Next, in Montevideo, an England side whose ranks had been laid low by food poisoning gave a credible performance but fell to a 1–2 defeat to world champions Uruguay. The tour was completed by a trip to New York where, in an almost empty Yankee Stadium, England gained some revenge over the Americans by recording a 6–3 win.

England's footballers had performed well in what was regarded by the players themselves as an exhausting finale to a tiring season. Yet Winterbottom had come to the realisation that, within the existing set-up, his was an impossible job. 'Some good players are coming through,' he confessed to those close to him, 'but in team play we are way behind. I'm still being prevented [by the selectors] from building a team. From match to match, there are too many changes to make planning possible. Stanley Rous is with me on this but he can't get through to the International Committee.'[24] Subtle attempts by the FA Chief Coach and Secretary to edge the International Committee aside were hamstrung by the knowledge that they owed their own positions to the FA hierarchy and could not afford to rock the boat, and the unshakable belief of its members – fishmongers, solicitors and whatever else – in their own righteousness.

While they remained obtusely deaf to Rous and Winterbottom's pleas, proof was to come in autumn 1953 that the FA would have to change its ways if England were to progress. First, on 21 October, came the anniversary match against the Rest of Europe. England instantly came unstuck, conceding a first-minute penalty, which Kubala converted; and while Mortensen equalised three minutes later, the Europe side, a hotchpotch of strangers not even united by a common language, took England apart. By the fortieth minute they were 3–1 in front, their hosts flagging. Jimmy Mullen pulled a goal back shortly before half-time and, as the game progressed into the second half, the input of Matthews began to take hold. Bamboozling the Europe defence with a mazy run he set up Mullen for England's equaliser; Mortensen hit the post; but Europe's quick, sharp passing time and again caught England out whenever an attack – usually prompted by a dribble, usually from Matthews – broke down. On sixty-five minutes Kubala put Europe back in front, and only Merrick's desperate dive a few minutes later prevented him from making it 5–3. Still the Europeans continued to outplay England, with only Merrick standing in the way of further goals. Then, with just seconds remaining, in one last-gasp attack, Mortensen burst into the Europe penalty area and was clumsily upended by Čajkovski. From the penalty spot Alf Ramsey coolly converted England's equaliser.

Watching the match that afternoon was Gustav Sebes, coach of the Hungarian national team, whom England were meeting the following month. Given the insularity and paranoia of the Soviet bloc in the fall-out from the Berlin blockade, the Hungarians knew almost nothing about the English and even Sebes had previously derived all his information from the London embassy's cultural attaché. The previous July, however, Imre Nagy had replaced Matyas Rakosi, Hungary's neo-Stalinist Prime Minister, heralding the start of the 'new course' programme, a more moderate, less repressive brand of communism, which opened the country to the west and allowed for hitherto banned scouting trips. The following day Sebes returned to Wembley to test the pitch. He noticed that the turf wasn't a springy surface with even high balls bouncing no more than a metre. He measured its dimensions, even tried to work out at which angle the sun would shine and asked Stanley Rous if he might have a match ball (English balls were harder and less sensitive than those commonly used on the continent). Rous gave him three. Back in Budapest, Sebes found a pitch of a similar size to Wembley and from early November, three times a week, the squad trained there using Rous's balls.

Perhaps surprisingly given the introversion of the Football Association, England responded with a scouting mission of their own. High up in ivory towers at their respective solicitors' offices and grocery shops, it seemed as if the International Selection Committee had heard excited whispers about this magnificent Magyar team. Although they had not entered the 1950 World Cup, Hungary were

1952 Olympic Champions (they were nominally amateur) and in November 1953 were three and a half years into a six-year run in which they would suffer just one defeat. Their two inside-forwards, Sandor Kocsis and Ferenc Puskás, would between them score 158 goals in a combined 152 appearances for their country and in the centre, Nandor Hidegkuti played in an otherwise unheard of 'free role', despite nominally taking the centre-forward's shirt. Yet on 15 November, when Hungary played Sweden at the Nepstadion, they drew 2–2 and were unusually unimpressive. Puskás missed a penalty and the band of English FA officials went home in a confident mood. 'Where's your fantasy team now?' one of them mocked the *Sunday People*'s Alan Hoby, who had been championing the Hungarians since witnessing their breathtaking football in Helsinki.

Ten days later the Hungarians were in London having travelled by train across Europe (stopping in Paris, where they warmed up against the workers of the Renault factory – turning out 17–0 winners). On the day of the match the press were typically confident that England would continue their 'unbeaten' home record against foreign opposition.

'Players out to slam Hungary – and critics,' the *Daily Mail* trumpeted. English 'character', it added, would prove superior to Hungarian technique: 'The Hungarians, Olympic Champions, who are rated in some quarters as a "wonder side" will today face a strong and determined England side. Their style will differ a lot from Hungarian play, but I think it will prevail . . . England should finish two or three goals to the good . . . but the Hungarians will not give in easily.' England's selectors had seen fit to make four changes to the forward line alone from the previous match, a 3–1 win over Northern Ireland and included four Blackpool players – Matthews, Mortenson, Ernie Taylor and Harry Johnston – who 'would provide some adhesion and coordination in our play'.

From the start it was obvious to the 100,000-strong crowd that this was mismatch of the day. Hungary completely defied any of the prevailing British notions of contemporary tactical orthodoxy. Nandor Hidegkuti was used as a deep-lying centre-forward and rather than deploying out-and-out wingers (like Matthews) the visitors used widemen to interchange with other members of the forward line. The very concept was alien to the England team, particularly the full-backs but none more so than the centre-half,

Harry Johnson. For him, the Hungary match was a catastrophe. Utterly baffled by Hidegkuti, he didn't know whether to stay with him and leave a gap at the back, or let him run free. He chose the latter and the Hungarian ran riot. Wright and his fellow half-back, Jimmy Dickinson, tried to help pick Hidegkuti up, but that merely left Kocsis and Puskás more space. 'It was a bit of a surprise that England were so unaware of our deep-lying centre-forward strategy,' the Hungarian goalkeeper Gyula Grosics revealed years later.

> We had been playing it for some time and their coaches must have seen us. But once the game started, it was even more of a surprise that their defence seemed so totally unable to adjust to it once it was apparent. They just kept on playing the same way and that meant that England's centre-half had no one to mark and didn't know what to do. It also meant that Hidegkuti was free to operate, and score, from midfield.[25]

But it wasn't just superior tactics that confounded England, it was a question of technical ability. Within a minute of kick-off, Hidegkuti, after playing a dummy of such sublimity that it wrong-footed the England defence in its entirety, thunderously crashed a shot past Merrick. On thirteen minutes Czibor and Puskás breath-takingly combined to set up Hidegkuti again but his shot past Merrick was disallowed for offside. Although they allowed England back into the game when Jackie Sewell equalised, hopes briefly raised that the visitors' stunning start had been an aberration were soon dashed. On twenty minutes Czibor and Puskás did what they had done seven minutes earlier but this time Hidegkuti stayed onside to make it 2–1. Moments later Kocsics fed Czibor down the right and he drifted past Eckersley with ease before playing the ball inside to Puskás. Wright slid in to tackle him, but the Hungarian pulled the ball back from his lunge with the sole of his boot and unleashed a goalbound shot in one movement. In *The Times* Geoffrey Green likened Wright's challenge to 'a fire engine going in the wrong direction for a blaze'. Before the half-hour-mark Bezsik furiously drilled in a free-kick that clipped Puskás' heel and diverted past the hapless Merrick to make it 4–1.

England rallied briefly, their main avenue of opportunity coming from the feet of Matthews and Mortensen, and when George Robb's shot was parried by Grosics, the latter was on hand to stab home England's second. The resurgence was brief. Before the hour-mark had been reached, Hungary's total was six: Boszik had hit a rising, swerving shot past the forlorn Merrick; then Puskás nonchalantly lobbed the ball over the England defence and Hidegkuti whacked a volley into the back of the England net. Ramsey scored a consolatory penalty to make it 3–6, but England's proud, unbeaten record had gone. Not only that, it had been obliterated. 'England were bewitched, yes, and bothered and bewildered, by a side of soccer sorcerers who, at times, seemed capable of reading each other's minds,' said Tom Finney, injured the previous Saturday for Preston, and watching from the stands. 'This was the nearest thing to telepathy on a football field, and doubt if its like will ever be reproduced again in my lifetime.'[26]

Most of the following day's newspapers magnanimously heaped praise on the victors. 'Billy Wright has never been given such a chasing in all his life as the one he got from Ferenc Puskás,' reported the *Daily Mirror*. 'We all know Wright is a world class defender, so what does that make Puskás? Collect all your money from your piggy bank and put in Hungary now to win the World Cup in Switzerland next summer. They made England look like second-class citizens.' Even the refuge of the little Englander – the *Daily Mail* – showed a picture of the England players saluting the Hungarians at the post-match banquet while its editorial saluted Hungarian greatness. There was some consolation, they added: England had beaten the Hungarians 5–4 in a table tennis international.

Some, like Alf Ramsey, were in denial. In a pique of ungraciousness, he wrote the result off as a fluke. 'Four of those goals came from outside our penalty area,' was his glib assessment of the debacle. 'We should never have lost.' The full-back's remarks notwithstanding, there followed another national debate about the state of the national team. As they had done after Belo Horizonte the FA set up various technical committees to undertake an autopsy, summoning club managers and former internationals Matt Busby, Stan Cullis, Arthur Rowe and Joe Mercer to come up with answers to remedy the malaise. There was an appeal to clubs to cooperate more closely in the building of the England side by releasing their players more and for longer periods so that Winterbottom could derive greater benefit from training sessions. But, by and large, the official response ended there.

Nevertheless, among clubs and players themselves there was a slow but increasing awareness of continental training techniques and pre-match preparation. It became widely acknowledged that the

Hungarians, in particular, led the way, and teams began to replicate similar advanced physical exercises and the use of scientific equipment to monitor the players. Elite footballers started to dispense with the clodhopping boots that had previously been the norm, using lighter, less cumbersome footwear that was more sensitively attuned to ball-play and allowed players to run faster. Bit by bit managers began to deploy more varied and interesting training routines designed to kill the tedium of the training ground by placing greater emphasis on ball practice. Slowly, the traditionally tedious training methods of 'lapping' and cross-country runs came to be supplanted.

Yet it would be nearly fifty years before the English training ground fully woke up to global innovations. In the short term nobody really knew how to react. If what was wrong was the anachronistic way that players were picked for their country, nobody came out and said so: it had always been like that; it would always be like that; therefore it was correct. If it was a matter of technical ability, that was down to the club's training routines, and, in any case, had not Winterbottom, in the other part of his multi-hatted job, laid down criteria for trainers? And if it was a question of tactics, well, most of the players simply didn't want to know. Matthews would later cause consternation by writing in his first autobiography of the 1950 World Cup:

> A will to win was sadly lacking in the England team . . . I blame this on the pre-match talks on playing tactics that had been introduced for the first time by our team manager. *You just cannot tell star players how they must play and what they must do on the field in an international match.* You must let them play their natural game, which has paid big dividends in the past. I have noticed that in recent years these pre-match instructions have become more and more longwinded while the playing ability of the players on the field has dwindled. So I say scrap the talks and instruct the players to play their natural game.

Instead, the inquest foundered on complacency, of pretending that what had happened was an aberration rather than treating it as a watershed, as Ralph Finn wrote: 'No one really considered we had lost very much. The tone of biased, misleading optimism laughed its way through the columns of our sportspages. We had been beaten, that was all. There was no lesson to be learned.'[27]

Indeed that seemed to be the case when England travelled to

Budapest the following May for the return match. The 3–6 defeat had spelt the end for Alf Ramsey, Bill Eckersley, Harry Johnston, Ernie Taylor, Stan Mortensen and George Robb, but there had been no radical attitude change in either the England team or press. The day before the match, the *Daily Mail* carried the memorable headline: 'England chance of revenge: Hungary worried.' Given the Wembley experience and what was to follow, it is difficult to tell quite what England's hosts might have had to be concerned about.

England came into the match on the back of a 0–1 defeat in Yugoslavia while in Hungary a million people (one in nine of the Hungarian population) had applied for one of the 100,000 tickets. Such was the insatiable demand for tickets from friends and acquaintances, Puskás claimed that he had had to change his telephone number two months before the return leg. The enthusiasm of his countrymen was no great shock but the naivety of his opponents was. 'Within minutes we realised that the English hadn't even changed their tactics since the last encounter, which was a big surprise,' he recalled. 'They just played the same; it was the only way they knew how to play and they stuck to it. Naturally, we knew what to do to take them apart.'[28]

Within an hour Hungary were 6–0 in front. 'I frankly wondered just how gigantic the catastrophe enveloping us would be,' Gil Merrick remembered.[29] Winterbottom cut a similarly forlorn figure. 'I felt helpless to do anything about it,' he would say. 'On that performance, Hungary would have overrun any team in the world, but sitting there, watching goal after goal go in, I could only bury my head in my hands.' After burying his head in the sand for six months that was probably the best he could do. Ivor Broadis pulled a goal back but Hidegkuti then made it 7–1, a record defeat for England and another humiliation. 'Defensively, we'd learnt nothing since 1950,' rued Billy Wright. 'We were still defending as individuals, not as a unit. The Hungarians were superb in both matches, but we made it easy for them.' With the World Cup finals in Switzerland only a month away, England would need a miracle to turn around their fortunes.

Qualifying for the 1954 World Cup finals had again been based on the Home Internationals, with the top two going through. Once more

Scotland finished runners-up. This time, however, they deigned to travel. If the organisation of the 1950 finals could be described as nonsensical, FIFA's rationale in 1954 was just baffling. It put four countries in four groups – admittedly an improvement on the previous tournament – but seeded two in each group and kept them apart. FIFA also laid down that draws after ninety minutes would mean extra time, even in the group stage. England were drawn in Pool 4, along with fellow seeds Italy, hosts Switzerland and Belgium, who had already eliminated the fancied Swedes in qualifying and beaten Yugoslavia along the way.

Interest in England was immeasurably greater than it had been four years earlier. Enraptured by the performances of the Hungarians, who had gained immense popularity despite twice mauling England, and the participation of the Scots, the presence of television cameras made the fifth World Cup finals the first to capture the British public's imagination. Fans even travelled over and were joined by Ralph Finn, who was writing his personal account of the finals – a kind of innocent precursor to Pete Davies's book on Italia '90, *All Played Out*.

England's involvement began on 17 June 1954 in the St Jakob Stadium against Belgium. The massacre in Budapest had done surprisingly little to dent the confidence of England's approach play, which was bright, breezy and, some observers suggested, took inspiration from the Hungarians. But the defence was no less porous, with Merrick and the centre-half, Syd Owen, in particular, singled out for their waywardness. ('Merrick, who has served England well in his time,' noted Finn, 'has become shaky and cannot be depended upon to pull off the brilliant out-of-the-bag save which can save a team by giving it confidence in its last line of resistance.'[30]) Belgium took a surprise early lead, which Ivor Broadis cancelled out in the twenty-fifth minute. Seven minutes later, Finney broke, hoodwinked his defender with his famous jink and sent in a centre, which Lofthouse raced in to smash home with his head. Shortly after half-time Broadis made it 3–1 and the recovery was seemingly complete.

Yet England sat back on their lead. Over-elaboration and profligacy in attack prevented them from increasing it and when the defence fell asleep, first Houf and then Coppens pounced on lapses to bring the scores level. At 3–3 Matthews almost restored the lead but Gurney stopped the ball under the crossbar and the game went into extra time. Moments into the additional period Lofthouse regained England's advantage after Broadis had set him up. Two minutes later a long, hopeful cross was inadvertently met by the head of Jimmy Dickinson and his own goal brought the scores level.

'Disgusting!' was Ralph Finn's forthright assessment. 'That's the only true comment I can make on the England display against Belgium.'[31] He had a point – it was a miserable result, but the wholly unfair seeding system, which meant they bypassed Italy, meant that the odds were still stacked in favour of England's progression to the next round. Most significantly perhaps, Billy Wright had spent the closing minutes in the problematic centre-half position after Owen was left limping on the wing with cramp. The unfortunate Owen had been the eleventh centre-back tried in the four years since Franklin's 'disgrace' but, like all his predecessors, had failed to successfully emulate the Bogotá Bandit. He never played for his country again, Wright permanently moved to central defence and remained there until his retirement after a further forty-five caps.

Three days later England met Switzerland in Berne. Already victors over Italy (they would beat them again, 4–1 in the play-off) the Swiss were more formidable than past form suggested and with home advantage against increasingly beleaguered visitors. Yet, under a burning sun, both sides were subdued. Matthews was injured, meaning Finney switched to his favoured right-sided berth, but it was on the left where England's best attacks came. On forty minutes Tommy Taylor headed a long ball into space and Jimmy Mullen – stand-in on the left – slid the ball into the net for England's first. Then midway through the second half, Dennis Wilshaw, who played his club football as inside-left for Wolves, dummied and feinted his way through the Swiss defence as if he were the absent Matthews himself, before crashing a shot past Parlier to give England an unassailable 2–0 lead.

It was enough to take England through to the quarter-finals where, six days later in Basle, they met the reigning world champions, Uruguay. Matthews returned in place of the unlucky Mullen and Lofthouse was restored ahead of Taylor. Uruguay had already sent the Scots home after handing out a 7–0 thrashing, leaving England's neighbours to return from their first World Cup finals without a point or a goal (a record they subsequently bettered . . . though never by much). Visions of Scotland's humiliation may well have come flooding into English minds when Borges shot expertly past Merrick after only five minutes, but encouraged by a 50,000-strong crowd who had not taken kindly to South American gamesmanship and backed the 'masters', England came back strongly. In the fifteenth minute Matthews sent Wilshaw clear, he laid the ball off to Lofthouse and the Bolton Bomber smashed in England's equaliser. Spurred on, wave upon wave of England attacks tested the holders' resolve: Maspoli's fingertips were just about enough to deny Lofthouse a second; he then palmed a loose ball into the path of Wilshaw and the inside-left tapped a shot the wrong side of the post; before Matthews set up Broadis, who finished tamely. Then Roger Byrne fouled Abbadie. Santamaria tapped the resulting free-kick to Varella and his shot fizzed beyond the grasp of Merrick, who had dived too late to stop it. Five minutes on the other side of half-time Byrne gave away another free-kick: this time the ball was worked from Míguez to Schiaffano, who came through a gap and hit a shot beyond the hesitant Merrick to make the score 3–1.

But England refused to give up. Urged on by Wright they drove forward in attack after attack. Matthews and Finney worked tirelessly and skilfully down the flanks, Wilshaw and Broadis provided diligent and dutiful support, while Lofthouse bobbed around the penalty area like a prize fighter looking for the kill. With twenty-five minutes to go Finney tapped home the rebound from a Lofthouse shot to make it 2–3 and give England hope. Almost immediately Matthews hit the post, before having another chance punched away by Maspoli. Others were even more profligate. 'Finney was our worst offender,' complained Finn. 'He would not shoot when well placed. He dribbled through, often from one of the inside positions and then, well placed, would hesitate or tap the ball to one of the dusky athletes waiting for it.'[32] Yet as a whole, England were playing well. 'We were knitting together as a side,' added Finn. 'Some of our moves were almost Hungarian in style. The Uruguayans were rattled. This was the crucial time, the testing time for England. If we could get into the lead before half-time, or even change over all square, we had more than a chance.'[33] And then . . . disaster. With thirteen minutes left, Mijuez's pass found Ambrois and he rifled a shot which Merrick, again, should have saved. At 2–4 a comeback was beyond England but they had lost with honour and shown that in the face of adversity they could still be heroes. 'This was the measure of our greatness,' concluded Finn. 'The indication that even in mediocrity we possess something of the true spirit which has made us supreme as fighters. This indeed was our finest hour. We went down, but how gallantly we went down. And we could easily have won.'[34]

England went home, West Germany – defeated 3–8 in the group stages by Hungary – emerged as champions, shocking the world by defeating the Magyars 3–2 when they met again in the final. Two years later, after repeatedly defying his masters in Moscow, the Soviet Union called time on Imre Nagy's 'new course', sending in tanks to depose the Hungarian Prime Minister. At the time Honvéd, the club of Puskás, Bozsik, Kocsis and Czibor were on tour in Spain. Offered sanctuary by their hosts, many of the Hungarians chose exile. Overnight one of the greatest teams the world has ever witnessed was broken up. Hungarian football – and the international game as a whole – would never quite be the same again.

If proof that method could be more than a match for magic had come in the World Cup final, for England this was scant comfort: they possessed neither in any great quantity. True, they could still call on players such as Matthews, Finney, Wright and Lofthouse, men whose names have become engrained in football legend; likewise they could claim a proud record in their twenty post-war internationals against non-British nations (won 14, drawn 2, lost 4); but lacking a sensible method of selection, a ready consensus as to whether players should be coached tactically or merely allowed to 'play' and the acceptance that what happened beyond the boundaries of the United Kingdom actually mattered, England would never succeed at the highest level of soccer. This was the crux of the problem: while the world had woken up to football, England had not woken up to the world. The FA's introversion, naivety and tactical and technical backwardness left it at the risk of slipping even further behind.

Yet the history of the game in England and the very fact that football was its unique gift to the world still gave Walter Winterbottom's men a unique air. If the perception of English football's more considered commentators placed it at a low ebb after the traumas of Belo Horizonte, Hungary and the relative failure at the Swiss World Cup, others still held it in far higher esteem.

Following the 7–1 defeat in Budapest, Geoffrey Green got talking to the Hungarian right-half and sometime politician, Jozsef Bozsik.

'In spite of our victory today,' he said, 'you are still *masters* of football.'

Green greeted his assertion with incredulity. 'How do you make that out after beating us hollow twice in six months and putting thirteen goals in all into our net in a space of three hours? You must be joking!'

Bozsik looked him in the eye with a serious air as he answered. 'But you will *always* be the masters. You fashioned the game, organised it and gave it to the world first of all. You were the original *teachers* . . .'

'At last I realised his meaning,' recalled Green. 'And it gave me the clue to the almost universal respect in which English football was held.'[35]

The challenge now was to match reverence with success.

6

BRIGHT YOUNG THINGS

Distraught in defeat, their standing diminished and disturbed by the notion that they were now only masters by dint of history, England's footballers flew home from Switzerland. For many of them failure would mark the final passage of their international careers; for others it was only the start. The inquests in the popular press, on the radio, in the pubs and social clubs throughout the country were brief, however, and lacking depth. No searching questions were asked of the selectors or Winterbottom, no one suggested that there was a fundamental flaw in the English game. If anything it was Billy Wright – as captain – who again bore the brunt of criticism, although even that was less stinging than it may have otherwise been as word slipped back about his sterling displays at centre-half.

Eight years earlier, Winterbottom had inherited the greatest pool of English talent ever seen. Now the international careers of much of that posse had run their course. Remnants still made up part of the England line-up: Wright's transition to centre-half marked the final part of his journey into the pantheon of England greats; Tom Finney and Nat Lofthouse, respectively thirty-two and twenty-nine, continued to excel domestically and on the international stage; while Stanley Matthews, in his fortieth year and on his way to becoming the first European Footballer of the Year, was – consistently – one of England's best players, continuing to defy the conception that football was a trade for the young.

Beyond those four Winterbottom and England's selectors could call upon the abundance of decent, though not exceptional, English talent that had made up the World Cup squad, or look to the future. They plumped firmly for the latter. Already, a programme of youth and 'B' internationals plus inter-league games had been established, providing in theory a system of promotion to the full England team.

In January 1954 the first match played by the England Under-23 team had taken place in snow-covered Bologna, with the eventual 0–3 defeat to Italy less significant than the very idea underlying the encounter. 'At last we had an opportunity to give our best young players experience of international football,' pointed out one of those selected. Winterbottom had also begun to call upon the resources of Matt Busby's brilliant young Manchester United team who would, over the course of the following few years, earn the tag 'the Busby Babes'. Already, United's centre-forward, Tommy Taylor, and full-back, Roger Byrne, had made the breakthrough to the England team and made the trip to Switzerland. More were to come.

Despite England's failure in Switzerland, at Lancaster Gate the pendulum swung back in Walter Winterbottom's favour. Following the World Cup his hand was strengthened when a new system of selection was arranged. Instead of the International Selection Committee debating a squad from scratch, Winterbottom plus two selectors put forward recommendations to a panel of five and the team was selected from the shortlist. Immediately, Winterbottom prepared a list of thirty players he felt were needed to mount a successful challenge for the 1958 World Cup in Sweden. When England played the first match after their return – against Northern Ireland – the changes were rung. Seven debuts were made and the emphasis placed firmly on youth. Alongside Byrne, Wright, Matthews and Lofthouse were Byrne's Old Trafford colleagues Ray Wood (in goal) and Bill Foulkes (at full-back); Bolton Wanderers' Johnny Wheeler (at half-back), West Bromwich Albion's Ray Barlow (also at half-back) and Burnley's Brian Pilkington (in the forward line); Manchester City's deep-lying centre-forward, Don Revie (who was famous for modelling his game on Nandor Hidegkuti – with predictably successful results against flat-footed First Division defenders) and, most notably, Fulham's nineteen-year-old midfield schemer, Johnny Haynes.

Born in Kentish Town in October 1934 and brought up in nearby Edmonton, the extravagantly gifted Haynes had been one of the most talked-about players in the country since making his league debut with Fulham at seventeen. A virtuoso, two-footed talent blessed with the technique and gracefulness of one of the new Hungarian masters and the sort of vision and passing abilities not commonly associated with English players (who, like Matthews and Finney, were generally better known for their ability to run with the ball), he had narrowly missed out on the squad for Switzerland after being included in the final forty and the pruned twenty-two before losing out when the FA decided to take just eighteen players. Under the eccentric tutelage of the Craven Cottage chairman, the music hall impresario and actor Tommy Trinder, Haynes had been hyped like a star of the screen, and by the time of his call-up, despite playing his football for a mediocre Second Division side, every self-respecting football fan's lips were moist with anticipation. Haynes did not disappoint, scoring the first and creating the second on his debut as England strolled to a 2–0 win. A month later, though, he was absent when England came from behind against Wales to win 3–2.

Victory over the Welsh set England up nicely ahead of a home friendly – and the first since the war – against the freshly crowned world champions, West Germany, on 1 December 1954. Ahead of it, interest was greater than for any match England had played in years: Wembley was a 100,000 sell-out (despite the game being played on a Wednesday afternoon); eight London cinemas were relaying live footage, as was the BBC on television and radio, and no fewer than 7000 Germans made the trip, the sort of visiting contingent not normally witnessed at Wembley unless the Scots were in town. Less than a decade after VE Day, contemporary experience might suggest that press and public would be imbued with triumphal and nationalist rhetoric, but a stranger to earth reading the pre-match publicity or attending the game itself would have struggled to conclude that the war had taken place at all. If the players had anything to say about it, their comments were not published; if journalists had their own take on things, their views were edited; and if some of England's fans had taunts for their rivals, they too were hushed by their more dignified compatriots.

West Germany, however, had been severely hampered by injury and even their manager, Sepp Herberger, was moved to admit: 'My team will have no chance but we hope to keep the score down to a reasonable size.' They started with just three of the players who had played against Hungary in the World Cup final – captain Josef Posipal, Werner Kohlmeyer and Werner Liebrich – but at centre-forward could boast a young Uwe Seeler, a man who had not even been born when Matthews had played against Germany in 1935.

As was so often the case, this was to be Matthews' day. After early English pressure had failed to yield a goal, Matthews set off on a march forward in the twenty-seventh minute, bamboozling and shimmying his way past opponents. Then, looking up, he spotted the run of Roy Bentley and swung in a cross that was met powerfully by the Chelsea forward's head and the ball crashed into the back of the West German net. Increasingly, England camped out in the German half with the visitors' outstanding centre-half, Liebrich – the star of the World Cup final – all that stood between respectability and a rout. Time and again Matthews cut inside, then outside and back in again, an untouchable presence serving up chance after chance. Three minutes into the second half, England doubled their lead. Len Shackleton scooped a pass over the German defence, which Finney ran onto and when his shot was blocked Ronnie Allen tapped home the rebound. Shackleton then missed the chance to make it 3–0 but, having skipped through the entire German defence, he let the ball overrun at the crucial moment.

After Beck had pulled a goal back for West Germany, Shackleton atoned for his earlier misjudgement. Picking up Allen's smart reverse pass he spotted the advancing German goalkeeper, Fritz Herkenrath, and delicately lobbed him to make it 3–1. England were 'on the way back to the top', according to the following day's *Daily Mail*, the victory bearing 'further evidence of the gradual restoration of our national football standards', added the *Daily Telegraph*. Later on that month Wolves defeated Hungary's leading club Honvéd – the team of Kocsis, Puskas and many more – in a dramatic floodlit friendly at Molineux broadcast on national television. Coming as it did three weeks after another victory over Moscow Spartak, the Midlanders were confidently hailed by the British press as 'Champions of the World'. English football could settle back under the rosy glow of self-congratulation.

Victory over West Germany had been good, but despite Winterbottom's investment of faith in youth and the revised selection procedures, the management of the England team in general and the selection of the players in particular continued to be a cause of consternation and confusion. Despite Haynes's impressive showing against Northern Ireland he was left out not just of the Wales match but also for West Germany and for the league representative sides. 'It lasted for a year and I did not like it,' he recounted. 'I was downright angry. I felt that to score one goal and make the other in my first international match was a fair contribution to what was, after all, a victory, and it was all too easy to convince myself that I had certainly not been the worst player.'[1] At the same time, Len Shackleton, Sunderland's engagingly eccentric inside-forward and sometime international, had received a recall to face the Germans at the age of thirty-three but, despite being overshadowed only by Matthews in his performance that day, never played for England again. His inclusion, it was suggested, was attributable to a selector from the north-east digging in his heels until his fellow panel members relented and named him in the side. Shackleton was unimpressed. 'There are so many things wrong with British football and so few things right that I can quite honestly state I have no desire to be capped again,' he raged in his infamous memoirs *The Clown Prince of Soccer*, published a year later. 'I believe, rightly or wrongly, nothing will be done to put our national team were it belongs – at the head of our class – until a few leading players withhold their support as a gesture against poor remuneration, poor team selection and the various other ills now afflicting our international soccer system.'[2]

The other great opponent of the selection system was the FA Secretary, Stanley Rous. Aware that the best way of controlling the selectors' excesses was by diplomatically edging them towards the dissolution of their quango, he maintained a public silence on the status quo but years later, in semi-retirement, when expounding on the after dinner circuit, Rous would recall the ridiculous nature of the International Selection Committee meetings:

Walter would hand in a list of recommended players to the chairman, and then a dozen selectors would tug and pull at his nominations like dogs fighting over a bone.

Chairman: 'Right gentleman, in goal our manager recommends Frank Swift. Those in favour . . .'

Eleven hands go up. The Rovers' chairman Bloggs, a retired baker, keeps his hand down.

Chairman: 'Who's your nomination Joe?'

Bloggs: 'Our lad Jones had a blinder against United on Saturday. He's in the best form of his life.'

Chairman: 'But you were beaten three–nil.'

Bloggs: 'Aye, and it were a bloody robbery. Two of the goals were offside and Jones had a forward standing on his toes when t'third goal went in.'

Following a ten-minute discussion on the merits of Jones versus Swift,

Bloggs would climb down after a promise that Jones would get serious consideration for the next match.

Chairman: 'Our manager suggests Ramsey for right back. Those in favour . . .'

Nine hands would go up and there would be a twenty-minute debate on the strengths and weaknesses of three other nominations. And so it would go on, with only a handful of Walter's nominations receiving one hundred per cent support.

There would be a distinct north-south divide, with the London selectors supporting each other's players and the north using their muscle to get their players into the team; and, of course, the Midlands would have their little clique. Sometimes a chairman would try to get his player out of the side because he wanted him for an important league match in the days when clubs had to play regardless of whether they had players on international duty. Smith, a retired shoe manufacturer from United, would say, 'I think it's time our lad had a rest from international football. Give someone else a chance.' The rest of the committee, knowing what he was up to, would vote to keep his player in. The meeting would drag on for two, sometimes three hours with each of the chairmen – retired butchers, greengrocers, builders, motor dealers, brewers and farmers – fighting his corner for a player from his own club. They would lobby each other before the meeting, promising support for a selector's choice in return for support for his own player.

Walter would sit listening to all this, sucking on his pipe and trying not to bite through the stem as the committee called for four or five changes to his selection. He would then, with the patience of Job, explain why you could not have two left-footed players together on the right side of the pitch, how player 'A' and player 'B' were too alike in style to fit in together, and he would quietly have to point out that one of the men recommended by the selectors was recovering from a broken leg. By the time the meeting was over he would have persuaded them to virtually accept his original nominations with perhaps one or two changes forced on him by selectors.[3]

Despite Winterbottom slowly gaining an upper hand over the selectors, Haynes didn't return to the England team for nearly a year. Without him Winterbottom's men continued to make steady progress, mixing good victories (Scotland 7–2; Denmark 5–1) with the introduction of some much-vaunted talent. Blackburn Rovers' fine half-back, Ronnie Clayton, made his international bow; likewise, on the other side of midfield, Duncan Edwards.

Like Haynes, Edwards was a teenage prodigy, albeit mixing it with the First Division's finest. Born in Dudley, he had been an early beneficiary of Matt Busby's extension of the Manchester United scouting system beyond the confines of Greater Manchester and Lancashire. Boasting the physique of a man while still a boy, he had made his first team debut at sixteen on Easter Monday 1953, and less than two years later he became England's youngest international when he played against Scotland in the 7–2 victory at Wembley. A tall, powerful and physically imposing figure who played with boundless energy and verve, Edwards was the lynchpin of a Manchester United side that would go on to take the League Championship in 1956 and 1957. 'His greatest asset was his strength,' Haynes was later to say of him.

> Not so much physical strength but a kind of dynamic strength which kept him endlessly on the move, covering, shadowing, backing up attacks, plunging through to finish off an attack with searing shots, as he did so often for his country. His defensive play was quite outstanding, his heading superb . . . we built up an acute understanding of each other's play, and a joy it was to play with this man, the most indomitable player I have known.[4]

Not until England played Scotland at Hampden on 14 April 1956 did the two young hopefuls play together. Then, England drew 1–1, a credible enough result which extended their unbeaten run on Scottish soil beyond nineteen years; a month later, a far sterner test materialised when Brazil came to Wembley for the first time.

England could justifiably claim to have their strongest side since before the 1950 World Cup. A balance of youth and experience, tenacity and skill had been struck in a team that represented the best of those steeped in the lore of the late forties combined with the new generation, whom it was hoped would bring glory through to the sixties. In defence Birmingham City's stylish full-back, Jeff Hall, lined up alongside Wright and Byrne; the half-back line could boast the contrasting talents of Edwards and Clayton and Tommy Taylor and Haynes linked up in attack alongside the old master, Stanley Matthews.

Yet again, England's fortysomething maestro seized the day. Just two minutes had passed when Edwards set him free down the flank. Matthews looked up, squared the ball to Haynes and he brushed a pass into the path of Taylor, who crashed a shot into the roof of the net. Three minutes later, Matthews was again in the thick of the action. This time he took possession by the corner flag, nonchalantly nutmegged Canhoteiro, passed to Hall who swerved in a long cross which Taylor flicked on and the debutant, Colin Grainger, slammed home the loose ball.

Brazil fought back strongly. Canhoteiro struck a post, then ten minutes past the interval Paulinho's shot cruelly deflected off Roger Byrne to bring the Brazilians back into the game. Two minutes later they were level after Wright lost possession to Didi who shot powerfully past Reg Matthews from twenty yards to equalise. Parity was brief. On the hour-mark England were awarded a free-kick just outside Brazil's penalty box. Seizing the initiative, Haynes quickly lobbed it in but, with the Brazilian defence unprepared, Nilton Santos caught the ball, insisting that there had been no whistle. The referee knew otherwise and awarded a penalty, prompting a scrum, jostling and arguments, which culminated in the Brazilian inside-right, Alvarao, picking up the ball and, like a piqued schoolboy, setting off for the touchline with it. On came the trainers, negotiations ensued and finally the matter was resolved. John Atyeo lined up the penalty... and missed. It mattered not. Shortly afterwards, Haynes threaded the ball through to Matthews, his centre was met by Atyeo's cushioned nod and Taylor crashed home England's third with his head.

England were then awarded a second penalty, again for handball. This time Roger Byrne claimed responsibility – and also missed. Again, it didn't matter. With ten minutes to go, England scored a fourth, decisive goal. Once more, Matthews was in the thick of the action, floating in a perfect centre which Grainger met with his head to make the score 4–2.

Little over a fortnight later on 26 May 1956 England met West Germany in Berlin. Cheered on by thousands of British servicemen, they reprised their 3–1 victory of eighteen months earlier, with Edwards, Grainger and Haynes scoring the goals. Edwards, in particular, showed his pedigree by adding one of the finest goals ever seen from an Englishman – marching through three tackles before unleashing a thunderbolt shot from twenty yards – to his man-of-the-match-winning performance. 'He tackled like a lion, attacked at every opportunity and topped it all off with a cracker of a goal,' remembered Billy Wright. 'He was still only twenty, and was already a world class player.'[5]

Although he didn't cap his performance with a goal, Edwards' Old Trafford team-mate, Tommy Taylor, also attracted high praise. Now aged twenty-four, some of his rougher edges had been smoothed and he had matured into one of Europe's finest front men and England's first choice centre-forward. A big, raw-boned Yorkshireman, Taylor's astonishing aerial prowess set him apart from all his contemporaries bar, perhaps, Lofthouse. But if his size sometimes obscured his many talents or made him appear ungainly, his ability as a prolific, instinctive finisher waylaid any concerns. Wherever he played, and for whatever team, Taylor scored goals with unerring regularity. With his inveterate workrate and sheer menace to opposing defenders, he was as crucial to his country's progress as he was to his club's.

If the emergence of Taylor, Edwards and Haynes spelt exciting times for England's followers, the mid-fifties can also be viewed as Billy Wright's heyday. In the absence of an adequate replacement Neil Franklin's fall from grace in 1950 had plunged the England team into a decline, and it was little coincidence that their revival in fortunes did not occur until Wright belatedly filled his mantle. Six months on from the 1–7 drubbing in Budapest in May 1954, England, with Wright marshalling the defence, beat West Germany with ease. His transformation from world-class half-back to world-class centre-half was an inspired one, and playing in a position where pace and acceleration were less necessary allowed the indomitable captain to prolong his international career. In 1956 Billy Wright had already won more than seventy caps, a record he was to extend further.

Longevity and greatness as a footballer are normally enough to write a player's name into the pantheon of legends, but Wright was also a captain of supreme virtue. On and off the field he led by example. Respected for being a great footballer and a good man, he never took recourse to yelling or barking at his colleagues – they simply followed his lead. He was also remembered fondly for welcoming new players and making them feel at ease. 'Billy made every player feel he could take any problems to the skipper,' Ronnie Clayton wrote in his autobiography. 'There were no cliques when Wright was around – everyone was part of a team; and he lost no time in driving the point home.'[6] Haynes, like Clayton, eventually succeeded Wright as skipper and took much from his mentor. 'Billy Wright captained by example,' he recalled. 'He was not a noisy captain; he sought to influence his team by the consistency of his own play. He could make points strongly enough, but he very seldom shouted at his players on the field. A captain has to dominate his team, but this does not mean he must browbeat them.'[7]

A year later Wright was to come second to Alfredo di Stefano in the poll for European Footballer of the Year, but it was his courtship of the singer Joy Beverley that saw him attain (unwanted) fame beyond his football achievements. Billy and Beverley became favourites of the popular press, the most famous couple apart from Queen Elizabeth and Prince Philip or as one writer dubbed them later, putting a contemporary slant on the pair: 'Posh and Becks in black and white'. The truth was rather more innocent. Wright may well have been England's captain, the winner of a multitude of honours with Wolves, but as a thirty-three-year-old bachelor who still lived in digs, he was not just unaccustomed to such attention, but embarrassed by it. Notwithstanding his initial unease, the two married in 1958 and the legend of the celebrity 'footballer's wife' was born.

England, led by Wright and spearheaded by a brilliant assortment of young players with the occasional cameo from an old master, marched on. They had shared the 1956 Home Championship in a four-way tie after losing their first game with Wales (1–2), beating Northern Ireland (3–0) and dramatically equalising to draw with Scotland (1–1) and save themselves from the wooden spoon. 'The silence,' recalled Haynes who struck the crucial goal, 'was almost louder than those pre-match roars.'[8] The following year England topped the Home Championship after wins over Wales (3–1) and Scotland (2–1) and a 1–1 draw with Northern Ireland.

World Cup qualification, meanwhile, now took the form of a three-country group. England, drawn with Denmark and the Republic of Ireland, got off to a winning start against the Danes in December 1956 with a 5–2 victory: Taylor grabbed a hat-trick, Edwards a brace. The following May, the Republic of Ireland were routed 5–1 (with Taylor again scoring a treble), Denmark 4–1 in Copenhagen and qualification to Sweden was secured with a 1–1 draw in Dublin on 19 May 1957.

For Matthews, Copenhagen spelt the end of a remarkable international career which had kicked off more than twenty-two years earlier when a teenager at Stoke. Age had made him more prone to niggling injuries and the unpredictable whims of England's selectors had seen him in and out of the national side. During one such spell on the sidelines he had accepted an offer to spend the summer of 1957 coaching in South Africa, and, after what he believed to be an unexpected recall for the Denmark game at the age of forty-two, he quietly withdrew from the England squad, missing the game in Ireland, and flew south. That wasn't the end of Matthews, though. Having played key roles in the victories over West Germany and Brazil, his belief that 'there was plenty of life in the old legs yet' was reinforced. For a further eight years he continued to turn out with distinction for Blackpool and Stoke, collecting the Footballer of the Year Award for a second time in 1963, the same year he won the Second Division Championship with Stoke. Frequently there were calls from the press and public for his return to the national team – never were they heeded. Finally, on 6 February 1965, five days past his fiftieth birthday, he called time on his playing career, having made nearly 800 first class appearances to add to the fifty-four he made for England (plus twenty-nine wartime and victory caps). Later that year he became the first professional footballer to receive a knighthood. 'He was one of the very few,' Ferenc Puskás pronounced, 'a football great blessed with genius and possessing the highest virtue of them all – humility.'

Even without Matthews England continued their impressive form. On 19 October 1957 Wales were humbled at Ninian Park, with the goals coming from Haynes (2), Finney and Hopkins putting into his own net. 'England, glorious England,' concluded one journalist, 'are good enough to reach the final of the World Cup in Sweden for the first time ever.' Three weeks later, though, Northern Ireland recorded only their second win on English soil with a 3–2 victory at Wembley. Gutsy defending and several strokes of luck had helped the Irish, but when England met France on 27 November, they set about proving that the defeat had been just a fluke deviation from their hot streak of form.

After years as one of the lesser lights of European football, France were exhibiting unmistakeable signs of revival. A year later they would reach the semi-finals of the World Cup when the Stade de Reims forward, Just Fontaine, would emerge from nowhere to score an unprecedented tally of thirteen goals. Against England there was no Fontaine, but there were several of his Reims colleagues who had reached the inaugural European Cup final in 1956 where they had been beaten by Real Madrid. Blackburn Rovers' Bryan Douglas had proved an adept replacement for the departed Matthews on the right wing and put in an exhilarating display thanks to the subtle link-up play and support of West Bromwich Albion's debutant inside-right, Bobby Robson. Just three minutes in Robson fed the ball out to Douglas on the right and he eased past Kaelbel before dipping in a near post cross, which the under-pressure Taylor looped with a flick into the corner of the net. On twenty-four minutes it was 2–0. Douglas weaved a path through the defence, took the ball around the goalkeeper, Claude Abbes, and unselfishly squared to Robson who scored easily. Six minutes later Haynes, who was dropping deep and spraying the field with devastatingly accurate passes, sent Taylor through with a glorious through ball and he raced clear to score England's third.

England continued to rain in chances on the French goal. Haynes, Taylor, Finney, Robson and Douglas each missed gilt-edged opportunities as no fewer than eighteen shots fell England's way in the last twenty-five minutes alone. Finally, with five minutes remaining, intricate build-up play orchestrated by the effervescent Edwards allowed Douglas to set up Robson with a clear chance, and the debutant took his tally to two and England's to four.

Reflecting on a year that had seen five wins, a draw, a solitary defeat and twenty-two goals scored, there was a growing realisation in the England ranks that, in the words of Haynes, they 'really had a very fine chance to do something in the World Cup finals'. Perhaps more importantly, players of genuine class had emerged to successfully fill the boots of some of the illustrious post-war team, with no fewer than six of the men who had beaten France graduating from the ranks of the Under-23 team Winterbottom had created. 'We never discussed it but I am sure we were all aware of it, and I am sure Walter Winterbottom was,' Haynes said of England's prospects in Sweden. 'He never made the point but I think he spent that winter waiting impatiently for the summer to come, to prove finally that the combination he had found would succeed.'[9] Unbeknownst to the Fulham man, Winterbottom had already reached that conclusion in the wake of the glorious victory over France. At the post-match banquet, he had pulled Billy Wright to one side. 'Bill,' he confessed, 'I think we have a team that could make a really telling challenge for the world championship.'[10] 1957 had been the year of promise: would 1958 be the year of fulfilment?

When Wolverhampton Wanderers had beaten Spartak Moscow and Honvéd at Molineux in November and December 1954, the very notion that the chauvinistic British press corps had proclaimed them the best club team in Europe had raised hackles across the continent. The deluded notion that they raised – that they could be the best on account of two friendly wins – was viewed outside England as wearisomely typical of a country still oblivious to the series of seismic shocks its footballers had suffered in the early 1950s. No one was more irked than Gabriel Hanot, editor of the influential French sports newspaper, *L'Équipe*. 'We had better wait until the Wolves travel to Moscow and Budapest to proclaim their invincibility,' he wrote in his editorial a few days after Wolves' win over Spartak. 'But if the English are so sure about their hegemony in football, this is the time to create a European tournament.'

Hanot was not just a man of words. Within days he had drafted a plan for a 'European Champions Cup' based around sixteen participants, who would contest a knock-out competition. Games would be played in midweek and in the evenings (still a rarity in the 1950s) to allow for working-class spectators to watch games which would be sponsored by a television station or newspaper of the participating country. When the proposals were put to UEFA the following March, European football's recently created governing body were hesitant in their support. But a month later, at a meeting convened by *L'Équipe* in Paris consisting of the chairmen and presidents of Europe's leading clubs, the plan met enthusiastic backing. When *L'Équipe* held another meeting with UEFA in May 1955, their proposals met greater support and UEFA agreed to organise the competition and respect all the decisions already approved. On 4 September 1955 in Lisbon, the European Champions Cup kicked off with a match between Sporting Lisbon and Yugoslavia's FK Partizan. Europe, in football terms, had suddenly become a smaller place.

Or so one would think, but Chelsea, champions for the first time in 1955, had withdrawn from the competition citing 'incompatibilities with the English league calendar' following pressure from the Football League and were replaced by the Polish side WKS Gwardia. A year later, when Matt Busby's Manchester United were crowned champions, it was immediately thought that they would follow Chelsea's lead. But Busby, a visionary who could see beyond the parochialism of the Football League, would not submit. Convinced that playing in Europe would only enhance his brilliant young team, Busby stood his ground under intense duress from the Football League and forced them to back down with the fervour of his impassioned obduracy. In September 1956 Manchester United kicked off English club football's involvement in European competition with a 12–0 aggregate win over Anderlecht, and eventually progressed to a semi-final against the reigning European champions Real Madrid the following April at which stage they were knocked out. As English title winners again in 1956–57 they qualified for the following year's tournament and, after a 3–3 draw against Red Star Belgrade on 5 February 1958 in Yugoslavia, progressed – on aggregate – to another semi-final. A day later the victorious squad embarked on its long journey home.

When Manchester United had won the title in 1956, they had boasted the youngest average age – at twenty-two – of any side ever to do so. Two years on, they were more mature, wiser, better footballers and promised to provide the strongest challenge yet to Real Madrid's hold on the competition; in the summer, Matt Busby's 'Babes' would be at the forefront of England's push for World Cup glory. Tommy Taylor had by now scored sixteen goals in nineteen appearances for his country; United's captain, Roger Byrne, had, over the duration of thirty-three caps, cemented a reputation as one of England's finest ever full-backs, and was tipped as long-term successor to Wright as captain; Duncan Edwards, still only twenty-one, needed only the highest stage of them all – the World Cup finals – to prove to the world what every English football follower already knew, that he was one of the best players on the planet. Meantime, several others including Jonny Berry, Ray Wood, David Pegg and Bill Foulkes stood on the fringes of the England selectors' plans.

United's charter flight was delayed several times on the journey home from Belgrade. First, Berry had mislaid his passport and the airplane hold had to be emptied while his suitcase was unloaded and the necessary documents recovered. Then there was a stop for refuelling in Munich, a city coated in the white of a heavy snowfall. As the players killed time in the airport's transit lounge, the snow continued to fall. Forty minutes later, as the party trooped back out through an icy wind, Roger Byrne noticed that the tracks made earlier by the plane were almost invisible. With the players on the plane, its pilot twice attempted to take off but each time 'boost surge' problems caused him to pull up on the runway. The passengers trudged back off the plane while the pilots consulted with an engineer. Barely had they made it back to the terminal than the party were called out once more. For a third time the pilot attempted to take off and at last the plane began to advance down the runway. Yet the sense of nervousness and foreboding that had pervaded amongst its passengers quickly turned to panic as the plane hurtled along. Ray Wood turned to Byrne, who sat with his hands tightly gripping the armrests, and asked: 'Roger, what's happening?'

'We're all going to be killed,' he replied. They were the last words he ever spoke.[11]

Moments later the plane ploughed through the airport's perimeter fence and skidded across a road. A wing struck a house, separating it and part of the tail from the fuselage which span on, hit a tree and a wooden hut, before coming to rest in a sea of flames.

In total twenty-two passengers were killed instantly or at the scene, including seven players and eight journalists. Amongst the dead lay Tommy Taylor, Roger Byrne and David Pegg, as well as Frank Swift, who was working as a journalist for the News of the World. 'I believe it was the most appalling moment of my life,' Johnny Haynes said of the moment he heard the news on his wireless. 'There was the first reaction of thinking that I had not quite heard the words that were being spoken. Then there was the realisation that it really was true. Then there was the moment of disbelief and finally out of the soulless, anonymous little box came the names, names that throbbed over and over again in my mind.'[12]

Duncan Edwards had, however, been pulled from the wreckage alive, although he had sustained severe internal injuries – a fractured leg, broken ribs and severe shock. For fifteen days he battled for his life with the world watching his progress as first he rallied, then deteriorated then seemed to be pulling through. But the extent of his injuries was too much even for such a colossus and he succumbed on 21 February. 'Duncan was a man in football but still a boy at heart,' recalled his United team-mate Jackie Blanchflower. 'His ability was good enough for England but his potential was good enough for heaven.'[13]

Two German inquiries attributed the cause of the tragedy to ice on the wings. Later, a separate British investigation blamed slush on the runway. Either way, the consequences were appalling for the families of the twenty-three dead. On a football level, the loss of eight of its players, as well as many others – including Matt Busby – who had suffered injuries of varying severity, savaged Manchester United's ranks. They conceded the title to Wolves, bowed out of the next round of the European Cup and cruelly lost the FA Cup final to Bolton Wanderers. It was to take them years to reach such heights again.

For England, in the short term at least, the blow was just as devastating. Byrne, Edwards and Taylor were simply not the sort of players that could be replaced overnight. Edwards, arguably, never has been. 'Over the years, I have played with and against many world-class players, but in my mind, Duncan Edwards is the greatest of them all,' one of his colleagues remembered. 'Pele and Di Stefano were marvellous, but they needed help to play. Duncan could do it all himself.' At the same time, less noticed, but no less inconsequential, Jeff Hall had been stricken by polio and died just two months later. Along with Byrne, according to Billy Wright, 'there were few better full-back pairings in English football history'.

Munich changed the history of Manchester United. Sympathy for the Old Trafford club attracted support way beyond its ordinary constituency and helped propel it to its current status as one of the world's biggest clubs. The legend of the Munich victims rightly lives on, their names immortalised in Old Trafford lore. Less remembered is their importance in the history of the national team. One could consider what might have been, even if one might be accused of being trite for doing so, but what was inescapable is that their memory was engrained on every footballer of that generation's mind. Almost every talent of the era had, in some way, crossed paths with those who had fallen or those who survived. They never forgot. In little ways and large, the ghosts of the past pushed England's footballers on.

Still strapped to his seat but thrown to safety on that terrible afternoon in Bavaria was Busby's latest fledgling, Bobby Charlton. Born in Ashington, Northumberland in October 1937, Charlton came from football stock and was part of a dynasty, which included several uncles who had played professionally, including Jackie Milburn, and a brother – Jack – who was centre-half at Leeds United. Like Milburn he was a forward but the similarities ended there. Like his friend Edwards, Bobby Charlton was a unique figure, impossible to readily categorise in one set position or another. In his early career, at least, he spent long spells out wide but he was always most effective when cutting inside and setting forth on one of his dashing charges into the heart of the opposition's defence, or firing an explosive shot in on goal, often from distance, usually with deadly, searing accuracy. Bobby Charlton was not a great goalscorer in the way that Mortensen or Lofthouse were, but he still scored plenty of goals. He was not a man to set up chance after chance like Matthews but he was invariably in the thick of the action when his team scored. Nor was he one to nonchalantly grace the field like Haynes – he could be as elegant as he was direct. Pinning down the essence of Bobby Charlton is no easy task but if something positive happened he would be part of it no matter which position he had nominally been assigned. In 1958, scarred by Munich though he was, the twenty-year-old was already an excellent player. Over subsequent years, however, he was to become a true great, greater perhaps than any other individual to set foot on an English football field in the latter half of the twentieth century.

After Munich, though, and even more so after the death of his friend Edwards, Charlton was ready to give up football altogether. He was coaxed back gently to the game. A month after the disaster he had returned for United; by April he was lining up for his country to face the Scots at Hampden Park. From the very minute he kicked off his international career, Bobby Charlton seemed hellbent on bringing the same sort of energy and verve to the England team once brought to it by Edwards. Twelve minutes into his debut, England were awarded a free-kick and Charlton lined it up before swinging a cross into the area with precision and pace where it was met by the head of Bryan Douglas, who pummelled it into the back of the Scotland net. Eleven minutes later, Derek Kevan made it 2–0 to England but it was Haynes and Charlton who were the dominant influences as England began to toy with the Scots.

'The dark blue of Scotland was once a proud emblem,' recorded *The Times*. 'But now the Scots move about like heavy cattle.' In the sixty-second minute Charlton rounded off a dream debut with a goal.

Finney picked the ball up on the left, completely perplexed Alex Parker – Scotland's elegant right-back – with a flurry of shimmies and feints, moved swiftly to the byline and cut the ball back deeply to be met by Charlton with such fury that it hit the back of the net before Tommy Younger, the Scottish goalkeeper, could even raise his hands. So impressed was Younger that he marched out of his area to congratulate the goalscorer. 'It was surely one of the finest goals ever seen at Hampden,' added the following Monday's *Times*. Kevan added a fourth with fifteen minutes remaining, but the talk afterwards was all about the debutant.

Three weeks later, and just four days after Manchester United had lost to Bolton Wanderers in the FA Cup final, Charlton scored both England's goals in the 2–1 defeat of Portugal at Wembley. Yet when England lost 0–5 to Yugoslavia in Belgrade four days later, the selectors (one or two of whom had already intimated to journalists that Charlton 'was not a ninety-minute player') made the Busby Babe the scapegoat and left him out of England's subsequent impressive 1–1 draw with the USSR in Moscow. If the dropping of the novice raised a few eyebrows, the real point of contention was about the centre-forward berth. The death of Tommy Taylor should, in most minds, have prompted the recall of Nat Lofthouse, scorer of twenty-nine goals in his thirty-two England appearances and both of Bolton's in their FA Cup triumph over United. Instead the selectors plumped for the doughty but questionable merits of West Bromwich Albion's Derek Kevan, a tall, sometimes ungainly presence whom England's followers were slow to warm to. Haynes did his best to state a case for him:

> Derek is not the most delicate player but then he has never pretended to be. I always took the view that he was selected to play for England for the qualities he has and not the qualities he should have. He is very strong, very fast, a good goalscorer and powerful in the air . . . He cannot be Derek Kevan in a West Bromwich Albion shirt, then become a Tom Finney as soon as he wears an England shirt.[14]

If England fans were not entirely convinced by Haynes' argument, the selectors patently were, even seeing fit to omit Lofthouse from the World Cup squad altogether.

The 1958 World Cup finals took on a similar form to the Swiss World Cup, with four groups of four countries and the top two progressing to the quarter-finals where the tournament took the form of a knock-out. This time, the ludicrous method of seeding had been dispensed with but goal average counted for nothing in the group stage, with teams on equal points going head-to-head in a play-off. England had been drawn in the toughest group of all with Austria, Central Europe's finest team following the decline of Hungary; the USSR who, with Lev Yashin and others, could comfortably claim to be the strongest Eastern Europe had to offer; and the mighty Brazil. For the only time all four home nations had qualified after England, Scotland and Northern Ireland had won their respective qualifying groups (with the Irish seeing off both Italy and Portugal) and Wales, who had finished second in their group, were drawn first out of the hat in a sweepstake of runners up to determine who should play off against Israel (all of whose Middle Eastern opponents had withdrawn in political protest). Wales duly beat the Israelis to make their only ever finals.

Once again, the thoroughness of England's preparations was a moot point. The squad only arrived in Sweden two days prior to the start of the tournament and the FA had decided against the luxury of a proper training camp. The players bedded down in the Park Avenue Hotel in central Gothenburg while Winterbottom went searching for somewhere to train. Amongst some of the players there was a mood that Sweden was an unfit venue for the finals. Certainly the tournament failed to drum up enthusiasm and attendances were often below 5000, with one scraping 2000. Tom Finney, for one, could not 'imagine why' Sweden was honoured with the World Cup: 'Attendances were bad, brightened only at times when the Swedes aroused themselves from their lethargy to cheer their own team or turned up to watch the English "masters".'[15]

England opened their group matches with a tie against the USSR on 8 June 1958. Pre-tournament hype echoing from the other side of the Iron Curtain – aided with tales of the astonishing prowess of Lev Yashin, 'the Black Octopus' – had helped create the myth that the Soviets were an even greater force than the Hungarians. Yet when England had met them a month earlier in the Lenin Stadium, the hosts had been lucky to gain a draw and Haynes had reached the conclusion that 'they were not supermen from outer space armed with some secret weapon that made them super footballers . . . [but] in short, human and, on the day, not terribly good footballers'.[16]

This time, though, the Soviets set the early pace, racing into a 2–0 lead within the hour. It was a hard, physical game, with Finney, in particular, on the receiving end of a kicking from various Russian defenders and Byrne's replacement, the Bolton full-back, Tommy Banks – a man famous for boasting that every winger who ever visited Burnden Park left with 'gravel burns' – especially revelling in the ruck. With thirty minutes left, Robson seemed to have scored after bundling the ball into the net but Kevan was adjudged to have fouled Yashin. The let-off unsettled the Soviets. Moments later, their defence failed to deal with Wright's long free-kick, Bryan Douglas touched on to Kevan, who repaid the selectors' faith with a goal.

England surged forward in search of an equaliser. Finney tore into his physical tormentors but could only watch as Robson and Kevan agonisingly spurned the opportunities he had laid on for them. Robson had a second goal disallowed but then, with six minutes remaining, Haynes ran onto a loose ball. As he approached the Soviets' penalty area, Yuri Voinov cut in front, sent him sprawling and conceded a penalty. A furious Yashin ran after the referee and span him around before hurling his cap at his feet in frustration. Finney claimed the ball. 'The tension was terrible,' he would write. 'I knew that Tom Finney from Preston could either keep England in the 1958 World Cup or see us halfway out of it after only one game in Sweden.' Even the normally unflappable Billy Wright could not bring himself to watch the spot-kick. With Yashin finally calmed, Finney placed the ball, walked back, ran up and struck the ball with his right foot to Yashin's right and into the back of the net. England were saved. 'What a wonderful feeling as I saw the net bulge,' he remembered.[17] Finney's penalty earned England a 2–2 draw but the next day the thirty-six-year-old was so sore that he was barely able to walk. Though Winterbottom tried to play down the injury, Finney's World Cup was over.

Into his place came Alan A'Court, Liverpool's reliable but inexperienced winger. He had just one previous cap and had played all his club football in Division Two and, though adept enough, was not of Finney's ilk. Three days after the opener he lined up against the formidable Brazil with Didi, Vavá, Nilton Santos and Gilmar amongst their number but not, on this occasion at least, their outstanding seventeen-year-old striker, Edson Arantes do Nascimento or, as he was to become better known, Pele. Yet it was the unlikely figure of A'Court – rather than any South American superstar – that was in the thick of the early action when he put Derek Kevan through to be denied by a fine diving save from Gilmar. The goalkeeper then outdid himself by turning Haynes's thunderous shot around the post after diving full length. Equally, Colin MacDonald, England's custodian, had his work cut out, but on the half-hour he could find no answer to Vavá's fierce drive from twenty yards which beat him all ends up. Fortunately for him, and for England, the ball crashed off the bar and back into play. Later Brazil hit the post but it was England who held more of the attacking possession, if not outright chances. With Didi marshalled superbly by the Wolves half-back, Bill Slater, the Brazilians were held to their first World Cup finals' blank.

If England emerged with credit from holding Brazil to a goalless draw, there were concerns about the lack of a cutting edge up front. Finney's injury had shown the thinness of the squad in terms of quality and experience. Beyond A'Court there was the uncapped trio of Peter Brabrook, Bobby Smith and Peter Broadbent, plus Bobby Charlton, who had briefly made such an impression in the white of his country. Back home, a nation watching the finals on television began to ask serious questions about his omission when an unchanged side was named for England's final group match against Austria. Winterbottom hid behind the veil of Charlton's inexperience and pledged his faith in those he had helped select.

England needed to beat Austria to progress to the quarter-finals, a draw would take them to a play-off with the USSR and defeat would send them home. Yet in the first half they were outthought and outmanoeuvred by an Austrian team who, after defeats in both of their previous matches, had little to play for but pride. Koller rifled a shot past McDonald in the fifteenth minute to give them a 1–0 lead and, but for the heroics of England's goalkeeper, they might well have held a greater advantage at the interval. Lame in the opening half – as they had been against the USSR – England played with renewed vigour in the second. Three times in its opening five minutes Haynes drove shots narrowly wide, before finally finding the net when he swept the ball home after A'Court's shot was parried into his path. The attacking impetus remained in England's favour but their build-up play was tame and finishing careless. Chances were spurned and then, with twenty minutes remaining, disaster struck when the unsighted McDonald was beaten by Körner's long-range shot. With the game in its final quarter, England were heading for an inglorious exit until Haynes and Robson combined to set up the much-maligned Kevan, and he finished smartly to make it 2–2. England pushed hard for a winner and thought they had it in the closing stages when Robson put the ball in the back of the net. Outrageously, Istvan Zsolt, the Hungarian linesman (who, when refereeing the USSR match, had *twice* disallowed Robson goals) ruled it out on account of handball. The game ended in a stalemate.

It was, by most accounts, a diabolical decision and one which left England with a play-off against the USSR just forty-eight hours later. It was the third time the two had met in the space of five weeks but in neither of the two previous drawn matches had Bobby Charlton played. Could he be the man to spring the deadlock? Apparently not. While in England a mystified nation pondered whether it was only the great unmentionable – the ghosts of Munich – keeping him out of the first XI, Winterbottom and his selectors alternatively batted away questions about his non-inclusion on account of his 'inexperience' and the idea that Charlton somehow wasn't 'a ninety-minute player'. Both suggestions were flawed. The inclusion of two debutants – Peter Brabrook and Peter Broadbent – in the side to face the USSR made a nonsense of Charlton's omission on the first count. As for the latter, it says more about the way that the England team was managed (and has often been since) than about Charlton himself. 'Even against Portugal,' Winterbottom would suggest later, 'when he scored both of England's goals, little was seen of Charlton as a footballer helping his team and being part of the team effort.' But had he not scored both goals and won the game? What more did they want? A three-minute mile to keep the crowd happy at half-time? Diligence was seemingly a virtue more highly valued than the ability to turn or transform the game with a moment of genius; the mundane were chosen over the magical if the former were prepared to track back and run themselves into the ground. Bobby Charlton wasn't the first victim of such an obtuse standpoint nor would it be the last time that England would stumble because of it.

At least England had Haynes and a well-organised rearguard to face the USSR. Against the odds, the right-wing partnership of Brabrook and Broadbent prospered too. Combining well, each set up the other to test the magnificent Yashin in the opening half, although on a chance-for-chance basis it was the Soviets who held the upper hand.

Fortunately, McDonald stood just as firm in England's goal and when the two nations came out for the second period the attacking advantage passed back to England. Twice Brabrook gained a clear sight of goal, both times he beat Yashin, and on each occasion his effort ricocheted off a post to safety. Then, typical of England's luck throughout the tournament, McDonald's poor goalkick was intercepted by Illyin. The Soviet winger switched play before having the ball threaded back through to him and he hit a low cross shot which hit McDonald's post and went in. With no one able to conjure an inspired or ingenious opening and Yashin being equal to Kevan, who spurned England's best chance of an equaliser near the end, it was enough to carry the USSR through. Mere inches had been the margin between success and failure.

Forty-eight hours later, the USSR fell themselves, to Sweden, who went on to reach the final with Brazil. The Brazilians' 0–0 draw with England earlier on in the competition had marked the tournament's turning point. Concerned about the failure to score, Brazil's manager Vicente Feola had called on Pele and Garrincha, neither previously considered ready, and the South Americans stormed through and eventually beat the hosts 5–2 for their first World Cup triumph. Back in England a country pondered whether more faith by its own selectors in the unorthodox might have yielded England greater reward. 'I want to know what every football fan in England wants to know,' wrote Desmond Hackett in the *Daily Express.* 'Why was Bobby Charlton missing from an England team that demanded a player who could shoot? I accuse the England selectors and team manager of deliberately killing the individual talents of the players they took with them.' Even Winterbottom had to put up with the admonishment of his family. Arriving back at Heathrow he was met by his wife, daughter and son. He greeted his wife and daughter with a hug and a kiss but stretched out his hand to his son who refused to shake it and, scowling, asked the question on the nation's lips: 'Why didn't you choose Bobby Charlton?'[18]

More imponderable was how England might have fared with a full complement of Busby Babes, not to mention Jeff Hall, Nat Lofthouse or a fit Tom Finney. Certainly their form leading into 1958 –

notwithstanding the occasional freak result – had been excellent, and the squad as a whole possibly the best in nearly a decade. In the finals themselves, luck hadn't been with England. Victory over the USSR would have led England to a quarter-final with an eminently beatable Swedish side. And then, who could predict what would have happened? But experience had shown that on their day, England could overcome each of the Swedes' semi and final opponents, West Germany and Brazil respectively. Further proof of the devastating impact of Munich came with the national team's recession that followed the disaster. In the twenty-five internationals preceding the crash, England had won sixteen, drawn five and lost just four. In the twenty-five that followed, they were to lose eight, draw ten and win only seven.

Neither Finney nor Lofthouse were to make heroic returns to the England team or spearhead its revival after another disappointing World Cup campaign. Both played twice more for their country and each took their haul of goals up to thirty, thus elevating themselves above Vivian Woodward's record of twenty-nine, but bowed out before the end of the year. Of the class of 1946 that left just Billy Wright still at the height of his powers. On his way to captaining Wolves to consecutive titles, one half of the most famous couple in the country became the first player in the world to win 100 caps on 11 April 1959, when England played Scotland. 'Billy Wright is our hero,' proclaimed Lord Brabazon on the day that Wright reached his century. 'It is his ability to use the inside of his head as well as the outside that has made him so remarkable. Not since Romulus and Remus has there been such a distinguished Wolf.' Similar plaudits came from across the football world with Wright the recipient of 'thousands' of congratulatory telegrams. The West German manager, Sepp Herberger, journeyed to England to present him with a giant silver candlestick; the city of Wolverhampton granted him a civil reception; each of the home Football Associations presented him with gifts and he was even invited to Buckingham Palace to attend a private lunch with the Queen.

Yet at the age of thirty-five, Wright had accepted that it could not last forever. Barring a Matthews-like run of form it was unlikely that he would partake in the 1962 World Cup finals, when he would be thirty-eight, and the now occasional exploitation of his declining pace would become commonplace. Some months later Wright met the

Home Secretary, R. A. Butler at the opening of a local football club in
the MP's constituency.

> 'The timing of retirement is so important,' the politician told him. 'I speak as
> someone who got it wrong. I had four years as chancellor of the exchequer:
> for the first three years I was proud of my record but then for twelve months
> I had to take unpopular measures. If I had stepped down after three years I
> would have been hailed a successful chancellor, but one more year changed
> many opinions about the job I had done. Take advice from me and don't
> leave retirement too late. You set standards that should never be lowered.'[19]

Wright paid heed to Butler's advice: at the end of the summer of 1959
he announced his retirement from international football.

Wright's retirement further confused England's state of flux. A
summer tour of South America that preceded his announcement had
been both a football and PR disaster. Before it even began England
had surrendered a 2–0 half-time lead to draw 2–2 with Italy at
Wembley and then things had gone from bad to worse. Matters
weren't helped when a hitherto benevolent press turned on the
players. Leading the charge was the *Daily Herald*'s new reporter, Sam
Leitch. In many ways, he could be seen as changing the entire
complexion of tabloid football reporting with his forthright attacks at
what he perceived to be the root of England's problems. His career
began with a report on England's 2–2 draw with Italy: 'Just forty-eight
hours before they fly off on their 20,000-mile tour of the Americas,
England plunged into pathetic depths of tame surrender . . . the full
list of England flops [was] headed by skipper Billy Wright whose
101st cap was his worst.' Things deteriorated from there on and
Leitch was joined by others at last ready to chastise the national team.
Suddenly gone, it seemed, were the days when the worst a player
could get was a gentle joshing from a journalist's pen. Now newspapers were increasingly filled with the kind of invective one would
formerly expect from only the most rabid fan. Expectation had not
just moved up a notch, it was suddenly screaming from the back
pages, particularly when it had not been lived up to.

Criticism tended to focus on Wright or Haynes and the latter, now
the chips were down, was increasingly seen as a moody, petulant
individual. An intolerant glare or even a volley of abuse would be
directed the way of any mere mortal who received one of his searching

passes and had the temerity to fluff the subsequent opportunity. 'It was myself I was getting the hump with for not getting the pass quite right,' he explained years later in retirement. 'I was a bit of a perfectionist; it was me cursing myself rather than a mate.'[20]

On 13 May 1959, in front of an estimated crowd of 160,000 in the Maracana, England fell to a 0–2 defeat to Brazil. If no disgrace had come from that, plenty was to follow. Four days later Peru beat England 4–1 in Lima and Leitch was apoplectic:

> Struggling, pathetic shame oozed out of every England football boot here at the foot of the Andes mountains tonight as a lightweight, slap-happy side from the ten first division teams of Peru thrashed us in a game which could so easily have ended 8–1. Beside me as I type, people jab at me through the twelve-foot high fence which protects us from the crowd. They beam and ask: is this really the first national side from England? Here tonight, as in Belo Horizonte nine years ago when America beat us 1–0, the great name of English football was reduced to futile palaver . . . to pathetic indifference . . . to sheer out of date fumbling.

The following week, the players exhausted and burnt out with altitude sickness, England were beaten 1–2 by Mexico and the response to the latest defeat took on a familiar tone: 'Beaten in Brazil, pulverised in Peru and now mauled in Mexico.'

By the time England reached Los Angeles, to face the United States it was openly suggested that the FA withdraw from the match lest there be a repeat of the 1950 fiasco. Journalists exercised their ire but, in particular, Leitch's typewriter keys must have taken a real battering:

> On this eighteenth day of the most disastrous soccer tour ever undertaken by an England team I AM SICK TO DEATH of using the words 'pitiful . . . pathetic . . . dismal . . . outclassed . . . outmanoeuvred . . . outfought.' I AM SICK of edgy England players saying to me: 'What are you worried about? You love to write this knocking stuff anyway.' This tour lies expressed for what it is – FIFTH RATE AND UNVARYING IN ITS MEDIOCRITY.[21]

In the event England prevailed as 8–1 winners in Wright's 105th and final match. On his return he launched into a heartfelt defence of his manager. 'Walter has been subjected to more criticism in the press and in a number of well meant but misguided books than most people,' he said. 'Walter is a warm-hearted person, a man of principles, and I know that some of this criticism hurt him deeply. Other stories have simply made him angry – particularly stories involving other people as well, which were not only unfair but untrue. It says much for his strength of character that his attitude to his job and the press has not been permanently scarred by this treatment.'[22] Maybe so, but with Winterbottom hamstrung by the whims of the selectors, was Wright's defence really aimed in the right direction?

Leitch's reports reflected a deeper cultural shift. Previously, England's troughs had been dismissed by the press as flukes, inevitable hiccups that would happen to any great side. There was little real analysis, anger was suppressed or occasionally heaped on the captain. Suddenly this changed. If the tabloid press can be seen as a vehicle that reflects its readers' wider anxieties and expectations, now they seemed to be saying, quite unequivocally, 'enough is enough'.

Predictably, the FA didn't like this new criticism. Joe Mears, Chairman of the International Selection Committee, took the unprecedented step of issuing a statement calling on the Press Council to intervene:

> Accompanying the FA party were journalists who, like some of the players, were experiencing their first long tour. Almost without exception their reports have been inaccurate, misleading, mischievous, and have been a great disservice to English football and footballers. It is our intention to recommend that the Press Council be asked to receive a deputation in order that a repetition of such conduct on future visits abroad may be avoided.

But little improved in the short term. In their first game back England drew 1–1 with Wales on 17 October 1959 and eleven days later fell to a second home defeat to a 'foreign' team when Sweden came away with a 3–2 victory. The malaise carried on into the summer of 1960. Twice against Yugoslavia, at Wembley on 11 May, England came from behind to draw 3–3; in Madrid four days later they lost 0–3 and also fell to defeat against Hungary in Budapest the following week, this time 0–2.

It meant that in the two years since exiting the World Cup, England had lost six matches and won only four. It was an unprecedented run of bad form and one for which Ronnie Clayton, Wright's successor as captain, took the rap. Four days prior to the Yugoslavia match, Clayton had captained Blackburn Rovers in the FA Cup final against Wolves. The Lancastrians had fallen to a 0–3 defeat and Clayton had been heavily criticised in the press for 'failing to rouse his colleagues'. In the build-up to the international journalists proclaimed that Clayton 'was on trial'. England drew, they opined 'Clayton must go' and go he did. He never played for his country again and Haynes succeeded him as captain.

Others had their own theories about England's slump. Tommy Lawton (ironically, given the way he had frittered away his own career in the pursuit of lucre) blamed it on the fixation for more money. 'People accuse the selectors, team manager and the system. The main fault is with the players, no matter what Jimmy Hill says. All they think about is: "What do I cop and how little do I do?"' His point of reference was a renewal in hostilities in the war between players and clubs over the outmoded contract and maximum wage status quo. In an effort to remove the maximum wage once and for all, the PFA led by Hill had astutely waged a campaign that garnered the sympathy of press and public. In 1960–61 it stood at £20 per week during the season and £17 in the summer, but by the end of that season the Football League came to the realisation that they would have to back down or else face a court case they had little or no prospect of winning. Finally, footballers could be paid their true worth: Haynes, famously, became the first £100 per week man.

As far as England were concerned, the press seemed content to chew on the sacrificial lamb of Clayton and focus on the iniquities of player power, rather than turn on the lame beast that was the International Selection Committee or its figurehead, Winterbottom. For Clayton the outcome had been most unfair. In thirty-five internationals he had barely put a foot wrong, and while he may have lacked some of Wright's leadership qualities, he was a man captaining England through a period of transition. Not only had the class of 1946 gone for good, but in the two years after Sweden, no fewer than twenty men had been handed England debuts, many of whom had graduated from the Under-23 team.

The most significant of these graduates were Ray Wilson, Jimmy Armfield and, most excitingly, Chelsea's brilliant young forward, Jimmy Greaves. He had made his league bow as a seventeen-year-old at the start of the 1957–58 season and ended it as Stamford Bridge's leading goalscorer with twenty-two goals. A year later he was topping the First Division scoring charts outright, a distinction he was to hold on an unparalleled six occasions. Essentially a penalty-box predator, Greaves was an instinctive, dazzlingly prolific finisher who would hit shots low, hard and powerfully, almost always on target, and very often beyond the reach of a despairing goalkeeper. Like Lofthouse, Lawton or Dean, he was a man born to score goals, but lacking some of their brute force, was more reliant on his whippet-like speed. Over ten yards there was nobody faster; beyond that distance Greaves seldom needed to tread.

The other Jimmy, Blackpool's Armfield, was a canny right-back who – with his fellow Seasider, Stanley Matthews – made up part of the country's best right-sided partnership. An astute tactician, tough tackler and, in his own right, a potent attacker on the overlap, he was to emerge as one of English football's finest ever full-backs, with only the cruel blight of injury ultimately barring him from football immortality.

On the opposite side of defence was a man who did reach such heights. Ray Wilson may well have played his football in the dreary hustle and bustle of the Second Division, but in a league full of yeomen he cut a positively aristocratic presence, elevating the role of left-back into an art form. Blessed with a change of pace more commonly associated with attacking players, he was a man who could successfully track then trap opposing wingers without having to resort to an ungainly hack, or simply slide in with the crispest of tackles. With precise and imaginative distribution, he was an asset to his winger and the team as a whole when striding forward on the overlap.

Sometimes in football a stroke of fortune is all that separates a team plunged into depression and one touching the very heights of glory. The width of a goalpost (as England knew only too well) could be the gulf between success and obscurity; a favourable refereeing decision the passage to ecstasy and a dodgy one the path to agony. When England met Northern Ireland on 8 October 1960, the luck was certainly not with the Irish. Led and inspired by Tottenham's great wing-half, Danny Blanchflower, Northern Ireland soon overcame an early goal by England's debutant striker, Bobby Smith. With the scores balanced at 1–1 Billy Bingham fired in a shot that was arrowing its way into the back of the England net, until it hit a fellow green shirt and bounced away to safety. Then Haynes broke clear and set Greaves up with an easy chance, which he buried to give England an undeserved 2–1 half-time lead. After the interval the Chelsea man capitalised on a rare error by Northern Ireland's goalkeeper, Harry Gregg, to make it three but still the Irish kept coming. McAdams made it 2–3; Dougan hit a post, as did McParland and McIlroy also went close. Just as it seemed as if Northern Ireland may find a way back and earn a draw, Haynes broke again and this time played in Douglas who made it 4–2. Shortly before full-time Bobby Charlton added a fifth. England had ridden their luck but victory was to serve as a prelude to an astonishing run of form.

First, eleven days later, England kicked off their World Cup qualification campaign in Luxembourg (who, along with Portugal, made up a three-strong qualification group ahead of the 1962 finals in Chile). England struck nine goals without reply: Greaves and Charlton each grabbed hat-tricks, Bobby Smith a brace and Haynes the other. If that result merely confirmed England's superiority against lesser football nations, when they beat Spain (3–0 victors in Madrid only the previous May) 4–2 at Wembley it added to the conviction that Winterbottom's latest batch of bright young things had begun to fit together. A 5–1 win over Wales on 23 November (which lifted England's goal tally to twenty-three in only four games) merely underlined it. 'The old guard had gone,' recalled Greaves, 'and Walter had created a young England team that was finely balanced and in tune with one another as players.'

More goals, however, were still to come. On Saturday, 15 April 1961 England met Scotland at Wembley for their annual Home Championship fixture. Winterbottom stayed loyal to the ten outfield players who had served him so well in the previous four goalfests, starting with a forward line that included Bryan Douglas, Greaves, Smith, Haynes and Charlton. Bobby Robson, who had returned to the national team after a gap of two years, now played as a wing-half. Playing in front of the Queen and Prince Philip, England stormed into a 3–0 half-time lead. First, on ten minutes, Greaves had picked up possession deep in the Scottish half. Shielding the ball from the attentions of several defenders, he held it up before releasing to

Robson with a pinpoint through ball, which the half-back struck first time past Frank Haffey in the Scottish goal. Nine minutes later Greaves latched onto Bobby Smith's pass and placed his shot beyond the reach of the Scottish goalkeeper; then, on the half-hour mark, Greaves was on hand to hit home his second after the hapless Haffey could only palm Haynes's cross into the Chelsea man's path.

Scotland were in disarray, but no side that could boast the likes of Dave Mackay, Denis Law and Ian St John amongst their number could be regarded an entirely hopeless cause. Davie Wilson had been slightly unfortunate to have a first-half goal disallowed, but three minutes after half-time, Mackay did manage to pull one back when his free-kick deflected past Springett. Seven minutes later Wilson dived heroically to meet McLeod's cross and crash the ball into the back of the net to make it 3–2. Game on.

The Scots' hopes, briefly raised, were soon dashed. Within a minute of Wilson's goal England had restored their two-goal advantage when Greaves's quickly taken free-kick found Douglas, who lashed in a shot that was too powerful for Haffey's fingertips to divert. England's fourth goal all but killed off Scotland's resurgence and in the last fifteen minutes the visitors' defence, which, in the opinion of the watching David Jack, 'had frequently threatened to cave in, was torn to shreds and exposed as just about the poorest to ever tread the Wembley turf'. Bobby Smith made it 5–2 on seventy-five minutes; Patrick Quinn pulled a goal back for the Scots; Haynes rounded off an excellent performance with goals six and seven on seventy-nine and eighty-one minutes; Greaves completed his hat-trick on eighty-two minutes and, with five minutes left, Bobby Smith made it 9–3. It was England's biggest-ever margin of victory over the Scots and the highest scoring game Wembley had ever seen. 'There was no suspicion of a weak link anywhere in England's ranks,' wrote Ian Wooldridge in the following day's *Sunday Dispatch*.

> But if I have to choose two men to honour individually then it must be the two inside-forwards provided by London clubs. Johnny Haynes, a magnificent general probing every weakness in Scotland's defence before deluging it with a stream of passes; Jimmy Greaves, a sprightly genius who gave a Stefano-class performance of ball control which made 100,000 fans gasp in disbelief.

Less than a month later the England bandwagon rolled on when they met Mexico at Wembley. Two years earlier defeat in Mexico City had caused consternation amongst British journalists; now, despite missing Greaves and Smith, England put eight goals past them without reply before flying out to Portugal for a World Cup qualifier, which they drew 1–1. The result set England up nicely for the home return in the autumn but the conviction was growing – as it had in the year prior to the previous World Cup – that England would not just qualify but stood a very real chance of winning the tournament itself. Victory over Italy (3–2) in Rome on 24 May merely deepened the belief that England stood on the verge of greatness, and qualification for the World Cup was secured with wins at home to Luxembourg (4–1) and Portugal (2–0). Would 1962 be England's year?

Four years earlier the awful events at Munich had done much to undermine hopes in the Swedish World Cup finals. Mercifully, no such calamity befell them in the run-up to Chile but progress was upset by the transfer of several leading players to Italian clubs at the end of the 1960–61 season. Shortly before the abolition of the maximum wage, hitherto untold fortunes had been offered to clubs and players to make the switch to the continent. Chelsea led the way by agreeing an £80,000 fee with AC Milan for Jimmy Greaves, who would receive a £15,000 signing on fee and £120 per week (as opposed to the £20 he earned at Stamford Bridge). Gerry Hitchens and Joe Baker, two men on the fringes of Winterbottom's plans, also followed the lure of the lire, as did Scotland's Denis Law. The departures of Greaves, Hitchens and Baker had a twofold effect on the England team. Firstly, because the three now fell outside the remit of the FA, their Italian clubs were not duty bound to release them for inter-nationals (Greaves, for example, didn't play for England once in his brief Milan career); secondly, Greaves and Baker were both deeply unhappy in Italy (Greaves lasted just four months, Baker not much longer) which naturally had an impact on the football of both, if only in the short term. As Haynes, lauded as a great patriot for rejecting the overtures of several Italian clubs, remembered, their departures were 'the small tragedy which hit the team and which it might not have thrown off in time for the matches in Chile in the summer of 1962. The rhythm was broken; the fast, open direct forward work was gone. Nobody seemed truly to understand this or remember it after Chile.'[23] By the time Greaves returned to the England line-up against

Scotland almost a year to the day since the famous 9–3 win, they were already on the wane, falling to a 0–2 defeat – their first at Hampden in a quarter of a century.

Meanwhile changes were afoot at Lancaster Gate. The death of the FA Chairman and FIFA President, Arthur Drewry, in March 1961 created two openings. As FA Chairman he was succeeded by Graham Doggart of Cambridge University; at FIFA, the FA's Secretary, Stanley Rous, became the third Englishman to hold the presidency (after D.B. Woolfall and Drewry). That left another opening and it was widely assumed that Winterbottom – who had worked closely with Rous on plans for the FA's centenary in 1963 and, further down the line, the 1966 World Cup finals which FIFA had awarded to England two years earlier – would follow in his footsteps and become FA Secretary following the 1962 World Cup. Within the FA head-quarters, however, there was a sizable faction, led by its charismatic and controversial vice-chairman, Professor Sir Harold Thompson, who maintained the belief that Rous had become too powerful and that the outgoing secretary's anointed choice – regardless of whom-ever it may be – should be vetoed. When the election was held by the FA Council, Thompson's choice, Denis Follows – the FA's Honorary Treasurer, and Secretary to the British Airline Pilots' Association – prevailed, by fifty votes to twenty. Winterbottom took the decision gracefully but plotted his departure from Lancaster Gate, accepting the post of General Secretary to the Central Council of Physical Recreation, which he was to take up in late autumn 1962.

First, however, he had to lead England through the World Cup finals for the fourth time. Chile had been awarded the World Cup even though the country was still recovering from an appalling series of earthquakes. It was precisely because they had nothing, argued the Chilean FA, that they should be given the tournament, though few would have described it as a success. True, there was a new national stadium in the capital but outside Santiago the facilities were primitive. Ludicrously high ticket prices in a poverty-stricken country meant that most matches were played in near-empty stadiums, while the long distances between the four playing centres – Santiago, Arica, Vina del Mar and Rancagua – meant that goal average would decide the first phase, or the drawing of lots would prevail if teams were still level. It meant that risks were plenty and, given the tension, violence frequently spilled over on the pitch.

England's base was the American Braden Copper Company high up in the mountains at Coya, which mined the 'El Teniente' mine – the world's largest underground copper mine, fifty miles up in the Andes from Rancagua. Coya was the company's guest camp and also where its executives lived, but to travel to the town of Rancagua, where England played their matches, the team had to journey down a miniature railway into the valley. 'To have our meals,' recalled Greaves, 'we had to walk from our barrack style quarters across a narrow, rickety wooden bridge with a 500 feet drop either side. It was great for building up an appetite. Bobby Moore and I shared a miner's shack that had a corrugated roof, and when it rained (which was often) it sounded as if the Grenadier Guards were marching above us.'[24] Not all complained and Greaves's chequered view ('even the dogs ran around with their tails between their legs') could, perhaps, be seen as typical of a man who rejected the splendour of Milan so that he could return to the more dubious pleasures offered in his native Essex. Yet there was also an indisputable sense that the FA, cack-handed in varying degrees when preparing for the previous three World Cups, had again overlooked several key components. For example, they had not even travelled with a proper doctor and Sheffield Wednesday's centre-half, Peter Swan, nearly died after he suffered a throat infection during the flight from London and then received the wrong treatment.

England played just one warm-up game, against Peru in Lima on 20 May 1962, which was won 4–0 with Greaves grabbing a hat-trick. Making his debut that afternoon was West Ham United's wing-half, Bobby Moore, who was considered a surprise choice despite adding some classy touches to a humdrum Hammers side. When Winterbottom named him in his final squad, the *Daily Mirror*'s Ken Jones privately pondered: 'Uncapped, pedestrian, not up to much in the air, suspect stamina – how could England select the twenty-one-year-old Moore for the 1962 World Cup finals?'[25] But Winterbottom evidently saw qualities in Moore not immediately obvious even to distinguished observers such as Jones. When England met Hungary eleven days later in their opening match, Moore retained his place ahead of the more experienced Robson.

Under a heavy drizzle, less than 8000 people were dotted around the Rancagua Stadium to witness the meeting of the two great rivals. Retirements and defections meant that only the Hungarian goalkeeper, Gyula Grosics, survived from the maulings of 1953 and 1954, but if the Magyars' reputation for greatness had diminished, their tactical nous was no less acute. Before the match their coach, Lajos Barotis, had pointed unashamedly as to how he intended to stop England: 'Number ten [Haynes] takes the corners, number ten takes the throw-ins, number ten does everything. So what do we do? We put a man on number ten. Goodbye England.' And so it came to pass. The Hungarians stifled the Fulham star; subdued, he began to hiss in frustration and, in the words of Brian Glanville, there developed 'a thin-skinned petulance about him which seemed to permeate the team'.[26] Hungary scored on either side of half-time, England responded with Ron Flowers's penalty but, lacking attacking verve, they were unable to overcome the deficit.

Next up were Argentina, who had brutally beaten Bulgaria – both physically and in the scoreline (3–1) – the day before England's opener. That match had seen sixty-nine free-kicks and one Bulgarian later showed reporters stud scrapes down both his legs and a broken nose. But it was not untypical: one of the blandest World Cups in the competition's history, it was memorable mostly for the physical violence on offer. Fortunately such an orgy of carnage failed to materialise when England met them and, perhaps surprisingly given that a win would confirm their progression to the next stage, Argentina packed their defence and offered virtually nothing in attack. On seventeen minutes Alan Peacock's goalbound header was illegally palmed off the line by the centre-half Navarro and, for the second game in succession, Flowers hit home the penalty. Before the interval Charlton added a second, striking home from twenty yards, then Greaves made it three in the second half with Sanfillipo grabbing a soft consolation goal. When Hungary drew 0–0 with Argentina on 6 June it left England needing just a draw with Bulgaria a day later to qualify by way of superior goal difference. In an utterly sterile encounter played out in front of just 5700 people ('I've played in front of more for Fulham reserves,' thought Haynes), England ground out a goalless draw to qualify for the quarter-finals. 'I had six cups of coffee during that match,' noted Frank Wilson of the *Daily Mirror*. 'But that still didn't keep me awake.'

Still, in progressing beyond the group stage, England had managed what they had failed to achieve in 1950 and 1958. But, as with their previous dalliance with the World Cup's latter stages, they suffered the misfortune of being drawn against the reigning holders – this time Brazil. When the two countries had met in 1958, Pele had been absent because he was considered too young; this time he was out with a groin injury but Brazil could still count on another individual who had made a telling contribution in the latter stages of the previous competition. Manuel Francisco dos Santos – Garrincha – had been born bow-legged and, as an adult, walked as if he still was. On the football field, however, he was a man transformed: a strong, quick, beautifully balanced player with one of the most explosive shots in world football. Winterbottom repeatedly warned his players about the threat he posed but, as one of them was to muse, 'how to stop the unstoppable?' Garrincha was to score twice, in the thirty-first and fifty-ninth minutes, with Vavá adding a third after Springett failed to hold onto a Garrincha free-kick; for England, Gerry Hitchens nabbed a consolation.

The Brazilians went on to retain the trophy, beating a well-organised but otherwise dour Czechoslovakia side in the final. England flew home and, like Ronnie Clayton and Billy Wright before him, captain Haynes ran the gauntlet of blame. Yet he remained defiant in the face of criticism: 'I am a footballer. This is my business. The World Cup is a part of it, a very big part of it. I want to win this thing to prove something which I know – that we can be as good as these other people at this old game.'[27]

Winterbottom, who made public his decision to move on at the start of August, was again absolved from culpability in the autopsies. His sixteen-year reign had seen one of the most radical periods of change in the history of the game. Floodlighting was introduced, club sides began to play on a European stage, baggy shorts and bulky, clodhopping boots were replaced by lighter, synthetic varieties, substitutes were allowed (albeit still not universally), training ground routines were improved and finally, in April 1961, the maximum wage had been abolished. Winterbottom had himself made several contributions to this period of revolution, not least the creation of the England Under-23 team, which provided a crucial stepping-stone between league and full international football for the country's best young footballers. Of the side that had lost to Brazil, the bulk of its members had progressed through its ranks, most notably Greaves, Charlton, Moore and, of course, one of the inaugural class of England's bright young things, Johnny Haynes. At the same time

England had slipped from masters to also-rans and arguably the finest-ever generation of its internationals had passed without combining to make a serious push for World Cup glory. Nations great and good had overtaken England on the football field and even the likes of Czechoslovakia and Sweden had outdone the inventors in challenging for the Jules Rimet trophy. In that respect Winterbottom must be viewed a failure, or at least a relative one. But then he had never been the manager in the modern sense of the word and, always answerable to the International Selection Committee in its various guises, he could only do what his job title stated for much of his reign – 'Chief Coach'. As Greaves later pointed out, Winterbottom 'had to do the job with his hands tied while answerable to football club chairmen blinded by vested interest and who had never kicked a ball in their lives. The farcical situation throughout most of his sixteen years in charge was that he *managed* the team, but did not *select* it.'[28]

And then there was Johnny Haynes. Always a man with an unshakeable belief in his own greatness, the criticism he received on his return to England was never likely to cause him sleepless nights. Always a virtuoso, all that was necessary was a moment of sublimity to serve as a salutary reminder to football followers that he was a man above the bog-standard cut and thrust of mere mortals. Still only twenty-eight, and with his future firmly pledged to a Fulham side that looked unlikely to have more than an outside chance of winning anything, his best stab at winning a trophy remained with his country. True, at the time of the next World Cup finals in 1966 he would be a roving veteran but sheer technical ability could keep him on a different plateau to his colleagues. He could still be a contender.

England's captain, however, wasn't to get the chance. In Blackpool ahead of a game with Bolton Wanderers in August 1962, Haynes was involved in a traffic accident on the promenade. Stretchered away with a fractured ankle, he would spend the following weeks in a hospital bed and months more convalescing. 'What rotten luck,' he complained in the following Sunday's *News of the World*. 'A wet road, a sudden gust of wind – and here I am in a hospital bed. It's a pretty frightening thing for a footballer to look down and see his leg in plaster. But I know my injuries aren't too serious and I'm determined to be back . . .'[29]

After a prolonged spell on the sidelines the 'king of the Cottage' did return but he was never truly the same player. He made more than

200 further appearances for Fulham but never played for England again. After fifty-six caps and eight years on the international stage, it was an outcome he remained philosophical about. 'Football has been good to me,' he reflected. 'But then,' he added, 'I have been good to football.'

7

ALF RAMSEY AND THE MAKING OF WORLD CHAMPIONS

For nearly a century the butchers, bakers and candlestick makers in charge of the Football Association had been virtually unchallenged in their control of the England team. They had run it like a gentlemen's club, blackballing players who fell outside their individual fiefdoms, capping inferior men to suit the needs of their own clubs, allowing personal rivalries and grievances to influence their rationale and allowing the destiny of English football to be shaped in a blasé, haphazard manner. They were amateurs, and so was the way in which they ran their organisation. The problem was that the game was no longer Corinthian at core and on a worldwide scale was less so than ever before. The longer, therefore, that the status quo prevailed, the more England fell behind. True, the FA had sometimes had to deal with piqued players, upstart journalists and aggrieved fans and indeed, more recently, had had to take into account some of Walter Winterbottom's opinions but, ultimately, it was their empire, and there were no checks on their rule. That was going to have to change.

The resignation of Winterbottom after sixteen years as England manager finally forced the hand of the FA. To attract the best candidate for the post, Winterbottom's successor would be tempted by the offer of a free hand in selection and that meant being unencumbered by the walking, talking anachronism of the International Selection Committee. For the FA's ruling council, this initially seemed an unpalatable option. A six-man committee was elected to choose the England manager but despite the publicly stated qualities for which they were looking in Winterbottom's successor (world knowledge; experience; success; star-finding ability; and discipline) their first two choices, Jimmy Adamson and Dennis Wilshaw, were both unproven quantities. Indeed at first sight it seemed as if the FA had merely plumped for suppliant individuals, whose inexperience could be manipulated, leaving control resting in the hands of the blazer brigade.

Adamson, Burnley's inspirational wing-half and captain, was the reigning Footballer of the Year and had accompanied the England party to Chile as coach that summer. In that sense his appointment would offer a direct link with Winterbottom's regime; but after a fourth, unsuccessful World Cup, was it continuity or change that England really needed? His limited experience begged a more funda-mental question: at the age of thirty-three and with no managerial experience or international playing career, was Jimmy Adamson really the man to command the respect of a nation and lead England to World Cup glory? Wilshaw, the former Wolves inside-right who had earned twelve caps in the mid-fifties, was Winterbottom's candidate. Like his former manager he was a football theorist and university sports science lecturer who lacked experience of the practice of his discipline beyond the corridors of his campus. Such inexperience had not stymied Winterbottom in 1946 but Wilshaw was not so keen and withdrew his name from the running, stating that he would prefer to continue teaching.

The public, however, were unimpressed by the direction in which the FA were moving. When the *Daily Express* ran a poll asking its readers whom they would like to see succeed Winterbottom, Adamson took just 1 per cent of the vote. Later, when the FA publicly toyed with the idea of a small panel of League managers picking the national team, the suggestion was met with derision. Bob Lord, the Burnley Chairman, spoke for many when he said, 'Make no mistake, I want England to win, but if they had eleven Di Stefanos they would have no chance with the present administration.'

Topping the *Daily Express* survey with 17.5 per cent of the vote had been Alf Ramsey, manager of Ipswich Town since 1955 and worker of miracles in East Anglia. In seven years Ramsey had led Ipswich from the Third Division to the League Championship on the sort of spartan resources one would expect from a club only elected to the Football League in 1938. His total outlay on signings had been £30,000, a sum that paled into insignificance when compared to his rivals: Spurs, for instance, Ipswich's main title challengers, had spent £100,000 on Jimmy Greaves alone. On winning the title, *The Times* had hailed Ipswich's achievement as 'the accomplishment of the impossible, beating the best that money could buy, cocking a snook at tradition and proving for all time that team spirit and the basically simple tactics of their manager, Mr Alfred Ramsey, probably the one great genius the game has produced in recent years, are an unbeatable combination'. The key to Ramsey's success had been simple: turning ordinary players into good ones and bonding these individuals into a unit good enough to take the title to East Anglia for the first and only time. They were a team of over-achievers, without stars (only Ray Crawford had made the breakthrough into Winterbottom's England, and even then had not made it to Chile), whose achievement was solely down to the tactical brain of their manager, so often in the face of his rivals' abiding naivety. Ramsey was 'a man who believes only in a team and not individuals, a man who is quiet, unassuming, strong and wholly confident in getting what he wants from his men,' according to L. Platt of Haverhill, Suffolk, when he wrote to the *Express* to back up his vote.

> Such a man made a happy winning team, a team from players who were unknown and misfits, he guided them swiftly and surely through the soccer divisions to the pinnacle of English football. What would this same man do with the 'pick' of his country? I say Mr Alf Ramsey as manager would take England just as confidently and just as surely to the top of world soccer.[1]

Yet when the *Daily Mail*'s Brian James interviewed him in September, Ramsey seemed to have alienated those at Lancaster Gate resistant to change. 'England should appoint a manager on exactly the same basis as a club appoints a manager,' he said.

> He must be allowed to pick his team alone and to decide how players will play . . . I think an England manager must make up his mind what players he has and then find a rigid method for them to play to. If any player, no matter how clever an individual, is not prepared to accept the discipline of the teams method, then I see no advantage in selecting him.

He went on to explain how 'great players' had failed to succeed in the past because England lacked method. While England's chances in the 1966 World Cup – without having to 'suffer' heat or foreign food – were excellent, he added, the League would have to help by giving extra preparation time. 'If we can work something out like this,' he concluded, 'I think we can win.'

When Adamson finally rejected the job at the start of October, there was increasing public disquiet about the protracted nature of the selection process, which had now taken two months. Moreover, looking ahead to 1966, there was very real concern that England might be embarrassed. Only in France in 1938 and Switzerland in 1954 had the host nation finished outside the top three places. Adamson's rejection of the job was an indictment. 'I want to go on playing for a few years yet, and my wife insists that I get a paper shop,' said the man who preferred the prospect of selling news to making it. 'I do not think I am equipped for the job.'

Who was left? The salary on offer for a new manager was thought to be an impediment to more experienced individuals such as Harry Catterick, Bill Nicholson or Arthur Rowe putting their names forward. Winterbottom's final earnings had been just £2000 or 'the equivalent of a local police chief' as he later liked to put it. Not much more was on offer to his successor. Given such a lack of munificence it would have to be a true patriot to take on the task, a man who would take literally the words of Joe Richards – 'It must be a case of country before club – country before everything' – when the FA had originally cast its net. Who else to take on such a task, but the man the people wanted: Alf Ramsey.

Ramsey's appointment was announced on 25 October 1962. It had been three weeks since Jimmy Adamson had turned the job down, and just short of three months since Walter Winterbottom had announced his decision to quit. The relief in Lancaster Gate was palpable. 'This is a first class choice,' said Winterbottom. 'I am sure he will do a wonderful job. He is a club manager with a wide international background and I have always found him a thoughtful and intelligent person.' He was to be paid £4500 per year and his duties would be fivefold according to the FA Secretary, Denis Follows: to produce the general England training programme; arrange training get-togethers; work with the FA's new director of coaching; win the World Cup and, crucially, be solely responsible for team selection. With Ipswich struggling at the wrong end of the First Division after a poor start to their defence of the championship, Ramsey said that he would not leave Portman Road until they were out of their current 'sticky patch'. He would arrive at Lancaster Gate on 31 December 1962, although he wasn't to take full charge until the end of the season.

Even before he thought about putting the England team in order, Ramsey had to sort out the way it was run. Having experienced first hand the disasters of 1950 and 1953, he had long raged about the meddlesome input of the International Selection Committee. As a man whose belief in the superiority of his country was unshakeable, he knew exactly where the blame lay for years of underachievement – and it wasn't with the men on the field. English players were the best in the world, according to Ramsey ('I believe in England, and Englishmen, as well as English football'): that they didn't live up to that billing was symptomatic of the way the game was governed and how they had been managed. 'The England team stumbled from one game to the next,' he would say later. 'Change after change to suit the whims of selectors, few of whom had a clue about football, I had no thoughts about managing England; however, I could see that unless one man was given absolute control over policy and selection there was little hope for the future.'[2]

One of the conditions of Ramsey's appointment was that he, and he alone, would be responsible for team selection. 'There are important duties for selectors other than picking teams,' said the FA Chairman Graham Doggart rather unconvincingly on Ramsey's appointment. 'They will support the new team manager.' Six weeks later the International Selection Committee officially disbanded. Yet with Ramsey still at Ipswich, England were without a full-time manager and Doggart spoke of a 'possible temporary appointment' to the England job for the first five months of 1963. Extraordinarily, late in January 1963 it was announced that the International Selection Committee would be reconvened under Joe Richards, the former chairman of the Senior Squad Committee, for the first three games of 1963, with Ramsey named as one of its members. Once the committee had picked the side, Ramsey would work with the players for three days before the match. Between games, he was free to continue introducing his successor at Ipswich, Jackie Milburn, to his managerial duties.

Even without the full attention of their manager elect, England entered 1963 in a kind of limbo. Britain was gripped by the coldest winter of the century, and beset by arctic conditions hundreds of people and thousands of livestock died. Road and rail transport was severely disrupted, the airports closed and the Thames froze over. The football programme was devastated by the weather with the FA Cup draw becoming a farce ('the winners of A or B will play the winners of

C or D' and so on). Without any stream of regular income, some clubs, notably Leeds, teetered towards bankruptcy. When England travelled to France at the end of February for a European Nations Cup tie, repeated postponements meant that many of Ramsey's squad had played but a handful of games each between them in the previous couple of months. The experience of England's Everton defender, Brian Labone, was typical: he went from 22 December to 12 February without playing a league game because of repeated cancellations. Any England fans expecting seismic changes to the first eleven were to be disappointed: eight of the players who had taken part in Winterbottom's last match, a 4–0 win over Wales in November, were included, with recalls for Bobby Charlton and Bobby Smith and a debut for Tottenham's Ron Henry.

The European Nations Cup was a newly constituted tournament which, in its early days, took the form of a straight knock-out competition with two-legged ties played in the two-year gap between the World Cup finals and the next round of qualifiers. England had suffered a disappointing debut, drawing 1–1 in the first leg of the tie with France when the two sides had met at Hillsborough the previous October. Then, with an almost completely new forward line and four new caps, they had lacked cohesion, created few chances and come out second best to the French in most departments, only being rescued by a dubiously awarded penalty. Come February, hopes of an English revival were soon confounded. Within three minutes of kick-off, they were a goal down, and by half-time the French were three goals to the good. Bobby Smith and Bobby Tambling pulled goals back, but slipshod defending and a nightmarish goalkeeping performance by Ron Springett saw further goals conceded. Eventually the French came away with a 5–2 victory.

'One does not expect five goals such as the French team got tonight,' said Ramsey afterwards. 'When we got our second goal I thought we were going to win. It was a magnificent effort to get back those two goals. But the fourth French goal a minute later was the killer.' It had been France's first international win since September 1961 and on the flight home Ramsey was berated by fans for not recalling Johnny Haynes (also present on the flight, having travelled as a supporter), who was returning to fitness following his road accident. The considerable burden of expectation was already weighing heavily.

In defeat, Ramsey was never a huffer or a puffer, a shouter or a bawler. 'If a player can't do what you ask them to,' explained his Ipswich centre-forward Ray Crawford, 'it's no good shouting and bawling at them – they can't do it. Alf never asked you to do something you couldn't. He'd never embarrass you . . . The way he worked and conducted himself brought the best out of us: we had a good team spirit, he welded us together as a team.'[3] Sometimes the new England manager would take this ethic to extremes, defending the indefensible, or making post-match pronouncements that flew completely in the face of what had just happened on the pitch. In many respects he was the perfect 'player's manager': he rarely criticised his teams, and never – not even in retirement – publicly berated one of his men. That his memoirs went unwritten was a mark not of a man who had no story to tell, but of a person devoted to a fault, who would never consider unburdening his opinions of those who had come under his management.

Yet Ramsey could be, and often was, ruthless. When England met Scotland five weeks later, Springett's porous display against the French saw him dropped. It had been an almost solitary aberration in thirty outings for his country, but thereafter he played just three more times for England. In his place came Leicester City's Gordon Banks. Born in Sheffield in 1937, Banks had kicked off his career with nearby Chesterfield in 1955, before stepping up to top-flight football with Leicester City four years later. For some, including Banks, his ascent was surprising: as a youngster he had been sent packing by Romarsh Welfare in the Yorkshire League following a two-game trial – having let in no fewer than fifteen goals! Despite playing for Sheffield Boys, Banks had given no thought to playing the game professionally when he left school. As he later put it: 'I was noted more for the alacrity with which I picked balls out of the back of my net than for any stopping ability.' Instead he became a coalman's mate, bagging and delivering coal, and later an apprentice bricklayer. Chance saw him pick up the green jersey again, when he filled in for another amateur side, Millspaugh, and his progression through the amateur ranks saw him picked up by Chesterfield in the Third Division North as a part-time professional. With Leicester he reached the FA Cup final in 1961, and was on his way to a second final in 1963, when he received his debut call-up. Little did the unassuming goalkeeper know then, but the step up to international football would mark the start of a meteoric rise to fame, fortune and adulation.

Nobody hated losing to England's 'Auld' Enemy more than the man who had called Banks up, Alf Ramsey. Scotland had come a long way since their 9–3 mauling at Wembley two years earlier and could boast a forward line strong enough to omit a player of the calibre of Everton's Alex Young. Even Ramsey was hesitant. 'We have a good chance of winning,' he said before the match, 'but the Scots are very well balanced.' Despite losing their captain Eric Caldow on six minutes after a collision with Bobby Smith (Smith himself was off the field receiving treatment until nearly half-time and thereafter was roundly booed by the visiting Scottish fans each time he touched the ball), England were torn apart by a rampant Jim Baxter, and got little change out of a makeshift Scotland defence, losing 1–2. The only crumbs of comfort came in the confident display of Banks and, as one FA denizen tried to point out to Ramsey, that it was 'only' Scotland and not in a World Cup match or anything important. He was telling the wrong man. 'I'd sooner anybody beat us than the bloody Scots,' came the manager's droll reply.[4]

A month later, on 8 May 1963, world champions Brazil came to Wembley. England gained a credible 1–1 draw; and Ramsey, who had finally left Ipswich Town that week, was able to dispense with the other two members of his selection committee and take complete control. Never again would management of the England team rest in the hands of amateurs.

Throughout his England managerial career Ramsey continued to reside in a modest home in Ipswich, commuting by train and tube to the FA's Lancaster Gate headquarters three or four times a week. Here he was allocated 'a stark office a little more spacious than a large cupboard on the third floor'. As his stock rose, he relocated to more salubrious surroundings on the ground floor, described by his first biographer, Max Marquis, as 'a sort of petitioned off cubicle in the middle of a large room, minimally furnished, with a table and two chairs. Most club football managers would use it for keeping suitcases in.'[5] England's new manager may well have seized full control of the team, but on a day-to-day basis his superiors clearly regarded him as a mere minion.

That summer Ramsey took his team on a three-match tour of

Europe, taking in Czechoslovakia, East Germany and Switzerland. After a protracted season with nearly half of its fixtures crammed into its final two and a half months, the sojourn seemingly offered little light relief. The Swiss and Germans were each useful opponents, while the Czechoslovaks had finished runners-up in the previous summer's World Cup. With a strong squad and an extended period of time for Ramsey to impress his ideas upon his players, England were to end their season in style and show glimpses of what could be expected under their new manager.

First up was the trip to Bratislava, where England's preparations were hampered by injury to Jimmy Armfield, captain elect since Haynes' enforced absence. Ramsey had a pool of experience to choose a deputy, including Ron Flowers, part of the England set-up since 1955, and the quiet but respected Bobby Charlton. Instead he surprised many by making West Ham's Bobby Moore England's youngest-ever captain. Born in Barking on 12 April 1941, Moore had been taken on by his beloved West Ham as a schoolboy and made his league debut in September 1958. As a teenager Moore had been instilled with the philosophy that you should know where you are going to play the ball before you receive it. Never the paciest of players, nor blessed with any great aerial ability, Moore's exemplary positional sense made him one of the First Division's most elegant defenders. His critics accused him of offering style over substance, but as his West Ham colleague Geoff Hurst later put it: 'They said he couldn't run, but he was rarely beaten to the ball. They said that he couldn't jump, but he was rarely beaten in the air. He recognised that he was deficient in some areas and compensated by working hard on the training pitch and focussing on his positional play.'[6] His international debut had come in Lima a year earlier, and he had been ever present in each of England's four games at the World Cup finals, but his promotion to captain – albeit on a temporary basis – came on just his eleventh appearance.

Like Ramsey, Moore hailed from east London. Both men were softly spoken, each was naturally conservative in his outlook and cautious in his outpourings, although Moore lacked his manager's prickliness. Like many of the great England captains – be it Wright, Haynes or Beckham – Moore was a leader by example: a shining infallible star on the field; a statesman and diplomat off it. 'Whatever you do on the field, whatever decisions you think are necessary,'

Ramsey told him that first day he captained England, 'you'll have my full backing.'[7] He meant every word.

Inept against the French, out of sorts against the Scots, but doing enough to hold the world champions, England were scintillating against the World Cup runners-up. On the first leg of their three-match tour, England withstood a barrage of Czechoslovak attacks in the first quarter-hour, deploying a cleverly retreating defence – a tactic often used successfully against them – and soaking up the pressure. After surviving the early onslaught, on eighteen minutes Moore intercepted a pass in midfield, found Bobby Smith, who played Greaves through; he wriggled his way past three defenders and placed a shot past Schroif. England held onto their 1–0 advantage until half-time, and two minutes after the interval doubled it: Gordon Milne, Charlton and Greaves combining to set up Bobby Smith from close range. The Czechs battled back strongly, and reduced the deficit when Scherer took advantage of a mix-up between Banks and Moore, but England soon hit back. Greaves set George Eastham free down the left and, when the Arsenal player's centre was too deep, Paine retrieved possession and his blocked cross fell into the path of Charlton, who smashed the ball home.

At 3–1 England looked good for their first win on the continent since beating Italy two years earlier. Yet Kadraba's contentious goal – after he seemed to impede Banks – brought a fresh battery of Czech attacks. Both sides continued to battle gamely – England for a deciding goal, the Czechoslovaks an equaliser – but a stroke of magic was needed to decide the contest. With twenty minutes to go Greaves provided just that when he pulled down Paine's cut back cross with his left foot and, in one sublime movement, shot home with his right. England played out the remainder of the contest with assured arrogance, stroking the ball around as if they were the side who had rushed to the summit of world football a year earlier, not fallen in its foothills. It was, reflected the watching Armfield, 'carthorses versus racehorses'. 'Today England played the football criticised as old fashioned,' said Ramsey after the match, 'but it was both entertaining and successful.'

As details of the Profumo affair were exploding onto the front covers of newspapers at home and across the world, the England squad journeyed across Soviet eastern Europe to Leipzig for a first-ever meeting with East Germany. Goals by Hunt and Charlton were enough to overcome an early German lead and secure a 2–1 win. 'The wingers in particular were the wonder men,' beamed Ramsey, pointing to the influence of the second goalscorer and also Southampton's Terry Paine on the right, who had again been impressive. Three days later, an inexperienced line-up rounded off their tour by putting eight past Switzerland: Charlton scored three, Johnny Byrne two and Tony Kay, Bryan Douglas and Jimmy Melia one apiece.

That same day John Profumo resigned as Secretary of State for War, and a month later the British establishment was shaken further when it was revealed that Kim Philby had spied for Russia. Indeed the summer of 1963 was momentous: Ronnie Biggs's gang seized £2.5 million in the Great Train Robbery; Martin Luther King told 200,000 marchers in Washington DC 'I have a dream'; the world fell in love with The Beatles and the sixties really began to swing. A more unlikely figure was also beginning to cause a stir. Humdrum, ordinary Alf from Dagenham, in his strange, stilted accent, had told a journalist from Ipswich that England would win the World Cup in 1966. Not could win it; *will* win it.

At an official FA press conference, on 21 August 1963, he was pushed for confirmation of his comments. 'I say it again,' said Ramsey. 'I think England will win the World Cup in 1966. We have the ability, strength, character and, perhaps above all, players with the right temperament. Such thoughts must be put to the public, and particularly to the players, so that confidence can be built up.'[8]

He meant it too, despite later admitting he had made a rod for his own back. 'I don't think I really meant it when I said it,' he confessed. 'The pressures at the time were enormous. It was probably a question of saying the first thing that came into my mind, something I don't normally do.' Ramsey was no braggart and only said things after careful consideration. While his belief in Englishmen to be the best in the world – simply on account of being Englishmen – counted for much of his thinking, he was not usually the sort to make such thoughts public. Instead it was a piece of kidology *par excellence* and shifted the burden of expectation onto his players. It was always an unspoken assumption amongst most fans that England should rule the world: now its manager was saying they would. This built a degree of pressure that would push his players forward, but also inspired confidence in them. What Ramsey was telling them was that they were capable of mounting a serious challenge, that they could be world beaters. And with each knock this pronouncement took over the following three years the spirit in his squad grew: they believed they would be world champions, they would show them.

In the short term, the remaining three fixtures of 1963 gave Ramsey's critics little call to question his proclamation. Emphatic victories over Wales (4–0) and Northern Ireland (8–3) as well as a 2–1 win over a Rest of the World select XI, staged to commemorate the FA's centenary, made it six wins out of six while in sole charge. But just as everything seemed to be going right – as every England manager has learned – everything seemed to go wrong.

On 11 April 1964 England were in Glasgow, needing just a draw to secure the Home International Championship. The squad had travelled up two days earlier when Ramsey had been greeted at the airport by a Scottish journalist. 'Welcome back to Scotland,' he said.

'You must be joking,' growled Ramsey.

If the manager set a hostile tone, his players were rather less convincing. On a wet and stormy afternoon England failed to create a single chance until the final moment when Maurice Norman went close with a header that could have cancelled out Alan Gilzean's seventy-second minute goal and saved them from the 0–1 defeat. The English press were stinging in their criticism. 'The manner in which their attack ambled and blundered through the opening period and subsequently showed no indication of being capable of beating a well-organised Scottish defence was pathetic,' wrote the following Monday's *Guardian*. The *Daily Telegraph* described how Ramsey and his side were booed and slow handclapped by a crowd 'whose patience had been tested beyond the limit by slow motion football'.

More bad news had by then come Ramsey's way. The day after the match the *Sunday People* printed allegations that a number of First Division players had received bribes to 'throw' games. The most prominent of the accused were Peter Swan, capped nineteen times by Winterbottom; his Sheffield Wednesday colleague David Layne and the Everton captain, Tony Kay, who had made his international bow against the Swiss the previous June. The allegations, relating to when the three had played for Sheffield Wednesday, were made by Jimmy Gauld, a one-time journeyman inside-forward who had turned out for Everton, Charlton and others during the 1950s. Gauld alleged that the three had accepted bribes to throw Wednesday's match with

Ipswich Town in December 1962. Kay reportedly told the *People* that he had been convinced that Ipswich would win anyway. 'It was money for old rope,' he allegedly said. Ipswich had won 2–0, but Kay had won the Man of the Match award and even the *People* noted that he 'put up a fine performance'. Ramsey, who was then in charge of Ipswich, was as shocked as anybody by the scandal. 'We had to fight hard to win that match,' he said. 'I remember feeling relieved to get the two points because we were at the wrong end of the table.'[9] The three were suspended pending investigation, the *People* passed their files to the Director of Public Prosecutions and the case was brought to court.

Nine months later, on 26 January 1965, Kay, Layne and Swan were sentenced to four months in prison for their parts in the scandal and subsequently banned for life by the FA. Gauld got four years. The sad irony was that the sums the players received – less than £100 – were the kind of figures that might have been tempting in the maximum-wage era, and in Kay's case would have been eclipsed within weeks by the signing-on fee, probably in the region of £3000, that he received on his arrival at Goodison.

For England it is difficult to tell what impact an international novice like Kay might have made (Swan's international career was by then all but over), but the indications were that Ramsey rated this tough, elegant midfielder highly and intended to take him to South America for the 'Little world cup' that summer. Given the way similar types of players became integral to his team, the indications are that his disgrace was a blow to the England manager. A midfield anchor would have to be found elsewhere.

Ramsey's men were again busy in the summer of 1964. They started a run of seven games in the space of a month with a match against Uruguay at Wembley. The South Americans were a pale imitation of the side that had twice won the World Cup, and only a week earlier had lost 0–3 to Northern Ireland in Belfast. In London their ambitions were seemingly limited to keeping the score down, and they lined up in an ultra-defensive formation with seven men behind the ball at all times. It was an approach that earned boos and slow-handclapping but ultimately the relative respectability of a 1–2 defeat. A last-minute winner by hat-trick hero Johnny Byrne sealed a thrilling 4–3 victory over the Portuguese in Lisbon on 17 May, but when England met the Republic of Ireland a week later in Dublin, it was an altogether more scrappy affair. Goals by Byrne, Eastham and Greaves secured a 3–1 win.

Prior to the trip to Portugal the squad had been based at Hendon Hall Hotel in north London. The hotel would become the regular base of Ramsey's team throughout his time as England manager, with training sessions taking place in Roehampton on the other side of the capital. A day ahead of their flight to Lisbon the squad were involved in a final work-out at Roehampton before heading back across the city for a meal and an early night. After dinner, six members of Ramsey's squad – Moore, Eastham, Byrne, Charlton, Banks and Wilson – retired to their rooms, changed, and slipped out for a night in the West End. At 11.30 p.m. Ramsey and his assistant, Harold Shepherdson, made a routine inspection of the players' rooms and found the miscreants' beds empty. When the six returned shortly after midnight they found their passports on their pillows – Ramsey's way of telling them that he knew.

Although the England manager was furious, he let the players stew. He also knew that he had to address the breach of discipline without causing resentment that could rend a split in the dressing room, or emitting a whiff of scandal to the press. The squad flew out to Lisbon, and still Ramsey said nothing. On the second day, after breakfast, he solemnly announced: 'There are some people I need to see. They know who they are.' Without a word, the six followed him out of the room. 'I don't admire what you've done,' he told them. 'If I had enough players you'd all be on the plane home, but I realise that I can't do this. Make sure it doesn't happen again.'*

Two days later all were picked, and they responded with the 4–3 win, with Byrne rewarding the manager's expedience with a hat-trick. It had been a superb piece of man-management. During the rest of his time as England boss no player had serious cause to call into question his authority; the players both feared and respected him.

Yet there was still a nagging unease in the manager's mind about his fellow east Londoners, not just Greaves, but Moore too. Greaves, an intelligent, humorous individual with a razor-sharp wit, was, in many ways, the antithesis of the more subdued Ramsey despite their shared background. Ramsey only had an elementary education, but

---

* Years later a friend of the late Bobby Moore told me that the England captain always maintained that this was the most terrifying incident of his professional life.

was comparatively well read – although there were times when he tried to appear the intellectual superior to his charges, a ruse which could backfire. For instance, after one training session the players were discussing who was the best club chairman. Greaves was unusually quiet on the subject, and Ramsey asked if he had any thoughts on the matter.

'Not really,' replied Greaves. 'There's small choice in rotten apples.'

Ramsey pompously upbraided him on his unimaginative response and clichéd use of the English language, which was, after all, 'the language of Shakespeare'.

'That is Shakespeare,' responded Greaves drolly.[10]

Greaves he could handle. Although the Spurs man was the best striker in the country and a regular in Ramsey's line-ups, he was not, as later emerged, essential to the England manager's plans. Moore was a different story. Seldom has a manager been more reliant on his captain than Ramsey was on Moore. On the pitch Moore's play embodied all that his manager stood for off it: assurance, control, quiet authority. While charismatic and influential players such as Alan Ball and Jack Charlton were to emerge over the following year, neither held the respect of their colleagues by sheer example. Moore, just like his manager, did.

Ten days after the rumpus over the trip to the West End, however, the two men came to blows again. This time it was in New York when Moore complained to Ramsey after the players had again been placed under curfew. Along with his earlier pique it seemed to contribute to unease in Ramsey's mind about the player's suitability, setting back the long-predicted announcement that Moore was to permanently succeed the seriously injured Armfield as captain until the autumn.

Was this the only reason for the delay? It has been suggested that Ramsey sensed he was being mocked by Greaves, Moore and others, particularly the east London contingent. Whether this was perception or reality is a different matter, but it was incontrovertible that Ramsey was prickly about his background. Could he have still been weighing up Moore's suitability as his lieutenant? Born in Dagenham, a tough, dirty, heavily industrialised town on the London–Essex borders, Ramsey was particularly secretive and sensitive about his roots, perpetually giving off the aura that he was somehow of a higher social standing than his forbears. Always smartly groomed and highly polished, the joke amongst the players was that Ramsey used to go to bed in a well-pressed suit. He took elocution lessons but ended up sounding like Dick Van Dyke; and his long, awkward sentences, often replete with mispronunciations, sounded exactly what they were: someone trying to climb the social ladder to middle-class respectability. Often he sounded vaguely ridiculous. When asked where his parents lived he responded, 'In Dagenham, I believe,' as if he were some aristocrat recalling a distant memory (albeit in a stilted cockney accent). Was there a sense of shame in his background? Jimmy Greaves, who grew up in nearby Hainault, once hinted that the Ramsey family were of gypsy stock. Given the social stigma attached to such antecedents, his secrecy is perhaps not surprising. On another occasion he asked Malcolm Allison (born in nearby Dartford): 'Tell me Malcolm, is Francis Lee a spiv?' 'Do you mean like your brothers, Alf?' was Allison's cutting reply.[11] Ramsey's family were no mob. But the proud man and inveterate social climber might have regarded certain members as ne'er-do-wells. To have been teased for his airs and graces would have been anathema to Ramsey; to have been mocked for his humble origins the cause of great discomfort. It may not even have been as complicated as that. It could simply be the fact that Greaves of Hainault, Moore of Barking and Malcolm Allison could see where he'd come from – dreary Dagenham – and who he really was: ordinary Alf, a clever man, though never intellectually so, a good sort, a loyal chap, a decent manager, but despite the posh inflections still just the Dagenham boy made good.

In New York, England put ten past the United States (whose Hamburg-born goalkeeper, Uwe Schwart, was a waiter at the England team hotel) in front of just 5062 spectators. Everton's Fred Pickering and Liverpool's Roger Hunt relived their Merseyside rivalry by trying to outscore each other – Hunt emerging the winner by four goals to Pickering's three.

The squad then flew south to Rio de Janeiro and after just thirty-six hours to recover from their ten-hour journey met Brazil in the splendour of the Maracana. The game, marking the start of a four-team tournament to commemorate the fiftieth anniversary of the Brazilian FA, began comfortably for the English with the defence holding up well against Pele, and Byrne testing the Brazilians with a couple of half chances. Just before the interval, however, Pele set Rinaldo free and the young winger shot past Tony Waiters, deputising for Banks in the England goal. It was a sucker punch, but shortly after half-time Greaves opportunistically equalised and, spurred on by his goal, waves of England attacks followed. Eastham saw his shot pushed onto the crossbar, and Byrne and Greaves both went close.

Then, on the hour-mark, Pele took control of the game. First, he put Rinaldo through and he cracked a left-footed shot past Waiters and into the top corner. England hit back, pushing for an equaliser, and Greaves saw a shot scrambled off the line, but the clearance only reached Pele and he span away, ran forty yards and rasped a shot past the hapless Waiters. Almost immediately the game was all but over. Cohen was fouled, England's free-kick was blocked and the ball fell to Pele, he played in Julinho, who made it 4–1. More followed. In the final minute Pele was fouled on the edge of the England area and from the free-kick Dias chipped home Brazil's fifth goal. 'England halted what is still the world's greatest team,' reported the *Daily Mail*, 'only to be finally humbled by the world's greatest player.'

Five days later, England met Portugal in Sao Paulo. On a ragged pitch the game ended in a 1–1 draw with Hunt's effort cancelling out a Ron Flowers own goal, but the game descended into anarchy. Colluda's seventieth-minute goal was disallowed for offside, the Portuguese players held up play for five minutes arguing, and when Torres was sent off for dissent the partisan crowd turned apoplectic, sending fireworks cascading onto the pitch and surging towards the wire fencing which, in the circumstances, was a necessity. Forty-eight hours later, England were back in Rio, rounding off their tour with a 0–1 defeat to Argentina, where, despite a spirited display by Peter Thompson – who earned comparisons of 'Garrincha, Garrincha' from an appreciative and largely Brazilian crowd – they proved disappointing.

On his return to England Ramsey admitted that there had been 'a gap in our respective standards of football' but didn't believe anything could be learned from the way the South Americans played. English football was still the best in the world, even if results had long since ceased to live up to such billing. Perhaps hoping to take advantage of the end of Ramsey's honeymoon period, John Cobbold, his old chairman at Ipswich, offered him his job back. Ramsey declined.

South America had been an important lesson, even if results had not entirely gone England's way. The Fulham right-back, George

Cohen, had made his debut against Uruguay and played in five of England's seven summer fixtures, impressing with his pace and composure on the ball. Born in Kensington six weeks after the outbreak of the Second World War, Cohen had signed professional forms with Fulham in October 1956 and made his debut the following March. A one-club man, Cohen embodied all the best attributes of a full-back: pace, attacking prowess on the overlap and solid defensive credentials. On the opposite side of England's defence was the well-established Ray Wilson, who had just completed a £35,000 transfer from Huddersfield Town to Everton. It meant that at the age of twenty-nine, Wilson, an international since 1960, could experience top-flight football for the first time in nine years. He had a change of pace and blend of precise, imaginative distribution more commonly found in attacking players but retained the crisp tackle and acute tactical awareness of a natural-born defender. The promotion to First Division football raised Wilson's game and he progressed in three years from being a top-class left-back to lay justifiable claim to be the best in the world.

In those three years Gordon Banks's exploits in goal would elevate him alongside Wilson in any putative world select XI but in 1964 he still had something to prove. Nevertheless, he had begun to enrich England with the sort of solidity lacking between the posts since the retirement of Frank Swift two decades earlier. True greatness was still to come the way of Moore too, but between himself, Banks and the two full-backs, Alf Ramsey had four-fifths of an enviably strong backline in place. It was in attack that England's problems seemed to lie. Although the quality of Greaves and Charlton was beyond doubt, their partners in midfield and up front meant that these two genuinely world-class talents could be infuriatingly enigmatic, brilliant one game, missing the next. Between the summers of 1964 and 1965, Ramsey tried no fewer than fourteen different forwards to partner Greaves or play wide on the right as he searched for the right blend.

Further evidence that all was not quite right came at the start of October in Belfast, when England met Northern Ireland for the opening salvo of the Home International Championships. If ever the cliché 'a game of two halves' had more resonance, this was it. For the first twenty-seven minutes England were supreme, tearing into the Irish with ruthless, brilliant efficiency stirred in with the occasional flash of flair. Greaves grabbed a hat-trick in the space of twelve minutes, Fred Pickering the other goal to put England 4–0 in front – a lead they held until half-time.

Come the second half, though, the fortunes of the teams were reversed. An early goal by Wilson gave the Irish encouragement and spurred on by an inspirational George Best they pulled two more goals back, and only the palms of Banks and, ultimately, the referee's final whistle maintained England's 4–3 advantage. To watching fans and commentators England needed more steel if they were to fulfil their manager's prophecy and win the World Cup. 'Ninety minutes of shambles in Belfast ought to be enough to end the eighteen month reign of amiable Alfred,' was one journalist's verdict. 'England's team manager should and must feel angry enough to become ruthless Ramsey.'[12] Further disappointing displays against Belgium (2–2), Wales (2–1) and Holland (1–1) merely deepened that conviction as England entered 1965.

Since taking sole charge against Czechoslovakia back in 1963, Ramsey had given debuts to a dozen players in his seventeen games at the helm. But of those twelve, seven were to share a total of only eleven caps while just three – Terry Paine, George Cohen and Peter Thompson – were to make more than ten appearances for their country. Of course, Ramsey had been instrumental in the decision to give Gordon Banks his chance, but beyond that there had been no great leap forward from the Winterbottom era, no individual who could claim to have come into the England side and fundamentally altered the way it played.

In February 1965 Ramsey convened an England training camp at Lilleshall. That he was able to do so said much about the changing attitudes in Lancaster Gate and among the clubs who had tradition- ally proved resistant to releasing their players for international duty. Nevertheless, both Bobby Charlton and Peter Thompson were prevented from attending because of FA Cup commitments. Without his preferred widemen Ramsey used the opportunity to play the Under-23 team, using a 4-2-4 formation against a senior side deploying 4-3-3. With a midfield triumvirate of Bryan Douglas, Johnny Byrne and George Eastham the seniors looked more defensively tight and won easily. They 'ran riot with the young lads,' Ramsey later reflected, 'they didn't know what it was all about. The senior team enjoyed it tremendously. They were full of enthusiasm.'[13]

This was all behind closed doors, of course, and for the paying public these developments lay further down the line. In the short term Ramsey had bigger surprises in store.

Since the retirement of the Comptons from top-class football in the early 1950s, the Milburn/Charlton sporting dynasty had become the nation's foremost football family. 'Wor' Jackie Milburn, hero of the north-east in the late 1940s and early 1950s, had been the cousin of four playing professionals: Jack, George, Jimmy and Stan Milburn – all full-backs – the first three for Leeds United, Stan with Chesterfield, Leicester and Rochdale. Their sister Cissie, herself soccer mad, had passed on the family passion to her three sons: Jack, Bobby and Gordon. While Gordon embarked on a career in the merchant navy, Jack and Bobby followed their maternal relations' football tradition and turned professional. With 'Uncle' Jackie Milburn trying to start a managerial career with Ipswich, cousin Bobby was chasing Jimmy Greaves for the England scoring record after both men surpassed Lofthouse and Finney's totals of thirty in 1964. Meanwhile, older brother Jack, until then utterly overshadowed by Bobby's achievements, was making his mark with a revitalised Leeds United side who had gained promotion to the top flight in 1964 and subsequently taken Division One by storm.

Bobby Charlton had been the schoolboy soccer prodigy with scouts from all over the country travelling to the north-east to vie for his signature. Jack, on the other hand, had been the steady, unspectacular stopper and occasional centre-forward who could not even get into the Ashington FC junior team, instead starting working life down the coal mine. It was some surprise when he signed for Leeds at fifteen, and even when he made it as a professional he plied his trade unspectacularly in the Second Division for the best part of a decade. He later said of Bobby's 1958 call-up: 'There was no jealousy. There couldn't be. He was the great player of the two of us, and I never in my wildest dreams thought I was good enough to play for England. I was just proud and thrilled for him.'[14] It was as if that was the accepted state of affairs for everybody, Jack included, until Don Revie, Leeds' brilliant and unorthodox young manager, came along and transformed both the club and Jack Charlton.

When Revie took control at Elland Road in March 1961, Leeds were perennial nobodies, a big city club with no trophies, no real top-flight pedigree, a 'yo-yo team', who seemed to be on their way down to the depths of the Third Division. Charlton was as well known for his vexatious temperament as he was for his under-utilised talents. Revie changed Leeds, halting their decline through a mix of shrewd signings, obsessive attention to detail and making hitherto under-achievers like Charlton perform. He improved attention to fitness and tactical detail and then added a further degree of ruthlessness to the team's play. Jack Charlton became the rock on which Revie built his Elland Road revolution and at the age of twenty-nine, when most players' best days lay behind them, his prime improbably lay ahead. Indeed when Alf Ramsey called him up in April 1965, the transformation from journeyman professional to top-class footballer seemed complete.

The contrast between Jack and Bobby could not have been greater, both on and off the field. Bobby was quiet, shy, polite; Jack loud, bumptious, sometimes rude. In one Liverpool–Leeds match, when a number of skirmishes were giving the referee much work to do, Jack sidled up to him, and asked: 'Excuse me, what would you do if I called you a bastard?'

'I'd send you off.'

'Okay, in that case I'll just think you're a bastard.'[15] The thought of the shy, reserved Bobby saying any such thing was inconceivable.

On the pitch Bobby was the most naturally talented and cultured English footballer of his generation; Jack, on the other hand, was tall, ungainly and hard as nails. The difference between him and his partner Moore was also enormous. 'Some days we'd be going out and I'd just look at him and wonder how this big giraffe played football,' Moore once said. 'We used to argue black and blue because I wanted to get the ball down and play the game and he wanted to hoof it to safety.'[16] In practice, though, Jack Charlton's blend of pace, aerial ability and ruthlessness in the tackle would complement Moore perfectly.

The other new call-up was Manchester United's midfield terrier Norbert (Nobby) Stiles. Standing just 5ft 5½in tall, this twenty-two-year-old, puny, bespectacled, toothless son of an undertaker, whose appearance evokes pictures of Woody Allen, seemed the most unlikely-looking lynchpin of any midfield. While it was easy to deride

Stiles as a mere scurrier, at Old Trafford he was the bedrock on which Matt Busby had built his team. His tenacity allowed the flair players to express themselves and his brutal streak put the fear of God into opposing mavericks. With Tony Kay disgraced and the First Division's other great hard men – Bobby Collins, Dave Mackay and Billy Bremner – excluded by birthplace, Stiles was the natural candidate for the role of defensive midfielder.

The two new selections were not without controversy. They were not England 'type' players, said their critics, not of sufficient pedigree to represent the country. Four years later, Roger Hunt would write, with some justification, that Stiles 'has made more enemies than probably any man in soccer over the past few years'. One First Division manager went further, declaring that he would jump off the skyscraper outside his ground if Jack Charlton ever played for England. Even Ramsey would later admit, when questioned by Charlton as to why he had ever picked him for England, 'I have a pattern of play in mind – and I pick the best players to fit the pattern. I don't necessarily always pick the best players, Jack.'[17] Others, however, welcomed the call-up of the pair. 'At last – Ramsey picks a real team,' ran a headline in the *Sun*.

And so it was to emerge as England strode out to face Scotland on 10 April 1965. Under a torrential downpour England were seeking to avoid a fourth straight defeat against their neighbours; not since the 1880s had Scotland had the upper hand for so long. The Charlton brothers were the first set of siblings to play for England since Frank and Fred Foreman in 1899 and it was Bobby who put England in front, opening the scoring just before the half-hour-mark. Using his turn of pace, he surged forward and hit a swerving shot into the corner of Scotland's net. England doubled their advantage shortly afterwards when Charlton Jnr, again in the thick of the action, sent Greaves through with a perfectly weighted pass, which split the Scottish defence, and the Tottenham man finished with ease.

There had been an element of fault in Bill Brown's attempt to save Charlton's goal but shortly before half-time it was Banks's turn to show a chink in his armour with an uncharacteristic error. When Law shot, England's number one misjudged the pace and was forced to try and save with his feet, but in doing so succeeded only in helping the ball into his own net to make it 2–1. Moments later Ray Wilson hobbled off with a muscle strain then, just after the interval, England were effectively reduced to nine men when Byrne pulled up with ligament trouble and played out the remainder of the game as a limping passenger. England reorganised with Bobby Charlton switched to left-back, but when Ian St John headed home on the hour-mark, further Scottish goals and eventual victory seemed all but inevitable.

Cometh the hour, cometh the men, in particular England's two debutants. Jack Charlton made himself an impregnable barrier, getting his head to everything that was thrown at England from the sky and a block behind everything that came lower. 'No one did better than Jackie Charlton in his first international,' opined *Soccer Star*. 'He was responsible for holding the defence together and made many fine sorties into attack, laying strong claim to that Footballer of the Year title.'[18] Yet it was in midfield, where Stiles dug in with the defiance of an entrenched gunner, that a point was secured. He was, said the *Sun*, 'the twopennorth of nothing who symbolised everything that was heart-stirringly magnificent about England . . . none was braver or more defiant than Nobby. None played better, worked harder or gave more.'[19] After ninety exhausting minutes and the score still deadlocked at 2–2, England's heroes left the Wembley pitch to a standing ovation. A moral victory had come out of the stalemate and Ramsey's selections were vindicated.

England finished the 1964–65 season with four matches against European opposition. First up was a meeting with Hungary at Wembley. Although the Magyars, through a combination of retirements and defections, lived in the shadow of their rampant predecessors, they could still count sublimely gifted talents like Nagy and Bene amongst their number. Prior to the match Ramsey had shown his squad a rerun of the 1953 encounter, but twelve years on there was to be no repeat of that traumatic afternoon. Greaves' seventeenth-minute goal was enough to give England their first win over Hungary in thirty years, a fillip ahead of the following weekend's visit to Belgrade where, on three previous visits, England had left with nothing.

For that trip, Ramsey included Blackpool's outstanding teenage midfielder Alan Ball. A fiercely driven, highly ambitious and, on the pitch, occasionally volatile individual, Ball carried a blend of ferocious aggression and delicate skill with distinction. A box-to-box midfielder who could score and create goals with the same ease that he could kill a game should he be deployed as a destroyer, he had vowed to his father (himself a former professional and coach of Stoke City) that he would play for England before he was twenty. Three days before that landmark birthday Ramsey included him in his side to face Yugoslavia. 'This is the first of ten caps you'll get for England,' he told him, 'and by that time we'll know how good you really are.'

In the Crvena Zvezda stadium in Belgrade England put on a display of maturity and control. The Banks-Cohen-Wilson-Charlton-Stiles-Moore defensive line looked as if it had formed an understanding over the course of two decades rather than two matches, while Ball – the man with the voice of a boy soprano but the heart of a lion – ran tirelessly, linking defence and attack, the centre and the flanks. But for some toothlessness in the forward line – Bobby Charlton was absent – England might well have come away with more than a 1–1 draw, yet it was still the first time that they had left that part of the Balkans undefeated and the following day's newspapers were fulsome in their praise. 'Ramsey was right,' ran the next day's *Daily Mirror* headline, 'England can win the World Cup – and this was proof.' Of Ball, Denis Law said: 'Alan Ball is the discovery of the season, an exciting player who can set any game alight.'

But, though Ramsey seemed to have formed a cohesive, composed defensive unit, the attack was a major cause for concern. For the meeting with West Germany three days later in Nuremberg, he gave debuts to Everton's wiry inside-forward, Derek Temple, and Sheffield United's bustling striker Mick Jones. England won 1–0 and gave another convincing display before rounding off their trip with a 2–1 win over Sweden. After the European tour, *Soccer Star* commented: 'Successes for England have been the normally inconsistent Paine, Ball and Stiles, but Jones is not yet the answer to the centre-forward position.'[20]

Jones would have to wait nearly five more years and join Jack Charlton at Leeds before making his third and final England appearance; Temple never got such an opportunity. When the international football season started again, with a fixture against Wales in October, it was 1962 World Cup veteran Alan Peacock, rejuvenated after his move to Leeds, partnering Greaves in attack. England lacked punch and sparkle as the veteran Welsh defender Ivor Allchurch rolled back the years, shutting out the England forwards in a dismal 0–0 draw. Three weeks later, Chelsea's Barry Bridges was given his fourth chance to stake a place in the forward line but Austria became only the third non-British team to come away from Wembley with a victory, winning 3–2, and Bridges never played for England again. 'We did not play well,' Ramsey admitted after the game. 'Unfortunately you people [the press] see everything in black and white. I stand by my belief that England will win the World Cup, but I didn't say I expect to win every match in the meantime.'

A month later, Ramsey ignored the growing clamour to include Chelsea's exciting young forward, Peter Osgood, when England met Northern Ireland on 10 November. Instead he recalled Joe Baker after a gap of five years. He celebrated his return with a goal after twenty-three minutes but despite that, and a strike from Peacock's overhead kick, there was little else to cheer in a dull 2–1 win.

With Greaves waylaid since October 1965 with hepatitis, Ramsey recalled Liverpool's Roger Hunt for a trip to Spain at the start of December. He also handed a first international call-up to West Ham's Geoff Hurst. Although he had been in the same age group at Upton Park as Bobby Moore, Hurst had been no more than a fringe player until 1962. A powerful, intelligent centre-forward, Hurst, like Ball, was the son of a professional footballer – Charlie Hurst, a centre-half who had plied his trade with Oldham, Bristol Rovers, Rochdale and Chelmsford. Born in Lancashire but raised in Essex, Hurst was a cricket professional with his adopted county, but it was on the football field that his performance attracted the most encouraging notices. 'If Hurst continues to develop along present lines he must surely attract the attention of the England selectors and will, I anticipate, be among our 1966 World Cup squad,' one magazine had written of him as early as April 1962. 'For polished style, ball distribution and command of a situation, Hurst has few peers.'[21] Yet even when the call-up came it had been something of a surprise, despite his position at the top of the First Division scoring charts. In the event he failed to make Ramsey's starting eleven and would have to wait ten weeks, when England played West Germany, before making his international bow. For Hunt, on the other hand, Spain was to prove a turning point. He had previously been on the periphery of the national team, playing only five internationals in four years, and Spain was to mark the real start of his England career.

Spain was a landmark game in Ramsey's career as England manager too. As his team lined up on a snowy night ('I have never felt so cold in all my life,' Bobby Moore complained) in Madrid's Bernabeu Stadium, their 4-4-2 formation looked conventional enough despite the lack of orthodox wingers in the line-up. But when play got under way, it was soon clear that something very different from the ordinary was taking place: instead of providing conventional support down the wings, England's four midfielders each took turns to support the strikers while a colleague would cover their position as they attacked. The Spaniards, particularly the full-backs, had no idea who to pick up as England swarmed forward in wave upon wave of attacks. It was less 4-4-2 than 4-3-3.

England took the lead on ten minutes. A cleverly worked free-kick between Bobby Charlton, Eastham and Wilson saw the left-back dip in a centre which Joe Baker touched home past Iribar. England continued to dominate, despite their scorer pulling up with a leg injury on the half-hour. A day earlier, when Ramsey had announced his selection to journalists, he had said, 'numbers on the back these days do not mean a thing – they are only useful for identification'. In doing so he had provoked puzzled frowns amongst assembled hacks; now, as players interchanged positions without regard for the numbers which traditionally denoted their roles, they knew what he had meant. England doubled their lead on the hour when Moore and Cohen combined, the captain squared to Hunt who lashed it home to make it 2–0. England laid siege to the Spanish goal in the final third of the match with Hunt twice going close and Ball also nearly adding a third.

England, according to the following day's *Sun*, were the 'Wingless Wonders'; the bookmakers' odds tumbled, making them 5–1 second favourites (after Brazil) for the World Cup and even Mrs Victoria Ramsey was backing her husband's team for glory. 'I wish he would let his hair down occasionally and throw his cap over the moon,' she told a journalist. 'It would do him a power of good. There is nothing spectacular in his reactions. But in his quiet way he's on top of the world. I can't think of any reason why he shouldn't bring the cup to England. He deserves it.'[22]

The system Ramsey had used was a variant of the *verrou* system (door bolt) first perfected by Switzerland in the 1930s and tried out at his training camp the previous February. It involved the deployment of a sweeper, speed on the break and players who could tirelessly track back. While Moore was not a *libero* in the classical sense, he was an orchestrator of attacks, while in Eastham and, in particular, Hunt and Bobby Charlton, Ramsey had the sort of quick, skilful, adaptable players who could instantaneously turn defence into attack. Charlton's move to a more central position from out on the left was to see him come in from the cold and finally attain greatness. He became the focal point of England's play; no longer a marginal player, flitting in and out of games, matching sparks of brilliance with spells of inactivity, he was now the fulcrum of the side – England's Puskás. 'He looked up,' Ramsey would say of Charlton's switch to the heart of the team, 'and at last became a great player.'

Over the first six months of 1966 the FA had organised a busy schedule of eight matches to warm up and make final adjustments ahead of the finals. It was a tough programme, taking in home and away games against Poland, visits to Wembley by West Germany and Yugoslavia, the Home International tie with Scotland and a tour of Scandinavia. Ramsey, it seemed, had found the right blend between flair and endeavour, youth and experience, defensive fortitude and attacking prowess. He had method and he had a nucleus of quality players, all he needed was to fine tune his charges. What happened in these final warm-up matches and the time the England squad spent together between them was to shape their destiny during the summer.

Evidence that the system deployed in Madrid still needed perfecting came in the opening two games of 1966, versus Poland at Goodison Park in January, then West Germany at Wembley a month later. Against the Poles, Burnley's Gordon Hill had been tried in place of Bobby Charlton and Joe Baker retained the centre-forward berth but, after a lively start, Baker faded and Hill lacked the all round sparkle usually brought by Charlton. The Poles, deploying a five-man defensive barrier, proved difficult to break down and when Moore's uncharacteristically lazy pass was blocked by Banaś, the Polish substitute seized the ball, cut back from the byline and his low, hard cross was struck home by Sadek to give the visitors a half-time lead. Taking heart from their advantage the Poles started the second half brightly and looked as if they had the stamina to hold on for a famous victory. Fifteen minutes from full-time, however, England summoned some inspiration. Cohen surged down the right, resisting three challenges, and sent in a deep searching cross which was met at the back post by Moore, who had charged in to score what was to be one of only two goals in a lengthy England career.

A month later, Hurst was given his debut against West Germany. Ramsey revealed the weight of importance he assigned to shirt numbers by handing Nobby Stiles the number nine shirt, briefly baffling the German manager Helmut Schoen. Again deploying a 4-3-3 formation, England lacked width and too much of their play was channelled unnecessarily down the centre, creating easy fodder for West Germany's best player, Franz Beckenbauer. Shortly before half-time, however, the hosts took the lead. Again, Cohen marched down the right flank and sent in a perfect centre but this time it was met by the head of Hunt; Tilkowski parried his effort but the ball span towards the goal line where – appropriately, given the number nine on his back – Stiles drilled the ball home. England held on to record their sixth victory in seven internationals against the Germans (the other being a draw), but it had been unconvincing stuff and they were booed off at the end. 'These new methods, which started so well in Madrid in December seemed to get nowhere,' wrote *The Times*. 'If England are to persist in the 4-3-3 formation, not only must they have finishing power but the finesse and ingenuity to go with it.' Others accused England of rough play. Bobby Moore admitted that there was 'a hardening process going on in the England team.' But neither he, nor the rest of the team, 'cared too much about whether we lived up to a "Good cricket, sir" image'.[23] Indeed, the toughening up of Alf Ramsey's charges would stand them in good stead come the summer.

Next, on 2 April came the biannual visit to Hampden Park. Ramsey was still to secure a victory as manager against his hated neighbours and England entered the usual cauldron of hostility deafened but unperturbed. Once again Ramsey deployed the 4-3-3 formation, but this time Bobby Charlton was used to the full, constantly in the heart of the action and pulling the strings of most of England's best attacking play. Yet the Manchester United star had no direct involvement in either of England's first two goals as they strode into a 2–0 lead after just twenty-six minutes. First, in the twentieth minute, Ball intercepted Baxter's aimless crossfield pass and broke quickly with Hunt and Hurst. The ball was threaded through to Hurst, who took his time and placed a shot past Ferguson for his first-ever England goal. Six minutes later it was 2–0. Stiles blocked Bremner's pass, broke with Hurst, who played in Hunt to ram a left-footed cross-shot into the far corner of the Scotland goal. With pace and power on the break, England were playing to the peak of their manager's ideals.

Less pleasing for Ramsey was the way in which England allowed Scotland back into the game, when, shortly before half-time, Law headed a corner past Banks. But England were indefatigable and continued to dominate much of the attacking play after the break. Unlucky not to get at least a penalty when McKinnon illegally palmed away Bobby Charlton's swerving shot off the line, England's third goal was not long in coming. Ball set Hunt away and he rocketed a strike past Ferguson to silence the Hampden roar. Johnstone pulled a goal back before Bobby Charlton seized the day. Picking up the ball midway in the Scotland half, he surged forward and let fly with a shot from twenty-five yards, which dipped into the corner of the Scotland net. Johnstone pulled another goal back but England held on to secure a 4–3 victory.

Five days later Ramsey released a 'provisional' list of forty players most likely to make up his final World Cup squad of twenty-two. FIFA's curious rules insisted they be provided with a list of possibles by the end of May and the final squad was to be submitted on 3 July, eight days before the first game, although the names of the twenty-two need not come from the forty already provided. Though Ramsey had used almost fifty players since 1963, several of the forty had never been capped, most notably Liverpool's Ian Callaghan and Tommy Smith, Chelsea's Peter Osgood, and West Ham's Martin Peters.

A subtle, elegant player, renowned for his late runs into the box, the twenty-two-year-old Peters was yet another member of Ramsey's squad to hail from east London. Although he had missed out on West Ham's 1964 FA Cup final victory over Preston, he had been a key member of the side that had beaten TSV Munich in the following year's European Cup Winners' Cup final. An important goalscorer for his club, he averaged a goal every three to four games. He was versatile too, playing in every outfield position in his 300 league games for West Ham, and his willingness and ability to adapt to any situation was to see him feature heavily in Ramsey's plans.

Not only was Peters included in Ramsey's line-up to face Yugoslavia at Wembley on 4 May, but England's manager also included two orthodox wingers – Terry Paine, and Chelsea's Bobby

Tambling – in his starting line-up. Also back in the white shirt of his country after a gap of seven months was Jimmy Greaves, recovered from hepatitis to stake his claim alongside Geoff Hurst, who was making his third straight start and striking favour with Ramsey when it mattered most. In a 2–0 victory England impressed enormously, with Greaves and Charlton grabbing, respectively, their thirty-ninth and thirty-seventh goals for their country and Peters making a strong case for inclusion among the pruned twenty-two. The successful reversion back to playing with wingers after a gap of six months had also given Ramsey more food for thought.

Two days after the Wembley victory Ramsey made another squad announcement. This time it was to name twenty-eight players who were to report for two weeks training at Lilleshall on 6 June ahead of the tour of Scandinavia and visit to Poland. They were Gordon Banks, George Cohen, Ray Wilson, Nobby Stiles, Jack Charlton, Bobby Moore, Alan Ball, Jimmy Greaves, Bobby Charlton, Geoff Hurst, John Connelly, Ron Springett, Peter Bonetti, Jimmy Armfield, Gerry Byrne, Martin Peters, Ron Flowers, Norman Hunter, Terry Paine, Ian Callaghan, Roger Hunt, George Eastham, Brian Labone, Peter Thompson, Gordon Milne, Keith Newton, Bobby Tambling and Johnny Byrne. The dozen players culled from the forty announced a month earlier were told to remain on standby but must have realised then that the expectations of England lay with their colleagues.

Formerly the country retreat and hunting lodge of the Duke of Sutherland, the Football Association's training centre at Lilleshall was the perfect base for Alf Ramsey's final preparations. Set in the lush countryside of Shropshire, with more than 100 acres of its own grounds and gardens, it was an escape from the intense pressure of the nation's football heartlands and the razzmatazz of its cities. There could be no subversive jaunts into the West End here. Instead the scene was set for a simple diet of training, bonding and resting.

There were few home comforts, though. The players slept in dormitories, stood in line for meals and took turns at doing the dishes. They queued to make phone calls from a coin-operated booth at the foot of its elegant period staircase and their one night out in a fortnight came when Ramsey took them for a beer at the local golf club. It was a 9 a.m. until 9 p.m. regimented routine of exercise, training films and practice matches. Alcohol was prohibited. When a small group did escape across fields to the local golf club they were caught by the England trainer Harold Shepherdson. 'You,' he said to Greaves, 'would manage to find a bar in the middle of the Sahara.' Ramsey warned them later: 'Gentlemen, if anybody gets the idea of popping out for a pint and I find out, he is finished with this squad forever.' Nobody went back after that.

Some loved the routine at Lilleshall, others weren't so sure. Jack Charlton described his time there as 'like being in a Stalag. Alf wanted to push us to the utmost limit of human endurance. It was a test of character as much as a physical training programme.' His brother took a different view: 'It was a monastic existence but I loved it. Football was my life and I was with footballers, playing football.' He told Ken Jones: 'The work was so strenuous that when the press lads were allowed in for a day they were convinced that a punishing session had been put on especially to impress them. That most definitely was not the case. Most nights we were looking for our beds long before lights out.'[24]

The players filled their spare time with darts, table tennis, five-a-sides, badminton, tennis and basketball. Ramsey would often referee these encounters, even games, such as basketball, for which he didn't know the rules – a weakness some players skilfully manipulated. Evenings would be passed watching films. Ramsey was a great lover of westerns and fed his players a cocktail of cowboy movies over the two weeks. Yet at bedtime, nine o'clock sharp, the projector would be switched off, no matter how far into the film they might be, and the order to go to bed would come. Geoff Hurst later claimed that he missed the ending of *Butch Cassidy and the Sundance Kid* three times during Ramsey's reign as manager. 'It wasn't until 1990 that I realised he got shot!'[25]

Some things, though, were harder to bear than missing the end of a movie. Several of the players' wives were expecting children at the time but such was the competition amongst the squad none ever felt they could apply for even a half-day's leave, no matter how deep their desire to do so. When Nobby Stiles's pregnant wife suggested that he should go and spend time with her at the birth of their child, he refused on the basis that even with Ramsey's blessing he might have slipped down the pecking order. Boredom played a part too.

Sometimes to kill it, Jack Charlton used to stroll down to the gate – a two-mile walk down a tree-lined avenue – with Stiles and Ball and appeal to passing traffic 'Let us out! Let us out!' The food could be monotonous too. 'Every lunch,' according to Banks, 'consisted of tomato soup, a side of roast beef with trimmings and apple pie with custard.' Welcomed by the players at first, the repetitive diet soon came to tire them. 'This chef's idea of a balanced meal,' quipped Ray Wilson, 'is a Yorkshire pudding on your dinner plate and one on your side plate.'

Yet Ramsey built up team spirit too. '[He] had a feel for players,' Jack Charlton wrote. 'In a real team you can't have shit-stirrers around. If there's someone you can't trust, get rid of them. They were totally absent in that squad. I never once heard any player questioning the merits of another, whether he should or shouldn't be in.'[26] If ever there were niggles, it was often the elder Charlton who was at the centre of them but Ramsey rarely intervened, seeing it as part of the team-building process. When a squabble between Charlton and Nobby Stiles blew up into a full-scale argument, it was the definitive sign that Ramsey had built up a team spirit. 'I was delighted,' remembered Geoff Hurst. 'I realised then that if we had players who felt they knew each other well enough to tear strips off each other's carcass, then we certainly knew each other well enough to sort out the problems and act together.'[27] Ramsey could have stopped them fighting at any time but let them carry on arguing until the insults were about to come round for a third time. 'It was, I now realise,' wrote Hurst a year later, 'a great piece of man management. If he had cut them short, the feelings would have bubbled along beneath the surface . . . resentment would have taken the place of reasoning. I go as far as to say if this squabble had not arisen and been allowed to blow itself out, England would not have won the World Cup six weeks later.'[28] The *Sun* even dubbed them 'England United' on account of the team spirit that had built up.

But the twenty-seven players present at Lilleshall (Brian Labone had already asked to be overlooked to get married) would soon have to be whittled down to twenty-two and Ramsey knew by the end of those two weeks who would survive the cull: there would be no more dry runs; any further games would be used to tweak his final plans. On the last full day at Lilleshall before the players briefly parted ahead of the tour to Scandinavia, Ramsey approached – one after another –

the unlucky five: Johnny Byrne, Gordon Milne, Keith Newton, Bobby Tambling and Peter Thompson. It was ten days before he had to submit his final squad to FIFA and Ramsey asked each man if they would mind training at their club in case of an emergency. With infinite sadness, each loyally agreed, wished him their best and trudged back to pack their things. 'I could imagine,' pondered Ray Wilson, who had briefly feared for his own place after missing several days' training with a pulled muscle, 'the emptiness I would have felt.'

A few days later the players regrouped, ready to fly out to Scandinavia. They were briefed by an FA official and told that they would each receive £60 per game plus £22,000 to be shared by the whole squad should England win the World Cup. They were then issued with heavy grey flannel suits – utterly inappropriate for the time of year – along with an FA enamel badge. 'The suit was just about acceptable,' recalled Hurst, 'but with the badge you looked like a school prefect!'

On formal occasions, Ramsey would call: 'suits please gentlemen'. The first time Hurst had to wear his suit, he decided not to wear the badge. Inevitably the first person he met was Ramsey.

'Geoffrey, where's your badge?' he asked. 'You're improperly dressed.'

'Sorry Alf,' he said. 'I think I've lost it.'

'Not to worry Geoffrey,' he said.

'Without a flicker of expression,' recalled Hurst, 'he reached into his pocket and pinned one on my lapel.'

'Now don't lose that one,' he told him. [29]

Ramsey himself still had nagging doubts about the concentration of his captain. At the time Bobby Moore was fishing for a move from West Ham to Spurs and refusing to sign a new contract to tie him at the Boleyn Ground, a situation which, in the event of it not being sorted, could make Moore ineligible for the finals. Concerned that his mind was not fully focused on the tasks that lay in store, Ramsey decided to give Moore a short, sharp jolt to focus his attention.

On the way to Helsinki, Ramsey hinted to some journalists that he was giving serious consideration to trying Norman Hunter in Moore's place. The Moore versus Hunter debate was a perennial one that emerged throughout the sixties and early seventies. Hunter was one of the First Division's most influential performers, playing an integral part in Leeds' relentless march to success. He was hard, competitive and highly consistent – better on a weekly basis than Moore – although he lacked some of his compatriot's finesse. Les Cocker was trainer for both Leeds and England and, whenever he returned to Elland Road after an international, he would get sucked into the debate. He later said that he would rather have Hunter week in week out, but when it came to England there was only one man. (Don Revie would later say as much to Moore: 'Had I been England manager earlier, I would have picked you in front of Norman because you can produce it for the big one. Week in, week out for Leeds, I would have gone for Norman. But it would have been you at Wembley.'[30])

Knowing Moore's importance to Ramsey, few of the assembled press took the manager seriously. But when Ramsey kept his word and played Hunter in Moore's place against the Finns the debate resurfaced. Though few doubted that he would return, it had the desired effect on Moore who lost any lingering complacency. 'From that day on,' he wrote, 'I never expected to be in the England squad until the letter from the FA dropped through my letter box. Alf was driving it home to me that there was always enough players for any team to get by without one player.'

England beat Finland 3–0 with goals from Peters, Hunt, and, in the second half, Jack Charlton. Three days later, on 29 June, Ramsey restored Moore to the side to face Norway, deployed two wingers, and England strolled out 6–1 winners with Greaves scoring four first-half goals.

Yet just four days after his blistering performance in Oslo, Greaves barely got a kick against Denmark. His forward partner Hurst fared even worse. 'I couldn't remember a match in my career either in West Ham's league side, reserves, or even A team when everything went so wrong,' Hurst recalled. 'It was embarrassing, I felt as though I had my boots on the wrong feet.' So bad was his display that Ramsey apparently considered sending Hurst home; he had never seen a worse performance by a centre-forward in his life. Jack Charlton and George Eastham eased the striking burden with the goals – met without reply – in a difficult, untidy game. 'It was a ragged match and there were glaring and elementary faults,' reported *The Times*. 'But it was also encouraging to see this England team work their way out of an unpromising situation.'[31] Yet Brazil's top tactical supervisor Carlos Nascimento, who had scouted England on tour, was impressed: 'England are a very strong side, physically and in organisation,' he said. 'They have excellent spirit and method: they are very safe in defence, active in midfield and should have won by more than two goals.'[32]

The three games in Scandinavia were relatively light fare compared to the threat posed by the Poles. The Slaski Stadium in Chorzow was one of Europe's most intimidating atmospheres: with a 70,000 capacity and a highly partisan local support, it was no stage for the faint of heart. 'This will give you all the chance to know what things will really be like in the World Cup itself,' Ramsey warned his players. 'You've had three comparatively easy games, and you know that – given the chance – you can score goals. Now the defence will get a real testing – the Poles will be all out to beat you and prove that they should be in the World Cup.'[33] He had previously hinted that he would choose his strongest side to face the Poles and there were few surprises as he read out to the press the names of Banks, Cohen, Wilson, Stiles, Jack Charlton, Moore, Ball, Greaves, Bobby Charlton and Hunt. But then, prior to reading out the final name, he paused mischievously.

'At number eleven – Martin Peters.'

The *Daily Mirror* correspondent, Frank McGhee asked Ramsey if he could tell him what role Peters could be expected to perform.

'No, Frank,' replied Ramsey, who got up and left the room with a smile on his face.[34]

Peters was the last piece in Ramsey's England jigsaw, slotting into place at the last moment. Described by Ramsey as being 'ten years ahead of his time', he was blessed with a blend of sound technical ability, pace, versatility and an eye for goal. In short, he had what it took to round off England's midfield and make the 'wingless wonders' work. 'The emergence of Martin,' said Moore, 'was the factor which settled us into a very efficient formation.'[35]

Against Poland, Peters was to put his worth to the England team beyond doubt with a tireless performance: getting the ball; giving it; moving into space and taking up possession again. It was a tight, efficient and mature all-round display won by Bobby Charlton's twenty-five-yard shot on thirteen minutes. The notices wired back to Fleet Street were overwhelmingly positive about the team as a whole, and *The Times*, pointing to the contribution of England's surprise inclusion, was moved to write that Peters 'was an outstanding success . . . So often when a player was in trouble tonight he looked for help: Peters was never far away; he came close to adding to his goal in Finland . . . and he was always ready to add his talents to an already massed defence.'[36]

On the flight back to London, journalists asked Ramsey to repeat his prediction that England would win the World Cup. 'I'll say it again now and really believe it,' he told them. 'I cannot think of a better defence than England's and all round we have more than a quota of very good players. It has taken three and a half years, but now the players believe in our way of working and are giving it all.'[37]

Amongst the players too, confidence was high. Few had seriously thought that England could win the World Cup when Ramsey had issued his statement nearly three years earlier, but just days ahead of the opening ceremony the realisation had emerged that they had a better chance than almost any of their rivals of lifting the Jules Rimet trophy. A settled squad; a solid new formation; a number of key players coming to the fore or to form at precisely the right time; two weeks of intensive training and a record seven consecutive wins behind them. It all contributed to an overwhelming sense of self belief, as Jack Charlton recalled:

> Among the England team there was a tremendous spirit of confidence as the aircraft skimmed through the skies towards home and the real thing at Wembley. Way back, when Alf Ramsey had made his famous prediction that England would win the World Cup, I had believed him implicitly. Then I had a few nagging doubts, when I considered how many slips there could be ''twixt cup and lip'; and now I was back to that abounding confidence which the boss had publicly proclaimed in us.

Their time had come.

8

'ENGLAND EXPECTS'

HAROLD WILSON WAS a man of many passions. He loved his wife (though some cruelly whispered that he was rather more enthralled by his secretary); his pipe; Paddy, his golden Labrador; and his frequent jaunts to the Isles of Scilly. He even, famously, when given the choice between smoked and canned salmon, admitted a preference for the tinned variety ('with vinegar' he added, no doubt trying to appeal to the common man's palate). Perhaps most interestingly, though, he also loved football. Wilson could be scheming and opportunist in pursuit of popularity – witness his taste in fish – but his passion for football was beyond question. Growing up in the West Riding after the First World War, he had been lucky enough to witness Herbert Chapman take his local team, Huddersfield Town, on an astonishing run of success in the mid-1920s. Twice in those years they had progressed to the FA Cup final, to which the young Wilson had travelled. 'We felt,' he wrote later, 'we were the lords of creation.' Even his official biographer was moved to admit: 'If the choice had been between Labour in office or Huddersfield for the Cup, he would probably have plumped for the latter.'[1] Later, as an MP, he would hold the constituency of Huyton, smack bang in the centre of England's Merseyside football heartland. Given the city's passion for the sport, it was probably fortunate that his loyalties lay beyond Goodison or Anfield. But his obsession with the game won him a universal affinity amongst Merseyside's populace. On Cup final day, if either of the city's two pre-eminent clubs were involved, fans would travel over to Downing Street to seek the Prime Minister out before the match. Unfailingly, Wilson would come down to greet them.

When the weight of the Profumo Affair, Harold Macmillan's ailing health, Britain's declining position in the world and the irresistible re-emergence of the Labour Party combined to bring an end to thirteen years of Tory government in October 1964, Harold Wilson became the first incumbent of 10 Downing Street who could genuinely claim to be a football supporter. By then, of course, the Football Association was a century old, and the game itself had been an integral part of national life for some eight decades, but no Prime Minister had ever taken the game to his heart. Wilson changed all that. He loved football and made certain that he was seen to love it, in the way that he was seen to embrace other popular causes, be it The Beatles, 'the white heat of technology' and, yes, tinned salmon.

Wilson had called and won a snap general election in March 1966, increasing Labour's majority from one to ninety-seven, but by July, as the World Cup was about to get under way, his government lurched into crisis. The seamen's strike worsened the critical economic situation; inflation led to a run on the pound and a strain on reserves; Wilson's cabinet became torn between those, such as his deputy, George Brown, who advocated devaluation, and those led by Wilson who rejected the notion. So dire had the situation become by the eve of the opening ceremony that there was talk of Wilson being usurped in a cabinet coup – provided of course that the government lasted that long.

In a last-ditch attempt to save the situation, Wilson flew out to Washington to plead with President Johnson to prop up the pound. In the meantime he desperately hoped that something, anything, would lift the mood of the country, divert attention from his government's woes and save his own job. Could Alf Ramsey's England help change the Prime Minister's fortunes?

Already World Cup mania had taken a grip on the national consciousness. Thousands of expectant fans had purchased 'season tickets' entitling them to see not just England, but nations whose football had previously been confined to the television set or the pages of *World Soccer*. 'World Cup Willie', the tournament's official mascot (a lion with a union jack emblazoned across his chest), found his image on all manner of merchandise from jigsaw puzzles and braces to glove puppets and money boxes, even World Cup cigars and beer. Designed by Reginald Hoye, an artist for Walter Tuckwell and Associates, and taking his name from Mr E.K. Wilson, the World Cup organisation's chief administrative officer (it was his nickname), World Cup Willie was the first serious stab at incorporating football across a wide range of consumer goods.

The build-up to the finals had not been without controversy. As early as 20 March the tournament had hit headlines when the Jules Rimet trophy had been stolen from Westminster Central Hall where it had been on public display. A massive police hunt ensued but intense police activity could find no trace of the missing cup. Calls were made to the home of Joe Mears, Chairman of the FA, in which demands were made for £15,000 in exchange for its safe return, lest it be melted down; and the detachable portion from the top of the trophy was even sent to Mears in the post. Eight days later, with a nation mystified by its whereabouts, a south Londoner, David Corbett, while walking his dog Pickles in Norwood, found it after the dog began scrabbling beneath a bush in a front garden. Corbett picked up a £6000 reward; the World Cup's kidnapper, Edward Walter Bletchley, an unemployed forty-seven-year-old, was arrested and jailed for two years. Pickles became a national hero.

As in Chile the sixteen teams who had made the finals were divided into four groups of four, with the top two from each group progressing to the quarter-finals. The qualifying tournament had been marred by controversy after virtually all entrants from the African and Asian confederations had withdrawn when only one place was awarded to the two continents plus Australasia combined. The only Afro-Asian nation to stay in the competition, North Korea, met Australia – who were expected to win comfortably – in a two-legged play-off in Phnom Penh, Cambodia. The North Koreans walked it – 6–1 and 3–1 – and Stanley Rous, who had travelled to see the two matches, warned that they were not a side to be taken lightly. Few, however, took notice of a team who were an almost entirely unknown quantity.

More controversy came when the refereeing arrangements were announced. Of the twenty-three referees chosen to officiate, seven came from England, three from other parts of the United Kingdom, five from northern Europe, three from southern Europe and five from Latin America. There was a clear predominance of those versed in a northern European style of playing – and intolerant to Latin gamesmanship – a trend accentuated by instructions to go easy on heavy tackling. They were appointed by an international committee consisting of one member each from Yugoslavia, Spain, the USSR, Switzerland, Malaysia and Britain; tellingly, if only for the conspiracy theorists, not a single South American nation was involved in the selection process.

At the England squad's base at Hendon Hall, the first serious piece of business needing attention was Bobby Moore's future. Still in the midst of a contractual dispute with West Ham, his hopes of a move to Spurs had seemingly begun to evaporate, but the situation had become complicated by Moore's unhappiness at the way West Ham had played the story out in the press. His contract expired on 30 June, meaning that from the start of July he was not attached to any club and was in turn not affiliated to the Football Association. As such he was technically ineligible to perform for the FA's national team. It was an unhappy situation and one that Alf Ramsey was more eager than anyone to redress. On the England squad's first day back together, the West Ham manager Ron Greenwood was summoned to Hendon. He arrived with a temporary contract that covered the month of July. Ramsey directed him and Moore into a private room and told them to re-emerge in sixty seconds with the contract signed. They promptly did and Moore was free to captain England again.

With that issue resolved the players returned to the routine they had known at Lilleshall: training, feeding, resting and an evening movie, once more unencumbered by the distractions of the outside world. At 10.30 p.m. on Sunday 10 July, as the players retired to bed, not even knowing who would be playing in the following afternoon's opener against Uruguay, they were all aware of just one thing: England expected.

At 11 a.m. the following morning, Ramsey read out the team to face Uruguay to his squad. There was one change from the side that had impressed so much against Poland six days earlier: Martin Peters, who had attracted such rave notices in Katowice, made way for Manchester United's John Connelly. Having seen the South Americans' defensive mindset when they'd met at Wembley two years earlier, Ramsey sought the same sort of width and spontaneity brought to the side by England's best player that day, Terry Paine. Hunt kept his place at centre-forward, instead of Hurst who was still to be forgiven for his display in Denmark.

The team arrived early at Wembley and Ramsey solemnly briefed his charges while the opening ceremony took place before the Queen. The flags of the sixteen competing nations rimmed the stadium; the bands of the Brigade of Guards played; and there was a march past of all the countries involved, made up of 320 London schoolboys representing the competing nations. Finally, the Uruguay and

England teams came out to a round of applause in a slightly less than full Empire Stadium. The two sides were presented to the Queen, Bobby Moore gave her a bouquet of flowers in the colours of the union jack, the Queen wished Moore luck, and the eighth World Cup finals were under way.

After all the attendant hype, hope and expectation, the match turned out to be a stinker. The Uruguayans massed ranks behind the ball and, apart from an early long-range shot from Cortés, offered nothing in attack, producing a stupefying spectacle for the watching crowd. England, despite sixteen corners and fifteen shots, never looked like scoring either. Charlton, Greaves and Hunt were repeatedly forced to resort to long-range efforts, and when England's best chance came on sixty-five minutes, after Bobby Charlton's left-foot shot was diverted goalwards, Mazurkiewicz dived expertly to turn the ball around the post. With the scoreline goalless, England trudged off at full-time, frustrated but crucially, in the eyes of their manager, unbeaten. 'You may not have won, but you didn't lose,' he told them in the dressing room. 'And you didn't give away a goal either. So whatever anyone says, remember that you will still qualify, provided you keep a clean sheet and don't lose a game.'[2]

Others were less impressed. It was the first time in fifty-two post-war Wembley internationals that England had gone without a goal. More ominously it was England's fifteenth World Cup finals match, of which they had now won just three. Travelling home to Essex, the *Observer*'s Hugh McIlvanney met two young men wearing huge England rosettes at Mile End tube station. What did they think of the match? 'Rubbish,' they replied in unison. And England's chances in the competition? 'Rubbish.'[3]

Ramsey was typically defiant. 'We can still win it,' he was quoted in the following day's newspapers. Yet at a press conference later that day he corrected himself: 'I was mistaken. I meant: we *will* win it.'

Back at Hendon Hall a television set had been provided complete with its own private BBC stream so that the players could tune into any match they wished to see, rather than whichever happened to be broadcast. Like all the best World Cup finals, 1966 was full of surprises, the first of which came on 15 July when Hungary beat Brazil 3–1 at Goodison Park. It brought to an end the Brazilians' unbeaten World Cup finals run that spanned some twelve years and eighteen days since Hungary had also defeated them in Switzerland.

The following morning at 11 a.m. sharp, Ramsey announced two changes to the England starting XI. Peters came in for Connelly and Terry Paine replaced Ball, who had picked up a knock to his ankle against Uruguay. Certain members of the press had already questioned whether Ramsey knew his best team, but England's manager was merely tweaking his plans, trying to find the perfect medium between endeavour – of which England's performance against Uruguay was not lacking – and attacking prowess.

But for the first half-hour against the Mexicans it looked like a similar story to the opening tie. Mexico kept eight or nine men behind the ball; England huffed and puffed, trying to break down the defensive barrier, but to little avail. At the other end, Gordon Banks's role was limited to the grand total of one save and a handful of goal kicks.

In amongst this dross, proceedings suddenly burst into life with a moment of inspiration. On thirty-eight minutes, Martin Peters intercepted a sloppy Mexican pass and played the ball to Hunt, who switched it to Bobby Charlton. Ignoring Stiles's run down the flank, Charlton surged towards Mexico's penalty area. Expecting a through ball, the Mexican defence stood off; then Charlton made that famous jinking movement – which had fooled so many opponents in the past – and changed direction from left to right. The Mexican players kept their distance but, as they weighed up the situation, their thickset defence revealed a glimmer of light and, in a single explosive moment, Charlton unleashed a bullet-like shot from thirty yards, straight past Calderon and into the net. Wembley stood to applaud one of the stadium's greatest-ever goals and an entire country heaved a collective sigh of relief.

The England players relaxed too, providing a more cohesive pattern of play as the game progressed into the second half. 'You can barely imagine the relief that overwhelmed us all,' Ray Wilson recalled, 'I could have turned cartwheels.' Though the game continued to be insipid entertainment for any watching neutral – largely because of the Mexicans' killjoy tactics – England continued to control affairs and with fifteen minutes remaining doubled their lead. Again Peters was in the thick of the action, combining with Bobby Charlton before sending Greaves clear with a perfectly placed through ball. Greaves hit a cross shot which was palmed by Calderon into the path of Hunt who tucked the ball home from close range.

It was Hunt's thirteenth goal in fifteen internationals. Greaves, by contrast, was still to open his account in the finals, and was without a goal in four games. It was an unwelcome and almost unknown position the Spurs striker found himself in, although he still had the weight of press and public support in his favour. 'Should England sack Greaves?' asked the *Sun* after the Mexico match, almost rhetorically. 'The answer is a thundering "No."'

The world, meanwhile, was either going football mad, or simply being driven mad by football. In Berlin, a twenty-three-year-old fan strangled his foster mother because she nagged him for staying at home from work to watch games on TV, then two of the giants of the game went into national mourning after they were unexpectedly knocked out in the opening stage. At Goodison, where they had already been beaten by the once-mighty Magyars, Brazil came up against their former colonial rulers, Portugal. Shamelessly, the Portuguese hacked Pele out of the game and, with the world's greatest player hobbled, the man who shadowed him as its best striker, Eusebio, took control of the game, scoring twice in a 3–1 victory. At Ayresome Park, Middlesbrough, an even bigger shock took place. Italy, like Brazil twice tournament winners, were up against little-known and less fancied North Korea, needing just a draw to progress to the quarter-finals. Four minutes from half-time Pak Seung Zin played the ball inside to Pak Doo Ik, who shot home from fifteen yards. North Korea maintained their lead and were rewarded with a quarter-final tie with Portugal, where even greater drama was to come. With Spain losing their third group match 1–2 to West Germany, the European Nations Cup holders were also absent from the last eight.

England, as Italy had, needed just a point from their last group match against France to be sure of progression to the quarter-finals. Having drawn 1–1 against Mexico and been defeated 1–2 by Uruguay the French were all but eliminated barring a sizable win over the hosts. Liverpool's Ian Callaghan came in for Terry Paine, who had played out most of the previous match as a passenger having been concussed early on, and Ball was again left out, despite recovering from his ankle injury.

Four minutes in, following a challenge by Moore, the injured Robert Herbin limped out of the fray to become a passenger but, despite their diminished potency, it was the French who brought dash and élan to the contest, a sharp contrast to insipid England, who lacked imagination or cohesion.

Slowly, surely, however, the hosts came into the contest. On the half-hour-mark Greaves was slightly unfortunate to be flagged offside when he fired home Peters's cushioned header, but ten minutes later the breakthrough came. Greaves and Stiles made a mess of a short corner but Stiles won the ball back and dipped in a back post cross that was met by the head of Jack Charlton. The ball bounced, hit an upright and rolled across the line where it was touched in by Roger Hunt. Wembley went wild; Yamasaki, the Peruvian referee, ignored French protests that Hunt had been offside and England went in at half-time a goal up.

Those members of the 98,000-plus crowd hoping at the interval that Hunt's opener might elevate the standard of play were to be sorely disappointed. Greaves, who had repeatedly struggled to find his best form in Ramsey's 4-3-3 formation, laboured ineffectually; Callaghan unsurprisingly struggled to invent a useful role on the wing in a side celebrated as the 'wingless wonders' and Bobby Charlton flitted in and out of the action, dazzling to deceive. Meanwhile France, knowing that their departure was imminent, threw everything they had at the England goal, providing Moore, Jack Charlton and in particular Banks with their sternest test yet. Wilson's last-ditch interception prevented Gondet from gaining a clear sight of goal; Bosquier fired a forty-yard shot narrowly over; Cohen got himself in front of Gondet's through ball; and Banks made a superb full-length save from Bosquier's chip, which prevented the ball from curling inside the goal post.

Yet the longer France went without scoring, the less likely they looked to do so. They had a let-off when Bobby Charlton's volleyed goal was mysteriously disallowed (which restored some justice after Hunt's dubious opener) and with fifteen minutes remaining, England sealed victory. It started ignominiously when Stiles ploughed wildly and late into the back of Jacques Simon on the halfway line, leaving the Frenchman prostrate, but the referee waved play on and the ball was switched to Callaghan. The Liverpool man crossed from the right and the ball was met by the head of Hunt, whose downward header slipped from the grasp of Aubour for England's second goal.

Simon was carried off and France, with Herbin hobbling around uselessly since his early injury, were down to nine fit players. Peters was twice expertly denied by Aubour in the French goal, and at the other end Banks's excellent save kept out Hausser's drive. Shortly after, the referee called time. The French were out; England through to the quarter-finals, but it had been – in the words of Ray Wilson – 'a hollow victory'.

Ramsey was not happy. In the dressing room he tore into his players, singling the out-of-sorts, though far from wholly culpable, Wilson. 'There were one or two people tonight who thought they were good players. And you were one of them.' Stiles's hack on Simon, which could at very best be construed as clumsy, was not mentioned. When Ramsey met members of the press he took the rare step of berating his players. 'England were not up to the standard of their two previous performances,' he said. 'Far too much casualness crept into their play. They were a little irresponsible. It started with two or three players and spread.'

England could be forgiven for a below-par performance, but Stiles's foul on Simon was treated with apoplexy. In the foreign press he was portrayed as a wild savage, while the conspiracy theorists saw it as an opportunity for his enemies to end his World Cup. Brian James of the *Daily Mail* had already written that there was a dirty tricks campaign among foreign journalists and officials to get Stiles barred even before the tournament had kicked off. 'It is a witch hunt, urged briskly by rivals trying to tame England by whispers in the hotels where FIFA officials gather . . . it is soccer's shame that the campaign seems to have succeeded so well.' FIFA added credence to his theories when its disciplinary committee immediately made it public that they had passed a note on to the FA, informing them that 'if this player were reported to them again by a referee, or other official, they would take serious action'. Pressure from the FA was in turn put on Ramsey to discipline or maybe even exile Stiles.

Back at Hendon Hall Ramsey asked Stiles about the Simon foul.

'Did you mean it?' he asked.

Stiles told him that it was an accident.

'I believe you,' said Ramsey. 'I take your word as an Englishman.'

Ramsey relayed Stiles's case back to the FA, adding that if any further pressure was put on him to drop Stiles, he would resign as England manager.

There was something definitively English about Ramsey's gesture. It was defiant, but also showed his deep-seated sense of loyalty in action. Ramsey was an undemonstrative man, but when questions were asked of his players he was always unstinting in their support. Of course, Stiles was also vital to the way in which his team played. 'Our game in defence before 1966 was not based on a sweeper as used in most European countries,' Ramsey later revealed. 'We had little experience of how to utilise a defender behind our four defenders. What I preferred in the case of Nobby Stiles was that instead of a sweeper at the back I would have a winner of the ball in front. I would have a man who would remain sitting in the centre of the field to win possession before any ball reached the back defence.' Later, when Stiles's heyday, and that of his heir to the number four shirt, Alan Mullery, had passed and Ramsey struggled to find a replacement of similar calibre, it was noticeable that England struggled too.

Knowing the intense pressure Ramsey had been put under, his backroom lieutenants, Les Cocker and Harold Shepherdson, paid Stiles a visit to tell him in no uncertain terms not to repeat his recklessness. Pinning Stiles up against a wall, they warned: 'Alf's stuck his neck out for you, don't let him down.'[4]

Stiles wasn't the only one to administer a rough challenge in the France match. Greaves had been the recipient of a late challenge from Jean Bonnel that had left him hobbling in the latter stages and later required fourteen stitches. With only seventy-two hours between the final group match and England's quarter-final with Argentina, Greaves was immediately listed as a grave doubt until, the day before, it became apparent that he would not be fit to play. Ramsey, nevertheless, seemed undaunted by the absence of his record goalscorer when he spoke to journalists twenty-four hours ahead of the tie. 'We have no fears,' he said. 'Argentina have an excellent defence and an excellent team. But our defence is equal to theirs – if not better.' Hurst, in any case, seemed better suited to Ramsey's wingless wonders, a system that preferred steady, well-rounded players like the West Ham man to mercurial figures like Greaves.

Argentina had progressed through their first-round group in second place to West Germany with a record identical – save for a conceded goal – to their hosts. If Stiles was painted as England's villain, Argentina had a team full of them. Although England had not been on the receiving end of their nastier side when they had met in Rio de Janeiro two years earlier, they had had a taster of what the Argentinians were about when they had watched them play Brazil.

Messiano had shackled Pele using fair means and foul to the extent that the Brazilian – purportedly one of the gentlemen of world football – was moved to attack his marker with a flying head-butt that smashed his tormentor's nose across his face. 'I think the way the Argentinians had played against Brazil that night – brutally cold and vicious – stayed imprinted on Alf Ramsey's mind,' Greaves said.[5] Any hope that they had improved had already been confounded after Jorge Albrecht had become the first man to be dismissed in the tournament, and the FIFA disciplinary committee subsequently warned the entire squad as to their future conduct.

What followed in the quarter-final came to be described in the immortal words of Hugh McIlvanney as 'not so much a football match as an international incident'. From the first attack, when Martin Peters was felled by a blatant, ugly body check, it was apparent that the Argentinians were out to stop England at any cost. Following the lead of their captain Antonio Rattin, they pushed, kicked, spat, wasted time, and tried to provoke England to sink to their level. 'They were always together and they always got the job done,' Bobby Charlton wrote. 'No fair races were allowed. Try to go past them and they would upend you. They spat. They were probably the meanest, roughest team I ever played against.'[6] The irony was that they were a good team and, according to a number of observers including Charlton, one with the ability to actually win the World Cup should they have gone out and tried to play.

Chances were few. Onega set up Mas with a beautifully placed pass, but his shot flew just wide of Banks' post. At the other end, Hurst watched in wonderment as Roma turned his thunderous shot over the angle of the crossbar and post.

In the middle, the referee, Rudolph Kreitlein, a forty-six-year-old tailor from Stuttgart who had refereed that year's European Cup final between Real Madrid and Partizan Belgrade, was struggling to control events. 'Kreitlein rushed hither and thither, an exacerbating rather than calming influence, inscribing notes in his notebook with the zeal of a schoolboy collecting engine numbers,'[7] noted Brian Glanville. Hugh McIlvanney concurred with his colleague's view, writing that the Argentinians had been 'needlessly provoked by inefficient and over punctilious refereeing'.[8] He also complained that as a reporter he had found it impossible to keep track of the bookings, as Kreitlein frequently took names without interrupting the play. Indeed, both

Charlton brothers were booked in the game, although neither knew anything about it until after the match.

In particular, Kreitlein was having problems with Rattin, who would tower over the German and argue and gesticulate whenever a decision went against his team. 'Whenever the referee intervened with free-kicks for us, Rattin would argue,' recalled Ray Wilson. 'He wanted to referee the match.'[9] Having already booked him for tripping Jack Charlton and warned him again about his conduct, Kreitlein finally had enough of Rattin's antics and sent him off ten minutes before half-time.

Anarchy descended. Rattin, the sort of player who would argue about the direction of a throw-in, now had a genuine grievance and was incandescent. He shouted at Kreitlein and jostled him before storming off to the touchline. Albrecht then took a voluntary exit and gestured to his team-mates to join him in leaving the field. Roma followed with two others, while Rattin stood on the edge of the pitch trying to argue his way back into the game. All the while Ramsey urged his players, who were limbering up, watching bemusedly, to keep away from the Argentinians lest they be spat at. When the police moved into advanced positions in readiness to intervene, it looked as though the game would be abandoned. Finally, after seven minutes, the Argentinians agreed to restart. Rattin sat provocatively on the sidelines, but the police, suspecting his presence might be incendiary, sent him down the tunnel and into the dressing room.

But that did not put an end to the controversy. Before the interval there was nearly a punch-up between Hurst and Ferreiro, after the England forward had mistimed a challenge. Ferreiro, nevertheless, noted McIlvanney, 'went down and turned over with a violent agility that would have been astonishing in a supremely fit man, let alone one who had been badly injured'.[10]

The tone of the game did not improve in the second half. Argentina continued to invest all their unquestionable talents in killing the game and England laboured in finding the piece of inspiration to break through their rearguard. The match was in desperate need of a goal and thirteen minutes before full-time it finally came. Wilson played Peters in down the left and he looked up and crossed a perfect, tantalising centre. For an instant the ball seemed to hang in the air, the whole world admiring its splendid, spinning curvature. And then Geoff Hurst's forehead met it like a hammer-blow, placing it wide of the sprawling Roma into the corner of the goal. 'West Ham United, united in thought and action, had done the trick for England,' mused the following Monday's *Times*.[11]

'Goal!!!' screamed 90,000 Englishmen packed into Wembley and a nation watching on television, enraptured that something so magisterial had overcome such malevolence. Hurst ran to the touch-line and stood, arms aloft, statue-like in his celebration. A nearby photographer put down his camera and patted the back of his head, while a small boy ran onto the pitch to congratulate the scorer but typically – given what had already passed – was cuffed around the back of the head by Mas.

It was a goal worthy of winning any match, and enough to settle this ugly affair. But there was yet more unpleasantness to come. When Kreitlein called time, Ramsey ran straight onto the pitch to physically stop George Cohen from swapping shirts. 'There is no dignity,' he explained later, 'in bare chested footballers parading on the pitch.'

The Argentinians made their disgust at the officials known. One of their number spat on a FIFA dignitary's blazer; another urinated on the concrete tunnel wall; Kreitlein left the field with his shirt torn away at the shoulder. Argentina's players hammered on the locked doors of the England changing room shouting insults and accusations. 'Send them in!' shouted Jack Charlton, 'I'll fight them all! Send them in!' Stiles and Ball were behind him echoing his words. 'I have refereed matches all over the world,' said Kreitlein, 'and this was undoubtedly the roughest.' Yet it had been England who had committed the most fouls: thirty-three to their opponents' nineteen. The main offence of the South Americans had been their games-manship and dissent. 'The look on Rattin's face was quite enough to tell me what he was saying and meaning,' added Kreitlein. 'I do not speak Spanish, but the look told me everything.' Kreitlein had to be smuggled out of Wembley's back entrance after the game.

Ramsey fanned the flames of controversy even further when he spoke to journalists afterwards. 'England play to win and win we did, which was important,' he said. 'We are afraid of no one. We still have to produce our best football. It is not possible until we meet the right type of opposition, a team which come out to play football, not as *animals*, as we have seen in the World Cup.' Understandably, his 'animals' allusion was seized upon by journalists across the world when the following morning's headlines were being written: 'Go home thugs', 'Animals!' and 'World Cup disgrace' captured English indignation perfectly.

The Argentinians pleaded they had been hard done by, even after FIFA fined them the maximum 1000 Swiss Francs (approximately £85), suspended Rattin for four games, Ferreira and Onega for three, and told the Argentinian FA to sort themselves out or risk expulsion from the next World Cup. 'I do not approve of the conduct of our players and officials yesterday, but they were provoked by the referee,' said Dr Mendez Bethy, President of the AFA. 'He was absolutely biased in favour of England. The referee and those who selected him were, in my view, responsible for the trouble. He was against Argentina. Argentines are not dirty players. They have never broken opponents' legs. Who was badly hurt in the England side after yesterday's match? No one!'

Hugh McIlvanney's assertion that the match had been an 'international incident' was a perceptive one. The British embassy in Buenos Aires received hundreds of abusive telephone calls and there was a small demonstration at a trade show where the British stage was invaded and vandalised, with one member of staff pinned into a corner by louts demanding to know if she had 'any referees for sale'. 'Neither the devotees of football nor the self-conscious nationalists will be inclined to forgive or forget,' reported the Buenos Aires embassy to London. 'It has left a scar on our popular image which we shall not fail to be reminded of whenever . . . in the future feelings become strained.'[12] Indeed the British ambassador, Sir Michael Cresswell, needed a special police guard in the aftermath, so badly did the Argentinians take Ramsey's statement. The inventors of 'the gentleman's agreement' and 'fair play' had perpetrated 'a double theft' wrote one Argentine journalist in an article that was typical in its level of anguish, also referring to the sovereignty of the Falklands.[13]

Amongst neutrals there was sympathy for Argentina's ire. In Italy, for example, identification with the South Americans' sense of grievance was widespread and there were protests made to the British embassy in Rome. Patrick Fairweather of the embassy staff mused that the World Cup 'has provided further proof if proof were needed, that a very good way to damage international relations is to have a really big sporting competition'.[14] The local press fuelled local outrage. 'It has already been decided the World Cup must be won by an English team,' opined Milan's *Corriere Della Sera*. 'It would have been enough to organise a ceremony at Wembley and deliver the cup to the English.' The Rome daily *Il Messaggero* described the defeat of Argentina as a 'colossal injustice' and attacked the 'incredible partisanship' of Kreitlein. 'How in a world championship, can one send off a player for protests, for insults (presumed) and thus condemn a team irremediably? How can one do it, especially when the possible insults were made in a language unknown to the object of the insults? And how can one accept a type of referee who lets Stiles play and does not even forgive a gesture of resentment from others.' The Czechoslovakia coach, Anton Malatinsky, said that if England reached the final 'football will go back a hundred years'. Even Lord Lovatt wrote from the Guards Club to *The Times*, 'any unbiased critic would agree that the Argentina XI were quite definitely the best footballers. England have got through to the last four by a lucky disqualification and the crippling of two Frenchmen in an earlier round. Is it too much to hope that when the might of England plays little Portugal tomorrow, Eusebio is not given the Pele treatment by Ramsey's defensive players who boast that they have not conceded a goal in all the matches played?'

The outrage quickly spread across South and Latin America and served to accentuate other grievances. In Mexico, where there was no indignation at the country's defeat by England (it was merely assumed that the best team had won), resentment had grown throughout the tournament at perceived British arrogance. After the Argentina match, the embassy received an anonymous threat to blow up the chancery should England win the World Cup.[15] In Uruguay, where there was already upset at the 'failure' of the British press to acknowledge its previous football achievements, the mood further soured when an English referee sent off two Uruguayan players in their quarter-final tie with West Germany, for which Kreitlein's performance was seen as 'repayment'. The British ambassador's residence, chancery and consulate were bombarded by 300 anonymous telephone calls – frequently abusive – and groups gathered outside the residence caused minor damage. The vice-president of the Uruguayan FA wrote 'this championship was prepared with great cleverness to ensure the English team the maximum number of advantages'. He wasn't alone in talking up a plot.

Perhaps most striking amidst this outrage was the view of the head of the Brazilian FA, Joao Havelange. Citing the fact that in Brazil's three matches seven of the nine officials were British and that the Brazilians had had two goals disallowed against the Hungarians, he claimed that an elaborate plot had been concocted – with the help of duplicitous refereeing – to further British political interests on the world stage by allowing England, Portugal, West Germany and the USSR a path to the semi-finals. The conspiracy went like this: Portugal would be allowed through so that the British government could regain a foothold in black Africa; the USSR to promote trade interests; and West Germany, who were the most important allies (and would therefore, presumably, be allowed through to the final), so that Britain could enter the EEC and gain a political counterweight to Charles De Gaulle's France. England's interests were, of course, paramount and their final victory would be a way of regaining national prestige after two decades of domestic and international decline. The notion that such a plan could come off was as absurd as the idea itself but Havelange, who was in search of a scapegoat to save his own position after Brazil's stunning failure, was a desperate man. Laughable though his assertions were, he held onto his job and later, in 1973, would succeed Stanley Rous as head of FIFA, a position he relentlessly clung onto for nearly three decades.

Not that Ramsey let any of this bother him or his side. If anything, the controversy knitted an already united England side even closer ahead of their semi-final with Portugal on Tuesday, 26 July – just three days after the Argentina match. Even in that short period there was room for another controversy to blow up. It had been expected that a semi-final involving England would be staged at Goodison Park. An FA booklet previewing the competition gave the impression that should England win their group they would play the quarter-final at Wembley and the semi at Goodison. It soon emerged, however, that no such decision had been made. In fact, FIFA's own rules made clear that it was up to the World Cup committee to choose the respective venues on a match-by-match basis. Stanley Rous, castigated by those parts of the European and South American media smelling a conspiracy, ironically led the discussion in favour of England playing on Merseyside. Other members of the committee argued on economic grounds that if England played at Wembley, it would be in front of a 90,000 crowd, whereas if the other semi-finalists played there, the crowd would be unlikely to be bigger than 50,000. On Merseyside, on the other hand, there would be a sell-out crowd, whoever played. Money won the day and England stayed at Wembley, but the whiff of scandal had become a stink.

With England and Portugal set to play on the Tuesday, the other semi-final between the USSR and West Germany was staged a day earlier. In a match dominated and dictated by early departures, the Germans beat the USSR 2–1 after the Soviets had lost Sabo through injury on fifteen minutes and Chislenko was sent off before half-time. It was to be a second final for West Germany after their 1954 triumph in Switzerland, and one in the eye for the bookmakers who had listed them as 20–1 pre-tournament outsiders.

If England were to meet them in the final they first had to overcome Eusebio. The reigning European Footballer of the Year and conqueror of the Brazilians had already scored seven goals in the tournament, including four against North Korea when Portugal had overcome a 0–3 deficit to win 5–3. Ramsey, however, could take comfort from the fact that when Eusebio's club side, Benfica, had come up against Manchester United in the European Cup the previous March, Nobby Stiles had completely nullified any threat from him.

England also had the historic edge. In nine previous meetings with Portugal they had lost just once, in 1955, and had also notched up their record post-war victory against them in 1947. Portuguese football had, however, come a long way. Spearheaded by Eusebio they had already scored fourteen times in the tournament, but their defence had proven suspect and was pierced three times in the opening fifteen minutes by the North Koreans. After Hurst's match-winning performance against Argentina, Alf Ramsey felt confident enough not to rush back Greaves and named an unchanged side.

When England had beaten Argentina, the match – with the exception of Hurst's moment of sublimity – had epitomised everything that was wrong about football. The semi-final, however, was its antithesis. Everything that was wrong became right. It was a perfect advert for pure, beautiful football, played in the right spirit and with the right attacking intentions, as Jack Charlton proudly remembered:

> The whole game was made up of moments that are magical in soccer. From the start both teams set out to win by enterprising, imaginative attacking football, without resorting to the rough stuff with which we had become so

disenchanted in earlier games. If, as some people had suggested, Portugal had brushed Brazil from the World Cup trail by physical endeavour, this accusation could certainly not be laid at their door in the semi final against us.[16]

Indeed it was not until the game was twenty-three minutes old that the French referee Pierre Schwinte blew for a foul, when Peters was adjudged to have obstructed Eusebio.

While England's West Ham triumvirate had claimed many of the accolades after the quarter-final battle, it was the Manchester United duo of Charlton and Stiles who took the plaudits after Portugal. Eusebio was neutralised with a triangular trap which involved one player – usually Stiles – sweeping in and closing him down, timing his effort so that Eusebio would have to commit himself. When he did, he would find two Englishmen, one on either side, backing up Stiles, ready to intercept as he attempted to break clear. Otto Gloria, the Portuguese manager would say afterwards, Eusebio 'paid the price of fame. He was closely marked all through. To do better than he did he would have to be God.' Outside the England camp, however, Stiles was merely the unsung star. For the rest of the world there was only one true hero. 'If Nelson's statue was not so firmly based on its foundation in Trafalgar Square, there would be a risk today that Bobby Charlton would be in its place,' was one assessment in the following day's newspapers. Charlton was 'in the mood where the splendours of the game approach fantasy'.[17]

England edged the first half. A handful of half chances that fell the way of Hurst came to nothing, but on the half-hour mark they took the lead. Ray Wilson, earning his fiftieth cap, sent a long ball forward which Hunt chased eagerly. Jose Pereira raced out of the Portuguese goal and blocked the ball with his knee but it only went as far as Bobby Charlton who hit it first time, low and through a gap and into the back of the net. Wembley went wild as England put one foot into the final. But the Portuguese began to battle back. Banks had to parry a Eusebio shot around the post and their giant forward Torres began to seriously test Jack Charlton. When Schwinte blew for half-time, it was to the relief of an increasingly besieged England team.

Wembley rose to applaud the two teams off at the interval for a spectacle that had been both compelling and fair. As for the side that had achieved notoriety for kicking Pele out of the tournament, they were seemingly absent. 'Portugal,' said the watching Brazilian, 'apparently irritated by the comments they had received in the press for the way Morais played against me, were on their best behaviour.'[18] In fact it would take them until the fifty-seventh minute to concede their first foul. Stiles, likewise, was a model of exemplary conduct. 'Not once did Stiles lay a boot on his opponent,' recalled Hurst. 'He relied entirely on the speed of his interceptions and the cunning positioning that lured Eusebio into positions where he could be robbed.'[19]

That isn't to say Eusebio and his team-mates didn't cause England problems. As the match moved into the second half, Portugal began to retain more and more of the possession, but seldom did they have the speed of movement and thought to turn their play into clear chances and goals. Too ponderous and too prone to over-elaboration in attack, Bobby Moore and Jack Charlton were able to stand firm at the back for England.

With twelve minutes remaining, Bobby Charlton – in the words of the watching Alfredo Di Stefano – gave a lesson on 'how to seize a game at the moment of truth'. George Cohen sent a long ball into the inside-right channel which Hurst chased. He took control of it on the by-line, beat Jose Carlos who had shadowed him, checked, and rolled the ball into the path of Bobby Charlton. Charlton connected with it perfectly and raised his arms aloft as the ball soared past Pereira into the back of the Portuguese net. It was another divine moment from the balding bomber. Even the Portuguese midfielder, José Augusto, in an incident that epitomised the spirit of the match, shook Charlton's hand as the players trooped back to the centre circle. England were edging ever closer to the final.

But two minutes later the game took another twist when Simoës swung in a cross from the right, Torres lost his marker and headed the ball past Banks, only to see it illegally palmed off the line by Jack Charlton. A penalty was awarded. Eusebio claimed the ball and placed it on the spot. As he limbered up, high behind the goal a white-coated attendant jumped and waved in an attempt to distract the taker. It made not the slightest difference and Eusebio scored. 'But what a good supporter,' thought Jack Charlton, who had noticed the distant figure.

Revitalised by the goal, Portugal tore into England. Simoës seemed certain to score from Torres's knock down until Stiles stole the ball off his toes. ('It didn't seem possible,' Alf Ramsey admitted, 'that anybody could get to him. I thought the ball was sure to finish in the back of the net. It had to. Then Nobby Stiles came from nowhere.') Torres shot wide after Jack Charlton and Wilson had collided; and Banks was unable to hold onto Eusebio's bullet-like shot, and Stiles, yet again, hacked clear. Then, in the dying seconds, Eusebio played in Coluña and his shot seemed destined for the top corner of Banks's goal – until England's number one acrobatically tipped the ball over the crossbar.

Finally, with three shrill blasts of Schwinte's whistle the match was over. England were in the World Cup final and Eusebio in tears after a contest neither side deserved to lose. As the Lisbon newspaper *A Voz* said afterwards: 'Why tears boys, unless you are out of emotion? You carried out your mission bravely and we are proud of you in this defeat, as we are proud of you in your triumphs.' The *Daily Sketch* eulogised the defeated heroes: 'These proud princes of Portugal, who have brought their intelligence to the magic of football, died like the knights of antiquity: fighting to the last breath. The final minutes of the game showed their true mettle.' The rest of the world was just as awestruck by what it had just seen. 'From the standard and correctness of the play it should have been the final rather than the semi-final,' opined the Turin daily *La Stampa*. 'This was a game based essentially on the technique of the teams and not the players' brute force, as in the semi-final between the USSR and West Germany.' It had been, noted the Soviet news agency *Tass*, 'a spring of clear water breaking through the wave of dirty football which has covered recent matches in the championship'. Even the normally inexpressive Ramsey was moved to say 'This was World Cup football as it should be played. Portugal were a great team, but one team always has to lose.'

Back in the England dressing room, Ramsey took the rare step of leading a round of applause for Stiles. Although his value to his manager had always been beyond question, he had also been redeemed in the eyes of the watching world. Yet it was his Manchester United colleague Bobby Charlton who claimed the eulogies. 'If Queen Elizabeth can knight Stanley Matthews,' wrote the Stockholm newspaper *Afton Badlet*, 'then it is her duty to give Bobby Charlton a knighthood too.' Their colleagues across the Swedish capital at *Dagens Nyheter* went one step further: 'It was England's day but above all it was Bobby Charlton's day. Thanks to his efforts he can eventually count on a knighthood. If he goes on to clinch the final against West Germany on Saturday, he may even get a seat in the House of Lords.' That same evening Eusebio was found waiting for Charlton outside the London cinema where the England squad had assembled so that he could present the victorious hero with a congratulatory bottle of wine. Two legends united by individual greatness, but otherwise separated by the spoils of victory: one magnanimous in defeat; the other humble in success.

Having faced nine-men defences, killjoy tactics, an off day against the French, cynicism, malevolence, criticism, the genius of Eusebio, foul play, sound play and the occasional onslaught on their path to the final, there was a feeling that England could take on all comers, not least West Germany, who had never beaten them and had been disposed of twice in the previous fourteen months. England were a team that had started slowly but still won games, and more crucially, were finding their best form as the finals reached their critical juncture. They were solid in defence – Eusebio's penalty being the only goal they had conceded all tournament – well organised in midfield and finally seemed to have struck the right balance in attack. They were a side at the peak of their form and almost on top of the world. What more could Alf Ramsey want? What else could be added to the mix?

There was always Jimmy Greaves. England's record goal-scorer and one of the finest strikers to ever grace the game could, at a push, have made the Portugal match. Having sat that out, he was more than ready to take on the Germans four days later. Yet he had never been comfortable with Ramsey's 4-3-3 formation, nor at his best after the bout of hepatitis that had seen him miss fifteen weeks of the league season. Later he would muse: 'That damned hepatitis attack robbed me of a vital half-yard of pace, but I still believed I was good enough and sharp enough to represent England better than any other striker around.'[20]

Jimmy Greaves's destiny became the talking point of the nation. The debate centred on whether he should come in in place of Hurst or Hunt. Neither was as gifted or prolific as Greaves, but both were in form and each had scored crucial goals in the finals, something Greaves had failed to do at all since single-handedly taking apart Norway a month earlier. The *Daily Express* asked its four chief football writers whether Ramsey should pick Greaves. They voted by three to one that he shouldn't, with the only dissenter arguing on the basis that Greaves would have something to prove while conceding that Hurst and Hunt fitted better into Ramsey's system. Others, by contrast, treated the notion that he might be left out as absurd.

Greaves himself already had a strong inkling that he would not be selected. 'At the end of the semi-final,' he wrote in his first auto-biography, 'I felt in my bones that Alf was not going to select me for the final.'[21] His conviction that Ramsey would pick an unchanged team deepened when, on the Wednesday and Thursday, Ramsey kept the semi-final team apart from the rest of the squad. By the time the squad were making the journey back from Roehampton on the Thursday Greaves knew, almost for certain, that he wasn't going to make the final eleven:

> I was sitting next to Harold Shepherdson, on the way back from training, and I said casually, 'I suppose it's going to be difficult to get back into the team' and he turned away and looked out of the window. I was close to Harold, he'd been there ever since I came into the squad. Alf had obviously confided in him, and he was too embarrassed to talk to me.[22]

But despite his inner turmoil, Greaves kept a positive outlook. When he faced reporters on the eve of the final, he said: 'It's agony waiting, I've never felt so full in all my life. I'd hate to be in Alf's shoes, but we've known the bloke long enough to realise he will only go for the team he thinks will have the best chance of winning. I am desperate to be in that side – but if I'm not, I'll understand why I've not been picked. Only the best is good enough tomorrow.'

Greaves's uncertainty was shared by Hunt and Hurst. 'For a couple of days, Alf didn't give the slightest hint,' recalled Hunt. 'Nobody knew who was in the side. Despite playing in all five games during the tournament so far, I wasn't convinced I'd be there. It kept going through my mind that Geoff had played in the last two matches and played extremely well, Jimmy was the star who could give the team an extra dimension. I could be the one to miss out, which would have been devastating after all that had happened.'[23] Hurst later likened the days leading up to the final to being given a death sentence; then on the Friday, at Roehampton, when Ramsey quietly sidled up to him and said, 'Geoff, you know you will be playing tomorrow. I thought you'd want to know . . . but please keep it to yourself. I am not telling the rest', it was akin to a last-minute reprieve.

'Knowing was almost worse than not knowing,' Hurst wrote. 'My reaction was to do three handstands, to kiss Alf firmly on the forehead and then run barefooted from Roehampton all the way back to Hendon, shouting to everyone I met on the way. Of course I did none of these things . . . simply muttered "thank you, I'll do my best" and turned casually towards the bath.'[24]

Hunt was in too. Ramsey told him that evening as the squad were getting off the coach to go to the cinema. In fact the England manager had broken precedent and told his starting line-up, one by one, that they were playing the day before the final. Everybody who was playing knew by the time they went to bed – though they had to keep silent about their inclusion – each man could relax and focus on the task in store, everybody, that is, except for Ramsey's captain, Bobby Moore. Thirty years later George Cohen would cause a stir by claiming to have overheard snatches of a conversation the day before the final, in which Ramsey was sounding out Cocker and Shepherdson as to whether he should drop Moore. Had that happened, and Moore's great rival Norman Hunter taken his place, it would have been the sensation of the tournament, easily overshadowing the controversy caused by Greaves's absence. The reality, however, was rather more mundane. Moore had come down with a bout of tonsillitis and might have missed the game were it not for the diligent attendance of the FA doctor Alan Bass. Come Saturday morning, however, the captain was deemed fit enough to play, and Ramsey told him he was in.

Greaves wasn't to find out until then either, but was magnanimous about his absence from the starting eleven. ('They'll win it for you,' he told Ramsey. 'I think so,' replied his manager.) Such generosity, according to Roger Hunt, was attributable to the team spirit of 'England United'. 'We had become a real team, in the true sense of the word, during that tournament,' he recalled, 'with the older players, like Jim Armfield and Ron Flowers, backing up the rest in everything, even though they knew that for them, there was only a little bit of glory. I sometimes think that those of us who played had the easiest job.'[25] Of course it was easy for Hunt to be so blithesome – he was in.

Bobby Moore, Greaves's closest friend in the squad, came to believe that his exclusion nearly destroyed the absent striker. 'That moment began Jimmy's disenchantment with football,' he said. 'I knew that if he'd stayed fit or got his place back the Germans would have been frightened of him. I believed Jimmy Greaves could have won us the cup. But I also knew that Alf Ramsey couldn't change the team.'[26]

As three o'clock approached England's finest killed time, steeling themselves for the task that lay ahead. A read over breakfast of that morning's papers revealed little of the grotesque nationalism that blighted later meetings between the two countries. The *Daily Express* was a rare exception and having decided that victory was a formality, concentrated on the details of the celebration. A drive of honour down The Mall and an appearance alongside the Queen on the balcony of Buckingham Palace would be the only satisfactory ritual to accompany the inevitable win. The Germans were unimpressed by this pique of nationalism. 'You would expect this from countries who have nothing else,' said Werner Schneider, the famous TV commentator, who had been a fighter pilot in the war. 'You could understand it in Ghana, or in the South American countries like the Argentine or Brazil where football is just about all they have. But in England it is strange and sad.'[27] Schneider had seen nothing yet, but the tone of the British press in 1966 was, as a whole, one of remarkable restraint.

After breakfast the players' relatives met them briefly at Hendon Hall ('the words flew in one ear and out of the other,' recalled Ball); they had a meal ('we managed to digest the food, but I doubt if any of us really tasted it'); and there was a final tactical talk by Ramsey, during which he went through the German team man by man. 'We were determined not to let HIM down,' said Ball. 'The partnership which had evolved was as close as any family relationship; the ties which bound "the boss" and his players were strong as tempered steel. Our success would be his success; his success would be ours. And failure by us would be his failure too.'[28]

The squad then went into their own routines, often dictated by a deep level of superstition. The devoutly Catholic Stiles went to mass. He also always wore a suit before the game, no matter what the occasion, and a special pair of cufflinks; he never wore his false teeth while playing – even though the thought of meeting the Queen made him consider it on this occasion. Ray Wilson and Bobby Charlton always shared a room, and before any match Charlton had to pack Wilson's boots. He would then carry their bags down to the lobby. In the dressing room George Cohen would always sprint around. Players always had to be massaged in the same order: Jack Charlton, the most superstitious member of the squad, was always last. As part of his routine he also put 'silver' (money) in his boot bag for luck, then with George Cohen always went for a pre-match walk. Finally, in the warm-up, he had to score past Banks. On the day of the final his first shot would sail over the bar. Mercifully the second went in.

Superstitions in tow, the players made their way across north London. Wembley was in a state of happy chaos. Union jacks fluttered all the way down Wembley Way; throngs of crowds, far more, seemingly, than the 100,000 the Empire Stadium could accommodate, filled every nook and precipice along it and around the concourse. As the team coach inched its way towards the twin towers chants of 'Eng-land! Eng-land!' filled the afternoon sky. All the members of Ramsey's team save for Cohen and Ball had experienced the unique atmosphere of a Wembley final before; none had seen the like. 'It was impossible,' wrote Hugh McIlvanney,

> to define the atmosphere precisely but it was palpable, and it was unique. It was like walking into an ordinary, familiar room and knowing instinctively that something vital and unbearably dramatic was happening, perhaps a matter of life and death. The people hurrying and jostling and laughing nervously inside had a flushed, supercharged look, but if they were high it was with excitement. 'It's bloody electric,' said one of the doormen. He had found the word.

If the players thought the dressing room would provide some sanctuary from this cacophony of mayhem and passion, they were mistaken. Photographers, journalists, officials, camera crews, stadium staff and assorted hangers on filled every inch of it. As late as 2.30 p.m. more than 100 people were in the room. Eventually it emptied and the players had some brief respite. Ramsey went around, shook each of the players' hands and wished them luck. One by one they stood, the signal came and they made their way out of the dressing room, studs clanking on concrete, along the tunnel and onto the pitch.

The bands of the Royal Marines marched off and the twenty-two players limbered up under the deafening din of the Wembley crowd. Then the Swiss referee, Gottfried Dienst, called Moore and the German captain Uwe Seeler over. They exchanged pennants, Moore called and won the toss and elected not to change ends. Moments later Siggy Held kicked off and the eighth World Cup final was under way.

The opening exchanges were tentative enough. Two heavy showers had fallen just prior to the start and the pitch had an awkward, greasy sheen which the players were only too aware of lest they slip. On twelve minutes Seeler took possession wide on the left in his own half and pumped a long, hopeful ball towards the far side of the England penalty area. With plenty of time and space Wilson rose to head clear, but his contact with the ball was weak and it skewed into the path of the surprised and grateful Haller. He shot – not with any great venom – Jack Charlton slid in to block, but pulled back at the last instant, thinking Banks had it covered. England's goalkeeper, sensing Charlton's imminent block, dived late and over the ball, which rolled into the back of the net. England were a goal down. 'This wasn't how we had planned it,' thought Ball. 'Indeed, Mr Ramsey had warned us of the danger of conceding an early goal.'[29]

It was a short-lived lead for the Germans. Six minutes later, Overath clattered into Moore forty yards from goal. Sensing a lapse in concentration in the German defence, Moore took the free-kick quickly, picking out the unmarked Hurst in the centre of the penalty area. He leapt, unchallenged and directed a downward header to the right of Tilkowski. Moore held one arm aloft in celebration while Hurst was showered with the congratulations of his team-mates and Wembley roared its approval.

1–1 after only eighteen minutes, but it was still a cagey affair with the two sides trying to get the measure of each other. Chances still went both ways though: Banks made a superb double-save from Overath and Emmerich while Tilkowski was forced to parry a left-footed drive from Hunt and then needed treatment after a twenty-yard shot from Charlton hit the post, bounced back and hit him flush in the face.

At half-time Ramsey told his men: 'You're doing all right . . . you're playing well . . . but you can play better than this. And if you play better, you will win.'

Yet the scores remained stuck at 1–1 with chances relatively few until thirteen minutes from the end. Ball, who had run ceaselessly all afternoon, forced a corner which he took himself. From it, the ball dropped to Hurst whose speculative shot was deflected by Höttges into the path of Martin Peters and he knocked the ball home. Wembley went wild, Banks ran the length of the pitch to congratulate the goalscorer, and the World Cup seemed to be heading for the first time to football's founding fathers.

For it to do so, however, with Peters as the scorer of the winner, would have deprived the World Cup of its most dramatic final. Indeed the rich tapestry of this match was still to fully unfold. As Jimmy Armfield was leading the reserves down to join in the imminent celebrations, a free-kick was harshly awarded against Jack Charlton. The concentration of the English defence momentarily lapsed as they hastily – too hastily – assembled the wall. Emmerich's free-kick deflected off Cohen into the path of Weber who smashed the ball past Banks for a dramatic equaliser.

As the German players celebrated their reprieve Jack Charlton held his head in his hands. 'I thought "oh God, I'm going to be the one who cost England the World Cup."'

With the referee calling an end to normal time, several of the England players looked crestfallen. Bobby Charlton admitted: 'Our spirits were sinking as we changed over.' It was a point backed up by Geoff Hurst: 'One or two of our team, especially the Charlton brothers, looked so sick you would have thought we had been beaten.'

It was the cue for some inspirational management. Purposely withholding his anger, Alf Ramsey ordered the England players to stand up to show how fit they were (the Germans by contrast were lying down being massaged) before addressing them. 'Alf was unbelievably good,' Bobby Moore recalled.

> He could have come on screaming and shouting, hollering and hooting, saying 'I thought you'd know better. I thought you'd have learned after all those years as professionals.' Instead he said, 'All right. You've won the World Cup once. Now go and win it again. Look at the Germans. They're flat out. Down on the grass. Having massages. They can't live with you. Not for another half-hour. Not through extra time.'

Stiles piped in: 'Look, they are finished, we can do this lot.'

Once play restarted the benefit of England's long training sessions began to take hold, while the huge dimensions of the Wembley pitch took their toll on the Germans. England stuck to their tight, efficient pattern of play and just before the halfway stage Stiles set Ball off on a lung-bursting charge into the German half. The Blackpool midfielder put in a cross which Hurst controlled, before spinning and smashing a shot against the underside of the German crossbar. The ball bounced down onto the line and back into play but Roger Hunt, searching for scraps, raised his arm, celebrating the most controversial goal in the history of the game. Chased by the German players, the Swiss referee Gottfried Dienst consulted with his linesman, Bakhramov, who raised his flag to indicate a goal. England were back in front.

It was, noted the following day's issue of *Bild*, 'the most discussed, most universally contested goal in the history of football'. Should it have stood? Probably not. As Bobby Moore said before his death: 'I've watched the film a million times. At normal speed it looks as if it might be a goal. In slow motion it's much more debateable. I don't know how the linesman could decide. At the time I had no doubt but on reflection I've got to say I wouldn't have liked a goal like that given against England.'[30] Indeed Bakhramov was level with the six-yard box, not the goal line. How could he have seen? Interviewed in 1989, Dienst said: 'I still don't know if the shot by Hurst in the 100th minute was in or not. I have to say I was standing in a poor position for that shot, exactly head-on instead of diagonal to goal. I wouldn't have allowed the goal if the linesman Bakhramov hadn't pointed to the middle with his flag.'

Even its closest witness, Roger Hunt, seems to have put forward a contrary account. In his 1995 autobiography he wrote:

> I was running in, sniffing for rebounds, and was about six yards out when the ball hit the ground. I saw the ball cross the line and I turned instantly to celebrate the goal. I believed at the time that it was over the line and I believe it now. If there had been the slightest shred of doubt in my mind I'd have followed it in.[31]

But he then seemed to contradict himself on the following page: 'I have seen so much film since and none of it is conclusive, but I am convinced I was right at the time. I sympathise with the officials though. It was an incredibly difficult decision, which had to be given instantly with the eyes of the world watching them.'[32] Eight years later he all but told Ken Jones that it hadn't been a goal and he wouldn't have scored the rebound anyway. 'I wouldn't have beaten Weber to the rebound, but show me a footballer who wouldn't claim a goal in those circumstances? It could have gone either way. The decision went for us, as it went against England twenty years later when Maradona punched the ball past Peter Shilton.'[33]

Either way, the controversy's protagonist – Geoff Hurst – was to make any debate spurious. With a minute to go Moore and Ball exchanged passes on the edge of the England penalty area.

'Kick the fucking thing out of the ground!' yelled Jack Charlton. Ignoring his colleague Moore took his time, dribbled into space, looked up, and played a perfect forty-yard pass to Hurst who lay in wait just inside Germany's half. Ball was on Hurst's heels, chasing hard to support him. 'Some people are on the pitch,' screamed the BBC commentator Kenneth Wolstenholme, 'they think it's all over.'

Hurst was exhausted and decided to hit the ball from thirty yards with his last ounce of strength. As he shaped to shoot, the ball hit a divot and bounced up a fraction higher than he anticipated so that he caught the ball hard on his instep. 'I knew I would never hit a better shot so long as I lived. The feel, the sound of leather on leather were exactly right. Over the tip of my left boot, raised chest high on the follow through I could see the ball speeding for the top corner. Tilkowski had no chance.'[34] Indeed he didn't.

'It is now!' hollered Wolstenholme as the ball hit the back of the net, almost bursting its strings.

4–2. The World Cup was England's. Moments later Dienst's whistle confirmed their victory. Jack Charlton knelt holding his head, and Ray Wilson slapped his hands on the floor of the pitch. Stiles and Cohen collapsed in an embrace and Alan Ball turned cartwheels, while the crowd chanted Ramsey's name. Bobby Charlton went over to his brother and tearfully embraced him.

'What else is there to win now?' asked Bobby.

'We shall have to win it again,' laughed his older brother.

Ramsey's success, was, according to David Miller in the *Sunday Telegraph*, 'the final rewarding vindication for one who has unwaveringly pursued his own, often lonely convictions'. Yet he didn't join in the celebrations, watching his players from the touchline, never wanting to steal their glory, even vigorously resisting their attempts to chair him off. 'It is not intentional,' he said of appearing so unemotional. 'But it was important that someone remained "sane" within the England party. That was me.'[35] Four years earlier it had been the same story after he had masterminded Ipswich's championship win. Then, Ramsey had gone to watch one of Ipswich's junior sides rather than join in the celebrations. Later, his chairman, the brewer John Cobbold, had found him late at night, sitting in the Portman Road stands. Ramsey handed Cobbold his jacket, climbed over the wall and started to run a lap of honour, with Cobbold his only spectator.*

One man's happiness, however, was tinged with sadness. 'I danced around the pitch with everybody else,' recalled Jimmy Greaves, 'But even in this great moment of triumph I felt a sickness in my stomach that I had not taken part in the match of a lifetime. It was my saddest day in football.'[36] Later he told Kenneth Wolstenholme: 'To play for your country in the final of the World Cup is the pinnacle of anyone's career, and I missed it. But only eleven Englishmen could make it on the day, and if you want to know whether they did a good job or not, look in the record books.'[37] As the celebrations got under way, Greaves quietly slipped away to Hendon Hall, collected his bags and went home. Late that night he went off on a family holiday. At the celebratory banquet Ramsey was puzzled about Greaves's absence. 'He's not bitter about it,' Moore explained. 'He just doesn't want to be here. He'd rather be away from it all.'

Then came the moment England were awarded the Jules Rimet trophy. Bobby Moore led his triumphant colleagues up the well-trodden steps to the royal box – in the space of two years, Moore had already walked them to collect the FA Cup and European Cup Winners' Cup – famously wiped his hands ('it had been a wet afternoon and when I got about two yards from the Queen I saw her lilywhite gloves. I thought: "My God, my hands are filthy"'), took it from Her Majesty, then held aloft the World Cup.

Back in the dressing room, Nobby Stiles sat on a bench repeating 'Bloody great! Bloody great!' Jack Charlton, meanwhile, had to give a

---

*Cobbold was the man who on Ramsey's first day at Ipswich in 1955 offered him a drink in the boardroom. 'This is the first and last time you will be offered a drink in the boardroom,' Cobbold told him and threw Ramsey two keys. 'From now on you are to come in and help yourself.' It was an unlikely but highly successful partnership.

urine sample for the fourth time out of England's six games.[38] His brother, amazingly given the circumstances, was criticised by Ramsey for not retaining possession while the game was still in ordinary time. 'What the bloody hell do you think you were doing out there,' he snapped. 'Shooting when you should have been looking around for other people. We should have had it sewn up.'[39]

England's win brought traffic in the West End to a standstill. Thousands of pedestrians crammed into Leicester, Trafalgar and Parliament Squares. Teenagers splashed in the fountains under Nelson's Column singing 'we gave them a bloody good hiding – and so say all of us'. A giant conga formed, led by a youth with a replica World Cup, singing 'we've got the whole world in our hands'. Cars were draped with flags, both those of St George and the union jack. In the East End of London West Ham supporters claimed that the score should have read West Germany 2 West Ham United 4. In Walton, fifteen-year-old Sandra Watt was crowned the World Cup queen following a World Cup carnival where the centrepiece was a 40lb cake featuring World Cup Willie. Muhammad Ali was at the final, ahead of his heavyweight title fight with Brian London a week later. He'd never seen a 'soccer match live' before but he'd 'enjoyed it'. In Johannesburg a man sporting a union jack in his buttonhole and shouting 'up the English' was thrown out of a bar and treated in hospital for a cut to his head. Banks was to be greeted by a civic reception in Leicester and, a day later, Roger Hunt was met by 600 people at his home in Culceth, near Warrington. Trees had been festooned with flags and decorations and much of his front garden had to be replanted after it was trampled by over eager well-wishers.

Harold Wilson had flown in from Washington at lunchtime to see the match. 'It was a marvellous game. I was a bit shattered when it went to extra time. I said before the game that it would be 2–1 and I was only a minute out!' Sterling was still under threat and Wilson had travelled to the US to enlist Lyndon Johnson's help in propping it up. His cabinet colleague Richard Crossman recorded in his diary:

> I must record a big change in Harold's position . . . tremendous help that we
> won the WC on Saturday . . . when I told [my wife] over lunch today that the
> World Cup could be a decisive factor in strengthening sterling she couldn't
> believe it. But I am sure it is. It was a tremendous gallant fight that England

> won. Our men showed real guts and the bankers, I suspect, will be influenced
> by this, and the position of the government correspondingly strengthened.

In the event Crossman was wrong. The Americans didn't bail Britain out, but Wilson survived despite being forced to devalue the pound a year later. Had England's World Cup victory saved him? Certainly it created a sense of optimism in the English part of the union and later he would boast: 'Have you noticed how we only win the World Cup under a Labour government?' Subsequent events were to show just how closely his political fortunes rose and fell with those of the England team.

Eventually the players made it aboard a coach and journeyed through the crowd-lined streets to Hendon Hall. When they drove past Hendon fire station, three fire engines were lined up on the forecourt flashing their lights and sounding their sirens in a guard of honour. The squad journeyed onto the Royal Garden Hotel on Kensington High Street, which was closed to traffic but packed with some 6000 well-wishers. The players tossed their red carnation buttonholes to the crowd and their supporters responded with choruses of 'ee eye addio England's won the Cup' and 'God save our gracious team'. There, the official banquet took place and the England squad were joined by the three other semi-finalists – the USSR, Portugal and West Germany – the Prime Minister, various other cabinet members and all manner of high, low and middle-ranking FA officials. Of course, none of the players' wives and girlfriends were invited to the official festivities and were shipped off to an ante-room before rejoining their menfolk much later.

Between courses the players made their way onto the balcony to greet the crowds assembled outside. Pickles the dog was held aloft on the balcony by Bobby Charlton and Bobby Moore to huge applause, but the biggest cheer of the night was reserved for England's reluctant hero, Alf Ramsey, when he was led out by Harold Wilson. Ramsey had not wanted to go out, but the Prime Minister insisted: 'It's only once in a lifetime you know.' The crowd chanted Ramsey's name, England's manager smiled, waved and modestly returned to the banqueting hall.

As events wound down in Kensington, the players hit the town. Hurst, Ball, Stiles and John Connelly went to Danny La Rue's club in Hanover Square where they sang 'When the Saints go marching in' and presented the players with a cake. 'Even at this point with the other revellers applauding this little knot of World Cup heroes,' Hurst recorded, 'it didn't strike me that we'd done anything special. It was all a bit unreal. We were back in the hotel by three.'[40] Most of them were anyway.

Jack Charlton, who had gone out with a card bearing the legend 'This body is to be returned to room 508, Royal Garden Hotel' in his top pocket, woke up on a random sofa in Leytonstone, east London. As he was having breakfast in the garden the next morning a woman put her head over the wall, to see what he was doing – it was one of his mother's neighbours from Ashington, staying with relatives!

Back in Kensington the players were reading accounts of the match in the Sunday papers. 'Pace, technical skill and whole-hearted determination gave this match its excitement and colour,' wrote Tony Pawson in the *Observer*. 'The goals gave it unbearable tension.'[41] 'In effect, England won the final twice,' said Brian Glanville in the *Sunday Times*. 'Won it, quite on their merits, in ordinary time, won it again in extra time, after a flagrantly illegal German goal had been allowed, inexplicably, in the last minute.' Across the world the press praised England's heroes. 'England were worthy winners, gaining their victory both convincingly and attractively,' said *Soviet Sports*. For *L'Humanite Dimanche* of Paris: 'It was a triumph of strength and determination.' 'The English not only built up a superior volume of play,' said *La Suisse,* 'but showed greater staying power.' *El Pais* of Montevideo was generous too: 'England's most glorious day – champions of football for the first time. The masters of football are now undisputed.' Others were less fulsome in their praise, focusing either on the disputed goal or simply their hatred of the English. Argentinian newspapers, for instance, spoke of the final as 'a farce' and one paper headlined its report 'Lucky Pirates'. In West Germany there was understandably some consternation about Hurst's second goal. 'Prevailing opinion of all eye witnesses: no goal,' said *Bild*; 'Linesman decides world championship,' wrote *Die Welt*.

By the following day though, much of the hype had died. There was some, but hardly saturation coverage in Monday's newspapers where the main news was the birth of Princess Alexandra's daughter – seventeenth in line to the throne, no less. By the Tuesday it might as well have been forgotten in the eyes of the media.

At lunchtime on the Sunday the squad went to a lunch at the ATV studios in Borehamwood, hosted by Eamonn Andrews. Ramsey took them aside, gave a short speech ('his words touched a chord of response in every one of the players,' recalled Ball. 'I know I had a lump in my throat as he spoke for there was no doubting his sincerity and it was a touching tribute he paid us all'[42]) and told them their bonus arrangements. And that was it.

'Apart from the odd weekend at home we'd been together for the best part of eight weeks. The spirit had been fantastic, I can't remember one moment of bad feeling,' reflected Bobby Moore. 'We'd all become part of each other. It was a funny, empty feeling.'[43]

It had been a tournament famous for the dashing talent of the once mighty Magyars; the astonishing prowess of Eusebio; the sad, injured figure of Pele; the giant argumentative presence of Rattin; the startling performance of the North Korean minnows; the Soviet linesman's flag; and ultimately made great by three men: Bobby Charlton, Geoff Hurst and Alf Ramsey.

Charlton brought illumination to the England side, even when his colleagues were at their most mundane. He did the easy things well and made the impossible look easy. His presence elevated others, provided a constant menace to his opponents and served as the fulcrum of England's play. At the critical juncture of the competition, though, his contribution had been overshadowed by Geoff Hurst's. He could – in common with most English players of the past fifty years – only dream of possessing Charlton's unique abilities, but his own qualities were beyond question and he added skill, endeavour and cutting edge to England's forward line when they needed it most. To score three goals in any football match is an achievement: to do so in the final of the World Cup is an awe-inspiring, incredible feat, and one that remains unparalleled. Rightly it has made Hurst a legend.

And then there was Alf Ramsey. The prickly, enigmatic mastermind of England's triumph had often flown in the face of purportedly wise opinion in his single-minded, sometimes stubborn and often lonely pursuit of football's greatest prize. To win a trophy that some still expected to be England's on account of birthright alone, he had brought tactical nous, strategy and discipline to the national team setup when there had previously been little or none. He spotted good players and made them great; and great players like Moore and Charlton he made immortal. Modestly, he played down his own part in England's triumph but it is unlikely that without him his country could have succeeded. Would success change him? Not a bit, he'd still be the same old Alf: cantankerous, stubborn, single-minded, a confirmed football genius, but, above all else, a winner.

9

THE BEST TEAM IN THE WORLD

IT WAS THE best of times; it was the worst of times. It was an age of war; it was an age of flower power. It was the epoch of ideologies; it was the epoch of indifference. It was a time of hippies, free love, combi vans; of Beatles, Monkees and Rolling Stones; when 400 million people in twenty-six countries were linked by satellite to witness John Lennon and friends perform 'All You Need Is Love'. It was an age of red-book-waving cultural revolution in China, of conflagration in Vietnam and Cambodia, and six-day war in the Middle East. It was the era of Mick Jagger and Marianne Faithfull, of John and Yoko, and Elvis and Priscilla.

In football, 1967 was the season of light and season of darkness: incomparable mavericks like George Best, Denis Law, Bobby Charlton, Alex Young and Jim Baxter bestrode the Football League; and others, such as Norman Hunter, Nobby Stiles, Tommy Smith and Ron Harris were increasingly blatant in their efforts to stop them. Manchester United were on their way to the League Championship, Spurs the FA Cup and Celtic were about to become the first British club to win the European Cup. Alf Ramsey had become soccer's second knight, when he was honoured in the 1967 New Year list ('I'm still Alf aren't I?') and though Bobby Charlton hadn't been given a place in the House of Lords, he was – officially – the best player in the world, winning both the English and European Footballer of the Year awards, and an OBE to boot. England, of course, ruled football. But on 15 April 1967, its capital was invaded by Scots.

Fuelled by Scottish nationalism and Scotch they came from Glasgow, Edinburgh and Aberdeen, from Montrose and Motherwell, Saltcoats and Stirling, Livingston and Lairg. They journeyed from the lowlands, descended from the Highlands, some even sailed from the islands. The dull, wan faces that disembarked from the overnight trains and coaches at Kings Cross and Victoria were soon re-energised by the intoxication of being on enemy territory. Chests swollen with pride, they swarmed down Piccadilly and Haymarket, taking over Soho's pubs with their singing and sheer weight of numbers. They spilled out into Oxford Street and its environs before heading north, to Wembley.

Interest in the Scotland–England match was far greater than it had been south of the border, with previews appearing in newspapers up to ten days beforehand. Perhaps it was attributable to the confidence generated by Celtic's inexorable march in the European Cup, but more likely it was the sense of expectation that came with the chance of knocking the world champions off their perch. 'The confrontation between England and Scotland has taken a strange twist,' one Scot wrote. 'It is regarded in Scotland not so much as a football match but more as a means of retribution. A new quality has been added to the rivalry, which has something to do with England winning the World Cup.'[1] The *Scotsman* added: 'They have an expectation that England's title of World Cup winners is a false one and that on Wembley's turf Scotland will demonstrate this to the world.'[2] Scotland, of course, had not lost at Wembley since 1961, although you could get odds of 4–1 against them winning, while England were 7–4 on. Desmond Hackett of the *Daily Express* pronounced it would be the day that England would 'firmly relegate Scotland to their minor role in international football'; and another critic confidently stated that even the 9–3 drubbing could not be repeated – on account of Scotland being incapable of scoring three times.

'Playing the Scots was a thing apart,' recalled Bobby Moore.

> For so long their football was retarded by the belief that beating England was all that mattered. They used to drop numerous daft results against foreign teams because they never charged themselves to play with the same heart as they did against England. In a way it was tremendous. The atmosphere was unique. It built up a magnificent tension and it took a while to come to terms with the experience.[3]

Sir Alf, of course, hated the Scots. As an Englishman, and an absurdly proud one at that, he abhorred the gloating, the half-baked historical analogies, and the ludicrous importance that was placed on the annual fixture. His team talks before Scotland matches would always be laced with a little extra emotion: 'You know I hate them. If

you don't want to beat them for yourselves, go out and beat them –
for me.' Maybe now it is easy to portray Ramsey as a 'little Englander',
but each year he had to face a team that had missed out on qualification to the latter stages of each European Nations' tournament
and every World Cup finals during his managership, but would
happily lay claim to every one of his achievements on the back of a
win over England. Little wonder he bore them such antipathy. 'Alf,
God bless him, was a real Englishman. I'm not saying he didn't like
foreigners, but,' said Brian Labone, 'he used to say, "I don't mind the
Irish, I don't mind the Welsh, but I hate the effin' Scots."[4]

In the three matches since winning the World Cup, Ramsey had
stayed faithful to the eleven men who had brought English football its
finest hour, but for the meeting with Scotland, he restored the inform Greaves in Hunt's place. 99,063 people – 2000 more than had
witnessed the World Cup final itself – crammed into Wembley, filling
the north London sky with a cacophony of shouting and singing. A
chorus of 'Eng-land! Eng-land!' did battle with the voices of 30,000
Scots high on national pride, excitement and drink singing 'Scotland!
Dear old Scotland! For-ever!' The air quietened to the hush of 'Abide
with Me', a roar then greeted the arrival of the two teams, followed by
another brief silence for the playing of the national anthem. With its
last note another great thunder emanated from the crowd. Then they
were under way.

After all the hope and hype, what followed was almost anti-
climactic. Scotland started at a frenetic pace, but seemed so wound up
and utterly set on winning at any cost that their glut of early chances
were taken too rashly. England's cause was not helped on fifteen
minutes when Jack Charlton's toe was broken – he said deliberately –
following a challenge by Bobby Lennox. Still without the luxury of
substitutes in competitive internationals, he was forced to hobble
painfully on, first on the right wing, then up front. Yet in an all-round
England performance notable only for its lack of lustre, Charlton
'played with a determination and a menace', wrote Brian Glanville in
the following day's *Sunday Times*, 'which put the two accepted
English strikers thoroughly to shame'. England's hopes were further
hamstrung when Ray Wilson picked up a knock, reducing him to half
pace, and Greaves too picked up an injury to his ankle.

Scotland took the lead on twenty-eight minutes. Wallace's shot was
saved by Banks but only parried into the path of Law – always deadly

from such close quarters – who fired in the rebound. The visitors continued in the vein they had started – 'spirit without subtlety', wrote Glanville, 'heat without light' – while England struggled to match the intensity of their passion, and could not overcome the injuries to key men. The score remained the same until twelve minutes from the end when Nobby Stiles missed a lob forward from Gemmell and Lennox was on hand to put Scotland 2–0 ahead.

With the match seemingly dead and buried, England mustered a thrilling finale. Jack Charlton poked home Ball's pass to reduce the arrears but almost immediately Jim McCalliog restored the two-goal margin. At the very death, Geoff Hurst headed in Bobby Charlton's cross to make it 2–3 but the referee's watch decreed a comeback was beyond the world champions. It was England's first defeat in twenty matches, a run stretching back to October 1965. It also meant that Scotland secured the Home International Championship and went into the lead for qualification to the European Nations' Cup finals.

For the Scottish players and supporters, though, victory meant much much more. 'They went absolutely mad over it,' recalled Moore. 'The eyes of some of the players were wild. Their supporters came pouring off the terraces to cut up the pitch, waving lumps of earth at us and saying this was the turf on which they destroyed the world champions. Some of them were seriously suggesting we ought to hand over the World Cup.'[5] Joyously they danced down Wembley Way and headed back into central London. Like the victorious England supporters after West Germany nine months earlier, they splashed in the fountains of Trafalgar Square, and marched around the capital demanding: 'Who won eh?' 'Whaur's yer World Cup noo?' 'Lacking a ready vocabulary of victory we continued to behave very badly very well,' wrote one fan, Samuel Hunter. When some Scottish supporters tried to climb Sir Alfred Gilbert's Eros statue in Piccadilly Circus, the police took umbrage, and circled the monument. 'They have a siege mentality about it,' added Hunter. 'Once it may have been like this in ancient Rome when word got around that Alaric was on the way with his Goths.'[6]

The Scottish press were just as vitriolic in their jubilation. The following day's headlines basked in their nation's glory: 'Just another Bannockburn', 'The great invasion' and 'England subdued, tormented and outclassed'.

'The score line,' reported the Glasgow *Sunday Mail*, 'is a laugh, a joke, a thing to ridicule in years to come. England didn't lose this incredible international by a goal – they lost it by the length of Wembley Way, Oxford Street and Sauciehall Street stretched from one end to the other.'[7] 'Now we know how Sir William Wallace felt after his success at Stirling,' added the *Scotsman*.[8] South of the border the *Daily Mail* put their own spin on things: 'Scotland have beaten England who are world champions, but the win does not give them the crown. The truth is this: in two years Scottish footballers have learned how to beat eight fit men, for in 1965 they could only draw against nine.'

Ramsey was magnanimous enough in defeat: 'It had to be a great team to beat us and Scotland were just that. But I still think that we are a great side ourselves.' And, pointing to the limited involvement of Jack Charlton, Wilson and Greaves, 'even with passengers'.

Managing the best team in the world was no easy task, and being world champions inexorably upped every Englishman's sense of expectation. Victory was a prerequisite; defeat a disaster. England were the team to beat and teams overachieved in trying to do so. Wholesale changes could not be brought about: who, even Sir Alf, could justify or get away with breaking up a team of world champions? But any new player introduced to the set-up had to live up to a predecessor bathed in the immortality of English football's greatest day. Sometimes victory wasn't enough: when England defeated Sweden 3–1 at Wembley in May 1968, England's dour but efficient and ultimately successful performance was roundly booed at the end.

Scotland didn't provide a wake-up call, despite repeated assertions that it should, or perhaps would. 'Now Sir Alf Ramsey must think deeply about some new blood in each department of his team,' Geoffrey Green had written in the following Monday's *Times*.[9] While several understudies – Peter Bonetti, Brian Labone, Keith Newton, Alan Mullery and Norman Hunter – were each given chances in friendlies with Spain and Austria at the end of the following month, Ramsey awarded only one debut cap, to Chelsea's John Hollins who never again played for his country. The situation was ripe for cribbing by fans of several clubs. Chelsea supporters bemoaned the absence of Peter Osgood; Manchester City fans the fact that Ramsey was so reluctant to make its two greatest-ever players – Francis Lee and Colin Bell – England regulars; while Evertonians could not believe that Colin Harvey and Howard Kendall, who, along with Goodison new boy Alan Ball, formed the finest midfield in the league – Goodison's 'Holy Trinity' – were never allowed to replicate their partnership in the white of England.

Ramsey, however, was not wholly resistant to change. Over the course of the 1967–68 season, injuries, creeping years, declining form and a piqued star saw several changes to the England line-up. First, when England beat Northern Ireland 2–0 on 22 November it marked the thirty-seventh and final cap of George Cohen's England career. A serious knee injury called time on not only his England days but his playing career at the age of just twenty-nine. Four decades later, his nephew, Ben Cohen, would – extraordinarily – follow in his uncle's footsteps, lifting the Rugby Union World Cup for England. Seven months later Ray Wilson also played his last international, against the Soviet Union. During pre-season training with Everton he would seriously injure his knee, limiting him to just a handful more games and precipitating the retirement of England's finest-ever full-back. By then Jimmy Greaves had also played his last game for his country. Fed up at being called up but left out of the starting XI, he told Ramsey that unless he was guaranteed a place in the side he should leave him out. Ramsey never selected him again, bringing an end to an international career of fifty-seven caps and forty-four goals, but one invariably tinged with the deep disappointment of missing out on the World Cup final.

The places of Jack Charlton and Nobby Stiles were no longer guaranteed either. For much of 1967 and 1968 Ramsey preferred Everton's Brian Labone or Manchester United's David Sadler to partner Bobby Moore in the centre of defence. Dubbed by his club manager 'the last of the great Corinthians', Labone had been an England cap, though never a regular, since the days of Winterbottom. An impeccable defender and one of the game's gentlemen, like Charlton he was an inspirational leader with the quiet authority of Moore. Sadler, likewise, was a model of composure with a bite in every tackle and extended Ramsey's defensive options. Alan Mullery matched the battling qualities Stiles brought to the team with an additional measure of finesse, and would come to take the Manchester United player's place on a regular basis. Blackburn

Football, by the early nineteenth century, 'was rough, tough, unruly and frequently disreputable. It was the sport of the mob, and in a growingly civilised society, was seemingly dying.'

Getty Images

Football may have been an English export, but in the game's early days it was the Scots who stumbled upon the game's secret success that was to remain elusive to their English counterparts for some years – teamwork.

Getty Images

SKETCHES AT THE INTERNATIONAL FOOTBALL MATCH, GLASGOW.

Football's founding fathers

Long-term FA Secretary
Charles Alcock

William McGregor, founder of the
Football League

Derby County's
Steve Bloomer,
soccer's first
superstar

Vivian Woodward, who held the
England scoring record until the days
of Lofthouse and Finney

Lord Kinnaird,
founder of the FA
Cup and one of the
leading figures
behind international
football

England pose ahead of their 3–1 win over
Wales in March 1905

G.O. Smith, a gentleman in name
and character

The dashing John Goodall

William Ralph 'Dixie' Dean (pictured with Spain goalkeeper Ricardo Zamora) was the dominant figure in English football at club and international level in the late 1920s and early 1930s, his goalscoring feats becoming part of football folklore.
Popperfoto

No one incident in the history of British sport has caused such consternation and controversy than the moment England's footballers gave the 'Heil Hitler' salute one May afternoon in 1938.
Empics

Without the pressure that came with being paid professionals, a more attacking, entertaining brand of football developed during the Second World War. Stanley Matthews, whose England career stretched for a record-breaking twenty-three years, was just one of the era's many stars.

Getty Images

England's first golden generation line up behind goalkeeper Frank Swift in 1946.

Getty Images

Billy Wright leads England out in Hungary in May 1954. Within an hour Hungary were 6–0 in front. 'I frankly wondered just how gigantic the catastrophe enveloping us would be,' pondered goalkeeper Gil Merrick. England lost 7–1.
Getty Images

Billy Wright (pictured with Tom Finney, Maurice Setters and Bobby Charlton) was an early, and reluctant, forerunner of David Beckham, catapulted to stardom through his football and marriage to singer Joy Beverley.
Getty Images

Walter Winterbottom, England manager from 1946 to 1962, was, according to one player, 'a distinguished, quietly spoken man who talked as if he had swallowed a dictionary and often sounded more like a university lecturer than a football coach'.

Empics

With their footballing uncles the Milburns, Jack and Bobby Charlton formed part of English football's greatest dynasty.

Empics

'There is no dignity,' said Alf Ramsey, 'in bare-chested footballers parading on the pitch.' England's manager gets to grips with Argentina's Alberto Gonzalez and George Cohen after the 1966 World Cup final.

Popperfoto

The ball bounced down onto the line and back into play, but Roger Hunt, searching for scraps, raised his arm, celebrating the most controversial goal in the history of the game. England go 3–2 up in the 1966 World Cup Final.

Getty Images

'It is not intentional,' Alf Ramsey said of appearing so unemotional at the final whistle. 'But it was important that someone remained "sane" within the England party. That was me.'

Getty Images

Hoisted by Geoff Hurst and Ray Wilson, Bobby Moore brandishes football's holy grail to an exultant Wembley Stadium.

Getty Images

After England lost 1–0 to Brazil in the 1970 World Cup group stage, Pele ran up to Moore – the victor and the vanquished – and embraced him. The two men changed shirts, and Pele, in his still rudimentary English, said: 'You no thief Bobby.'

Colorsport

'Leave me alone. I have had a very long journey and I'm tired. No autopsies.' Alf Ramsey turns on the charm after returning home from the 1970 World Cup finals in Mexico.

Popperfoto

Margaret Thatcher inherently misunderstood football. Her ill-judged war on the game almost brought the game to its knees in its birthplace.

'I have no hesitation in describing Bryan Robson as a "great player",' Bobby Robson would say. 'A fighter with a desire to be perfect and to do things the right way on the football pitch.' Captain Marvel puts England in front in Bobby Robson's first match as England manager, against Denmark in September 1982.

The onslaught of vitriolic criticism suffered by Bobby Robson during his managership from 1982–1990 was virtually unparalleled in the undistinguished history of the British tabloid press. But his critics were ultimately proved stupid, mean and wrong.

Wrist clad in plaster after sustaining a pre-tournament fracture, Gary Lineker, the newly crowned European Golden Boot winner and pictured here scoring in the second round tie against Paraguay, set the 1986 Mexico World Cup alight.

Terry Butcher after a 0–0 World Cup qualifying draw against Sweden in September 1989. 'This was the Dunkirk spirit in action, the sort of gutsiness adored by the English support.'

Colorsport

'I put my own arm around him trying to keep away my own tears,' Bobby Robson recalled of Gazza's tears in Turin after his second yellow card in Italia '90. 'I felt so sorry for him . . . my own eyes were filling up.'

Getty Images

An inherently decent individual and capable club manager, Graham Taylor, England manager 1990–3, always seemed to be a man wading out of his depth in the ocean of English fans' expectations.

After scoring one of Wembley's finest goals, against Scotland at the 1996 European Championships, Paul Gascoigne celebrates in typically exuberant fashion.

September 2001. 5–1 winners against Germany... in Germany. As one newspaper asked, was it all just a 'magnificent, ridiculous dream'?

Colorsport

David Beckham's sending off against Argentina at the 1998 World Cup finals saw him transformed into a pariah by the English press and public. But within a year he would fashion an astonishing reversal of fortune.

Getty Images

Sven-Göran Eriksson, England's first foreign manager in 2001–6, suffered from astonishingly xenophobic attacks in the press but over time, particularly in his private life, the nature of his defects became apparent.

Colorsport

Three of England's latest golden generation, Michael Owen, Wayne Rooney and David Beckham, celebrate Owen's late winner in a friendly against Argentina in Switzerland in November 2005.

Getty Images

Rovers' full-back, Keith Newton, came in on the right, then left of defence and he was eventually joined in the side by Bob McNab of Arsenal, Terry Cooper of Leeds and Everton's Tommy Wright as Ramsey sought replacements for Cohen and Wilson.

The 2–3 defeat by Scotland in April 1967 was not as devastating as fans of England's Auld Enemy may have hoped. The Scottish propensity to shoot themselves in the foot struck again on 21 October when they lost 0–1 to Northern Ireland in Belfast. The same day England beat Wales 3–0 in Cardiff, putting them a point ahead in the race for a European Nations' Cup quarter-final place, which was secured with a 1–1 draw in Glasgow the following February.

The format of the European Nations' Cup meant that England next had to face Spain in a two-legged quarter-final in April and May 1968 with the winners progressing to the semi-finals – then final or third-place play-off – in Italy that summer. The first leg was played at Wembley on 3 April, where England had the historical edge. Spain had never escaped defeat on English shores despite being the first continentals ever to beat them, in Madrid in 1929. A full house greeted the two teams, but England lacked panache and ideas in attack and struggled to break down the Spanish defence. With Hurst injured, Greaves an outcast, Bobby Charlton looking jaded, and Manchester City's Mike Summerbee the latest unlucky winger to have to invent a wide role for himself in Ramsey's wingless wonders, it was difficult to see where England's attacking inspiration was going to come from. Almost inevitably Bobby Charlton came to the rescue. In the eighty-fifth minute a foul was given against Zoco for an infringement on Jack Charlton thirty-five yards from goal. From the resultant free-kick, Moore tapped the ball to Charlton junior and he glided past one defender and veered a cross-shot past Sadurni and into the corner of the net for the tie's only goal.

A month later England journeyed to Madrid for the second leg. Hours before the game England's chances took a blow when Hurst pulled out with an injury and Hunter took his place. In the face of such adversity and 120,000 passionate Spanish supporters, England provided one of their best performances since the World Cup finals. After surviving some early defensive scares, Moore took steely command of England's rearguard and the teams went in goalless at half-time – a scoreline, which, if it stayed the same, would see England through to Italy.

Three minutes into the second half, however, Spain took the lead. Hunter's crossfield pass was intercepted by Gento who took the ball forward, beat Newton and squared it to Amancio to fire a shot past Bonetti. England, nevertheless, held their nerve, and Spanish elation was soon replaced by silence. Six minutes later, Hunt's shot was parried away for a corner, and from it Peters stole in unmarked to head home England's equaliser. Eight minutes from the end the visitors secured their path to Italy: Mullery's long throw sent Hunt chasing down the right; he pulled the ball back diagonally and, although it evaded Bobby Charlton, Hunter was on hand to send a shot wide of Sadurni and into the net. 'I was very pleased with the team and the result,' said Ramsey after the final whistle. 'We did very well, although it wasn't an easy game.'

Four days later, on 5 June, England were in Florence playing Yugoslavia. In a rough and tumble contest that would see forty-nine free-kicks, England had the edge in possession, packing the midfield and using Hunt as a solitary striker. Chances were few though, and Bobby Charlton went closest with two spectacular second-half efforts that both just went wide of the post. Then, in the eighty-sixth minute, disaster struck. Trivic and Holcer combined on the wing and, when the cross came in, Džajić beat Moore to the ball, crashing a shot past Banks to give Yugoslavia a 1–0 lead.

England had no time to get back into the game, and thereafter tempers boiled over. Not for the first time Trivic hacked Mullery, the Tottenham man retaliated, and the Spanish referee, Mendibil, made him the first England player to be sent off in an international. 'I don't think anybody, if they were any sort of man, could have stood for much more of what you had to put up with,' Ramsey told him later. 'If you hadn't done it, I would have.'

Afterwards, Italian journalists blamed Ramsey for setting the hard tone of the game, but the England manager laughed them off. When they asked him about a brutal fifth-minute challenge by Hunter on Osim, which had effectively handicapped the Yugoslav playmaker, Ramsey referred – with typical diplomacy – back to a challenge by Trivic on Ball two minutes before that: 'I am sure that Alan Ball was at least as badly hurt as Osim. The difference is that Alan Ball has more courage.' He added that having seen other teams in action, 'when it comes to rough play we have a great deal to learn. But I don't think we wish to play that way.' 'They say we're hard and we are at times,' added Moore. 'But at least it's a fairly open kind of hardness, man to man.'[10]

England won the third-place play-off 2–0 against the USSR (who had lost their semi-final to Italy only by the flip of a coin) with Bobby Charlton and Geoff Hurst scoring the goals in a performance described by one Italian newspaper as 'Senso Unico' (one-way street). 'England are still world champions and worthy of a higher place in Europe,' said Ramsey afterwards. Others, however, were less convinced. After Yugoslavia, Hugh McIlvanney had written that England would have to attempt an 'almost miraculous feat of retaining the World Cup',[11] and his conviction would have deepened over the autumn of 1968 after three unimpressive displays against Romania (in Bucharest, then Wembley) and Bulgaria, which ended 0–0, 1–1 and 1–1 respectively.

Still, in mitigation, it was a time of transition for England. As well as experimenting with new full-backs Ramsey gave debuts to Gordon West, Francis Lee, Paul Reaney and John Radford. The second tie with Romania also marked the end of Roger Hunt's thirty-four-game England career. Having scored fifteen goals in his first sixteen internationals, he had managed just three in his last eighteen – a pointer to the evolving nature of the game rather than any dramatic collapse in his own standards. Since 1962, when Hunt had made his debut, defences had become meaner, attacks leaner; less goals were conceded and fewer scored. It was a truism for the whole of football, not just on the international stage.

When England met France at Wembley on 12 March 1969, however, Ramsey's men answered those who accused them of a defensive mindset in resounding fashion. Having scored just four goals in their previous six matches, and deprived of players from Everton, Manchester United, Arsenal or Chelsea due to club commitments, the portents for victory were not great. England put in a display imbued with style and attacking verve, scoring five without reply and Hurst grabbed a hat-trick. It was, nevertheless, worth noting the words of one reporter that this was, after all, 'the shadow eleven of England against the pale ghosts of once great France'.[12]

At the end of the 1968–69 season the Home Internationals were compressed into a single week in an effort to alleviate the perennial club versus country disputes. First up was a trip to Windsor Park where England overcame several early scares to emerge 3–1 winners.

Martin Peters, Francis Lee and Geoff Hurst got the goals. The following Wednesday Wales visited Wembley and, in one of the best meetings between the two countries in years, England overcame a 0–1 half-time deficit to win 2–1, after goals by Bobby Charlton and Francis Lee. Three days later the Home Championship was sealed in emphatic style with a 4–1 victory over Scotland. Martin Peters and Geoff Hurst claimed England's goals with a brace apiece.

Two weeks later England flew to Mexico where they were to play the national team and a representative side, before travelling to Montevideo and Rio de Janeiro for fixtures against Uruguay and Brazil. After the continent-wide consternation caused by Ramsey's 'animal' comments three years earlier, not to mention the perceived 'conspiracy' which had, in farcical allegations, seen England lift the Jules Rimet trophy, the trip was viewed as much as a public relations' exercise as preparation ahead of their defence in the following year's World Cup finals. Yet fears of a hostile reception initially seemed to be without foundation. 'The greeting was compelling and contagious as we carved a path through the dark sea of smiling faces to our transport, to which the younger ones clung like flies on a wall,' wrote Geoffrey Green in *The Times*. 'In their eyes there was little difference between Bobby Charlton and the least of the rest of us. We were all in the act, each a champion.'

It wasn't to last. Alf Ramsey, it seemed, was continuing his one-man mission to alienate the Spanish-speaking world. Although a 0–0 draw in the gargantuan splendour of the Azteca Stadium passed peaceably enough, he had already gaffed. Asked if he had a word for the Mexican press he replied afterwards:

Yes. There was a band playing outside our hotel until five o'clock this morning. We were promised a motorcycle escort to the stadium. It never arrived. When our players went out to inspect the pitch, they were abused and jeered by the crowd. I would have thought the Mexican public would have been delighted to welcome England, then when the game began, they could cheer their own team as much as they liked.

Mexican sensibilities were wounded, the slur stored in offended minds, but things got worse. When an England XI played a Mexican XI in a representative friendly, the visitors were soon in a commanding 4–0 lead and playing with imagination, zest and flair when

Mexican frustration bubbled over. In the closing minutes a mistimed tackle by Everton's Colin Harvey on Gonzales saw the game erupt: Gonzales reacted by kicking at the floored Harvey; Mullery piled in, grabbed the Mexican by the neck and pushed him away and, for the second time in a year, Mullery was sent off. The crowd bayed its disapproval at their increasingly unpopular guests and Ramsey sealed the grudge at full-time when a flock of Mexican journalists tried to follow the team into their underground dressing rooms. Ramsey shooed them away: 'You've no right in here!' They wouldn't forget Sir Alf in a hurry. Even in the more relaxed climes of Uruguay the charm offensive continued. Introduced to a local journalist by his English wife, Ramsey responded: 'Yes, I know you. You're a pest.'

Even with English journalists Ramsey could be, and usually was, a tough cookie. Some who had got to know him over a matter of years overlooked his more prickly moments and respected his sharp football mind; others, put off by his awkward persona, didn't take the trouble and became increasingly scathing of this overtly sullen man. While England were winning it wasn't a great problem; but grudges were beginning to be stored.

Part of Ramsey's problem was his perpetually solemn demeanour. It meant that when his dry sense of humour did surface, it was usually met by puzzlement rather than laughs. On one occasion Geoff Hurst gave Ramsey a lift from Heathrow after England had played Northern Ireland. When they pulled up to Lancaster Gate, Hurst let him out. 'There you are Alf, see you at the next game.' 'Yes,' deadpanned Ramsey, without a flicker of a grin, 'I'll send over some tickets.' On another, Allan Clarke was making his first trip with the England team when Ramsey sidled up to him. 'Enjoying yourself Allan?' asked Ramsey. 'Yes boss, loving every second,' replied Clarke. 'Nobody fucking enjoys themselves with me,' was his reply to a startled Clarke. Amongst his players he could just about get away with it – 'that's just Alf,' they'd say, shaking their heads with a wry smile – but with journalists and the public at large, the impression could be more damaging. 'As a public relations man,' Bobby Moore memorably quipped, '[Ramsey] would have made a splendid concentration camp commandant.'[13]

In Uruguay Ramsey had it the way he liked it best: he let his team do the talking. Unbelievably England had never recorded a victory over a South American host nation but began the contest in the

Centenario Stadium – venue of the first World Cup final some four decades earlier – superbly after Lee put them in front with an early goal. With the defence expertly marshalled by Moore and Labone, and the ceaseless running of Ball and Bell keeping tight rein on the midfield as well as providing fast breakaways on the attack, England were good value for their half-time lead. After the interval they were slightly unfortunate to concede an equaliser: Tommy Wright was adjudged to have fouled Morales and from Mujica's free-kick Cubilla was on hand to head past Banks.

The goal invigorated the South Americans and the England rearguard had to work hard to repel their attacks. Conversely England looked even sharper up front when they could counter-attack from deep. Ten minutes from full-time the ball was fed to Colin Bell who passed it to Ball. Everton's white-booted warrior played in Lee who galloped down the flank, crossed at pace and watched in delight as Hurst volleyed the winner past Maidana. England, said the watching Brazil manager Joao Saldanha, were 'a better side now than in 1966'. He particularly admired Brian Labone ('a sounder player than Jack Charlton in your triumph three years ago') and the sense of teamwork made for 'A combination that offers little space for manoeuvre for the opposition . . . There can be no doubt that they have maintained their position in the world game. Tactically they are supreme; they lead the world in this respect. It will be difficult for us to beat them in Rio on Thursday because they are so well organised.'

Fireworks, whistles, the ceaseless beat of the samba drum and the song of 125,000 men, women and children made for a carnival atmosphere in the Maracana Stadium four days later. Rockets lit the sky and the illuminated statue of Christ bore down from the top of Corcavado Mountain, watching his sons at play in one of soccer's great temples. If England was the birthplace of football, few of Ramsey's men could have doubted that Brazil had become its spiritual home. In the face of all this, and against the side most likely to rival their mantle a year later, England started impressively. On fifteen minutes, neat interplay instigated by Moore saw the ball threaded out of defence, into midfield and on to Peters hugging the left flank. He swung in a cross from the wing and when Bobby Charlton dived unsuccessfully towards the ball he seemed to take half of the Brazilian defence with him, allowing Bell to come in unchecked and slam the ball into the roof of the net.

For the next sixty-five minutes, Pele, Tostão, Gerson and the man they called 'the new Garrincha', Jairzinho, threw what they had at England. Shepherded with calm and courage by Moore and protected at the last line by Banks, England held onto their advantage. Charlton missed a fine chance to double the lead just after the interval, but with his defence in fine form it looked like a goal would be enough. Then, with just ten minutes to go, Tostão turned the game on its head. First, a loose ball span away from Peters on the edge of the England penalty area and seemed to be covered, but through the crowd of players Tostão's left-footed drive flashed and crept past the unsighted Banks. Moments later Tostão shimmied past Newton on the right and sent in a low, hard, diagonal pass across goal which was glanced in by Jairzinho for Brazil's winner. England left the Maracana proud but defeated. 'We were lucky in the end,' admitted Saldanha. 'If Charlton had scored just after half-time to put you two up we would have been finished.'

Ramsey had come to believe that he had a better squad of players than in 1966 – an opinion that was gaining wide currency. 'We all believed we had the best squad in England's history,' Moore agreed. 'We all believed we were going to win the World Cup again.' Domestically English teams' progress in Europe gave cause for optimism and of the core of the 1966 squad, only George Cohen (retired), Ray Wilson (at the end of his career at Fourth Division Oldham), Jimmy Greaves (retired from international football) and Roger Hunt (who had stepped down a division to join Bolton) were out of contention. Yet other worthy stars had come in their place. Manchester City's re-emergence as a football power had been spearheaded by the rise of Colin Bell and Francis Lee, who matched their excellence at Maine Road with impressive early displays in the white of their country. Bell had been picked up for a veritable song from Bury as a twenty-year-old in 1966 after Malcolm Allison had been so desperate to sign him that he would sit in the directors' box at Gigg Lane and criticise the inside-forward in the hope that his comments would dissuade other watching managers and scouts. Fortunately for him – and City – the ruse worked. He was, in the words of Allison's boss Joe Mercer, 'the best player since Peter Doherty [a City legend of the 1930s]. He has got fantastic stamina, and this unusual combination of speed and stamina. He is best when he is given a free rein and coming from deep. He is a good tackler and covers every inch of the pitch.' He was joined at Maine Road in October 1967 by Bolton Wanderers' prolific forward Francis Lee. With a devastatingly powerful shot and a deceptive turn of pace that left opposing defenders flat-footed, comparisons with his Old Trafford rival, Bobby Charlton, were inevitable. While the two men played together for England, long term it seemed that Ramsey was grooming Lee as the ageing Charlton's successor. In the more immediate future he bolstered Ramsey's options in an England forward line now deprived of Greaves and Hunt.

Of central importance to the way that England had developed tactically was the role of the overlapping full-back. Of the four that Ramsey seemed to have settled on – Terry Cooper, Tommy Wright, Emlyn Hughes and Keith Newton – it was telling that Cooper, Wright and Hughes were all converted inside-forwards while Newton was no slouch on an attacking run. With the emergence of these players, the 4-3-3 formation of 1966 had evolved into something more akin to a conventional 4-4-2 line-up with midfielders dropping back to cover the marauding runs of the defenders. Whether the problems caused by heat and altitude would render high workrate and lung-busting overlaps impossible in Mexico, though, was another matter.

Others were less convinced of England's development. Bobby Charlton, in particular, was thought to be a declining force. 'Charlton, it seems, had talismanic qualities for Ramsey,' wrote the journalist Max Marquis early in 1970.

> For some time now – a season and a half or more – Charlton has been struggling as an international player. His courage and devotion are enormous; his prestige and influence unparalleled. If sentiment is to overrule grim necessity, then Charlton is the first player who deserves the benefit of it. But long since Charlton has looked mentally and physically tired to the very marrow of his being. Whether Ramsey realises it or not, he makes allowances for him.[14]

Even Bobby Moore publicly expressed concerns about Charlton's capacity for the campaign, given the problems of heat and altitude likely to be experienced in Mexico. 'He is so willing, so eager, that he tends to take more out of himself than he needs. He cannot help it. This is the part and the style he has played for both Manchester United and England for the past five years, and it is difficult to get out of a habitual groove. Can he do this in this air? If only he were lazier, it might be better for him.'[15] Other options in attack – beyond Lee and the continually excellent Hurst – were few. Indeed, so limited were the England manager's alternatives that he was forced to plump for the doughty but questionable merits of West Bromwich Albion's Jeff Astle.

Ramsey's relationship with the British press had also started to falter. Although England won three of their four autumn and winter games, after the one game they drew, 0–0 at home to a Dutch side that could boast the likes of Krol, Jansen, Van Hanegem and a certain Johann Cruyff, the team had been slow handclapped and greeted with jeers of 'What a load of English rubbish.' The reaction of the following morning's headlines was scathing: 'Dismal show by England', 'Sad flop by side that promised so much' and, remarkably, 'Rubbish'. Ramsey was defiant. 'If you want me to win unimportant matches I will pick teams to do so . . . surely they were slow handclapping the Dutch team?' Alas not. The heady days that followed 1966 when 'Saint Alf' could do no wrong had come to an end and criticism of the knight had begun to creep into assessments of his running of the England team.

The 1969–70 domestic season had been one of the most closely fought in years. Its outstanding force, Leeds United, had led the charge to League and FA Cup glory but wilted as winter became spring and ended it empty-handed. At the start of April the season concluded (more than a month early) with Everton League Champions and Chelsea FA Cup winners following a bitter, bloody final against the Yorkshiremen. Once more the Home Championship was compressed into a week, and ended in a three-way tie with England, Scotland and Wales locked on four points after England had drawn 1–1 with the Welsh, 0–0 with the Scots and beaten Northern Ireland 3–1.

Nine days after the final Home International, on 4 May 1970, the England squad met at Heathrow Airport, where they boarded a Boeing 707 – flight number 675 – to take them to Mexico City. They were the first of the European nations to depart, twenty-nine full days before their opening match with Romania, time that would largely be spent getting used to the thin air. Ramsey was in a confident mood: 'I have said before that we have a stronger party than in 1966. This is not sales talk, I really do believe it. Provided we can acclimatise properly I really do believe it.'

Mexico was the first truly 'modern' World Cup. On the pitch it saw the introduction of red and yellow cards, as well as substitutes; off it, it marked the start of a television revolution. The rapid ascent of satellite technology meant that games were beamed across the world in glorious Technicolor, vanquishing memories of the turgid Chilean World Cup of eight years earlier to a bygone era of black and white and transmission delays. The England players also realised their commercial value. Last time they had won the World Cup and made just £1000 apiece; four years on they organised themselves. They employed – collectively – the agent Ken Stanley, a former table tennis international who represented George Best. They forewent sponsorship deals, instead striking up arrangements whereby certain products – Findus, Ford and Esso – were able to sport the lion rosette logo and the slogan 'Chosen by England'. It netted the squad an estimated £5000 each. Fans, hitherto largely impervious to lengthy and expensive transatlantic trips, also travelled in relatively large numbers. It was possible to fly to Mexico first class for £245 with James Vance Travel of Fulham for a twenty-four-day trip. In all, some 3000 England fans ventured over. ('The sort of magnificent obsessionists who suspect that when Jesus performed the miracle of walking on the waters he was bouncing a ball on his instep at the time,' wrote Hugh McIlvanney.[16])

The football record was also born. In March the squad had been approached about the possibility of producing a 'team song' by Bill Martin, a songwriter/producer who, with his partner Phil Coulter, had produced hits such as 'Puppet on a String' and 'Congratulations'. He spent a day with the squad recording an album entitled *The World Beaters Sing the World Beaters* at London's Pye Studios. Even Ramsey encouraged the project. Among their repertoire was a catchy tune by the name of 'Back Home'. It was released as a single on 18 April and was to spend sixteen weeks in the charts. Within a fortnight of its release it had climbed to number three; a week later it dislodged Norman Greenbaum's 'Spirit in the Sky' from the top spot and stayed there for three weeks.

Elsewhere Bill Shankly's defining belief, that 'football was not a matter of life and death, but more important', seemed to be borne out. The game seemed to take on a greater importance than ever before. The previous June, a qualifier between El Salvador and Honduras in San Salvador had ended in a violent riot which in turn led to the break-up of diplomatic relations between the two countries, then war. In four days of fighting 3000 people (80 per cent of them Honduran) were killed and $50 million of damage caused. Then, on the day the finals opened, with most of the nation listening to the opening ceremony, a devastating earthquake hit Peru, killing thousands. The Peruvian team, with little or no news about the fate of their families, were ordered by their president to play on.

Altitude would invariably have an impact on proceedings one way or another. It would make the players short of breath, affect their recovery time and the flight of the ball. Even the pitch at England's base, the Jalisca Stadium in Guadalajara (the lowest of the five World Cup stadiums), was 5212 feet (around a mile) high. At that level the oxygen content of the air was 20 per cent less than at sea level: the resultant lack of oxygen put lungs into overdrive which in turn put strain on the heart. Along with the notoriously smoggy air of Mexico's cities, plus the 100° heat of noon, a debilitating, if not dangerous, climate was in place. Roger Bannister, breaker of the four-minute mile record and now a practising doctor, warned that someone might die as a result of the problems caused by altitude (a suggestion that met howls of anguished derision in Mexico). Two years earlier the Mexico Olympics had yielded all manner of strange results in the field events. Numerous throwing and jumping records were set, including, most famously, Bob Beamon's astonishing long jump record. Although the lack of oxygen was not a problem in an event that required minimal breathing, such as sprinting, the middle- and long-distance runners – like footballers, aerobic athletes – had struggled. The marathon had been the slowest in modern times and officials had to be on hand every stretch of the way, ready to dispense emergency oxygen. Conversely, the Olympic football tournament had passed by without serious incident and the final had been contested by two European teams, Bulgaria and Hungary.

The truth was that nobody really knew what to expect. It was anticipated that the tournament would be played at a slower pace, and it was seen as a necessity that the players had at least three weeks to acclimatise fully so as to allow the blood to produce the additional cells necessary for top-class athletic performance.

After ten days of preparation the English players were becoming used to the problems posed by altitude. David Sadler told *The Times*:

> At first I was blown after five minutes of practice. Now I get a second wind very quickly and can sustain it more and more. We cannot play as we do at home, however. It is a case now of short bursts followed by periods of possession play. But accuracy must be up to the last refined inch. The ball runs away like a mad thing on the ground and does not die in thin air.[17]

'I found a noticeable difference at first, especially balls being played to the chest,' said Geoff Hurst. 'I found it bouncing away. The ball seems so damned lively as well, quite apart from the velocity, just like cricketers playing on soft and hard wickets.'[18] Gordon Banks, tellingly, added, 'The ball comes much faster, more unexpectedly than it does at sea level and it's not sure to stay true. Sometimes it's going all over the place. Things I'd eat up at home I may find myself scrambling to hold. It may be safer at times to push them away and the lads will have to be ready for that situation.'[19] Later, much later, his words were to have particular resonance for his understudy, Peter Bonetti.

The level of preparation undertaken by the England team was the envy of all the other managers. Not only were England the best team in the world, but no other European team had been so thorough in readying themselves to contest their crown. Their planning went beyond the training pitch too. On 7 April Sid Brown, the England coach driver, set off from Lancaster Gate with the England team bus boasting a 'Willie for Mexico' logo (the World Cup Willie lion of four years earlier sporting a sombrero) emblazoned on the side. The bus had been fitted out with tea and coffee making facilities, fridges for iced drinks and a built-in hi-fi system. The move soon stoked the embers of resentment still burning from the previous summer's gaffe-ridden tour, and 1966 before that. 'Do you think we have not yet discovered the wheel or the internal combustion engine?' one Mexican daily harrumphed. In the event it proved self defeating: not only were the Mexicans piqued, but the coach couldn't cope with the heat and in the end the squad had to use a local model.

The mood of England's hosts soon turned to apoplexy. Findus, one of the team's main sponsors, exacerbated existing tensions with a well-meaning but naive newspaper advertisement campaign. Under a picture of a befuddled-looking Bobby Charlton and Norman Hunter, with an apprehensive Ramsey in between, they asked the question: 'What happens if foreign food gives our boys a bellyache?' ('Don't worry, it's no risk a team manager will take in a foreign country.') It said more about common attitudes to 'exotic food' in Britain (where chicken kiev and arctic roll were seen as the cutting edge of culinary chic) than about Ramsey's in particular, but the perception it cast was nevertheless a bad one. England were due to take all their own provisions, including an array of Findus products, but again the plan was thwarted. When their supplies arrived the Mexican authorities decreed that all dairy and beef products were to be destroyed on the quayside. England's footballers were left to live off ready meals and fish fingers and, worse still, local produce. The whole situation caused more outrage in the Mexican press. As one headline wittily proclaimed: 'If you are going to throw fruit at the England team, remember to wash it first'.

Why was there such antipathy to England's methodical but otherwise harmless preparations? Certainly memories lingered from 1966, and the 1969 tour, but Mexican ire extended beyond the great 'fix' of the World Cup or anger at Sir Alf Ramsey's brusqueness. For instance, British journalists had caused consternation during the 1968 Olympic Games when they had 'dared' to focus on the Mexican government's brutal suppression of student demonstrations rather than the sport that was on offer. After the World Cup finals C.P. Hope, British ambassador to Mexico City, wrote a confidential report entitled 'The World Cup 1970: The Politics of Football'. In it he concluded that England's problems were multifaceted:

A mixture of past history (imagined slights during the 1966 World Cup in England, recollection of the attitude of the British press to Mexico during the 1968 Olympics and student riots, lingering resentment at the opposition of the FA to the choice of Mexico as the venue for the Championship); Mexican chauvinism; the failure of the Mexican organisers to cope adequately either with the administrative or the press relations problems; an unduly one-sided attitude by British press commentators; the refusal of the Mexican media to come to terms with the ground rules for contact between themselves and our team manager and players – rules reasonable in themselves but more restrictive than those of most other teams participating in the tournament.[20]

The Mexican press, he wrote, 'were sometimes bent on mischief, but also with plenty of space to fill and happy to print idle chatter so long as it filled the pages of their newspaper'. Hope added: 'Sir Alf Ramsey is seldom at ease with the press. Although trying hard he does not look at ease with them and rarely gives them a felicitous phrase. In the long run he will show the quality of his defects.'[21] Ramsey had pleaded indifference, stating that he didn't see or care what difference the hostile attitude of the Mexican press made, an attitude with which the British embassy had begged to differ, eventually making him consent to having a Spanish-speaking press officer.

After more than two weeks' acclimatisation and intense training in Mexico the England squad flew to Bogotá – 'a sombre city of thieves and criminals' according to Brian Glanville – on Monday, 18 May for a friendly match against Colombia. The game offered valuable pre-tournament experience, but there were other dangers involved. It was a time of civil unrest, not just in Colombia but across South America, and the FA had received warnings of kidnapping and terrorist activity from the Foreign Office. They weren't without foundation either: the German ambassador had recently been assassinated in Guatemala and an Israeli official murdered in Paraguay. 'You are all valuable property,' Ramsey warned his players. 'Go out in groups and lock your doors at night.'

Against the Colombians Ramsey put out a strong side and they recorded a 4–0 victory thanks to goals from Martin Peters (2), Bobby Charlton and Alan Ball. Indeed the wilds of Bogotá seemed to have passed almost without incident, save for a minor commotion the day the players checked into their hotel. Killing time in the lobby, the two Bobbys – Moore and Charlton – went into a small gift shop, the Fuego Verde, looking for gifts for their wives. Several other players and Dr Phillips, the England team doctor, drifted in and out disinterestedly, put off by the prices or simply the sheer gaudiness of some of the wares. Eventually Moore and Charlton came out too and joined the rest of the squad.

Suddenly a commotion broke out. An alarm bell sounded and out came the Fuego Verde's shop assistant shouting in a mix of broken English and Spanish that something had gone missing. Seeing

Moore and Charlton she jabbed an accusing finger at the England captain.

The police, hotel manager and Ramsey were soon on hand. The assistant repeated her accusation; Moore, utterly bemused, denied it and even offered to be searched, but the hotel manager told him it would not be necessary. Moore made an official statement, accepted an apology for the inconvenience and the matter was seemingly laid to rest.

The England squad had already had a foretaste of the Bogotá incident the night before they had flown out of Mexico. A jewellery salesman had turned up with bags of watches, diamonds, pearls and emeralds to be reserved and paid for on the players' return. Some bought items, most didn't and, as they wandered back out towards the pool, Ramsey summoned the squad together. There had been a problem. An Omega watch had gone missing and the salesman was accusing the England players of stealing it. To waylay any trouble Ramsey suggested that the players held a collection to cover the cost – a suggestion they initially baulked at, before relenting after Ramsey had offered to cover the cost himself. With that, and then the Fuego Verde incident, it seemed that extortion was a way of life in the Americas.

After Colombia, England flew to Quito for a final warm-up match against Ecuador. More controversy and upset was to come. The whittling down from twenty-eight to twenty-two players was set to be announced after the match – on the Sunday – but the press set up a bargain with Ramsey that he would tell them in the strictest confidence on the Saturday afternoon so that they could make their Sunday deadlines. The rest of the country would therefore read the news over breakfast or, because of time differences, at around the same time that the players would hear it. Given the isolation of their Quito training camp, Ramsey thought that he could tell the journalists in confidence, and, as agreed, on early Saturday afternoon Ramsey sat down with members of the press in a conference room, and solemnly informed them of his squad. 'It was a difficult job, it had to be a difficult job,' he told them. 'For those who have been left out, being with us will have been an invaluable experience. In any case they may be in a position no different from some who are already in the twenty-two.'

The assembled journalists restated their commitment to treat the privileged information as if it were a national secret. But they, and Ramsey, were let down by their news desks. As soon as London had the information, the families of the six discarded players were contacted by hacks seeking disparaging remarks about Ramsey. The tabloid rotter had been born. One of the unlucky six, David Sadler, learnt from his wife, who had made a late-night telephone call to the England team hotel to inform him. At breakfast the following morning he stormed into the hotel dining room and furiously demanded to speak to Ramsey. Nobody spoke to the England manager like that, but Ramsey went outside and there followed a confrontation with the justifiably angry Manchester United defender.

Ramsey then walked back into the hushed dining room and summoned the five other unlucky players – Peter Shilton, Brian Kidd, Ralph Coates, Bob McNab and, as in 1966, Peter Thompson. He apologised, told them that he had been let down but that they were not included, adding that they could stay on if they so wished. Sadler and Thompson did, the rest returned home. 'The thing that gets me most,' said Sadler after he had calmed down, 'is that this lot are going to win it and I won't be taking part.'[22]

After that rumpus, an uneventful game was won 2–0, with England's goals coming from Lee and the discarded Kidd. More crucial perhaps, was the fact that England had played 9300 feet above sea level and felt no ill effects. The final twenty-two now had nine days to fine tune their fitness ahead of England's opener in Guadalajara with Romania.

The following day's journey back to Mexico was, however, convoluted. Instead of travelling back directly, the squad had to return via Bogotá. Once there, they were taken back to the Tequendama Hotel where, to kill the four-and-a-half-hour wait, the screening of a film had been laid on. While in the darkened room, two detectives turned up and discreetly tapped Moore on the shoulder and asked him to go outside. There, he was arrested for the theft of an emerald bracelet from the Fuego Verde the previous Monday. When the film was over nobody wondered where Moore was: they merely expected he was giving an interview. It was only an hour later, when Martin Peters was asked to carry the captain's hand luggage onto the waiting plane, that there was an inkling that something was awry. On the plane Ramsey, Moore and several FA officials were missing too. Finally, the manager turned up in time for the flight, which then took off without Moore. Once in the air, Ramsey grimly announced to the players that their captain had been left behind.

The case against Moore had reopened after an antiques dealer, Alvaro Suarez, had come forward as a witness and, based on his testimony, charges had been made. At first it had been suggested that Moore would be released within an hour and be allowed to travel on with his team-mates, but when that deadline passed, he found himself being led to a cell. Shuttle diplomacy between anxious FA officials and Colombian police ensued and a compromise was reached: instead of being left in a local jailhouse, Moore found himself placed under house arrest at the suburban residence of the chief of the Colombian FA. He was then brought before a judge, Justice Pedro Dorado, who informed Moore that he did not like football, that there was no agenda and that he would judge the case purely on its legal merits. Colombian law, nevertheless, warned the British embassy in Bogotá, 'puts a premium on indecision'.

The following day, Moore was brought to his office and interrogated for a further four hours. The judge was not impressed by the conflicting information brought before him and requested to see the scene of the crime. As news filtered through to London, deep anxieties were expressed by press and public and, away from their glare, in Westminster. In 1966, England's World Cup success had provided the perfect antidote to the problems enveloping Harold Wilson's government. Four years on, campaigning for the general election, scheduled to take place just days ahead of the World Cup final, was well under way. Wilson knew full well the importance of England's progress to his own prospects; and, as a football fan himself, how central Bobby Moore was to England's hopes. With that in mind, the Prime Minister gave the British ambassador to Bogotá an informal undertaking to deliver a personal message from him to the Colombian foreign minister to ensure that Moore's case was dealt with the utmost urgency. The Colombian President, Misael Pastrana Borrero, dispatched an emissary along with the head of the notorious Colombian Security Service DAS to put pressure on the judge to release Moore quickly, but farcically couldn't find him at home. At the same time, the Foreign Secretary, Michael Stewart, attending a NATO summit in Rome, also took his own action, telexing the Colombian ambassador to London, requesting 'anything that can be done to ensure that the case is resolved as speedily as possible'.

Meanwhile contradictory stories from the store assistant, Clara Padilla, had emerged. First it was a £600 eighteen-carat gold bracelet that had been stolen; next it was one encrusted with diamonds and emeralds worth £5000. 'It all happened very quickly,' she told reporters in proficient, accented English. 'Bobby Moore and two of his team-mates came to the counter and started talking to me. Then I saw Mr Moore open a glass case, take out the bracelet and put it in his pocket.'

The next day, Wednesday, Moore, Padilla, their lawyers and a further 300 people including police, journalists and photographers, visited the Tequendama Hotel. After swearing on oath, Moore and Padilla went through a ninety-minute-long reconstruction. Here the case against the England captain started to unravel. After already stating that she had seen Moore take the bracelet, Padilla then confessed that she hadn't actually seen him take the bracelet from the wall cabinet because it was obscured by his 'wide shoulders' but deduced it was a bracelet from Suarez's say so.

When Suarez was asked why he took four days to come forward, he mumbled excuses about not getting around to it, though he might not have done anyway (the policeman whom he claimed to have reported his accusations to also claimed he had never spoken to Suarez). Then, it emerged that far from being an impartial witness, Suarez was actually an associate of the shop's owner, Danilo Rojas. It was hinted that Rojas, who was claiming £6000 in 'moral and material compensation' for the bracelet, was, in the ultimate of ironies, trying to extort money so that he could take some friends to go and see the finals.

All the while Bobby Moore remained utterly unflappable. Padilla claimed that she saw Moore put something in his left jacket pocket; Moore showed the judge his blazer: there was no left pocket. Moore was led away to cheers of 'Viva Bobby' and Padilla fell into floods of tears. Nevertheless, Judge Dorado informed Moore that it would take up to five days for that stage of the investigation to be concluded, and even then he might not be released straight away. Unhappy at the procrastination, Michael Stewart took a harder line, sending a note to the Colombian ambassador that threatened 'a potentially delicate decision might develop; and we should have to consider carefully the form of our further representations to the government of Colombia'.[23]

Finally, on the Thursday, Moore was summoned to another meeting with Judge Dorado, where he was told that the case was to be dropped due to insufficient evidence. Technically it needed the opinion of a second arbiter so that it could be officially dropped, but it meant that he was free to go.

Within hours he was on a flight bound for Mexico City. That evening, before flying on to Guadalajara to be finally reunited with his team-mates, Moore was joined for a drink by an unexpected friend. Having driven 16,245 miles in the London to Mexico rally, Jimmy Greaves had arrived in Mexico City a day earlier. Hearing the plight of his friend he had gone over to see Moore and, evading the attentions of embassy staff not to mention a police cordon, called by to see him. 'Come on Mooro – what you done with that bracelet?' he asked the startled England captain. 'I told you that I'd see you in Mexico – well here I am!'[24]

What Moore didn't know then was that his release was conditional and that the British embassy in Bogotá had withheld some of the possibilities of Moore's discharge. 'We should try to steer the press away from any speculation on these imponderables,' reported the ambassador, 'which could affect the climate of opinion at home and in Mexico with risk to the team's morale.'[25] Indeed the case reopened in the autumn and Charlton and Moore had to give additional evidence at a special hearing at Bow Street Magistrates' Court which were passed onto Mexican police. It wasn't until 1972 that the case was finally dropped.*

Ramsey, meanwhile, had given a press conference at which he refused to answer questions about Moore and instead stayed focused on the task ahead. 'I insisted in 1966 England would win the World Cup. Without wishing to appear repetitive, I say in 1970 England will win the World Cup. This squad contains all the abilities to do it again. Their enthusiasm, skills and, above all, their peak physical fitness command the respect of the rest of the world.' Nevertheless, the

---

* It was later suggested that a third player may have been in the shop and have removed an item as a practical joke which then backfired, and Moore covered up to protect the younger player. Moore, before his death in 1993, told close friends as much, adding that the player 'never thanked him'. Nevertheless he swore under oath at the Bow Street hearing: 'As far as I know no other member of the team entered the shop, but I had my back to the door the whole time.' If that left some doubt, Bobby Charlton's statement cleared up any suspicion of a cover up: 'It is possible that there were other members of the English team standing by the door, but not in the shop itself.'

England manager had been having more problems with the Mexican press. Leading the anti-English assault had been Fernando Marcos, Mexico's leading political and football commentator, who had described England as 'the champions of antipathy' and called them 'arrogant and inaccessible'.[26] Marcos and his colleagues had been given even more ammunition by Moore's arrest and other incidents that had since occurred.

On the flight back from Bogotá Jeff Astle, a nervous flyer, decided to indulge in a couple of beers to quell his anxiety. In the event he consumed more than a few and by the time the plane landed in Mexico City, with the Mexican press swarming around, needed to be helped off the plane and sat in a chair in the arrivals lounge. Stiles did his best to smarten his colleague up, and a *Daily Mirror* photographer disguised him in a cape, but it was to little avail. Ramsey, with his mind elsewhere, may not have caught wind of his drunken striker, but the Mexican newspapers did. The next day *El Heraldo* carried a picture of the intoxicated player and described England as 'a team of thieves and drunks'.

While Astle was drunk, Ramsey was fielding questions about Moore from the Mexican press. He told them that he would make a statement at a later date, if he felt it necessary. Yet when he had to repeat his position, in the same terms, six or seven times, the England manager snapped.

'Why do you people do this to us?' Ramsey demanded.

'Don't you think the way you are treated is the result of the way you treat people?' he was asked in response.

There followed a pedantic argument which a Mexican journalist sought to defuse.

'Anyway, we welcome you now with open arms.'

'Surely you must be joking,' sneered Ramsey.[27]

Mindful of the troubles that had repeatedly followed England, on the Friday, ahead of Tuesday's opening match with Romania, Ramsey went on yet another PR offensive. It started well enough with him holding court with some of the 2000 locals watching the training session at Club Atlas. Mexico, he said, was 'wonderful', adding – without irony – that in four visits each welcome was even better than before. He could not name his favourite player ('do you want me shot!?!') and rounded off his publicity assault by telling British journalists: 'You'd all like to see me fired, I know.' If that had escaped the notice of some of his Mexican followers, his vigorous complaints about the state of the Jalisca Stadium pitch didn't. 'What can you expect?' he said. 'I am told that the Brazilians have been training on it. The grass is in poor condition and the pitch is very bumpy.' England were even more unloved than ever before. Two days later at the opening ceremony, the schoolchildren parading in England shirts were roundly booed by the majority of the 107,000-strong crowd.

Whatever else was going through the minds of the best team in the world, England's footballers couldn't deny that the build-up to the finals had been eventful. They had experienced scandal, framing, subterfuge, universal hostility, heat and acclimatisation difficulties, press leaks, foreign food and were still, even after all that, to kick a ball in anger. But forty-eight hours after the opening ceremony they were finally able to concentrate solely on defending their crown when they met Romania at the Jalisca Stadium, Guadalajara.

Six men – Banks, Moore, Ball, Hurst, Peters and Bobby Charlton – survived from English football's greatest day. They were grateful for the added, belated, bonus of two substitutes since Romania were a rough side. Setting the tone, Dumitru cut down Mullery, then Mocanu hacked Newton so badly that he had to be replaced by his Everton team-mate, Tommy Wright. Although Dumitrache caused a few early problems, England soon settled and quickly grew in confidence: Bobby Charlton went close with two of his long-range rockets; Lee smashed Cooper's cross against the bar and Peters headed narrowly over from Newton's cross. Then, on sixty-five minutes, came the breakthrough. Ball lifted a high cross that Hurst trapped, took around a defender and slammed home from an acute angle. It was enough to seal a successful start to England's defence of the World Cup.

Back home, the anti-English sentiment in Mexico had built up a siege mentality in the press. 'Triumphant England . . . they're on the way,' thundered the *Sun* after the Romania win. 'Hurst's super goal beats the hate,' thought the *Daily Mail*. A *Daily Express* cartoon summed up the nature of the match and the loyalties of the Mexicans by portraying an English gentleman with a union jack sitting in a crowd of sombreroed Mexicans who were all cheering as a white-shirted player is kicked in the air. 'Come in our sweep,' said the caption. 'The one who getta kicked the highest into the air is the winner.' Peter Batt in the *Sun* compared Ramsey's composure to that of Churchill.

The Mexicans did, however, have some praise for their guests. Bobby Moore was 'the king of world football', as one newspaper put it. 'He shone with gold. For a man who has been burdened with vile accusations and imprisoned, he commanded the game like an emperor.'[28] Bobby Charlton, meanwhile, had earned himself the nickname 'Il Calvino Divino' – The Divine Baldy. Another attempt to rationalise the antipathy towards England came in *Excelsior* – a 'quality' newspaper – when it defined the psychology of the man in the street: 'The Mexican subconsciously identifies himself with the weak. While the Mexican male sees the English team as the brutal conqueror who has to be deposed, the Mexican woman admires the arrogance of the England team, disregards its lack of sympathy towards the public and, as women, falls for the *triumfadores*.'

A successful start was an important boost ahead of what was likely to be England's sternest challenge: Brazil. All the while the England squad hoped that the rainy season would start and the unexpected heatwave that had gripped the country and started to dog their efforts would come to an end. Ramsey trained his players at the same time of day as their next match, typically in temperatures in the late eighties, although with a noon kick-off to accommodate the European TV audience, against Brazil they would play in a ninety-eight-degree furnace. 'I was better off in jail,' Moore complained.

Prior to the tournament Ramsey had given the players a choice between a rural retreat and the Hilton Hotel in town. They chose the latter, against Ramsey's better instincts. It was a bad call. The night before the Brazil game, the Guadalajara Hilton was besieged by locals cheering 'Mexico!' and 'Brazil!', blasting car horns, beating bin lids and making as much noise as they possibly could to upset their ungrateful guests. The Mexican police, previously so diligent, seemed quite impotent in stopping them and at one stage some fans even made it as high as the twelfth floor, reserved for England, and started banging on doors. In the middle of the night some of the players were switched to rooms at the back, although as three-quarters of the hotel was exposed to the road it offered little respite. Frustrated, some of the England players resorted to pelting the Mexicans with milk cartons. Few got much sleep.

With Newton still injured, Wright took his place in an otherwise unchanged line-up. Given the intense heat the game was to be about possession football: taking the sting out of the game; dictating the pace; playing carefully. 'Do you like gold, boys?' asked Ramsey before the game. 'Well the ball's a lump of gold today.' As the players came out, the size of the task facing England struck Ball. 'I looked across at the Brazilian side and thought, you'll not get a much better side than this ever, ever, ever.'[29]

Yet it was England who controlled the early stages. Peters, Ball and Lee each had half chances, but the Brazilian goalkeeper, Felix, was equal to them. Then, on eleven minutes, the ball was played out to Jairzinho. Deceptively languid at first, he showed a turn of foot that took him past Cooper. He looked up, and then hung a centre, perfectly, into the middle of the England penalty area, seven yards out. Soaring in, unmarked and at pace was Pele, the word's greatest striker. He outjumped Wright, meeting the ball flawlessly, his head striking it with power, pace and precision downwards towards the bottom of Banks' right post. On his descent he started to shout 'goal!' and the crowd stood to applaud.

Nobody, however, had counted on the miracle of Jalisca Stadium.

Caught out by the initial cross, the six-foot frame of Gordon Banks seemed to defeat the laws of physics and physiology. Arrowing down towards the corner, his right palm, with every sinew in his arm stretched, somehow, incredibly, made contact with the ball and scooped it over the bar.

Pele stood there unable to believe exactly what he had seen. The crowd, who had risen to applaud his goal, instead directed their applause at Banks. Pele came up to him and patted him on the back.

'I thought that was a goal,' said Moore, smiling, as Banks got up.

'You and me both,' he replied.

'You're getting old Banksy,' laughed Moore, 'you used to hold onto them.'[30]

In spite of the midday heat, the two teams continued to provide an engrossing encounter. Labone effectively shackled Tostão, the man whose contribution had proved so destructive to England's hopes a year earlier in Rio, and Moore kept tight rein on Pele. For England, Francis Lee went closest to scoring, but was denied by Felix's exemplary double save. As the game progressed into the second half, Brazil had more and more possession, and with it chances. Paulo

Cesar's long-range shot was tipped around the post; Banks blocked Jairzinho's through ball to Pele, then fisted away Rivelinho's bullet shot and Mullery blocked Pele's final path to goal after he had beaten four defenders. 'Even *we* were impressed,' said Bobby Charlton later. 'You could take that film and use it for coaching. That is what the game at the top is all about. There was everything in that, all the skills and techniques, all the tactical control, the lot. There was some special stuff played out there.'[31]

The decisive goal came on the hour. Tostão took possession and, creating space where none seemed to exist, turned and chipped the ball square to Pele. Heavily marked himself, he held off the attentions of the England defenders long enough to slide the ball into Jairzinho's path, and he hammered it past Banks.

Ramsey changed his tactics, bringing the burly presence of Jeff Astle on in place of Lee and replacing Charlton with Colin Bell. The more direct approach immediately caused the Brazilian defence problems and they struggled to contain Astle, who thrived on long, high crosses to the back post. Ball miskicked when he should have buried a knock down; then hit the crossbar, and Astle missed a virtually open goal; while at the other end Moore tackled Jairzinho with the sort of textbook perfection which would be used as an example to budding defenders a million times. And then it was all over.

After shaking hands with Labone, Pele ran up to Moore – the victor and the vanquished – and embraced him. The two men changed shirts, and Pele, in his still rudimentary English, said: 'You no thief Bobby.'

Ramsey took the defeat badly. 'The difference was that Brazil took ONE of their chances and we took none of ours. I think it would be inaccurate to say that the better team won. All you can say is that Brazil got the goal.' As if to attest to how closely run the game had been, the Brazil manager, Mario Zagallo, admitted: 'At no time did I think victory was certain until the final whistle. We were always evenly matched.'

It had been one of the World Cup's great contests, an encounter of passion, panache and, above all else, enduring images and memories: Moore's famous block on Jairzinho; Pele and Moore swapping shirts; and, more than anything, Banks's save. 'I've never seen a save like the one Banks made from me in the first half,' said Pele after the game. 'It was impossible. As soon as I headed the ball I thought it must be a goal. Yet Banks still got it with his wrist. The greatest save I have ever seen.'

Back in England, a nation was bleary-eyed after often staying up through the night to catch games. The World Cup finals were set against the background of not only the general election but also widespread strike action. Industrial action by printers had meant that there was no national press coming out of Manchester or London, while a strike at Tetley's brewery had left many pubs without beer. Some towns were nearly dry. In the north-west there was no ITV either, again because of a walkout. Nobody was very interested in the hustings. When Michael Stewart spoke in Cambridge on the night of the Brazil match, fewer than fifty people turned up. When the Chancellor, Roy Jenkins, and the Minister for Sport, Denis Howell, attended a similar function in Birmingham on the same day, they wisely brought forward the time of their addresses so that the audience – and they – could get back home to watch the game. Labour were overwhelming favourites having gained more than 400 seats in the May local elections, but there was widespread disillusionment at the two main parties.

It was the England football team who carried the attention and hopes of most of the country though, not Harold Wilson or Edward Heath. To qualify for the quarter-finals they had to focus on the difficult task that lay ahead when they met Czechoslovakia in their final first-round match. England's group was loaded with possibilities. Czechoslovakia were already out, but if they beat England by two goals then Romania, on the strength of a four for and five against scoring record, would go through. If England lost by one, they would draw lots to decide who had qualified. Ramsey's overriding concern was therefore to avoid losing.

With only seventy-two hours between the group game and a possible quarter-final, Ramsey made five changes. Jack Charlton replaced Labone, Colin Bell came in for Alan Ball, Astle and debutant Allan Clarke of Leeds were preferred in place of Hurst and Lee, while Newton returned for Wright. Sporting a new light-blue change strip, England had even more of an unfamiliar look, and indeed when play got under way seemingly played like strangers. Goalless at half-time, shortly after the interval luck fell England's way: Bell burst into the penalty area after a one-two with Newton, Hagara challenged the

Manchester City player but, in doing so, fell and handled the ball. The referee, Roger Machin, was on top of the incident and pointed to the penalty spot.

England, with Hurst and Lee missing, were without either regular penalty taker, but the debutant, Clarke, boldly collected the ball. As the Leeds striker lined up the ball Ramsey turned to Les Cocker, Clarke's coach at Elland Road.

'Will he score Les?' asked Ramsey.

'Put your mortgage on him.'

Calmly he slotted the ball into the back of the net, low, hard and to Viktor's left, as if he had been taking penalties for England all his life.

It was enough to settle a turgid game (it was 'the least impressive of the three matches played', noted Ramsey in his private report to the FA afterwards. 'England strived to find their rhythm and touch and were fortunate to win by a goal scored from a penalty.'[32]). England's progression to a quarter-final meeting three days later in Leon was assured. There they would meet the vanquished finalists of 1966, West Germany.

Given the traumatic prelude to the tournament, it may have been hoped that England's problems were over. It was an optimistic thought. Surprisingly, particularly since everything else had seemingly been thought through for once, the possibility of a quarter-final in Leon had been overlooked. No hotel rooms had been booked there and the only available accommodation was a roadside motel – Motel La Estancio – which the England squad found themselves sharing with the wives and girlfriends of the West German team. It seemed as if the age-old expectation that England merely had to turn up to win had prevailed again. To make matters worse, the Mexican authorities refused the England team permission to fly into Leon on account of the size of their aircraft, this despite the fact that the Germans had flown there just two weeks earlier. Ramsey was furious, bleating conspiracy theories, but it made no difference and his squad were forced to travel 170 miles by coach on bumpy roads while the Mexicans turned around the hotel issue to portray it as an implicit attack on their organisation.

On the coach was a stricken Gordon Banks. A day after the Czechoslovakia game Banks had reported a case of diarrhoea to Dr Neil Phillips. Phillips administered the necessary medication and sent him to bed. In his mind there was little to worry about: Allan Clarke had missed the Brazil game with a similar complaint, but had been fine in time for Czechoslovakia; likewise, Bobby Charlton and Keith Newton had reported the same symptoms a day earlier and both were okay. Indeed by the following morning Banks seemed much better as the team embarked on their journey to Leon. His woes were not over, though, and within an hour he was doubling up with stomach cramps. Phillips administered more medication while Banks's thoughts centred entirely on getting there, as he later put it, 'without disgracing myself'. On arrival, Banks was sent straight to bed and the team undertook a training session.

Back in England excitement was building to a fever pitch. In 1966 the majority of the press had shown enough restraint not to mention the war at every turn; four years on, most, but not all showed such enlightenment. The *Liverpool Echo* reported:

> England's World Cup convoy advances to the field of Leon today with the field marshal of football, Sir Alf Ramsey, wondering if the time has come to change his strategy and call up the artillery. While West Germany, encamped sixteen miles from here in a desert dug out that might have been a relic from Rommel, await the world champions, England have some thinking to do. [The Germans] are confident, almost arrogantly so . . . Walking around the one-horse, leather manufacturing town of Leon – the speciality is, aptly, gun holsters – one would think that the Germans had already won the World Cup, as well as the last one and the war.

If England expected in 1966, they positively demanded success four years later. Twenty-nine million had tuned into England versus Brazil – by contrast twenty-seven million had watched the World Cup final in 1966. More still were expected to watch the quarter-final.

In Leon there was some good news. By the Saturday evening Banks was much better and by the Sunday morning, the day of the match, he seemed to be back to normal. He had some breakfast and went through some stretching and catching exercises with Cocker. At ten, Ramsey named his team – with Banks in it – and the squad got ready to board the coach to take them to the ground for their noon kick-off.

But once on the coach, Ramsey sat next to Peter Bonetti. 'You're in,' he told him.

Banks had had another relapse and stayed at the hotel.

It was a blow but all the same England, it seemed, had little to fear. Bonetti had already played six times for his country, proving an able deputy to Banks and conceding just one goal in all that time. High on confidence having brilliantly helped Chelsea win the FA Cup against Leeds, he was, in the words of Hugh McIlvanney, 'by all acceptable standards of comparison among the best half-dozen goalkeepers in the tournament'.[33] It was a point validated by his Stamford Bridge colleague, Peter Osgood: 'Peter was the best professional I ever played with, bar none. He trained right, ate right, drank right, he was a good family man, never went out late, a model pro. He was second best in the world behind Banks.'[34]

When the two teams entered the Guanajuanto Stadium each could boast five veterans of 1966 on either side: Moore, Bobby Charlton, Hurst, Peters, Ball; Beckenbauer, Seeler, Höttges, Schnellinger and Overath in the German line-up. As in 1966 England wore red, the Germans white, though this time it was England who deployed a more conventional 4-4-2 formation against the Germans' 4-3-3.

The extra man didn't allow England to swamp the midfield, but they did possess greater pace on the break, which in turn gave them an early attacking edge. From one such attack, on thirty-one minutes, they took the lead. Mullery swept the ball out to Newton on the flank, and the full-back hurtled down the wing, with Mullery running up through the centre. Looking up, he chose not to play the obvious near-post cross to Hurst and, spotting Mullery continuing his run, swept a pass in space ahead of him, which the Spurs man took on the half volley, hammering it hard past Maier. It was his first goal for his country.

Things got even better at the start of the second half. Moore's tackle robbed Seeler of the ball, and he passed to Alan Ball who switched it to Hurst. Picking out Newton galloping down the right wing, Hurst played in the full-back whose far post cross was met by the head of Peters for England's second goal. Back home, a television audience of nearly thirty million went wild as Peters was congratulated by his team-mates and Ball ran around the Germans taunting 'Auf Wiedersehen! Auf Wiedersehen!'

On fifty-seven minutes Helmut Schoen brought on the pacy winger Grabowski for Libuda, who had been subdued by the impressive but tiring Terry Cooper. Ramsey also started warming up his own substitutes, Bell and Hunter. With another – seemingly inevitable –

match to play midweek, he had no intention of taking any risks with his first eleven in the soaring heat of the midday sun.

Almost immediately Lee was painfully caught in the groin by Fitchel's shot, causing him to double over in pain. Overath retrieved the ball and played it to Beckenbauer on the right, midway through the England half. He took the ball past Mullery and, with his options limited, stabbed a hopeful shot at Bonetti. It bobbled along the pitch and agonisingly slipped under the goalkeeper's body. With twenty-one minutes remaining Germany suddenly had a lifeline.

For one man the pressure became too much. Jack Charlton, who was watching from the stands, left his seat, left the stadium and walked away down the road, where he found a café and ordered a beer.

Back in the Guanajuanto Stadium, England still looked most likely winners. Ramsey called for Bell and, with the game into its last twenty minutes, brought him on for Bobby Charlton. 'I could hardly believe it was me who was to come off,' he said later. 'I was only disappointed in that I felt fantastic. It was so hard playing in Mexico, and when you did feel well you really wanted to enjoy it. I was full of running that day.'[35] Bell's introduction initially added some fresh impetus to England. From one of his early runs down the right he hit a cross, met at the near post by Hurst, who touched it past Maier but onto the outside of the post, and it rolled wide for a goal kick.

Ramsey then made his second substitution, bringing on Hunter to replace Peters and shore up the midfield. The substitute's first touch was not a good one, though, and the Germans won a throw-in. From it, Labone cleared but only as far as Schnellinger and the German defender lofted in a cross that caught the England defence square. Seeler, running backwards, lost his balance, but made contact with the ball which looped over the head of the stranded Bonetti and into the England goal.

In the Mexican café, the locals were not watching the match, but knew that their unexpected customer was *Il Calvino Divino*'s big brother. While he was sipping his beer a Mexican walked in and announced that West Germany had equalised. Jack, uncertain, thought they were teasing him and walked back to the stadium at exactly full-time. Seeing the scores at 2–2, he felt sick and knew then that England were going to lose.

After nearly seventy minutes, extra time had seemed an

inconceivable prospect, but here the two sides were, 2–2 after 90 minutes, the same as it had been in 1966. This time, however, it was the England players lying on the pitch. There was no standing, no psychological battle with the Germans.

After play had restarted, however, it looked as if the game was to be decided by that most dreadful of outcomes – the flip of a coin – as both teams battled gamely, but failed to make headway on either's goal. Not until just after the midway point in extra time did the game burst back into life. The fresh-legged Grabowski, a stern challenge for the tiring Cooper from the minute he first bestrode the field, left the Leeds full-back trailing in his wake but overhit his cross, which looped high over the danger area, though only as far as Lahr on the other side of the penalty box. He arced a header back across the face of the England goal, in between Moore and Labone, to the waiting Gerd Müller. Having done nothing all match long, Müller, scorer of 138 goals in five years of league football, including thirty-eight in the 1969–70 season, span to volley the ball past the helpless Bonetti for West Germany's third. Nobody could believe it.

England had eleven and a half minutes left to try and fashion an equaliser. Lee cut in from the byline to cross for Hurst, who hit the ball home, only to see that Lee had been adjudged to have taken the ball out of play; Bell was brought down by Beckenbauer in the penalty area but the referee played on and Ball shot wide from Hurst's nod down. None of it was good enough. England had been felled, and West Germany had wreaked their revenge.

After the final whistle Ramsey went around consoling his shattered players. 'He never said a great deal about what went wrong,' recalled Moore. 'He just went round trying to console this player and that player. He was more worried about consoling people than reasons.'[36] There was a minor pitch invasion by jubilant German supporters, one of whom trailed a banner saying, 'This is revenge for the robbery of 1966.'

Ramsey was unrepentant in the post-match press conference. 'He lost his last chance of a moment of grandeur,' recorded one Latin American journalist.

He was ill-mannered to Mexican officials and the press alike. He dismissed the German victory as a lucky one, saying their first two goals came from defensive mistakes. He said he had never seen England give away goals like that. He hinted that no tactical instructions from him could have averted defeat. All of this most of us believed to be true, but it was not for him to say it. It was as if he was disowning his team in defeat.[37]

Yet as Gordon Banks later put it: 'The Mexican press had done their worst to blacken our reputations both as footballers and private citizens. They had been antagonised by Alf's cold manner towards them and got their own back with a procession of wicked lies, exaggerations and innuendoes in their own newspapers.'[38] Indeed the response of the Mexican newspaper *Esto* said it all: 'The champions are dead. Go home England.'

Later, in his private report to the FA, Ramsey explained that the substitutions were an attempt to stabilise the team and ensure that nobody burned out. 'England were represented by the best players available and, indeed, were one of the strongest teams in the competition,' he wrote. 'The changes made were understandable when climatic conditions were taken into consideration. Thirteen players were used in each game and nineteen throughout the four matches.'[39]

Back at the hotel the stricken Banks was still watching the match in bed in his hotel room. There had been a one-hour delay on the broadcast and when his room-mate, Alex Stepney, came back England were still in front. His joy soon turned to sadness.

The rest of the players were meanwhile allowed to indulge in previously forbidden pleasures: drinking beer and swimming in the pool. Ken Jones, the *Daily Mirror* correspondent, went down to join them, and hunt out Ramsey. He found him in his chalet with the Thomas Cook representative, Cyril Broderick, and a clutch of champagne bottles.

'I don't know what to say,' said Jones.

'Do you want a drink?' asked Ramsey.

'Please.'

'Pour it yourself,' he said morosely, then looked at him. 'It had to be *him*. Of all the players to lose, it had to be him.'[40]

Back in England, Harold Wilson had intervened to resolve the printers' strike. 'It was a battle of wits, will-over and stamina,' wrote Albert Barham in the *Guardian*. 'And it was stamina which perhaps lost this game.' Other newspapers were generous about the Germans. 'West Germany emerge worthy winners,' said *The Times*. Even the *Daily Mail* echoed their sentiments. 'If it had to be, then better to lose to such fighters.' The *Sun*, on the other hand, chastised the 'Millionaires who threw away their fortune . . . Now for the big inquest.'

On the plane home Ramsey apologised to Bobby Charlton for taking him off. 'I was thinking about the next match. That was a mistake I shall always regret,' he said. 'Now I'd like to thank you for all that you have done for me and England.' Charlton knew then that it was the end of his England career. Twelve years, four World Cup finals, 106 appearances and a still unsurpassed record of forty-nine goals made him one of the greatest – if not the greatest – players to turn out for his country. He was vital to England and Ramsey. What would they do without him? Mexico didn't just mark the end for the Divine Baldy, it also meant the end for Newton, Labone, Jack Charlton, Bonetti, Wright and Astle.

At Heathrow Ramsey was asked if he was glad to be back. 'If you ask a stupid question, you'll get a stupid answer,' he barked. 'Leave me alone. I have had a very long journey and I'm tired. No autopsies.' Yet a press conference had already been arranged. 'I am rude,' he replied, when it was suggested that he was being uncooperative. 'They stick these things in front of me and so forth and so forth [waving angrily at the microphones and cameras], and I'm being rude? There isn't a word invented that would describe some of the people I've been confronted with and yet I'm rude.' Asked what he had learned from Brazil, who were on their way to winning the trophy, he replied 'Nothing.'

Four days after losing to West Germany Britain went to the polls. The day before the election *The Times* gave Labour an 8.7 per cent lead over the Tories; and the *Daily Express* and *Daily Telegraph* both put it at 2 per cent. The *Sun* backed Labour: 'Not because the government has been a scintillating success – it hasn't. But because all things considered we think that Harold Wilson has a better team.'

After the defeat Wilson had telegrammed Ramsey offering his 'congratulations on the magnificent effort England put up . . . Hard luck, but well done.' Little did he know then that he too was set to receive an avalanche of commiserations. Making a mockery of the polls, Edward Heath's Conservative Party upset the odds and ended six years of Labour rule. Members of the outgoing Labour government would later joke that Ramsey had lost them the election by bringing off Bobby Charlton. As in 1966 football had had a decisive impact on British politics.

Dejected England players, meanwhile, were still coming to terms with the defeat. Some had stayed on in Mexico; others, like Bobby Charlton, had returned and were watching the remainder of the tournament on late-night television. 'We lost,' mused Charlton, 'but I still believe we are the best team in the world, despite everything. No team worked harder or longer. We were better prepared than anyone.'

☺ ☺ ☺

Along the length of Fleet Street sports editors, piqued by Ramsey's abrasiveness and peeved by the capitulation against West Germany, began to sharpen their knives in preparation for the scalp of the England manager. The public, however, voted with their feet. Five months after the Mexican adventure, 93,000 people turned out to watch England's first match since the summer, a friendly against East Germany on a grimy November night. England ran out 3–1 winners with goals coming from Francis Lee, Martin Peters and Allan Clarke.

Since the last round of matches in Italy, the European Nations' Cup had been renamed the European Championship. Rather than quali-fiers being decided on the basis of two years' Home Championship results, England were put into a four-team group with Greece, Malta and Switzerland, with the winner progressing to a two-legged quarter-final ahead of the semi-finals and final to be staged in Belgium. England were expected to qualify easily, but as Geoffrey Green warned on the morning of England's opener away in Malta in February 1971: 'Malta may seem a small obstacle in the big world of football but even a gnat can bite and raise a bump.'[41] England struggled to a 1–0 victory. 'Certainly Malta played above themselves,' said Ramsey afterwards. 'The conditions of the pitch were obviously difficult, but I was disappointed that we failed to rise above them. Nine times out of ten the run of the ball was untrue. Even so we could have done better, though in the circumstances, I would hesitate to criticise any of the players.'

Against Malta, Ramsey made four new caps, and in the eighteen months following Mexico would hand out a total of twelve debuts. While there was no doubting the value of these men to their First Division sides it would be difficult to compare the likes of Chris Lawler, Larry Lloyd or Alan Brown favourably with the class of '66. In the midst of this transitional period, perhaps the most significant debut given by the England manager was to Leicester City's goal-keeper, Peter Shilton. Born in Leicester in 1949, Shilton was an individual with an obsessive dedication to his craft: as a child he had hung from banisters to stretch his arms and increase his reach, and later his devotion to the training ground was legendary. He had emerged through the ranks to make his league debut for Leicester aged only sixteen, and so good was the teenager that when a year later Stoke City made a comparatively small offer of £52,000 for the man he was understudying at Filbert Street, they felt able to accept the bid. The prodigy replacing the seasoned pro is a perennial tale in football, but this time it rightly attracted attention – Shilton had succeeded the greatest of them all: Gordon Banks. By his twenty-first birthday it only seemed natural that Shilton should be shadowing Banks on the international stage too. Though not the tallest of goalkeepers, Shilton commanded his penalty area with supreme self-assurance, plucking crosses from the air with an almost arrogant coolness. A reflex goalkeeper, his agility and famous long reach made him one of the best shot stoppers in the country and, eventually, the world. In the early 1970s, however, Shilton's finest days were still ahead of him.

Despite the slow start against Malta, England eventually qualified for a two-legged European Championship quarter-final with their old foes West Germany, to be staged in April and May 1972. They also won the 1971 Home Championship but were failing to convince, failing to entertain and the mantra, worryingly, seemed to be to win at all costs. While Shilton was one for the future, none of Ramsey's other new boys could claim to be an unqualified success, with the exception of Derby County's elegant centre-half, Roy McFarland. Perhaps of even greater concern was that Ramsey's stalwarts – Peters, Moore, Ball and Hurst – were not only struggling at club level, but replicating their declining form in the white of their country. Ramsey's England were on the wane, and were heading for something they had never experienced: a sound thrashing.

If England's match against West Germany in Leon had marked the start of a steady decline, the meeting between the two countries in what was billed as 'the Match of the Century' two years later marked just how far England had fallen. They had eight survivors from the thirteen who had played in Leon, and still had five from 1966, but perhaps crucially no longer had Bobby Charlton or a figure of his ilk to occupy Beckenbauer, whose marauding runs had previously been curtailed by his having to shackle Charlton. Likewise, there was no longer an anchor of the calibre of Stiles or Mullery to break up attacks in midfield. Yet West Germany were also missing men too. Players of the calibre of Schnellinger, Vogts and Overath were all absent and the team as a whole had not played well since Mexico. Their manager, Helmut Schoen, bemoaned the fact that both teams wouldn't be at full strength.

From the outset it was obvious that England were in for a difficult afternoon. Their build-up was slow, ponderous and lacking in spontaneity, while Germany's playmaker, Günter Netzer, ran everything: tilling the flanks, dictating from the middle and proving deadly at set pieces. Ramsey paired Moore and Hunter in defence, but without a midfield destroyer it effectively gave Netzer the freedom of the park. 'He hated being marked tight,' recalled Moore. 'But in the circumstances he found at Wembley his skills and brain could take any team to the cleaners. He was just allowed to carry the ball from his own half at our defence.'[42]

West Germany took the lead on twenty-six minutes when Uli Hoeness robbed Moore of the ball and hit a shot past Banks. Unexpectedly, given the deluge of German attacks and level of their possession, England held on to a single-goal deficit and even equalised through Lee. West Germany's class, however, showed through in the final stages: Moore's clumsy tackle resulted in a penalty, which Netzer converted; then Müller finished expertly to bring the scores to 3–1. 'The magnitude of our performance was really just like a dream,' Beckenbauer said later, 'I have never shared in a finer West German performance. Everything we wanted to do we did. The moves, the idea and the execution all happened.'

The following day those tabloid knives were out for Ramsey: 'The axe is out for Ramsey', 'Germans in takeover', and 'The man ten years behind the times' were just three of the vituperative headlines.

'Sir Alf Ramsey's team selection is the starting point for the witch hunt,' said the *Sun*. 'Never before has his loyalty to men like Bobby Moore, Geoff Hurst, Martin Peters and Alan Ball been so sorely tested by poor club form.' The *Sunday Express* asked:

Have the methods of the only man to win the World Cup for England become as dead as a dinosaur? . . . does not Ramsey's ponderous system based on prodigious work rate, no wingers and endless top speed running also burn up players? . . . A crushing load is placed on England's full-backs . . . 'I learned nothing from Mexico,' said Ramsey incredibly . . . well, West Germany certainly did!

Letters rained into the *Sun*. 'Sir Alf is out of date with his team selections and seems more concerned with his personal record as England manager than with English football's future,' wrote P. Marshall of Oxford. 'The England performance against West Germany was the worst show of football put up by our national side for many years,' claimed A.J. Harris of West Bromwich. 'If Sir Alf cannot or will not recognise the new talent available he should resign and make way for a new manager.' 'England won the 1966 World Cup but they sacrificed the greatness and spectacle that made British football the finest entertainment in the world,' said J.J. Purdie of London, 'either Alf brings back ball players and fast wingers or he should fade out of the international scene.' D. Tweedale of Blackpool was seemingly a sole voice of dissent amidst the onslaught: 'England lose and everybody gets at Alf Ramsey. Perhaps there could be a few changes. But take away those three mistakes and one goal for England and then what would the papers have said?'

Many of the calls from fans and journalists were for Queens Park Rangers' maverick forward, Rodney Marsh, to be given a proper chance by Ramsey. Championed as the heir to Bobby Charlton, like many of his contemporaries the weight of expectation heaped on him was ludicrously high. Putting it bluntly, Marsh was simply not in the same class as his illustrious predecessor. He was, nevertheless, included to play in the second leg two weeks later, the solitary allowance to flair in a hard, workmanlike team that battled and bruised the Germans without once looking like it had come for anything but to escape defeat – this despite the necessity of winning by a three-goal margin to progress. The game ended 0–0 and the heavily marked Netzer complained, 'Every Englishman except the goalkeeper has autographed my legs.'

In a newspaper interview around this time Joe Mercer pointed to some of the problems Ramsey was facing. He spoke of a growing gulf between his generation and the new showbiz type players, who had never known the maximum-wage era, as more senior players had – or at least nearly – done. He also said that the longer a manager stays with a club, the further he grows apart from his players. 'You suddenly realise that you're dealing with players thirty years your junior. How can you hope to understand them? They have entirely different values, an entirely different lifestyle.' The same was, of course, true of Ramsey, who had begun to lose many of his old guard. Not only that, but he had difficulty in relating to the new era of 'celebrity footballers' who wore their non-conformity with pride. These were the days of what one contemporary described as 'coffee house jugglers' – court jesters, who would play a few tricks on Saturday and live the high life the rest of the week; it was a time when George Best was in the drunken death throes of his playing career; Jimmy Greaves, retired, and tragically, a washed-out alcoholic in an east London bedsit; but others – Stan Bowles, Frank Worthington and even, occasionally, his beloved Bobby Moore – were becoming as well known for their antics off the field as on it. The over-riding sense for an old-timer like Ramsey was that players were getting too big for their boots. When, for instance, Ramsey told Rodney Marsh before a game with Wales that if he didn't work harder he'd pull him off at half-time, Marsh responded: 'Christ, at City we only get a cup of tea and an orange!' Ramsey never picked him again.

Ramsey's predicament worsened on 22 October 1972. A day after Stoke had lost to Liverpool at Anfield, Gordon Banks, the reigning Footballer of the Year, visited the Victoria Ground for treatment on the minor injury he had picked up a day earlier. Driving home he was dawdling behind a slower car. He went to overtake, but came up against an unseen vehicle coming from the opposite direction. 'There was an almighty bang,' Banks wrote. 'There was a sound of glass shattering. Then there was nothing.'[43]

He had more than 200 stitches from his face to his scalp, a further 100 micro-stitches inside the socket of his right eye and around the periphery of his retina. He was partially blinded in his right eye and never played at the top level again.

Ramsey's drunkenly uttered words in Leon thirty months earlier – 'it had to be him' – rang truer than ever.

To qualify for the 1974 World Cup finals in West Germany, England had to top a three-country group made up by Wales and Poland. It was a harder task than many gave them credit for, and it was also England's first World Cup qualifying campaign since they had battled their way to Chile in 1962. A winning start was nevertheless attained in November 1972 with a 1–0 victory over the Welsh in Cardiff. Two months later they played the return at Wembley. Wales had three First Division reserves, three Second Division players and one from the Third in their line-up: 'We're on a wing and a prayer,' said their manager Dave Bowen before the game. Yet England were crab-like and uninspired against this assortment of journeymen and triers and, ultimately, slightly fortunate to come away with a 1–1 draw. 'It is a terribly disappointing result,' said Ramsey. 'I don't think a team can have worked any harder in their efforts to win. The Welsh team made it extremely difficult for us to play. They played above themselves and certainly gave the best performance I have seen from a Welsh team.' Perhaps he should have checked his list of excuses: he had said almost exactly the same words after the narrow win over Malta.

If England had been the proverbial champagne cocktail in the five years from 1965, since Mexico they had been rather more like a warm, weak martini. When they travelled to Scotland on St Valentine's Day 1973 they had scored just thirteen goals in their previous eleven matches. Yet on the day of Bobby Moore's 100th cap, England surprised everybody by streaking into a 3–0 lead in the first quarter-hour, and eventually emerging 5–0 victors. 'The difference between success and failure in football is paper thin,' said Ramsey. 'We took our chances, which hasn't been happening lately.' The 1973 Home Championship was then won with a 100 per cent record, but if Ramsey thought that his, and England's, luck was changing, he was mistaken.

Next England journeyed to Prague for a friendly with Czecho-slovakia (1–1), then on to Chorzow for a crucial World Cup qualifier with Poland. Eight years earlier England had come to this latter-day coliseum for a final, crucial World Cup warm-up match before going on to win the competition; now they needed a draw or win to stand them in good stead for a place in Germany. The day before, Ramsey sought to curry favour with an increasingly antagonistic press. 'The England team will not be announced at present,' he told them. When asked if it was being delayed because of injuries or as a tactical move, he replied sniffily: 'Do I have to give reasons?'

In the event, his line-up – a defensive 4-4-2 formation – indicated where his priorities lay: a point. Such hopes took a sucker punch when Poland took the lead after just seven minutes from a Bobby Moore own goal, a lead they doubled just after the interval when Lubański stole the ball off the unusually ponderous Moore and hit it low and hard past Shilton. Ramsey defiantly and obtusely refused to bring on an attacking substitute and the defensive formation lacked the invention or ideas to improve the scoreline. Shortly before the end Alan Ball clashed with Cmikiewicz and was sent off by Schiller, the Austrian referee. It rounded off a rotten evening for England, one that was so unlike Ramsey's England: undisciplined, bereft of ideas, and with Moore – utterly dependable on so many previous occasions – culpable for both goals.

Again the headlines were vociferous in their condemnation: 'England's horror show', 'Alfred you're up the Pole' and 'World Cup is a sick joke' were festooned in forty-eight point high letters across the back pages. 'The nation awoke yesterday morning with a sense of embarrassment, if not shame, after TV watching that World Cup qualifying match against Poland,' wrote the *Daily Mail*. 'It is time Sir Alf came out of his ivory tower, stopped talking in riddles and told the people who pay his wages what the hell he's trying to do.'[44]

Not only did Ramsey have the press on his back, but he had increasingly lost the confidence of many within the FA. Its vice-chairman, Professor Sir Harold Thompson, was a maverick figure within Lancaster Gate and as renowned for making enemies as he was friends. Born in Wombwell, Yorkshire in 1908, he was a distinguished Oxford scientist and teacher who made exceptional contributions to international science. He founded Pegasus, a combined Oxford and Cambridge XI, who twice played in the FA Amateur Cup final. An FA Council member from 1941, he would rise through the ranks of committees and sub-committees to the highest position of all – that of Chairman, in 1976. He was a hugely influential figure and had, of course, played a key role in blocking Walter Winterbottom's appointment as FA Secretary a decade earlier. Known affectionately as 'Tommy' to his friends, but perhaps more aptly as the 'atom bomb' by those who were not, it was not difficult to see why he and Ramsey did not get on.

One of the things Thompson sought was greater professionalism in the way the FA was run. Part of this came down to public relations and Mexico had been a PR disaster. In 1972 he wrote a confidential paper entitled 'The Function and Policy of the FA' which was circulated around the upper echelons of the organisation. In it, Thompson wrote:

> The wave of euphoria which followed England's World Cup victory nearly six years ago has long since passed . . . [While] the enormous popularity of the game is still beyond argument, its image has become rather blurred, almost tarnished. This was attributable to a number of factors including the bad behaviour of players, crowds and supporters, prima donnas in our leading teams, high wages and transfer fees, and *the idiosyncrasies of the England team manager.*[45]

The witch hunt was on.

The FA's counterparts at the Football League hardly made Ramsey's cause any easier. With England's do or die return fixture against Poland to be staged on Wednesday, 17 October 1973, Ramsey had called for the previous Saturday's fixtures to be postponed to give him a full week to prepare. The Football League, however, wouldn't accommodate him. Alan Hardaker, the League Secretary, was typically obtuse in his assessment: 'If England do lose this game the country is not going to die. It will be a big thing for about six weeks and then everyone will forget about it.'[46] The decision provoked fury in the England camp and criticism from across the English football fraternity. Brian Clough spoke for most people with any interest in the national side when he wrote in his Sunday newspaper column that the Football League had 'cheated' the public by not postponing the league programme the Saturday before.*

Ramsey was further undermined by the attitude of various members of the fourth estate. 'I honestly hope to see England get beaten,' wrote Peter Batt (who had compared Ramsey to Churchill three years earlier) in the *Sun*. 'Euthanasia is the only course left to put us all out of our misery. We must blow soccer up and build on the ashes.' The rotter journalist born in Mexico three years ago had taken spite to another level.

Some of the *Sun*'s readers may well have agreed with Batt's assessment, but when the big night came there was no doubting where the

---

* Clough would actually be forced to resign his post partly on account of the pressure put on him by the Derby board after his outburst. It wouldn't be the last time old big 'ead's big mouth would get him in trouble . . .

Wembley crowd's feelings lay. 'In all my years of covering sport I had never seen or heard anything to compare with that experience,' wrote Vic Ziegel of the *New York Times*. 'It was a statement of nationalism beyond anything I'd known, and few American sports watchers would have understood.'[47] One hundred thousand people packed the famous stadium and watched a side full of the sort of attacking players – Mick Channon, Tony Currie, Martin Chivers and Allan Clarke – for whom they had wished for so long.

From the outset England flung chances at the Poles as if their football lives depended on the outcome. Unfortunately, the Polish goalkeeper Jan Tomaszewski – previously dismissed as a 'clown' by Brian Clough – was in inspired form, getting a palm, fist or other body part in front of everything that was thrown at him. He was, wrote *The Times*, 'like a windmill caught in a gale as he flapped his arms and feet in every direction. But with it all he made four dazzling saves which clearly made him the Polish hero of the occasion.'[48] Even when he was beaten, after nineteen minutes, the goalpost rescued him. Unbelievably the interval came with the scores still level. The unthinkable, however, was still to come.

On the hour, Hunter backed out of a challenge with Gadocha, Hughes mistimed his tackle, the ball was played inside to the unmarked Domarski, who hit it low past Shilton. Wave upon wave of England attacks followed, and they drew level six minutes later when Peters was pushed in the area and Clarke coolly buried the penalty.

But England still needed another goal. Currie struck the crossbar then Clarke, Channon and Currie were each thwarted by Tomaszewski's heroics. As the game entered its final ten minutes it was in dire need of fresh legs but Ramsey, always a reluctant gambler and turned by the experience of Leon even further against substitutions, stuck with his original picks. Bobby Moore, for once alongside his manager on the bench, frantically tried to persuade Ramsey into bringing on a substitute. 'It's getting desperate Alf,' he said. 'Don't you think it would be a good idea to get a left-sided player on?'

'I've pushed Norman forward on that side,' Ramsey replied. A minute later Moore tried again.

'It's too late,' said Ramsey.

The crowd began to scream for a change. 'Stick a left-sided player on,' said Moore. 'We might get them down that side. It's never too late. Get Kevin Hector on for two minutes and see what he can do.'[49]

With precisely two minutes to go on the clock, Ramsey relented and brought Hector, a prolific goal-scorer with Derby County, on in place of the ineffectual Chivers. Almost immediately he made a difference, seeing his goal-bound header from England's twenty-third corner of the match cleared off the line. But it was too little, too late. England were out of the World Cup.

'I don't think I have seen a better performance by a visiting country at Wembley,' Ramsey said afterwards. 'You have seen a great performance by England. I do not think they could have played better.' Asked about his future, he said: 'I have to work to live, my life is football.' Ramsey told the players: 'You couldn't have done any more. I'm sorry you're not going. Pick up your heads. Let me do the worrying.'[50]

Almost exactly twenty years earlier, defeat by Hungary had prompted a period of soul-searching. Now, an exit from the qualifying stages of the World Cup set in motion another re-evaluation about the future of the England team. 'A disaster, but not the end of the world,' said Bill Shankly. 'When you have a disaster you have to rebuild brick by brick, as they rebuilt San Francisco after the earthquake. The only thing to do now is get a young team together for the future.' 'It's how we react now that counts,' added Joe Mercer. 'We, the professionals in the game, must take a careful look at the situation and decide where we go now. We learned from the Hungarian humiliation. This wasn't humiliation. It was a freak.' Tony Waiters, the Plymouth Argyle boss and one time Ramsey international, argued for an overhaul of English football:

> The result could snap people out of their complacency and allow us to have a critical look at our game – not just the players who faced Poland but the whole structure of football. This was not a defeat just for eleven Englishmen but for English football. If we see the present situation as an opportunity to examine everything in the game from the top shelf to the schoolboys, England can become a top soccer nation once more.

Jimmy Armfield, now Bolton Wanderers manager, continued in a similar vein: 'The game illustrated once again that we have never been good at taking chances. Where do we go from here? I believe that if we are to have any success in international football we must develop our ball skills.'[51]

A month later England played Italy at Wembley. There were recalls for Osgood and Moore who, for his 108th and final international match, played as a sweeper. In Italy's tenth consecutive match without conceding a goal, they seized a 1–0 victory – but England had most of the attacking play, with nineteen corners to Italy's one and only the inspired form of Dino Zoff several times rescuing the Italians. Yet the conclusion drawn by most members of the crowd was that England lacked not mere luck, but imagination and verve. Moreover, they lacked the sort of players who could produce it.

In February 1974 an FA sub-committee was set up 'to consider our future policy in respect of the promotion of international football' under the leadership of Sir Harold Thompson with Bert Millichip, Brian Mears, Dr Andrew Stephen and League President, Len Shipman. Ramsey saw just where this consultation was leading – namely his sacking – and pre-emptively laid out his own three-point plan 'Club or Country', asking for three days' preparation for friendlies, a week for competitive games and at least one international get-together during the season.

At the beginning of April 1974 Ramsey led England to Portugal for a friendly and took the unprecedented step of handing out debuts to six players: Phil Parkes, Mike Pejic, Martin Dobson, Dave Watson, Stan Bowles and Trevor Brooking. England drew 0–0, but it was clear that Ramsey's thoughts lay in the future. Indeed, on 28 April, when Ramsey announced his summer squad for the Home Championship and a tour of Eastern Europe, it was replete with novices and youngsters.

He never got the chance to use them. A day later, Thompson's committee announced its findings which included 'a unanimous recommendation that Sir Alf Ramsey should be replaced as England team manager'. It added: 'The FA wishes at this time to record its deep appreciation for all that Sir Alf has accomplished and the debt owed to him by English football for his unbending loyalty and dedication and the high level of integrity he has brought to world football.' A 'close associate' of Ramsey at the FA HQ said: 'He was badly shaken. He has cleared his desk and said he will not be coming back.' Later Ramsey described it as 'the most devastating half hour in my life . . . I stood in a room almost full of staring committee men. It was just like I was on trial. I thought I was going to be hanged . . . typically I was never given a reason for the sack.'[52]

The committee hadn't been unanimous. Len Shipman said, 'I am very upset. It is very disturbing. But what can you do when your hand is forced?' Brian Mears agreed: 'I'm ashamed to say that I allowed myself to be forced into it. I left that room thinking that I'd done a wicked thing. I've never forgiven myself.[53] Thompson, despite his avowed intention to 'professionalise' the FA and bring it into line with the public's expectations of a modern organisation, had only been interested in sacking Ramsey, not finding a replacement. Joe Mercer was given caretaker charge.

Sir Alf Ramsey was, wrote Geoffrey Green, 'always much his own man; in personal terms he was curt, at times almost to the point of rudeness – frequently to the foreign press – autocratic, distant, a dictator behind a mask'. Yet he was also, and above all else, a players' man. 'Few could call Ramsey a friend because friendship didn't come easily to him,' wrote Ken Jones, who knew him better than most journalists. 'But no player who turned out for England under Ramsey's management ever uttered a bad word about him or had cause to question his loyalty.'[54] 'We all loved playing for Ramsey and he managed to produce a club-style atmosphere within the international set up,' eulogised Alan Mullery. 'The players were as close as team-mates, we knew each others' styles and outside the regular team there were others bursting to play.'[55]

It was irrefutable that he had been treated badly by the FA – his salary alone pointed to that. At the end of his England days it was only £7200 – about a third of what some First Division managers were earning – and his golden handshake (he called it 'a tissue') was just £8000, plus a pension of £1200. Everton's Harry Catterick, who had been 'moved upstairs' a year before, by contrast, received £50,000 over two years.

Ajax, Athletic Bilbao and Second Division Aston Villa all reportedly made advances for him to take up managerial positions, but nothing materialised thereafter and the offers started to dry up. It was not for another twenty months, in January 1976, that he returned to football, when he joined the Birmingham City board, although it was in a non-executive capacity and he had no say in team affairs. 'It seems Birmingham City have taken on Sir Alf to do nothing except be there,' said one local newspaper. His sojourn at St Andrews lasted thirty months, and thereafter, unbelievably, he never had another role in the game, eventually falling out of love with the sport he had given so much to.

A quiet, decent man, a stranger to almost all he met, but loved and respected by those who knew and worked with him, he had been the mastermind of the England football team's finest hour and many great afternoons besides. 'Have I failed?' he pondered shortly after his dismissal. 'Remember that England had never won a World Cup until 1966.' Nor have they since.

10

KEEGAN'S RUN

IT WAS 4 MAY 1974 and an hour into the ninety-first FA Cup final. Liverpool, favourites, league runners-up, a side full of stars, had subdued the underdogs, Newcastle United, but were without a goal to show for their dominance. Bit by bit, however, the screw was being turned. Then Liverpool's full-back, Tommy Smith, burst down the right. Looking up he pumped a cross into the Newcastle penalty area. Brian Hall threw himself at the ball and failed to make contact, but it fell kindly for Kevin Keegan, Liverpool's twenty-three-year-old forward. Turning sharply, he hit a clean shot on the spin that bulleted past the Newcastle goalkeeper Iam McFaul and into the top corner of the net. Liverpool finally had their 1–0 lead. 'This was the beginning of the end,' reported Geoffrey Green, 'and the end of the sparring.' Fifteen minutes later, Steve Heighway doubled the advantage, Bill Shankly danced a jig on the touchline, Liverpool had all but won. Victory, however, was still to be crowned. Two minutes from the end, Keegan ensured that it was with a magnificent third goal. First, he sent a beautifully flighted crossfield pass to Smith. The right-back played the ball to Hall, who touched it back in a one-two; Smith passed it to Heighway, who passed it back. Up the flank the full-back surged, before playing in a diagonal cross, and there was Keegan, in a flash, rounding off the move he had instigated. 'Keegan 2 Heighway 1' roared the crowd; 'Liverpool 3 Newcastle 0' beamed the Wembley scoreboard in confirmation.

Winning the 1974 Cup final completed a remarkable three years in the life of Kevin Keegan. The period had begun with him plying his trade with lowly Scunthorpe United, where his performances had attracted the attention of Bill Shankly who brought him to Anfield in May 1971 for a fee of £35,000. Compact, energetic, prodigious and diligent Keegan might have been, but not even the

Liverpool manager could have envisaged the impact his new signing would have.

Dedication to his craft, bucket-loads of self-confidence and relentless efforts to improve his shortcomings were the defining characteristics that would elevate Kevin Keegan to greatness. In many ways he was a man of his time: clever, canny, hard-working – the very sort of individual who, a few years later, would come to succeed in and epitomise Margaret Thatcher's Britain. While, say, Bobby Charlton or Tom Finney had dripped with natural ability, Keegan became the best English player of his generation through a mixture of hard work, self improvement and resolute belief in his own destiny. Those who had written him off had said that he was too small, yet he learned to jump; that he was too slight, but he built himself up; that there was no role for him to play, yet he crafted himself a position (a sort of old-fashioned inside-forward, remoulded for the orthodoxies of the modern game). None of this is to say that on his own merits Kevin Keegan wasn't a very good player – he was. However, by the 1970s, natural ability and instinct alone were not enough for a footballer to succeed at the highest level. What set Keegan apart from the 'coffee-house ball jugglers' and playboys of his era was his dedication to succeed: devotion off the field led to divinity on it.

Given such qualities, Keegan should have been tailor-made for Sir Alf Ramsey's England, where the prodigious were frequently pre-ferred to the prodigal. In happier times he probably would have been, but Keegan's ascent with Liverpool coincided with the sad final days of Sir Alf's reign, when the pressures of the job offered scant opportunity to introduce new players gradually into his set-up, as he had done so successfully with the likes of Geoff Hurst and Martin Peters. Twice he tried Keegan in the senior side – both times against Wales in World Cup qualifiers – but he failed to gel successfully with Martin Chivers and Rodney Marsh in the England attack. Later Keegan suggested Ramsey hadn't known where best to play him and, consequently, had never rated him. More likely was that Ramsey had simply never known how to best use him in a side struggling through a transitional period.

As with his first couple of caps Keegan's third international appearance came against Wales. This time, of course, the squad fell under the caretaker stewardship of Joe Mercer, who had greeted his players with the words: 'I didn't want this bloody job in the first place!' After his international playing career had ended in 1946, he had left Everton for Arsenal and enjoyed his most successful years as a Highbury veteran, captaining the Gunners to Championships in 1948 and 1953, and the FA Cup in 1950. A broken leg in 1954 saw him switch to management, first with Sheffield United, then Aston Villa, and later Manchester City where, with Malcolm Allison, he master-minded Second and First Division title wins, as well as FA Cup and European Cup Winners' Cup successes. In 1974, after a spell as Coventry City's General Manager, Mercer was in semi-retirement and his appointment as England's caretaker boss had been a surprise. His cheerful presence provided a welcome antidote to the troubled final days of the Ramsey regime and his managerial style had the welcome whiff of a bygone era. 'I call 'em all footballers,' he once said of his football philosophy. 'If they're good enough, I pick 'em. If not, I leave 'em out.'

Although it was expected his caretakership would only last the duration of the summer, it was a period that would take in some seven matches: three home internationals, a Wembley friendly against Argentina and a three-match tour of Eastern Europe. With Bobby Moore's distinguished international career at an end following a record-breaking 108, mostly exemplary, appearances, the Liverpool full-back Emlyn Hughes was given the captaincy. Brash, sometimes pugnacious and often a rabble rouser, the squeaky-voiced son of a rugby league international, Hughes' leadership style could not have been further removed from his illustrious predecessor, but he got his captaincy off to a winning start by leading England to a 2–0 win over Wales at Ninian Park. Kevin Keegan notched his first goal for his country, Stanley Bowles the other. Four days later at Wembley, Keith Weller's goal was enough to see off Northern Ireland. But the following Saturday, England were unable to tie up the Home Championship, falling 0–2 to Scotland at Hampden.

The Scots flew off to West Germany for the World Cup finals, leaving England – winners just eight years earlier – as mere warm-up material for other finalists. Argentina visited Wembley for the first time since the infamous World Cup quarter-final eight years earlier and so fresh in their minds were memories of Rudolph Kreitlein's performance that the Argentinian FA had only agreed to the friendly on the condition that one of their countrymen officiate. Just one survivor from 1966 – Roberto Perfumo – made either side, and he made explicitly clear that he had neither forgiven nor forgotten the great 'fix'. Shortly before half-time he became embroiled in a tussle with Hughes and Ruben Glaria intervened, punching the England captain; Hughes went down but the referee, surprisingly (or perhaps not), didn't see fit to send off his compatriot. England, by then, were a goal to the good having put in an impressive, attractive first-half performance imbued with the sort of attacking impetus and flair that evoked memories of Mercer's own playing days. Ten minutes after half-time England doubled their advantage when Colin Bell's shot crashed off the underside of the bar and was met by Frank Worthington who hooked the ball home.

Within two minutes, Argentina were back in the game. Ayala broke down the right and, losing his marker, sent in a searching cross that Shilton could only palm away. Meeting the ball was Mario Kempes, who rifled it past England's goalkeeper, to make the score 2–1. Despite the setback, England continued to search for a third, decisive goal in the face of escalating gamesmanship from the South Americans. First Bell's volley hit Argentina's otherwise oblivious goalkeeper Daniel Carnevali in the chest and bounced harmlessly away, then Keegan went close and, at the other end, Alec Lindsay cleared a goalbound shot from Ayala off the England goalline. With the match drifting towards an England victory, it needed a crucial intervention to change its destiny and a minute from the end the referee stepped up. A left-wing cross was floated in to Kempes, Hughes tackled him easily but, with all the grace of a ballerina floating to earth, the South American striker fell. It was a beautifully executed, perfectly timed dive, but it was the cue the referee had been looking for. He pointed to the spot, Kempes converted and the remainder of the match was played out to the familiar chorus of 'Animals! Animals!'

England then flew out to East Germany to begin a three-match tour of Eastern Europe. The positive performances of this youthful-looking, reinvigorated England team continued with a 1–1 draw in front of a crowd of 100,000 in Leipzig. Next, a 1–0 victory over World Cup qualifiers Bulgaria in Sofia was followed by a journey to Yugoslavia for the last leg of the tour where, at Belgrade airport, there were chilling echoes of the Bobby Moore incident in Bogotá. After several players had been caught playing around on the baggage conveyor, the innocent Kevin Keegan was hauled away by a group of zealous guards and presented with a list of trumped up charges that included the 'sexual assault' of an air-hostess on the flight from Sofia, the 'assault' of a security guard, disturbance of the peace and causing an obstruction. Still mindful of having abandoned Moore to his fate, this time the squad refused to leave the airport without Keegan. Shuttle diplomacy between FA officials, embassy staff and Yugoslav bureaucrats eventually secured Keegan's release and he emerged bruised, but without charge. Two days later he played a starring role in an exhilarating match and his diving header fifteen minutes from the end secured a deserved 2–2 draw.

Again Mercer's men had impressed and the players enjoyed the caretaker's tutelage. 'A wonderful friendly atmosphere prevailed throughout the home internationals and the tour,' Hughes said.[1] Yet there was no question of Mercer taking the job permanently. Sciatica, which affected the middle of his right leg, left him in agony for much of the time and – on a longer term – put the uniquely pressured role beyond his capabilities. Although his approach had been popular, his team's decent results should be viewed in the context that they only came against opposition who were looking to warm up gently for the World Cup. While the players were allowed to play almost as they wished under his charge, as Hughes pointed out, 'it's doubtful that England could ever have approached World Cup or European Championship matches with such a cavalier attitude'.[2] In any case, debate about Mercer's future was spurious: by the time the squad had returned from their tour England had a new manager.

Donald George Revie was the most controversial figure in English football. Loved by an Elland Road faithful to whom he had brought an unprecedented glut of success during the 1960s and early 1970s, he was loathed by practically everyone else in the game. To his followers he was a charismatic, unorthodox genius who would do anything for his players to bring victory, and for whom his players would do anything to help achieve that success. Others viewed his every move with scepticism: distrustful of his methods and disdainful of his rough and ready teams, his many detractors saw Revie as representing the ugly face of English football. But by 1974 he had evolved into the most successful, and probably best, manager in the country.

To reach such heights of fame and notoriety, Revie had come a long way from his humble beginnings and even his own relatively successful playing days. Born on 10 July 1927, Revie was the son of an unemployed joiner in depression-hit Middlesbrough. He grew up under the shadow of Ayresome Park at a time when Wilf Mannion was starting to provide a ray of light to the impoverished town's football followers. Like most of his contemporaries he was as a boy fixated by the magic of football, but at the age of twelve he happened upon the key influence behind his football development. Playing for a junior side – Middlesbrough Swifts – he came under the charge of Bill Sanderson. A train driver by day, Sanderson had an obsessive interest in the tactical minutiae of the game: he held regular meetings in his council house living room; prepared dossiers on Swifts' local rivals; and in formulating tactics showed more nous than most First Division managers. Sanderson's ideas were to remain deeply engrained on the adolescent's mind. Revie left school at fourteen, worked as a bricklayer for two years and joined Leicester City, for whom he made his debut at sixteen. With Leicester, then Hull City, he was an intelligent, diligent, but not especially quick player. A transfer to Manchester City brought him to national prominence, specifically for his mastery of a deep-lying centre-forward role modelled on the revolutionary Hungarian system made famous by Nandor Hidegkuti. Using the so-called 'Revie Plan' City won the FA Cup in 1956 and he was voted Player of the Year (1955) and won six England caps. A move to Sunderland came in November 1956 and then, two years later, though he may not have recognised it at the time, the crucial move in his career: a £14,000 transfer to Leeds.

Leeds United were a nothing sort of club in 1958. They had never won any trophies (save for a Second Division title in 1924); they had never been noted for anything save for mediocrity in their inter-mittent brushes with the top flight; a ramshackle Elland Road was testimony to the second fiddle football played to rugby league in the city's affections; and worse still, its greatest player, John Charles, had just left for Juventus. The sense of despair deepened in 1960, when they were relegated to Division Two. The following year they seemed to be in freefall, plummeting towards Division Three, nearing bankruptcy, and with crowds sometimes as low as 8000. When Jack Taylor quit the Elland Road hot seat in March 1961, devoid of ideas how to bring deliverance the Leeds board gambled and took the radical option, appointing Revie, their thirty-three-year-old captain, as player-manager. It seemed to be one final attempt at salvation, but Revie saved Leeds that season and thereafter revolutionised them. Obsessively, he built a sense of community at Elland Road: he changed the Leeds strip to all white (like the European champions Real Madrid), involved the players' families to heighten the sense of togetherness, and would famously organise social nights for the players involving rounds of carpet bowls, dominos and games of bingo. The bonding of his squad would be completed each Thursday when he would give them a soapy massage.

On the field Leeds were a brutal, win-at-all costs side imbued with a relentless will to succeed. Often they took the game to extremes: they were notoriously hard tacklers, feigned injuries, harassed officials, pinched, kicked and hit opponents. Revie himself was not above such gamesmanship. Implicit approval came by way of a lack of criticism for such heavy-handedness; sometimes, it was alleged, he used his own underhand methods to determine results.* Revie's Leeds were hated, but they were winners. From the brink of relegation to the Third Division in 1961, they won the Second Division title in 1964, and almost won the League and FA Cup double in their first season back in the top flight. Over the next decade they never finished lower than fourth in the league, winning the title in 1969 (with a record 67 points and without defeat in their last 28 matches) and 1974; were runners-up a further four times; won the League Cup in 1968; and the FA Cup in 1972, and were runners-up three times. In Europe they won the Fairs Cup in 1968 and 1971, were runners-up in 1967 and also lost out in the 1973 European Cup Winners' Cup final. 'We want to win everything there is to win,' said Revie's long-term captain, Billy Bremner, of the obsessive quest for success. 'And we will not rest until Leeds are acknowledged around the world as one of the greatest teams of all time.'

Yet on his appointment as England manager, Revie had taken just two days to clear his desk and leave Elland Road. He would reveal at

---

*In 1962 he was accused of trying to bribe opponents by the Bury manager, Bob Stokoe. Tellingly perhaps, Stokoe never retracted his accusation, and Revie never sued. A decade later, after Leeds lost the title by losing the last game of the season to Wolves, similar accusations surfaced when three Wolves players claimed to have been offered £1000 apiece to relax their efforts. FA and police investigations proved inconclusive, but the taint of scandal never went away.

the press conference: 'I made the first move. They did not contact me. I fancied being England manager.' Loyalty, that core value of Alf Ramsey, was never one shared by his successor. Several times in the years leading up to his England appointment he had come close to leaving Leeds after embroiling himself in secret negotiations with other clubs. Equally, tellingly, he never let the truth get in the way of his outpourings. The FA had in fact approached Revie through an intermediary, initially making contact through Tom Holly, a *Sunday People* journalist who relayed Revie's eagerness for the job to the Chairman of the International Committee, Dick Wragg. Obviously Revie could hardly go revealing his new employer's subterfuge, but why the blatant lie? Maybe it was a symptom of modern football, but Don Revie's struggle with the truth and the expectation that as England manager he would act with probity would eventually undermine both him and his managership.

Despite the controversy that dogged him wherever he went, in July 1974 Revie's appointment as England manager can only be seen as a real coup for the Football Association. Not only was his record at Leeds one of repeated success, he was also the sort of charismatic individual who would bring to Lancaster Gate the sort of increased professionalism and commercial awareness Sir Harold Thompson had so long sought. Indeed, Revie and the FA Secretary, Ted Croker, were soon involved in discussions with Austin Reed, Courtaulds, the Milk Marketing Board and Stylo boots about various endorsements, and a deal with Revie's contacts at Admiral to take over from Umbro as official kit suppliers substantially boosted the FA's coffers. England's new manager also drew up a list of ideas to boost flagging international attendances, which were also worked upon. His efforts on the commercial side were, however, commensurate with his wages. His annual salary of £25,000 was three times that of his predecessor, though for his efforts in waking the FA from their commercial sleep he was probably justified in saying that he was worth it.

Charged with the task of reversing English football's malaise, Revie sought to inspire the Wembley crowd ahead of his first international with Czechoslovakia on 30 October 1974 by insisting that 'Land of Hope and Glory' song sheets were distributed before kick-off. Cannily cautious, the new manager warned the England fans to expect no easy task: 'I don't think that people who come along to Wembley expect miracles, but they might be expecting something special. I hope that you remember the old saying in football that you only play as well as the opposition will allow you. Nevertheless, there is a lot of skill in the side and I hope it's a win for England.' There was no radical overhaul of the team that had done so well on the summer's tour. Queens Park Rangers' midfield tyro, Gerry Francis, was the solitary new cap and his clubmate, Dave Thomas, a winger, made the bench. A crowd of 85,000 welcomed in the Revie era, but after a flurry of excitement in the opening stages, with Bell, Channon and Worthington frequently combining to make chances for each other, the game began to slip towards a stalemate. Goalless at half-time and bereft of inspiration in the second half, with twenty-five minutes to go Revie pulled off his masterstroke. Thomas came on for Worthington, Trevor Brooking for Martin Dobson, and England were transformed. Obstructed when trying to tease his way past Vojtech Varadin, Thomas, within five minutes of the switch, won a free-kick from which Channon headed home. Ten minutes later it was 2–0: Channon stole down the left, played a diagonal pass across the penalty area, Keegan dummied intelligently and Bell broke in from the rear to score a wonderfully crafted goal. Almost immediately, the Bell–Channon partnership combined again. This time Bell set Channon free down the left and his cross was met beautifully by the head of Bell, who had run at full speed to meet it. 3–0 and England supporters were able to leave Wembley with smiles on their faces.

Nearly five months later, punctuated by a goalless draw with Portugal and a squad get-together, England met their great foes and newly crowned world champions, West Germany, at Wembley. In the hope of seeing revenge for Netzer's destruction three years earlier, a full house turned out. The Germans were without Müller, Grabowski, Overath and Hoeness in attack, and Breitner and Netzer at the rear. 'We are the world champions only on paper,' Franz Beckenbauer pointed out the day before, but for all their inexperience they could still count on eight men who had played a part in winning the World Cup. 'This is one of the most experienced German sides I have seen in my life,' Revie countered. 'We are the experimental team.'[3] Indeed it was. Revie made no fewer than seven changes to the side that had been unable to break down Portugal, bringing back Alan Ball, Colin Todd, Malcolm MacDonald and Keegan. Ball, in his tenth year as an England international, was promoted to the role of captain, a decision that prompted outrage in some quarters owing to his poor disciplinary record. 'For Revie to choose a man like this with his record – however good a player – is a bloody disgrace,' said Walter Johnson, MP for Derby South. Ball, he added, was 'a bad example'. Revie made light of the controversy. 'I read that there was scuffling in the Commons over the recent finance bill, but I don't think it's my place to comment on that . . . I would never dream of trying to show him how to do his job. I do what I think is best for English football in my knowledge. Ball won't let me down or disgrace England.' Revie also handed debuts to Ian Gillard, Steve Whitworth and, most interestingly, Alan Hudson. Stoke City's midfield wizard had several times (while still a Chelsea player) taken Revie's Leeds apart – a rare achievement for any player – and his individual skills frequently earned him comparisons to the likes of Johnny Haynes. In the dull and dreary drudgery of the First Division his talent provided a rare light and his elevation to the England team was seen by many fans as long overdue. Could his unique talents raise England out of the mire of mediocrity?

Emphatically yes, at least against these West Germans. In England's 100th Wembley international, Hudson did to the visitors exactly what Netzer had done to them in 1972, controlling the midfield, orchestrating attacks and majestically destroying his opponents. He was, wrote Geoffrey Green, 'a tour de force, a mercurial player, poised, assured, polished as a nugget and even at times arrogant'.[4] Netzer recognised the talent, if not the face: 'Who is this man Hudson,' he asked, 'and for whom does he play? He *can* play.'

England took the lead in the twenty-fifth minute: Hudson cleverly floated in a free-kick from the right, Bell met it on the volley, and the ball – assisted by a deflection – crashed past Maier. Keegan – the game's other outstanding presence – then set up MacDonald, whose bullet-like effort was parried by Maier, and the Newcastle forward then chipped narrowly over after Hudson had threaded him through. Midway through the second half, England doubled their lead. Mick Channon flicked the ball out to Ball on the right, he marched to the byline, cut inside and sent in a teasing cross to the far post, which MacDonald rose to power home. Thereafter England controlled the game, and nearly added a third in the final minute when Keegan's chip hit the bar. 'Keegan,' commented the *Daily Mirror*, 'showed all the aggression, intricate skill and willingness to go in and finish that in the past he has reserved for Liverpool. It was the finest game this little man has ever played in an England shirt.'[5]

Revie was ebullient. 'This is the best performance by an England team since I took over as manager,' he beamed. 'I cuddled everyone of my players when they got back to the dressing room. They proved we have the players in this country who can really play. There is a lot to do yet, but at least the foundation is there.' He picked out Ball ('I could hear him from the touchline shouting encouragement non-stop for the ninety minutes'), Todd ('his reading of the game was so quick and alive') and Hudson ('proved he has the arrogance and individual flair of a top class player') for special praise. 'That was only for starters,' proclaimed Tony Waddington, Hudson's manager at Stoke. 'I have seen the main course many times and he can play even better than he did at Wembley.'[6] When England played Cyprus in a European Championship qualifier at Wembley a month later (MacDonald scored all the goals in a 5–0 rout) Hudson retained his place in Revie's line-up, but thereafter never played for his country again. Later, he claimed that Revie held the bitterly contested 1970 FA Cup final (even though he had been injured and not played in Chelsea's victory over Leeds) and his failure to conform to Revie's rounds of carpet bowls and bingo against him. 'I was playing against West Germany and Leeds United rolled into one,' he would write in his memoirs.[7] This may well have been true, but Hudson, like so many before and since, seemed illogically drawn to bad habits and, ultimately, self-destruction. Most likely Revie simply viewed him a disruptive influence – he wouldn't be the first – and thereafter his multitude of football gifts flickered in the wind before dying under a fug of excess and argument, leaving English football to lament another lost talent.

England won their return match with Cyprus 1–0 in Limassol on 11 May 1975 before embarking on the Home Championships. For Keegan it was a traumatic time. He had once innocuously expressed sympathy for Ulster's Catholics, which earned him a death threat in the run-up to the tie at Windsor Park. In the event he played, and alongside him, Colin Viljoen, the brain that made Bobby Robson's Ipswich tick, was given his first cap along with Dennis Tueart, Manchester City's potent winger. England, however, were unimpressive and the game fizzled out in a goalless stalemate. Four days later at Wembley, they drew 2–2 with a Wales side that came within five minutes of recording their first win on English soil in thirty-nine years until David Johnson restored parity with a late far-post header.

Keegan, who had walked out on the squad in a sulk after Revie had 'rested him' without proffering an explanation, was restored to the side three days later when Scotland were the visitors to Wembley. Within just seven minutes of kick-off England had raced into a two-goal lead after goals by Gerry Francis and Kevin Beattie and were thereafter able to relax somewhat – although more goals came. Francis, who dominated the game with an exquisite range of passing over both short and long range, set Bell up to score with a twenty-yard shot shortly after half-time. Francis then claimed his second and England's fourth with a deflected free-kick, midway through the second half, and the 5–1 rout was completed by Johnson, who fired home from close range after Keegan's header had been palmed onto the bar.

It was the eighth consecutive year that England had won (or shared) the Home Championship and it brought to an end a satisfactory first season for Revie, which had consisted of five wins, three draws, eighteen goals scored and just three conceded. The new manager had continued the refurbishment of the England team begun under Ramsey, and set in place by Mercer, introducing much-needed new talent and bedding-down others. While the international careers of England's key men had begun in the Ramsey era (the likes of Alan Ball, Colin Bell, Colin Todd and Keegan), others had since emerged under Revie's charge. Keegan's Liverpool team-mate Ray Clemence was a tall commanding goalkeeper – Anfield's finest since the legendary Elisha Scott – who had supplanted Peter Shilton and would vie with him for the number one jersey for the remainder of the decade. The Sunderland centre-half, Dave Watson, was a stern, influential figure at the heart of the England defence, resolute in the tackle, dominant in the air. Gerry Francis brought the sort of sharp edge to the England midfield lacking since Stiles's heyday, but enhanced it with the sort of gritty elegance that often brought comparisons to Alan Mullery. Also adding finesse to the England midfield was West Ham's Trevor Brooking, a polished, composed player, an accurate and imaginative passer and one with an eye for goal. Impeccably mannered, articulate and good natured, 'Hadleigh' (as he was known by his colleagues) was to emerge as one of English football's finest ambassadors. Southampton's Mick Channon had first come to prominence under Ramsey but attained a regular berth under Revie after the goals began to dry up for Malcolm MacDonald. A well-rounded figure, a consistent player and scorer of goals, he was one of England's brightest performers then and over following years.

Ostensibly Revie was building well for the future, but behind the scenes all was not well. The tang of controversy that had first clung to him at Elland Road had followed him to Lancaster Gate. He was admired but never universally respected, as if he confounded the expectation of what an England manager should represent: loyalty, honesty, integrity. His team-building exercises – usually consisting of carpet bowls, indoor golf or some other game – were widely disliked by many of the players who branded them patronising and anachronistic. Often they proved self defeating anyway as half the squad would skulk off to bed rather than sit through a round of bingo. 'You don't have to be playing particularly well or score many goals,' went the joke amongst some of the players. 'But if you are putting well and can win a few houses of bingo, you've got a great chance!' The other famous procedure Revie carried over from his Leeds days – the dossiers on opponents – were disliked too, couched in overly technical language and laced with too much attention to detail as they were; what was the point, as one player later argued, of a dozen pages on a Cypriot amateur? Suspicions were also aroused by Revie's apparent obsession with money. After MacDonald had scored his famous five goals against Cyprus – only the second man to do so since the turn of the century – Revie summoned him to one side. 'The television and radio boys want to see you,' he said, adding, 'don't worry about the fee . . . leave that to me.' An incredulous MacDonald told him not to worry about it.

What grated most, though, was Revie's obsessive changing of the line-up. It wasn't so much that the England manager refused to persevere with players in the way that Ramsey, sometimes obstinately, had done; more that he was irrational in his selection. In excess of five changes, even to a winning side, was not uncommon. As Keegan put it: 'I could be captain for one match and not be sure of my place in the side in the next, which was a diabolical situation for a player to be in.' Ironically Revie's changing of the team was wholly at odds with his time at Leeds, when he would even play unfit players. He was also seen as being too close to certain journalists, particularly the *Daily Mail*'s

Jeff Powell and the *Sun*'s Frank Clough, who would frequently print important information before it was officially announced. 'We'll read Frank and Jeff in the morning to see if we're in the team,' went another joke. 'With Alf Ramsey, it was more difficult to get out of his side than in, but it was completely different with Don Revie,' Alan Ball would recall. 'Even the Leeds players in the squad were scratching their heads to explain what was going on. No one could understand it.'[8]

In late August 1975 Ball himself was to fall prey to Revie's inconsistent selection policies. Captain in the 5–1 win over Scotland, he was not even included to face Switzerland in a friendly in Basle at the start of September. Worse still, Revie never deigned to tell him of his omission and the first Ball heard was from a journalist calling to get his reaction. In the following morning's post a letter arrived from the FA telling Ball that he was no longer considered part of the England squad. It contained no explanation, nor even Revie's signature, and was signed *in absentia*. Ball was furious, Revie unrepentant and unwilling to offer an explanation, and so the England career of the last surviving member of the 1966 team came to a shabby end.

Ball may have derived some *schadenfreude* from the subsequent decline of Revie's England. Against the Swiss a promising start after goals from Keegan and Channon (Keegan also missed a penalty) dried up, and England were ultimately lucky to squeeze through as 2–1 winners. More disappointing was their 1–2 defeat in the European Championship qualifier in Czechoslovakia, which left England needing a win in Portugal to keep their chances of qualification alive. When they were unable to gain more than a 1–1 draw in Lisbon they became reliant on the unlikely event of Cyprus beating Czechoslovakia in Limassol; but the Czechs strolled through 3–0 victors, England slipped out of contention, and their conquerors eventually went on to win the finals.

As England moved into 1976, again without a major tournament to look forward to, Revie brought in ten new caps over the duration of two games with Wales (a friendly in March and the Home Championship match in May), both of which England won, as they did against Northern Ireland (4–0 on 11 May). Yet when Ray Clemence let an innocuous Kenny Dalglish shot slip through his legs and give Scotland a 2–1 win at Hampden (and the Home Championship) four days later, it seemed proof positive that England had not moved on nor even halted their decline.

Revie's growing discomfort was not eased by his relations with pompous and simpering FA officials, not least Sir Harold Thompson, who had succeeded Dr Andrew Stephen as FA Chairman. Their relationship had started in a congenial enough manner, but Thompson was keen to cut down on Revie's expenditure, which had risen substantially since the Ramsey era. A year after his own appointment Revie had admitted in a letter to his chairman: 'There is still a lot of work to be done with individual skills and teamwork in the very limited time we have the England players together. Our four day get-together . . . I felt was money very well spent as we got through more tactical work and dead ball sets.' Revie went on to request another training camp at the end of the season. Thompson's reply paid lip service to Revie's 'gruelling and complex regime' and the effort he was putting in, but made reference to the FA's increased expenditure, and was non-committal about 'unnecessary extravagances'.[9] Inevitably the get-together never happened.

The dispute soon became personal. At an official dinner, when Revie and his wife were sat on the same table as Thompson, the England manager objected to Sir Harold's habit of referring to him by his surname. 'When I get to know you better, Revie, I shall call you Don,' Thompson responded with a sneer. Revie retorted: 'When I get to know you better, Thompson, I shall call you Sir Harold.' Thompson did not like that, nor did the FA councillor C.D. Bullen also present ('I was at once left with the impression he felt he was more important than the position he was appointed to do,' he unctuously wrote in a letter to the chairman).[10] Just two years after his high-profile succession of Ramsey, rumblings of discontent about Revie began to reverberate around Lancaster Gate.

Revie had other problems too. The qualification group for the 1978 World Cup finals in Argentina was absurdly tight: just one country would qualify from a group consisting of England, Finland, Luxembourg . . . and Italy. It was a stupid system and made the fixtures between England and Italy not just significant, but do or die.

England's manager could, however, take some encouragement from a 3–2 friendly victory over the Italians in New York. That came a fortnight before England kicked off their World Cup qualifiers in Helsinki on 13 June 1976, with a 4–1 win. Pearson, Channon and Keegan (2) claimed England's goals. In October, England took the return match 2–1 at Wembley in front of 87,000 people. In theory it set them up nicely for the following month's crunch match in Rome, but in practice the boos that rang around at the final whistle said much about how the support were coming to regard the way that Revie's England played its football.

At the heart of the problem was Revie's constant tinkering. It still seemed as if he didn't know his best side nor even how they should play. Even in the run-up to the crucial World Cup qualifier with Italy he played a cat and mouse selection game. Would he, for instance, deploy a playmaker, like Stanley Bowles; or an anchor, such as Brian Greenhoff? In the end he plumped for the worst of both worlds and used both. Not only did that upset the balance of the team, so too did the six changes he made to the side that had beaten Finland. The result was a mess of a line-up that was lacking experience and cohesion. In defence, for example, Dave Clement, Roy McFarland and Mick Mills had never played alongside each other before; Italy, by contrast, had seven Juventus players in their starting line-up.

From the outset, England set about containing and frustrating the Italians. Yet they were up against the masters of *catenaccio* and, despite having more attacks in the first half at least, they lacked the soaring power and intensity of the hosts' forays. Bettega, Tardelli and Causio each tested Clemence and gave the pocket of England followers cause to quiver. Then, on twenty-six minutes, a free-kick went the Italians' way: Causio nudged the ball to Antognoni and his fiercely driven shot was deflected by Keegan under the despairing dive of Clemence. From then on, England seemed ready to cut their losses and all but set out to keep the deficit at a minimum. Indeed, it took the Italians until the seventy-seventh minute to add a second, decisive goal in a move that showed the abundant gulf in skill between the two sides. Benetti and Causio combined on the left wing, the latter took it past Mills with consummate ease, centred low and hard, and Bettega headed waist-high past Clemence. Several times in the closing stages Italy almost added to their tally but McFarland's experience repeatedly rescued his team-mates.

England had been unconvincing, incoherent and their per-formance should have yielded a heavier defeat. Afterwards, Revie almost accepted that England's World Cup destiny lay not against Italy at Wembley the following autumn, but in the amateur hands of Luxembourg or Finland. 'Naturally, I am disappointed. I thought we played as well as could be expected,' he said. 'It's now out of our hands. We can only hope Finland or Luxembourg upset the Italians. The goals came at critical times, especially the first.'

If Revie had any doubts about the size of his task, they were blown away when England met Holland at Wembley in a friendly on 9 February 1977. Again, he made drastic changes to his line-up: five alterations to the team that had fallen to Italy, including a debut for Birmingham City's exciting young forward, Trevor Francis, who could lay claim to being the most eagerly anticipated English goal poacher since Greaves. 'If he is going to be a good international, he has got to show me 75 per cent of his ability in his first match,' said Revie before the game. But not even Francis's inclusion was able to stop what followed. From the opening kick, Holland ripped England apart, dominating possession, wowing with their skill and making a nonsense of the solitary method of English attack – hoofing and hoping that Keegan, one of the shortest players on the field, would somehow get on the end of it. Just ten minutes in Johnny Rep walked past Keegan and called, 'Kevvy, this is the worst England side I have ever seen. You have problems here.'[11]

Indeed they did. Johann Cruyff did to England what Netzer and Puskás had done at Wembley before him: he destroyed them. 'Cruyff was brilliant,' Jan Zwartkruis, the Dutch manager said. 'He was like the Scarlet Pimpernel: You saw him here, you saw him there, you saw him everywhere . . .' The final scoreline – 2–0 to Holland – flattered England in a match where the sheer gulf in ability dealt a cataclysmic blow to the dwindling confidence of the hosts. Norman Fox, *The Times*' new football correspondent, likened the defeat to that earlier defining one against the Hungarians in 1953. 'If anything,' he added, 'this latest embarrassment was even more revealing than that first opening of our eyes. At once it deflated and inspired. It increased existing doubts over the whole range of English football and, because it was watched by 90,000 at the stadium and a wider television audience, it highlighted the inadequacies for all to see.'[12] Revie himself admitted that it would take ten to fifteen years for English football to reach such a zenith. 'There is no point in kidding ourselves,' he said. 'We just couldn't cope. It was a lesson in control and passing and not giving the ball away. It was not just a lesson to the England international side but to all of English football. This was one of the best international performances I have ever seen.' Zwartkruis concurred: 'The Dutch game is different. It is a fantasy. We use our imagination. We create. We take risks.'

Against Luxembourg a month later Revie made six changes and, though at times England looked disjointed, they ran out 5–0 winners. Yet the old problems resurfaced in the Home Championships. England scraped past Northern Ireland 2–1, but then lost to Wales at Wembley for the first time, falling to a Leighton James penalty. In a television interview Revie stated in unequivocal terms that he had given no thought to resigning:

> You have just got to be big enough and strong enough to stand up and be counted when things are not going well. Everyone in the country is ready to judge you on the last result . . . It has been suggested I will be regarded as a failure if England do not qualify. I would not agree. I think I have given something to the game and five defeats in twenty-six matches is hardly failure.'[13]

Perhaps if England had beaten Scotland the following Saturday things may have turned out differently for Revie. Maybe, if the eventual nature of Scotland's victory had been less vitriolic, Revie's mind might not have set so firmly on the conclusion that his was an impossible job. If 1967 marked the year that the Scots invaded London, 4 June 1977 was the day they sacked Wembley. Details of the game itself are almost immaterial: Gordon McQueen headed home Asa Hartford's fortieth-minute free-kick to give Scotland the lead; Kenny Dalglish doubled it after the interval; and three minutes from the end Trevor Francis was hauled down in the Scotland area and Mick Channon converted the resultant penalty. On ninety minutes the sound of the Hungarian referee's whistle marked the signal for a large part of Scotland's 30,000 followers to make their way onto the Wembley pitch. They ripped up the turf, danced around the penalty areas and snapped the goalposts. 'Behaving very badly very well' had been the order of the day ten years earlier in central London; now they celebrated England's 'humiliation' in the self-styled 'home of football' in front of the world.

This author's own father had travelled down from Liverpool to support England with his Scottish Uncle Bertie and several of his mates, and been in the unusual position of seeing events from the Scottish part of the Wembley terraces. On the journey back, at a motorway service station, Bertie – a sort of cross between Rab C. Nesbitt and Arthur Daley – pulled up his battered Cortina next to a brand-new Volvo estate and got out at the same time as the Volvo owner, a cerebral-looking man with a pristine moustache, tweed jacket and kilt. Eyeing Bertie's car and its intoxicated occupants (and my subdued father) dubiously, he asked in a cut-glass Edinburgh accent: 'Did ya go to the game today lads?'

'Aye,' responded Bertie, and gave him a detailed itinerary of his pre-match misdemeanours, which centred mostly on boozing and baiting their hosts.

'And did ya go on the pitch lads?' he asked, still looking at the Cortina with a hint of suspicion.

'Oh aye,' responded Bertie, who without a second thought gave an account of various transgressions. (My father had waited in patient misery for his elders on the terrace.)

'And did you steal any of the pitch?' asked the Volvo owner.

'Och noo.'

'That's a shame,' he responded. 'Wid yers like some?' he asked, opening his boot to reveal a substantial hunk of the Wembley centre circle.

If my father, in the midst of his long miserable journey home, could see the funny side, Revie almost certainly couldn't. England had to fly out immediately for a three-match tour of South America – a dry run ahead of the following summer's World Cup finals, a tournament for which it was looking less and less likely that England would qualify. Indeed there was the very real prospect that the Home Championship humiliation might deepen. Yet the England manager would not be flying out with his team: Les Cocker was taking charge of the side when they played Brazil in Rio, while Revie was in Helsinki watching the Finns' qualifier with Italy. Afterwards he would fly directly to Buenos Aires and rejoin his squad ahead of England's friendly on 12 June.

Or so everybody thought. In March, Revie had been privately approached by the United Arab Emirates Football Association about the prospect of his taking over as national coach and developing the game across their kingdoms. It was the sort of multi-faceted role that Walter Winterbottom had once enjoyed at Lancaster Gate – albeit with tax-free personal terms that would offer him wealth beyond his dreams. Revie had turned them down flatly, stating that he had to focus on England's qualification for the 1978 World Cup finals. Something, somewhere down the line, however, caused him to change his mind. After watching Italy emerge victorious in Finland (and deepen his predicament), instead of flying straight to South America, Revie had journeyed in the opposite direction, in disguise and under an assumed name, to Dubai where he held brief, top-secret talks about the earlier offer. He then flew back out, directly to Argentina.

Under Cocker England had gained a creditable 0–0 draw with the Brazilians by defending stubbornly and methodically, although Stuart Pearson and Trevor Francis had ultimately been unable to finish the game's best chances. Revie, however, had other things on his mind. On meeting up with the party in Buenos Aires he had demanded a meeting with Dick Wragg, the Chairman of the International Committee. Without mention of his clandestine negotiations in the United Arab Emirates, he told Wragg that he believed there to be a conspiracy in the FA to oust him, that it was making his position untenable and that he would agree to go quietly on payment of £50,000 compensation, justified on the basis of improved gates at Wembley. This perceived conspiracy centred on the FA's 'attempts' to replace Revie with the Ipswich Town manager, Bobby Robson, allegations that they and Ipswich subsequently denied vigorously.* Wragg discarded Revie's claims out of hand, but privately discussed the situation with other members of the FA hierarchy, including Sir Harold Thompson.

In the short term, Revie turned his attentions to playing matters. In front of a largely hostile Argentinian crowd, England took an unexpected lead when Stuart Pearson flicked home Channon's near-post cross. The South Americans upped the tempo and twelve minutes later levelled the scores when Bertoni curled a free-kick past the grasp of Clemence. The scoreline remained the same, but the antics of the South Americans revealed that little had really changed since Rattin's heyday. Ten minutes from the end, Trevor Cherry tackled Bertoni and as the Leeds player pulled away, the Argentinian turned and hit Cherry in the face, knocking out his two front teeth.

*Robson himself has never given any indication that there was any basis for the claims, yet given the way that Revie himself had been approached in 1974, it was not beyond the realms of possibility that the 'feelers' had been put out.

Barreto, the Uruguayan referee, consulted his linesman, and then, unbelievably, sent off both men.

Three days later, in Montevideo, against an appalling Uruguayan side (whose own manager admitted that he expected to be beaten by 'four or five goals'), England drew 0–0 in an encounter that was surprising only for the fact that Revie, for the first time as national manager, named an unchanged England team. The squad flew home with some pride restored, although Kevin Keegan, who had just agreed to a £500,000 transfer from Liverpool to SV Hamburg, sensed that all was not right with his manager. 'On the flight home, I sensed that something was afoot with Revie,' he wrote two years later. 'I had felt a closeness to him ever since my walkout, and I was one of the players in whom he confided. I guessed that he wanted to get out of the job; I didn't realise that, in his own mind, he was out already.'[14]

Indeed Revie's mind was made up, but having had his efforts to extract a pay-off from the FA rebuffed, the England manager went in search of an alternative source. In Fleet Street he found it. The *Daily Mail*'s Jeff Powell arranged a reported £20,000 deal for Revie to tell his story to add to the £60,000 annual salary and signing-on fee he would receive from the £340,000 six-year deal he was about to sign in the Gulf.*

At Lancaster Gate, Sir Harold Thompson sought to clarify Revie's position. Having heard Wragg's account of what had happened in Buenos Aires he tried to meet the England manager at the FA's summer conference on the weekend of 24 June, but Revie was continually busy, then left early. Next he missed a meeting with Thompson on 4 July at Bisham Abbey and thereafter avoided subsequent attempts by Thompson to get hold of him. What would Thompson have said had he met Revie? Correspondence hints that the FA Chairman may well have been willing to come to some sort of compromise to allow Revie's departure (and save the FA a considerable amount of money if and when they sacked him when the seemingly doomed qualification programme concluded). A letter to Thompson dated 30 June 1977, from the International Committee member, Peter Swales, is ambiguous, but reading between the lines

---

* In addition to this he was to receive accommodation, a car, medical care and air travel for him and his family.

hints that the FA may have been willing to sit it out to see if Revie lessened his demands to be released. 'I have, of course, strong opinions regarding the Don Revie affair – but would certainly prefer to air them to you personally rather than in letter form,' he wrote. 'Your idea of being noncommittal at this stage is certainly the best. However, I think the matter needs discussing amongst whoever you decide at the earliest opportunity.'[15] Either way, Revie's hard-nosed machinations were viewed with disdain, as if he belonged to a different world to his predecessors, Ramsey and Winterbottom.

Thompson wasn't to get the chance to meet Revie. A week after he had dodged his appointment at Bisham Abbey, the England manager flew out to Dubai via Switzerland and Athens with Powell, who had left two sealed envelopes at the *Daily Mail* offices. One contained the story of Revie's decision to quit, the other gave details of his move to the Middle East. Copies were delivered to the Football Association that evening (11 July), but arrived after its headquarters had shut for the night. Revie's employer first read about his resignation in the *Daily Mail* the following morning.

Initially Revie claimed that the pressures of being in a job when 'nearly everyone in the country seems to want me out' were simply too unbearable for him and his family. Being England manager had simply brought 'too much heartache to those nearest me'.

But in his letter to Sir Harold Thompson he was rather more scathing:

You and your committee are aware of the many reasons I have found the job intolerable. I was aware of the difficulties when I accepted the post and did not expect it to be an easy job. I realised that help and co-operation from all sections of the FA would be necessary if we were to progress in present day football and I naturally assumed that this would be given. This was not the case. The job of England manager is a difficult enough one when everyone is pulling in the same direction. It is an impossible task under the present set up.

The constant criticism I have had to withstand has not only affected my wife and family but has also, I fear, rubbed off on the players. They have been magnificent. Many of them have been upset on my behalf and have tried too hard to get results for me, and the pressure has sometimes produced the wrong results.

In addition to all these facts, it has been brought to my notice that enquiries have been made of another manager and his club concerning the England job.[16]*

In the following day's *Daily Mail* he attributed England's failures to his being the veritable child in a sweet shop:

> On reflection I was too conscious of public opinion, too keen to satisfy people. All the critics have their favourite players and I wanted to give them all a go . . . men like Alan Hudson, Charlie George. It was a mistake to keep changing the side to give players like that a chance. The day I took the job, I was excited by the prospect of having the pick of the country. But I'd been spoiled for choice at Leeds and I realised there are no more around like Billy Bremner and Johnny Giles. As soon as it dawned on me that we were short of players who combined skill and commitment I should have forgotten all about trying to play more controlled attractive football and settled for a real bastard of a team.[17]

It was a valid point. Over the course of twenty-nine internationals, on five occasions Revie had made seven changes to his line-up, six times he made six, five times four, and only one or two on five occasions. Ironically, of course, it wasn't until his last match in charge that he named an unchanged side. 'His biggest problem,' Mick Channon diagnosed, 'has been that he has not had a settled side. He did everything he could for the players and it's worth more to play for England now than when he became manager. He couldn't have done more for us in that respect.'[18] Likewise he suffered the same problems as Ramsey: he had no top-class hard man; he had lost the gritty Gerry Francis to serious injury; beyond Keegan and Hughes he had no real leaders; nor did he have one single player – as Ramsey had Moore, and Winterbottom Wright – on whom he could rely unfailingly.

Over the days that followed, details emerged about Revie's fabulous tax-free salary.† 'I will return to England and find some part-time involvement in football,' he boasted, 'perhaps as a consultant. I will

---

* The FA have always maintained it was short and terse – 'It is with deep regret that I tender my resignation as England team manager to take effect forthwith' – presumably as a public relations cover-up.
† By contrast the British tax system was almost punitive, with a ruinous top rate of 83 per cent meaning Revie would have to have had a contract worth £2 million to earn a similar wage.

travel to the great sporting events of the world . . . the major golf tournaments, the Olympics, World Cup finals – whatever takes my fancy.' He claimed that he had turned down big money offers from Barcelona, Atletico Madrid, Roma and Everton. A series of sycophantic articles saw him try and justify his defection. 'I am not pretending we're poor,' he told Powell, 'but I'm not the wealthy man people try and make out.'[19] The reality was that the more he talked about his earnings the more that any sympathy he might have still had eroded. A survey of national earnings published the same week that Revie was complaining about his 'meagre' £25,000 annual salary reported that teachers earned £90 per week; busmen £71; nurses £65; and farm workers just £46.[20]

In recession- and strike-hit Britain, his gloating left a bitter taste, not least at Lancaster Gate. Thompson wrote back to him on 18 July, 'I had the impression that you had been well paid, had received liberal expense allowances, and certainly the FA has never before spent such a large sum on the general preparation and costs of an England team squad.'[21] Revie ignored him.

The jilted chairman, meanwhile, plotted his revenge. Thompson liaised with Chethams, the FA solicitors, to find out what legal recourse the FA had against Revie, but the lawyers advised against proceedings. The FA, they said, was essentially powerless to force Revie to 'see out his contract'; FIFA had no jurisdiction over him; and in terms of demonstrating financial loss 'there is none I can envisage'. They suggested that Thompson let the matter rest and 'issue a dignified statement to the effect that having carefully considered the matter and the legal implications and costs involved, they prefer to get on with the problem of endeavouring to qualify for the 1978 World Cup and allow Mr Revie to carry on in the hopes that he will have greater success in his new vocation than he had in the past'.[22] Instead, Thompson, explicitly ignoring their advice, summoned Revie to an FA disciplinary hearing. He refused to turn up, saying that they no longer had any jurisdiction over him – which they didn't. Revie was lording it up in the sun, earning more than £1000 a week tax-free: why would he want to go back to have his knuckles rapped by a man who didn't even address him by his first name?

Still they leant on him and, perhaps surprisingly, more than a year later, on 18 December 1978, he agreed to face his former employers at a disciplinary hearing. At the same meeting the FA hauled in Alan

Ball, who had wreaked some revenge on Revie after claiming in his autobiography that in 1966, while still Leeds manager, Revie had paid illegal inducements to Ball – amounting to £300 – in an effort to sign him from Blackpool. With this charge and his 'desertion' to face, Revie's QC, Gilbert Gray, argued that the Football Association could not ban his client from football as they had no jurisdiction over him while he was in the Middle East; he also asked how they could possibly expect a fair hearing given that Sir Harold Thompson had presided over it. But Thompson scornfully steam-rollered his arguments and at the end of the five-hour meeting the punishment was predictably onerous: a ten-year ban from English football – its intention effectively to prevent Revie ever resuming his career in England, should he ever decide to return.

'The FA are talking about the disgrace to football,' said a visibly angry Revie at the end of the hearing, 'but this ban is one of the most disgraceful things I've ever heard of in the game.'[23] For once, however, the weight of public opinion was behind the FA. Revie's disloyalty and greed were disliked intensely by the English public. Venality was a trait deplored more than any, something considered almost 'foreign'. Yet Revie had shamelessly displayed it while he was supposed to be leading his country. Donald Saunders spoke for many when he wrote in the *Daily Telegraph*:

> English soccer will shed no tears for Don Revie . . . As manager of England, the motherland of soccer, Mr Revie had a special responsibility. He accepted it willingly, in return for twice as high a salary as any of his predecessors had enjoyed. Then, the burden became irksome, he tossed it casually aside and picked up another, lighter, richer package, caring nothing for the consequences to be faced by those whose international careers had been entrusted to his safekeeping. Can anyone seriously argue that this did not bring the game into disrepute or realistically complain that Mr Revie has been harshly treated?[24]

A year later, in November 1979, Revie returned to Britain – and the High Court. For Thompson, the case had become a personal obsession with the FA chairman making copious notes and keeping folders packed with cuttings about the dispute. 'I never called people by their Christian names until I knew them reasonably well,' he noted when the 'call me Don' incident resurfaced in the press. 'I was fair and my colleagues were fair. I did all I could do to give Mr Revie a chance to explain and justify his conduct . . . I really tried to lean backwards to be fair.' Perhaps his anxiety was due to the realisation that he had tripped up badly by ignoring legal advice and pursuing Revie in the first place. Chethams had, after all, not only advised against taking further action, but also, when he did, explicitly counselled *against* banning Revie from an affiliation with an English club as he had recourse to appeal under the Right to Work Act. Again Thompson had ignored them.

Justice Cantley presided over an appeal case during which the great and good of English football came to testify over the course of eighteen days. During his testimony Revie revealed how he had developed insomnia while in charge of the national team after suffering the insults of the fans. 'You cannot sleep too well,' he said, 'and you get up in the middle of the night and make cups of tea and talk things over with your wife.'[25] He admitted his hurt when his famous dossiers had been used by the players as scoresheets for card games and claimed that he had turned down other offers out of loyalty to England prior to his Dubai defection. That had only come, he said, because he was fearful for his future and protective of his family's interests and security. He also alleged that Thompson had criticised his selections of Gerry Francis, Malcolm MacDonald and Allan Clarke and on another occasion told him that Kevin Keegan 'did not look very sharp and should have been rested'.[26]

Revie's QC, Gilbert Gray, focused on Thompson, saying that Revie had met his hostility from an early stage. He had resigned only when the criticisms and whisperings about his management had mounted and 'it was obvious that some sort of scapegoat was being sought'. Given such unremitting opposition it was wholly inappropriate for Thompson, claimed Gray, to sit on the FA Disciplinary Commission which had imposed the ban on Revie. 'Sir Harold, in his own court, was effectively prosecutor, witness, judge and jury,' he said.[27] The FA ban, claimed Gray, was not just a restraint of trade, but 'a more tightly closed shop, one fancies, than a trade union could devise'.[28]

Obliged by legal precedent, Justice Cantley upheld Revie's bid to have the ban lifted and agreed with the view that Thompson had not been in a position to take an impartial view of Revie's case. However, summing up, he expressed grave reservations about Revie's integrity.

'Mr Revie is a very prickly man and I think that he has been brooding on imagined wrongs,' he told the court.

> Mr Revie was the English team manager. He held the highest position of its kind in English professional football and he published and presented to the public a sensational and notorious example of disloyalty, breach of duty, discourtesy and selfishness. His conduct brought English football, at a high level, into disrepute. As a mode of resignation it was utterly selfish and was discourteous in the extreme. It inevitably and naturally caused a sensation in the football world. It was, of course, a glaring and flagrant breach of contract.

As regards Thompson, he said: 'I am glad to be able to wholly acquit Sir Harold of bad faith. He is an honourable man who deplores the coarse comments, materialism and selfish greed which, from time to time, obtrude in professional football.' Revie's claim for damages was dismissed out of hand.

Defeat left Sir Harold and his allies in pensive mood. Justice Cantley's words had been scant consolation after a long and exhausting legal battle. As Stan Cullis wrote to Thompson, 'the judge's ruling gives us all a salutary reminder of the complexities of the law and the inescapable fact that having moral right on your side is not always sufficient to win your case'. It was a fair point, but Thompson's crusade had lasted more than two years and cost the Football Association £150,000 in legal bills. With football about to lurch into recession, even the mighty 'Atom Bomb' must have had the humility to ask himself: was it all really worth it?

In the eyes of the Football Association, Don Revie's three greatest failings had been his lack of success, his ultimate betrayal and the perception that he had become 'too big for his boots'. In appointing a successor Sir Harold Thompson intended to give a narrower range of responsibilities than those enjoyed by Revie. 'I want somebody who has character and principles of honesty, devotion and can cooperate dutifully,' he had written to Dick Wragg in July 1977. 'The new man should deal with the team and its coaching. He should not have authority to commit the FA financially or otherwise as has been happening recently. He should not assume duties and responsibilities which are rightly those of other appointed members on tours, get togethers etc.' Two days later he wrote to FA Council members canvassing views on Revie's successor. From Westmorland, Somerset, Surrey and across other such football hotbeds (not to mention the Royal Navy, RAF and, most bizarrely, the New Zealand High Commission) came replies. The FA Deputy Head of Coaching and England Amateur manager, Charles Hughes, 'has the virtues which you yourself have said are necessary both in conversation and to the press,' wrote Lt.-Cdr H.A. Sheppard (Retd.) of the Royal Navy FA. Dick Sale, headmaster of Brentwood School in Essex, said that 'Tommy' should avoid appointing a foreigner ('I don't think they transplant well'), a controversial loudmouth ('Like Clough or Docherty'), or a limited ex-player ('Like Jackie Charlton'). 'The more amateur, part-time approach of Wales, for example, would seem to be just as, if not more, successful than the current role [which is] too highly paid, and too much expected of.' Charles Hughes 'has the necessary qualifications to do the job and could eventually prove to be the man who we are looking for', wrote L.G. Webb of the Somerset County FA and member of the International Committee. Others suggested Joe Mercer, Lawrie McMenemy, Brian Clough and Jack Charlton.[29]

Yet in the immediate wake of Revie's departure Ladbrokes had made Bobby Robson, who was one year into a ten-year contract at Ipswich Town, 4–5 favourite to succeed him; Brian Clough 9–4; Jack Charlton 5–1; Ron Greenwood 10–1; Ron Saunders 25–1 and Terry Venables 50–1. The *Daily Mirror* held a snap poll and found 84 per cent of its readers backed Clough. Yet, with clubs in the midst of pre-season training, few, if any, were willing to countenance a disruptive departure so close to the start of the 1977–78 campaign. With that in mind and with one eye on England's friendly with Switzerland on 7 September and the remaining World Cup qualifiers after that, the FA again opted for a caretaker manager. Once more they chose someone widely respected in Lancaster Gate, a man able to calm the storm, and, in the words of Thompson, bring 'honesty, devotion and cooperation' to the job. Their choice was Ron Greenwood.

Announced as caretaker boss on 17 August 1977, Greenwood had a reputation as one of the game's great thinkers. The possibility of him becoming England boss had first arisen in 1960, when he was coach at Arsenal and Walter Winterbottom had entertained hopes of succeeding Stanley Rous as Secretary of the FA. Then, Winterbottom had told Greenwood that he would be first choice to follow in his footsteps should he succeed Rous, but when Denis Follows usurped Winterbottom, Greenwood went to West Ham. At the Boleyn Ground he had a pedigree for producing good cup sides, winning the FA Cup in 1964 and the European Cup Winners' Cup in 1965. In the league, however, West Ham were perennial underachievers.

Greenwood's first task was the home friendly against Switzerland. For it, he sought a return to basics with the emphasis on trying to replicate some of the glories enjoyed by English clubs in European competition. His great friend Enzo Bearzot had brought much success to Italy by building his team around Juventus players and Greenwood sought to mirror some of that continuity by building around the European champions, Liverpool. Some argued that he took the 'one club' idea to extremes: against Switzerland Greenwood selected no fewer than six Liverpool players, including Ian Callaghan – aged thirty-five and without a cap since the World Cup finals eleven years earlier – plus Keegan. England ambled to a 0–0 draw and a month later, without Keegan and Callaghan, managed only a 2–0 win over Luxembourg – a result that was to prove costly.

Meanwhile the race for a permanent successor to Revie was on, and for once it was hotly contested: a job treated as the pinnacle of English football management rather than a poisoned chalice. The FA had advertised the position in newspapers, letting it be known that if Revie was worth £25,000 per year, so too was his successor (by comparison, Dave Sexton, the recently appointed Manchester United manager, was earning a salary of £20,000). Jimmy Armfield, John Bond, Jimmy Bloomfield, Jack Charlton, Charles Hughes, Harry Catterick, Lawrie McMenemy, Bertie Mee, Tony Waiters and Dennis Wilshaw all applied for the position. Perhaps most interesting were two applications from former England captains. Joy Beverley Wright wrote on behalf of her husband:

> I feel that I would always regret it if I allowed this opportunity to pass by without putting forward the name of Billy Wright in connection with the England manager's vacancy. It seems to me that he has so much of the quality needed. He is far too modest to approach you himself . . . He still has a great heart for football and a great deal to offer.

Whether her husband ever found out or what he would have said if he did is another matter.

Bobby Moore wrote:

> Although my playing commitments have prevented me seeking a managerial position before this summer, I have gained considerable experience in assisting with coaching both with my clubs in England and abroad during the latter stages of my playing career. I know you are aware of my international playing record and how proud I was of my years with the England team . . . I feel that the experience and knowledge I have gained at this level of football over the years have provided me with the ideal background for the specialised demands of the job.[30]

Neither made the shortlist: Wright never returned to football; Moore subsequently struggled to find a meaningful role within the game.

The majority of the public were in no doubt as to whom they wanted: Brian Clough. Nottingham Forest's brilliant, eccentric, ferocious, idiosyncratic manager was everything that the diplomatic, decorous Greenwood wasn't. Already a championship winner with unfashionable Derby County, he was on his way to taking Forest to the same unprecedented peak – and, later, as double European champions, even higher. He was the sort of uncompromising figure to rock the foundations of Lancaster Gate and revolutionise English football. The public loved the idea, the FA weren't so sure. Yet they could be in no doubt that the weight of opinion was with Clough and, after the Luxembourg match, they were inundated with letters championing his cause. John Feast of Blackburn wrote that Greenwood was a 'has-been manager who would do well to return to the boardroom from whence he came and hand over his office to "The Man", namely Brian Clough'. Ken Pearl of Nuneaton wrote that 'the whole of the football fraternity in this country want Clough and Taylor to get us out of this mire or die in the attempt. There is no way that England will win the World Cup finals in 1982 without a strong personality who can tell every manager of every club what he wants and get it.' 'Stop sitting in FA HQ like little tin gods,' added D.J. Saunders of Market Harborough, '[and] start doing something constructive for the 1982 finals by appointing Brian Clough, who instead of being your slayer could become your saviour.'

The following month, though, the advantage began to slip from

Clough when England met Italy at Wembley. The disappointingly small win in Luxembourg had practically extinguished any remaining hopes of qualification and salvation would only come if England trounced the Italians and hoped that they didn't do the same in their remaining group match with Luxembourg. If dreams of Argentina had all but died, there was always pride to play for. Greenwood picked three debutants: Everton's prolific, physically imposing striker, Bob Latchford; and two wingers from either side of the Manchester divide: Peter Barnes of City and Steve Coppell of United. Kevin Keegan was to play in the 'hole' behind Latchford. It was a bold, attack-minded formation and one that immediately captured the imagination of the crowd of 92,000, who roared on their compatriots from the off. On eleven minutes England took the lead. Trevor Brooking, a pivotal figure throughout, found space on the right and sent in a fast, telling cross that the head of Keegan glanced, sending the ball looping over the head of Zoff and into the far corner of the Italy net. Wembley erupted, and, spurred on by the vociferous encouragement of their countrymen, Greenwood's men continued to tear into the clearly unsettled Italians. Coppell and Barnes in particular provided a constant menace, perplexing Benetti and Gentile, who were each booked when foul means of stopping the England wingers proved more straightforward than fair.

Ten minutes from the end, as Trevor Francis was warming up to replace him, Keegan had the last laugh, sending Brooking clear with a devastatingly accurate through ball that the West Ham player slotted past Zoff with all the composure of a training ground exercise. 'The players said it was nice to be cheered off the Wembley pitch,' said Greenwood afterwards. 'We set out to restore pride and respect in our football and we got the verdict from the crowd at the end. We played with a lot of emotion and freedom for the first time in a long while. I am proud of English football and proud we showed millions of people up and down the country we are not down and out as people seem to think we are.'[31] Ultimately a 2–0 win was not enough. After England's lacklustre display in Luxembourg, Italy needed just a 1–0 victory over the duchy to surpass the English goals for tally; they scored three and England's slim hopes of qualification were at an end.

For Greenwood, who had previously ruled himself out of taking the manager's job permanently, victory over the Italians brought a change of heart. 'Perhaps this isn't the last supper after all,' he told the players as they sat down for their post-match dinner. A day later he publicly threw his hat into the ring, adding that if he were to continue as England manager, his ambition was to destroy what he described as 'the age old bugbear' that results count above everything else. 'This has been the ruination of English soccer,' he said, 'and the public have been largely to blame for demanding it, but now they are demanding something better.'[32] It was an optimistic thought.

Greenwood was joined by five other candidates on the FA's shortlist: Dave Sexton, Jack Charlton (Sheffield Wednesday), Lawrie McMenemy (Southampton) plus Clough and Bobby Robson, both of whom the FA had approached via their clubs. Despite victory over Italy, it was still effectively deemed a two-horse race between Clough and Robson, even though Robson was reluctant to leave Portman Road. The odds swayed even further in Clough's favour with the revelation that Peter Swales (one of the five-man selection committee with Sir Harold Thompson, Bert Millichip, Dick Wragg and Matt Busby) had promised Clough his vote. Indeed with Nottingham Forest top of the league (and on their way to the title) it seemed inconceivable – to the public at least – that anyone but Clough could permanently succeed Don Revie. When the interviews were held in December, so confident was he of 'winning' over the interview panel with his charm and Busby, in particular, with his football knowledge, that he rang his assistant, Peter Taylor, to tell him that he'd got the job.

Clough had been premature in his celebrations. Later that afternoon, Ron Greenwood, who had been interviewed earlier, tuned into Radio Two's sports news and the dulcet tones of Bryon Butler informed him – and the rest of the country – that he had become the new England manager.

Old 'Big 'Ead' was as perplexed by the announcement as his adoring public. 'I was at my peak then – building a good side, winning things, happy and fulfilled,' Clough would say. 'I was absolutely ripe for the England job in 1977 . . . I had a superb interview and should've got it. You always know if you've had a good match as a sportsman without anyone telling you, I assume you know when you've done a good interview. I was spot on that day.'[33] Spot on he may well have been, but Clough was a man of many enemies. Certainly the timing had been inopportune for him, despite Forest's lofty league position. A few months earlier he had publicly criticised West Bromwich Albion for not offering their manager, Ronnie Allen, a new contract.

Albion's chairman, Bert Millichip, a doyen of the FA, on the interview panel and to later succeed Thompson as head of its Selection Committee, was the wrong sort of man to dabble with. It wasn't just Millichip who had an axe to grind. The FA as a whole, after some of their experiences with Alf Ramsey, were wary of Clough's loose tongue. For instance, when his Derby County side had played Juventus in the semi-finals of the 1973 European Cup – a match tainted with the whiff of corruption (Derby lost 1–3) – he had begun the post-match press conference with the immortal line: 'I don't talk to cheating bastards,' before giving his observations on Italy's performance in the last war. After the return leg, and a goalless draw, the frenzy restarted: 'You tell those fucking cheating Italian bastards . . .' He could barely get away with such outbursts at Derby, but to come out with something similar while England boss would have resulted in nothing short of a diplomatic incident. Even when waiting for his interview, he couldn't keep his mouth shut. Looking at photographs of England teams past and present, he told Ted Croker, the FA Secretary, that the new kit was hideous. Croker responded that the FA were merely moving with the times. 'Bullshit,' retorted Clough. 'A Rolls Royce is always a Rolls Royce and it's the same with the England shirt.'

A loose cannon without friends in high places is one thing, but though 'Reverend Ron's' many abilities were beyond question, his managerial record was not in the same league as Clough's. Clough had a proven record of taking teams with good, but not exceptional players, to the summit of the First Division. By contrast, Greenwood's successes were limited to cup competitions (and even they had come in the mid-sixties). His West Ham sides – despite boasting a triumvirate of World Cup winners in Peters, Hurst and Moore – for much of his time at the Boleyn Ground were nothing more than mid-table fodder in the First Division. Surely, then, Clough was worth the gamble?

Damaged by the Revie affair, the FA's desire for a 'safe pair of hands' was at the top of their recruitment criteria. Revie's venality was despised because it seemed so 'unEnglish', but the eccentric Clough also seemed to embody characteristics not expected of a typical representative of Queen and country. What the FA wanted – although they may not have recognised or admitted it at the time – was a man who brought the same inherently English qualities to the job as Sir Alf

Ramsey had done: decorum, integrity, loyalty. None of these were particularly synonymous with Cloughie.

With commercial interests rapidly taking on a greater importance within the FA, Clough was also seen as a liability. Bert Patrick, chairman of England's shirt manufacturers Admiral, wrote to Ted Croker at the end of October 1977 pointing out vaguely libellous comments Clough had made in a magazine interview which inferred that his company had paid backhanders to Revie when securing the deal. 'I thought you would wish to make a note of these irresponsible comments from Clough,' wrote Patrick, 'which have absolutely no foundation.' At first sight Bert Patrick's comments seemed innocuous enough, but coming as they did when the FA were not only shortlisting candidates for the manager's position but preparing to put out a tender for a new shirt deal they imply a vague threat. At the time the FA's bank account was depleted following the successive failures to qualify for the 1974 World Cup finals, the 1976 European Championship finals and, still to be confirmed but all but certain, the 1978 World Cup. They were also threatened with the loss of the annual sell-out fixture with Scotland after the trouble in May. The lucrative deal struck with Admiral, therefore, assumed enormous importance. To put it into perspective, when the tenders came in, in mid-1978, Admiral's closest rivals, Umbro, initially offered just £50,000 per year over five years, and when they upped it, their offer was still worth only £130,000 per year – or just over half of the million plus that Admiral guaranteed the FA over the same period. Could it have been that commercial interests and financial necessities provided the final confirmation for the FA that Clough should not become England manager?

The fears over Clough's volubility were soon realised. One of Ron Greenwood's first actions as permanent England manager was to implement a structure that introduced club managers to the England set-up. Geoff Hurst, then managing non-league Telford United, was to act as his assistant and help plug the gap between generations; Bobby Robson and Don Howe were given control of the B side; Dave Sexton, Terry Venables and Howard Wilkinson the Under-21s (which had superseded the Under-23 team in 1976); Clough and Taylor the youth side. With Greenwood in his mid-fifties and already interrupting his retirement to take on the England job, time was not on his side and it was thought unlikely that he would manage England beyond the 1982 World Cup finals. For Clough then, the chance to manage the England youth side was a perfect opportunity to prove his 'good behaviour' ahead of the next vacancy.

It was a test he failed miserably. Seldom were Clough and Taylor seen on the training ground at youth team get-togethers and their mere presence seemed incendiary. Things came to a head at an international youth tournament in Las Palmas in October 1978. Little was seen of either and they attended just one training session; Clough was then rude to a Spanish interpreter, leaving her in tears, leading to his exclusion from an invitation to a party at the Spanish FA. He then compounded matters by turning up late to a British embassy reception. The whole affair left the FA intent on sacking him at the end of the 1978–79 season, but, knowing the scorn they would attract from Clough and in the popular press, they came to an 'arrangement' and prematurely released him from his duties, ostensibly so that he could focus on Nottingham Forest's European Cup campaign. Never again would Brian Clough come even remotely close to landing the job he coveted so badly.

Ron Greenwood was acutely aware of the unique pressures that came with managing England. 'Cats will be kicked in Ipswich or Leeds or east London if the local side goes down, but who else cares?' he reflected in his memoirs. 'But if England lose it is a national disaster.'[34] The former apprentice signwriter, who had once painted hoardings at Wembley, also knew that he wasn't the people's choice to manage England and that he had arguably the weakest pool of talent to choose from in more than a century of international football. His core group of players was able enough, but injuries would stretch his options and undermine progress. In defence he could count on two steady, unspectacular, but utterly dependable defenders in Phil Neal and Phil Thompson, who would replicate their fine form for Liverpool in the white of England over a number of years. Alongside them stood the imposing pair of Dave Watson and Ipswich Town's Mick Mills, and behind them either Ray Clemence or Peter Shilton, each of whom could justifiably lay claim to be the best goalkeeper in Europe. Chelsea's Ray Wilkins, a young midfielder who did the simple things well and brought a stabilising influence to the heart of the England team, was rewarded with a regular berth. If occasionally his preference for the simple over the spectacular prompted frustration amongst supporters, his mere presence allowed other, more attacking players to prosper. Trevor Brooking, always a quick thoughtful player, had become an integral part of the England midfield; Peter Barnes and Steve Coppell provided dash and élan down the wings with the latter, in particular, proving integral to the new manager's plans.

Yet it was Keegan who was the key figure: when he hummed, England ticked; when he faltered, his country struggled. Between late 1977 and 1980 Keegan was at the absolute peak of his game. Self made he may have been but for SV Hamburg and England he was untouchable. Twice, in 1978 and 1979, he was crowned European Footballer of the Year; at club level he inspired Hamburg to the Bundesliga title in 1979 and a year later spearheaded their march to the European Cup final (which they lost, ironically, to Clough's Nottingham Forest); on the international stage his often sublime presence aided the re-emergence of his country. 'When Keegan returned from Germany the whole place lit up,' Greenwood would recall. 'He excited the crowds and lifted his team mates. He put his stamp on every occasion and I cannot speak too highly of this man in terms of his application, sense of responsibility, personality and ambition. He is a rare and brilliant little chap.'[35]

Greenwood's first full game in charge, away against West Germany in Munich, saw England lose 1–2 after holding a half-time lead. There was no disgrace in losing to the world champions and it was to mark the start of a run which would see just one defeat over the following twenty-eight months, taking in some twenty-two matches. Starting with a 1–1 draw with Brazil on 19 April 1978, England went on to win all three of that year's Home Championship ties, secure friendly victories over the likes of Hungary (4–1) and Czechoslovakia (1–0), take the Home Championship again in 1979 and top the qualification group – consisting of Denmark, Bulgaria, the Republic of Ireland and Northern Ireland – for the 1980 European Championship finals in Italy, having dropped just a solitary point. After England beat Bulgaria 3–0 in June 1979, their manager Izvetan Ilchev proclaimed: 'This is a new England. They are still physically strong but they no longer concentrate on power. They have ideas, sophistication, a team who play modern football.'[36]

Pride had unquestionably been restored, but if England needed an indication as to how far they had progressed since the death throes of the Revie era, it came in spring 1980. On 26 March England travelled to the Nou Camp for a friendly with Spain. Only 29,000 turned out – an indication perhaps of Catalan indifference to the Spanish national team, rather than their English opponents in particular – but they witnessed the visitors tear Spain apart. Only twenty-five seconds had passed when Keegan forced Luis Arconada into the first of many saves, handing England an attacking initiative they never once looked like surrendering. Two minutes later Ray Kennedy set up Tony Woodcock whose shot glanced wide; Francis was hacked when running through on goal; the same player's free-kick was dropped by Arconada; then he missed after being set up by Keegan when it seemed easier to score. On sixteen minutes England went in front: Coppell's flick set Woodcock chasing after the ball and despite the close attentions of a huddle of defenders – and Arconada – he lunged for the ball, injuring himself in the process, and successfully managed to steer it into the back of the net. The Spanish defence, at last, began to gain a tighter rein on the England attack but the visitors continued to control proceedings and, twenty-five minutes from the end, sealed victory: Wilkins sent Coppell on a run down the right and he managed to hold off the attentions of his markers and play in Francis. His pace took him past the Spanish defence and as Arconada advanced, hit an unstoppable shot into the far corner to make it 2–0. 'Giants and Dwarfs' was how the Barcelona paper *Sport* described the difference between the two sides. 'It could almost be measured in light years,' they added. Europe took notice too: 'The English amazed me with their strength and fine conception of football,' said Enzo Bearzot, who had been so dismissive of Revie's side. 'They appear well prepared and I think they will be the most dangerous side in Italy. In this side, every player is phenomenal.' Fifteen years earlier a 2–0 victory on Spanish soil had marked the arrival of Alf Ramsey's England as genuine contenders. Was the same true of Greenwood's England?

Six weeks later – on 13 May – it seemed to be the case. 1978 world champions Argentina were the visitors to Wembley in a contest described by the *Sun* as the 'War of the Wondermen' – Kevin Keegan versus nineteen-year-old superstar Diego Maradona. Maradona was just reaching world prominence, but Argentina had known about the phenomenon since he was just eleven. Then, he had appeared on national television juggling footballs, tennis balls, satsumas, even golf balls. His team, Los Cebollitas (the Little Onions), were so good that Argentinos Juniors signed them *en masse* and used them as one of its youth sides. By the time Maradona was fifteen he was playing in the Argentinian First Division; then, a year later, in 1977, for his country. He was to become an immortal figure, but in 1980, precocious, chubby, often brilliant, he was still not quite as good as Kevin Keegan.

Chances were to go both ways, with Maradona providing several breathtaking moments, but England stood firm and when Steve Coppell ran to the touchline and pulled the ball back, David Johnson was on hand to head home powerfully and give England a one-goal half-time lead. Six minutes after the interval Johnson doubled England's lead, striking home the rebound after Fillol was unable to keep hold of Ray Kennedy's shot. The game continued to ebb and flow, the Wembley crowd roaring on the home side as well as applauding intermittent flashes of Maradona's repertoire of genius. On fifty-four minutes he set off on one of his dribbles, testing and teasing Kenny Sansom before the befuddled full-back upended him. Daniel Passarella slammed home the penalty and the attacking impetus passed back to the Argentinians, who probed and tested an increasingly over-burdened England defence.

2–1 in front, but more and more under pressure, it was time for a captain's intervention. Keegan played in Johnson down the left, he ran with the ball before switching to Coppell, and the Manchester United winger laid it off, back into the path of Keegan, who shot home. 3–1 to England, victory was theirs. 'We said that we would see whether when Maradona had the ball he could beat four or five men,' said Greenwood of his decision to play Thompson as sweeper. At nineteen it was beyond him; six years later England were to find him a different proposition.

Expectation invariably rose out of all proportion to their albeit excellent achievement. It had been a great win, but nonetheless only a friendly victory and one on home soil to boot. Four days later England were to get a rude reawakening.

At the Racecourse Ground, Wrexham, a side without Keegan or most of the Nottingham Forest contingent – rested ahead of the European Cup final – faced Wales in the first Home Championship match of the season. On fifteen minutes England took the lead through the Ipswich forward, Paul Mariner, but thereafter things fell apart. Five minutes later Micky Thomas equalised; Walsh gave them a 2–1 lead; Leighton James made it three; and a Phil Thompson own goal completed the rout: 4–1 to Wales, and England's heaviest-ever defeat to its neighbours. If anything the loss, a freak result though it was, showed the thinness of quality in the England ranks. For instance, Dave Watson had been rested to allow Larry Lloyd to regain some international experience after a gap of eight years, but the plan had backfired horribly and James had run him ragged. Lloyd never played for England again.

The following Tuesday – and only a week after beating Argentina – England drew 1–1 with Northern Ireland. Then, needing a win to avoid the ignominy of the wooden spoon, they travelled to Hampden. Goals from Coppell and Mariner sealed a 2–0 England victory; the Scots took bottom spot and, for the first time, the Home Championship went to Belfast outright.

From scaling the heights against the world champions, it could scarcely be said that England had immediately sunk to the depths of football despair. Nevertheless, on the eve of the European Champion-ships in Italy, the Home Championship had been an unsettling affair, and hopes in Italy were further stymied by the news that Trevor Francis would be missing after sustaining a severe ligament injury. Despite all that, England had suffered just three defeats in nearly three years under Ron Greenwood's management. He was able to take a side high on confidence – despite the troubled Home Championship campaign – full of experience and packed with players who had just tasted success in European club football. (As well as Nottingham Forest and Keegan's Hamburg just contesting the European Cup final, Arsenal had also finished runners-up in the European Cup Winners' Cup.) Although Greenwood's squad had its limitations, on its day it had proven a match for anybody: could they rise to the challenge in their first tournament appearance in a decade?

Since England had last qualified for the final stages of the European Championships, the tournament had come to assume two four-team groups with the top two countries from each going on to contest semi-finals. England were drawn with the hosts, Italy; Spain, who had been beaten so memorably in Barcelona four months earlier; and Belgium, against whom England opened the competition on 12 June. Things began promisingly: Keegan's darting runs provided an early menace; Woodcock headed narrowly wide from Wilkins's cross; a fine centre from Woodcock narrowly evaded Johnson's lunge; then, on twenty-two minutes and to the consternation of the England players, Keegan's goalbound shout was disallowed for an offside call against Woodcock. Three minutes later though, Wilkins broke the deadlock in quite brilliant fashion. Picking up the ball in the heart of the pitch he chipped it over the advancing Belgian defence and displayed the pace and presence of mind to run onto his own pass and, spotting Pfaff off his line, send a delicate lob over the Belgian goalkeeper to put England in front.

England's fans went wild with delight, but four minutes later some of them simply turned wild. Van Moer's corner caused all manner of problems in the England penalty area and, when the ball wasn't cleared properly, Ceulemans scored from close range. Furious at Italian fans celebrating the Belgian goal, a section of the England support in the sparsely populated stadium attacked them. Fighting broke out, which left one Italian stabbed, seven in hospital and, when carabinieri intervened with batons and tear gas, one England fan seriously injured. The tear gas then drifted onto the playing area, affecting the players and overcoming Ray Clemence, who had to receive lengthy treatment. When play restarted five minutes later the intensity of the encounter had diminished and neither side thereafter looked remotely like winning the game. Later, Greenwood suggested, when interviewed by the BBC, that the troublemakers be put on a boat, and 'someone should pull the plug'. Michel Daphinoff, a senior UEFA official, was in less of a mood for joking. 'There is a recurring pattern of violent behaviour by English football supporters. It cannot go on. We are alarmed because the rest of society cannot be expected to tolerate it.' UEFA slapped the FA with an £8000 fine for its supporters' excesses.

Three days later England met Italy, again in Turin, knowing they had to avoid defeat in order to remain in control of their own destiny. For the first half they marshalled the Italians efficiently, making light work of Bettega's pace and Tardelli's skills, and prompted frustration in the home ranks. As the game progressed into the second half chances went both ways, most notably for England, when Keegan smartly dummied Wilkins's centre and Ray Kennedy's half-volley crashed off the post. Then, on seventy-eight minutes, came the game's decisive moment. Francesco Graziani broke free, Phil Neal dived into a futile tackle, the Italian flew past him, crossed, and Tardelli swept home the winner.

England travelled south to Naples for their final group match with Spain, needing a win and Italy to beat Belgium in order to progress. Greenwood made several changes to his line-up, recalling Brooking and also giving Tottenham Hotspur's twenty-two-year-old mid-fielder Glenn Hoddle his fifth cap. Born in Hayes, Middlesex, in October 1957, Hoddle had made his league debut for Spurs at the age of seventeen and established himself as a White Hart Lane regular before his twentieth birthday. A tall, slim, leggy player, whose elegance was immediately obvious from his very first touch in a game, he seemed a throwback to a bygone era when playmakers played and mere mortals did the tracking back and tackling. 'People talk about character,' he once complained. 'But what is character? Is it tearing around at 100 miles per hour? It makes me laugh – If I thought defending was important I could improve my game by 50 per cent. But it isn't.'[37] If his critics derided him as a 'fancy Dan', the Tottenham faithful were in no doubt of their affections: 'Hoddle is God' proclaimed a 1980s graffiti campaign. Ron Greenwood was inclined to agree: 'His ability is prodigious: there is no question about that. On the ball he is a delight. His control is of Brazilian quality. He is a living, breathing denial of the charge that British football cannot produce players with great technical skill. He also has balance and a feeling for the unexpected.'[38]

Against Spain the inclusion of Hoddle and Brooking provided England with a greater cutting edge to their attacks. A frenetic opening reaped reward in the thirteenth minute when Brooking slid in to convert Wilkins's header across the face of the Spanish goal. England maintained their lead until shortly after half-time when two dubiously awarded penalties went Spain's way. First, Clemence's challenge at the feet of Zamora was adjudged to have been illegal and Dani converted the contentiously awarded spot-kick; six minutes later, Dave Watson challenged Saura in a crowded penalty area first fairly, then, a second time, not so. Dani again fired past Clemence from the penalty spot, but this time the referee spotted an infringe-ment and ordered him to retake the kick. When he went to hit it in the opposite corner, Clemence guessed the right way and palmed his shot away to safety.

Justice restored by the goalkeeper's heroics, on the hour-mark England deservedly regained the lead. Brooking played a corner to the unmarked McDermott, who was lurking on the edge of the penalty area, and he struck a sweetly volleyed shot that Arconada could only palm into the path of Woodcock, who tapped home to make it 2–1, a lead England held until the game's conclusion. In Turin though, events at the Belgium–Italy encounter had taken a turn against England. Indomitable Belgian defending earned them a 0–0 draw, England were out, Belgium through and eventually on their way to the final, which they lost 1–2 to West Germany. 'We lost none of our honour,' reflected Greenwood. 'I am pleased to have been part of a gem which showed the best of football.'

England's manager had little time to dwell on the relative failure of the 1980 European Championships as attention turned immediately to the qualifying campaign for the 1982 World Cup finals in Spain. It had been twenty years since England had successfully progressed through a World Cup qualifying group (having turned up in 1966 as hosts and 1970 as winners) and to make it to Spain they first had to overcome Norway, Switzerland, Romania and Hungary, a set of teams which initially seemed to throw up few problems.

As well as Glenn Hoddle, Greenwood could look upon a few other up and coming young players to help spearhead England's efforts. Nottingham Forest's right-back, Viv Anderson, had, in November 1978, become the first black footballer to pull on the white of England. A fine pacy player blessed with the knack of getting one of his long spindly legs wrapped around the ball at the most opportune moment, Anderson, fresh from his European success at the City Ground, was an excellent addition to the national squad. Equally so was West Bromwich Albion's midfielder, Bryan Robson. In many ways he was the antithesis of the ever-elegant Hoddle: where the Spurs man tried the extraordinary, Robson kept it simple; when Hoddle faded, Robson was still there hurrying, scrapping, fighting; if Hoddle scored a beautifully flighted volley, Robson would match it with a well-timed stab at the ball through a crowd of players. While

Glenn Hoddle could be seen as the rightful heir to Johnny Haynes, Robson was a more than worthy successor to Alan Ball. Despite being devastatingly prone to injury, his battling qualities, leadership abilities, boundless energy and knack of scoring crucial goals were to be vital to England over the following decade.

England still, of course, also had Kevin Keegan. The European Footballer of the Year was now nearly thirty and had, to the surprise of many, left SV Hamburg to join unfashionable Southampton. Injuries, age and the toll of decades of relentless training-ground toil were to make him a lesser force for his country, if only because he found himself sidelined so often. Indeed, when England got their qualifying campaign off to a winning start against Norway at Wembley on 10 September 1980, injury kept Keegan out of the side which won 4–0.

A month later in Romania, Keegan was still missing, but so too, seemingly, were many of those who had made the trip. A day before the qualifier, the Under-21 side had been thrashed 0–4 in what was a worrying portent. Indeed when play got under way in the senior match, Romania's passing was just as slick, imaginative and cutting as it had been twenty-four hours earlier and England got away lightly with a 0–1 half-time deficit. In the second half they played with greater composure and were rewarded with an equaliser from the boot of Woodcock. It was short-lived. In the seventy-sixth minute Crişan took a tumble in the England box, the Swedish referee pointed to the spot and Iordanescu scored from the penalty kick. 'I felt we did not deserve more than a draw,' said Greenwood afterwards, 'but we did deserve that on our second half performance.'

Two points were taken in an uneasy 2–1 win over Switzerland at Wembley on 19 November, but England's worrying form carried on into 1981. Spain, twice conquered a year earlier, left Wembley with a 2–1 friendly victory on 25 March, even with Keegan restored to the line-up for the first time since Italy; five weeks later, in the crucial match with Romania, injury again precluded his inclusion and England failed to break down their opponents' rearguard, drawing 0–0. Brazil came away from Wembley with a 1–0 victory on 12 May, and the depression continued the week after against Wales (0–0) and Scotland (0–1).

Gloom pervaded the England ranks. Defeat against Scotland had been England's fifth straight match without a victory and fourth without a goal. They had struggled to link the endeavour of the midfield with attack and their attempts at using a target man – Peter Withe – had not reaped dividends. England still played like an archetypal Greenwood team, building from the back, retaining possession, using space intelligently, waiting patiently for chances to come, but when they did they were not being taken. More philosophical commentators began to muse, yet again, on the decline of the England team; others pointed to the paucity of talent Greenwood had at his disposal. His best players were either advancing in years, like Keegan and Brooking, or frustratingly prone to injury such as Robson, Wilkins and Francis. Glenn Hoddle was still not deemed ready for a regular international berth: against Scotland Greenwood had given him a free rein but on the day he had lacked influence beyond a few graceful touches.

Things were to get worse. Following defeat to Scotland, Greenwood's men steeled themselves for two crucial World Cup qualifiers, first against Switzerland, then Hungary. To regain the impetus in their group England needed to win both; defeat in either, not least against the early pacesetters, Hungary, threatened to fatally tip the balance against England's qualification hopes. The first encounter, in Basle, looked the easier of the two: the Swiss were bottom of the group and gleefully described by the *Sun* as 'a bunch of cuckoo clock makers and waiters' (although all but two of their team were professionals); whereas the Hungarians had not lost to England in Budapest since 1908. A measure of Greenwood's travails came on the eve of the match when Dick Wragg felt the need to deliver a personal vote of confidence. Greenwood joked: 'If I had heard that at club level I would be worried.' Still, he finally had Keegan back from injury, and his ranks were boosted on the eve of the Switzerland game by the return of the Liverpool players (excused from the Scotland and Wales debacles) following their European Cup final victory over Real Madrid. Not that it helped. Greenwood rested the Anfield contingent while Keegan spent more time arguing than playing. A spell of early pressure failed to end England's goal famine, then, on twenty-eight minutes, Alfred Scheiwiler all but walked through the England defence and fired a shot past Clemence. Moments later, Sulser repeated the feat to give the Swiss a two-goal advantage. While England's footballers were embarrassing themselves on the field, some of their inadequately policed fans were adding to the national shame by ripping out seats to use as missiles and provoking the small, local gendarmerie into deploying the tear gas they had stockpiled since the events in Turin.

At half-time Greenwood brought on Terry McDermott for the subdued Francis and within nine minutes of his introduction he had pulled a goal back, and then twice more sent efforts narrowly wide. None of it, however, was enough: England fell to a 1–2 defeat and their World Cup dreams seemed to have died. 'We just haven't got the quality any more. We just haven't got good enough men to take the opponents out of the game,' Gordon Banks lamented. 'While the rest of Europe has advanced tremendously in the last ten years English soccer has declined,' added the Argentina manager Cesar Luis Menotti. 'I won't be at all surprised if they now fail to reach the World Cup finals.' England's odds to win the World Cup halved to 40–1 and not for the last time the *Sun* implored of an England manager 'For God's sake go'. In *The Times* Norman Fox accused Greenwood of allowing 'his loyalty to extend international careers (notably those of Keegan and Watson) to which there is little justification for selection. Both could play well [against Hungary] but their appearance would confirm that England have failed to build for the future.'[39] Others focused on the appalling behaviour of England's supporters. FIFA observer Jacques Georges commented: 'The English supporters were a disgrace to their country. There is no danger of England being banned from the World Cup, but their fans – that is something different.'[40]

Defeat by Switzerland spurred Greenwood to make four changes for the Hungary match: Neal and Thompson came in for Sansom and Osman, Brooking replaced Wilkins and McDermott's goal in Basle won him a starting place ahead of Francis. Defeat in Budapest would almost certainly bring an end to any lingering hopes of qualification – ambitions only still intact because no one country in England's group had been good enough to establish an unassailable position in a mediocre pool – and Greenwood's four-year-long stewardship. 'This is a game for character, attitude and experience,' he told his players before the game, 'and we're going to need a lot of it.' Indeed they were. 70,000 people packed into the Nepstadion, a ground where memories of England's demolition by the Puskás-inspired Magyars twenty-seven years earlier were still vivid and the early indications were that England were in for a difficult night. On thirteen minutes

Nyilasi shot weakly when put through by Fazekas, and four minutes later only Dave Watson's last-ditch tackle prevented the same player from gaining a clear sight of goal. Only a minute had elapsed since that let-off when England broke swiftly and concisely through Neal and his cross was switched to Brooking, who rounded off a well-worked move by drilling a low, skimming shot between post and goalkeeper: it was the sort of cleverly orchestrated goal which Puskás himself would have been proud of conducting.

Hungary came back strongly. Clemence did well to save Kiss's header, then block Fazekas's shot; Nyilasi's thunderous header rebounded off the bar; and Törőcsik twice opened up the England defence, only to find his colleagues lacking his same speed of mind. Then, just before the interval, came the hosts' elusive equaliser. Kiss was set free by Garaba, he played in Törőcsik and, although Clemence dived bravely at his feet, the loose ball fell to Garaba, who scored easily.

England, however, were indomitable. As the game moved into the second half they managed to contain the Hungarians and on the hour-mark retook their lead. Neal broke and, seeing Keegan, played in his former Anfield colleague. Immediately, intelligently, Keegan sensed Brooking on the right and switched play to him: he cut inside and let fly with a stunning shot, hit with such ferocity that it wedged in the top corner between the stanchion and post. 'It was,' mused Brooking, 'the finest shot I have ever struck.'[41] Fifteen minutes later McDermott sent Keegan clear, who was crudely chopped down for a penalty. England's captain claimed the ball and fired his country into an unsurpassable 3–1 lead. The win, conceded Monday's *Times*, 'was a remarkable recovery of confidence and as complete a performance as has been seen under the stewardship of Ron Greenwood'.[42]

For Greenwood, though, the traumas of the previous year had become too much. On the plane home Greenwood took Keegan to one side, and told him – as captain – that he was going to announce his resignation at a press conference to be staged on their return to Luton Airport. With the press pack at the back of the charter flight and the players at the front Greenwood then ordered the intersecting curtains to be closed, and proceeded to tell the rest of his players of his decision.

Keegan, who was as distraught as he was shocked by the announcement, gathered the senior players – Brooking, Mick Mills and Ray Clemence – and they went to Greenwood's seat and told him that he had the backing of the entire squad and that they didn't want another manager. Greenwood demurred, but they were insistent. Only inside the terminal building at Luton, while waiting for the bags to appear on the carousel, did Greenwood finally change his mind. 'I have to admit that I'm feeling good right now,' he told the assembled journalists just minutes later. 'The thought of resignation never came into my head. It has been a difficult week, a traumatic week, but I said some time ago that England would qualify for Spain and that's where we're going.'

Or so he thought. Hopes that victory in the Nepstadion had marked a change in fortunes were soon confounded. On 9 September 1981 England travelled to Oslo to take on the part-timers of Norway in their penultimate qualifying match. Anything but a win was deemed an inconceivable notion: as one reporter noted in his preview – 'Pitch more of a worry than Norway.' If that glib assessment evoked memories of previews of one of England's more traumatic days in Belo Horizonte, no one could have imagined that such horrors would be repeated, not least after Bryan Robson fired England into a seventeenth minute lead. Chances, thereafter, began to dry up, as Norway began to threaten on the counter-attack and when Mills failed to clear Lund's corner on thirty-seven minutes, the ball fell to Albertsen and he shot an equaliser past Clemence. Five minutes later Larsen-Økland's cross was missed by McDermott and Thoresen stole in to grab Norway's second. England spent the second half camped out in the Norwegian half as the hosts' area bulged with players alternatively trying to force the ball into the goal, or away from it. Desperately, forlornly, they battled until the legendary words of the Norwegian commentator, Bjorge Lillelien, sang out across the globe: 'We are the best in the world! We have beaten England! Lord Nelson . . . Lord Beaverbrook . . . Sir Winston Churchill . . . Sir Anthony Eden . . . Clement Attlee . . . Henry Cooper . . . Lady Diana . . . We have beaten them all! Maggie Thatcher, can you hear me? Maggie Thatcher, your boys took one hell of a beating! Your boys took a hell of a beating! Norway have beaten England at football!'

And then, a miracle. On 10 October Romania met Switzerland in Bucharest needing just a win then, or in the return fixture a month later, to qualify for Spain. On fifty-seven minutes Romania scored directly from a free-kick by Balaci and seemed to be cruising to the World Cup finals. Astonishingly, they imploded. Gianpietro Zappa equalised eleven minutes later, then with thirteen minutes to go Luethy came on as a substitute and scored Switzerland's winner, stunning the 80,000 crowd. Four weeks later in Berne, Romania dropped another point, leaving the door open for England. A win against Hungary at Wembley on 18 November would put England into the World Cup finals for the first time in twelve years.

Nothing, however, could be taken for granted, not least given the stumbles England had already made on their way to the finals. Hungary were already there as group winners and England could expect no easy passage, not least since they had failed to score a single goal in the previous six hours at Wembley, and no England forward had found the net there since Mariner had scored against Switzerland a year earlier. Greenwood picked a side full of experience: the squad's average age was twenty-nine and had a combined total of 316 caps; Keegan was the most experienced player with fifty-eight caps, West Ham's centre-back, Alvin Martin, the least, with just two.

Wembley was packed to capacity, its terraces bedecked with flags, the north London air filled with noise. The vociferous mass of Englishmen were immediately encouraged by their team's positive start. Keegan had a header saved; Neal and McDermott both hit shots wide; then, on sixteen minutes, Martin headed down a McDermott cross, Brooking miscued his shot into the path of Mariner who rammed the ball home. Wembley roared its relief and England pushed for a second goal: McDermott volleyed narrowly over and Keegan twice went close. Half-time brought respite for the Hungarians, the second half brought a more measured approach from the hosts. England began to close the game, hitting the Hungarians inter-mittently on the counter-attack, but Mariner's goal was enough to secure the once elusive goal of qualification. A joyous Keegan, whose absences and below-par performances had attracted criticism throughout the qualifiers, beamed: 'We never gave them a yard and did all the things English football is renowned for. Let's hope the twenty-two in Spain do us as proud as the crowd did tonight. Let's hope it was not my last appearance for England.'

If victory in Budapest in June 1981 had initially brought a false dawn, England's second win over the Hungarians the following November marked a genuine turning point. Their confidence restored by qualification, England slotted back into the sort of fluent, patient, passing game that bore all the hallmarks of Greenwood's management. The goal famine ended and England began winning again. The 1982 Home Championship was won in emphatic style (Northern Ireland 4–0, Wales 1–0, Scotland 1–0) and England's renaissance was capped with an excellent 2–0 win over Holland on 25 May. The Dutch may well have been a team in transition, the '82 vintage falling as it did between two great sides, but on the eve of England's first foray into the World Cup finals since 1970 it was an excellent fillip.

For Greenwood, though, the World Cup was to mark the end of the line. Cajoled out of resigning a year earlier, he announced at the age of sixty-one that he would be stepping down after the finals. Eight years earlier, after Ramsey had been sacked, Greenwood, then West Ham manager, had leapt to his defence. 'It wasn't Alf's fault we haven't succeeded. Blame me – and the other ninety-one League club managers – for not producing players of the quality required for success at international level.' Eight years on his assertion held truer than ever. Of the Football League's three outstanding teams – champions Liverpool, UEFA Cup winners Ipswich and European champions Aston Villa – two of Ipswich's best three players were Dutch (Arnold Muhren and Franz Thijssen), the other a Scot (John Wark); at Liverpool, three Scots (Graeme Souness, Kenny Dalglish and Alan Hansen) and a Welshman (Ian Rush) provided Anfield with its core of world-class players; while Villa contributed just one player – Peter Withe – to Greenwood's twenty-two-man squad for Spain. Perhaps blessed with more of the sort of players he had himself nurtured at the Boleyn Ground – a Moore, a Hurst or a Peters – he may have been more inclined to stay.

The media, as one would expect, went into a spin about Greenwood's likely successor with all the usual suspects championing the 'people's choice' Brian Clough. But 'old Big 'Ead' had already burnt too many bridges during his brief, inglorious spell as youth team coach and it would have taken a radical and unprecedented bout of forbearance at FA headquarters to seriously consider his application. Nothing, however, changed very often at Lancaster Gate. That left Liverpool's Bob Paisley and Ipswich Town's Bobby Robson as the leading contenders, but with Paisley himself pushing on in years, the path was left open for Robson.

Born in Langley Park in 1932, Robson, like many footballers of his generation, was versed in realities of normal working life, having spent three years as an apprentice electrician down the pit before embarking on a professional football career. As a stylish wing-half cum inside-forward with Fulham and West Bromwich Albion he had already served his country with distinction, earning twenty caps and taking his place in the World Cup squads that travelled to Sweden and Chile. His early managerial career at Vancouver Whitecaps and Fulham had been inauspicious enough but, if they were false starts, he could claim to be grateful that the Ipswich chairman, John Cobbold, saw beyond them and appointed him manager in 1968. With little money at his disposal, over his fourteen-year spell at Portman Road he fashioned an attractive side that seldom left the upper echelons of the First Division, qualified for Europe nine times, won the FA Cup in 1978 and UEFA Cup in 1981, and narrowly missed the title when Ipswich finished runners-up in 1981 and 1982. If Ramsey had performed a miracle in taking the championship to Suffolk in 1962, Robson, although he never reached that pinnacle, arguably outdid even him. Certainly, over the course of the 1970s and early 1980s he outstripped each member of the so-called 'Big Five' bar Liverpool. With this in mind the FA offered Robson, who was assisting Greenwood in Spain, a five-year contract and £50,000 annual salary, which he accepted during the course of the tournament.

England were drawn in Group Four which was based in and around the Basque city of Bilbao. Since they had last taken part in Mexico, the finals had been expanded to include twenty-four countries and the tournament now consisted of six groups of four with the top two progressing to a second group stage of four groups of three. The winners of each of those groups would then go through to the semi-final stages, which finally assumed the form of a knock-out competition. It was a convoluted method that was open to abuse, put a premium on not losing and meant that the better teams – as England found out to their cost – didn't always get the reward that early success merited.

Greenwood's squad also had to contend with the backdrop of a rapidly developing conflict between Britain and Argentina in the wilds of the South Atlantic. Argentina had invaded the Falkland Islands at the start of April, prompting trade sanctions, diplomatic appeals and the dispatch of a naval task force to liberate them. The crucial battle at Goose Green was fought on 28 May, and the surrender of Argentina's forces was secured two days before England kicked off their World Cup matches. Nevertheless, across the Spanish-speaking world sympathy lay with the defeated South Americans and protests about British 'imperial' injustice (at holding the Falklands) were widespread.

The welcome the England party enjoyed in the Basque country would be in sharp contrast to this prevailing mood. Their base, the Los Tamarises Hotel ten miles outside Bilbao, was a complex located against the side of a cliff where no prying lens or irate local could upset the players' routine this time, although there was a certain amount of tension throughout. Armed guards prowled the complex, worried about attacks from Basque separatists, and boredom inevitably soon set in. The players broke up the dull routine with pool and table-tennis competitions while Bryan Robson was crowned the Pacman champion after spending so long playing the arcade console that the controls gave him blisters. Where others had feared or resented the English, the Basques – perhaps sharing the mentality of the outcast – embraced them. Jesus, the Los Tamarises' genial proprietor, for instance, presented each person in the England party with a bottle of wine from the year of their birth. The thought of Alf Ramsey attracting similar affection was almost inconceivable.

A few days prior to the opening match Keegan was awarded the OBE for services to football. With his room-mate Trevor Brooking already an MBE their bedroom became known as the 'royal room'. Neither, however, was in a particularly congenial mood: on their door Keegan had daubed a red cross. Both men were injured. The Southampton star had suffered a recurrence of an old back injury; Brooking was laid low with a groin injury. Both men missed England's first group game, with France on 16 June.

So often the opening group match is a subdued, tentative affair with both teams trying their utmost to get the measure of the other, but ultimately intent on avoiding defeat. With England drawn against tough European opposition – France and Czechoslovakia – plus World Cup first-timers Kuwait, avoiding defeat was surely the key to progression. Yet England got off to a flyer. Just twenty-seven seconds had passed when Steve Coppell's long throw-in was flicked on by Terry Butcher across the goal and met by the onrushing Robson, who hooked the ball past Ettori and into the French net.

France's response was robust. Spearheaded by Michel Platini they maintained much of the possession and tested England's tactical nous like a grand master mustering an offensive onslaught. On twenty-five minutes it came. Trevor Francis lost possession and Larios found Soler; the Frenchman was too fast for Butcher and he left the centre-half flagging in his wake before hitting a clean crisp shot past Shilton to level the scores. If Platini was the artist it was Alain Giresse who made the team tick. More and more he began to dictate the pattern of the game in midfield and France were unlucky to go in after forty-five minutes without more to show than Soler's equaliser. By contrast, half-time had come as a relief for Ron Greenwood and the England manager used the interval to modify his tactics. He did so astutely. Graham Rix dropped back into a more defensive position and England came alive. Francis headed Mills's cross narrowly over and then went close after good work from Rix. Then, on sixty-six minutes, he turned provider, breaking clear on the right before flighting a cross into the heart of the French penalty area. Surging in stealthily from midfield was Bryan Robson and at full length he dived, pummelling the ball with his head and into the back of the French net. England were rolling and seized the moment. Shortly after, Rix, Wilkins and Francis combined to create a chance for Paul Mariner and he made no mistake in making it 3–1. It was Mariner's fifth goal in successive matches and enough to secure victory.

But Keegan and Brooking were still causing Greenwood concern as neither's injury had cleared up, despite the attentions of a groin specialist summoned from England to treat the West Ham man. Keegan was also itching for specialist treatment. He knew a doctor in Germany who was familiar with his condition and he tried to persuade Greenwood and Vernon Edwards, the England team doctor, to let him consult the Hamburg physician. The idea itself was desperate, but then so was Keegan to finally get a run out in the World Cup finals. Edwards talked him round and persuaded Keegan to have an epidural, which meant he sat out Czechoslovakia, resting in the hope that it cleared up.

If the French were all flair and attacking verve, Czechoslovakia were altogether different. A tightly disciplined, well-organised side, England had already come unstuck against them under Revie when they were heading towards a surprise victory in the 1976 European Championships. Six years on, however, they were a lesser side, devoid of several stars that had brought them their most famous victory. Once more England got off to a good start: Coppell's cross kissed the crossbar before being cleared; Mariner's header was hacked off the line; Wilkins' fierce volley hit an otherwise oblivious goalkeeper and Robson twice went close. But when half-time came, the scoreline remained goalless.

Hoddle came on for the injured Robson and then, on the hour-mark, came the stroke of luck England had needed. Rix was fouled on the right, Wilkins took the free-kick, the Czechoslovak goalkeeper Stanislav Semen fumbled and Francis volleyed the loose ball into the empty net. Three minutes later England doubled their lead when Josef Barmos tried to intercept with a slide in an attempt to block build-up play between Mariner and Francis, only to put the ball past Semen. England were in an unassailable lead and through to the second group stage as group winners. A 1–0 win over Kuwait who, despite the scorching heat, refused to take water because of the strictures of Ramadan, meant England qualified for the second round with a 100 per cent record.

Meanwhile, although Brooking had proven slowly receptive to his treatment, Keegan had had no such luck. At 11.30 p.m., the night before the Kuwait game he had confronted the England manager.

'I'm letting everyone down. D'you think it would be better if I went home? Would I be best out of the place?'

Greenwood tried to calm him, but it was to little avail.

'I've got this specialist in Hamburg . . .' he told Greenwood, adding that it was pointless staying if he didn't think he'd be fit. 'I'm really frustrated. I feel bloody useless. And if I don't go to Hamburg I might as well go home. I know I could get to Hamburg . . .'

Finally his manager relented and Keegan went straight to the hotel reception to try and book himself a cab to Madrid. Unable to find a taxi driver prepared to make a five-hour journey to Madrid, the quick-thinking Keegan persuaded the hotel receptionist to lend him her tiny, two-seated Seat 500 – what Greenwood described as a 'toy-sized car'. 'I would not have let anyone else make the journey,' he later wrote. 'But Kevin was such a man of the world that I knew he would be all right.' Forty-eight hours later Keegan was back . . . and recovered. All that was left was for him to regain his match sharpness after three weeks without a game.

England's second group stage pitted them against Spain and old adversaries West Germany. It was as tough a draw as they could have possibly envisaged, while the French, who had finished runners-up in the initial stage, only faced Northern Ireland and Austria. The Germans had not been beaten by another European team since Jupp Derwall succeeded Helmut Schoen as manager after the 1978 World Cup, but they were an average side that had already been beaten by the Algerians and only scraped through thanks to a disgraceful draw with Austria – the so called 'Anschluss agreement' – when both teams conspired to allow West Germany a 1–0 win in order for both to qualify at Algeria's expense. Hugh McIlvanney had written that 'if this non-contest had been a horse race the stewards would have held an instant inquiry', while Pele memorably described the Germans as 'Rummenigge and ten robots'.

And so it came to pass when the two countries met at the Bernabeu Stadium in Madrid on 29 June. West Germany were ultra cautious, offering nothing in attack and reduced England's attacking options to long-range pot shots. Still without Keegan and Brooking, their opponents lacked the inspiration to break them down. 'Germany played like frightened sheep,' Trevor Francis propounded, 'and England had not the inventiveness to shear them as naked as they deserved to be.'[43] Rummenigge had the best chance five minutes from the end when he lost his marker and crashed a shot past Shilton and against the England crossbar. Had it gone in the outcome would have been a travesty, but the deadlock left England needing to better the scoreline achieved in the game between West Germany and Spain, which the Germans won 2–1 three days later.

That result left Spain with nothing to play for but pride against England, who needed to win by two clear goals. Attention focused on the two walking wounded, each just about recovered from injury, but lacking match sharpness. Two days before the game Keegan declared: 'I am fully fit for the first time. I am 100 per cent and my old confidence is back.' It was a view immediately contradicted by Trevor Francis: 'Kevin hasn't played for a month. He can't be match fit.' That same evening Greenwood staged a short practice match at England's training ground next to the hotel. Brooking was in the second team – an indication that he was unlikely to play – but Keegan was included in the first team in place of Coppell. The second team won, Brooking grabbing the decider, yet when Greenwood named his side to face Spain, neither he nor Keegan was named in the starting XI. Both were included on the bench and, to the surprise of many, Tony Woodcock was named to partner Francis up front. It marked the first time that the two men had played together since both had scored in the 2–0 win at the Nou Camp two years earlier.

Inspired by a sense of patriotism that had been all but invisible when progression to the semi-finals had actually been at stake, Spain lined up against England prepared to fight for everything. They had been utterly lacklustre hitherto in the second stage, woefully falling to defeat (as they had when Northern Ireland beat them in the first round), but now they chased every ball, harried, tackled and played as if it were they – and not England – with a semi-final to play for. Luis Arconada, whose mistake had given away the first goal to Germany, was in fine form, saving fierce drives from Francis and Robson early on, but otherwise remained untroubled by English advances, most of which came down the left through Graham Rix, but were easily cut out.

Disappointing in the first half, England were just as poor once the second got under way. After an hour Greenwood shuffled his pack, bringing off Rix and Woodcock and finally giving Keegan and Brooking a run out. Within minutes of his arrival Brooking gained possession and ran at the Spanish defence, before letting fly with a shot that Arconada tipped around the post. Then Bryan Robson broke down the left, looked up and sent in a perfect dipping cross. Keegan rose, watching the arc of the ball, and struck it with the flat of his forehead – and wide.

Time ticked away, but England were unable to add to their tally of attacks and once more the game fizzled out to a goalless stalemate. England were out, West Germany through to a semi-final against France. That was won on penalties after the world had watched aghast when the German goalkeeper Toni Schumacher had lunged high and with his feet at the French defender Patrick Battiston, almost decapitating the Frenchman in the process. The moment encapsulated the ugly, relentless manner of this German team; few mourned their demise when Italy defeated them 3–1 in the final.

Ron Greenwood left the England manager's job stating: 'The earth will be flat and the moon made of cheese before England's manager is given all he needs to do his job properly. We are talking about the impossible.'[44] Maybe he had a point. The resources he had at his disposal – both in terms of his largely undistinguished squad, and his modest backroom staff (who were largely part time and borrowed from First Division clubs), were inadequate to meet the insatiable expectations of England's fans. Yet Greenwood returned to retirement after a gap of five years able to reflect that he had restored dignity and pride to the England set-up when its reputation had never been so low. Later he admitted that had Brooking and Keegan been fit, England would have gone all the way to the World Cup final; in the semi-final they would have met a French team they had already beaten, and thereafter? Who could possibly say?

Keegan, nevertheless, remained convinced that he and Brooking could and should have started the Spain match. 'Leaving us on the bench was Ron Greenwood's biggest mistake,' he wrote in his 1998 autobiography. 'We were his two best players, we were very influential in the way England played and I do not believe any other country in the world would have made that decision, even if the team had done all right without us.'[45] In fact, Brooking's injury would keep him out of club action until the following March. Then aged thirty-four, he never got the chance to add to his forty-seven caps.

Keegan still had brushes with individual glory. He left Southampton that summer after two successful years at The Dell, and, to much excitement and fanfare, dropped down a division to try and help rescue ailing Newcastle United. On Tyneside, an area plunged into economic and football depression, he was an overnight hero, hailed as a messiah he would inspire the Magpies' return to the top flight. Keegan also hoped for a complete return to fitness and the chance to prove as indispensable to Bobby Robson as he had been to Greenwood and Don Revie.

Past his thirty-first birthday and playing at a lower level, he wasn't to get the chance. Robson, who had witnessed at close quarters Keegan's occasionally disruptive behaviour in Madrid and Bilbao, was looking to the 1986 World Cup finals. When he named his first squad, to face Denmark in a European Championship qualifier in September 1982, Keegan's name was omitted. Worse still, in the player's opinion, Robson hadn't deigned to tell him of his omission. Somewhat arrogantly, the new England manager claimed to owe Keegan nothing, having never previously managed him, adding, however, that the door was closed on no player.

If it wasn't, Keegan soon ensured that it was slammed tightly shut. 'I'm finished with England. I'll never kick a ball for my country again,' he told the following day's *Sun*. 'There has never been a more delighted England skipper than Kevin Keegan. Nobody has ever worn an international shirt with so much pride. And I never thought I'd see the day when anybody would sour my ambitions to play for England until I dropped. But Bobby Robson has done just that.'

After sixty-three caps and twenty-one goals, Keegan's run was at an end. Little did he know then that he would – much further down the line – return to the national fold in the most dramatic fashion.

11

THE EFFLUENT TENDENCY

THE GAME WAS done. Players were showered, liveried in official garb, hoping to be in bed before the small hours became the wee small hours. Officials, tired and disappointed that victory hadn't been secured, were also anxious to get back. With them assorted journalists, their stories long since wired or phoned through to London, mingled loosely and amongst themselves; others rounded off a long day with a beer or two, killing time, fighting back fatigue. Then came the call. The plane was ready, the gate open. Would passengers ensure that they had their boarding cards and passports at the ready? Together they trooped to the waiting charter plane: superstars, honest pros, a few journeymen, coaching staff, pompous functionaries, judicious apparatchiks, hacks, rotters and one or two more noted scribes; a motley divergent assortment certainly, but all players in little ways and large, apparent or otherwise, in the great game that they and millions more loved.

It was late in the evening of Wednesday 22 September 1982, hours after the conclusion of Bobby Robson's first game as England manager, a European Championship qualifier against Denmark. For him and many of the others who made up the party, the week had begun on Sunday afternoon at Bisham Abbey. A meal, a meeting, an early night and a training session had followed, before they'd flown out to Copenhagen early on the Tuesday. Robson had been able to put his players through their paces at the Idraetsparken stadium later that afternoon, and again on the morning of the match, before letting his squad relax into their pre-match routine at the hotel. It was brief, all too brief, but such are the woes of an international football manager.

For some of England's fans, Sunday had also been their starting point. Like a flock of migrating geese they had started to hit

Copenhagen in groups of two or three, mostly arriving at the city's main railway station; others, however, came by coach, some, but not many, flew. Before long there was a mass of more than 300 supporters. In the context of a football crowd it was not many, in the milieu of a relatively small city centre, and with seventy-two hours to kill, it was enough to ensure that the people of Copenhagen would not forget them in a hurry.

Many spent the dead time before kick-off by interspersing drinking sessions with tours of Copenhagen's sex shows, shoplifting raids and befouling the city's walls. 'On the Perspex surrounds of a number of cafes on Vesterbrogade,' noted one witness, 'one could read references to the "Blackburn NF", the "Manchester Nazis" and so on. Slogans like these came with hastily fashioned swastikas and the nicknames of the artists.'[1] Many fans had arrived with little or no funds and sustained themselves by stealing from supermarkets and market stalls. Others were more organised and took advantage of comparatively lax security arrangements to undertake targeted shoplifting raids. Six Liverpool fans were arrested for stealing clothes and jewellery valued at 75,000 Kroner (£4000), but many more got away with similar crimes, such as a mob of thirty to forty fans who spontaneously raided a jeweller's store. 'We couldn't fuckin' believe it,' boasted one of them. 'They had it [some unidentified object] through the window, and they were in. We all fucked off out of it before the coppers came.'[2]

When Wednesday came and the bulk of England's 2000 followers arrived in the Danish capital, one of the first sights that greeted them was a union jack with 'Chelsea' stitched across its centre flying from the first floor window of a hotel above Copenhagen's largest 'sex supermarket'. By four o'clock, the bars were filling up, reverberating to the strains of 'Rule Britannia' and 'We're on the March with Robson's Army'. While that may have been good-natured enough, the actions of some of those there since the weekend had already been noted disdainfully by the locals. The Copenhagen daily *Ekstra Bladet* reported: 'We sent the Vikings but now, after 1000 years, they are paying us back. The English football fanatics – called hooligans – hit Copenhagen yesterday. They are feared all over Europe. There isn't any other country where football fans run amok when they are following their team.' For those short on funds the notoriously potent Scandinavian lager 'Elephant Beer' was the drink of choice, with fans drinking from six packs as they made their way around. During the day Danish fans began to arrive from around the country and embark on their own drinking sessions. Sporadic fights broke out in and around the Central Station, home to many England followers who had come with insufficient funds for accommodation. They 'were vocal in support of the home side and, in many cases, no less the worse for drink than their English guests', noted one observer.[3]

It would be quite wrong to convey the impression that all of England's followers that day in September 1982 were thieves, drunks and racists. They weren't. Most were in Copenhagen simply to enjoy foreign climes, watch Bobby Robson's debut as England manager, before heading home without trouble. For the majority, the very idea of fighting had been left on the school playground years earlier.

Nevertheless, a significant minority were bent on causing chaos. For instance, mid-afternoon on match day, a group of around thirty, wrapped in flags, arms bristling with tattoos, marched noisily and menacingly through Copenhagen's main shopping area, singing, swearing, some carrying out thefts or assaults on Danish fans. Later, outside the Idraetsparken before the match, a group of supporters from London goaded and jeered passing Danes, some throwing beer over them and lashing out with their feet. If their hosts stopped to remonstrate they were urged to 'C'mon and have a go'; if they backed down they were met with jeers of derision and flashes of the English invaders' buttocks. Displays of mooning proved a popular and reliable shot for photographers and cameramen.[4]

Inside the stadium there was no proper segregation and, where they existed, seating arrangements were not properly enforced. When some England fans refused to use the seats designated for them and insisted on trying to join friends in different parts of the ground, pushing and shoving broke out when they were challenged. Meantime in the seats in the upper deck of the main stand, Danish fans provocatively threw a barrage of beer, cans and plastic cups on their visitors below. As kick-off approached the strains of 'Rule Britannia' became intermingled with references to the Falklands War, with a variation of the 'Sparrow Song' being a particular favourite:

> The Argies they went to the Falklands
> They said that they wanted to ruck.
> So the Argies went in.
> And the English moved in.
> And kicked all the Argies to fuck.

This was the cause of some consternation amongst Danish youths, who used pro-Argentina slogans to bait England fans. Invariably they reacted in kind. As one of them told the *Daily Star*, such verbosity provided cause for him to stand up for himself and his country. 'I'm very patriotic and when they started calling me an English bastard and chanting "Argentina, Argentina!" because of the Falklands War I thought it was about time I started to defend myself,' he said. 'A couple of them got cut up a bit, but there was no bottles or knives. All the continentals want to do is to give us a good thumping.'[5] Amongst some misguided sections of the England support, it seemed as if there existed a belief that they were standing up for 'national pride' as much as Bobby Robson's team. The Nelsonian sense of 'duty', it seemed, manifested itself in many strange ways.

As to the football, there were several significant changes brought by England's new manager. Obviously there was no Kevin Keegan; Trevor Brooking was injured, never to play for his country again; and Bobby Robson had left out Mick Mills – once his captain at Portman Road – as he looked to the future. 'I've got to start somewhere as England manager. I have to map out a five-year programme,' he had explained. 'I'm not saying this is the end for Kevin Keegan and Mick Mills – you can never write off players of true international class. I might well decide in the future that I need to turn back to more experienced players to steady the younger element.' Neither Keegan, infamously, nor his fans at Newcastle agreed: later on in the season, when Robson visited St James' Park, supporters verbally abused and spat at him.

Against Denmark England's footballers got off to a solid start. Ranussen's full-length save was enough to block Graham Rix's early long-range volley, but after only seven minutes he was picking the ball out of his net when Francis's shot slipped wide of his grasp. Denmark came back strongly, dominating long stretches of possession and were unlucky not to have more to show than a sixty-ninth-minute equaliser, and unluckier still to fall behind again, when Francis stabbed home his and England's second.

On the terraces and in the stands only a handful of minor scuffles took place once play had got under way as fans concentrated on the unfolding spectacle. Indeed the only incident of any great note came when a smoke bomb was thrown onto the field from the Danish section after the referee had refused to give a penalty. As the game seemed to be fizzling out towards a 2–1 win for England the Danish police began to leave, readying themselves for the dispersal operation. Then, in the final minute, the Ajax winger Jesper Olsen weaved his way through the England defence before sliding the ball past Shilton for Denmark's equaliser. Across the Idraetspark bedlam broke out as Danes celebrated a deserved draw. Not everyone shared their elation. In one corner minor mayhem ensued as around 200 England fans began to provoke celebrating Danish fans. As fighting broke out police surged back into the stadium, heightening the sense of drama for watching TV crews, although the violence quickly died.

Following the final whistle, however, a series of fights broke out down the main thoroughfare back into the city centre. 'The English kicked everybody and everything which came in their way,' reported *Aktuelt*. 'A taxi-driver who was stuck sent an SOS to the taxi headquarters because he feared for his life and car. The local police station received assistance from all stations in the city and they tried – as far as they could – to follow the English fans around the city.'

Things soon calmed again and the England supporters went back to the bars or – like the official party – simply returned home on late-night charter flights. According to one Dane, large numbers of Denmark fans usually converged on Copenhagen for internationals, many of whom drank heavily prior to matches. However the extent to which they contributed to the disorder this time around was unusual, he said: 'The English, say the newspapers, have the vandals, so the Danes who want to fight, they come to see the English.'[6] Indeed a team of leading experts on football hooliganism who had charted the events concluded that supporters of both countries had been culpable: both had provoked; each had risen to provocation. 'Much of the hooligan behaviour in Copenhagen was co-produced,' they said, 'a consequence of the interaction between them and their Danish counterparts.'[7]

Still, more than 100 England fans were arrested, although just six were held for more than a day. All the rest were fined and released. By contrast only fifteen Danes were detained by police. Leslie Walker, the

FA's security liaison officer, reported 'Denmark was not a major incident in terms of misbehaviour abroad. It was very limited. It was after the match and, indeed, I think the press and the media did a disservice because it was nowhere near as bad as people thought it was by the pictures.' He had a point. Most of England's 2000 travelling fans had played no part in the disturbances; many who had, had not pre-arranged it, but had become embroiled in violence simply because it was there or they themselves had come under attack. Very few had journeyed to Copenhagen with the express purpose of finding trouble. Nevertheless, as TV pictures were beamed across Europe and beyond, it reinforced the rising consensus that English fans were the hooligan kings of the world.[8]

Football and violence seemed to be intrinsically linked. Even when the game assumed its most basic form in the Middle Ages, it had attracted trouble. Between 1314 and 1660 football was banned by national and local authorities on no less than thirty different occasions, and outright by James II of Scotland. In 1608 The Court Leet Manchester complained of 'disorder, crude language, broken windows and damaged property by lewde and disordered persons using that unlawful exercise of playing with the football in the streets of the town'. In 1638 on the Isle of Ely several hundred men gathered together to play football and then proceeded to 'destroy the drainage ditches'. The advent of a proper set of rules did little to move things on. In 1884, a match between Preston and Bolton Wanderers at Deepdale saw the visitors win, a result that irked the locals: 'Orange peel and cinders were thrown at the goalkeeper,' noted one eye-witness. 'Stones, kicks and blows aimed at players and away spectators at the end of the game, hardly a member of the Wanderers party, i.e. players and spectators got to the station intact.' At Everton there was a riot in 1895 when a match was abandoned; a year later serious trouble at a Scotland v England match, and so it went on. Between 1895 and 1915 the FA closed grounds on eight occasions and issued seventeen cautions to clubs as to the future conduct of their fans. Between 1921 and 1939 there were eight closures again, but this time sixty-four cautions.[9] In the fifties and sixties, trains were wrecked by travelling fans, bottles thrown onto pitches, fighting broke out on the terraces, opposing supporters were often ambushed or simply terrorised and pubs were ransacked. Then, it was less prevalent, and though fans frequently stumbled on trouble, it was by no means all pervading. By the 1970s and early 1980s the wrong coloured scarf at the wrong time or place would make almost any fan a target, sometimes with appalling consequences. For visiting supporters it was a no-win situation. 'If you ran,' one fan said, 'you got caught and were given a good hiding and if you stayed and fought the local police would try and arrest you.'[10]

With domestic football attendances in a steady decline since the early fifties, the inhospitable climate on the terraces merely added to the fall. By the early eighties football grounds had become, in the words of the writer Russell Davies, 'Cockpits of Ignobility'. He argued that 'the game drifts slowly into the possession of what we are now supposed to call the underclass; and a whole middle-class public grows without ever dreaming of visiting a Football League ground'.[11] The drop in gate revenues left English football in a financial recession, leaving once proud grounds standing only as nearly empty, dilapidated carcasses of their former heyday. Unable to match salaries offered on the continent, and in need of additional revenue, clubs began to allow their best players to leave for foreign teams. Kevin Keegan, Tony Woodcock, Ray Wilkins, Trevor Francis, Glenn Hoddle, Gordon Cowans, Laurie Cunningham, Mark Hateley and Luther Blissett were just some of England's stars to opt for different climes during this period. English football, it seemed, was slowly dying, hooliganism merely pushing it closer to its grave.

English hooliganism had been exported to the continent since the mid-sixties when Manchester United fans – boosted by a complement of British soldiers stationed in West Germany – fought running battles on the terraces with SV Hanover in 1965. But it wasn't until 1974, when Spurs fans were reported as having 'gone on the rampage' in Rotterdam and Manchester United fans fought with local youths in Ostend, that football hooliganism by 'civvies' in Europe really kicked off. A number of Liverpool fans following their team's extraordinary success on the continent paid for their travels and gave birth to the cult of the football casual by emptying poorly policed boutiques of their Lacoste, Benetton and Henri Lloyd wares and exporting them back home. For England fans, the scenes in Denmark in September 1982 were reminiscent of Luxembourg in 1977, Turin in 1980, and Basle and Oslo in 1981.

Certainly the perception cast by English supporters at home and abroad was a bad one. Yet, while they were regarded by themselves and others as the 'hooligan champions of Europe', this was by no means an English disease. In Lima in 1964 at an Olympic qualifier between Peru and Argentina the referee refused to allow a goal to the home side and in the riot that ensued 318 people were killed and more than 500 injured. Forty-eight people died after a riot at a club match in Turkey in 1967, seventy-four in Argentina in 1968 and so it continued throughout the 1970s and on into the 1980s: sixty-nine were killed after a match in Moscow in 1982 and twenty-nine in Colombia in the same year. Even as early as 1965 *The Times* had gone so far as to recommend the wholesale withdrawal of British clubs from European competition until the 'continentals had put their house in order'.[12] Trying to portray yourself as the least worst is no sort of absolution but, as one academic study showed, English fans were certainly not always to blame, despite their reputation as King Rats of Europe. Looking into reported incidents involving either English clubs playing in Europe or the national team it came across twenty-one when English fans had initiated violence, but found a further fourteen in which English supporters or players were the victims.[13] The very fact that out of hundreds of visits to the continent only thirty-five had seen trouble seemed proof positive that most English fans who followed football abroad would see their visit pass peaceably and without incident. The conclusion was inescapable: perception was usually worse than reality.

Nevertheless, when skirmishes, such as those in Copenhagen, did occur, no matter how over-magnified the actions of the few may have been by press or television coverage, it merely added to a prevailing sense of 'moral panic' back home. Just as bank robberies in the sixties and muggings in the seventies provided fodder for an over-anxious population, football hooliganism in the eighties seemed to be the latest symptom of national decay. The reality, though, was that the problem was little worse than before and certainly nowhere near as bad as popularly perceived. At the worst club (Millwall) in its worst season (1986–87), only thirty-nine in every 10,000 fans was arrested. Of these, the majority were released without charge, and of those that were, most were charged only with drunkenness or 'threatening or abusive words or behaviour' rather than assault and violence itself. A study into the mugging 'crisis' published in 1978 had suggested that the moral panic about the subject was an expression of wider anxieties about changes in British society and asked: 'Could it be possible that a societal reaction could precede the appearance of a pattern of crime?' [14] Was the same true about football hooliganism?

It didn't really matter if it was. Few people read academic studies; everybody read newspapers or watched television. Those who weren't at football grounds to see the reality for themselves were able to draw their conclusions from the increasingly skewed media coverage: football was violent; football was dangerous; football was rotten to the core.

Taking a lead from all this was the Prime Minister. Armed with a mandate for deflationary cuts, incentives for private enterprise and a tough line on the unions, Margaret Thatcher had come to power in 1979. Her government propagated a two-thirds/one-third society, in which the two-thirds of the population eventually benefited from lower taxes, share and property ownership and fewer constraints as employers; the remaining third, mostly northern (or from Scottish and Welsh parts of the union), mostly working class, mostly unskilled or semi-skilled, were simply left to rot. The woman who castigated her predecessor Jim Callaghan as the 'Prime Minister of Unemployment' presided over a doubling of the jobless (to two million) in her first two years as premier, and would see the figure top three million by 1986. Popular discontent with her government had already bubbled over in the spring and summer of 1981 when inner-city riots in Brixton, Toxteth, Moss Side and St Pauls brought violence, arson and looting. The poverty and unemployment induced by the government's deflationary policies was widely regarded as being responsible. Mrs Thatcher's reported reaction? 'Oh those poor shopkeepers.' Her declining fortunes were only reversed by victory in the Falklands War and the subsequent tide of jingoism would help her overcome a pitifully weak opposition and seal a second term in June 1983. But as her arguments about the economy began to lose more votes than they gained, she began to diversify her obsessions into public order issues, which offered an easy route to votes at a time when public concern was running high. Tackling football hooliganism was to become a cause célèbre.

Margaret Thatcher's two defining beliefs meant an inherent lack of understanding for football as a whole was inevitable. If she declared that 'there is no such thing as society – only individuals and families' – how then could she comprehend the unique community of football supporters? Given that her other great maxim was that 'the lady is not for turning' – could she ever? With football-related violence a deeply unpopular (albeit exaggerated) phenomenon and the Prime Minister in the hunt for votes, it was an issue she could pursue with impunity. The game became one of several political footballs to which she would give a thunderous toe-poke when seeking to divert attention from her political woes. The Iron Lady's contempt for not just the problem of hooliganism but the sport as a whole were to eventually threaten the very future of the game in its homeland. In the three years that followed the Denmark game, with English football at home and abroad continuing to be tainted by violence, the government continued to intimate that it would crack down hard if the trouble didn't stop. Still it went on: football and politics were seemingly set on a collision course.

For Bobby Robson, more pressing problems came on the pitch. Results in his first year at the helm represented patchy progress for England's new manager as his team struggled to match the pace set by the impressive Danes in the European Championship qualification group. An away win in Greece (3–0) and a victory over Luxembourg of the magnitude not witnessed since Robson's own international playing days (9–0), set England on a positive course as they entered 1983. Yet when they failed to turn dominance into goals in the return meeting with Greece at Wembley at the end of March and only managed a goalless draw, the advantage fell firmly into the hands of the Danes. Success in the 1982–83 Home Championship, following victory over Wales (2–1), Scotland (2–0) and a goalless draw with Northern Ireland, was more impressive. Less so was a ludicrous 30,000 mile round trip to Australia in June 1983 which saw three games played against the hosts over the duration of a week in three cities. First, in Sydney England drew 0–0; then, in Brisbane (in front of less than 10,000 spectators) they mustered a 1–0 win; before drawing 1–1 in Melbourne.

Insipid though the antipodean results were, more worrisome still was the paucity of talent emerging through England's ranks. In his first year in charge Robson handed out no fewer than fourteen debuts but it would be difficult to categorise the majority of them as anything other than good club players, and some of them weren't even that.

Ricky Hill, Mark Chamberlain, Gordon Cowans, Derek Statham, Graham Roberts, Danny Thomas, Steve Williams, John Gregory, Nick Pickering and Nigel Spink came, saw, played without any great distinction and faded from the consciousness of most England fans. Only Gary Mabbutt, the Tottenham Hotspur centre-back, who went on to make sixteen appearances in a stop-start international career that spanned a decade, and, most significantly, John Barnes, could claim to have left a lasting impression.

Barnes represented a unique addition to the history of the national team. In many ways his background was more reminiscent of some of the generation of 'gentlemen footballers' who had preceded him a century earlier than their twentieth-century successors. Born in Jamaica in 1963, John Charles Bryan Barnes (he took his name from the Welsh football legend) had come to England as a teenager with his father, the Jamaican military attaché, and had spent adolescence amongst London's diplomatic set. It was a background of com-parative privilege and prestige, in which he enjoyed some of London's smarter addresses, rather than the council houses and terraced streets that usually provided the breeding grounds of England's footballers. Less worldly was the country he had become part of: Barnes pur-portedly had the wrong coloured skin in the wrong neighbourhoods. Invariably this caused him problems. Police seeing the black teenager training on the fashionable streets of St James' or Hampstead would approach him assuming him to be a burglar. By his own admission he would hear worse. Graham Taylor signed him for Watford as a sixteen-year-old, and the unusually tall, burly, left-flanker was instrumental in helping Watford to promotion to the top flight in 1982, and then the unparalleled heights of First Division runners-up a year later. At the end of that season Robson made him one of the growing number of black players to have followed Viv Anderson's lead and played for England, when he brought him on as a substitute against Northern Ireland. Three months later, on 21 September 1983, he gave him his third start, in the crunch European qualifier with Denmark.

The Danes, however, had their own teenage prodigy. Michael Laudrup, son of Finn Laudrup, a Danish international star of the late 1960s and 1970s, was a sumptuously gifted winger-cum-striker whose exquisite football talent had already earned him a big money transfer to Juventus. Mindful of Laudrup's presence, that of Jesper Olsen –

who had been so deadly a year earlier – and the former European Footballer of the Year, Allan Simonsen, Robson put out a defensive formation, keeping Glenn Hoddle on the bench and playing Queens Park Rangers' unspectacular defensive midfielder, John Gregory, because he wanted someone 'a bit spiky'. Yet by placing Denmark on a pedestal, Robson handed them the initiative and England never once looked like gaining the win they needed for qualification. As early as the first minute, when Simonsen robbed Barnes and lobbed the ball through to Laudrup, the ponderous nature of the England backline was exposed. As the game progressed the Danes grew in confidence, as did their tally of chances: Shilton did enough to distract Laudrup into putting his shot in the side-netting; minutes later, only the profligacy of Bergren saved England after Olsen had run through the defence with ease to set him up; then, on thirty-seven minutes, Laudrup evaded the attentions of Butcher and Sansom before sending in a cross testing enough to force the normally immaculate Phil Neal to handle. Simonsen converted the penalty to give Denmark a 1–0 lead, an advantage England never looked like challenging. For the tabloid press it was a disaster to lose to a country of purported football no-marks (even though the Danes would emerge as one of Europe's finest up-and-coming teams); for Robson it meant that hopes of qualification for the following summer's European Championship finals in France were all but extinguished. When confirmation of that came, just prior to England's final qualifying match in Luxembourg on 16 November, Bryan Robson could never remember a dressing room being so low. 'The news killed us all, and – for twenty minutes or so – nobody said a word. All you could hear was the clatter of boots on the floor as the players went through their usual rituals of getting ready.'[15]

Disappointed though he unquestionably was, it had been his own prolonged absence through injury, along with Ray Wilkins and Glenn Hoddle, that had done much to undermine England's qualification campaign. Robson, who was now a Manchester United player, would be plagued with ailments throughout his international career and the only factor more surprising than the frequency with which he was on the treatment table, was his ability to overcome them. A broken cheekbone suffered by his Old Trafford colleague Wilkins meant he took the captain's armband for both club and country and, as England captain, Robson was arguably more vital to his namesake than even Bobby Moore had been to Sir Alf Ramsey. He scored frequent and usually crucial goals, defended with tenacity, led like a king and, without fail, always played with pride, verve, guts and skill. 'Great is a word too lightly used in the football parlance,' Bobby Robson would write of him later. 'But I have no hesitation in describing Bryan Robson as a "great player" – a fighter with a desire to be perfect and to do things the right way on the football pitch.'[16]

Conversely the presence of this great box-to-box midfielder hindered the blossoming of Glenn Hoddle. For Spurs he was often magnificent; for England he was frequently enigmatic. His champions said that the fault lay with the way England played, that Bobby Robson preferred industry over craftsmanship. In a way he did: given the choice between Hoddle and Robson, England's manager would always choose the latter; given the option of both, he would often overlook Hoddle. Hoddle's one possible weakness was his positional play. He never hid from the ball, but getting it to him posed a problem. Spurs dealt with it collectively: everything went through Hoddle – when he played, Tottenham played. At international level England didn't have that luxury. It was not that England would have been one-dimensional playing such a way – how could any team be with a player who possessed such a repertoire of passing and skill? – more that Hoddle needed the proverbial water-carrier to do the hard work, to get and give. Bryan Robson could play that role, but to do so would have subdued his own extraordinary attacking prowess. It is no coincidence that Hoddle's best games came, when Robson was injured, playing alongside more defensive players such as Peter Reid or Ray Wilkins.

Proof positive that Bobby Robson would be better served by a different midfield pairing came when both played in England's first match of 1984 against France in Paris. Up against the bulk of the side they had beaten so convincingly in Bilbao two years earlier, after a pleasing start by the visitors Michel Platini took control of a game in which he was the dominant influence in a French side whose performance was rampant. Time and again they overran England, easing paths through to Shilton's goal, with only the excellence of its custodian and the profligacy of their finishing sparing England a half-time deficit. In the second half Platini put paid to that. First, he ghosted away from his marker to head home Giresse's cross; next, he blasted a gloriously taken free-kick beyond the reach of Shilton to give

France an unassailable 2–0 lead. While England's footballers were adding to their burgeoning reputation for mediocrity, on the terraces their fans were adding to their own rising notoriety, fighting with French fans and police.

The disturbances in Paris brought the inevitable angry reaction from the British government, but by then they were about to be faced with another social order problem to which they gleefully dealt a heavy hand. A 1983 Monopolies and Mergers Commission report on the coal-mining industry had suggested that 75 per cent of pits were making a loss. Thatcher said they must go; the response of Arthur Scargill, leader of the National Union of Mineworkers (NUM), was straightforward: 'uneconomic pits' did not exist. Confrontation was inevitable and it came in April 1984 when the NUM called a national strike against pit closures and in favour of a vastly increased basic wage. Having seen how the unions had undone her predecessors, Thatcher was determined not to lose the battle. The result was a long, bitterly contested dispute that split families and communities, for which the government was patently better prepared than the miners, whose families were often forced to subsist on less than £12 strike pay per week. Violence frequently spilled out in pickets; people talked of 'class war'; the Prime Minister spoke of 'the enemy within'. Decimated and divided, almost a year later, in April 1985, the miners ended their struggle. The Iron Lady had prevailed; she could now focus her attention on other popular scapegoats – like football.

By then she had claimed first blood in her war on the game. In its centenary year, an otherwise dismal Home Championship (Northern Ireland won it with a goal difference of one, after all four countries had tied on three points) had been notable only for it being the last. After years of governmental pressure, the four British Football Associations relented and put an end to a national institution. Ironically, the annual tournament had a relatively mundane history of violence, the worst of it coming in the biannual England v Scotland fixture at Wembley when the spectre of drunken Scots 'desecrating' English soil provided the perfect ingredients for a fight. That it was mostly nothing more than stupid exuberance on both sides, and that the majority of matches passed peaceably didn't matter: it was highly visible, abhorrent to those in Westminster and, from 1984, it was no more.

England's dreary performances in the Home Championships

increased the pressure on Bobby Robson. When England met the USSR at Wembley a week later on 2 June 1984, the manager had been greeted by a 'Robson Out' demonstration organised by the *Sun*, who had even produced 'Robson Out, Clough In' lapel badges. Maybe they had a point. England put in a performance as woeful as they had against France, falling to a 0–2 defeat and, at the game's end, Robson was jeered and spat at by a section of England's supporters. 'Success brings you all the friends and allies you could ever wish for,' philosophised his captain, 'while anything short of the best makes you the most beleaguered man in football.'[17]

And then, quite remarkably, something changed. With no European Championship finals to compete in, England's beleaguered footballers crossed the Atlantic for a three-game tour of South America. First came a meeting with Brazil in the Maracana Stadium. Robson named a line-up bold enough to be mocked by the Brazilian press for its temerity: as well as handing a debut to Norwich City's centre-back, Dave Watson*, he gave only a second start to Portsmouth's tall powerful centre-forward, Mark Hateley ('he is a classic example of the old-fashioned English centre-forward in the mould of Nat Lofthouse,' Robson would say of him. 'He leads the line superbly; he's tenacious, fast, brave and bursting with confidence.'[18]). More radical still, he abandoned the twenty-year-old tactical mantra by deploying two out-and-out wingers in Barnes and Mark Chamberlain. 'I wanted some imagination,' he wrote of his decision. 'I wanted England to attack, be exciting and brighten things up generally and to get rid of some of that gloom and despondency that surrounded all of us.'[19]

It worked too. After holding firm in the face of some early Brazilian attacks, Wilkins and Robson gained control of the midfield and Barnes began to impress the home crowd with several assured runs. Then, just prior to half-time, Hateley won a header and the ball fell to Barnes wide on the left, slightly beyond the halfway line. Instantly he took it past one man, Woodcock ran into space expecting the pass, but Barnes maintained possession and suddenly he was away. Accelerating past a second marker, he cut inside a third and, as he bore down on the Brazilian penalty area, left a perplexed Junior

---

* Later of Everton and not to be confused with his recent predecessor and namesake, by then retired.

sprawled on his backside. Feigning to shoot, he fooled the Brazilian goalkeeper Costa, indolently rolling the ball into the back of the empty net. In the Maracana, the home of the sublime and the spectacular, an England player had scored one of *the* great goals. 'But for his all white strip,' joked his manager later, Barnes 'might have been a Brazilian himself.'[20] (Barnes was altogether more modest: 'I don't honestly remember much about it,' he said later. 'I just put my head down and went and went and went.') On sixty-five minutes Barnes turned provider, cutting in from the left and sending in a testing cross for Hateley to power home and seal a famous 2–0 victory.

Not all of England's followers saw it as a cause for celebration. A small section of the travelling support had refused to acknowledge Barnes's goal on account of the colour of his skin – a notion even more extraordinary than the goal that they had just witnessed; then, on the flight between Rio de Janeiro and Montevideo, four England 'fans' travelling on the same plane as the players continued the abuse by singing racist songs and berating the FA Secretary, Ted Croker. ('You fucking wanker, you prefer Sambos to us.') Later, there was a suggestion that England's supporters had been infiltrated by the National Front and the abuse of Barnes had been a 'political act', but either way it was indisputable that there was a faction of Englishmen not willing to accept black players.* The problem wasn't exclusively England's, more a reflection on football crowds of the era. In the mid-1980s, one only had to visit a ground – any ground – on any given Saturday, and if a black player was on show, they could virtually be guaranteed an earful of the sort of bile that would make even Alf Garnett blush. Like those who perpetrated violence in the name of club or country, it was a minority who uttered such hatred, but still a minority sizeable enough to further sully football's name.[21]

The remainder of the South American tour fizzled out with a 0–2 defeat in Uruguay and a 0–0 draw in Chile. Yet for the previously forlorn Bobby Robson, it represented a turning point. 'Looking back, that was the moment our team spirit began to develop,' he recalled. 'The players had been drawn together in adversity and had come

---

*As James Walvin put it: 'A political organisation which could never expect more than minimal coverage by the media at home – and a mere handful of votes at national elections – had secured massive, albeit notorious, coverage by the simple tactic of racial abuse.'

through the ordeal together. It produced a common bond and a shared pride that was heightened when the compliments and good wishes began to come in.'[22] Prior to the England squad's departure he had been approached by Barcelona who wanted him for their vacant manager's position. Motivated by an overwhelming desire to succeed and also determined to tread a different path than that taken by the disgraced Don Revie, Robson rejected their overtures. Instead, he recommended Queens Park Rangers' young manager, Terry Venables. For him it was to act as a springboard that set his career on an upward trajectory that would eventually lead him to Lancaster Gate.

To qualify for the 1986 World Cup finals, which were to be staged once more in Mexico, England had to finish in the top two of a five-nation group that included Finland, Northern Ireland, Turkey and, as in the run-up to 1982, Romania. The latter, boasting the emergent genius of the 'Maradona of the Carpathians' Gheorgie Hagi, posed the greatest threat to England's progress, but Robson could offer few complaints about the draw. Indeed before his men had even kicked a ball he could note with satisfaction that the Finns had beaten the Irish and the Irish had gone on to defeat Romania 3–2 in Belfast. England themselves got off to a perfect start, beating Finland 5–0 at Wembley on 17 October 1984 and then winning 8–0 in Turkey four weeks later, a win which was followed by a 1–0 victory over Northern Ireland at the end of February 1985. Even when they could only draw 0–0 in Bucharest on 1 May, and after a 1–1 stalemate in Helsinki on 22 May, it left England needing just three points from their remaining three qualifiers, all of which were at home.

The remarkable rise of Howard Kendall's Everton, from First Division also rans to record-breaking league champions over the course of the 1984–85 season, provided Robson with a previously untapped pool of talent. During the course of that campaign the England manager would hand out debuts to a quartet of Goodison men: Gary Stevens, Trevor Steven, Peter Reid and Paul Bracewell, and establish Gary Lineker (signed from Leicester City at the end of the season) in his forward line. Serious injury limited Bracewell, a tough but classy midfielder, to just three caps, but the other four were to be vital to Robson and their country. Stevens and Steven, respectively a right-back and right midfielder at Everton (and later Rangers), provided an excellent partnership in defence and attack, each complementing the other as a potent attacking force and, when called upon, steely defensive cover. Their team-mate Reid had overcome an appalling catalogue of injuries, which had seen him written off in his mid-twenties, to become the 1985 Player of the Year, win a multitude of trophies and finally emerge – at the age of nearly thirty – as one of the country's best players. Like that other great English defensive midfielder, Nobby Stiles, his technique was simple – get it, give it, move into space and demand it back – but devastatingly effective. Age and injury were to limit his international career to thirteen caps, but his presence was to be crucial at several vital junctures.

And then there was Lineker. One of England's great problems, dating all the way back to the end of Mick Channon's international career in the late 1970s, had been a lack of a natural goalscorer. True, Keegan had scored many important goals, but he was hardly prolific, while Robson had experimented with more than a dozen different forward permutations in his first three years in charge without ever really finding the right mix. In the twenty-four-year-old Lineker he had someone with pace, intelligence, perhaps not all the elegance of a Greaves or Lawton, but with an intuitive grasp of being in the right place at precisely the right time. Arguably nobody with Lineker's sense of timing or occasion – he had that wonderful knack of scoring crucial goals in vital matches – had worn the famous three lions before. He was to make himself a legend.

English football was dominated by Everton and their Merseyside rivals Liverpool in the mid-1980s. While Everton were sweeping aside all comers in the league, Liverpool, reigning European champions, had progressed to their fifth European Cup final, against Juventus in the Heysel Stadium, Brussels on 29 May 1985. A win – and they had never lost in the final before – would put them just one title behind Real Madrid's record of six. But what could, and should, have been one of English football's great days was to be its nadir.

In Brussels the build-up to the match had been characterised by heavy drinking amongst Liverpool supporters, and had, by the end of the afternoon, turned into an orgy of obscene drunkenness. Newspapers reported Liverpool fans urinating openly in bars where they had stood drinking for seven or eight hours and a jewellery shop was looted by passing supporters. As kick-off approached and fans left Brussels' main square, a trail of broken glass, scattered chairs and debris littered the city's streets.

In the stadium itself Liverpool and Juventus fans had not been properly segregated and at one end all that separated them was an empty area marked out by flimsy temporary fencing. As kick-off approached, hails of bottles and other missiles were showered on the Italian supporters from across this no man's land, to which they responded in kind, only serving to further provoke the hordes of drunken Liverpool fans. Soon the fencing – which only consisted of four-foot-high poles joined with wire – was broken down and a mob of Liverpudlians charged across the open terrace towards the Juventus section. The Italians panicked, turned and ran towards an exit. In the chaos that ensued many were trampled underfoot in the rush to escape. Worse was to come. Under the pressure of thousands of fleeing supporters a wall collapsed causing Juventus fans to fall on their fellow spectators and crush dozens to death. The suddenness of events overwhelmed the emergency services and they struggled to help save the injured and contain the rioting hordes. Even the Liverpool manager, Joe Fagan, failed to quell the fighting when he appeared on the pitch and desperately appealed to his fans, who had by then turned on riot police.

Incredibly the match went ahead, albeit some eighty-three minutes late. The result – a 1–0 victory to Juventus – was immaterial. The deaths of thirty-nine Italian fans and the shame that Liverpool supporters had heaped onto the English game were what figured most prominently. Disgust at the drunken mob was universal. 'After years of punishment which never fitted the crimes of English soccer thugs abroad, Brussels was the ultimate shame,' wrote the *Daily Mirror*. 'We gave football to the world. Now we give it our national disgrace.' *The Times* wrote: 'England's involvement in European competition can surely not continue.' The rest of the world united in its condemnation of the rioting supporters and the poor policing. *Corriere dello Sport* spoke of 'assassins on parole and absent police'. *La Derniere Heure des Sports* castigated the 'Liverpool Animals' and added that the tragedy could have been avoided if police had reacted more quickly and there had been better segregation between rival fans. Signor Agnelli, the Juventus President, said: 'the first thing to do to prevent such dreadful incidents to happen again is unfortunately ban English fans from European soccer'.[23]

Politicians back in London moved quickly. Margaret Thatcher bustled out of an emergency cabinet meeting to tell reporters that her blood had boiled at the scenes shown on television. 'It isn't that we're numb, we're worse than numb. Everything, but everything must be done.' She summoned the FA Chairman, Bert Millichip, back to London from England's North American tour. He returned immediately and gave journalists who greeted him at Heathrow Airport a portent of what was to follow. 'I believe the behaviour of hooligans over the past year culminating in the terrible events in Brussels may well mean that we may not see our football in Europe. Enough is enough and we cannot put up with these problems any longer.'

She spoke in the Commons later that day about how 'these violent people must be isolated from society' but linked the violence on the terraces with violence in Northern Ireland and on the picket line. Her attitude to these matters had always been of the sledge-hammer variety – would it be the same for football? 'There is violence in human nature and there are three ways of trying to deal with it,' she proclaimed, 'persuasion, prevention and punishment.' In doing so she neatly reduced a previously complicated social problem into a simple and straightforward moral issue. Everything connected with football was sullied; her assertion that 'everything but everything must be done' might as well have meant everything to everybody – even if it was to the detriment of the almost unanimous body of supporters who watched the game peaceably and respectably.

Privately she questioned whether football could simply be played behind closed doors. Whether even the 'Iron Lady' had such power is another matter, but such a sequence of events would have spelt the death knell for top-class football in England. Taking the lead from the Prime Minister's stance and acting under intense pressure from her ministers, just forty-eight hours after Heysel the FA announced that it would not be entering English clubs into European competition the following year. That wasn't enough. The government then conducted consultations with UEFA and gave the green light for the European governing body to make an example of all English clubs by taking an intractably hard line. Two days later, just ninety-six hours after the tragedy had happened, UEFA announced that they were banning all English clubs from European competition indefinitely, although they did stop short of banning the national team. Jacques Georges, the UEFA President, said, 'The decision to ban English clubs from UEFA

Club competitions for an undetermined period of time was made deliberately to give flexibility. We suspect the ban will be for two or three years, but it could be moderated because obviously some clubs may prove that they have civilised supporters and could be allowed to participate in European events.'[24]

Heysel had come at the end of a grim few months for English football. Chelsea fans had been involved in several violent incidents, leading to the installation of electric fences at Stamford Bridge to try and contain the hooligans. Eye-catching though the idea was to the government, they were never turned on. Then, on 11 May 1985, a terrible fire during a game between Bradford City and Lincoln City at Valley Parade incinerated the main stand within minutes. Fifty-five people died. Although the blaze had absolutely nothing to do with crowd violence and everything to do with the failure of the club to make their ground safe, the same afternoon fighting had broken out at a Birmingham City game, leaving a teenage spectator dead.* Showing utter ignorance and a failure to comprehend how the fire at Bradford demonstrated how a well-behaved crowd was fatally imperilled by negligent management, the government ordered a single inquiry into *both* tragedies. Given the political climate in which it was written, the subsequent report by Lord Popplewell almost inevitably overlooked virtually all safety issues thrown up by Bradford and focused instead on disciplinary issues. As a result the report, according to one expert, 'finished up reading like a contribution to the debate, which was then current in England, on the Police and Criminal Evidence Bill and the extension of police powers of search'.[25] The principal recommendations were: the introduction of CCTV; half the crowds to fall under a membership scheme; the hurling of physical objects and obscene or racist abuse to be made a punishable criminal offence and the introduction of a 'standard, efficient perimeter fence with proper exits'. What did it have to do with the Valley Parade disaster? Not a lot. What would it do to halt the hooligan menace? Not a lot.

Applying simplistic solutions to complicated issues was the defining

---

* Bradford City had repeatedly ignored warnings from the local authority about the potentially hazardous accumulation of rubbish under the seats in its wooden stand. A final warning sent a week before the tragedy informed them that fire inspectors would be visiting the club a week after the eventual disaster, which had occurred when a cigarette butt lit the debris and set the wooden stand on fire.

method of policy-making for Thatcher's Conservative Party: if the coal pits weren't profitable, you closed them; if a prisoner went on hunger strike, you let him starve; if some football supporters couldn't behave, you banned the lot of them. Visiting Liverpool after the Toxteth riots, the Bishop of Warrington had spoken to the Prime Minister of the need for compassion. 'That's not one of your words is it?' joked her husband Denis. 'I find it so condescending,' she replied. 'Compassion? That's not a word I use.'[26] Football didn't need compassion, but its problems did require some understanding. Unfortunately, no homogenous group could put their hands up and claim to be hooligans so everybody who watched the game took the collective rap. Yet as with everything, every large dissolute group had its miscreant fringe. Indeed Mrs Thatcher only had to look at the behaviour of some of the Young Conservatives at their conference that year at Loughborough University (which included the distribution of 'Hang Nelson Mandela' badges, drunken fights aplenty and one Tory leaving his mark by shitting in a communal shower) to see that there was no fair way of legislating against the repugnant actions of the few.[27]

In Margaret Thatcher's mind England supporters abroad were as much representatives of their country as the teams they followed, and as Prime Minister she saw it as her 'duty' to ensure her countrymen lived up to foreign expectations of Englishmen and women. It was a different sort of interference to that which the game had suffered at the hands of the appeasement politicians in the 1930s, but its motives were essentially the same. Nor was her interference in sport unprecedented. Five years earlier, in the run-up to the Moscow Olympics, she had successfully withdrawn the Great Britain team as a protest against the Soviet invasion of Afghanistan (they subsequently competed under the flag of the British Olympic Association).

In 1985 football was easy fodder and the European ban added to the malaise of the English game. The loss of the distraction of competing with Europe's best and the inevitable end of season race to gain qualification for the following year's competitions via a high league position saw the domestic programme stagnate. Crowds dropped, sapping revenues further. More players, without the additional challenge of European football and with clubs unable to match salaries offered by their continental rivals, began to move overseas or even to Scotland. The decline of English football seemed an inexorable circle.

The national side had, of course, escaped the ban, but the Football

Association knew that they needed to tread with extreme caution to avoid entering the abyss. In a cruel twist, England met Italy just eight days after Heysel in an end of season tournament in Mexico. Acutely aware of the sensitive nature of the game and the low esteem in which not only English football but the country in general were held, in a show of sportsmanship the two countries came out in mixed ranks, and played the match in a fair, if not wholly tame manner. England gave a good account of themselves against the world champions, although, as Mark Hateley put it: 'The Mexican referee had seemingly decided that England had to lose for the sake of football.'[28] With the scores balanced at 1–1, in the last minute he inexplicably awarded a penalty against Stevens for a tackle on Vierchowod, which Altobelli dispatched past Shilton. England lost their next match to Mexico (0–1) before meeting an exhausted West Germany at the Azteca, who had travelled to Mexico just four days after the end of their domestic season and two before the match with England. The Germans' new manager, Franz Beckenbauer, described the decision to travel to Mexico as 'foolishness', adding: 'If the question had come up before I was appointed, we would not be here . . . I'm told Bobby Robson is under pressure. If so, we have done him a favour.' Chelsea's centre-forward, Kerry Dixon, scored twice in only his second international appearance, and Bryan Robson grabbed the other goal as England strolled out easy 3–0 winners, and the tour was completed with a 5–0 win over the United States in Los Angeles.

World Cup qualification restarted a month after the 1985–86 season commenced with a home tie against Romania. A win would have secured qualification, but Hoddle's elegantly curled shot from the left edge of the penalty area was enough only to earn a 1–1 draw. It mattered not. A month later, on 16 October, Northern Ireland earned a 1–0 win in Bucharest, which made England untouchable at the top of their group. Later on that day, Turkey were crushed 5–0 at Wembley, with Lineker grabbing a hat-trick, and qualification was concluded on 13 November with a 0–0 draw against the Northern Irish, which also secured the province's progression.

When Joao Havelange had succeeded Sir Stanley Rous as President of FIFA in 1974 the organisation had changed rapidly. Gone was its congenial image as an amateurish *laissez-faire* organiser of internationals and overseer of infrequent rule changes and in came a hardnosed, businesslike mentality that relentlessly sought alliances with multinational companies and marketed the game itself as such. Corruption was often whiffed; vested interests frequently exposed in all their naked notoriety; Havelange seldom far from controversy. Colombia had originally been nominated hosts elect for the 1986 World Cup finals, a decision even more appalling than that which had seen Chile stage the competition in 1962. It was a politically unstable, poverty-ridden society without the infrastructure to cope with the visit of twenty-four countries and their attendant entourages of fans, press and various other hangers on, and even more perturbing was the penetration of the drug cartels into Colombian football. Bribery, violence and an appalling level of intimidation were the order of the day in Colombian football – how could this possibly be a fit stage for the World Cup finals?

Whispers that it wasn't became a crescendo of calls (many indiscreetly coming from FIFA headquarters in Switzerland) when Havelange fell in with Emilio Azcarraga, a Mexican media tycoon, whose empire included the Televisa and Spanish International Networks in the United States. Unceremoniously Colombia were dumped in early 1983 – a decision mourned by few – and the United States and, perhaps surprisingly (though maybe not at all), Mexico emerged as contenders to take over. Despite the 1970 World Cup finals being one of the great tournaments, the multitude of problems posed by high altitude and the nation's reputation as international football underachievers (not that the US had any greater pedigree) worked against them. In any case, no country had ever hosted the World Cup twice: was it not inherently unfair that Mexico should do so, and within the space of sixteen years? Apparently not. Contention and speculation abound as to what went on between Havelange and Azcarraga – but the suggestion that the Mexican 'was a man with much in the gift' was telling.[29] When the FIFA World Cup Committee met in Stockholm in May 1983, America's bid was not even discussed. 1986 was to be Mexico's year – again – and Azcarraga's television companies could look forward to lucrative days.

The prevalent mood of controversy did not end there. Two years later, in September 1985, a massive earthquake devastated huge parts of Mexico City. While the Mexican government begged the world for humanitarian aid, FIFA gave its full support to the rebuilding of the country's telecommunications facilities. As one correspondent, who witnessed untagged bodies thrown into trucks as the ground was cleared for reconstruction, reported: 'In view of what has happened there is no moral justification for holding the World Cup in Mexico.'[30] Tens of thousands of survivors were left homeless while the race to rebuild stadia and television facilities moved on apace. Within four months of the earthquake Mexico's television links were restored. West Germany – the tournament's substitute venue – was told to stand down.

The seven-month interval between qualification and the finals was spent fruitfully by Bobby Robson, as he watched his team extend an unbeaten run which, by the time of the opening ceremony, spanned a year. Wins over Egypt (4–0), Israel (2–1), the USSR (1–0), Scotland (2–1), Mexico (3–0) and Canada (1–0) boosted a burgeoning reputation, and inspired real confidence ahead of a major tournament. The build-up also allowed several players to stake claims for places in the final twenty-two, although the bulk of its members – if not the best eleven – had seemingly been decided upon by England's manager. Only three players, two of them fellow Geordies, progressed to the international stage. Chris Waddle, a former sausage factory worker, had been plucked from non-league obscurity by Newcastle United in the early 1980s and shone in an attack-minded side, boosted by Kevin Keegan's presence, before a move south with Spurs beckoned. A tall, gangly winger, he would drift past opponents or tie them in knots with his elegant long legs before sending in a testing, teasing cross or fizzing in a shot on goal. Alongside him and Keegan at St James' Park had been Peter Beardsley, an intelligent, diligent deep-lying forward – a latter-day Mannion – who always seemed to play the right pass or make room for his colleagues by running into the correct gaps. A clever, modest man who always turned out with a smile on his face, he made the step up to the England team in January 1986, despite playing for a poor Newcastle side, perpetually struggling at the foot of the First Division. Later, when the extended squad were getting measured up for their official suits, the unassuming Beardsley thought that he was only being included to avoid embarrassment. Also making the step up was Nottingham Forest's Steve Hodge, a hard-working, tough-tackling midfielder, a good passer and a man with an eye for goal.

Hodge's presence became vital because, yet again, Bryan Robson had been cut down by injury. Outstanding in the first half of the 1985–86 season as Manchester United at last looked to be marching to their first Championship in nearly two decades, when they slipped after Christmas the coincidence of their fall and Robson being tied to the treatment table was lost on nobody. His predicament – a shoulder that kept 'popping out' of its socket – was as painful as it was persistent. Even when it seemed to be on the mend it dislocated again during the friendly with Mexico, but so crucial was Robson to his namesake that the England manager lied to the assembled press corps about the extent of the ailment and crossed his fingers, hoping that it would mend in time for the start of the tournament.

Twenty-four countries in six groups of four made up the finals, but only eight would be eliminated at the first stage, with the top two from every group qualifying along with the four best third-placed teams. Unnecessarily convoluted? Certainly, but it was a good deal fairer than the double group stage of previous years. England were based in Monterrey, an industrial town 500 miles north of Mexico City, and pre-tournament preparations paid as much attention to detail as those prior to the last Mexico World Cup. Four thousand tea bags, 500 bars of chocolate, 108 bottles of HP Sauce, dozens of jars of English mustard, 144 tins of beans and so on, made up the party's inventory. This time however, with no Ramsey to antagonise the locals, England's footballers were left in peace.

England were drawn in Group F with Portugal, Poland and Morocco. For the tabloid press, basking in the success of eleven matches without defeat, these teams were mere fodder on England's march to the next round – although that notion, as ever, ignored the realities of each side's true standing. Portugal were full of promise and had reached the semi-finals of the 1984 European Championships only to lose to the eventual winners, France; Morocco were one of the leading lights in African football, a continent whose stock as a football power was rising all the time; and Poland, who had not played England since that infamous night at Wembley in October 1973, could boast a number of stars, most notably AS Roma's Zbigniew Boniek, amongst their number.

Hype and expectation soon gave way to disappointment. In England's opener against Portugal on 3 June, early pressure failed to reap dividends, chances passed without being taken, and fifteen minutes from the end disaster struck. Diamantino cut in from the right and struck a low, hard cross to the far post, which Carlos Manuel tapped home easily to give Portugal a 1–0 victory. It was, complained Lineker later, 'just one of those days.' He added: 'If we were still playing now we still wouldn't have scored.'[31] Pressure was, nevertheless, turned up a notch for England's two remaining group matches.

Against Morocco three days later events didn't go as badly for England, although they barely fared much better. Bobby Robson named an unchanged side to face a country that had already held Poland to a goalless draw, but in the early stages they made little headway against a determined defence. In particular the 'big man, little man' combination of Hateley and Lineker was toothless, while Hoddle was wasted in a right-sided role. England's prospects took a nosedive in the thirty-eighth minute when Robson tumbled in the Moroccan penalty area painfully clutching his shoulder. It had dislocated again. Hodge replaced him, Robson's World Cup over. Wilkins took the captain's armband, but a few minutes later he too was handing it on. Uncharacteristically he had reacted to an offside decision by throwing the ball at the referee, and the Paraguayan gave him a red card. Shilton, England's third captain of the afternoon, led his country out in the second half and his colleagues played out a goalless draw. 'Well done. We've got a draw and we're still in the competition,' Bobby Robson was able to tell his players afterwards. 'If we beat Poland we're through to the next round.'

The reaction of the tabloid press was characteristically well considered. 'Bring them home,' demanded the *Sun*, whose chief sportswriter described Robson as 'the fool on the hill'. They chauvinistically added: 'England are the big name jokes of the World Cup – the mugs of Monterrey. They still have a chance – as slim as a wafer – of qualifying from this group. But that will not wipe out the humiliation of this result against a team with no pedigree and no tradition from the Third World.' The draw, added the *News of the World*, was 'disastrous', although they admitted fortune had again not been on England's side. Bobby Charlton told them: 'It's just a matter of time before our luck changes and we score.'

Robson reacted by summoning his players to a meeting. At it a chorus of dissenters led by Terry Fenwick and Peter Reid openly questioned his tactics. It was hardly mutiny but after further consultation with his backroom team he heeded their advice, dropping

Waddle and picking more orthodox wide-midfielders in Steven and Hodge. He also replaced Hateley with the creative skills of Beardsley, whose sharp football brain could create the passes to fully utilise the pace of Lineker; switched Hoddle to the centre of midfield and brought in Reid for a straight swap with the suspended Wilkins. The changes finally freed up Hoddle's creativity and fully exploited Lineker's deadly finishing. With his wrist clad in plaster after sustaining a fracture against Canada, the newly crowned European Golden Boot winner and scorer of forty domestic goals the previous season had previously looked uneasy alongside Hateley and was seemingly crying out for a colleague to pick holes in opponents' defences.

Seven minutes into the Poland match Robson's overhaul won its reward. Hoddle's loping pass smartly found Lineker, he raced clear switching the ball to the right, where Gary Stevens, on the overlap, played a low cross into the danger area and Lineker swept a shot home from close quarters, raising his strapped wrist in celebration. Exactly seven minutes later Beardsley played Hodge into space down the left flank, he centred first time and Lineker tapped the ball into the back of the net from close range. On twenty-six minutes the rout was complete. Poland's goalkeeper, Josef Mlynarczyk, failed to deal with Trevor Steven's corner and the unmarked Lineker completed his hat-trick with a shot into the roof of the net. Thereafter England closed the game down, easing their passage through to a second-round tie with Paraguay.

Progression meant a switch from the relatively peaceful climes of Monterrey (where crowds had barely topped 20,000) to the searing intensity of Mexico City. Unwisely, the Football Association had elected for the appalling Valle de Mexico Hotel, which was situated on a main road with beds too small for the taller players and catering akin to a prison camp. Terry Butcher described the main meal as 'a small piece of fried fish, one boiled potato and six slices of carrot each, followed by a slim wedge of dried cake for dessert'.[32] The arrogant expectation – witnessed on countless occasions before – that England's footballers could simply turn up and win, whatever the prevailing conditions, had reared its head again. Disgusted, many of the squad went in search of sustenance from a nearby burger bar. At night, traffic kept them awake – Peter Reid likened it to 'sleeping in Bolton bus station' – and after forty-eight restless hours, Robson saw sense and switched to more comfortable accommodation.

Rest was likely to be necessary. In the second round were the unknowns of Paraguay, unbeaten in the group matches and complete with Julio Cesar Romero, reigning South American Footballer of the Year, in their ranks. Robson had been forewarned that they were likely to test England with power, pace and attacking verve, but were not above mixing it with the sort of rough and ready play that gave aspects of South American football its more notorious reputation.

Back home, the changes overseen by Robson against Poland had transformed the national mood as the England team began to recapture the public's imagination. One fan, Mrs Porter, a pensioner from Newcastle, was so taken by Bobby Robson's inclusion of her favourite player, Peter Beardsley, that she would call Mexico on the day of every match, somehow circumventing accommodation changes, language barriers and hotel switchboards to personally speak to the England manager and wish him and Beardsley luck. 'I've been dithering all day whether to ring you,' she explained on the morning of the Paraguay game. 'I can't really afford it, but if it didn't go well I would think it was my fault for not wishing you luck.'[33]

Shortly afterwards, Robson and his men were on their way to the Azteca Stadium for their noon kick-off. Boasting just one change (Alvin Martin in for the suspended Fenwick), England started shakily with early defensive lapses letting in Cañete and Mendoza for half chances but both finished lamely. Then England broke free, the ball was played out wide to Hoddle, he chipped it across goal but for once Lineker failed to connect. Hodge claimed possession on the left and sent in another cross. This time, though, Lineker made no mistake and met the ball, tapping it past Fernandez from close range. Again the bandaged arm punched the air: England were on their way.

Almost immediately Lineker nearly made it two: Beardsley sent in a first-time cross, the Everton striker volleyed from eight yards, and Fernandez's acrobatics diverted the goalbound shot away. 'The South Americans were shaken,' recalled Bobby Robson. 'Suddenly they were no longer the happy, smiling, devil-may-care players.' As the game progressed into the second half, the Paraguayans heightened their efforts to intimidate the Syrian referee and their opponents. Reid, who had suffered a hard, late challenge early on, was substituted and Lineker was chopped down by an ugly elbow to his throat, which saw him leave the field to receive treatment. It mattered not. While he was receiving attention on the touchline, Beardsley assumed Lineker's normal corner kick position and when the ball fell loose, he smashed it home with all the conviction of his absent team-mate. Lineker then returned to head home the decisive third goal, putting him at the top of the World Cup goalscorers chart, and England firmly into a quarter-final meeting against Argentina.

Questions of Maradona and questions of war inevitably pre-dominated in the four days leading up to the tie on 22 June. The former had been the tournament's outstanding presence, setting an otherwise workmanlike Argentinian side apart as one of the com-petition's favourites. Certainly on a man-for-man basis it would be difficult to compare the South Americans favourably to Italy, France or Brazil, or arguably even dark horses like England. But Maradona was playing like a man possessed, as if he alone could claim World Cup glory. Brian Glanville wrote of him: 'In an era when individual talent was at a premium, defensive football more prevalent than ever, Maradona – squat, muscular, explosive, endlessly adroit – showed that a footballer of genius could still prevail.'[34] As to the treatment of the war, there was no question that the British media would show any sort of dignified restraint. With Fleet Street dominated by a ratings battle between the Rupert Murdoch and Robert Maxwell newspaper empires, the tabloids seemed bent on outbidding the others' nastiness and the rest of the press and broadcast media took their cues – with varying degrees of virulence – from them. As the headlines were printed in the days leading up to the match, there was something wearyingly predictable about them: 'Bring on the Argies'; 'We're coming to get you Senors'; 'It's war Senor'.

But for once, the British press weren't alone in stirring things up. Their Argentinian counterparts retorted by comparing Maradona to José San Martín, Argentina's nineteenth-century revolutionary hero, who had led the struggle against the Spanish colonialists. 'We're coming to get you, pirates' was the battle-cry of *Crónica* – mirroring almost word-for-word some of their British counterparts. Groups of *Barras Bravas* – Argentinian ultras – flew into Mexico City vowing revenge for their fallen brothers. Inevitably the sight of union jacks being burned provided excellent photo opportunities for the English media. Maradona was as bemused as anyone. 'When we go on the field it is the game of football that matters and not who won the war,' he said. When pushed, he responded: 'Look mate, I play football. About politics I know nothing. Nothing mate, nothing.'[35] Later he asked,

'Why is it the English always want to talk about that?' Another player suggested: 'Because it's easy for them to talk about it. They won.'

At noon on 22 June 1986 the two countries met at the Azteca Stadium: the tournament's finest player against its leading goalscorer; its most splendid ground and, at 114,580, one of its largest crowds. Two nations divided for twenty years by one of football's most bitter rivalries, war and political differences; its peoples united in the sense of expectation that it would be their team that would prevail. In fact the only mismatch of the day seemed the choice of referee – the Tunisian, Ali Bennaceur. FIFA's desire to fully globalise the sport by sharing its spoils was seemingly unrelenting, even if it meant giving a lesser man a disproportionate amount of influence. Bennaceur, it seemed, had only been given charge of the match on account of his nationality, rather than any great contribution to the art of refereeing. Already, against Paraguay, a similarly appointed Syrian referee had put in a patchy performance, missing several key decisions including the ugly, throttling blow to Lineker's throat. It hadn't been conclusive proof that FIFA's policy had failed, but it had been enough for Bobby Robson to voice concerns.

The opening stages of the encounter provided Bennaceur with several early tests. Tackles flew in thick and fast as both countries sought to nullify the threat of the other. Reid crunched Brown, Fenwick was booked for fouling Maradona, while the Argentinians hurried and harried the referee in a manner that was sometimes reminiscent of 1966. When half-time came, without either goalkeeper having been offered too stern a test, Reid was able to noisily conclude to his team-mates: 'If that's the best they can play, we can win this game . . . come on, let's have a go!'

He had a point, but Maradona was still to wake to the task. Five minutes into the second period, he picked the ball up just past the halfway line and ran at the England defence. Looking up, he went to play a one-two, but Steve Hodge intercepted and sliced a high clearance, clumsily, but seemingly within the reach of Shilton, who was running to the edge of his area to claim it. With a hint of hesitation as to whether he should punch or catch, he elected for a fist as Maradona went up to challenge him. It should have been no contest: Shilton towered above the diminutive Argentinian, but at the crucial moment Maradona flicked the ball out of Shilton's grasp with his left hand and it dropped into the empty England net.

To virtually everyone within sight of the incident it was clear what had happened. As Maradona celebrated wildly, the normally unflappable Shilton chased after the Tunisian referee with several others, protesting furiously. It was to no avail. The man who mattered – Ali Bennaceur – signalled to the centre circle: the most contentious goal since Geoff Hurst's second in the 1966 World Cup final had been allowed. England had it all to do.

Four minutes later Maradona matched deception with divinity. Collecting the ball just inside his own half, he skipped past Beardsley, drifted inside Reid and set off on a dribble that carved through the heart of the English defence. Wrong-footing Butcher and evading the tackle of Fenwick, it left him one on one with Shilton. For England's goalkeeper there was to be no atonement: Maradona dropped his shoulder and rolled the ball past him and into the empty net. 'Diego felt so bad about the first goal,' said his team-mate Jorge Valdano afterwards. 'That's why he had to come up with his great second.'

Needing three goals to win, two for salvation but without a shot on target all afternoon, Robson gambled and threw on his two wingers, John Barnes and Chris Waddle for Steven and Reid. Barnes, once scorer himself of a goal of similar magnitude to Maradona's second, transformed England and almost the entire match. From his first moment on the field his directness and skill caused panic within the South American defence. Argentina had no contingency for the type of genius that was occasionally redolent of Maradona himself. With ten minutes remaining, he waltzed past two defenders, sent in a perfect cross and Lineker headed home the goal that would secure him the World Cup Golden Boot. Bolstered by his strike, England suddenly had the momentum as Barnes wreaked more havoc. Shots flew in, were blocked and clearances scrambled as England laid siege in Argentina's half, searching for an equaliser. Three minutes from the end, Barnes cut in from the left and sent in a cross of such teasing precision that it needed the merest of touches to find the net. Lineker slid in, entangling himself in the net and the ball rebounded out of the melee . . . and past the wrong side of the post. Forty-five seconds into stoppage time, which should have been protracted by Argentina's time-wasting, Bennaceur blew the final whistle. England's World Cup dreams were over for another four years, killed by a goal of intense dubiousness and a miraculous one.

'We were so near – yet in football that can be so far,' Robson told reporters. 'I'm sick for the players. They have given everything they had. They have made terrific sacrifices and worked like Trojans. You can't ask any more from human beings.' On entering the dressing room he found 'tears, anger and annoyance. [The players] were sick and bitter and nothing I could say could help them. I was in a trance myself and the coach seemed more like a hearse on the return trip. There was no blame attached to anyone. We had done all we could. They had their Maradona – we did not have our Bryan Robson.'[36]

Much of the post-match attention obviously focused on the errant genius of Maradona. When asked about the first goal, he merely smiled and said it was scored a little 'by the hand of God and a little by the head of Maradona'. Others hinted more darkly at a fix. Butcher was one of three England players to be dope tested, along with José Luís Brown, one of the Argentinian substitutes and Maradona. As they waited in an anteroom to give their samples, a FIFA official came in and embraced Maradona. Such views gained more currency a month later when *FIFA News*, the official publication of the game's governing body, published a provocative article, which exonerated the goalscorer and proclaimed 'Diego Maradona's football in Mexico was honest.'

By then, of course, Maradona was a World Cup winner. He had inspired a 2–0 semi-final victory over Belgium and in the final set up a 2–0 lead over the West Germans. With seventeen minutes remaining the Germans mounted a comeback with Rummenigge and Völler bringing the scores level. Then, with only six minutes left, and West Germany pressing strongly for a winner, he made a final contribution to a tournament he had dominated, releasing Jorge Burruchaga with a perfectly placed pass, and he slipped the ball past Schumacher for the winner. 'Maradona's genius goes beyond the simple realisation that he is indisputably the best and most exciting player now at work in the game,' Hugh McIlvanney wrote of the man who destroyed England and left everyone else in his wake. 'It is inseparable from the potent sense of declaration inherent in almost everything he has done in the field here in Mexico, from his vast public's conviction that he has chosen the Aztec Stadium as the setting for the definitive statement of genius.'[37]

Back in England the progress of the nation's footballers in Mexico lifted the respectability of the game from its post-Heysel low. Having suffered the lowest aggregate attendance in living memory, the dwindling halted, in part because of the enthusiasm generated by the World Cup run, but also because clubs began to battle back against the hooligans, introducing a raft of measures aimed at winning back local communities. Nevertheless, the fight to reclaim the game was a multi-faceted one. Police improved intelligence gathering, serving preventative measures, but sometimes simply using common sense on occasions when it hadn't previously been applied. Alternative cultures emerged, giving different vent to emotions. The birth of acid house culture – 'raving' to synthesised music in nightclubs or sometimes more spontaneously in disused warehouses or factories – at first sight seems irrelevant to football, but it drew from the same sort of constituency as those who had once fought, bringing the people of different towns and cities together. At football matches they might have brawled, but fuelled by hallucinogenics ('happy not hard drugs') casuals and skinheads, who had once derived their kicks from violence, often became as 'loved up' as the flower power generation that had preceded them. For them, football hooliganism became a thing of the past. Football fanzines – amateurly produced magazines written for fans by fans – from numbering just a handful at the time of Heysel exploded in numbers, so that there were more than 200 by the end of the decade. Not only did they provide a different means of pledging allegiance, they also gave an outlet to challenge the preconceived stereotypes of the day. Allied to this was the establishment of the Football Supporters Association (FSA). Founded by the Liverpool supporter, Rogan Taylor, in the wake of Heysel, it claimed to provide a voice for the hitherto unheard millions of fans and, like fanzines, enjoyed a remarkable rise in size and influence.

For years though, they battled unsuccessfully for proper recognition from the government which, the FSA believed, perceived them as barely more respectable than the thugs themselves. Such a prevalent attitude was telling of where the government's sympathies lay, despite football's – albeit tentative – renaissance and Thatcher's brief détente in her war on the sport. But then her need to give it a good kicking in 1986 and 1987 – the high tide of her premiership – was less insatiable than before. Spurred on by the privatisation of British utilities and swathes of industry, the sale of council houses, cuts in taxes (and, rather more substantially, public spending), Britain, or at least a considerable portion of it, was booming. No longer did she need a scapegoat to divert attention from her shortcomings, and in June 1987 she won a third term in office.

Bobby Robson was also thriving. In the wake of his relative success in Mexico the incredible weight of media and public pressure had lifted, for a period at least, affording him the rare opportunity of actually enjoying the role of England manager. He knew it couldn't possibly last, but he was aided by an impressive record for qualification for the 1988 European Championship finals in West Germany. In a difficult four-team group, which included Yugoslavia, Northern Ireland and Turkey, England topped it easily, conceding just one goal, dropping a solitary point and, most impressively, beating Yugoslavia 4–1 in Belgrade.

For the most part Robson remained faithful to the men who had served him so well in England's last three World Cup matches, skippered by a revitalised Bryan Robson. In two years the England manager handed out just seven debuts (notably to Arsenal's centre-half, Tony Adams; the Nottingham Forest left-back, Stuart Pearce and his City Ground colleague, Neil Webb, who became England's 1,000th international). After ten years and eighty-four caps, Ray Wilkins was edged out of contention; while Lineker, after his Golden Boot-winning exploits, earned a £2.2 million move to Barcelona, whose lucrative personal terms set him along the way to becoming the first English footballer to become a millionaire from his playing exploits alone. Contrary to suggestions that the money might go to his head, in the two years following Mexico he scored fourteen goals in fourteen games for his country. Such prolific returns had not been seen since Jimmy Greaves's heyday.

Lineker wasn't the only one on his way to wealth and fortune. The country he had left behind had gone money mad. This was the era of the yuppie, of wheeler-dealers, spivs and brazen city boys bedecked in pin-striped suits and loud braces oikishly shouting down brick-sized prototype mobile phones. House prices were up, stocks and shares were up, consumer spending was up. Vulgarly, millions gorged on this Thatcherite boom, buying into the mantra of the great cultural icons of the day, Gordon Gecko ('greed is good') and 'Del Boy' Trotter ('this time next year we'll be millionaires'). Spectacularly, the bubble was pricked on 19 October 1987 – 'Black Monday' – when a huge stock market crash wiped 24 per cent off share prices in a single day, and over the following months interest rates and inflation soared, and unemployment began to rise. With it the popularity of Margaret Thatcher amongst the public and even within the government itself began to spiral downwards. How to redress this collapse in confidence? In the same way she had previously reacted when economic policies had brought her to the brink of political failure: hitting the whipping boy hard and firm. This time, however, there were no miners, no 'enemy within', just football fans. As the *Economist* was to encapsulate her attitude: 'Those close to Mrs Thatcher have always seen measures to change the nature of football as guaranteed vote winners. Their convictions reflect a common view that the game is irredeemably tied to the old industrial north, yobs and slum cultures of the stricken inner cities – everything, in fact, that modern Britain inspires to put behind it.'[38]

After Heysel, the government had mooted the idea of a national identity card scheme in which every single supporter would have to possess a card to gain admission to a ground. Those convicted of hooligan offences would have their cards rescinded and would therefore be excluded from the ground – or so the theory went. In partnership with her new Minister for Sport, the former Olympic rowing cox Colin Moynihan (a man who would later describe his country's football supporters as 'the effluent tendency'), Margaret Thatcher pushed in earnest for the ID scheme. Opposition came from almost every quarter. The police were against it on the basis that it would unnecessarily delay entry into stadia, exacerbating tension, creating overcrowding and providing greater opportunity for confrontation outside; the clubs, the FA and Football League were opposed on the grounds of cost, implementation practicalities and the lack of promised results; fans were opposed to what amounted to a gross imposition on their civil liberties. But the ID scheme wasn't really about them: it was a headline-grabbing, vote-winning 'solution' by people who knew nothing about football and cared even less, to satisfy those similarly inclined, terrified by the 'moral panic' of hooliganism.

Its effects would be far-reaching. In real terms what it meant was that in addition to all the impracticalities it threw up, casual fans would be shut away from the game; the imposition of having a card would put off those who had slowly started to return to football and the sport as a whole would be stigmatised by the very fact that a government otherwise bent on deregulation sought to regulate watching it in the same way that it would later control gun ownership and the possession of a dangerous dog. The slow, steady revival of football in general, and Bobby Robson's England in particular, would almost certainly be halted and resume its decline. Indeed slipping from such a low position of strength might well have made further regression terminal.

Thatcher's hand was strengthened when scattered disturbances broke out between English and Dutch fans at the end of a friendly at Wembley in March 1988 (the game ended 2–2) and two months later, after a Rous Cup match with Scotland. In turn the press whipped up the forthcoming European Championship finals as the 'Hooligan Championship of Europe'. Some published league tables of hooliganism prior to the tournament, provocatively establishing the Dutch, and not the English, as European football's *betes noires*.[39] What all this seemed to imply was that some felt it was as much the 'duty' of England's supporters to defend the honour of their country off the pitch as it was for Robson's to do so on it. Others carried stories about what Dutch and German fans, preoccupied with testing the strength of the 'professionals' from England, intended to do to their rivals. Research by Leicester University revealed that three-quarters of England fans believed 'provocation of the English by foreign fans' to be highly significant in contributing to violence. Given their standing, or at least their perceived reputation, trouble seemed inevitable when the tournament got under way. At the same time it was made clear by UEFA that the behaviour of England's supporters in West Germany was the key to the readmittance of clubs into European competition.

With such a build-up to the European Championship finals it seemed to have been forgotten that there was football to be played. England were drawn in a group with the Republic of Ireland – now managed by Jack Charlton – Holland and the USSR, and went to West Germany as one of the favourites following their impressive post-Mexico run. Victory, however, in England's first match with the Irish on 12 June was still deemed almost a prerequisite to progression given the reputation of their latter two opponents. Under their World Cup winner manager, the Irish had begun to wield a reputation rather more formidable than their previous status as also rans. They were tough, they were gritty, some of them weren't even discernibly Irish (Charlton plundered players' family trees in search of Irish parents or grandparents, which would confirm eligibility for a non-native) and one or two were actually quite good. Amongst his number he could count three of Liverpool's excellent championship winning team (Ronnie Whelan, Ray Houghton and John Aldridge), the First Division's best centre-back (Paul McGrath) and the league's finest left foot (Kevin Sheedy). With characteristic naivety, nobody in England gave Charlton's men a chance. It was a dreadful misjudgement.

From the outset the ever wily Charlton outsmarted Robson tactically. England had deployed two wingers, Ireland two wide-midfielders to nullify their threat, plus an extra central-midfielder to swamp the heart of the pitch. It wasn't pretty in the least, but Ireland totally upset England's rhythm. Every time the ball came near an Irish defender, it would be hit hard and high, leaving their opponents to crane their necks while the Irish surged forward chasing the loose ball and unsettling the English defence. On six minutes it paid off when Houghton's header looped over Shilton. Thereafter the Irish retreated to their own half, killed the game and reduced England to a series of half chances, none of which were taken with success. 'Lineker did everything but score,' remembered Robson. 'Beardsley side-footed wide from in front of goal and a shot from substitute Hoddle slipped through Bonner's hands only to run wide of the post . . . It was a bad result, but at that stage not a disaster.'[40] The tabloids didn't see it that way, summing up the national mood with their customary brevity: 'Disgrace to the name of England'; 'Shame of Stuttgart' and, most succinctly, 'On your bike Robson'. If anything, the tone beneath the straplines was even worse.

'England were stuffed like Fourth Division nobodies here,' raged the *Sun*, 'their European dreams in tatters if not yet totally destroyed. This wasn't just defeat, it was a disaster and a national disaster at that.' Robson retorted: 'We know we haven't been scoring as often as we would like or indeed need to do. A goal a game isn't really good enough. We should be looking for two or three. We've got to get it right against the Dutch.'

For that must-win tie England moved from Stuttgart to Düsseldorf. Off the field rumour insisted that this would be the ultimate clash of Europe's football hooligans. In Stuttgart there had been some skirmishes, although most were relatively minor and the trouble had centred on those fans whose budget was reserved for beer and tickets and had given little or no thought to accommodation. When they congregated around the train station or shop doorways late at night, local youths taunted or attacked them, which met an inevitably angry, violent response.

By far the worst violence in Düsseldorf was to come the night before England played Holland. At around 9 p.m. around 150 Germans, including right-wing skinheads from the extremist 'Gelsenszene' (Schalke) and the 'Borussiafront' (Dortmund) gangs, arrived from the West Germany v Denmark game. Armed with bricks, the Germans stampeded through the railway station (where as usual many England fans had taken up residence), smashing windows and furniture. English and German fans then fought a running battle from the station through to the town centre, breaking more windows and seriously damaging or wrecking cars. Fighting escalated as more German fans returned from the match and other England supporters, hearing their compatriots were under attack, rushed to defend them. Several bars were blitzed and bricks were thrown through ransacked shop fronts, with looting also taking place. The German police struggled to come to terms with the trouble and as they gained control of one street, fighting would break out in another. Eventually, as England fans gained the upper hand the locals began to disperse. By that time police had arrested 130 fans, ninety-five of them English. Estimates put the damage at between £150,000 and £500,000.[41]

It had been a serious incident captured on film and broadcast across the world. England's football fans were again in disgrace, or so it appeared. In fact they had been far from wholly culpable: winning the fight is hardly the same as starting it, and the level of violence was not as serious as it had first seemed. 'It was bad,' concluded Bernard Abetz, a Düsseldorf city official responsible for public order, sport and transport. 'But they [the media] gave the impression that Düsseldorf was burning, which was totally untrue . . . We have the same problem in Germany, and we expected worse from the Dutch fans.'[42]

Of course, Margaret Thatcher's ailing government didn't see it that way. The same evening six people had died at the hands of the IRA but when, the following morning, an emergency cabinet meeting was called – it was to discuss the Düsseldorf 'riot' in which the two most serious injuries were a slashed face and a broken finger.[43] It had hardly been a Heysel, but as then, the heavy hand of government came down on the Football Association. A few weeks later, under political duress, they made the 'noble gesture' of withdrawing their application for readmittance into European club competition. It was a hasty move. Shortly after that announcement, the publication of the official report into the Championships included UEFA's favourable comparison of the disturbances with any ordinary weekend in the Bundesliga. Quite unnecessarily, as it transpired, English clubs' exile from European competition continued.

If events off the pitch before the Holland match overshadowed Peter Shilton's hundredth cap (an achievement matched only by Billy Wright, Bobby Moore and Bobby Charlton), events on it certainly did. Robson brought in Glenn Hoddle in the knowledge that on the opposite side of midfield, one of his former Ipswich charges, Arnold Muhren, would not provide too physical a confrontation. In the early stages, at least, the additional creativity gave England the attacking advantage. An early mix-up between Ronald Koeman and the Dutch goalkeeper, Hans van Breukelen, allowed Lineker through, but he took the ball too wide and his shot from an acute angle hit the base of the post. Then Robson's tapped free-kick was struck cleanly by Hoddle, the ball hit the inside of the Dutch post and rolled agonisingly along the line before being cleared to safety. Holland battled back and a minute before half-time took the lead. Frank Rijkaard robbed Lineker, played in Ruud Gullit, whose cross was met by his Milan team-mate Marco van Basten, and he turned and shot past Shilton.

England began the second half in determined mood, spurred on by the inspirational efforts of 'Captain Marvel', Bryan Robson. Indeed it was he who pulled England back into the game, almost charging into the net with the ball like a latter-day Nat Lofthouse to bring the scores level. 'Any gambling money would have had to go on us at that stage,' recalled Bobby Robson. 'We were exhilarated and lifted. We had the impetus and we were going to win it.' England cranked up the pressure, storming forward in search of a winner, but against the run of play Gullit again set up Van Basten and he put the Dutch back in front. Van Basten completed his hat-trick with fourteen minutes to go; England were finished.

In Frankfurt three days later, a subdued, despondent, England team put in an abysmal performance against the USSR and slumped to another 1–3 defeat. For Hoddle, in his last international, the afternoon was a personal disaster. Just three minutes had passed when he tried to nutmeg Aleinikov, lost possession and the Soviet went up the field and scored. In many ways the moment summed up Hoddle's fifty-four cap career: for all his skill and ability, in an England shirt it never quite came off. For Kenny Sansom, Dave Watson and Mark Hateley, West Germany also effectively spelt the end of their international careers.*

The press assault was inevitably vigorous, but it was Bobby Robson who carried most of the blame as England fell from heroes to zeroes and the sub-editors got to work: 'Stuffed'; 'A gutless spineless shower' and 'Robson twenty years out of date' were reflective of the tabloids' increasingly strident disdain for the manager. The *Sun* portrayed him in a dunce's cap and invited its readers to phone in with their 'best' Bobby Robson jokes. England's manager was alternatively 'naïve', 'second best' and 'a flop'; his squad was 'both badly picked and badly prepared' and showed 'a disturbing lack of pride in pulling on that famous white shirt'. For Robson it was to be 'the worst summer of my life', but even then he knew the press were hypocrites. As he wrote in his autobiography: 'As it was the media who had tipped us to win I thought maybe one or two of their jobs might be in jeopardy. Not likely . . .' Robson offered his resignation to the Football Association; they declined it and he was able to take solace from their loyalty. Even that would prove to be tentative.

Mrs Thatcher used the off-field events in West Germany as an excuse to renew her campaign to introduce the hare-brained identity-card scheme. Ugly though that night in Düsseldorf may have been, even if it had been half as bad as portrayed in the media it would have flown in the face of prevailing trends. Football-related violence was down by more than a third in the three years since Heysel, despite increased attendances. To put it into context, less than one in 5000 people attending football matches was ever arrested and even then the overwhelming majority of those arrests were for minor public-order offences. A 1989 FSA survey found that 77 per cent of respondents agreed or strongly agreed that there was not as much hooliganism at football as there had been five years earlier. Only 3 per cent agreed or

---

* Hateley made one further appearance, in 1992, when Graham Taylor was England manager.

strongly agreed that the government's ID scheme would reduce hooliganism. More than 90 per cent were opposed to it and just 1.5 per cent thought it would 'eventually attract more fans back to football'.[44] Still the crusade went on. The attitude of the government was, in the words of one magazine: 'If you can't beat the hooligans, kill football instead.'[45]

And then, on Saturday 15 April 1989, the Hillsborough disaster. At an FA Cup semi-final between Nottingham Forest and Liverpool, overcrowding in the streets outside the ground before kick-off led a senior police officer to order a gate to be opened. This allowed hundreds of Liverpool fans crowded outside the ground to move inside, but they were funnelled into a central pen in the Leppings Lane End, where thousands of supporters were already crammed. As hundreds of expectant fans entered the ground there was a surge forward crushing those at the front into the metal fences at the bottom of the terrace. Unaware that their fellow fans were dying at the front, latecomers pushed forward, trampling more people underfoot and causing those at the front to suffocate. By the time the game was abandoned at 3.06 p.m. and the gates opened onto the pitch, nearly one hundred Liverpool fans had died.

Early suggestions hinted at the culpability of drunken Liverpool supporters with the *Sun* 'reporting' that they had urinated on the dead, attacked ambulance men and stolen from the stricken. They were outrageous lies, of course, but given the continual attacks the game had received over previous years, many believed them. The government appointed Lord Justice Taylor to head an inquiry into the tragedy, but if they were expecting a green light for their ludicrous identity card scheme, they were sorely mistaken. This time there was no fudge and Taylor was damning of just about everybody in authority. In his interim report he was highly critical of the police officer in charge, Chief Inspector Duckenfield, whose actions, he said, had been dictated by prevailing attitudes. Taylor said that Duckenfield had 'continued to treat the incident as a threat to the pitch and public order' until 3.06 p.m., when the gates were opened. He added that fear of hooliganism had 'led to an imbalance between the need to quell the minority of troublemakers and the need to secure the safety and comfort of the majority'. The judge also pointed at the link between poor facilities and hooliganism.

In his final report, published in January 1990, he concluded that the British game was suffering from a 'general malaise or blight' reflected in the often 'lamentable' facilities offered to fans which are 'below the basic decent standard necessary to give spectators dignity, let alone comfort'. Allied to this was the organisation of crowd management at matches which meant that 'the ordinary, law-abiding football supporter, travelling away, is caught up in a police operation reminiscent of a column of prisoners of war'. In total he made seventy-six recommendations to promote better and safer conditions at sports grounds, the most important of which was the requirement for all-seater accommodation in the top flight by the start of the 1994–95 season. It specifically recommended *against* a national membership registration, which would have exacerbated the Hillsborough disaster.

After several false starts Taylor's report precipitated the real renaissance of English football. For the first time a person of power had spoken with authority for the fans. Shiny new stands and sometimes new grounds helped bring back its missing millions, and though football-related violence has never entirely gone away, it has declined inexorably and certainly ceased to be a national preoccupation. In 1990 England's strong showing at the World Cup finals reignited the nation's obsession, seemingly dwindling since the latter days of Alf Ramsey. Indeed at the start of the 1990–91 season, a campaign which would see English clubs competing in Europe again, the *Daily Telegraph* was able to proclaim: 'In the dark days after Bradford, Heysel and Hillsborough, it was hard to imagine that football would ever be greeted with the anticipation which heralds the 102nd League season.'[46] The game's strength grew and grew from thereon; never again would English football's very future be threatened by a hostile and intolerant government.

In November 1990 Margaret Thatcher was ousted from office by her fellow MPs, bringing an end to the eleven-year reign of the century's most influential British peacetime politician. It is an oft-misused and lazy caricature to portray everything that happened under her rule as inherently wrong or evil. She was certainly no Beelzebub. In 1979 she had inherited a forlorn, inefficient, heavily subsidised, class-ridden society prone to every whim of the trade unions and seemingly set in an endemic state of decline. When she left office, the face of Britain had altered fundamentally – not always for the better – and the changes wrought by her premiership are still very much in evidence today. The Marxist historian, Eric Hobsbawm, conceded that 'even the British left was eventually to admit that some of the ruthless shocks imposed on the British economy by Mrs Thatcher had probably been necessary'. Hugo Young added that 'in the estimation of the world, Britain was now among the strong economies. Productivity in particular, was dramatically higher than a decade before . . . The over manning was a thing of the past . . .'[47]

Economics aside, she was in essence a populist politician, a rabble rouser, a woman of action. If there was a problem she would always involve herself in trying to rectify it, even if her actions were deeply unpopular or simply plain wrong. English football in the 1980s had a number of problems, one of which – but by no means its only blight – was hooliganism. When nobody had the knowledge or intent to tackle it, Thatcher stepped into the breach and met fire with fire. But not knowing her enemy, her approach was inherently flawed from the outset. A football crowd is very often a reflection of society. Except for an allegiance to a club or country, it is a disparate mass. A community of fans is unique, incongruent and almost impossible to categorise readily; like any such gathering – even a political party (as the Conservatives knew only too well) – it invariably had its own 'effluent tendency'. Thatcher's fatal error was to tar every football fan with that same brush. In doing so she threatened to bring the game to its knees.

In her place came the Chancellor of the Exchequer, John Major, a Chelsea fan who, like Harold Wilson a generation earlier, liked to portray himself as an ordinary man. Football was a way of connecting to the electorate, but this time to the part of it which loved the game. 'Supporting Chelsea over the years has been a roller coaster ride,' he once wrote, 'but it has been a great aid in developing a philosophical view of life.'[48] He wasn't perfect, but at least he understood. Moynihan was pushed aside and David Mellor, another Blues fan, eventually took up the government's remit on sport under the auspices of the Department of National Heritage. Where once it had been confrontational, the government now became co-operative. The flagging expectation, first expressed by the organised game's founders more than a century earlier, that it could be a force for national good returned. Football, finally, was once more a positive influence.

12

THE GREAT WHITE HOPE

AUTUMN 1984 AND Jack Charlton is manager of his hometown club, Newcastle United. Eleven years earlier, after 773 club appearances, all of them for Leeds United, he had called time on his playing days and embarked on a managerial career first with Middlesbrough, then Sheffield Wednesday, followed by a year long sabbatical before taking charge at St James' Park in July 1984. His teams had a reputation for defensive play, big hard strikers and long, direct balls. Newcastle fans, however, did not take kindly to the World Cup winner's purportedly crude football ethos. Indeed his return to Tyneside was to be brief and unhappy; in August 1985, after just a year in charge, he walked out on Newcastle, for a while turning his back on club football altogether.

Throughout his managerial career Jack Charlton would repeatedly tell football purists that he could only use the tools that he had at his disposal. Yet at Newcastle he had, in Chris Waddle and Peter Beardsley, two of English football's finest up and coming talents, both of whom he exiled to the flanks with the express purpose of hoofing in crosses for his lumpen centre-forwards. Further down the ladder, he had an even more extraordinary talent: a local teenager, chubby, precocious, with a love of practical jokes and Mars bars, but blessed with an incredible gift for football. His name was Paul Gascoigne.

Charlton had seen and heard much about Gascoigne, some good, some bad, but a mixed enough bag to make him unsure whether the teenager would make the grade. Concerned about his progress, or rather lack of it, the Newcastle boss decided to give Gascoigne an abrupt wake-up call and hauled him into his office.

'I hear you're a cheeky chappie,' said Charlton, 'There's a lot of fat there but I'm told underneath you've got a bit of skill. I'm giving you two weeks to get yourself fit. If you've not made it by then, I'll show you the door.'

Gascoigne heeded Charlton's words. Soon he was captain of the youth team and within months was leading Newcastle out at the FA Youth Cup final against Watford. In that match came the realisation for Charlton that he had a truly unique talent on his hands, the sort of ingenuity that no English footballer had displayed perhaps since his own brother's heyday. Eight years later he would describe it to the *Sunday Times*:

> Thirty yards out he checks, sees the goalie off his line and instantly digs the ball out with his right foot and it sails clean over the top into the goal and the keeper turns flat on his arse. I turned to my assistant Maurice Setters and said, 'You'll have to wait a thousand years to see that again.'[1]

Soon Gascoigne had made the step up to the first team. Newcastle lost Waddle, then Charlton, then Beardsley, but there was always Gazza, as he liked to be called. The team was mediocre, not good enough to ride the peaks, but not quite bad enough to sink to the depths, packed full of journeymen and also-rans, yet occasionally illuminated by the podgy, precocious, curly-haired Geordie at its heart. A central-midfielder, Gascoigne possessed a range of passing that was occasionally reminiscent of Hoddle; he could shoot, he could finish, sometimes he could tackle too. His bulk gave him the sort of upper-body strength that enabled him to ride challenges, while his turn of pace and close control were key facets to his game: getting the ball, running, dribbling, swerving, bursting into the box to set up a colleague or shoot himself.

Off the field there were tales of wild drinking sessions, elaborate practical jokes, japes with his mates. Nobody worried too much. The media loved him. He'd crack jokes on *Saint and Greavsie*, pull faces at cameras and dress up in costumes for the tabloids. Soon he had his own column in the *Sun*, a hark back to some of the seventies' court jesters.

On the pitch he could be wayward, go missing or simply lose interest. Sometimes colleagues weren't on his wavelength. Other times, too often said his critics, he'd be caught out of position, trying to do everything himself or simply going where it took his fancy. He could be stupid, but he could be brilliant too, more brilliant, in fact, than any other young player in English football. Nobody matched his potential, no one seemed more destined for greatness.

In July 1988, Gascoigne left Newcastle for Tottenham Hotspur in a £2 million deal. Having lost Hoddle a year earlier, he was seen as a saviour of Spurs, the man who would help bring championship glory to White Hart Lane for the first time since the days of Bill Nicholson. Yet England's failure at that summer's European Championships saw those expectations rise tenfold. Limited, luckless, lacklustre England also needed a saviour. Who other than Paul Gascoigne could, or would fill that void? Previous murmurings that Bobby Robson might give Gascoigne a run out for the senior side became, in the aftermath of Euro '88, a clarion call. Suddenly Gazza, who a few months earlier had been playing for unfashionable Newcastle, was thrust firmly into the limelight. Not only was Gascoigne Spurs' redeemer, he was now England's great white hope.

Bobby Robson heeded the media's calls for England's first match back after Euro '88 against Denmark at Wembley. As well as the absent Hoddle, Kenny Sansom made way for Stuart Pearce; Arsenal's excellent young midfielder, David Rocastle, was handed his debut, Nottingham Forest's Neil Webb was given a run out in midfield and his club team-mate, the centre-back Des Walker, a place on the bench. Gary Lineker was rested and Luton Town's Mick Harford given a chance up front. Gascoigne was named as a substitute.

The sense of anticipation was, nevertheless, stupefying. Only 3000 tickets were sold prior to the match and FA officials feared that England would suffer their lowest-ever attendance. In the event 25,837 turned up to watch Neil Webb's twenty-ninth-minute goal defeat the Danes in a performance that marked an improvement on the summer's displays. Walker made his debut, coming on for Adams, as did Gascoigne, when he replaced his former team-mate Beardsley. Winning, however, was not enough for the press and in the post-match press conference there were shades of Ramsey at his most volatile when Robson was put under pressure by their questioning. 'You have slaughtered me because of the only match England have played badly in two years,' he barked, alluding to the horror show against the USSR. He left the platform and refused to answer any more questions: 'And you wouldn't let it go. I've said enough. The team's won – the team's said it all.'

England's qualifying group for the 1990 World Cup pitted them against Albania, Poland and Sweden. It was a tough quartet and decent home results were deemed a pre-requisite for qualification. Yet when England met Sweden at Wembley a month after the Denmark win, they could manage only a 0–0 draw. 'Shilton is too old, Adams and Pearce are inadequate and Barnes too much of a luxury,' was *The Times'* glib assessment of Robson's selection.[2] England were booed off the field, and there were cries of 'what a load of rubbish.'

A month later England were lured to Riyadh by the promise of oil-dollars to play a prestige friendly with Saudi Arabia. Earlier that year Saudi had failed to take a point in their Olympic qualifying group and had lost all their games in the bicentennial tournament. Failure to win convincingly was not an option. As the *Sun* warned: 'Win or get the hell out of it.' But after only fifteen minutes of play Abdullah put the Saudis in front. In response, England were unable to muster anything more than Tony Adams' fifty-fourth-minute equaliser, despite Gascoigne's introduction as substitute.

'We are discovering the days of winning 4–0 every time you play one of these matches are long gone,' said Robson on his return to Heathrow on Concorde. 'I am pleased with the result. I am pleased with the experiment and with what we learned . . . The engine is spluttering but we just need the spark plugs to be polished.'

Invariably, the tabloids had other ideas: 'Bobby's desert disaster – even Saudis kick sand in our faces'; 'England mustafa new boss' and 'In the name of Allah go!' led the calls for his dismissal. 'We want Clough' said the *Daily Star*. 'We know you want Cloughie. So don't ring us. Tell the FA. We're sure they're dying to hear from you. Give them a buzz on . . . 01 262 4542.'

The *Sun* were slightly less direct in their approach, and ran a hotline for their readers to vent their spleen at the England manager. 'I saw Robson at a fag machine the other day, trying to get out ten Players,' said C. Merchant of Grays. 'We have as much chance of winning the World Cup as the Pope has of getting married.' 'Bobby Robson is a nice man,' opined D. Wilkinson of Coventry. 'He would suit Brazil because he's nutty enough.' 'Bobby Robson MUST stay,' said S. Kidd of Newcastle, with a sense of irony that would only be fully appreciated more than a decade later. 'If he goes he could get the manager's job at Newcastle and we don't want that.'

Yet many readers ran to the England manager's defence. Given the nature of the *Sun*'s kangaroo court, the fact that a quarter of callers vigorously defended him was impressive. 'All criticism fired at Bobby Robson is on a personal level without any constructive or intelligent comments,' said A. Hill of Cambridge. 'Robson has done a great job for England,' argued P. Lewis from Grimsby. 'If critics would get off his back and leave him alone he would have more chance of winning.'[3]

The Football Association also stayed loyal and Robson went on the offensive. 'In May we had what everybody recognised as a good team,' he said.

> Six months later they can't all have become bad – they can't all have nose-dived . . . They are our best players who simply didn't get the result they deserved . . . I experimented with new players in a friendly and found out a good deal about them. That's what you've been telling me to do. You said the results won't matter – that makes me laugh. As soon as we lose you go berserk. Anybody who says England results don't matter is talking rubbish. I'll soldier on until we put right our old failing of wasting chances we create.

After the slating he received for his Riyadh experiment, Robson relaunched the England B team as a stepping stone to the full side. 'If I were a club manager,' said Robson when he unveiled the plan, 'with around sixty matches a season, it would be easy to introduce bright young kids, but with just eight internationals a season, I'm restricted in how much I dare experiment. I'm in a cleft stick, particularly as players can't increase their education in Europe because of the ban.'

Between Robson and his backroom staff debates were constant about England's great white hope. By turns Gascoigne was dazzling and anonymous for Tottenham. An impudently brilliant goal against Arsenal in September won him the affection of White Hart Lane, but many of his best moments came from spectacular free-kicks, which were often executed with the aplomb of a Brazilian. Questions of application and consistency were always foremost in the mind of the England coaches. 'It was always a question of the talent and the discipline,' recalled the England Under-21 manager, Dave Sexton.

> We would ask ourselves if by playing him, it would be a case of 'strengthen or disrupt'. Experienced players do not like a young boy to come in and take

liberties. The A-team needs stability and when young fellas come in, the first question the senior players ask is, 'Is this kid reliable or flash in the pan?' Paul could be brilliant. But he could also be unreliable. He needed to be both brilliant and reliable to be in the England team.[4]

As Bobby Robson later put it: 'Gazza was a rich, rare talent and I was sure his time would come. But only when I thought he was ready. He certainly wasn't then. He was fat and played only twenty minutes in each half before fading out of games. He would make a clever pass or score a goal and the papers would scream, "Pick Gazza!"'

Robson, however, had more pressing problems with the tabloid press than Gazza's destiny. When England travelled to Greece in February 1989 for a friendly match, Nigel Clarke of the *Daily Mirror* announced the press corps' intentions when interviewed on TV: 'We are here to fry Robson.' The rotters were certainly given ammunition by England's poor start when Butcher's clumsy challenge resulted in a penalty and from it Saravakos became the first Greek to score against England. John Barnes' free-kick and Bryan Robson's volley dampened the tabloids' incandescence as England emerged 2–1 winners.

Four weeks later England returned to the eastern Mediterranean to meet Albania. The Albanians had scared Sweden three months earlier before falling to two late goals and succumbing to a 1–2 defeat. Fears of an upset proved unfounded and Bryan Robson, in his fiftieth game as England captain, fulfilled his manager's maxim that he was in fact 'three players in one: a tough tackling defender, a midfield player of vision and a phenomenal goalscorer'.[5] He was England's most potent attacker; when the Albanians put England under pressure following Barnes' opener he provided a cool head; and rounded off his performance with his twenty-fourth goal for his country. England were impressive in their 2–0 win and Bobby Robson was delighted with the victory: 'It was a marvellous game and particularly in the first half there was plenty of action at both ends. It was cut and thrust with both teams going for each other's throat.'

Proof that winning wasn't everything came in the following day's newspapers, and it wasn't just the tabloids that were gunning for Robson. The *Times* football commentator, David Miller, was a particularly ardent – and ultimately pedantic – critic of Robson's management. Thus, while the back page headlines which accompanied the main report after the Albania win read 'Sunny side up for England' and 'Performance for a manager to relish', Miller was moved to snipe in his comment piece: 'The lesson of the match is that England need at least two new defenders, and that there is certainly not room for both Waddle and Barnes in the same attack.'[6]

The woes of the England team were put into stark perspective by the following month's disaster at Hillsborough. The football programme was suspended and Liverpool, along with their Merseyside neighbours, Everton and Tranmere Rovers, were given indefinite leave to postpone their fixtures. Eleven days later in London, English football kicked off again with the return match against Albania. Wembley's 60,000 spectators stood in silence for a minute before watching England take apart their opponents. Lineker took just five minutes to score his first goal in eight starts for his country; Beardsley, bravely turning out despite the traumas he had faced with Liverpool, added a second seven minutes later; then in the second half, Neil Webb and Lineker combined to set up Beardsley for his second.

With twenty-five minutes remaining Gascoigne came on for Rocastle. Robson gave him express instructions to get as much of the ball as possible *but* to stay in position on the right. Gascoigne came on to applause, but the first thing he did was head over to the left side of the pitch. 'It probably wasn't so much disobeying me – more a case of everything I'd said going in one ear and straight out the other,' recalled Robson. 'He just forgot everything about my instructions.'

Robson turned to Don Howe and said, 'Look at that silly bugger. He's daft as a fucking brush, isn't he? I told him to play over here and now he's gone to play with his mate. He's daft as a brush.'[7] Eventually Gascoigne heeded his manager's advice and returned to the right from where he set up Waddle for England's fourth, before, brilliantly, scoring England's fifth and final goal.

The press were in raptures but Robson wasn't entirely convinced. Three weeks later he put him in the England B team to face Switzerland. Gascoigne played on the right and put in an impeccably disciplined performance, weighing in with another superb individual goal. It was enough to earn him a first start for England, in a Rous Cup match with Chile at Wembley seven days later. 'We'll have to nail him to the ground,' joked Robson, but Gazza wasn't in the mood for repartee. 'Please take me seriously,' he pleaded. 'I know what I've got to do and I'll play any way and anywhere the boss asks me to. Against

Albania I got carried away. I wanted the ball all the time and felt tremendous. But I know what to do this time. I'm not in the team to put smiles on people's faces – I'm in because of the way I've been playing for Spurs.'

The Chile match was an apology of a game. On his debut Wimbledon's thuggish centre-forward, John Fashanu, arguably the worst player ever named in an England side, was lucky not to be sent off when he brutally elbowed Astengo in the face. Only 15,628 watched the match which ended 0–0, the Chileans were booed off and the players didn't shake hands at the end. 'Far too many of their players fell over for no reason,' Robson complained later. 'But that is their game. They break the flow of the game and the momentum. That's part of their tactics.'

Seventy-two hours later it was revealed that Don Revie had passed away. After walking out on the England job he stayed in Dubai until 1982, doing much to develop the game in the Arab kingdom. Later, he managed Al Nasr, one of the leading Emirates clubs, did some consultancy work at Leeds and managed the Cairo side Al-Al FC. In the summer of 1986 he was diagnosed with the terminal neurological illness motor neurone disease and declined quickly. He was last seen in public in May 1988 for a benefit match at Leeds. Jeff Powell, who had broken the story of his defection twelve years earlier, wrote movingly of a side of Revie seldom acknowledged outside his extended family at Elland Road: 'A friend of mine died yesterday . . . a big lovable bear of a man . . . released at last from the controversy that clouded the summit of his career.'

For the second time in consecutive months England donned black armbands, this time when they marched out against Scotland at Hampden Park. Goals by Waddle and Steve Bull, who plied his trade in the Third Division with Wolves, were enough to secure a 2–0 win.

Gascoigne had come on as a substitute for Tony Cottee, but when Robson named his side to face Poland in a crucial World Cup qualifier a week later, the England manager made it clear he had not done enough, by omitting him. England took a large step towards World Cup qualification with a 3–0 win that was harder to gain than the emphatic scoreline suggested. Des Walker, a fast strong centre-back and as good a reader of play as England had counted amongst their number since the days of Bobby Moore, announced his arrival on the international scene with a monumental performance which included a series of superb blocks, most notably on the stroke of half-time when he got in the way of a potentially psychologically damaging strike to maintain England's one-goal advantage, gained by Lineker. Not until Barnes struck in the seventieth minute, though, was the game put beyond doubt and Neil Webb rounded off the scoring with seven minutes remaining.

England still had to travel to both Sweden and Poland in the autumn of 1989 and come away without losing to be assured of qualification for Italia '90. Their prospects were hampered in Stockholm by the loss through injury of Bryan Robson, on whom his namesake was so traditionally reliant. In his place came Liverpool's capable bruiser, Steve McMahon, while Terry Butcher donned the captain's armband. Few people could claim to match Bryan Robson's courage or charisma in an England shirt, but Butcher was one of them, which was as well, given that the meeting with Sweden turned out to be a whole-hearted, gutsy affair. Shortly before half-time, the stand-in skipper was involved in a crunching aerial collision with the Swedish centre-forward, Johnny Ekström. He signalled immediately that he had been cut, confirmation of which came when his white shirt was bloodied, but he refused to leave the field for treatment until the half-time whistle had blown. When it was time for the second half, Butcher was last out of the tunnel, complete with a bandage around his head that covered seven hastily inserted stitches (all that there had been time for) and a fresh shirt. Clapping his hands he urged his team-mates on. His shirt was soon crimson again, but he gave an imposing performance along with Walker, as England battled to a 0–0 draw. This was the Dunkirk spirit in action, the sort of gutsiness adored by the English support. It emerged later that Butcher had suffered two wounds, one across his eyebrow and another in his forehead, which required a total of seventeen stitches. The display of monumental courage transported Butcher – a steady and effective but by no means world-class performer – into the hall of England legends.

'The skipper was absolutely marvellous,' Robson lauded. 'It was the sort of courageous performance that one expects from an England captain . . . It was massive . . . I knew he could see the match out and he was never going to come off.'

Mrs Thatcher was less impressed with what she had seen. One hundred England fans had been arrested (though none were charged) and deported from Sweden, and the Prime Minister urged the FA to 'consider very carefully' pulling England out of the World Cup finals. England, of course, still had to get there.

At the start of October England travelled to Poland. The country in which they arrived was in the midst of intense social and political unrest. Parliamentary elections the previous June had started to unravel more than forty years of single-party communist rule, which had served as a beacon for dissidents across the Warsaw Pact. All over Soviet eastern Europe governments teetered on the brink of collapse and, after the fall of the Berlin Wall a month later, fell like dominoes, culminating in a violent revolution in Romania on Christmas Day and, eventually, the break-up of the USSR. Little did England's footballers know it then, but this was to be the last time they stepped behind the Iron Curtain.

As for the match itself, those doomsayers who prophesied a repeat of the nightmare of 1973 were almost, but not quite, proved right. Shilton, who had kept goal that fateful night sixteen years earlier, put in an imperious performance, several times denying Dziekanowski, while the remaining parts of the defence constantly had to work hard to stay equal to the Polish attack. As the clock ticked away, with the scoreline goalless, England looked as if they had done enough to just about secure qualification. Then, in the final minute, out of nowhere Tarasiewicz fired in a shot from thirty-five yards. Shilton remained rooted to the spot and a nation watched momentarily aghast as the ball rocketed past him, before mercifully crashing off the crossbar to safety. The Pole had hit his shot so hard that it rebounded as far as the halfway line. Shortly after, the referee blew the full-time whistle, and a visibly relieved Robson was able to reflect on England's quali-fication. 'We defended like men,' he said. 'It was a night for men and we had a lot of men out on the pitch. It's thanks to them that we survived. We are going again to the World Cup finals and that's a tribute to the players. We are just looking forward to going to Italy and doing as well as we can.' In particular, he praised Shilton, who had finally exorcised the nightmare of 1973. 'I have never doubted that Shilton is the best. It's other people who have questioned his ability . . . When we were under siege, he made four or five top-class saves. It only needed one mistake from Peter and we could have lost. His presence and stature stands out a mile. I am immensely proud of him.' On the flight back, Bryan Robson briefly took over the steward's tannoy and told the plane, 'The stick the boss took was unbelievable.

On behalf of the players we want to thank him for standing by us.'
England's manager was roundly applauded.

The press had a different spin on events, and there was no euphoria
or even praise at qualification. 'England showed all the failings they
displayed in the catastrophic European Championships,' moaned the
Sun, 'a lack of both pattern and inspiration.'[8] The *Daily Star* warned:
'Unless Bobby Robson has a miracle up the sleeve of his Savile Row
suit, England will become the laughing stock of next year's World
Cup finals . . . At the moment, there are so many donkeys in his side
that they should open an animal sanctuary and dispense carrot juice.'[9]

Robson had no miracles, but the press were willing to invent one
for him: Gazza. With each passing game for Spurs the calls increased
for his automatic inclusion in Robson's first XI. Every pass, shimmy
or dribble was hyped beyond recognition; everything Gascoigne
touched turned to gold, according to some anyway. Robson didn't
seem entirely impressed. He had brought him on against Sweden, but
only because his hand had been forced by an injury to Neil Webb.
'Gazza's such a wonderful talent, that he's worth persevering with,' he
had said then. 'He's coming through, but he must have the maturity
to go with the skill.' Yet when England met Poland it was David
Rocastle named in the team not Gazza. 'From what I hear, I'm not
going to get the chance because I can't be trusted,' said the excluded
midfielder. 'Well, if people think I'm going to let England down, I
shouldn't be in the squad, full stop. It seems there is almost a
campaign to keep me out of the team.' There was no vendetta. Indeed,
as Robson would say later, 'I was watching him more than any other
England manager had ever watched any player, and out of all those
games I didn't ever . . . think Gazza was not going to make an England
player. But I did keep wishing he would master two aspects of
football: what do you do when you've got the ball, and what do you
do when you haven't.'[10]

When he named his squads for the friendlies against Italy and
Yugoslavia in November and December 1989, Gascoigne was named
in the B squads rather than the senior side. Dave Sexton, who was in
charge of the B side, warned Gascoigne not to lose his temper. 'Paul
simply cannot afford to lose his cool. He has listened and responded
since he came into the Under-21 side and his fuse, which was very
short, is now longer. But he must learn to walk away – an ability likely
to be tested by the Italians.' He had a quiet match in front of 16,000

people at Brighton's Goldstone Ground (its biggest crowd in three years). Yet a week later, in the white of Spurs, he was making headlines again, and once more for the wrong reasons. Before a match with Crystal Palace, he interrupted a pre-season kickabout sponsored by the Post Office between actors dressed up as Jess the Cat, Postman Pat and a teddy bear, head-locking the bear and kicking the cat in the backside. He then went out and committed what he later described as the worst tackle of his life, precipitating an eight-man brawl. The Post Office complained to Spurs about the incident, and Terry Venables had barely stopped trying to laugh it off when another complaint was levelled, this time after Gascoigne was accused of deliberately kicking the ball in a cameraman's face and breaking his glasses prior to a League Cup tie with Tranmere.

When he played the second B international he impressed and Robson seemed happy, but then the England manager told the press, 'The man who plays alongside Bryan Robson has to have a brain and discipline. He has to be able to work out when to go and when to stay, when to take chances. I'm not saying Gascoigne has not got a brain. But he still has to learn when to use it.' The following day's headlines were achingly predictable: 'I can't trust Gazza' and 'Brainless Gazza? No Bobby's barmy', summed up the manager's many doubters.

Maybe Gascoigne was bent on self-destruction. On New Year's Day 1990, again the red mist descended and a clash with Coventry City's Lloyd McGrath left him with a cracked bone in his left hand, which left him sidelined for six weeks. Robson went to see his return at Chelsea, but the great white hope put in another performance of exasperating petulance, punching Chelsea's John Bumstead right in front of the East Stand where Robson was sitting. 'What can you do?' asked Robson. 'Of course he's still in the reckoning, but I want to see no more of what he did at Chelsea. The boy still has a lot to learn what he can and can't do. Retaliation – he won't get away with it in the World Cup . . . and he must just learn not to bite.'

In terms of England's midfield, the friendlies with Italy and Yugoslavia seemed to provide Robson with more answers than questions. Against the Italians he brought on Aston Villa's midfielder David Platt as a late substitute, completing a remarkable turnaround in the player's career; less than two years earlier he had been playing for lowly Crewe. In January 1988 the one-time Manchester United reject was the subject of a £200,000 transfer to Aston Villa, precipitating a remarkable rise for the midfielder. Already on his way to winning the PFA Player of the Year award in only his second top-flight season, Platt combined the blend of tenacious skill, sound technical ability and eye for goal displayed so consistently by Bryan Robson. As for 'Captain Marvel', he twice proved why he was so important to the England team. In the 0–0 draw with Italy he gave a strikingly authoritative performance of calm composure and tactical organisation; against the Yugoslavs he matched that with two goals, which brought England a 2–1 victory. 'His immense quality declares itself not, as with other supreme footballers, in stunning flourishes of grace, but in the persistent application of a powerful armoury of high skills,' wrote Hugh McIlvanney afterwards. 'He may not always look like one of the giants of the game, but that is what he is. At his best, he is a class above anybody else now plying the same trade in this country.'

Bobby Robson also seemed to have settled on the core of his defence. Des Walker had edged out Mark Wright, Dave Watson and Tony Adams from contention as Terry Butcher's central defensive partner, while Stuart Pearce had made the left-back berth his own. Pearce was a late starter. Having trained as an electrician with Brent Council he was picked up by Coventry City from non-league Wealdstone in October 1983. Twenty months later Brian Clough signed him for Nottingham Forest for £250,000, where he became captain. A strong, hard left-back, he added grit and steel to the back line and, though he was portrayed as a quiet man by the press (largely because Clough embargoed his outpourings), on the field he was a shouter and a leader. As for Peter Shilton, the man whom Robson had considered putting into international retirement after the European Championship debacle, he had become teetotal, redoubled – as if it were possible – his efforts on the training ground, and rolled back the years to prove why he was England's finest goalkeeper and still amongst the best in the world. Gary Lineker was invariably assured of his place in Bobby Robson's first XI and he was usually joined in the England forward line by a combination (or sometimes all) of Beardsley, Barnes and Waddle. While these individuals were virtually cast-iron certainties, as England went into 1990 a handful of places were still waiting to be claimed in Robson's final twenty-two for Italy.

With Neil Webb injured and a doubt for the finals, at the start of March Robson all but confirmed that it was a straight fight between

Gascoigne and Platt for the place alongside Bryan Robson. He asked his assistant Don Howe to keep his eye on both players when they came up against Queens Park Rangers (who he managed in his day job). 'They had such contrasting styles,' Howe would later say. 'Platt hadn't got the skills and grace, but was reliable and would get in the box, then get back in position. Gazza had all the flair and imagination, but would go missing. On league form, I was more impressed with Platt.'[11] When England played – and beat – Brazil at the end of the month, Platt had started his first international and impressed, while Gascoigne only had a cameo role in which to make his mark after coming on as a substitute for Beardsley. It was clear that any further chance he got would have to be devoured greedily.

A month later, on 25 April 1990, Czechoslovakia visited Wembley. Only 21,342 people turned out to watch what, for Gazza, would be a make or break match. A week earlier he had come face to face with Bryan Robson when Spurs met Manchester United at White Hart Lane and Gascoigne destroyed United with a virtuoso display. That game added to his burgeoning reputation, but Czechoslovakia was to be Gascoigne's ticket to the World Cup finals. Only seventeen minutes had elapsed when, barely looking up, he played an instinctive, forty-yard pass, straight to Steve Bull who was charging clear of his marker on the edge of the area. Bull chested the ball down in front of him, waited for it to bounce, and then hammered it into the back of the net. Seven minutes later he swung a corner into the Czech goalmouth, Butcher headed on and Pearce hit the knock down into the back of the net. Gascoigne was spraying passes hither and thither, controlling the game. On fifty-six minutes, he set off with the ball at his feet, left two men standing in his wake, and landed a cross onto Bull's head. 3–1. Fiorentina's Lubos Kubick curled a free-kick to make it 3–2 and suddenly the interest of the Czechs returned. In the last minute Gascoigne took the ball from Dorigo, surged forward, feinted past a Czech defender and let fly with an unstoppable shot from the edge of the area that soared into the roof of the Czech goal.

As the players came off the pitch Robson congratulated Gascoigne.

'Well done Gazza – that was super stuff son. You were bloody great and involved in three of the goals. Good lad.'

'Fou-wa.'

'What do you mean four?'

'The second was off my corner.'

'Any bugger can take a corner.'

'Yeah, but not the way I take them!'

At the post-match press conference Robson was asked why he hadn't picked Gascoigne more often. In other words, the press hounds were asking for an admission that he had been wrong. 'You were clamouring for him a year ago, and he wasn't ready a year ago,' responded Robson. 'I'm a football manager, I managed a club for fourteen years on the development of young players. I couldn't go out and buy people, not at Ipswich – so don't talk to me about developing young players. And all right, tonight he's passed the test – and they've done well at Tottenham, he's slimmer, fitter, he's matured, far better discipline . . . but you're still not a player after one match.'[12]

Despite masterminding England's qualification to the World Cup finals without a goal being conceded; although he had sated demand and introduced Gazza; despite bringing dignity to the English game when, through a combination of the European ban on clubs, the sullied reputation of its fans and a catalogue of defections to continental and Scottish clubs, it stood at its lowest ebb, Bobby Robson could never ever do enough for a press who not just criticised him, but outbid each other in trying to persecute him. Earlier on in the year Robson's marriage had been hauled under the limelight when revelations emerged about an extra-marital affair a decade earlier when still Ipswich manager. Various other indiscretions were trawled up, inflated and exaggerated before being thrown at him from the front covers of various red tops. Amazingly he remained a dignified figure in the face of such unremitting hostility and, even more remarkably, he kept smiling and stayed sane. As Peter Beardsley put it:

I'm surprised he's not in a box. With gold handles. [Robson's] just took so much stick it's unbelievable – but he comes back for more. And that's why we love him. Because he's never slagged us off, he always tries to defend us as much as he can. Sometimes he's defending us and he's cut his own throat. But that's the sort of man he is – he tries to be so fair to the players, when in the end it's down to us.[13]

Robson, like Ramsey before him, was instinctively loyal and dedicated to his men, the embodiment of what England expected. For large sections of the press, however, it wasn't enough; nor was it for the FA on 15 May 1990. England played their first World Cup warm-up game against Denmark at Wembley. They were unimpressive, despite winning 1–0 thanks to Lineker's thirty-first goal for his country, an accomplishment which lifted him above Nat Lofthouse and Tom Finney in the ranks of England's all-time goalscorers. Questions were invariably asked about the way England had played, but more pressing it seemed was Bobby Robson's future. His contract expired in January 1991 and when asked about it, the FA Secretary, Bert Millichip, had effectively told the press that Robson would either win the World Cup or go. In light of that the England manager then had a tentative approach from the Dutch club, PSV Eindhoven, whom he was told he could not speak to on account of his being under contract to the England team. On trying to clarify his future with Millichip prior to the Denmark game, Millichip would not promise anything and gave him permission to speak to PSV. Somehow, somewhere along the line, between England's match with Denmark, and their meeting with Uruguay a week later, the story leaked.

Despite nothing being formally agreed, and Robson being sold up the creek by the FA, the headlines that announced Robson's likely departure to PSV were typically vitriolic: 'I quit!'; 'Raging Robson Blasts Smears'; 'I'm off before I get sacked'; 'Robson sells out for a pot of gold' and 'PSV off Bungler Bobby' were as misleading as they were malevolent. *Today* was unquestionably the most vindictive in its coverage. Under a headline pronouncing Robson 'A liar, a cheat . . . and not fit to lead England' it said that this 'shambles of a man . . . stands accused of being a liar, a cheat and a traitor. He has been all these to his wife for many years and now to the England team which was entrusted to him and to the nation . . . Tomorrow he takes that team to Italy for the World Cup. He is not fit to lead it. There can be no confidence in him from the players or the millions who hope for a successful England performance.' Making reference to his move to PSV, it wrote: 'In previous centuries, a man who has committed such treachery would have been sent to the Tower. In these civilised times, the least we can do is not send him to Italy.'[14]

Given the persistent incandescence of the press, the sly manoeuvring of the FA (not to mention their reluctance to make a pledge of loyalty to Robson), small wonder that he eventually signed a contract with PSV. In doing so his salary was said to have risen fivefold to £500,000, a reflection not of Robson's greed – as some newspapers liked to portray it – more of his true value. As with their treatment of Sir Alf Ramsey before him, the FA's lack of munificence was notable. At PSV Robson would be the man who brought Ronaldo to Europe when other top managers would not take the gamble on the teenager, and his Indian summer would continue right throughout his sixties and on into his seventies with Sporting Lisbon, Barcelona and Newcastle. Like Ramsey, he too would be knighted for his services to football.

The press weren't just out to get Robson, they were out to get the fans too. Egged on by Margaret Thatcher's hyperactive Minister for Sport, Colin Moynihan, and doubtless with memories of Heysel still fresh in the mind, the Italians had put England on the island of Sardinia in an effort to try and contain their supporters. 'Sardinia,' John Sadler gleefully wrote in the *Sun* when the arrangements were announced, 'will become a kind of leper colony.'[15] Even if Sardinia wasn't contaminated, the tabloids were certain to be like a vial, ready to inflict their own brand of poison. The story from Monterrey at the previous World Cup, about a *Sun* journalist travelling around with a brick tied up in a note saying that it was 'a gift from England' and offered to fans for a couple of hundred pounds to put through a shop window, may have been apocryphal but it said much about expectations of 'rotter' journalists. Fresher still were lies in the same newspaper about Liverpool supporters pissing on the dead at Hillsborough. 'It makes you wonder,' questioned Steve McMahon, 'are these English people? Do they really want you to win the World Cup? Or would they rather you lost it, so they can sell loads of papers?'

England's World Cup preparations continued to be dogged by the hostility of the press, indifferent performances and poor results in their last two warm-up games. First, their seventeen-match unbeaten run came to an end after a 1–2 home defeat by Uruguay on 22 May three days before they flew out to Italy. A week after their arrival in Sardinia, England flew south for a first-ever meeting with Tunisia. Robson had by then named his final twenty-two with both Platt and Gascoigne making the cut, but in Tunis things got off to the worst possible start when a wayward Gascoigne pass inadvertently set up Hergal, who volleyed past Shilton from thirty-five yards. Shortly after the break the deficit almost doubled when Neji's shot hit the side-netting. Frustrated by England's ineptness and the North African heat, a piqued Terry Butcher headbutted a Tunisian defender, fortunately (for him) out of the sight of the referee. Robson, despite later denials, evidently saw the incident and promptly substituted Butcher, who responded furiously, ripping off his shirt, flinging it at the bench and sitting in simmering solitude under the shadow of an advertisement hoarding. Parity was only restored in the last minute when Barnes got around the back of the Tunisian defence and whipped in a waist-high cross that was met by Bull's stooping header.

If it had been enough to save England's blushes, it could not prevent the ire of the press. 'Pathetic! Arrogant! Smug!' the *Sun* fulminated. 'It was worrying that England, apart from the opening and closing fifteen minutes, showed no more collective understanding than opponents who had not played together since losing to Cameroon six months ago,' added *The Times*.[16] Elsewhere Butcher's head-butt attracted consternation, not least from the *Daily Star* who demanded he be sent home – this despite Butcher being one of its columnists!

England had been poor, but as Bobby Robson wrote in his diary: 'Most of my problems seem to stem from the media these days and I find myself waiting in dread to see what falsehoods they've been writing this time. Not the sports pages – I can take that – but the constant assault and assassination of my personal character. Why can't they just leave me alone?'[17] Robson's critics accused him of focusing on the role of the media rather than the deficiencies of his team, but it was a moot point. Football is a game of many parts, but to succeed at the highest level individuals need to make it their own magnificent obsession. Robson was one such man, but the press had their own unique passion: persecuting the England manager. As if to exemplify the extent of the media campaign against him, back in England Robson's brother had just suffered a heart attack and, while recovering in hospital, a tabloid journalist had been caught trying to photograph him.

In Sardinia the England team had taken over the Is Molas hotel complex, although the players weren't allowed to use its golf course until the day after a game and were restricted to half an hour's sun each day. They soon grew bored of life there and David Platt later described the highlight of the day as lunchtime when Brian Scott, the FA's travel representative, would bring in the morning's English newspapers – this despite the less than complimentary coverage usually meted out. They broke up the boredom with bets on videos of horse races or the other matches and by letting themselves be entertained by the antics of Gazza. Daft as a brush, Gascoigne would co-opt a golf buggy and race it around Is Molas like a dodgem, or play tennis in the midday sun. Full of nervous energy, he never stopped. ('He couldn't sit still for two minutes,' recalled Pearce. 'He'd be up and down, here and there.'[18])

From the luxury of Is Molas the England team watched with satisfaction as their conquerors of 1986, Argentina, were beaten 1–0 in the opening match by minnows Cameroon in a tough, exciting game. The Africans attacked with verve and tackled like barbarians: the world immediately fell in love with them. A typical example of their spectacular and violent defending came when the South Americans' speedy forward, Claudio Caniggia, had set off on a run just past the halfway line and was charging towards their goal. One Cameroonian slid in with a leg-breaking tackle, but pulled out at the last second and Caniggia went hurtling on; a second defender tried the same at full pelt, but Caniggia hurdled over him. The third man, Massing, was to show no such discretion. 'He executed a kind of full-pelt, waist-high, horizontal flying body check,' recorded Pete Davies in the definitive account of Italia '90, *All Played Out*. 'The general intention seemed to be not so much to break Caniggia's legs as to actually separate them from the rest of his body.'[19] In 1962 Walter Winterbottom had said that an African nation would win the World Cup before 2000. With a victory over the world champions already under their belt, would 1990 be Cameroon's year?

As in 1986 the twenty-four finalists were split into six groups. From these the top two would qualify for the second round with the four best third-placed teams also progressing. Two points for a win remained in place. While it would be wrong to categorise England's group – Group F – as a 'Group of Death', it was probably the toughest of the competition. As well as European Champions Holland, England were also drawn against the 1986 winners of the African Nations Cup, Egypt, and Jack Charlton's Ireland, who had continued their remarkable rise by qualifying for their first World Cup finals. Playing dour, defensive and sometimes downright dirty percentage football, Ireland weren't pretty on the eye – it was, noted one of the Egyptians, 'contagious crap' – but were nevertheless tough to play against.

Ireland's fans didn't seem to care. They drank, partied and cheered their team on as if they'd already won the World Cup. When the two teams came out on Monday, 11 June, the Irish boasted five men born in England, one in Wales and a Glaswegian in their starting XI, not to mention their English World Cup winner boss; yet were greeted by their fans with unconditional enthusiasm. England could boast players in their own starting line-up with the skill of Waddle, Barnes, Beardsley and, perhaps surprisingly, the great white hope himself, Paul Gascoigne, yet Ireland's hotchpotch of hackers and cloggers almost completely suffocated them. On one of the few occasions – after just nine minutes – when they didn't, Waddle shimmied past Staunton, played a diagonal ball into Lineker, who controlled it with his chest past McCarthy and scrambled it into the net.

Jack Charlton's gameplan was seemingly consigned to the dustbin by England's early goal. With the Irish devoid of attacking ideas and seemingly happy to nullify the game, England seemed content to battle out a 1–0 win and on sixty-nine minutes Robson took off Beardsley and sent on Steve McMahon to beef up the England midfield. It looked like a sensible move, but the Liverpool player had been on for just four minutes when he lost control of the ball and it rolled over to Kevin Sheedy, who hit it home first time. Ireland's fans went mad, and so did England's journalists.

The following day's headlines had a familiar air: 'Eire we go again'; 'Laughing stock of the world' and 'Our World Cup dream looks just like a bad Irish joke' hit the newsstands. The *Sun*, however, went the furthest: in a front page diatribe entitled 'Bring 'em home', it wrote:

> A sense of shame fills the heart of every right-thinking Englishman this morning. How COULD our lads play like that? How COULD they let us down so badly?
>
> It was truly the most appalling performance by an England team in living memory. And how the whole World must have watched and laughed.
>
> Maggie Thatcher has hinted darkly that if our fans got out of hand she would call the whole team home.
>
> Don't wait, Mrs T. We can't face another night like that.

'I thought the game was won, but we made a crucial mistake,' explained Robson afterwards. 'I made a substitution to nullify the Republic's substitution, but in the end it cost us the game. We had it won – then lost it.' The hysteria that accompanied the draw gave the impression that England was the laughing stock of planet soccer. As one of the Scottish players asked a *Guardian* journalist in the build-up to their opener with Costa Rica, 'Just one thing. Don't say we were as bad as England.' The Scottish player was right, his country weren't as bad as England – they were far, far worse, losing 0–1 to a cacophony of cackling the world over.

Not content with haranguing Robson on a daily basis, the press turned on the players. The *Daily Mirror* printed lurid allegations about Isabella Ciaravola, a World Cup hostess, alleging she was involved in a lurid foursome with three members of the England squad after a late-night disco, adding that Ciaravola's brother was going to wreak revenge to restore her honour. The allegations were complete nonsense of course, and after the story the players refused to talk to the press, walking out in silence after a training session. 'The players do not want to share the same ground as people who have written such garbage,' Robson told journalists. 'It was abusive and scandalous rubbish. That is why they have gone.' Indeed the attitude of the English press mystified their foreign counterparts. Why, one Italian journalist asked Robson at the pre-Ireland game press conference, are they all against you? Robson told them that he was the wrong person to ask, why not ask the other journalists in the room? No response was forthcoming.

The daily kicking in the press turned the squad inwards, creating a siege mentality which bonded the players even further. By contrast England's next opponents, Holland, were in a state of disarray. They had drawn their first match with Egypt, which was, according to Ruud Gullit, 'the result of two years of bad work, bad football and bad coaching'. The Dutch malaise went deeper than that, though. The players had wanted Johann Cruyff as coach but instead got Leo Beenhakker, towards whom some squad members barely disguised their contempt. As one Dutch journalist, pondering the outcome, put it: 'It depends on which team turns up. Will it be the team that can take your breath away? Or the team that sulks?'

Having been turned over by the Dutch in 1988, Robson reverted to a sweeper system, bringing in a third centre-back – Mark Wright – in place of Peter Beardsley. Peter Shilton had won his 100th cap against Holland two years earlier in Germany, when Van Basten had slammed a hat-trick past him, but against Holland in Sardinia he passed another, far greater, milestone in winning his 120th cap, which took him past Northern Ireland's keeper, Pat Jennings, to become the most capped international footballer of all time.

With the new system England put in a vastly improved performance. The three centre-backs looked at ease with Van Basten ('everyone felt so comfortable, and it worked so well that we ought to keep that formation,' said Butcher later), Barnes and Waddle were a constant menace, while Paul Gascoigne finally came of age. Up against the Milan duo of Gullit and Frank Rijkaard, not once did he look out of place, constantly probing the Dutch defence with his passing and runs. Twice he nearly created goals for Robson and Lineker on either side of half-time, and with sharper finishing England would have gone ahead. The judgement of the referee and his linesmen also went against England. Lineker had the ball in the net, only to be harshly adjudged to have handled it; Pearce also briefly caused excitement when his free-kick arrowed into the Dutch goal, only for it to be disallowed after the referee claimed to have originally awarded an indirect free-kick.

Although the match ended goalless, England had finally impressed. Leo Beenhakker acknowledged that England were by some stretch the best team on the pitch and Ruud Gullit added, in a rare moment of empathy with his manager, 'It was difficult to control them, and we were lucky to get a draw.'

The draw gave Robson some respite from the press, who now focused their fiction on England's fans. After the match there was meant to have been a riot between Dutch and English fans in the streets of Cagliari. 'WORLD WAR', reported the *News of the World*. 'Rampaging English soccer thugs turned the streets of Sardinia into a bloodbath last night . . . More than 500 Brits were arrested . . . It happened after 1,000 angry fans hurled rocks . . . The arrested yobs – many of them drug crazed.' 'The essence of what happened,' wrote Pete Davies, 'is that – again – a small number of yobs got a large number of others mixed up in an upheaval; and it grew larger (albeit fairly briefly) than it need have done because, trembling with hooligan psychosis, the Italian security forces violently over-reacted.'[20] Les Walker, the FA's head of security, put the hard core at around sixty; there were five reported arrests.

Reality, however, was not given a helping hand by Colin Moynihan. While other countries had their kings and presidents travelling around with their teams, England had a Tory minister who described his country's supporters as 'the effluent tendency'. Thatcher's hyperactive lieutenant instilled a sense of fear of the English supporters into the foreign authorities that went beyond all reason and justified any action deemed necessary to put them in their place. So, when several innocent English bystanders were beaten by brutal *carabinieri*, Moynihan praised the 'tough and decisive action' of the Italian police. He had, wrote the lawyer Mel Stein in a letter to *The Times* after the finals, 'done everything in his power to talk English football out of Europe. One can only assume that this stems from his basic lack of understanding of our national game and his reluctance to meet any of the problems involved in the sport headlong in a constructive rather than a destructive manner.'[21]

While Paul Gascoigne had been one of England's great successes against the Dutch, that other great stalwart of the England midfield, Bryan Robson, had limped off injured. A ruptured achilles tendon was diagnosed, and despite receiving heavy treatment and even the attentions of a faith healer, he was to play no further part in the competition and little more for his country there on. It was a hammer blow to England's chances, and to Robson, who had missed out through injury in the previous two World Cups. 'Somebody up there doesn't like me,' he complained, 'Why is it always me?' He had featured in sixty-two of Bobby Robson's eighty-eight internationals prior to Italia '90: with him in the side England had lost only ten and had been defeated seven times in the other twenty-six matches. 'He is as good a player as we've ever produced,' Bobby Robson said of him before the tournament. 'He is the bravest player I've ever seen . . . he opens the game, he performs non stop and, above all, he scores vital goals.' To his colleagues too, his importance as a player, captain and motivator was crucial. A decade later Stuart Pearce recalled in his autobiography:

> He scored goals at one end and cleared them off the line at the other. When you played in the same team as him and he shouted at you to get tight on your man, you would want to do it for him because you didn't want to let him down. That's a mark of a good captain. You upped your standards because he demanded it of you. He talked sparingly on the pitch but led massively by example. Sometimes you can just look at someone and respect them, him more than most.[22]

He would be sorely missed.

In England's final group match against Egypt Steve McMahon was recalled in Robson's place, ahead of Platt. Bobby Robson also reverted back to a flat back four dropping Terry Butcher for the first time in thirteen years of managing him, and drafted in Steve Bull, a brusque, combative forward. 'We think we're due a goal, and we think they're due to concede one,' said England's manager before the match. 'If we get in front we'll be okay – but they have one or two that need looking after. If he gets a draw he'll be satisfied – but I won't be. We need our boys to be world class, not club class. Some threaten, some deliver . . . I wish the skipper was in, I'll tell you.' A draw would probably see England through, although with all four teams in Group F balanced on the same points and goals (for *and* against), if the result and score of the Holland v Ireland game were the same, it would mean the unedifying prospect of drawing lots for second round qualification.

Before the match, while still at Is Molas, Robson received a telephone call. It was Mrs Porter, the Newcastle pensioner who had called every morning before games in Mexico wishing Robson and her favourite player, Peter Beardsley, good fortune. 'I couldn't let it go,' she said. 'I am going to bring you luck.' They would need it.

Like Ireland before them, Egypt set out to suffocate the England attack, and in the first half almost completely succeeded. With both defences pushing up, the midfield – where most of the play took place – was crammed into a tiny portion of the pitch. Lineker and Bull spent large chunks of the match as spectators. On fifty-nine minutes, with the game slowly heading towards stalemate, Des Walker was fouled in one of his rare forays into the opposition half. Gascoigne stepped up to take the free-kick, weighted a perfectly flighted ball onto Wright's head, and he powered it past Ahmed Shobeuir in the Egypt goal. England were through. 'England Give 'em a Pharaoh Stuffing' reported the *Sun*. 'Our soccer heroes shook off the Sphinx jinx and anNILEated the Egyptians . . . as England stormed to victory in Cagliari, Sardinia.'

With Ireland and Holland having drawn their match, Wright's goal proved the difference between England playing Belgium in the second round and facing West Germany. It also meant that England journeyed to the Italian mainland and the ancient university town of Bologna.

Belgium had finished third in the previous World Cup and in Enzo

Scifo had an attacking midfielder with the finesse and prowess to pull even the best opponents apart. Robson dropped Bull and reverted to the sweeper system that had served England so well against the Dutch. Though the gritty presence of McMahon was scant compensation for the attacking qualities of Bryan Robson, there was always Gazza. 'Whenever he crosses the halfway line, you feel as though something is going to happen,' Robson had said after the Egypt game. His progress had been steady rather than spectacular in England's group matches, but creeping into Gascoigne's game was the sort of maturity, discipline and work rate that his critics had so often claimed he lacked. True, he sometimes got caught wandering, but equally he could conjure the impossible. Who else was capable of producing such magic?

Not John Barnes. A Liverpool player since July 1987, the winger had been in scintillating form for the Anfield club, picking up the 1988 PFA and Football Writers' Player of the Year Awards, consistently producing the sort of brilliance that his goal at Maracana had promised. Like Gascoigne, he was the sort of technically gifted attacker Robson so loved to have in his side. Yet for England the John Barnes question was one which perennially reared its head: incomparable for his club; inconsistent, nay, invisible for his adopted country. 'I fully believed that John could be our match winner in Italy,' Bobby Robson wrote in his World Cup diary. 'Maybe because it is because the game at international level is played on a different plane, at a different mental pace. Maybe it is that he cannot raise the tempo within himself. I don't know. It is baffling because he is such a high-quality technical player.'[23]

Still Robson persisted with him and yet again a nation was left collectively shaking its head. In the first ten minutes a languid pass by Barnes was picked up by the Belgians, who nearly scored from the resulting break. He wasn't the only one at fault in the early stages: Butcher had given the ball away to Scifo in the first minute and, but for some tidy defensive work by Gascoigne, might well have punished England more heavily; Versavel's shot was palmed away by Shilton, then Ceulemans hit a post. England eventually settled, and the open, attacking play of their opponents suited their own style. Waddle and Barnes started to attack down the flanks, jinking, shuffling, dribbling their way past defenders. There were chances at both ends. Pearce's free-kick screamed just wide; Scifo volleyed high and wide; Belgium were denied a penalty appeal; then Lineker found the net, only to be dubiously denied by the linesman's flag; Pearce's header landed on the roof of the Belgium net. Then a Belgium attack broke down, the ball was played to Pearce, who crossed it to Barnes, but he – seemingly inevitably – finished lamely. Again Barnes had blown cold, but he could blow hot too. Moments later, Waddle played Lineker into space, he crossed and this time Barnes met it with a glorious first-time volley that scorched past Preud'homme and into the Belgian net. But again it was called offside – England's fourth disallowed goal of the finals – although replays showed that it should have stood.

All this engrossing action had taken place in the first forty-five pulsating minutes. The pace continued into the second half. Scifo's free-kick hit the post, minutes later the same player played the ball across the England six-yard box but mercifully no one was there to pounce. Gascoigne tried to weave his way through the entire Belgian back line and almost, but not quite, pulled it off; but it was Belgium who looked most lively and most likely.

With nineteen minutes left, Robson added fresh attacking impetus by bringing on Platt for McMahon. Two minutes later Barnes pulled up with a groin strain and Bull took his place. Walker and Butcher each picked up knocks but both substitutes were already on and they had to soldier on. It was win or go home. As extra time loomed, Gascoigne lunged in needlessly on Scifo. A yellow card was produced and Gazza shrugged his shoulders. Little did he know then the price of his recklessness.

Ninety minutes came and still the match was goalless. As the game moved into extra time, tiredness and injuries took over and chances were rarer. More and more the defenders simply lumped the ball clear, too exhausted to set up attacks. England, with Walker virtually a passenger, were out of ideas and began to knock the ball around their defence, waiting for the inevitability of their first-ever penalty shoot-out.

With a minute of extra time remaining, Gascoigne picked the ball up on the edge of his own penalty area and surged forward, seemingly impervious to the fact that he had just played two hours of football in energy-sapping humidity. And then he was fouled. England's big men pushed forward for one last desperate attack before being thrown to the lottery of penalties. Gascoigne stood over the ball, surveyed the

Belgian penalty area and looped a cross just out of Preud'homme's reach, on an angle, over the heads of the defenders. Platt read the ball perfectly, surged through and, with his back to goal, span and struck the ball first time into the roof of the Belgian net. Goal!

There were just thirty-two seconds remaining. England played the last few moments out before exploding into another bout of celebration. Butcher and Waddle danced a jig in the centre circle and Gascoigne – who had manically kissed his manager when Platt's goal went in – ran around simultaneously taunting the Belgians with mock violin gestures and raising his hands aloft.

'It was my 108th match and unquestionably the best,' said Guy Thys the Belgium manager. 'We played very well. We worried about our game, not our opponents, and if we had to do it again, I'd play it the same way.' Bobby Robson dedicated Platt's goal to Bryan Robson. 'That goal was especially for him. It was a wonderful goal to win a wonderful match. The next one will be for ourselves. I said before the game that we would give a bit more for the skipper and we showed a lot of fighting spirit. We didn't die even though we were playing at the end with only nine fit men.'

It was, wrote *Il Corriere dello Sport*, 'the most exciting and dramatic 120 minutes of this World Cup'. Yet not everybody agreed. Pointing to a minor incident involving Gascoigne prior to the match (the midfielder had thrown a cup of water at Paul Parker, which had missed and hit a journalist), and Waddle and Butcher's (understandable) celebrations in front of the continually maligned England spectators, David Miller carped in *The Times*: 'The off the field behaviour of the England team has been childish and irresponsible and a poor example to younger professionals and the many misguided spectators from England in Italy.' It was difficult to see where he was coming from, and almost all of England – including, finally, the bulk of the tabloids – were now firmly behind the nation's footballers.

Next up, after their 2–1 extra-time win over Colombia, were the tournament's surprise package, Cameroon. After beating Argentina they had defeated Romania and topped their group. Matching tenacious – and occasionally over enthusiastic – defending with speed and skill on the break, the Africans had been an unexpected light in one of the dullest World Cup finals in history. Not only could they boast a forward of rare, raw all-round ability in Francois Omam-

Biyik, they had in Roger Milla an exciting wildcard to summon from the bench for a twenty-minute burst of often prolific attacking verve. Officially aged thirty-eight, but rumoured to be up to a decade older, the 1976 African Footballer of the Year wowed with his predatory instinct and won hearts with his elaborate celebratory dance, which involved a jig around the corner flag and an Elvis-esque pelvic thrust. No one quite knew what to expect from Cameroon. Certainly, on their day, they were good enough for anyone – as the world champions had discovered – but there was frequent sniping at the naivety of African defending, a point proved when they had fallen 0–4 to the USSR in their final group match. That said, no African country had ever progressed so far, they were playing well, and looked more likely than anyone to fulfil Winterbottom's prediction.

Howard Wilkinson didn't think so. The Leeds United manager had been carrying out scouting work for Robson and, having witnessed Cameroon's capitulation against the USSR, advised the England manager that a tie with the Africans was 'effectively a bye'. Robson passed on this tip to his players but was under no illusions about the task that lay ahead. With Barnes and Walker recovered from their knocks, Robson made just one change, starting with Platt instead of McMahon. It gave the England side even more of an attacking complexion, but as the game got under way they seemed to miss the presence of a holding man in midfield, and time and again proved too easy to break down. Pagal's dummy befuddled Walker and set Omam-Biyik free, Shilton blocked his shot, but only as far as M'Fede who shot wide with the goal at his mercy.

England looked good in possession, vulnerable when not. Gascoigne was lively, Waddle bright and busy, but all too often England lost the ball and, when they did, the Cameroon players ran at them, causing panic in defensive ranks. Then, on twenty-five minutes, Butcher sent Pearce scuttling down the left. He beat his man and sent in a deep cross to the back post, which Platt headed powerfully into the back of the Cameroon net. Advantage England, but Cameroon kept chipping away. Their defence looked solid, far more so than their critics would ever have envisaged, and their potency in attack made nonsense of Wilkinson's assertion.

Half-time came with England a goal up, but in the dressing room Robson was not pleased with his team. 'You may think you are one up and on the way into the semi-final,' he said, 'but I'll tell you that if you carry on playing like that we are on our way out.' Barnes, again impersonating the invisible man, was taken off and Beardsley brought on in his place.

Cameroon, meanwhile, had made their own substitution, bringing on their talisman, Milla, in place of Mabeang. The game restarted with the Africans briefly losing their ascendancy. Lineker shot over the bar; then Gascoigne wriggled his way past two men, switched to Waddle who played in Pearce. He crossed, Platt tumbled, no penalty, and the ball was played up field to Milla. Suddenly England were caught out. As the veteran surged into the penalty area, Gascoigne hauled him down. This time the referee gave the penalty. Kunde, the sweeper, stepped up and hit the ball emphatically past Shilton. 1–1 and an hour gone.

Cameroon brought on another substitute – Ekeke for M'Fede – and almost immediately the move paid dividends. Milla chipped the ball through and his fellow substitute raced clear and hit a shot cleanly past Shilton. The jubilant scorer ran to the corner and was submerged under a mass of joyous green-shirted players, including N'Kono, the goalkeeper, who had run the full length of the pitch to join them. Having led at half-time, England now had just twenty-six minutes to turn around a game which had evolved into one of the most compelling in tournament history. Cameroon searched for a killer goal, England salvation. Pearce blocked a Makanaky shot and Shilton saved from Omam-Biyik, then Makanaky. Pearce was booked; Trevor Steven came on for Butcher; Wright and N'Kono squared up. Gascoigne then put Platt through with a defence splitting pass, but the England goalscorer shot wide. Next it was Omam-Biyik's turn again, and he almost killed off England with a back-heeled shot that Shilton blocked.

Redemption, so elusive, finally came when Wright's flick sent Lineker through and Kunde sent him crashing to the ground as he was shaping up to shoot. This time there was no doubt about the outcome: Penalty! It was England's first since February 1986, when Bryan Robson scored against Israel. Now there was no Robson, but Lineker took the ball. With only eight minutes to go and the world watching him, Lineker stroked his penalty past N'Kono as if it were a training ground exercise.

2–2, and the game went into extra time. Mark Wright picked up a nasty cut to his eye, but with no more substitutes left he had to carry on, heavily bandaged like Butcher in Sweden, switching to right midfield, with the diminutive Parker covering at centre-back and Trevor Steven at right-back. (Later he would muse: 'I was keen to get on just to make up the numbers. We didn't want to be down to ten men at that stage but when I went down to the touchline, the reserve referee said that I couldn't see. I told him that didn't matter . . .'[24]). England battled on – like Wright – sometimes desperately, as the Cameroonians laid siege to the England goal. Omam-Biyik tested the England goalkeeper yet again; then shot over after racing past Platt, as if the England player wasn't there. Balls continually bobbled around the England penalty area, were sliced clear or hacked away. It seemed as if England had nothing left, as if they had expended every last ounce of energy keeping the Cameroonians out. And then Gazza transformed the game.

Socks around his ankles, red faced and glistening with sweat, as extra time reached its halfway point suddenly he took off and was away. Looking up he saw Lineker racing free and with inch-perfect precision played the ball into his feet. Mercilessly, desperately, N'Kono brought him down. It was another penalty. After just two penalties in eight years and ninety-two matches England had had two in the space of twenty-three minutes.

Lineker received attention for the foul; N'Kono was booked for protesting; Lineker composed himself; ran up and fired England into a 3–2 lead. But still it wasn't over. Parker, another of England's heroes, was tested to the limit by more attacks from an increasingly exhausted Cameroon side; Platt and Lineker conspired to miss the easiest chance of the night after Steven had beaten two and dipped in a cross; and then, finally, the referee called time.

'No one on the African continent could remain indifferent to the battle waged by the Indomitable Lions against the English,' wrote the Ivorian newspaper *Fraternité Matin*. 'Roger Milla and his comrades have permitted us to vibrate to their rhythm for three weeks, taking us on board with them for this wild adventure.' They weren't the only ones: the world had fallen in love with Cameroon, more so for pushing England to the absolute limit. They had been the better side and contributed more than their share to the best contest of the finals. 'It was nail biting,' a rueful Robson noted in his diary, 'heart-rending, like riding the roughest of roller coasters as it ebbed and flowed and changed course in crazy fashion.'[25] On the night itself, breathless, delighted, in awe of what he'd witnessed, he faced journalists.

> We've got good players, players who fight. And yes, we had luck – you need luck. But it's about players and they had some good players too. They did to us what we thought we'd do to them. So we've been party to an outstanding game – and I applaud them. They were excellent. Everybody had a bit of sympathy for Cameroon today – I know I did. When I saw them beat Argentina I was delighted for them. They've done very well here, like Morocco four years ago, and Algeria eight years ago – African football has to be respected. And they will get better . . . We pulled it out the fire. Sometimes I don't know how we do it but we showed a marvellous will to fight to the bitter end.

The nation shared his elation and even those who had rooted for the Africans could manage a wry smile at the awesome display of football provided by the two countries. Everybody, that is, except David Miller. Even the tabloids – perhaps hypocritically – had dropped their vehement anti-Robson stance. Not in *The Times*, though, where Miller continued to berate Robson.

> The only person the England manager is deluding is himself, and possibly one or two of his players, when he asserts, 'We're in the top four in the world'. The only aspect in which England stand in the top four is that referred to by the eager and enthusiastic Platt, when he sat with his manager at the post match interview: not throwing in the towel, the Dunkirk bit.[26]

Yet the hard facts spelt out the truth: England were one of the four best teams at the World Cup, and for all the sniping it was impossible not to admire their progress. Certainly, the entire country back home was united behind their TV sets.

After the exhausting intensity of their quarter-final England had just seventy-two hours to recover before meeting West Germany in the semi-final in Turin. England expected. The country's largest-ever television audience – some thirty million people – tuned into the match; the demand for electricity hit an eight-year high and the country's roads and public places emptied. Meanwhile rumours were flying around that Robson was staying. Still to sign a contract with PSV, the FA were supposed to be reconsidering their position and

Robson fanned the flames of speculation when he refused to state unequivocally what was happening. 'It is not my decision whether I stay with England. The subject is not open for discussion.'

England had Beardsley in for the injured Barnes, but were otherwise unchanged, Wright was heavily bandaged but otherwise indomitable: 'I'm confident, I've played with cuts before. All I can do is make it worse, maybe.' Fifteen thousand England fans converged on Turin, prompting the biggest fears of trouble to date. This was, after all, the home of Juventus, the victim of the excesses of English hooliganism only five years earlier. Add to the ferment anything up to 40,000 Germans and it seemed a recipe for disaster. In the event there was antagonism, stand-offs and the inevitable heavy hand of the *carabinieri* on the streets of Turin, but no war as the doommongers had prophesied, and nothing in any way resembling a riot to satisfy the rotters.

In the municipal magnificence of the Stadio delle Alpi, England seemed to be inspired by the attacking lessons taught them by Cameroon. The initiative was theirs right from the first minute when, from a corner, Gascoigne's goalbound volley was parried away by Illgner. A second, third and fourth corner went England's way, but the attacks were varied, ranging from the rampant charges of Gascoigne and Waddle to the overlaps of Pearce and Parker and darting runs of Lineker. The Germans were conspicuously on the back foot. Beardsley went through; Pearce shot wide; Waddle's cross only just evaded the head of Lineker; Gascoigne nutmegged Matthaüs, making purportedly the best midfielder in the world look strikingly ordinary. Then Waddle quickly took a free-kick from thirty-five yards, and, catching Illgner unaware, audaciously lobbed a shot in, which had the German back-pedalling furiously to touch over the bar.

Slowly the Germans came back into it. Karl-Heinz Riedle came on for the stricken Völler and brought some attacking impetus to his team. Shilton saved Thon's shot; then clawed away an Augenthaler free-kick. After forty-five breathless minutes it was goalless but, following the interval, Germany looked the more composed. England weren't allowed to settle and the attacking dominance of the opening half seemed a distant memory. On fifty-nine minutes Pearce brought down Hässler on the edge of the England penalty area. The England wall formed to defend the free-kick, with Paul Parker standing a yard wide on the right-hand end of it. Hässler tapped the ball square to Andreas Brehme, who shot. The advancing Parker charged, the ball ballooned off him and looped – almost in agonising slow motion – over the England defenders and above the head of the furiously back-pedalling Shilton and into the England net. It had been the cruellest twist of fate, and Shilton sat in his goal with a look of disbelief and disgust. 'If the Germans had taken it a hundred times again it would never have been repeated,' recalled Robson.[27] Platt ran back to pick up the ball from the net and get the match back under way.

It was time for Gascoigne to reassert his authority on the game. He sent a free-kick just wide; Illgner saved Wright's header from his cross; then Gazza sent Waddle scampering clear with a superlative through ball but his fellow Geordie failed to find the finish. Robson shuffled his cards, bringing Trevor Steven on in place of Butcher again, and switching to a flat back four with Steven as a right-midfielder.

With ten minutes to go, Parker surged down the right and sent in a long looping cross. The Germans failed to deal with it, Lineker charged in, controlled it with his thigh, simultaneously wrong-footing Augenthaler and Berthold and crashed a low left-footed shot past Illgner and into the far corner. England were saved.

Lineker's eyes bulged with elation, his mouth contorted with joy screamed 'Yeeesss!!!' as he was mobbed by his team-mates, but nobody, not even the forlorn Illgner, could hear him over the din of the Stadio delle Alpi.

Extra time came and the Germans attacked with force again. Walker's last-ditch tackle denied Klinsmann, then Shilton saved acrobatically from the same striker and the third time Klinsmann went through he dragged his shot wide. In midfield the ball – and tackles – fizzed around with the pace and intensity of a game that was ten minutes old, not a hundred.

Then Gascoigne clattered Berthold. It was a clumsy, pretty innocuous challenge, but Berthold made the most of it, writhing around as if Gazza had broken his leg, not brushed his ankle, while the German bench protested angrily. The referee held up the yellow card, Gascoigne would miss the final. A look of demented anguish washed over his face and it reddened even further, as if he was about to burst into tears. Lineker tapped his finger to his forehead, warning the England bench that Gazza might have lost the plot and could be on the verge of doing something stupid.

Chris Waddle hit the inside of the post and Lineker's lunge at the rebound missed the ball by inches when the slightest of touches would have resulted in a goal. Brehme hit Gascoigne with a hard, ugly challenge, sending him down in a crumpled heap. The German was booked and the England fans booed him furiously. Gascoigne got up and shook the German's hand. 'He'd been threatening to grow up all this time,' recorded Pete Davies. 'But there was the moment, booked himself and heartbroken, that he proved that he'd done so. Six months ago he'd have hit him, and got himself sent off.'28

From the free-kick, Platt put the ball in the net, but the linesman called offside. It was the fifth time in as many games that England had had a goal disallowed, a fact that pretty much summed up Italia '90 as a spectacle. Indeed when full-time was finally blown, at first sight the 1–1 scoreline seemed indicative of the sterility that had pervaded the fourteenth World Cup finals. The result, however, didn't tell half of the story.

So, for the first time in England's history, a match went to penalties. Gascoigne, who was in floods of tears, was nominated for the sixth penalty, should it go to sudden death. 'I put my own arm around him trying to keep away my own tears,' Robson recalled.

> I felt so sorry for him. It was so emotional out there on the pitch, feeling what he was feeling . . . my eyes were filling up. I said, 'You can't play in the final Paul. But what you can do is to make sure everyone else can, son. You've done great to get us here. Now see it out. Do it for us.' I kept saying these things, and Paul, hardly able to look at me through his tears said, 'Don't worry . . . don't worry about me. Trust me. I'll do it.'29

The world gazed on through the gaps in their fingers as Lineker, Beardsley and Platt converted their penalties and Brehme, Matthäus and Riedle responded for West Germany. Bobby Robson had specifically requested that Stuart Pearce take England's fourth penalty since the full-back boasted the best spot-kick in the First Division and Robson realised the fourth was the most important in the sequence.

Pearce ran up and shot hard, low, but too centrally and Illgner saved with his legs. 'My world collapsed,' recalled Pearce. 'I had been taking penalties for as long as I could remember but now I'd missed the most important penalty of my life, in the semi-final of the World Cup finals.'30

Olaf Thon scored West Germany's fourth penalty, meaning Chris Waddle had to score simply to keep England in the game. But when he shot, he hit the ball high, like a rugby place-kick, over Illgner's bar. England's World Cup dream was finished, and so too was Bobby Robson.

⚽ ⚽ ⚽

With tears of sadness and tears of regret, floods of saltwater washed over the country. England's epic World Cup adventure had come to an end. There were plenty of tears in Turin too. In the dressing room, Robson pointed out to his players that nobody deserved to lose like that. Gazza was still crying, as were Stuart Pearce and several others. But Robson's most vivid memory was Peter Shilton's look of dejection that said: 'I'm forty and I am going to retire, and I could have finished as a World Cup winner.' Indeed Pearce couldn't stop crying. He had to take a dope test but it was ninety minutes before he could urinate and he sobbed all the way back to the hotel. England played a third place play-off against Italy in Bari three days later, which was lost 1–2 in large part because of the scandalously poor refereeing.

Nobody really cared by that stage, although it did mark Peter Shilton's 125th and last international appearance, a game he distinguished by a string of saves from Roberto Baggio. Starting out as a young pretender, Shilton had been party to some of the England team's most traumatic nights but had grown in stature with the renaissance of the national team under Ron Greenwood and Robson. A supremely fit, infinitely dedicated athlete, he had repeatedly proved his critics wrong in the twilight of his career, and proved he was still amongst the best in the world. Terry Butcher had also played his last game for his country against the West Germans, bringing an end to a decade-long international career.

The following day the squad, triumphant despite defeat, flew into Luton Airport and a heroes' welcome. Pearce and Waddle had heard rumours that they were about to be lynched on their return and initially sat nervously on the lower deck of the bus, but their concern was surely a symptom of an age when the very worst was always expected of England fans. They need not have worried as 200,000 appreciative people greeted the England team in and around the airport and it took the players four hours to reach their hotel two miles away. The biggest cheer of the afternoon came for English football's darling, Paul Gascoigne, who repaid the compliment by flashing a pair of plastic breasts at the crowd.

Bobby Robson, so often and unfairly a pariah, was able to reflect happily on eight relatively successful years that had taken him, and England, so close to glory. 'We have competed with the best and only once were we awful,' he said. 'That was against the Soviets in the European Championships two years ago. Other than that we have had a fair share of success and maybe our performances here will, as in 1966, stimulate the domestic game.'[31] He was right. Italia '90 marked the end of more than a decade's domestic decline and the start of football's renaissance. Attendances went on a continual upward curve, the quality of fare improved dramatically, and England fell back in love with the game that had so often been a dirty word in the seventies and eighties.

Robson had also exacted a dramatic re-evaluation in the media of his own character and abilities as a manager. From being May's charlatan and June's villain, he had become July's hero. In years to come he would be regarded as a veritable 'national treasure' – once an inconceivable notion. *Today* made the most dramatic about turn. A few weeks earlier Robson, according to them, had been an adulterous, incompetent 'shambles of a man'. Now, in a piece entitled 'Robson's Supermen' it declared 'Bobby Robson can walk away from the England manager's job in the knowledge that he has raised the stature of our national game to its highest point since the World Cup triumph in 1966.' It was monumental hypocrisy, of course, but no less than he finally deserved.

One man, however, stuck to his guns. Two years earlier, after the European Championships, David Miller had written that he never expected England to reach a semi-final if he lived to be eighty: 'England's success was welcome,' he wrote, teeth no doubt gritted, fist invariably clenched angrily around a pen, furious at the notion that Robson's achievements may finally have to be acknowledged, 'but do not let us be deluded into thinking as the manager was eager to claim, that England stand among the best four in the world. They have simply improved.' Later, he described England's performances against Italy and West Germany as 'tolerably encouraging'. His snide disregard had gone beyond the point where it could be attributed to frustrated expectation; it was personal and epitomised the treatment meted out to Robson during his tenure from the press as a whole. In a way Miller deserved some credit for keeping a consistent line, but his arguments were ultimately mean and stupid. As Gordon Taylor, the Chief Executive of the PFA, put it in a riposte to *The Times*: 'To add that England cannot consider themselves in the top four in the world but merely as having "improved" is tantamount to telling Franz Beckenbauer that West Germany are not world champions but merely World Cup winners.'[32]

Robson's replacement-elect was the Aston Villa manager, Graham Taylor. As a player, the forty-five-year-old had been an ordinary left-back with Grimsby Town and Lincoln City in the Third and Fourth Divisions during the 1960s. He took charge of Lincoln City at the age of just twenty-eight in 1972 and within three years had led them to the Fourth Division title with a record haul of seventy-four points and 111 goals. Watford's eccentric pop-star owner, Elton John, had seen Taylor's potential and lured him to Vicarage Road in 1977. There he took Watford from the Fourth Division to runners-up in the First and the 1984 FA Cup final. Later, as manager of Aston Villa he had won promotion back to the top flight in 1988 before taking them to the verge of the title in 1990. He was a disciple of the FA's Director of Coaching, Charles Hughes, who extolled the virtues of an unsophisticated brand of direct football and playing by percentages to the disgust of many of those involved in the British game. Despite the assertions of the likes of Brian Glanville that Taylor's appointment was 'an abysmal decision', his record supplied the evidence that Hughes's methods could bring success: his teams were functional, hard-working and highly successful, given the limited resources he normally had at his disposal. He had also 'discovered' a number of young players from lower league sides or even more opaque obscurity and helped elevate them to international stardom. David Platt and John Barnes were his two greatest successes then, and Dwight Yorke was on his way to fame thanks in large part to Taylor.

Taylor had been offered and accepted the post at the start of June, but six weeks of tortuous negotiations followed between the FA and Aston Villa chairman, Doug Ellis, which delayed the appointment until the middle of July. The FA had offered Villa £90,000 – which was more than the amount owing on Taylor's contract – but Ellis was holding out for £200,000. 'Graham is the best manager in the country,' said Ellis. 'Villa are entitled to compensation. Graham has also brought his own staff to Villa Park. Our new manager will probably want his own men and we will have to compensate Graham's.'[33] Eventually a compromise was reached and Ellis backed down. With it, hopes of a dramatic reprieve for Robson finally died.

'I am relieved that the waiting is over,' said Taylor.

> And keen to lay my plans for the future. Very few managers get the chance to lead their country and I feel very honoured to have been offered the position. I'd like to be the most track-suited manager England have ever had. My worst fear is that we might get back to the situation where football is nobody's friend. The game does not deserve the hammering it has had, English clubs out of Europe and the game bashed politically.

Taylor's target was to set England the same standards as the West Germans. 'We ought to be able to put ourselves on a par with them. Are they that much better?' He named Gascoigne, Platt, Walker and Wright as the nucleus of players capable of helping England challenge for European and World Cup honours.

England, meanwhile, was gripped by Gazzamania. For the two months after Turin his face was in the newspapers almost every day, on the back and front pages. There was an unprecedented demand for him to endorse products and take part in commercial activities, which his two advisers – the London-based lawyer Mel Stein and accountant Len Lazarus – seized upon with gusto. Soon the midfielder's name was appearing on everything from Gazza footballs to shinpads and toothpaste. There was a Gazza LP and his cover of the Lindisfarne hit 'Fog on the Tyne' topped the charts in October. Lazarus sought to register Gazza and his signature as a trademark. 'He's such a popular figure at the moment he could be used to endorse just about anything,' John O'Donnell, creative director of Collett Dickinson Pearce advertising agency told the *Sunday Times*. 'We're going to float him,' joked Mel Stein. 'I could have him opening supermarkets, record shops or pizza parlours four times a day.'[34]

Yet while Gazza was king of the back pages, he was King Rat of the garbage printed beneath the mastheads. After Italy he took a holiday with his childhood sweetheart Gail Pringle. It turned out to be a disaster, with Gascoigne constantly besieged by autograph hunters, and signalled the end of their relationship. Shortly afterwards, Ms Heidi Shepherd, a Dunston neighbour of Gascoigne, appeared on the front of the *Sun* replete in suspender-belt, g-string and 'provocatively opened leather jacket'. Heidi, according to the *Sun*, was Gazza's new love (largely an invention it emerged). Speculation about the great white hope's love life was one thing, but this appeared in the same issue as Gazza promising that he wanted to be the 'best in the world'.

A few days later, Gail Pringle sold her sob story to the *Mail on Sunday* ('How I lost Gazza to the world'). Gascoigne appeared bemused by the attention. After Tottenham's first game of the new season, he announced: 'I'm fed up with all this girl-talk. I have split up with Gail but I don't want to have another girlfriend. It took me twenty-five minutes to get going playing football because of all this hype about a new girlfriend. It seems the only place I am safe these days is out there on the football pitch.'[35]

Yet when a newspaper flashed its chequebook at him – or his family – he seemed to love the attention. The *Sun* had him under contract for £120,000, which meant that the other three tabloids had to appoint full-time 'Gazza watchers' to steal their rivals' thunder. Everyone was grabbing a piece of the action. For £3000 you could get to photograph his mother; for £1000 she would give an interview – about herself. For talking about Gazza she charged extra. His sister Anne-Marie charged £2000 to talk about her acting career; the same for a photo. To get Gazza himself a premium rate was obviously charged: £10,000 for an interview. Professional footballers' obsession with money had seemingly reached a new level.[36]

Conversely Gascoigne claimed to hate the press. His interviews seldom consisted of more than a 'daft as a brush' pose and a few monosyllabic answers to dull questions. In October, though, when he was promoting his record, he opened up to a journalist from *Time Out*:

The English press treat football like a joke. All they do is look for bad bits; every week bad bits. You never see the good side of it. They've been writing great about me but people should realise that I had nearly two years of shit off them. Nearly two years of absolute crap, slaughtered by them.

With myself they've been really good. But the news people, the news guys, have been right bastards. I'd love to see some of them come into the local pub I go to in Newcastle and see how brave they are then. They're all soft: all they can do is write the front page of the newspaper and give somebody stick. They're cowards . . .

They camp out at the end of the drive in cars, like little kids. I mean those people have got to go back to their families. Imagine one of them going home and his wife saying, 'How did your day go?' 'Great. I sat outside Gascoigne's house all day and all night waiting for him to come out.' His wife must say, 'What do you want to do that for, you prick?'[37]

England's first international after Italia '90 was a home friendly against Hungary on 12 September. Taylor named Nigel Winterburn, Lee Dixon, Gary Pallister and Nigel Martyn in his first squad and Lineker was appointed captain in place of the injured Robson. With Butcher and Shilton now both retired, the only player who had captained England before was Beardsley, once, against Israel, and his place was by no means secure. 'He has the status and he takes a wide view of football,' explained Taylor of Lineker. 'As well as being the leader on the pitch, he can be the link between the squad and the media.'[38]

England drew 1–1 with the Magyars then began their qualification campaign for the 1992 European Championships the following month. To make the finals in Sweden England had to get past Poland, Turkey and, yet again, Jack Charlton's Ireland. The campaign got under way against Poland at Wembley, which was a sell-out of 77,000 now that the shabby stadium's capacity had been reduced. Again Taylor preferred Bull over Beardsley to partner Lineker, a statement, if ever there was one, about his preferred methods. Bull's partnership with Lineker had done little to impress in its previous four outings and meant that Lineker had to drop deeper. Even the Wolves man seemed surprised about his inclusion. 'I thought that Peter Beardsley would be in because he has had such a good run at his club,' Bull remarked on the eve of the match.

Gazzamania, meanwhile, had reached silly proportions. Gascoigne had revealed that in the days leading up to the start of the 1990–91 season, he was having to be smuggled out of Spurs' training ground in the boot of his car: 'To be honest, the last few days have made me think – is all this fame stuff worth it? I just want to be one of the lads.'[39] The *Sun*, of course, couldn't possibly let Gazza be just 'one of the lads'. Had they not just paid him £120,000? A day later they kindly published Gail Pringle's photo album, introduced with their characteristic decorum: 'My Gazza-nova. Ex-love Gail opens up her photo album.' Then, the following morning, for anybody who might have missed the previous weekend's *Mail on Sunday*, the *Sun* generously syndicated Pringle's lament from their colleagues at Associated Newspapers with the catch-all caption: 'Why I gave boot to my Gazza'.

But it wasn't just the tabloids: Gazza's name was on everybody's lips. Writing in the *London Review of Books* Karl Miller described him as 'a highly charged spectacle on the field of play; fierce and comic, formidable and vulnerable, urchin-like and waif-like, a strong head and torso with comparatively frail-looking breakable legs, strange-eyed, pink-faced, tense and upright, a priapic monolith in the Mediterranean sun'.[40] Later, the poet Ian Hamilton would write an essay entitled 'Gazza Italia' in the literary magazine *Granta* that would later be expanded into a full-length biography. There was nothing unusual in a biography, or a rhapsodic eulogy about a footballer – but a homoerotic tribute from the (Scottish) editor of the *LRB* or a book by a distinguished poet? This was extraordinary stuff. Never before had the chattering classes taken a footballer so closely to their hearts.

When the two teams came out to rapturous applause, Gascoigne lingered in the tunnel like a true showman and emerged to face Poland last. Yet after the match – a 2–0 win – Graham Taylor said that England had been playing with ten men, and it was obvious to those watching who had been the missing figure: Gazza had made little impact.

A month later England played Jack Charlton's Republic of Ireland, who had become the bogey team for the English. Three days prior to the match, *The Times* asked: 'What should Graham Taylor do with Paul Gascoigne?' The question would have been unimaginable a few months earlier, yet Gascoigne was in and out of form and Taylor dropped him. It was not, he said, a Gazza sort of match; nor were a team of clod-hopping destroyers like the Irish the sort of side he thrived against. Indeed, so workmanlike were the Irish that Charlton left out the elegant Sheedy, the goalscorer in Cagliari. In a pique of nationalism in Dublin, the Irish refused to play the English national anthem. (Perhaps their anti-English sentiments were a result of the national self-confidence that came with now boasting 'just' four English-born players in their starting XI, although they still, of course, had Charlton, plus another two English-born men on their substitutes' bench.) Platt scored for England on sixty-nine minutes when neat interplay between himself, Lineker and Pearce found Dixon on the right and his low cross was touched home by the Aston Villa player. Ireland's only previous chance had come on the hour-mark when McCarthy, from just inside his own half, took a free-kick that was carried by the wind, over the head of the stumbling Woods and kissed the top of the England bar. His fifty-five-yard shot was typical of Ireland's approach to the game, but late on Cascarino hoofed an equaliser and Ireland's twenty-two-match unbeaten home run was extended.

At the start of February 1991 Cameroon became the first African nation to play at Wembley. The occasion marked the England debut of Crystal Palace's Ian Wright, a former apprentice plasterer who, over a period of six years, had graduated from amateur ranks to the top end of the First Division scoring charts. His debut was marred by financial bickering when Roger Milla tried to claim a 'premium' of £30,000 after he claimed that most of the 61,000-strong crowd were there simply to see him and eventually refused to play when the bonus was not forthcoming. Playing in sub-zero temperatures Gascoigne was subdued, then substituted and England won 2–0 courtesy of two goals from Gary Lineker.

The following month Ireland came to Wembley for an eagerly awaited European Championship qualifier. There were record receipts of £1.25 million with demand at three times Wembley's 80,000 capacity, forcing the FA to return £2 million to disappointed supporters. 'I don't think there's a voodoo,' said John Barnes of the recent luck of the Irish. 'Even if there is, it is about time it was laid to rest.' Lee Dixon's deflected shot gave England a tenth-minute lead, but the Irish hit the long ball and harried and eventually their persistence won them an equaliser and draw. 'It was my most disappointing day since I became England manager because we didn't win,' said Taylor. 'It was a point lost, but we got what we deserved.' Charlton jibed in return: 'They were doing exactly what we do. They played two men wide and started knocking the ball behind the full-backs, and it worked for them.' He wasn't far wrong.

The result left Ireland at the top of the group on goal difference, and meant that England went to Turkey five weeks later, needing to go some way to emulating Ireland's earlier 5–0 win over the Turks to pull clear of their neighbours. England were all but unrecognisable from the team that had almost conquered the world ten months earlier. Not only were they sporting a new kit ('a horrendous pale-blue fruit-salad design that looked as though it had been knocked up from curtains removed from a kitchen window at a seaside boarding house', according to *The Times*[41]) but included two debutants – Dennis Wise and Geoff Thomas – plus a recall for the Arsenal striker Alan Smith. England's display bordered on the inept, with the Turks having two goals disallowed for offside, and England only getting their winner – with more than a hint of handball – when Wise scrambled home after a long-range free-kick. When Taylor re-emerged pitch side for a post-match interview he had insults hurled at him by England fans who also chanted the name of Waddle, omitted from the squad, despite being in mesmerising form that had seen his club, Marseille, reach the European Cup final. 'England are still expected to go around the world beating everyone in sight, but that is a silly thought,' said Taylor. 'We got a result today, and if we win our next two games we will go to Sweden for the finals next year and that is all that matters.'

England's messiah had been absent with injury, but having helped save English football he was turning his redemptive qualities to his club. Spurs were crawling in £15 million of debt with interest running at a further £3 million per annum and teetering towards bankruptcy following a series of disastrous investments and business diver-sifications in the late 1980s. Their best way out of the mess seemed to be by selling, but who to sell? Waddle had been shipped out to Marseille for £4.5 million eighteen months earlier, which left Lineker and Gascoigne as their most saleable assets. Lineker, at thirty, was probably not worth much more than a million, but Gazza could be worth anything. Prior to the World Cup, Roberto Baggio – the same age, but a lesser light at the finals – had cost Juventus a shade under £9 million; estimates put Gazza's value between £5 million and £15 million.

The question was how to get Gascoigne into the shop window so as to optimise that value. Spurs were never going to win the title, or even mount a serious challenge for it. The FA Cup was their best route to success, and Gazza their best chance of winning it. Yet he was also struggling with a groin injury as the 1990–91 season moved into its second half. The answer the Spurs management seemed to arrive on was for Gazza to win the FA Cup for them. So they rested him from the grim grind of the league programme, and unleashed him on opponents almost solely in the FA Cup. It worked too. His free-kick set up the third-round winner against Blackpool; he ran the game against Oxford in the fourth; scored twice against Portsmouth in the next round; won the quarter-final against Notts County in the last minute and then, most spectacularly of all, scored an astonishing free-kick against Arsenal in the fifth minute of the semi-final at Wembley. All the while talks were going on with Lazio, who had tabled a £5 million bid prior to the Notts County match, an offer Spurs had rejected. Shortly after Gazza had helped clinch Spurs' place in the final, a fee of £8 million had been agreed. It was a done deal, England's Great White Hope would be returning to Italy after the FA Cup final.

Still, he had resolved to give the Spurs fans a farewell gift – their first FA Cup since 1982.

At Wembley, on 14 May 1991, Tottenham Hotspur and Nottingham Forest are preparing to come out for the 111th FA Cup final. A TV camera catches Gazza in the tunnel, twitching, perspiring; he looked wired, not unlike he had after being booked against West Germany when Lineker had signalled that he had lost it. 'Gazza was too wound up,' one witness told the *News of the World*. 'The occasion had his eyes popping out. He was like a stone age man in for the kill.'[42]

The two teams came out, and at the pre-match presentation Gascoigne looked more relaxed, kissing the hand of Princess Diana instead of shaking it. But as play started it was clear that Gascoigne was wild, running around the pitch with reckless abandon, not holding his position, snatching at the ball. In the fifth minute he launched a chest-high kick at Gary Parker, a foul serious enough to have warranted a sending-off in some games. Gascoigne was booked, but it didn't settle him. A couple of minutes later, Gary Charles was running at the edge of the Tottenham penalty area, about to be closed down by the Spurs left-back, Pat Van Den Hauwe, when, seemingly out of nowhere, Gazza launched himself at full pelt. He caught

Charles, the two men went down, Gazza underneath, his right leg twisting as it fell. A free-kick to Forest (which Pearce scored) and the £8 million man got up and was okay.

Or so it seemed. The game restarted, Gascoigne ran a few paces and fell. This time he stayed down. He had snapped his cruciate ligament. Stretchered off, he was rushed to hospital in tears where he underwent an emergency operation. The next day he told reporters from his hospital bed, 'God knows what was in my head when I made that tackle. But don't write me off, I'll be back better than ever.'[43] Not everyone shared his optimism. Mr William Miller, Gascoigne's surgeon, said: 'It is early days yet, but his career is in jeopardy. The chances of him playing again at that standard are not at all great . . . Only a lunatic would pay big money for him now.'[44]

Without him, Spurs had gone on to win the FA Cup. The divergent outcomes for him and his club seemed depressingly familiar. Gascoigne, the man kissed by greatness, had turned the other cheek. Indeed it could be said to be the story of his life: following every moment of sublimity would be one of stupidity. Sometimes, often in fact, fortune didn't favour him; at others he had nobody to blame but himself.

Gazzamania had come, in large part, because English football needed a saviour. The success of its clubs in European competition in the 1970s and first half of the 1980s had patched over the repeated failures at international level, where the technical failings, tactical naivety and sheer blandness of its players had seen progress halt at the 1970 World Cup finals. Gascoigne's explosion onto the international scene and his realisation of other people's hopes in Italia '90 had changed all that. Expectation had never been higher for any single individual; never had the hopes of England rested so heavily on one man's shoulders. Yet hope bred hope. With Gascoigne in the side, England seemed capable of anything; without him, and without anybody, bar perhaps Platt, Waddle and Lineker (the latter two of whom were at the end of their international careers) threatening to match his world-class status, England seemed destined to remain in the thrall of mediocrity. The sad reality was that after that fateful FA Cup final England's great white hope would never be the same again. Would England?

13

THE IMPOSSIBLE JOB

NOBODY, IT SEEMED, would miss Paul Gascoigne more than England's football followers. Ostensibly there had been little to detract from the results of Graham Taylor's first year as England manager. Nor would there be for much of the next: qualification was secured – with an unbeaten record – for the 1992 European Championships in Sweden, and England would suffer just one defeat (to world champions Germany in September 1991) in the period leading up to the tournament. Yet the sense that there was something fundamentally wrong with the way in which England were playing their football deepened with every game that they played. Frequently torpid, wins were hard fought, results ground out, but seldom was the way in which Taylor's men played pleasing to the eye. Too often the tactical options pursued were one dimensional, reliant on a long quick ball over the top and the muscular qualities of a centre-forward to hold the ball up. In many ways Taylor's England followed directly along the tactical path he had trodden at Aston Villa and Watford. His two previous clubs had typified what English football had been good at in the 1980s: robustness, abrasiveness, forcing errors and playing the percentages. Without more accomplished opponents in the First Division, such basic attributes were enough to succeed and even push for trophies; on the international stage, however, faced with more technically gifted opponents and teams extolling a more thoughtful brand of football, the thought that England's shortcomings would be exposed, perhaps catastrophically, was impossible to shake.[1]

Part of Taylor's problem was a paucity of talent. When Bobby Robson had first taken the job eight years earlier he had initially doled out caps with abandon but only really discovered two men in his first couple of years – John Barnes and Gary Lineker – who would go on to make a real impact in international football. The same was true for

Taylor. Between his first match in charge against Hungary in September 1990 and the start of the European Championship finals twenty-one months later, Taylor awarded no fewer than twenty-two first caps. Often, however, these ghosts of England's past – the likes of Geoff Thomas, John Salako or Earl Barrett – have been dragged up to haunt him. Combinations of ill luck, injuries or more general shortcomings may well have seen the aforementioned drift into obscurity, but at the time Taylor's choices generally represented the cutting edge of English talent. Not all would fade so ingloriously either. Chelsea's tough but technically accomplished midfielder, Dennis Wise, would be one of the England squad's more dependable players for much of the 1990s and beyond; likewise, Leeds United's midfield anchorman, David Batty. Arsenal's full-back, Lee Dixon, never received the international recognition his continually excellent performances in a trophy-studded Highbury career deserved but his club mate Martin Keown (formerly of Everton) did enjoy international success, earning forty-three caps at centre-back over the course of a decade. Arsenal's greatest English goalscorer, Ian Wright, like Dixon, arguably never received the international recognition his club form merited, but this quick, decisive finisher and vociferous member of the dressing room would still go on to earn thirty-three caps, scoring nine goals.

At the same time, though, there was a suspicion that Taylor had been hasty in ousting some of the old in order to blood the new. Although age and that devastating blight of injuries had all but forced Bryan Robson into international retirement in October 1991 (after just three further caps since his exit from Italia '90), some of his contemporaries also cast into the wilderness had more to offer. The 1991–92 season would see Peter Beardsley's best domestic campaign in years when he shone in an otherwise sterile Everton team; Chris Waddle had been a mainstay of the Marseille side that reached the final of the 1991 European Cup while Mark Hateley scored a creditable twenty-one goals in thirty appearances for Glasgow Rangers. And what was the reward for their fine form? For Beardsley it was just two starts and two substitute appearances (the last of which came in May 1991); for Waddle, just one start and two as a substitute (and none after October 1991); and Hateley got just one run out.

Still, Taylor could look to the form of Gary Lineker and David Platt as a cause for optimism. The latter, like Gascoigne, had burst onto the international scene in spectacular fashion during the Italy World Cup, and his stock had continued to rise from there on. A £5.5 million transfer from Aston Villa to Bari in the summer of 1991 would be the first of a series of big-money moves that eventually earned him the status of the world's most expensive player (based on an aggregate of fees), and on the field he continued to grow in stature. Though perhaps lacking some of Bryan Robson's charisma, he would follow in his footsteps by captaining England, weighing in with a ratio of goals even more prolific than his forebear in the number seven shirt. Lineker too was adding to his tally of strikes, and creeping up on Bobby Charlton's record of forty-nine England goals. Goal forty-eight had come against the CIS (brief successor of the USSR) on 29 April 1992 and, although he had announced his international retirement that summer (which would coincide with another personally lucrative move, this time to Japan's formative J-League), it was widely reckoned that with three warm-up games and at least three matches in the Championships themselves, England's hot-shot striker would at least go on to match Charlton's tally.

Though mourned, Lineker's impending departure was viewed with less trepidation than it might have been in previous years because of the emergence of a worthy successor. Southampton's Alan Shearer had exploded onto the English football map as a seventeen-year-old, after marking his full league debut with a hat-trick against Arsenal in April 1988. If his progress at The Dell had been rather more gradual after that, few doubted that he would develop into an excellent player. Standing 5ft 11in tall, Shearer's relative lack of height was belied by model aerial ability; he was strong, he was quick, he could strike the ball with magnificent ferocity, his positional play showed his intelligence, his movement was good: in short, he had all the essential attributes one could possibly hope for from a centre-forward. By the 1991–92 season he had emerged as a very real contender to succeed Lineker as England's lead striker and Taylor rewarded him with a call-up for the friendly with France in February 1992, an occasion he marked with a fine goal as England won 2–0. He had subsequently played against the CIS, but despite being named by Taylor in the squad for the European Championships, England's manager seemed unsure alternatively as to whether Shearer was ready for the step up to international football (in which case he would use Arsenal's less accomplished centre-forward, Alan Smith, in his place) or whether he was better advised deploying Lineker as a lone striker.

With good results, but patchy form, how Taylor's men would fare at the finals could not be predicted with any great certainty. Bookmakers priced them 5–1 fourth favourites after Germany, Holland and France, the last of whom joined England in a four-country group with Denmark and hosts Sweden. The Danes had only been invited to the tournament days before the opening ceremony after UEFA had belatedly decreed that Yugoslavia be excluded on account of its murderous civil war; the French, though impressive in qualifying, were lesser lights than in the playing days of their manager, Michel Platini; while England hadn't beaten the Swedes since 1968 and had found the hosts in recent meetings to be well-organised, hard-to-beat opponents supplemented by stars like Anders Limpar and Tomas Brolin. Some, such as the exiled Waddle, castigated Taylor in the run-up to the tournament for his preference of the steady over the spectacular and even suggested that English football had regressed by 'five years' under his watch. Others were more optimistic about prospects of English success. 'It will be England against Germany for the title of European soccer kings in just over two weeks' was the self-styled 'expert-verdict' of the *Sun*'s chief football writer, Alex Montgomery. 'And just like the classic meeting back in 1966, it will be an England triumph: winners for their first major championship in twenty-six years.'[2]

England opened the tournament against the unfancied Danes on 11 June at the Malmö Stadium. Lineker, who had been unable to dent Bobby Charlton's scoring record in England's three warm-up games (even missing a penalty in a 1–1 draw with Brazil), partnered Alan Smith up front; Smith's Highbury colleague, the attacking midfielder Paul Merson, was a rare indulgence of flair in an otherwise workman-like England team (still without the injured Gascoigne); and the defence included Keith Curle, a centre-back, deputising in the right-back position. Within twelve minutes his name, along with that of Keown, had found their way into the Dutch referee's notebook, adding individual uncertainty to an uneasy first-half performance. Much of England's most positive play came via Merson, and he combined with Lineker to set Smith up for England's best chance but, though his shot evaded the grasp of Peter Schmeichel, it also went wide of the Dane's post. Goalless at half-time, the standard of play limped from the staid to the insipid in the second half. Curle, clearly uncomfortable in his unfamiliar berth, was wisely substituted after narrowly avoiding a red card; John Jensen hit the inside of the England post after being played through by Christensen and, in the last minute, mere inches separated Kim Vilfort's lunge from the ball and a certain goal. 0–0 at the final whistle and the stakes were suddenly upped for England's remaining two games. Defeat in either would almost certainly spell disaster.

Three days later, England lined up against France with three changes to the side that had played out the bore-fest with Denmark. Andy Sinton, nominally a right-winger, took over from Curle in the troublesome right-back berth; Batty replaced Merson; and Shearer came in for Smith. It looked a distinctly uneven line-up, particularly when compared to the French, who could boast six of Waddle's Marseille team-mates, including the reigning European Footballer of the Year, Jean-Pierre Papin; and though the partnership of the master Lineker and his apprentice Shearer looked promising, the two had started just one previous match together. Even the talismanic elder was without an England goal in 430 minutes. In the event neither country played with any great cohesion or verve; each had but fleeting chances (Sinton cleared Angloma's header off the England line; Shearer's diving header went narrowly wide) and when Basile Boli headbutted Stuart Pearce in the face, the game looked as though it might bubble over angrily. Missing that incident, Boli went unpunished by the Hungarian referee, who ordered Pearce to leave the field to have his wound treated. He returned minutes later to smash a thunderous free-kick against the underside of the French bar, which bounced to safety, and with it went the game's best chance of a goal.

Achingly dull again, the stalemate left England needing a win against Sweden three days later in order to progress to the semi-finals. Taylor tinkered with his line-up once more, bringing in Aston Villa's speedy winger, Tony Daley; deploying Batty in the problematic right-back berth; moving Sinton up the flank and adding another midfielder – Neil Webb – in place of Shearer. With David Platt playing off Lineker, the changes immediately reaped dividends. Four minutes in, Batty's flick header set Lineker free and, looking up, he played a centre into Platt's path. Though his connection wasn't clean he did enough to bundle the ball home. England's goal drought was over. Twice Daley had the opportunity to increase England's advantage: on thirty-four minutes he broke clear and tried to play in Lineker – without success – when he should have shot himself; then, a minute later, when unmarked, he finished weakly from Pearce's cross. Cursing his profligacy, England held on for a half-time lead, but when Johnny Ekström replaced the ineffectual Limpar at half-time, the Swedes matched England's directness and began to cause Taylor's makeshift defence problems. Territorially the hosts began to dominate and chances rained in on Chris Woods' goal. From a corner, Jan Eriksson headed Sweden's equaliser as the hosts began to turn the screw, prompting Taylor's notorious response in the face of this onslaught – off came Lineker and in his place trotted Alan Smith ('Because,' explained Taylor later, 'I felt we needed someone who could hold the ball up'). England's second-greatest ever goalscorer could only watch as Tomas Brolin extinguished England's hopes with a Swedish winner eight minutes later. With it died England's European Championship hopes and Lineker's ambitions of surpassing Charlton.

The image of a forlorn Gary Lineker, head down, a look of dejection washed across his face, ambling sadly towards the touchline, has come to characterise England's decline and the dismal year under Taylor that followed. 'When the dust has settled the more immediate memories will disappear and I'll forget about this tournament,' Lineker reflected. 'I'll look back over my career and how good it's been, how enjoyable playing for England was. I'll want to remember all the good times and, yes, this was a bad one.'[3] The tabloids were rather less forgiving, slamming Taylor with such force that even their earlier treatment of Bobby Robson looked generous. The following day's headlines screamed with indignation: 'Go now'; 'English football RIP' and 'Swedes 2 Turnips 1'.

The latter was the assessment of the *Sun*, who memorably morphed Taylor's face into an image of a turnip. But then wasn't this the same newspaper that had tipped England for glory just days earlier? Apparently this was beyond the average memory span of a *Sun* hack and, presumably, reader. Now they implored Taylor to resign: 'Graham Taylor should do himself and England one big favour today – QUIT . . . Taylor's dummies are back home in England after losing to Sweden in what was our last chance to grab victory . . . [He said] "I can see a team forming in my mind." Oh yeah, Graham . . . and can you see fairies at the bottom of your garden too?'[4] Ninety-four per cent of its readers agreed that he should go. Of course, he didn't, but long after the outcry had died, the memory of England's 'vegetable' manager lived on. Indeed, when international football returned in September and Spain beat England 1–0 in Santander, the *Sun* marked the occasion with a less inspired twist of their famous headline: 'Spanish 1 Onions 0'. There were no prizes for guessing who the onion of the piece was.

Football, as a sport, continued to evolve. At the 1992 Olympic Games in Barcelona, FIFA launched an experiment to counteract the sterile defensive play at Italia '90 by preventing goalkeepers from handling backpasses. What looked like only a slight adjustment to the laws had a huge influence, primarily on the pace of games, which went on a steep upward curve from there on. The beginning of the 1992–93 season also saw the inception of the Premier League. After years of talks and procrastination, English football's elite clubs finally broke away from the rump of the Football League, having submitted their resignations *en masse* some twelve months earlier. The original vision for this 'Super League' envisaged an eighteen-team elite division replete with minimum standards for pitches, floodlights, stadium facilities and so on, but actually emerged as little different from the old Division One, albeit with twenty teams (instead of twenty-two) from the start of the 1994–95 season. The influx of money into clubs' bank accounts was, however, enormous. From numbering just a handful of millions under the Football League, television money was suddenly worth hundreds of millions and within a decade a broadcasting deal worth more than a billion pounds had been agreed with Sky. 'I'm getting increasingly embarrassed when people say "what is the difference between the Premier League and the old First Division?"' the Arsenal vice-chairman, David Dein, admitted shortly after the Premier League's formation. 'I have to face them and say: "Nothing, except there's more money swishing about."'[5]

The influx of big money into the upper echelons of the English game had enormous repercussions. As it filtered into the transfer market, the value of players rose hugely. Alan Shearer, subject of a record £3.6 million fee when he moved from Southampton to Blackburn Rovers in the summer of 1992, would, just four years later, cost Newcastle United some £15 million. Five years after that benchmark deal, in July 2001, Manchester United would pay close to £30 million for Juan Sebastian Veron. Players' wages increased just as dramatically. In 1992 only a handful of footballers at the very peak of the sport – the likes of Lineker, Gascoigne and Platt – could boast contracts worth in excess of £1 million *over their duration*. By the end of the decade it was not uncommon for even journeyman footballers to earn in excess of that amount in a single year. Clubs also began to invest large amounts of money in their coaching facilities, youth schemes and scouting networks. Attention to improving players' technical ability, fitness and other previously ignored aspects, such as diet and psychology, increased greatly. All this was complemented by the influx of foreign footballers into the English game. Previously a net exporter of its best talent, the Football League clubs had until now limited their imports, with one or two notable exceptions, to largely ordinary Scandinavian players. Leeds United's fabulously talented French international forward, Eric Cantona, had bucked that trend, and over subsequent years he would be joined by such exquisitely gifted footballers as Jürgen Klinsmann, Gianluca Vialli, Dennis Bergkamp, Gianfranco Zola, Thierry Henry and many, many others. Some argued that the domestic game was being submerged by foreigners at a cost to English talent, but at the very highest level the influence of overseas stars pushed the frontiers of English football ever further forward.

Sky TV's infiltration of football also fundamentally altered the way people watched football in England. Its slick presentation of live matches helped to rejuvenate the sport and the limitations of the old-style terrestrial coverage were plain for all to see once Sky made football a seven-days-a-week phenomenon. It also helped create a new breed of football supporter – the Sky fan – who was suddenly able to follow a chosen team live on TV most weeks. Increasingly such a person had none of the local or familial bonds that normally tied an individual to a club, and the local pub with its big screen or living room with its Sky decoder became a substitute for a real-life theatre of dreams, but it expanded football's reach into the national consciousness. Rightly or wrongly, such new fans are usually dismissed as Manchester United-supporting glory-hunters, but this condescending line is not always true (Aston Villa fan Prince William is proof that ridiculous measures of success aren't the only motivation for the armchair supporter) and the most natural inclination is to follow the national team, particularly during tournament time. In short, Sky had added another dose of expectation to the nation's unyielding swell of hope.

Much of this, however, lay in the future. Under Taylor, England's depression continued. To qualify for the 1994 World Cup finals in the United States they had been handed a tough six-country qualification group consisting of Holland, the minnows of San Marino, Turkey, up-and-coming Norway and Poland, of whom dark memories lingered from 1973. First up, though, on 14 October 1992, were Norway at Wembley, a nation which promised to 'out English the English'. Managed by Egil Olsen – a wondrously eccentric figure who peppered his outpourings with references to Marx and Engels, bestrode the touchline in Wellington boots and cited Wimbledon as his 'dream team' – Norway took the directness of Taylor's side one step further. They played a hard, relentless game in which chances were few, and if they couldn't snatch the odd goal, were happy to play out a goalless draw. Like Charlton's Ireland their football was not in the least bit attractive, but Olsen had already overseen Norway's transformation from international whipping boys into contenders. They had already amassed six points from their first two qualifiers and put ten goals past San Marino. 'People said it was nothing,' said Olsen ahead of the meeting with England, 'but have England ever scored ten in a World Cup tie?'

Of course, on a man-for-man basis, England had little to worry about. Up front, they could boast the likes of Shearer and Wright; in midfield, Paul Gascoigne, finally fit after his long absence, and David Platt, now a Juventus player; while in defence was Des Walker, himself amongst the world's most expensive players after a summer move to Sampdoria. Added to the England set-up a month earlier had been Paul Ince, Manchester United's abrasive midfielder and self-styled 'guv'nor' who added the sort of spark to the England midfield once brought to it by Mullery and Stiles. Norway, by contrast, had no one of such calibre, yet on a wet Wembley night they held England to a goalless half-time stalemate and though Platt later put the hosts in front with a strike from a well-worked free-kick, profligacy and bad luck prevented England from increasing their advantage. When Kjetil Rekdal's twenty-five-yard volley beat Woods thirteen minutes from the end, it was enough to earn the visitors a 1–1 draw.

Less problematic, however, were Turkey and San Marino. England beat the Turks 2–0 in Izmir the following March and, although it took until the latter stages to bring the emphatic result that was expected as a matter of course, San Marino were defeated 6–0 at Wembley that same month. Had Graham Taylor's England turned the corner?

When they met Holland at Wembley a month later on 28 April 1993, the early indications were that they had. Only a minute had passed when Paul Ince was fouled on the edge of the Dutch penalty area by Richard Witschge. John Barnes, again plagued by enigmatic form in recent games, responded to his critics in mesmerising fashion, hitting a rocket-like free-kick that flew past the Dutch goalkeeper, Ed de Goey. England dominated proceedings from there on, wowing Wembley with some of the best football the famous old stadium had seen in years. Platt blasted Barnes's cross into the side-netting; Gascoigne was inches away from giving the same player a clear chance and then, when Les Ferdinand's shot struck a post, Platt was on hand to touch home England's second.

From such a position of ascendancy, England were struck by two shattering blows shortly before half-time. First, on thirty-five minutes, as if from nowhere, a Dennis Bergkamp wonder goal brought the Dutch back into the game; then Jan Wouters deliberately smashed Gascoigne in the face with his elbow, fracturing the midfielder's cheekbone. Gascoigne went off injured; Wouters escaped unpunished.

England continued to play well after the interval, but were never quite the same force without Gascoigne's élan. Ince and Carlton Palmer, who had largely subdued the visitors' midfield, began to tire and four minutes from the end disaster struck. Marc Overmars, who had switched wings, lost Walker and he panicked and pulled the flying Dutchman down just inside the England penalty area. Peter Van Vossen equalised from the penalty spot; Taylor told reporters that he felt like crying.

Inroads made over previous months were swept away; England's fragile confidence was shattered and Taylor was largely portrayed as the tragi-comic fool of the piece. In some quarters the treatment of Taylor stopped barely short of outright character assassination. It was an unfair outcome for a good man who was probably the most open and honest national coach England had ever had, an individual who would freely give of his time to pressmen and even hand out his home telephone number 'in case of emergencies'. These desperate months would come to be immortalised in the extraordinary fly-on-the-wall Channel Four film *The Impossible Job*, whose makers were afforded unprecedented access to the England squad. The portrayal, while not unsympathetic, was of a man struggling to save his career, doing his best but swimming out of his depth.

Summer 1993 was to mark Graham Taylor's Passion, seeing him crucified by the press but still standing at its end. The media would thereafter pick at his remains like a pack of dogs until his management finally died a death. The demise of his regime started in Poland on 29 May when, in the simmering cauldron of the Slaski Stadium, England's footballers looked both daunted by the occasion and confused by the instructions given by their manager. Ten minutes from the interval Lesniak cut through the England defence to set up Adamczuk, who lobbed Woods to give Poland a 1–0 half-time lead. It could, and should, have been a greater margin for the hosts, while England offered almost nothing in attack. As the second half ticked away and the Poles passed up chances with regularity, England undeservedly retained a chance of salvation. With just six minutes remaining, the substitute Ian Wright capitalised on poor defending to fire a shot which slipped through Bako's hands and over the line. 1–1; England were saved.

Four days later England were in Oslo to face Norway, who had blazed a trail to the top of the World Cup qualifying group. Taylor changed the tactics that had failed so miserably in Poland, deploying a quasi 3-4-3 formation, with Gascoigne playing off the forward pairing of Teddy Sheringham and Les Ferdinand. The overhaul was an unmitigated disaster. Channel Four's unforgiving cameras would show Taylor giving instructions to patently incredulous players and then desperately trying to amend them thereafter, which only seemed to compound matters.[6] Twice Norway scored, through Jan Age Fjortoft and Lars Bohinen – two frankly average Premiership players – and England offered scant resistance in a game in which they were outfought, outplayed and ultimately outclassed. Moreover the result left their sinking hopes of qualification resting on England's ability to win each of their remaining three games. Worse, however, was to come Taylor's way.

From Oslo the England squad journeyed to the United States to take part in a four-team mini-tournament, which was to act as a test-run ahead of the following year's World Cup finals. Also making the trip were Germany and Brazil, but first, on 9 June England had to face the United States, who boasted the usual array of stringers and semi-professionals – including Alexi Lalas, a university student and sometime rock musician, whose lurid orange goatee beard made him a target for the gently condescending British press corps. What followed had an aura of inevitability. England were wretched. Thomas Dooley put the United States ahead; Lalas added a second, his beaming village idiot's visage beamed across the globe, laughing at English football's latest humiliation. 'There can't be a lower point for any manager and, yes, it is a national disgrace,' admitted Taylor. 'But I accepted the job. I knew I was putting everything at risk and will continue to battle. You have to pick yourself off the ground and battle on. Don't look around, don't make excuses, get in there and fight.'

England's footballers eventually returned home having put in two rather more creditable performances against Brazil (1–1) and Germany (1–2), but the damage had been done. The national team had never stood at a lower ebb. Humiliated by the United States in 1950 and by Puskas et al in 1953 and 1954, their subsequent embarrassments in failing to qualify for the 1974 and 1978 World Cup finals had been tempered by the realisation that fortune had, by degrees, stood in the national team's way or, in the case of Hungary, they had simply been undone by genius. None of these factors came into play in 1993. Whatever the feasibility of English fans' expectations that, as football's founders, their countrymen should be the best in the world, none could counter or accept standing on the verge of being dumped out of the World Cup by Norway, or being humbled by the Americans. Clueless in their displays, Taylor's England were not just an embarrassment to the nation's proud football heritage, they were quite simply abysmal.

Yet when qualifying resumed in September 1993 with a Wembley tie against Poland, England perversely put in their best performance under Graham Taylor and won 3–0 with goals from Gascoigne, Pearce and Ferdinand. Suddenly, the question on everybody's lips was could England somehow still fluke qualification for USA '94?

The answer came a month later in Rotterdam. As Norway had already qualified as group winners, slogging it out for second place was now the best that these two purported giants of European football could hope for. For England, little else but a win would suffice.

Taylor, perhaps understandably, was tetchy in the days leading up to the match and at one press conference became embroiled in an extraordinary exchange with a journalist, whom the England manager berated for being pessimistic about England's prospects. 'I am literally staggered that you should think there is any apprehension in the England camp,' he announced, 'I am greatly disturbed that people will think this is a Norwegian situation.' Outwardly Taylor seemed on the verge of losing the plot: David Lacey, in the *Guardian*, likened his performance to Basil Fawlty reacting to the news that one of his guests was a psychiatrist.

England's footballers justified their manager's show of faith. This was no Oslo: Taylor's men gave him guile, spirit and fight; and while the attack was still too one-dimensional in the absence of Gascoigne's sparkle and invention, for long stretches they were the better side. Twice the visitors hit the post only to see the ball ricochet to safety, and though Frank Rijkaard had a perfectly good goal disallowed for offside shortly before half-time, it seemed as though the gods were smiling on the Dutch. On the hour-mark David Platt was put through on goal, with only the flagging Ronald Koeman impeding his path to goal. As Platt approached the penalty area, Koeman cynically scythed him down. Was it a penalty? Very possibly, and later the referee – bizarrely – admitted that he would have given it had he not been 'overruled' by his linesman. Should Koeman have been dismissed? Almost certainly. Incredibly, Koeman received just a yellow card, and the referee only awarded a free-kick. The consequences were dire and almost immediately fatal.

Two minutes later Ince fouled Wouters on the edge of the penalty area. Who better to take the free-kick than Koeman, who had scored the winner for Barcelona from a similar position in the previous year's European Cup final? Back home a nation sat on the edge of their seats as he lined the ball up but when the shot finally came Ince blocked it and the danger seemed to pass. But no, the referee called Ince over and booked him for encroachment, handing Koeman a second chance. As he prepared to take it a second time, back in England the unforgettable words of Brian Moore boomed out to viewers: 'He's going to flick it, he's going to flick it.' Flick it he did, over the top of the wall and beyond the grasp of the poorly positioned Seaman. Instead of taking an early bath, Koeman was running the length of the pitch in celebration.

Moments later Merson hit a post, the ball bounced to safety and with it went England's best chance of deliverance. On sixty-eight minutes Bergkamp sealed a Dutch victory and Graham Taylor's end. On the touchline the death throes of his stewardship were played out with a heart-rending monologue to an impassive match official:

> You know we've been cheated don't you, then he [Koeman] goes and takes a free-kick at the other end . . . Even if he [the referee] doesn't see it as a penalty, he has to go. You know that, I know you know it, and the fella goes and scores the free-kick. You can't say anything. I know you can't say anything. I know that. You see at the end of the day I get the sack now. [Taylor walks over to the linesman and pats his shoulder.] I was just saying to your colleague that the referee's got me the sack. Thank you ever so much for that . . .

Afterwards some in England sought solace in a sense of deluded optimism that the team could still make the finals if results went their way in the final round of matches ('If Holland lose to Poland and England win by at least seven goals to San Marino . . .' and so on). Like so much of Taylor's reign, such hopes were to end in farce. San Marino went in front after just eight seconds, scoring the fastest-ever international goal, and though England responded with seven of their own, the 7–1 result, on its own merits, wasn't enough. Either way, Holland beat Poland 3–1 to take the second qualifying berth. Six days later, on 23 November 1993, Graham Taylor tendered his resignation. An inherently decent man and a highly proficient club manager, Taylor always seemed to be wading out of his depth in the ocean of English fans' expectations. Lacking the authority of a Ramsey, or charisma of a Robson, Taylor also suffered from a shortage of talent to equip him to build on England's relative success at Italia '90. He had also suffered horrendously at the hands of the press, a harsh and undeserved outcome for a good man.

'I've been betrayed by people in my profession and even by some of my friends,' he said.

> If I'd known what I do today, I wouldn't have taken this job. I wouldn't have put myself through this. I'm deeply hurt to the depths of my soul. I went from

being a respected manager at Aston Villa to an England manager without an ounce of credibility. I've been called useless, stupid, thick. I've been told I'm no good and I don't know what I'm doing by people who've never played a game in their life. But I don't want anyone to think I'm a broken man. I will be back and I will be fighting.[7]

Four years on from missing out on the World Cup final by a mere penalty kick, England entered 1994 weak, demoralised, lacking direction and, of course, without a place in the forthcoming World Cup finals. As hosts of the 1996 European Championships England also had more than thirty months without a competitive international, which offered an opportunity for a new manager to regroup and reorganise. From being the pinnacle of football management, the England manager's job now seemed a kind of purgatory, impossible in the sense that expectation remained relentlessly high, but the players were not even of sufficient quality to qualify for a major tournament, much less win one. England fans weren't so deluded that it escaped their notice that their national team was average, and sometimes not even that. Not that this served as any disincentive to the notion that England *should* win every match. Unreasonable expectation plus a lack of tools equalled hopelessness. Who on earth, everyone asked, would want what had become known as 'The Impossible Job'?

Initially, the FA seemed predisposed to an old hand – as they had after the departures of Ramsey and Revie – with the respected rather than revered names of Don Howe and John Lyall appearing amongst the lead contenders. Howard Wilkinson, Steve Coppell and Gerry Francis (respectively of Leeds United, Crystal Palace and Queens Park Rangers) were amongst the bookmakers' favourites, but it was the 25–1 shot Terry Venables, initially priced alongside a Scot (Kenny Dalglish) and a man without any prior managerial experience (Bryan Robson), who would move to an odds-on certainty.

Venables' sharp wit and easy manner offered a welcome contrast to some of the confrontational farce that had plagued the latter Taylor era. As a player he had been on the fringes of Ramsey's England squad, picking up two caps, and played out a solid if not wholly successful career with Chelsea, Tottenham, QPR and Crystal Palace, managing the latter two in a convincing enough manner for Bobby Robson to recommend him for the Barcelona job in 1984. He was a popular coach at the Catalan giants, leading them to their first league title in eleven years in 1985 and to a European Cup final a year later. He returned to England to manage Spurs in 1987, guiding them to the FA Cup in 1991 and then helped stave off bankruptcy by buying a stake in the club as part of Alan Sugar's consortium. That 'dream ticket' would fall apart in the midst of bitter recriminations within two years, with Venables exiled from White Hart Lane and faced with a catalogue of accusations of financial wrongdoing – and not just from his former business partner.

Two BBC *Panorama* investigations in September 1993 and October 1994 also made allegations about the way that Venables had raised capital to buy into Tottenham, accusing him of selling assets which he never owned and of consequently obtaining £500,000 unlawfully.[8] At the same time police were investigating accusations that Venables had paid a £50,000 bung to Brian Clough. That case was eventually dropped through lack of evidence and the Football Association later exonerated him. Venables, for his part, claimed to be the victim of a 'concerted and organised' campaign aimed at discrediting him. He may have had a point, but in many minds mud stuck.

For nearly a month the FA procrastinated over his suitability for the England manager's job. Uneasy about the trail Venables' business dealings had left, the FA initially offered him only a one-year contract then, when he refused, a two-year deal. When he accepted the FA also insisted that the title of the post be changed from 'manager' to 'coach' as they did not like the suggestion that Venables was involved in management *per se*. They also loaded his contract with get-out clauses allowing for his speedy release should his managerial reign become submerged in legal issues.

Despite the apparent misgivings of his new employers, Venables was exultant about his appointment. 'I want a team that can stop goals, create in midfield and finish well,' he told journalists. 'I also hope to be able to take the pressure off players. There is enough of it on them already. We have potential and I have been pleased with a lot of the football I have seen this season, but turning potential into reality is never easy . . . Our target,' he added, 'is 1966.' 'You made a mistake Terry,' someone pointed out. 'Oh what,' came the response, 'a Freudian slip?'

Yet the whiff of scandal never seemed to leave him. Just days before he was appointed national coach, the *Financial Times* printed further allegations of malpractice. Matters thereafter descended into a fug of claim, counter claim, libel actions and out-of-court settlements, until finally, in January 1998, Venables was disqualified as a company director for seven years. In an agreed statement of facts, Venables admitted accounting irregularities at Scribes West, the members' club he co-owned, and acknowledged receiving 'unwarranted benefits' from the nightclub at a time when it faced grave financial difficulties. He admitted causing Edenote – a company used for property and financial deals – to continue trading whilst insolvent and failing to keep proper accounts.[9]

By then, of course, Terry Venables' time in the sun had come to an end, but what of the football? A crowd of 71,790 had launched the Venables era on 9 March 1994. They saw three debutants: Blackburn Rovers' classy left-back Graeme Le Saux; Spurs' elegant flanker Darren Anderton, and, as a substitute, Southampton's hugely gifted, if occasionally erratic, forward Matthew Le Tissier. Peter Beardsley, seemingly impervious to the passing years and in fine form at Newcastle United, received a deserved recall and partnered Alan Shearer up front. England played in a 'Christmas tree' formation; their build-up was patient, forward play thoughtful and measured, movement off the ball intelligent, and they ran out worthy 1–0 winners over Denmark. The first of many scars left by Graham Taylor had been healed.

As he rebuilt England's tattered reputation over subsequent months, Venables would introduce twenty-six new international caps to the fray. Some were inevitably more successful than others; seldom, however, were his selections subject to the barely suppressed sniggers that had so undermined many of Taylor's choices. Amongst the pick of them was Gary Neville, the first of an outstanding crop of Manchester United youngsters who would come to dominate the England squad to make the breakthrough to the international team. Unspectacular but dependable, Neville would make the right-back slot his own for a decade, later often joined in the party by his younger brother Philip. Darren Anderton, who would later visit the treatment table more often than the pitch, would enjoy his best years on the international stage under Venables, providing a calm measured influence to the team, adding potency from set pieces. Gareth Southgate had started out as a midfielder with Crystal Palace, but successfully converted to central defence after a 1995 transfer to Aston Villa. In many respects he represented the antithesis of the traditional English centre-back: cool, unruffled, thoughtful and with the ability to pass rather than hoof and hope, Southgate came to typify the new England Venables was trying to build. There was room for some exciting youngsters too. Liverpool's Steve McManaman was the country's best exponent of the forgotten art of dribbling: a tall, shaggy-haired rake, he could unlock defences with a mazy dribble or slip through the most telling of passes.

In the early stages, at least, the principal concern lay with reorganising the defence. Too often Taylor had chopped and changed, not just individuals but formations also, leaving his players scant opportunity to build up solid partnerships. Initially the new manager alternated his goalkeepers, trying out Arsenal's David Seaman and Blackburn Rovers' Tim Flowers, before plumping for the Gunner. The imposing Yorkshireman had earned his international spurs under Bobby Robson and had also been used by Taylor – though never quite enough, according to those who despaired at some of Chris Woods' more unconvincing displays. Like Seaman, Tony Adams, his Highbury colleague, had spent much of his early international career in and out of the England team, but Venables invested his faith in him as England's foremost centre-half. As rocks go, Adams was a granite-like presence on which to build a defence. Hard, dependable, a good leader and excellent organiser of the defensive line, Adams had been the mainstay of an Arsenal backline that was the foundation stone of a multitude of Highbury trophies. Could he replicate that form in the white of his country?

In Venables' first year in charge, England conceded just a solitary goal, and if there was a problem it came in converting possession and chances into goals. Part of it centred on Alan Shearer who, after a brace against the United States in September 1994, failed to score again for England for nearly two years. Form is temporary, preached Venables of the man who would plunder more than thirty league goals in each of three consecutive seasons for Blackburn, class is permanent. Shearer's time would come.

Without a competitive international in more than two and a half years, England fans soon bored of the humdrum routine of friendlies. No one, however, was more desperate for the European Championship finals to come than Venables. Still dogged by accusations of financial impropriety, the manager had many points to prove, not least to the FA with whom talks over a contract extension had broken down. In December 1995, with just seven months left on his existing deal, Venables had sought to clarify his future with his employer and met with its Secretary, Graham Kelly; Chairman, Bert Millichip; and the Chairman of the Senior International Committee, Noel White. White, who had made unfavourable remarks about Venables in the press, told the 'coach' that he was unproven in 'competitive games' – a maddeningly unfair assertion given that England had not played a competitive international since the farce in Imola two years earlier when Taylor was still at the helm. Venables reportedly responded: 'You don't want to place your bet until the horse crosses the line.' The inference to the England manager was clear: he had to prove himself at Euro '96 before his future could be assured. 'I don't do auditions,' a furious Venables told the delegation and left the meeting. As far as he was concerned, his sojourn as England manager would conclude in the summer. Just two years after scrabbling around for a replacement for Taylor the FA began searching for another England manager.

Venables, however, readied himself and his team ahead of the forthcoming tournament. The preparations entailed a warm-up tour of the Far East where the England manager hoped that his squad would be able to concentrate beyond the prying eyes of the press. Fat chance. First, pictures of players adorned in ripped shirts brandishing beer bottles in a late-night Hong Kong bar were wired back to England and splashed across the front pages of newspapers. If that wasn't enough fodder for the tabloids, rowdy squad members celebrating Paul Gascoigne's twenty-ninth birthday on a Cathay Pacific flight back to England were accused by the airline of causing £5000 worth of damage to the cabin. Again the team were pilloried. This time, however, Venables neutralised the hunt for villains by claiming that his squad would be taking 'collective responsibility' for their actions. It was a master-stroke, and one that created a renewed sense of solidarity amongst the team.

Given the often dour tournaments that had preceded the 1996 European Championships, UEFA had wisely decided to expand the finals from eight to sixteen nations. Far from diluting the standard of the football on offer, the expansion was to be a resounding success: the football was more flowing, less tense, the drama heightened by several glorious upsets; and played out against a classic addition to the hitherto dubious art of the football record: 'Three Lions'.

England were drawn in a four-nation group with Switzerland, Scotland and Holland. First up on 8 June were the Swiss, widely regarded as the easiest of England's first three opponents. The hosts got off to the best of starts when Gascoigne, full of willingness and invention, carefully built an attack with Shearer before Ince played the killer ball, slipping a short pass through the Swiss defence. The centre-forward, marginally onside, touched the ball forward, then hammered it home off the near post. Without a goal in fourteen previous internationals, spanning nearly two years it had taken Shearer just twenty-three minutes of Euro '96 to break his duck. Twelve minutes later he should have made it two when he headed Pearce's carefully dangled cross just wide. Thereafter, however, the Swiss gained a tighter rein on the England midfield, chances became fewer and, when on 83 minutes Türkyilmaz stroked a penalty past Seaman after Pearce had handled, few could have argued that the Swiss didn't deserve at least a point.

A week later it was Scotland's turn to visit Wembley. Venables named an unchanged side but pushed Southgate into midfield, where he formed a triumvirate with Ince and Gascoigne. Yet, in the initial stages, the additional beef in the heart of the pitch made scant difference. Scotland settled more quickly and England struggled to attack with any fluency. After a sterile forty-five minutes which failed to bring any clear-cut chances, Venables introduced the Liverpool midfielder, Jamie Redknapp, in place of Pearce, and ordered McManaman and Anderton to switch flanks. The move yielded immediate dividends as McManaman began to run and skip around the Scottish defence with all the thrilling prowess he had so often shown in the red of Liverpool. Straight away the match started to open up. First, McManaman let fly with a dipping shot that fizzed inches past the left-hand angle of Scotland's goal; then, on fifty-two minutes, he released Gary Neville on an overlapping run down the right. The Manchester United full-back kept his composure and sent in a perfect far-post cross that was met forcefully by the head of Shearer, who gave Andy Goram no chance. England almost scored twice more in the wake of their opener but Anderton shot narrowly over the crossbar and a marvellous reflex save from Goram prevented Sheringham's diving header making it 2–0.

Just as England threatened to run riot, Scotland fought back strongly. Seaman clawed away Durie's header and, with a hint of desperation, the ball was hacked to safety; substitute Ally McCoist went flying under a challenge from Neville but the Italian referee was not conned; yet on seventy-six minutes he proved more amenable to Scots appeals when Durie was caught by Adams's sliding tackle. For the second match running England had conceded a late penalty, but this time they were not to be undone. Gary McAllister struck the ball firmly but too straight and Seaman's stiff jab parried the ball to safety.

Shortly after, England broke forward. Anderton fed Gascoigne and the peroxided prodigal left his unique mark on the game and entire tournament. Flicking the ball up and over the head of Colin Hendry, he left the Scottish defender flagging before sending a hard, low volley beyond the grasp of Goram. It was one of Wembley's greatest goals and the crowd roared its approval as Gascoigne celebrated in typically exuberant fashion. 'It's coming home, it's coming home, football's coming home,' resounded around Wembley, pubs, bars and homes across the nation.

'If we think we are through now, it is a big mistake,' said Venables after the 2–0 victory had been secured. Looking forward to the final group match with Holland he said: 'You don't play for a draw. I can't think for one moment they [the Dutch] would.' A draw, nevertheless, would be enough to carry England through to the quarter-finals – and keep them at Wembley. Achieving that in itself would be no easy task: having proven so troublesome to Graham Taylor's England, the class of '96 boasted the core of Ajax players who had won the European Cup so brilliantly in 1995 and only been beaten in their second final on penalties a month earlier. Mindful of what lay ahead, Venables counselled caution on the eve of the match: 'We are inclined to be a nation [which thinks] we are the worst team in the world or the best. Neither is true.'

But what followed a day later suggested that the pundits should err towards the latter school of thought. England were outstanding, more outstanding perhaps, than in any performance over the previous three decades. Only seven minutes had passed when Anderton's chipped corner found Shearer on the edge of the penalty area and he connected with a thunderous half-volley. As the ball raced goalwards, a nation braced itself for the breakthrough, but it was not to be. Richard Witschge blocked his shot on the Dutch goal line but the tone of the evening had been set.

With the Dutch wings checked, England pushed and probed and on twenty-three minutes a goal came their way. McManaman slipped through a pass to Ince on the edge of the Holland penalty area and his neat touch took the ball past Danny Blind. The Ajax captain, completely fooled, responded by ending Ince's progress with a blatant trip and conceded a penalty. Shearer claimed the ball, jogged back, turned, ran, and drove the ball between Edwin van der Sar and his right post. England were rolling.

A constant menace in the first half, England were rampant in the second. Sheringham's head powered home Gascoigne's corner on fifty-one minutes, but the best was still to come. Six minutes later McManaman swept down the left, played in Gascoigne, who tricked Winter, before squaring the ball inside to Sheringham. He shaped to shoot, but instead cleverly rolled the ball to Shearer who blasted an emphatic shot past Van der Sar for his fourth goal of the tournament.

There was still more. Five minutes later Anderton's twenty-yard shot glanced off Blind, momentarily throwing Van der Sar. When he failed to hold onto the ball, Sheringham was on hand to make it 4–0. A jubilant Wembley rubbed its eyes with disbelief, singing England's footballers home until vocal chords could only croak tired, euphoric words of victory. Not even Patrick Kluivert's late consolation goal (which prevented Scottish progression to the quarter-finals) could dampen one of England's finest evenings.

England 'gave us a lesson in every department', concluded the Dutch coach Guus Hiddink. 'Our commitment to the game was not as good as most of the England players. The way England are playing now, England are favourites. People considered us the favourites before but I think that, after their win over us, they could be unstoppable.' Venables, visibly exultant, was nevertheless modest about his side's dazzling display. 'I was very, very pleased with the result. The players did exceptionally well. But now,' he added, 'we've got to do it all over again.'[10]

The quarter-final threw up a meeting with Spain four days later. Though their status as international football's perennial under-achievers had long been a pre-tournament cliche, the Spaniards were unbeaten in twenty matches extending back to the 1994 World Cup and promised to be well-organised and highly experienced opponents. Yet after the excitement of the Holland game, this was to be a damp squib of a match dominated by poor refereeing decisions. Twice Spain had goals disallowed in the first forty-five minutes, only one of which deserved not to count, and were also later denied two good shouts for penalties. The first appeal, five minutes into the second half, suggested that fortune may well have been shining on England, after Gascoigne seemed to bring down Alfonso as the Spanish substitute swept past him in the penalty area. Television replays confirmed the suspicion, but Marc Batta, the French referee, not only refused to give a penalty but interpreted Alfonso's fall as a dive and booked him for it. With luck against them, David Seaman imperious and the home defence resolute, the game drifted into extra time. Like the Arsenal goalkeeper, Andoni Zubizarreta was in fine form, palming away Gascoigne's curling shot, which represented England's best chance of summoning a so-called 'golden goal'. When Shearer was unable to keep the ball down after lunging at Gascoigne's floated pass, penalties seemed the only way to separate the two countries and after 120 minutes of tense, tightly matched football, Batta's whistle signalled that the game would become a goalkeeping duel between Seaman and Zubizarreta.

England were first up, and Shearer made no mistake in striking his effort past Zubizarreta. Next was Fernando Hierro, and he hit a shot hard, high of Seaman, and, to the delight of most of Wembley, against the crossbar. Platt made it 2–0; Guillermo Amor pulled a goal back; before Stuart Pearce picked the ball up for England's third penalty. In 1990 his miss had spelt the beginning of the end of England's World Cup run in Italy and for six years he had borne taunts, teasing and the knowledge that he had contributed to his country's demise. Could he exorcise the ghosts of his and England's past? Damn right he could. Pearce struck the ball cleanly and firmly past Zubizarreta to make it 3–1. Above the tumult of the Wembley crowd one could almost hear Pearce's roar of elation. Belsue made it 3–2; Gascoigne made no mistake in restoring England's advantage, which left Barcelona's Miguel Angel Nadal the responsibility of delivering Spain from elimination. He ran up, struck the ball firmly, but Seaman, for the second time in the tournament swooped low and palmed the ball away to a deafening roar from the massed ranks of England fans.

England were through to a semi-final . . . with Germany.

Terry Venables and England expected. 'This is a chance for us to do something for the country,' he said ahead of the crunch match four days later. 'It's very rare in your life when you can forget selfishness and give something to someone else. We know we've got a tough game. We know how hard it's going to be. But we think we can do it.'[11] Germany, physically battered after a bruising quarter-final against Croatia, would be missing Jürgen Klinsmann and Fredi Bobic for the tie. Several others, including Jürgen Kohler had already gone home injured. After thirty years of mastery over England there was a definite sense that this Germany were eminently beatable. What hadn't changed was the rancid attitude of the British tabloids. Already the *Daily Mirror* had caused a furore prior to the Spain game with a series of jokes so lame that even Bernard Manning aficionados would have struggled to muster a laugh. 'What do you call a good-looking girl in Spain?' the newspaper had asked. 'A tourist.' If that hadn't had its readers clutching their sides with laughter, it had gone on to provide a list of 'ten nasties' Spain had given Europe. This included syphilis, which had been brought back from America by Columbus, paella and the carpet-bombing of Guernica. Of course, Columbus was Italian and the Germans had bombed Guernica but since when had the facts ever stood in the way of good old xenophobia?

The onslaught continued ahead of the semi-final. Two days before England met them the *Mirror*'s front page had portrayed Pearce and Gascoigne in 'Tommy' helmets under the headline 'Achtung! Surrender!' followed by a trite parody of Chamberlain's declaration of war in 1939. Venables was positively embarrassed by the coverage. 'It's gone beyond rivalry in a football match and it's not funny. It's a football match not a war,' he said. 'The rest of Europe is envying the wonderful atmosphere we have created, so let's not spoil it. Let's respect the opposition, starting with their national anthem. If you don't hear a pin drop when it's played, that would be ideal.'[12]

Venables' appeals were ignored by a significant minority. No matter. When England came out, it was to a riot of noise and white and red flags waved in the night sky, to painted faces and choruses of 'It's coming home, it's coming home . . .' Regardless of what happened on the pitch, of whether a bunch of idiots would boo the German national anthem, this proud, vociferous mass would ensure that Wembley would revel in one of its greatest nights.

With Gary Neville suspended, pre-match talk had been of whether his brother Philip would replace him or whether Venables would plump for a three-man defence. The England manager left his decision to the very last moment and when he heard that Germany had plumped for three men at the back, went with the latter. His selection got off to a flyer. Two minutes in, Ince shot from twenty-five yards and the goalkeeper Andreas Köpke elected to punch the ball over rather than try and claim it outright. It was a mistake. From the corner, Gascoigne turned in a near-post cross, Adams' flick header clipped the ball across the six-yard box, and there was Shearer, stooping low to head the ball through Köpke's legs.

Lesser sides might have folded there and then. But not Germany. They stuck rigidly to their game plan and began to piece together the sort of powerful and committed play that had reaped them so much success in the past. On sixteen minutes Thomas Helmer charged down the left, played a one-two with Andreas Möller and burst unmarked into the penalty area. Adroitly, he turned and cut the ball across to Stefan Kuntz, who beat David Seaman from close range.

Briefly the momentum was with Germany, but Sammer and Scholl were unable to craft further opportunities and the impetus ebbed back to England. Shearer headed too high from Anderton's cross; Sheringham's fiercely driven volley drive from a corner was goal-bound until Stefan Reuter blocked it and, shortly before half-time, Shearer headed powerfully and beyond the grasp of Köpke, but wide.

As the game moved into the second half, both sides closed the other down and chances became fewer. Only when sudden death extra time came did the tempo reach fever pitch again. Three minutes in, McManaman ran and fed Anderton in the box, he went wide of Köpke but shot against the post; Kuntz missed with the goal begging on ninety-four minutes; 120 seconds later the same player found the net – but mercifully it was disallowed after Adams had been fouled. On ninety-nine minutes Shearer's powerful volley was only parried the way of Gascoigne but, with the goal at his mercy, his lunge couldn't quite reach the ball. Five minutes later, McManaman set Gascoigne up again, and once more he missed; Anderton's volley glanced past the German post; Ziege missed when one-on-one with Seaman and McManaman shot weakly after Shearer had set him up. And then it was over.

Reverberating with excitement after a tantalising, terrifying half-hour of high drama, once more the game would be decided by penalties. Again England went first, and once more Shearer took the opening shot, sending a forceful strike under Köpke's crossbar. Hässler levelled with a shot to the left of Seaman. Platt made it 2–1; Strunz sent a shot down the centre but Seaman dived early and couldn't stop it. Pearce, to huge applause, struck a powerful shot into the left corner; Reuter made it 3–3; Gascoigne restored England's advantage; Ziege made it 4–4; and Sheringham and Kuntz ensured that each country had a perfect five.

Sudden death. Who was left? England still had an array of defenders, Steve McManaman and Darren Anderton – neither of whom took penalties at club level – and Paul Ince. The 'guv'nor' seemed the natural choice given his experience – though, admittedly, not at taking penalties – and self-professed fearlessness but he could barely look and clearly wasn't volunteering.[13] Instead, up stepped the deceptively meek figure of Gareth Southgate. He claimed the ball after the long walk from the centre-circle, placed it on the penalty spot, walked back, ran, and shot . . . but his effort lacked pace and precision and Köpke saved easily. Southgate hung his head; Andreas Möller claimed the ball; and did what every German international who had taken a penalty in the previous twenty years had done, and scored.

'We felt we were the better team but Germany have shown in the last thirty years how strong they are and we wish them well. All that mattered on the night was that England got there. It didn't matter who scored the penalties and who missed them,' said Stuart Pearce, a man who knew all too well about slipping under the unbearable weight of expectation dangled by a shoot-out. 'I wish I could say I don't know how it feels to miss a penalty in these circumstances but I do . . . I am convinced that his [Southgate's] personality – which is a bit like mine – will make him bounce back a better player next season. It will stick with him a while like it stuck with me.'[14] Sir Bobby Charlton said: 'I am as disappointed as everyone, particularly because it was penalties. But we have come a long way, we have won respect and as a team given a lift to the whole country.' His old sparring partner, Franz Beckenbauer, added: 'England can hold their heads up. There is no disgrace in losing on penalties.'[15] Terry Venables could reflect on leaving the England job with pride intact – a rare achievement for a former England manager. 'We played Spain, Holland and Germany, three of the four favourites in the competition, and we have competed tactically and technically with them,' he said. 'There is nothing to be downhearted about, apart from the result. We just fell at the last hurdle. I felt that we were the better team over ninety minutes, and I am very proud of my team. I have made them do things they haven't done before at the highest level and it proved everything has been well worked out by the coaching staff.'[16]

Turning points are often spoken about in football. A game, a season, a career can hinge on one moment, an instant that historians will later describe as 'defining', 'historic', 'momentous'. Euro '96 was a turning point for the England team only in the sense that the belief returned that they could actually win a tournament (the unshakable belief that they *should* win – despite everything – had never really died). Yet it held deeper significance for English football in general. Largely unsullied by trouble, it represented the conclusion of the game's shift back to respectability initiated in the wake of Italia '90. Even the endless chants of 'Football's coming home' had more resonance than appeared on first hearing. Here is the home of football, England fans were shouting, and what a show we've put on. The Premiership – increasingly the most cosmopolitan league in the world – provided the perfect backdrop to the thousands of visitors who swarmed on England for the tournament. On the day of the Scotland game I had been in Manchester, a balmy June morning rudely interrupted by a massive IRA bomb that rocked the city, amazingly not killing anyone. As police evacuated the centre of Manchester, I and thousands of others ended up in Moss Side, cordoned off until the police declared the city safe once more. A pub was found and a jovial afternoon spent watching the football with fellow England supporters, a few Scots, Russians and Germans in the city ahead of their own matches. Later, on the train back to Liverpool, I reflected that such a scene would have been inconceivable even a few years earlier. Football had finally grown up.

Within days of England's defeat to Germany Venables had packed up his office at Lancaster Gate and moved on. Later he would hold down roles at Portsmouth, Crystal Palace, the Australian FA, Middlesbrough and Leeds United, but the golden touch seemed to have left him and when the latter sacked him in spring 2003 it effectively spelt the end of his managerial career. Well liked by players, press and public; highly respected as a coach and successful, Terry Venables had been the perfect coach. As a businessman, by contrast, his reputation cast him as a dark figure: duplicitous, shady and thoroughly untrustworthy. His main fault may well have been limited to keeping the wrong company or merely following bad advice, but the murky accusations that repeatedly plagued Venables contributed to the image of the East End wide boy, constantly on the take. With hindsight, that perception seems unfair even if it remains true that his focus – dogged as it was by scandal and legal battles – could not have been occupied by football alone. Ultimately, it was that which cost him his job as England manager and curtailed what should have been a glittering career at Lancaster Gate and elsewhere.

Terry Venables had created a new England based on technique, flair, thoughtful build-up play and skill. So far removed from the Taylor era was the brand of football played at Euro '96 that the mindless clogging of his predecessor's team seemed to belong to a different century rather than the thirty-two months that separated the San Marino debacle and the agonising defeat to Germany. It was as if England's footballers had made the seismic leap from the stone age to the modern world and Venables' successor, Glenn Hoddle, seemed perfectly placed to carry on the revolution.

After a successful spell at Monaco Hoddle had become player-manager of Swindon Town in April 1991, aged thirty-three, and led them via the play-offs to promotion to the Premiership two years later. Hoddle left that summer to take the manager's job at Chelsea, and Swindon went straight back down. His three years at Stamford Bridge were to be a qualified success, but as one writer suggested 'the qualifications were arguably more telling than the successes'.[17] The season before Hoddle took over, Chelsea had finished in eleventh position; in his first season he took them to fourteenth; and eleventh in both of the following years. If his league record was hardly a glittering one, he took Chelsea to their first FA Cup final in years (thrashed 0–4 by Manchester United) and on a creditable European run. His signing of Ruud Gullit in the summer of 1995 heralded the start of Chelsea's transformation into a multinational squad of superstars. Moreover, his teams played good, passing, patient football, almost like a continental side; if that didn't always bring success that was sometimes attributable to the rough and tough nature of the league – in which physical strength was still usually more than a match for individual technique – and the more general shortcomings of his squad.[18] Some also raised concerns about his man management skills. The 1980s maxim that 'Hoddle is God' had been taken too literally by its subject said some; 'If he was ice cream he would lick himself,' was one player's memorable description. Other former players would lay charges that he was arrogant, aloof, intolerant of those who didn't share his own unique gifts as a player, never wrong. 'He made grown men feel as if they were treated as children,' Tony Cascarino wrote, 'If the team won, it was because his decisions were correct. When we lost, it was our fault, never his. He was always right. When he asked for opinions . . . he says they are wrong. It was him and us.'[19] At Chelsea and Swindon he could get away with such criticisms; placed in the uniquely pressured England manager's seat, he would be under rather more intense scrutiny. Would a lack of humility come back to haunt Glenn Hoddle?

England's new manager offered 'continuity', said the Football Association's new Chief Executive, Graham Kelly, and his teams promised to echo those of Venables. 'Terry and I are very close in principle to how the game should be played,' Hoddle told reporters when his appointment was announced. 'The way Terry has been playing recently has been very brave at times, but he knows exactly what he wants. For me it's exciting. If Terry had been manager when I was playing, I think I would have won a lot more caps; he would have brought out the best in me.' Venables, who had direct experience of Hoddle when managing him in the England Under-21 side in the late 1970s, added:

> He was always keen to look at new things. While others may have shied off a bit, he could never get enough. He had a good knowledge of the game and I feel he is one of the best players we've ever had in this country. He's now taken that a step further. He has turned his talent into reality. He's had two jobs and done very well for them. I have said it's an older man's job, but only as a rule of thumb. When you get into personalities, I think Glenn is a good choice.[20]

Indeed there seemed every hope that Hoddle could move the progress of the Venables era on a level. Certainly, his England would be aided and invigorated by the emergence of an outstanding group of young footballers at Manchester United. In the summer of 1995 their manager, Alex Ferguson, had sold three of the club's star players – Paul Ince, Andrei Kanchelskis and Mark Hughes – and staked the future of the club on youth. On the opening day of the 1995–96 season, after United had been beaten 1–3 by Aston Villa, BBC TV's *Match of the Day* pundit, Alan Hansen, had mocked Ferguson's temerity with a damning verdict: 'You'll never win anything with kids.' Nine months later as 'Fergie's Fledglings' stormed to a League and FA Cup double, becoming the first team to win the 'double double', Hansen's words were thrown back to ridicule his earlier 'expert' opinion.

The Neville brothers had already made the step up to the England team under Venables, but pushing strongly for international recognition by the time Hoddle had succeeded him were the outstanding midfield triumvirate of David Beckham, Nicky Butt and Paul Scholes. Each would get their chance in Hoddle's first year as England manager, Beckham in his first match against Moldova after petitions for his inclusion became a clarion call when he scored an incredible goal from the halfway line in the opening fixture of the 1996–97 season.

Although all were products of the Old Trafford youth programme and separated in age by just six months, each player was wholly different in terms of technique and personality. While Butt and Scholes each hailed from Greater Manchester, Beckham was born in Chingford, East London, but had been a Manchester United-mad kid spotted by Bobby Charlton at a soccer school. Courted by his boyhood heroes, Beckham had been transplanted north and lived, worked and breathed with the most promising set of youngsters seen in English football since Matt Busby's 'Babes'. With model looks and a pop-star girlfriend (whom he would later marry) Beckham would become in his own right a fashion icon, celebrity and eventually the most famous Briton on earth. Though more physically adept at the hustle and bustle of top-class football and usually deployed on the right flank, his technique was not dissimilar to that once showcased by Hoddle: long rangy passes, excellence at set pieces, a powerful shot and a tireless training ground ethic. Gifted, dedicated, far more intelligent than his nasal east-London tones suggested, he would develop into the star around which the team was built come the turn of the twenty-first century. Butt and Scholes were the antithesis of Beckham in personality if not character: where he courted publicity, they actively eschewed it; where he revelled in being an A-list celebrity, football was the only path they sought to tread. Despite their common ground, the two flame-haired midfielders could not be more dissimilar as players. Butt, a defensive box-to-box midfielder, would for much of his Old Trafford career be cast in the shadow of Roy Keane and suffer in comparison; Scholes, by contrast, was an attacking midfielder, not only an excellent finisher and prolific scorer, but also a schemer and creator *par excellence*. Each would be vital to Hoddle and his successors.

The Hoddle era kicked off on 1 September 1996 in Chisinau, Moldova. It was the first game in England's five-nation qualifying group for the World Cup in France; two men – Beckham, and the Everton full-back, Andy Hinchcliffe – made their debuts; and England strolled out 3–0 victors after goals from Barmby, Gascoigne and Shearer. Subsequent wins over Poland (2–1) and Georgia (2–0) put England in a strong position going into 1997 ahead of the first of two crunch games with their strongest rivals Italy on 12 February.

Just one team would automatically qualify for the finals from Group Two. Unlike the last time Italy and England had met in World Cup qualifying twenty years earlier, however, there was scope for redemption in the lottery of a two-legged play-off for the group runners-up. Of course, given the rising pressure of the fixture list, it was obviously desirable to go through at the first time of asking.

Ahead of the Wembley meeting with Italy, Hoddle was faced with all manner of injury problems, but still managed to produce a few surprises in his selection. In place of the injured David Seaman he promoted Tottenham's Ian Walker – a veteran of two substitute appearances – ahead of the more experienced Tim Flowers and Nigel Martyn. Inexperienced and unexceptional as Walker was, it was to be a costly error. The other surprise choice (or perhaps not, given that his brother had leaked news of his selection to the press ahead of the game) was Matthew Le Tissier. Magical at club level, hitherto mercurial in an England shirt, like Walker he had previously been limited largely to substitute appearances. Le Tissier toiled in isolation throughout, given neither the space nor service to prove a threat, and was substituted after an hour and never played for his country again. By then England were a goal down, conceding an early goal to Gianfranco Zola after the Italian had cut in and driven a fierce shot beyond the despairing lunge of Sol Campbell and through Walker's grasp. Italy immediately closed the game up, cherishing possession, stroking the ball around and providing a constant threat on the break. Not once did England threaten to break the visitors' rearguard and not once did they do so.

If that display was the worst of the still nascent Hoddle regime, when England travelled to France for a four-team summer tournament with the hosts, Italy and Brazil, there was strong evidence that his side could still blossom. Boosted by further World Cup qualifying wins over Georgia (2–0) and Poland (2–0) going into *La Tournoi de France*, England's first opponents were Italy, upon whom Hoddle set the youth of Old Trafford. The two Nevilles, Beckham – in central midfield – and Scholes playing in a floating inside-forward's role all played a part in a performance as far removed from the dour night the previous February as seemed conceivable. Beckham sprayed the pitch with passing long and short, but always with supreme accuracy; Scholes, a constant menace, lurked with deadly intent; Ian Wright, given a rare start, span and ran and probed like a tyro rather than the roving veteran he had become; and the performances of all in England's white shirts were underpinned by the control, experience and solidity of Paul Ince. It was Scholes, though, who was at the heart of England's best moments. On 25 minutes he threaded a ball through to Ian Wright and, with all of the icy composure he had shown on countless afternoons with Arsenal, he tucked a shot beyond Angelo Peruzzi. Shortly before half-time Stuart Pearce found Wright down the inside-left channel, and he returned Scholes's earlier compliment, hooking the ball across for the United player, who struck a first-time volley past Peruzzi. Gary Neville and Andy Cole each nearly increased England's advantage in the second half, while Italy remained unable to offer a substantial response. 'That game showed Italy we really can play,' said Gareth Southgate later. 'The Italians may dismiss it publicly, but privately they know they have a lot to worry about.'

Next up were France. In 1996 they had been tipped for European Championship success but had fallen at the same stage as England – in the semi-final, on penalties. Ahead of the World Cup they were hosting they were already fancied amongst the favourites, but England put in another display of control and élan and won 1–0 courtesy of an Alan Shearer goal. By the time Hoddle's men met Brazil (against whom they would lose 0–1), England had already won

La Tournoi and plaudits were coming in thick and fast. 'According to Louis Van Gaal . . . the essence of the modern game is circulation,' wrote Patrick Barclay in the *Daily Telegraph*, '"The team that moves the ball around the field the quickest," he says, "is the best." So step forward England. And hail Glenn Hoddle, who has completed the task begun by Terry Venables and brought football's founders up to date.'

'I congratulate England,' added Rene Simoes, the Brazilian coach of Jamaica.

> For the first time I cheered England. This was real football. You cannot play all the time through channels, going for the second ball. In Brazil sometimes we joke: 'How can you play with the second ball? There is only one ball.' But England have learned about possession . . . I noticed them begin to improve in the European Championship, especially against Holland, when the ball had been stroked across the penalty area [it] made me so happy, because football to a Brazilian is like a bullfight. You don't shoot the bull. You play with it. That is what gives the joy.[21]

It had been no more than a dry run, but it gave England a psychological edge over Italy ahead of their concluding World Cup qualifier in Rome in October. By September, the advantage had incontrovertibly passed to England after the Italians failed to do what Hoddle's men had already done and beat Georgia in Tbilisi. With only a draw to their name in Poland too, it put England at the top of the group after beating Moldova 4–0 at Wembley. A draw in Rome, therefore, would see England through to France.

On 11 October 1997 the England party journeyed to the Italian capital for the key meeting. Perhaps surprisingly, David Beckham was the only member of 'Fergie's fledglings' included in a side otherwise packed with experience. Paul Ince and David Batty provided a tough, workmanlike core to the team; Sheringham and Wright intelligence and pace in attack; and David Seaman one of the safest pairs of hands in Europe. In a night of high tension, England gave a methodical, authoritative performance, locking out the hosts until the dying seconds, when Christian Vieri contrived to send a header over from close range. Moments later the Dutch referee called time on a 0–0 draw. England had confirmed their place in France; Italy consigned to an unwanted play-off with Russia.

Already boosted by the brightest contingent of English youngsters in forty years, Glenn Hoddle's hand was further strengthened in the months leading up to the World Cup finals by the emergence of Liverpool's Michael Owen. The son of a journeyman player – Terry Owen – who had trawled the lower divisions in the 1970s, Owen junior had been given his Anfield debut in the latter stages of the 1996–97 season, and burst into prominence early on in the next campaign. Like Lineker and Greaves before him, he boasted whippet-like pace, speed of thought, agility and an excellent finish. As doubts about whether the eighteen-year-old was up to the physical rigours of the Premiership passed with every scoring display for Liverpool, calls for his inclusion in the England squad became more vocal. His international debut came as a substitute on 11 February 1998 in a 0–2 defeat to Chile but, though glimmers of promise were shown in subsequent cameos, only his first goal in England's penultimate warm-up against Morocco on 27 May and injury to Ian Wright secured his place in Hoddle's twenty-two.

After a glorious run of form in the last six months of 1997, England's performances dipped in the opening half of 1998. The defeat to Chile was but one of a series of torpid performances that included a goalless home draw with Saudi Arabia and a 1–1 stalemate with Switzerland. Hoddle, revered as a coaching genius for his part in England's ascent, suddenly began to have questions asked of his judgement and some of his pronouncements. According to him, Michael Owen, the Premiership's joint leading scorer, was apparently not a 'natural goalscorer'; others began to suggest that Hoddle treated them with barely suppressed contempt. Duplicitous statements and bare-faced lies to the press did little to add to his stature. Suggestions that everyone else had accepted that Hoddle was no longer God but Glenn had yet to catch on began to re-emerge.

These were brought into sharp focus in the days immediately leading up to the World Cup finals. First, Hoddle needed to shed five players from the twenty-seven hopefuls he had taken to Morocco. In the days leading up to the announcement, rumours – presumably leaked by a member of Hoddle's management team – were floating around the England camp and the press that one high-profile player would be excluded from the twenty-two. The suggestion was that it would be Paul Gascoigne. After a gap of nearly seven years Gazza had returned to England in spring 1998 to join Middlesbrough. Age and injury had subdued some of his once extraordinary talents, lessened his pace and made him more prone to all manner of niggles and knocks; but he was still a supreme passer, still an effusive character, still able to instigate the impossible, still a contender. Unfortunately, the years had not dampened Gascoigne's self-destructive bent. Tales of marital problems, wife beating, alcohol abuse and depression had long emanated from the Gascoigne camp; less dark, but no less damaging to his prospects, as a top-class footballer, were recurrent stories about his antics with fellow celebrities. Just days before England's trip to Morocco he was photographed with the broadcasters Danny Baker and Chris Evans in the midst of a boozy night out in Soho eating a kebab. The press frothed into frenzy. Initially Hoddle stood by Gascoigne, but pointedly made reference to his fitness and lifestyle. If there was going to be a 'big name' fall guy, it did not look good for Gazza.

Come the day of reckoning, Hoddle had set up five-minute slots to tell each squad member their fate. In truth, according to Beckham, it was 'a bit like a meat market: "You're in, you're out."' He, of course, was in but his Old Trafford colleagues Philip Neville and Nicky Butt were not. Nor was Gazza. Left out because of concerns about his fitness and drinking, by his own admission he went 'berserk' on being told by Hoddle, and later trashed his hotel room in a rage. Hoddle remained tight-lipped on what occurred between the two men, saying only that 'there were tears in his eyes'. This was not some dignified courtesy, though: as it would emerge, Glenn Hoddle had his own agenda for remaining silent about the moment that he had ended the international career of England's great white hope.

But what of Paul Gascoigne? He spent another two years at the Riverside troubled by injury, personal problems, rumour and counter-rumour. In July 2000 he joined Everton, where he was reunited with his former Rangers manager, Walter Smith, the one man – along with Venables – who had been able to curb the midfielder's excesses and get the best out of him on the pitch. Hopes that this final chance for Gascoigne would see an Indian summer in his story came to nothing. He spent twenty months at Goodison, interspersed with spells in rehabilitation clinics and lengthy periods on the treatment table. On his infrequent appearances it was like a tragedy watching a once extraordinary player try tricks he was no longer able to physically pull off. A brief, unhappy spell at Burnley followed, and then a humiliating world-wide search for a club, any club. Eventually he ended up in the second division of the Chinese league, but this was no worthy stage for him and he soon left for home. In February 2004 he announced his retirement and, despite various coaching roles in football's lower reaches, Gascoigne has struggled to carve out a role for himself in the game he graced. Top-class football is all the poorer without him.

Barely had the controversy over Gascoigne subsided than another had emerged. Hoddle, naming his line-up for England's opening game against Tunisia, left out Owen and, more surprisingly, Gazza's heir apparent, David Beckham. The Manchester United midfielder was apparently 'not focused'. What that meant, nobody quite knew – including Beckham. Matters were subsequently compounded when Beckham was forced to attend and answer questions at the very same press conference at which his manager justified the player's omission. If Beckham had entertained doubts about Hoddle's assessment before, all uncertainty was banished afterwards. Events clearly threw the player, and he looked decidedly uncomfortable as the England manager told the world's press why Beckham – the player he had selected most in qualifying – was not ready for World Cup action.

Despite not being seeded (owing to FIFA's legendarily baffling ranking system), England had earned a generous draw alongside Tunisia, Colombia and Romania. First, on 15 June, were the North Africans, managed by the Pole Henry Kasperczak, a man who had haunted England once before when playing for his native country in the 1973 games that had spelt the end for Sir Alf Ramsey. 'I embarrassed England twenty years ago and I hope my players can do it again,' he bragged. 'My players are competitive, combative and full of team spirit. We're well prepared. The game will be tight. There will not be much difference between the teams' styles. The English have changed their style. Their play is much more varied now. The Tunisians have become more European in fashion.'[22] There was, however, to be no shock this time around: Hoddle's selection was vindicated, in his eyes at least, as England put on a prodigious, dashing performance – their best since the draw in Rome – running out 2–0 winners, after goals by Alan Shearer, and the game's outstanding presence, Paul Scholes. 'He is a player that loves being out there, playing his football,' enthused Hoddle. 'He played a super role for us today and he gets his foot in well. The boy is confident in his own ability; he doesn't particularly like all the razzmatazz that goes with it so he does all his talking on the pitch.'

Seven days later against Romania, though, England contrived to put on a display that was the absolute antithesis of their earlier performance. Where they had been commanding against Tunisia, England were jittery, uncertain; where once they had lurked with perpetual intent, here they were one-dimensional, impotent. Beckham was still an outcast to Hoddle, at least until Ince limped off injured thirty minutes in and the Manchester United star made his finals' bow. Not that he made much difference. Viorel Moldovan put the Romanians in front on forty-seven minutes, and it was a lead they never looked like conceding until Michael Owen came on with eighteen minutes to go. His pace and verve transformed England and, were it not for some of his more flat-footed defensive colleagues, would have changed the game. Within minutes a move flowing from Beckham to Shearer found Scholes. Under pressure, he slowed the ball and rolled it to Owen, who did the rest, shooting home from close range. As England fans celebrated an undeserved draw, Dan Petrescu carved a path through the England rearguard and, with defenders looking on like life guards at a cesspool, slotted a cool shot past Seaman to make it 2–1 to Romania. Still Owen might have salvaged a draw, firing a shot against the Romanian post, but it was not to be.

Four days later, when England met Colombia in Toulouse, Hoddle rang the changes. Beckham and Owen replaced Batty and Sheringham in a game where defeat meant elimination. Vibrant against Tunisia, inept against Romania, England were back on song against the South Americans. On twenty minutes Darren Anderton's strike put them in front; ten minutes later Beckham's exquisitely curled free-kick sealed a 2–0 victory and England's progression to the second round. It had been Beckham's first goal for his country and one of the best of his career. 'Part of me wanted to run over to the bench to Glenn Hoddle,' he recalled in his autobiography *My Side*, '"There you go. What do you make of that?"'

Failure to get a result against Romania had, however, cost England dear. Instead of a second-stage meeting with an accomplished but beatable Croatia in Bordeaux, England had to go to Saint Etienne to face Argentina and all their Maradona and Malvinas baggage. Hoddle had of course experienced the 'hand of God' at close quarters and the iniquity of that hot afternoon in Mexico City bristled through the room when he was asked about it a day ahead of the tie. 'Revenge is a horrible word,' he said.

> Redress the balance is what I would say. I'm sure players like Peter Reid would love to be in the camp now. That stayed with us for a long time. For the football people in the country, we've got a chance of getting that result out of our system. I felt it was an injustice. It was a sickening blow we had to take. We couldn't believe how we went out.[23]

Resisting the temptation to bolster his midfield with a scrapper like Batty, Hoddle named an unchanged side – 'sometimes you don't have to change the team,' he said, 'just the shape at certain times in the game.' The game dominated the agenda back home and, when asked whether she would be cheering on England, even the Queen said: 'Well I think one should. They're going to have a very difficult job, I think.' Tony Blair was more optimistic. 'The whole country is right behind the English team and we are going to have our fingers and everything crossed. I am sure they will go out there and be a credit to the whole country.' Even Sir Alf Ramsey, who had recently suffered a stroke, wished Hoddle's team 'every success' from his Ipswich hospital bed.

Ramsey had, of course, experienced the gamesmanship of the Argentinians at close quarters on his way to leading England to their finest hour in 1966, and it would be no less evident on this searing night in France. Only five minutes had passed when Diego Simeone was chasing onto a through ball, away from goal, but in the confines of the England penalty area. David Seaman dived, so too did Simeone – seeking to profit from the goalkeeper's rashness – and the Danish referee, Kim Milton Nielsen, pointed to the penalty spot. It wouldn't be the last time he was conned, nor the last faulty judgement he made.

Seaman was booked, Gabriel Batistuta fired home the penalty and England looked as if they were rocking. Four minutes later Michael Owen repaid Simeone's dubious compliment. Released into Argentina's penalty area by Scholes's clever header, he tumbled under the faintest of touches from Robert Ayala. Another penalty. Roa guessed the right way, but could not keep out Shearer's resounding finish. Having not conceded a goal for eight matches, Argentina let in a second after fifteen minutes. This time there were no doubts about the way Owen earned it. Beckham lifted forward an immaculate looping pass that the Liverpool striker raced onto. His first touch was sublime. Losing Jose Chamot, he sped up the field and into the penalty area. Touching the ball past Ayala – the South Americans' penultimate line of defence – he cracked a supreme shot past Roa. Owen and 28 million Englishmen and women watching in France and at home were in heaven.

Suitably rattled, Argentina's players showed their frustration. Officials were berated, so too were some of England's players. They quickly regained their composure and rhythm, though, battling back strongly and repeatedly testing the excellence of Sol Campbell and Tony Adams. On forty-five minutes a free-kick was awarded on the edge of the England penalty area. A huge wall was formed to protect Seaman's goal, attackers were picked up – except Javier Zanetti, who hovered around the ball with Juan Sebastian Veron. When Nielsen's whistle blew, Veron slid the dead-ball forward to Zanetti, who impeccably dragged it forward with his first touch and fired home with his second to equalise.

Minutes after the interval, English hopes were dampened further. Simeone backed into Beckham, sending the midfielder falling. Patting the forlorn midfielder on the back of the head, he gave Beckham's blond locks a tug. Immaturely and irresponsibly – not least given that the Argentinian had already shown all the poise of a one-legged elephant when under pressure – Beckham flicked out his boot. Simeone went down as if he'd been knee-capped, out came Nielsen's red card and England were down to ten men.

In the teeth of such adversity England excelled. With Owen and Scholes dropping back and Shearer providing a solitary presence up front, England's ten men defended like lions, obstinately frustrating the South Americans and producing glimmers of hope for themselves. Owen flashed a shot wide, and late on Sol Campbell's header found the net but his effort was disallowed after Shearer was penalised for fouling Roa. Video evidence showed that it was another harsh – if not dubious decision – by Nielsen. The game went on into extra time and the Danish referee again caused consternation in the English ranks when he missed Chamot's blatant handball in his own area. As with the 'hand of God' everyone but the referee seemed to see what had happened.

Extra time yielded no further goals and so, once more, the game went to penalties. Berti and Shearer scored the opening salvoes; then came Hernan Crespo – but Seaman saved. Next was Paul Ince. Heavily criticised for not stepping up in Euro '96, could he give England the lead? No, like Southgate two years earlier his shot was poor and Roa saved. Veron made it 2–1, substitute Merson equalised; Gallardo scored, likewise Owen, before Ayala made it 4–3. It meant that England's fate rested with David Batty. Head down, he trudged forwards, his demeanour seemingly betraying a lack of confidence. As he placed the ball, millions looked away from their television sets, unable to watch, and the silence that greeted his kick indicated that it was all over for another four years.

Gallant losers again, England's footballers returned home. Despite their worst World Cup finals showing since 1958, Hoddle arrived back in England with his reputation enhanced. In the way his team had performed, bristling with youth, battling to the end, there was room for optimism in spite of the early exit, and widespread praise for the manager throughout a media who had not always received courteous treatment from him. David Beckham, on the other hand, was a pariah. Newspapers harangued him, leading from the front rather than back pages. For the 'rotters' who had lurked in the background since the demise of Graham Taylor, it was a field day. The *Daily Mirror* printed Beckham's face as a dartboard, the *Sun* carried pictures of an effigy of the player hung from a lamp post, all the tabloids fulminated with ire and indignation. When Beckham played in the second league game of the 1998–99 season for Manchester United against West Ham, he ran a gauntlet of hatred unlike anything witnessed in English football's recent past.

A season is, nevertheless, a long time in football. By the campaign's end, Hoddle and Beckham were to experience quite stunning reversals of fortune. Indeed, the tide had already started to turn against the England manager by the time that Beckham had made his infamous appearance at the Boleyn Ground. At the start of August Hoddle's World Cup diary had been published and serialised in the *Sun*, for which deal he was said to have been paid £250,000, or the equivalent of a year's salary from the Football Association. In 1986 and 1990 Bobby Robson had published similar books, but what separated the two managers' tomes was their tone and content: where

Robson shirked from offering criticism in his anodyne accounts, Hoddle never shied; when Robson would offer gentle anecdotes, Hoddle gave insights so explicit and sometimes unnecessary that he seemed to undermine the very essence of squad solidarity. Indeed, over a period of days *Sun* readers were treated to stories of Tony Adams swearing on his way to the shower, Alan Shearer lying naked on the floor and jubilant Argentinian footballers taunting Hoddle's players. He informed Chris Sutton that he would never play for England via his book, and cited his principal mistake in France in leaving his faith healer, Eileen Drewery, behind rather than the failure to rehearse spot-kicks. 'Practising [penalties] until kingdom come is not necessarily the answer,' he wrote, 'in fact it might just make things worse.'

But what irked most was his blow-by-blow account of Gascoigne's omission. When Hoddle had initially dropped him he had received broad public support, despite Gazza's popularity; with the publication of his diary, however, by flagrantly sweeping aside the unwritten rule that what passes between a player and his manager stays in the dressing room, he provoked outrage. According to his diary Hoddle 'already knew that the meeting was going to be stormy. I had received a phone call from one of my staff marking my card that Gazza was half cut. Again.' Having removed a bottle of wine from sight, Hoddle put on a tape of Kenny G to provide some background noise. When the manager broke the news, at first Gascoigne started to cry, but then composed himself and shook Hoddle's hand, wishing him and the team 'all the best'. As he moved to leave the room though, the midfielder suddenly flew into a rage, kicking a chair. 'He was a different person now,' wrote Hoddle. 'He had snapped. I stood there and he turned as if to go again, then came back with a barrage of abuse. He was ranting, swearing and slurring his words, not making much sense.' Gascoigne, according to his manager, was like a 'man possessed' and Hoddle feared that he would hit him. Instead he smashed his fist into a nearby lamp, sending shards of glass across the room. Hoddle's assistants, John Gorman and Glenn Roeder, then ushered the distraught player out of the room.

What made the affair all the more extraordinary was that the book had not only been published with the consent of the FA, but that it had been ghost-written by *its very own* Director of Public Affairs, David Davies. Gordon Taylor, the Chief Executive of the Professional

Footballers Association, lambasted Hoddle, calling him 'unpro-fessional'. 'Players in the squad will be very wary of Glenn. They will be worried that their discussions are going to reappear somewhere down the line. This is not the sort of thing we should expect from an England coach.'[24] He had a point. Indeed, the contrast with someone like Sir Alf Ramsey, a disciplinarian like Hoddle but a man unfailingly loyal to players present and past, could not have been greater. Could Hoddle regain the respect of his squad? Could he even restore credibility?

His troubles continued on into the autumn. European Champion-ship qualification saw England pitted with Sweden, Bulgaria, Luxembourg and Poland, but when England visited Stockholm at the start of September they fell to a 1–2 defeat, and in the following month's encounters with Bulgaria (0–0) at Wembley, and in Luxembourg (3–0), they were twice deeply unimpressive. With contract negotiations between Hoddle and the FA stuttering, the long-term future of England's manager began to be called into question, even by more considered commentators. 'This is certainly not the time for Glenn Hoddle to be negotiating a pay rise under terms of his contract,' wrote Patrick Barclay in the *Daily Telegraph* on 11 October. 'Rather it is time to ask if he should be national coach at all. Even those of us who have always supported him must concede that the argument has become thinner since England's dramatic, frustrating but generally promising World Cup.'

Hoddle eventually got his contract complete with substantially improved terms, but barely had the ink dried than the England manager had stumbled into another controversy. This time, however, it was to fatally imperil his reign as national coach.

On Saturday, 30 January 1999 an extraordinary interview Hoddle had given to *The Times* was published. It included the subject of reincarnation and Hoddle was quoted as saying: 'You and I have been physically given two hands and two legs and half-decent brains. Some people have not been born like that for a reason. The karma is working from another lifetime.'[25] The inference was clear, even if Hoddle's words weren't entirely: if you were handicapped or disabled, you were paying for sins from a former life. The view was as stupid as it was offensive to those he impugned: what was he thinking? Hoddle had previously publicly espoused views on matters of faith and religion, but where he had been ignored, laughed at or simply viewed as a crank in the past, his latest pronouncement seemed to suggest that he had lost the plot altogether.

At lunchtime the England manager appeared on BBC1's *Football Focus* saying he had been 'misconstrued, misinterpreted and misunderstood'. He apologised for any hurt he had caused, but did not deny what *The Times* had claimed. As the press and the great and good of British public life went into overdrive, Hoddle waged his own PR offensive, appearing on national television and radio, reiterating what he had already told *Football Focus*. By doing so, Hoddle merely deepened the chasm into which he had fallen. The problem was that the England manager – who had always liked to portray himself as the bright young thing of football management – was simply not that erudite. Lacking the gumption or verbal felicity to defend the indefensible, or at least deflect attention away from his comments, he began to be swallowed up by waves of consternation and anger. His repeated contention that the disabled were suffering in this life for wrongs committed in a previous existence was, as one commentator rightly put it, 'medieval', but rather than backing down he alternately tried to justify his beliefs – which heightened the sense that Hoddle inhabited a different planet from most Englishmen – or deny what he'd said, which assumed that the public were even more stupid than he was. Even those not directly touched by disability were likely to find Hoddle's preaching anathema. This, after all, had become a country where questions of personal belief are deemed deeply private matters rather than something to be worn on one's sleeve. It was not something expected from a national figure, much less a football manager, and by the end of the weekend Hoddle was a target of barely suppressed derision. As the (blind) Education Secretary, David Blunkett, reportedly joked: 'If Hoddle is right, then I must have been a failed football manager in a previous existence.'

Blunkett wasn't the only political heavyweight sticking the knife in. On the Monday morning, the Prime Minister appeared on the *Richard and Judy* television show. When asked about Hoddle, Blair said that it would be 'very difficult' for him to stay. 'If he said what he is reported to have said then I think that was very wrong,' he added. It was becoming increasingly obvious that it would be unviable for the 'impossible job's' incumbent to carry on. David Davies – Hoddle's partner in crime just months earlier and now (unbelievably, given his part in the diary furore) acting FA Chief Executive – emerged from

Lancaster Gate at lunchtime to tell waiting journalists that there would be a decision on Hoddle's future within thirty-six hours. Senior FA committee members entered into a flurry of meetings, while Hoddle again went on the offensive. Within hours he had appeared on ITN news saying he would not resign because 'I didn't say them things.' Later on that evening he announced that he would issue a writ against *The Times*, but in the following morning's *Daily Mirror* he said: 'The reporter from *The Times* did not misquote me but he did misrepresent me.' At the same time the Sports Minister Tony Banks called for Hoddle's resignation on BBC Breakfast News, saying: 'Quite frankly, I don't think he can effectively do his job.' By then, most of the country, baffled by Hoddle's initial comments and simply bemused by what followed, were inclined to agree.

By the evening of Tuesday, 2 February Hoddle had gone. David Davies told reporters that Hoddle's position had become increasingly untenable. 'He accepts he made an error of judgment and he has apologised,' his erstwhile 'ghost' confirmed. 'The past few days have been painful for everyone involved. [But] the past few days have been as of nothing compared to any offence that may have been caused to disabled people in our community and in our country.' Hoddle later read a brief statement in which he accepted that he had 'made an error of judgement in a newspaper interview. This was never my intention.' He thanked friends, colleagues and players before beating a hasty retreat. He would return to football eleven months later at Southampton where his reputation would enjoy a partial revival. Yet when he walked out on the south-coast club to become Spurs' manager in March 2001, his name became sullied once more, this time by accusations of disloyalty. Tottenham, who had floundered in dire mediocrity all the way back to the days of Gascoigne and Venables, would not be revived by their prodigal son. Tales of backroom discord predominated, there was no improvement in playing standards and, less than thirty months after Hoddle's return to White Hart Lane, he fell victim to the sack once more.

A week after Glenn Hoddle's exit from Lancaster Gate, England played world champions France at Wembley. Taking charge of the team was the FA's Technical Director Howard Wilkinson. Highly regarded by the FA, even if that respect wasn't widely shared amongst the general football-watching public, he had emerged as the front-runner to succeed Hoddle. Ninety minutes later, after a pallid England performance in which the gulf in class and tactical nous was not ultimately matched by the magnitude of the 2–0 French victory, even Wilkinson's most ardent admirers at Lancaster Gate would have struggled to state a case for him. In the days that followed some fancifully suggested that the Arsenal manager Arsène Wenger or the Manchester United boss Alex Ferguson might be interested in succeeding Hoddle; others that Terry Venables or even Bobby Robson could make a return. This time, however, the denizens at the FA headquarters held their ears to the ground and plumped for the public's choice.

Kevin Keegan had called time on his playing days in 1984, two years after Bobby Robson had heralded the end of his international career. His departure was marked with the sort of dramatic flourish that had characterised his extraordinary career: a helicopter came down from the Northumbrian skies and lifted this latter-day football god into the heavens. Rich beyond the dreams of many of his contemporaries, Keegan took extended leave from England, soaking up the sun in Spain, spending time with his family, working on his golf handicap. Football, it seemed, was consigned to his past.

In February 1992 he made a dramatic return to the game, when he was appointed manager of Newcastle United, a team struggling in the lower reaches of the Second Division. The galvanising effect Keegan would have was remarkable: not since Don Revie had transformed Leeds United from no-hopers into a dominant force in the 1960s had a manager so single-handedly changed the direction of a club. Drifting towards Division Three, with crowds sometimes teetering towards just four figures when he took over, Newcastle stormed back into the top flight in resounding fashion fifteen months later, winning the First Division championship.* Playing a free-flowing, attacking brand of football more reminiscent of a less cynical era, Newcastle

---

* The inception of the Premier League had, by then, seen the Second Division become the First Division, the Third Division the Second, and so on.

won hearts if not trophies. Twice, in 1995–96 and 1996–97 they would finish Premiership runners-up and in 1993–94 – their first season back – third. Goals were scored by the hatful; stars of the ilk of Peter Beardsley, Andy Cole, David Ginola and Alan Shearer were brought to the north-east; even St James' Park was rebuilt.

But if there were doubts amidst this north-eastern football revolution, they concerned Newcastle's staying power and Keegan's temperament. Certainly the former was not helped by defensive frailties which, when dissected, made them look guilty of tactical naivety. On the latter point, the impetuous, volatile streak that had occasionally surfaced in Keegan the player had not left him in middle age. On several occasions he let out furious outbursts on live television, most infamously during the climax of the 1995–96 championship race after Alex Ferguson had intimated that Leeds United – one of Newcastle's forthcoming opponents – would not try as hard as they should. A wild-eyed Keegan then appeared live after his side had won at Elland Road and announced that he would 'love it, just love it' if they beat United to the title. It was hardly comparable to some of, say, Brian Clough's more explosive moments, but nor did it befit one of football's so-called ambassadors.

Less than a year later, in January 1997, Keegan finally carried out the threat he had made privately on several occasions, and resigned from his job. Difficulties over the club's transition to PLC status were cited, but on earlier occasions lack of transfer funds and a perceived lack of boardroom support had unsettled Keegan. Sixteen months later, in May 1998, he was appointed manager of Fulham, freshly promoted to Division Two, by Mohamed Al Fayed, who craved Premiership football at Craven Cottage and picked Keegan to effect his dream. When Hoddle fell from grace midway through Keegan's debut season at Fulham, with the Cottagers riding high and the rehabilitation of their manager well under way, the press and public focused their desire on him. They weren't the only ones. The FA also cast a seductive eye over Keegan, like a cad regaining the affections of a lost lover. They announced that the successful candidate must be a man capable of 'inspiring' the country, from players to public. Whoever could they mean?

Al Fayed, however, was insistent that Keegan was going nowhere. 'Kevin will not leave us,' he said. 'He loves us, he's married to Fulham. How can he divorce us? It's impossible. He is a man of integrity, of loyalty and I don't need to do anything to keep him. The club is his club, it's not mine. He runs it himself.'[26] Keegan, perhaps conscious of the bad light cast by his departure from Newcastle, pledged allegiance. 'Whoever it is who eventually gets the job, I wish him good luck and I mean that,' he told reporters. 'It's nice of people if they think you've got something to offer, but those who really know me know I want to see the contract out. At a time when loyalty is under question it would be nice for some of us to show that contracts count.'

The FA, for once however, knew the man they wanted. When the acting Chairman, Geoff Thompson, met journalists ten days after Hoddle's departure he made it patently obvious who their number one target was. 'He's got to be the best available coach at international level,' Thompson said. 'He's got to be a good man-manager as well. And he's got to have integrity. We're under the microscope. You can't have the first two without the third because eventually the third overrides them – as we've seen in the past. It's not Utopia. There are a lot of capable people who have got all three. How many parts would Keegan fit into? He'd fit into a few wouldn't he?'[27] For all the talk of integrity and honour, it was clear, however, that the FA were not-so-subtly tapping Keegan up.

It worked too. Keegan revealed that should he be given the opportunity to speak to the FA, he would be 'happy' to do so. What followed over the next few days was a gentle tug-of-war between Lancaster Gate and Fulham with an end result that seemed to suit everybody: England got Keegan – with Peter Beardsley as his assistant – for the remaining four international games of the season; Fulham got to keep their manager – in the short term anyway; and Al Fayed, a man whose futile quest for a British passport had obsessed him for years, was portrayed as the magnanimous hero of the piece, a true 'patriot' who had allowed English national interests to override his own.

Kevin Keegan's second run began on 27 March 1999 with a 3–1 win over Poland at Wembley that set England's European Championship hopes back on track. Steve McManaman was restored to the side, so too was one of Keegan's Newcastle apostles, Andy Cole; but it was Paul Scholes who stole the show, hitting a superb hat-trick. Afterwards Keegan hinted that there might be a 'solution' to the logistical problem of managing club and country, and Mohamed Al Fayed also suggested that he would be willing to permanently release

Keegan from his duties at Fulham. It was only a month later, however, after a 1–1 draw in Hungary, that Keegan explicitly made clear that he wanted the job on a long-term basis. At the end of the domestic season, which ended with Fulham crowned Second Division champions, Keegan relinquished his role at Craven Cottage, and England's first millionaire footballer became the first million-pound-a-year England manager. 'Not bad for someone who started at the Football Association as a temp ten weeks ago,' mused Henry Winter. 'Not bad too, for a position that paid Terry Venables £150,000 five years ago. Even Glenn Hoddle had only renegotiated up to £350,000 before his demise.'

Just what Sir Alf Ramsey would have made of this latest chapter in football's era of excess is anybody's guess. Little over a fortnight before his former charge signed his latest lucrative deal, England's greatest manager passed away, aged seventy-nine. After his brief spell at Birmingham City, Ramsey had returned to his adopted home of Ipswich where he lived in almost reclusive retirement, occasionally making forays into journalism. His observations were not always popular, nor welcomed, and some accused him of bitterness and holding old grudges. Perhaps he was justified to do so. After all, in an age where even the most ordinary of past players were feted as legends, Ramsey was a figure whom a nation had first shunned, then blithely forgotten. It was a small tragedy that he was so rarely revered as the man who put England on top of the world and a sad indictment that he never felt able to luxuriate in the glory of its finest hour.

Ramsey had, of course, given Kevin Keegan his international debut. Six unsuccessful England reigns separated their managerial careers, and while Keegan sought to be the lucky seventh, by autumn 1999 hopes of glory in the following summer's European Championship in Holland and Belgium had become complicated. Unable to overcome Sweden in the June qualifier at Wembley, or make substantial headway on the group leaders in subsequent qualifiers in Bulgaria (1–1) and Poland (0–0), England's fate was left to rest in a two-legged November play-off – with Scotland.

England's Manchester United contingent had enjoyed differing fortunes that summer. Against Sweden, Paul Scholes had rampaged around the pitch in the first half, lashing out hither and thither, like a school bully fighting for dinner money. Eventually, yet another careless challenge shortly after half-time cost him a second booking and Scholes became the first England international ever to be sent off at Wembley. As for Beckham, himself foolishly sent off a year earlier in Saint Etienne, he too was a premature departure, this time, however, limping off with an injury that would keep him out of the subsequent meeting with Bulgaria four days later. If that brought disappointing conclusions to both players' international seasons, each man could still bask in the glory of extraordinary domestic seasons. Already league and FA Cup winners, a week earlier they had crowned an unprecedented treble by winning the most dramatic European Cup final in the competition's history. Even the most ardent Manchester United hater could not fail to be impressed by the club's spectacular achievement in beating Bayern Munich. For Beckham, in particular, it completed his rehabilitation from pariah to national icon. He is yet to look back.

England travelled to Scotland on 13 November 1999 for the first half of their two-legged showdown. It was the first meeting between the two countries at Hampden in more than a decade and the hosts were as imbued with their desire for pantomime English bashing as ever before. 'I reckon there's one or two of their players who will crack under pressure,' Johnny Marr the 'general' of the 'Tartan Army's Edinburgh Battalion' told one newspaper. 'We've got more soul than England. They just take it for granted that they'll come up here, do the business and go away again. It's not like that for us.'[28] As so often, such optimism was wishful thinking. Twice in the first half Paul Scholes penetrated the Scottish defence: first, on twenty-one minutes, he chested down a searching pass from Campbell, strode past Hendry and calmly turned a shot past Neil Sullivan; then, on forty-two minutes, he stole in between two Scottish defenders and headed Beckham's free-kick into the back of the net. A dull second half passed, with Billy Dodds' shot against Seaman's crossbar causing English hearts a solitary flutter, but after ninety minutes Keegan could reflect on a job well done, if only half completed. 'It was a good game,' he told reporters, 'We had goals in us, they played well and hit the bar. In the history of England v Scotland it was probably one of the better games. Now we've got to finish the job off in front of our own fans.'

Four days later at Wembley, Don Hutchison's goal earned Scotland a 1–0 victory and salvaged some Caledonian pride, but for the hosts, Scholes's Hampden brace had been enough to win through to Belgium and Holland.

Losing to Scotland at Wembley may well have brought an unsatisfactory close to the twentieth century for England's footballers, but they could rest in the knowledge that they had secured qualification for another major tournament. The early days of the new millennium brought backroom changes aplenty at the FA. A new Chief Executive, Adam Crozier, a slick, smooth-talking, former marketing-man, was appointed with the intention of helping the FA finally reach its commercial potential. After seventy years and two different offices there, the FA abandoned Lancaster Gate and returned to its West End roots, taking up residence in Soho Square. And the very home of English football – Wembley Stadium – would be brought up to date at last. Erosion caused by its age and a botched modernisation job brought by the Taylor Report had not been kind to the famous old ground, which by the turn of the century existed only as an uncomfortable, dirty, decrepit wreck, with bad seats and out-of-date facilities. The FA announced that it would close by the end of 2000 with a brand new stadium rising out of its ashes.

Ahead of the 2000 European Championships, England enjoyed satisfactory Wembley draws with Argentina (0–0) and Brazil (1–1), a comfortable win over Ukraine (2–0) and a rather patchy one in Malta (2–1). If praise for the performances of Keegan's men was not always universal, many believed he had a side capable of winning the tournament. When his team lined up for their opening first round match against Portugal in the Philips Stadium, Eindhoven on 12 June 2000 he could count on four individuals – the two Nevilles, Beckham and Scholes – who had played parts in Manchester United's unprecedented successes of the previous year; and a fifth – Steve McManaman – who had played a starring role in Real Madrid's European Cup final win a month earlier. He could boast a core of immense experience – Seaman, Adams, Ince and Shearer – running through the heart of his team and, in Michael Owen, a world-class youngster with whom anything might happen.

His men set off in blistering fashion, taking the lead on three minutes with a fabulous flowing move. Phil Neville fed Shearer, who spread the ball to the far flank; Beckham dispatched a cross with pace and curve; and Scholes's head met it perfectly, powering the ball past Victor Baia. Within fifteen minutes England had doubled their advantage. Michael Owen laid off Gary Neville's throw-in into the path of Beckham; again he struck a cross of supreme accuracy, Scholes's dummy run fooled the Portuguese defence and McManaman met his cross thunderously to make it 2–0. England were outstanding, and playing with the sort of thrilling football reminiscent of Keegan's Newcastle in their prime. But just as Newcastle could delight, so could they frustrate, and so it was with Keegan's England . . .

On twenty-two minutes, the English defence were struggling to keep track of Luis Figo and, in trying to close him down, Tony Adams left a glimmer of light between himself and the goal, and Figo punished him, sending a right-footed shot – with a touch off the defender – past Seaman. With that goal the momentum passed to the Portuguese. Time and again they pushed and probed the English defence and eight minutes from the interval earned an equaliser when Joao Pinto's diving header met Rui Costa's cross.

England's malaise deepened in the second half. With Owen and McManaman withdrawn because of injury, their once vibrant team-mates looked flaccid, subdued and shaken. Just before the hour-mark Adams was caught out by Rui Costa's pass and Nuno Gomes arrived to lift the ball over Seaman. England's collapse was complete. 'It was disappointing that at 2–0 we didn't think, "Wow, let's sit back and let Portugal really work for ten to fifteen minutes,"' said Keegan afterwards. 'The players got carried away with the euphoric atmosphere and went looking for a third goal. You'll probably say that's typical Kevin Keegan. I'm not against that. But believe it or not, I do like to see teams play with their head at times. I felt we should have steadied ourselves.'

Five days later, England had their showdown tie with Germany. To lose would mean not just an ignominious early return – met with the inevitable outraged reaction – but would let the Germans' unbeaten run in competitive matches since 1966 endure. In October England would play the first of two World Cup qualifiers against the Germans: did Keegan really want his team going into those matches with the jinx extended?

Castigated for their carelessness against Portugal, England responded with a performance of composure and conviction against the Germans. Superficially they provided a display wholly uncharacteristic of a 'Kevin Keegan side': there were none of the dashing charges which had provided the two outstanding goals early on in the opening match; but nor were there the sort of lapses that had seen them so miserably surrender that advantage. Owen and Scholes were each denied by the excellence of Oliver Kahn in an untidy first half, and the standard of play scarcely improved in the second. Seven minutes after the interval, however, Beckham was fouled near the touchline, about twelve yards inside the German half. Taking the free-kick himself, he span a cross into a crowded penalty area. Owen and Jens Nowotny rose together, though failed to make contact, but the ball fell at the back post and Shearer headed powerfully home for the game's only goal.

The result left England needing only a draw when they met Romania three days later in order to make the quarter-finals. Few doubted they could do it, despite fresh memories of defeat in the France World Cup and the knowledge that England were without a victory over them since long before Keegan's playing days had started. In a compelling first half Christian Chivu gave Romania a twenty-first-minute lead when his cross shot rebounded in off Martyn's far post. England looked stunned, though drew on their reserves and showed the mettle to claw their way back. Twice in the final five minutes of the half they found the net. First, Shearer played Ince in through the middle, and his dash into the Romanian box was stymied by Chivu's foul to give away the penalty that Shearer duly dispatched. Soon, England were in front. Owen chased onto Scholes's cleverly lifted pass, took it around the goalkeeper and struck home from a tight angle.

2–1 up at half-time and firmly in the ascendancy, would England show the sort of resolve displayed against Germany, or the recklessness that had ruined their hopes against Portugal? Initially the former looked the more likely, but England were incapable of holding onto the ball for more than fleeting passages of play. The more possession Romania had, the more chances went their way and the more vulnerable England looked. Dorinel Munteanu capitalised on Nigel Martyn's weak punch to make it 2–2 but even that, surely, would still be enough to ensure England's progression. Then, in the final minute, a moment of madness ended it. Viorel Moldovan raced into the penalty area and, though not in a position to place England in imminent danger, Philip Neville came from nowhere and crudely crashed into him. Ioan Ganea stroked home Romania's winner from the penalty spot; England were finished.

Four months later, so too was Kevin Keegan.

Euro 2000 had marked the end of the line for Ince and Shearer, two of the cornerstones of England's mid-1990s resurgence, as well as the arrival of storm clouds over Keegan's managerial reign. Notwithstanding the victory over Germany, it had been one of England's worst-ever showings in a major tournament. In the face of this, Keegan's England visited the Stade de France on 2 September and earned a creditable 1–1 draw with the world and newly crowned European champions. A month later, Germany were the visitors to Wembley for a match to mark the start of England's World Cup qualifying campaign, and the last action that the Empire Stadium would see ahead of its demolition and rebuilding. At the end of its seventy-seven-year life it seemed apposite that it was Germany – opponents on the stadium's greatest afternoon – whom England were facing; and that the captain, Tony Adams, should be making his sixty-sixth international appearance. Leading England out, however, was Sir Bobby Charlton under driving, ceaseless rain. On an emotional afternoon, that was probably the high point. What followed was a mess of flaccid, untidy, technically inept football played out by a poor England side and the shadows of once great Germany. Dietmar Hamann's fourteenth-minute goal was enough to settle a deeply unsatisfactory encounter and bring a blisteringly disappointing conclusion to Wembley's life.

No one was more dissatisfied and disappointed by England's defeat than Kevin Keegan. In the dressing room immediately after the match the England manager told his players that he did not believe that he was the man to bring back glory to the national team and that he was resigning with immediate effect. Adam Crozier, perhaps hoping that this was just another Keegan tantrum, desperately tried to persuade him to reconsider, but he would not be moved. Barely an hour after his team had trooped off Keegan appeared on television and told the country of his decision to resign. 'I have had all the help I have needed but I have not been quite good enough,' he said. 'It's the end of the road for me. I have wished the players the best and I know it's not good timing but there's never a good time. I look forward to a life outside football.'

The forty-five years that had followed Walter Winterbottom's appointment as England coach had seen just five men fill what has been termed 'the second most important job in the country'. By contrast, within little over a decade after the departure of England's fifth manager, Bobby Robson, the FA were left looking for manager number ten. The conclusion seemed inescapable: this had become an impossible job. The pressures on its incumbent were, after all, intolerable. To be England manager meant, it seemed, not only that every tactical decision, selection or result came under the microscopic scrutiny of an entire country, but likewise every outpouring, transgression and personal conviction. Even if success was brought, immortality was not assured – witness the quiet, final years of Sir Alf Ramsey, ignored by the football establishment and media; failure, however relative, brought insults, mocking and demonisation. Given such unique pressures and expectation, who could possibly thrive in such a position? Who could ever want such a role?

But was it an impossible job? After all, Sir Alf Ramsey had brought World Cup glory to England in 1966; could it simply have been that his successors were not blessed with his talents or a similarly gifted squad? Don Revie and Ron Greenwood had each, by degrees, been let down by weak teams; Bobby Robson, twice – when Diego Maradona blew his side away with a flick of the hand of God and, four years later, after an unsuccessful penalty shoot-out – by ill fortune. His successors, though, had more fundamental flaws. Graham Taylor and Kevin Keegan were simply not equipped with the tactical skills to succeed at the highest level; Terry Venables and Glenn Hoddle were, but each was undone by conditions of human fallibility: avarice and poor judgement in the former; obtusity, arrogance and, ultimately, 'medieval' views in the latter. Only Venables left with dignity intact, and even that was undone by later disclosures about his business dealings; the unlamented exits of the others added to the perception that managing England was a hopeless task. Of course, it wasn't, but who could succeed?

14

SVENGLAND

THE EIGHT YEARS that followed the inception of the FA Premier League (later the Premiership) in 1992 marked the most rapid period of change in the history of English football. In 1992 it was still taking the first steps out of the post-Heysel slump, with a turgid national side the laughing stock of Europe, and lack of outstanding prospects ready to drag the game out of the mire; it had become a national pastime to cast envious glances elsewhere. The French and Dutch were envied for their outstanding youth development schemes; the Italians the technical excellence of their players; even the Americans for their stadia and marketing nous.

Few fans could have imagined the impact that the breakaway of the elite clubs would have on English football, much less that within a few years it would incorporate so many of its neighbours' long-coveted attractions. Ostensibly it looked like a rebranding in name alone and, to all intents and purposes, it was: the top flight's size was trimmed down by two clubs but virtually everything else remained the same. Yet it was phenomenally successful. Football's new core sponsors sold the game as a lifestyle choice, something that could be neatly summed up by one of its key sponsors' slogans: 'Eat football, sleep football' ('. . . drink Coca-Cola . . .'). Not only was this accompanied by an exponential growth in attendances, but a vast number were suddenly willing to pay to watch live football at home. Above all else it was the huge revenues earned from BSkyB and other broadcasters that drove English football's revolution.

The money went in many directions: to stadia, training and scouting infrastructure, and over-inflated players' salaries. But arguably the most significant impact these vast revenues had on weekly Premiership fare came as a result of the large-scale recruitment of foreign players. Previously, each generation of British football had speckled the old First Division with a dusting of home-grown giants; now legends of the game – from France, Holland, Italy, Spain, Brazil and even further afield – vied with each other not just for the top teams, but in humdrum middle of the table clashes too. Some complained that home-grown talent was being suffocated but the reality was that the bar was being raised for native players, as were fans' expectations of what their heroes could produce.

If anything, the biggest problem created by the new-found cosmopolitanism of English football affected the managers. Foreign players and the new generation of home-grown superstars carried baggage both on and off the field that many bosses failed to deal with. Those who succeeded in combining the extraordinary array of available talent on the field; and could temper the inflated egos off it; blend the variety of nationalities and keep rich young men away from trouble, became 'superbosses' – as well rewarded and highly revered as the megastars they managed. These men numbered barely a dozen within the entire football world and the Premiership had just two: Sir Alex Ferguson and Arsène Wenger. No Englishman, however, came close to fulfilling such criteria. Indeed, in the days following Kevin Keegan's departure, the FA Chief Executive, Adam Crozier, made quite clear that there was no Englishman of sufficient talent (or unsullied by previous relations with the FA) who could take on the vacant manager's job. Only two Englishmen – Howard Wilkinson and Howard Kendall – had won the championship in the previous fifteen years and besides Terry Venables, only Joe Royle had lifted the FA Cup in the previous decade. None of these was deemed a serious candidate. 'There is not a huge abundance of English coaches now,' said Crozier. 'If we are going to get the right man we're going to have to cast the net wider.' He foresaw the need to pay top wages to bring in the right man, and spoke of the necessity of appointing someone on a long-term basis. 'We'll get the right person,' he promised, 'whatever that ends up costing.'

Arsène Wenger, the FA's preferred choice, quickly distanced himself from the running, opening up the way for Sven-Göran Eriksson, manager of Serie A champions, Lazio. The Swede, whose contract was due to expire at the end of the 2000–01 season, was not only an experienced and highly successful manager, as much a 'superboss' as Wenger or Ferguson, but available too. Tord Grip, Eriksson's assistant in Rome, told the press just three weeks after Keegan's resignation: 'The English have contacted Sven. He is very flattered by receiving their offer but he will probably not leave before his contract here runs out in the summer.' Forty-eight hours later it was announced Eriksson would take over as England manager the following summer, a move that was eventually moved forward by more than six months.

'England haven't performed well,' Crozier admitted when he unveiled the new manager.

> We needed to do something dramatic. Sven is one of the best coaches in the world. It definitely is a new beginning. He has the respect of coaches across the world. He understands the world game, he has seen it from different perspectives, he can bring a whole new dimension to our football. He is very aware of English football, having grown up watching it. As professor of football across the world, he is very aware of what goes on here.

Eriksson was given a six-year contract, worth a minimum of £2 million per year plus substantial performance-related bonuses. It made him comfortably the highest-paid manager in Britain, if not the world.

Inevitably, not everyone greeted the arrival of a foreigner to the top job in English football with enthusiasm. In part it was the defiance of a nation that had never been invaded: now a Swede was taking the so-called 'second most important job in the country'. And derision came mostly from those who believed in the outmoded expectation that Englishmen could take on the world, simply on account of being Englishmen. 'We've sold our birthright down the river to a nation of seven million skiers and hammer-throwers who spend half their lives in darkness,' thundered the *Daily Mail*'s Jeff Powell. Gordon Taylor, Chief Executive of the PFA, slammed the appointment as a 'betrayal of our heritage'. He warned that there would be 'tears at the end of the day'. When Eriksson turned up for his first day at Soho Square he was greeted by a man dressed in a John Bull uniform bearing a placard that read: 'Hang your heads in shame. We wanted Terry Venables.'

For once John Bull seemed to speak for the minority only. Anyone with a passing interest in the game could not have failed to have been impressed by the football revolution instigated by Wenger in north London. A number of clubs had tried to replicate Arsenal's success by bringing in foreign managers of their own, but nobody of Wenger's pedigree or genius had been found. In Eriksson, by contrast, the FA had a man whose achievements at the time outstripped even those of the Arsenal manager. Indeed, not only did Eriksson fulfil the description of 'world class', no Englishman could come near to the standard he had set.

Much like Wenger, Eriksson had never made much of an impression as a player, calling time on his career due to a knee injury aged just twenty-seven. He started out as a coach at Swedish part-timers Degerfors a year later in 1976, before moving up a level three years later when he was appointed at IFK Gothenburg. There he enjoyed much success before joining Benfica in 1982. Consecutive Portuguese championships and a UEFA Cup final place led him to Roma in 1984 and he won the Coppa Italia in only his second season in charge. Later, he managed Fiorentina, Benfica again (whom he took to the 1990 European Cup final, where they lost to AC Milan), Sampdoria, and finally, in 1997, Lazio. In Rome he won trophies in each of his three years: Coppa Italia and the Italian Super Cup in 1998; a European Cup Winners' Cup and UEFA Super Cup in 1999; and the Italian league and cup double in 2000. Crozier had hired a man absolutely at the top of his game.

Eriksson launched his England career with an impressive 3–0 friendly victory over Spain at Villa Park at the end of February 2001. It was the first fixture of an England roadshow that would last five years, taking in all points from Ipswich to Southampton and Newcastle, Leicester and Liverpool. Although the stuttering World Cup campaign was put back on track with consecutive victories over Finland, Albania and Greece, by the start of September 2001, when England travelled to Germany for the return qualifier, their hosts were still in the driving seat of the qualification group and it still looked as if it would be England who would have to go to a play-off with another runner-up to ensure qualification for the following summer's World Cup in Japan and South Korea.

Despite the European Championship win in Charleroi, the sense that Germany still had the mark over England was palpable. Keegan's unhappy exit the previous autumn had been merely the latest in a series of unhappy adventures against England's greatest rivals and 1970, 1990 and 1996 all hung heavy in the minds of even those too young to remember them. When England arrived at the Olympic Stadium in Munich, few gave them a chance. The age-old rivalry, combined with a disappointing 0–2 friendly defeat to Holland a month earlier, had dampened some of the excitement that accompanied Eriksson's honeymoon as England manager. The hosts, on the other hand, had lost just one home qualifying game in their history, and had never lost a competitive match against England in Germany. They approached the match with a confidence that bordered on arrogance.

Indeed, as early as the sixth minute there was a definite sense of 'here we go again' after Carsten Jancker thundered Oliver Neuville's cushion header past David Seaman. The Germans were in control again, the same old story looked as if it was being played out: German efficiency and English frailty – with a conclusion set for Minsk or Kiev, where England seemed to be heading for a play-off.

Yet, quite amazingly, the very act of falling behind seemed to wake England from their thirty-four-year-long slumber. Eriksson's men dropped their defensive mindset and began to attack. Six minutes after Jancker's goal they equalised. A free-kick by Beckham looked to be drifting out of play when Steven Gerrard stopped the ball and crossed it back across the German area. Gary Neville headed it forward into the goalmouth, Barmby beat Oliver Kahn to the ball with a flick header and Michael Owen struck the ball home on the volley. Twice more in the following twelve minutes the Liverpool striker went close to scoring again; but it was a gloriously open game and Germany, equally, could have regained their lead.

But it was the hosts left trailing at the interval, after another uncharacteristically poor free-kick from Beckham was only half cleared. Again Gerrard picked it up, before sending a crashing shot into the far corner of Kahn's net from just outside the penalty area. Three minutes after the restart Beckham muscled in from the right and crossed with his left foot to Heskey who headed into the path of Owen, and he made it 3–1 with a flick home from close range.

England were rampant, and, inspired by the apparent exorcism of nearly four decades of pain, went in search of further goals. Owen completed his hat-trick on sixty-six minutes when he ran on to Gerrard's through ball and blasted his shot past Kahn. Seven minutes later Heskey made it 5–1 after Beckham and Scholes combined to send the Liverpool striker clear.

'Blitzed!' screamed the front page of the following morning's *Sunday Mirror*, while the *News of the World* picked up on a similarly familiar theme under the headline 'Don't mention the score'. This time, however, writing about the unfamiliar story of an English victory over Germany, the press didn't seem to know how to express their praise. As the *Sunday Telegraph* asked, was it all just a 'magnificent, ridiculous' dream? Eriksson was similarly bewildered. 'I can't believe that we can beat Germany 5–1 away, it seems like a dream, it's unbelievable,' he said. 'I said to the players: "I don't know what to say to you." I told the players before the game, if you play football as you can play we can beat any team, even Germany away but I can't believe it was 5–1. I don't think they deserved to lose 5–1, maybe 2–1, maximum 3–1, it was a great evening for England.' Magnanimous in defeat and with a deeper understanding of great, good, and plain poor England teams of yesteryear, Franz Beckenbauer said: 'I have never seen a better England team and I have never seen an England team playing better football. They had pace, aggression, movement and skill. It was fantasy football with England on a high.'

Eriksson's men were feted not only for their performances, but because they had eradicated so many demons in one astonishing night. Not just because they had thrashed a team that had previously lost just a single World Cup qualifier in its history; but because they were young, dashing, exciting and glamorous, representatives of a new golden generation in English football. Germany had just two players under the age of twenty-seven while England had just one outfield player – Nick Barmby – who had reached that birthday, and who had done so only seven months previously. Beckham and Owen had long excited England fans in the same way that the likes of Jimmy Greaves, Paul Gascoigne and Duncan Edwards had done in past generations; but the Germany match also represented the arrival of Ashley Cole, Steven Gerrard and Rio Ferdinand as players of genuine world-class potential. The victory suddenly left England in pole position in their World Cup qualifying group; the Germans, meanwhile awoke to one headline that held greater resonance with British tabloids than anything previously published in one of their own newspapers. The single word said it all: 'Debacle'.

A few days after England's great triumph, they eased past Albania 2–0 at St James' Park, a scoreline that left them only needing a result equal to Germany's in their final qualifier against Greece at Old Trafford on 6 October to make it straight through to the 2002 World

Cup finals. But this qualifying group still had a few more twists and turns. At the team hotel the day before the Greece match, Eriksson warned that his men still faced 'ninety minutes of hard, difficult work'. And so it proved. Five weeks after looking like world beaters in Germany, England produced a performance that was at best mundane and could have been far worse.

Owen, the hero of Munich, was missing through injury and replaced by his Liverpool colleague, Robbie Fowler. Nigel Martyn came in for the injured David Seaman. A packed Old Trafford, glowing in the autumn sun, had been in carnival mood before kick-off; the national anthem sung with particular gusto and resounding around the Salford sky. Once play got under way, however, England were disappointing, struggling to make headway against an efficient and tightly knit Greek team. Gerrard, so often the driving force behind England in Germany, was far from his best, giving away too many errant passes and caught out of position too often. The most England could muster in terms of first-half attacks came from set pieces; while Greece shaved the crossbar though Charisteas, who was several times wasteful in front of Martyn. Nevertheless he made the breakthrough on thirty-six minutes when Rio Ferdinand's poor clearance found him on the edge of the box and he drilled the ball into the back of the England net.

Eriksson responded by bringing on Andy Cole at half-time, but England still dithered, were ineffective in front of goal while looking susceptible to Greek counter-attacks. Only David Beckham, celebrating his first anniversary as England captain, was anything other than ordinary. Single-handedly he dragged England back into the game, willing on his team-mates, taking the game to the opposition and rattling the Greek defence with his deadly right boot. On sixty-six minutes Eriksson withdrew the ineffective Fowler, bringing on Teddy Sheringham. Almost immediately the substitution paid dividends. A minute later, Beckham dipped in a free-kick and Sheringham glanced home England's equaliser.

But the joy was short-lived. A couple of minutes later, more suspect defending let Dabizas flick on a free-kick and Nikolaidis restored Greece's lead. England began to look increasingly desperate as the clock ticked down. The frantic efforts of Beckham and Sheringham became increasingly forlorn as ninety minutes, defeat, and a play-off edged ever closer.

Then, in injury time, one final opportunity presented itself when a free-kick was awarded just outside the Greeks' penalty area. Beckham picked up the ball and placed it in position. Sheringham, his former Manchester United colleague, offered to take it but Beckham, by far the best England player on the day, held onto it. 'I was feeling exhausted and a little desperate that it had to go in,' Beckham revealed. 'I'd been taking free-kicks all afternoon and it wasn't like me not to hit the target and make the goalkeeper work. Every time I missed it I was just waiting for another chance, and another one and another one. I knew that it was our last chance . . .'

This was Beckham's ninth free-kick of the afternoon and as the England captain stepped up an entire nation expected. Striding up to the ball, he struck it beautifully and in less than half a second it had rocketed into the top corner of the net. An exultant Beckham, his face contorted with absolute joy, ran towards the crowd, punching the air in celebration. The iconic image of this latter-day Adonis, clad in white, hand reaching for the sky, facing thousands of fans, their faces framed in ecstasy, was a timely reminder of what makes this game so glorious.

'David was the driving force today so he deserved the goal,' said Beckham's colleague and close friend Gary Neville afterwards. 'You'll have to ask him if it was his finest moment, but right now I can't think of anything better than taking your country to the World Cup finals. It doesn't happen every day that's for sure.' Sheringham, who had wanted to take the free-kick and had brought England back into the game, said: 'The captain led by example. He was magnificent. He was the one who dug deep, who took the game by the scruff of the neck and drove us on.' When the midfielder went up to the press room, one after another the assembled journalists stood up and started clapping. 'That's something that never happens,' recalled Beckham in his autobiography. 'Thinking back to after France 98, it's certainly not something I'd have ever imagined happening to me. I hope those guys know how good they made me feel that afternoon.'

Sven-Göran Eriksson and his captain were – for a few months anyway – deified figures who could do no wrong. In football, however, such goodwill is usually temporary, not least at national level, where expectations are always high and the competing fancies and opinions of such a vast array of supporters so diverse. Eriksson, untouchable in his first year as England manager, soon learned of the fickle side of the English public, and particularly the press. A number of lukewarm performances in friendly matches left many followers pondering whether England had peaked too early.

Certainly, in the run-up to the 2002 World Cup, England had at least four stars of world-class standard, and the same number with the potential to match them. But this talent was spread in patches across his squad. England could count on no fewer than three top-class midfielders – Beckham, Steven Gerrard, and Paul Scholes – but no naturally left-footed midfielder of any sort of quality, nor the sort of midfield destroyer that those same men relied on at club level to allow them to prosper so magnificently. Michael Owen could unquestionably claim to be one of the top strikers in the world but lacked a decent foil, leaving Eriksson to alternate between the questionable qualities of Emile Heskey or the veteran, Sheringham. England could count on a number of excellent defenders, but when Gary Neville became injured on the eve of the World Cup finals, it was left to the limited Danny Mills to fill the vacant right-back position. And was there really no better English goalkeeper than David Seaman, who at the age of thirty-seven combined the mesmerising with the mistakes of a man past his best?

England's friendly matches were no real way to find out. Eriksson regarded them as little more than training exercises, regularly bringing on eight or more substitutes over the course of ninety minutes. These turgid encounters frequently lacked flow and excitement and worse still made a mockery of football. The crowd of 36,000 who turned up to Elland Road to witness no fewer than eleven substitutions and a 1–2 defeat to Italy at the end of March 2002, could surely not have come away feeling anything less than short changed.

Questions about Eriksson's personal and professional trustworthiness began to proliferate. Rumours linking him to the Manchester United job surfaced when author Michael Crick revealed in his biography of Alex Ferguson, published in April 2002, that negotiations had taken place between Eriksson's representatives and the Old Trafford board for him to replace Alex Ferguson as manager at the start of the 2002–03 season, when Ferguson was due to retire.

(Ferguson later reversed his decision.) The press also ruminated on the fact that Eriksson, so circumspect at FA press conferences, was freely available to endorse various products, which netted him, it was believed, £1.3 million in the run-up to the World Cup.

His image portrayed him as the apotheosis of everything that was mild-mannered and discreet, but Eriksson had gone into the England job with a little-known – but eventful – past as a 'ladies' man'. When Sampdoria manager he had left his wife for another woman; then at Lazio had cuckolded a wealthy Rome lawyer and prominent fan, whose wife Nancy Dell'Olio became his glamorous partner. It was with her that he moved to London, yet it didn't take the manager's roving eye long to settle on Britain's other prominent Swede, the television presenter Ulrika Jonsson. The inevitable explosion of tabloid headlines that greeted their affair was accompanied by suggestions that the invasion of his private life would precipitate his early departure from Soho Square. Always guarded about personal matters, Eriksson retained a dignified silence, treating the intrusions with a barely suppressed bemusement.

In any case he had bigger worries by then. The perception was that Beckham and Eriksson had the potential to form the sort of captain–manager relationship which had characterised the managerial reigns of Alf Ramsey and Walter Winterbottom. Just as Ramsey had built his great sides around Bobby Moore, and Winterbottom his around Billy Wright, so it was believed that Beckham would be the lynchpin of the squad that would travel to the Far East. Less than two months before the start of the tournament, however, disaster struck when Beckham, playing for Manchester United in a Champions League match against Deportivo La Coruna, was the subject of a late tackle that saw him carried off the pitch. Updates on the injury led the news agenda over the following week with speculation that the blow – a broken metatarsal in Beckham's foot – would keep him out of the World Cup altogether, speculation which later focused on the precise schedule of his recovery.

As it happened Beckham missed the remainder of Manchester United's season, and all of England's remaining warm-up games, but was ready for England's opening World Cup game against Sweden on 2 June 2002. Certainly he was fit; whether he was match fit would be open to question for the remainder of the tournament.

It was as well that he was able to make it as Eriksson's plans had already been upset by injury. Gary Neville was ruled out of the tournament after suffering a similar fracture to Beckham; and Steven Gerrard would miss the finals because of a groin injury. Owen was also nursing a thigh strain and the promising young midfield tyro, Kieron Dyer, who it was hoped would slot in on the problematic left flank, was also injured. To add to England's problems, FIFA's ludicrous seeding system (which ranked Ireland ahead of England) had placed them in the so-called 'group of death', the sort of nightmarish draw that seems to crop up in every tournament. As well as Sweden, who England had a miserable record against, they had been drawn against Argentina, who were by some distance the strongest nation in the South American qualifiers (Brazil, by contrast, had barely squeezed through) and Nigeria, widely regarded as the strongest African nation.

But it was against Eriksson's compatriots that England opened the 2002 World Cup finals. In the searing heat and humidity of south-east Asia – which would make this World Cup amongst the dullest in memory – England looked well off the pace. Despite taking the lead through Sol Campbell, they let the Swedes attack them and on several occasions were rescued by Seaman's heroics. Eventually a mistake by Danny Mills, who lost control of the ball outside his own area, led to a Swedish equaliser. Beckham had by then been substituted and was clearly not fit. By his own account, after a draw had been secured, he reckoned he was '90 per cent' although Eriksson observed that he would be stronger for having played the game and would be fully fit for England's next match against Argentina.

England had been lucky to come away with a draw. That the only man who came away with any praise was Seaman said much about the way the game had panned out. 'It's ridiculous that people say David Seaman is not the best goalkeeper in England,' said his Swedish counterpart Magnus Hedman. 'He is. He kept England in the game. He stopped us from winning 3–1. If England had lost it would have been very difficult for them to go through.' It certainly would have been, given that England were next up against Argentina. Could Eriksson exorcise more ghosts in the same fashion achieved so thrillingly in Munich nine months earlier? Boasting a core of players of immense experience, Argentina had emerged as pre-tournament favourites, eclipsing the achievements of all their rivals in South America's elongated qualification campaign. With a savage economic recession threatening to plummet the country towards Third World poverty-levels, success in the World Cup – as had been the case under the military junta in 1978 and after defeat in the Falklands War, in 1982 and 1986 – was more than just about football. 'Our country is in a very tough situation and we have the duty to do everything we can during this World Cup to restore its pride,' insisted the midfielder, Marcello Gallardo.

Added to these high stakes was the mutual antipathy which had characterised the relationship between the two teams all the way back to Antonio Rattin's antics in 1966. The revelation, in the days leading up to the match, that Argentina's players had goaded their English counterparts after England's exit from the World Cup in 1998 heightened tension. England's qualification for the knock-out stages hinged squarely on this match. To get past Argentina would not just add monumental impetus to England's chances but, in the context of the national team's history, it would also represent an historic achievement. In each of the genuinely big showdowns in every World Cup since their victory in 1966 – West Germany in 1970, Argentina in 1986, West Germany in 1990, and Argentina at France '98 – England had failed. Here now was a chance to stake their claim to resume their place amongst world football's aristocracy.

On a night of high tension and drama England put in a performance of consummate maturity that belied the relative youth of their side. Utilising the searing pace of Michael Owen, Eriksson's team allowed Argentina to weave pretty passing patterns in the heart of the pitch – they were to control much of the possession throughout – but tried to exploit them on the break. On twenty-five minutes Owen broke past two defenders on the right side of the pitch before letting fire with a shot from fifteen yards that found its way past Walter Samuel, but could not stay inside the far post. The ball cannoned back to the England forward but was cleared away for a corner. Seaman saved well from Batistuta and González, and as half-time approached it looked like this tightly balanced and intriguing battle would stand at a deadlock. Then, with a minute to go before the interval, Owen again found space and, as he brushed past Mauricio Pochettino into the penalty area, fell. The Italian referee, Pierluigi Collina, made no hesitation in pointing to the penalty spot.

Beckham claimed the ball and placed it. With nerves of steel, and ignoring the attempts of Diego Simeone to distract him, he walked up and drilled a withering shot into the centre of the Argentine net. England's considerable travelling contingent, and thousands more locals who had pledged allegiance to the team (and particularly Beckham), almost lifted the roof off the Sapporo Dome in celebration. Although he had proved himself many times over since that night in St Etienne, personal redemption was finally Beckham's. 'In those few seconds after the ball settled in the back of Argentina's net, I could see flashbulbs fire off around the ground,' he recalled. 'As each little explosion died against the blur and colour of the stands, it took everything that happened, everything that had been said or written since my red card in Saint Etienne, away into the night sky with it . . . The film that had been running in my head for so long stopped dead. Burnt away. Out of my mind for the first time in four years.'[1]

As the second half progressed, England cemented their grip on the game, reducing Argentina to long-range efforts which seldom seriously threatened Seaman's control of the goalmouth. Still England kept coming. On fifty-eight minutes Sheringham latched onto a cross on the right side of the penalty area and hit a venomous volley from twenty yards that was acrobatically punched away by the goalkeeper. No more goals, however, were to come and the win was England's.

It represented a stunning victory, upsetting one of the tournament's genuine contenders. 'The victory,' surmised Ashley Cole, 'made us realise we are a great team.' In the press conference afterwards Eriksson was reminded of the fact that in the space of just nine months he had led England to their two biggest results in years. 'They were two very good victories,' he said with characteristic understatement. 'It wouldn't be easy for any team to go to Germany and win 5–1, and Argentina were favourites for the World Cup when we played them.'

For one man, there was no mistaking the depth of England's achievement. 'It was the sweetest moment in my career,' David Beckham said of the match-winning penalty. 'After what happened last time, that game meant so much to me, and my family. To the whole country, in fact. As a footballing nation, we have been waiting for that result for a long time, and it was so nice that it came at the World Cup finals.' Asked by journalists how it compared to the 5–1 drubbing of Germany in Munich, Beckham was emphatic in his response. 'It definitely beat that,' he said. 'Germany was a massive result for us, but there is a lot of history to England v Argentina.'

The captain went on to add that impressive though England's result was, it would stand for nothing if England lost or even drew to Nigeria in their final group match. In the event England drew 0–0 in a pallid performance, but the failure to make the necessary breakthrough and take victory cost them winner's position in their group. This was more damaging than at first seemed. From eyeing a segment of the draw that would include a second-round tie with Senegal and potential quarter-final with either Turkey or Japan, England were instead left to face Denmark in round two with Belgium or Brazil to follow.

Denmark were tough, well-organised opponents, much along the lines of their Scandinavian counterparts Sweden, against whom England had laboured in their opening match. Indeed Denmark had already contributed to France's fall at the first stage, beating the reigning champions 2–0 in their final Group A match. With five Premiership players in Denmark's starting line-up and a sixth – Claus Jensen – coming on in the second half, the game could have been mistaken for a typical Saturday afternoon Premiership clash. Indifferent and disappointing against both Sweden and Nigeria but outstanding against Argentina; which England would come out against Denmark?

As early as the fourth minute, they dropped an almighty hint. Beckham's left-wing corner was headed across the face of goal by Rio Ferdinand, Owen stole in unnoticed at the far post and the goalkeeper, Thomas Sorensen, fumbled the ball over his own line. England could have added to their lead in the next ten minutes. Owen failed to connect properly with Beckham's chipped reverse pass; then Heskey's shot was well saved by Sorensen. England's second goal wasn't long in coming, however. On twenty-four minutes Butt flicked Sinclair's low centre through the legs of Thomas Gravesen and Owen turned a left-footed shot into the far corner. As half-time approached England confirmed their progress to the quarter-finals, when Danny Mills's throw-in was headed straight back to Beckham and his cross was rifled home by Emile Heskey. But victory had come at a price. Three of England's players – Beckham, Heskey and Owen – had picked up knocks. Attention was paid to the captain's troublesome left foot, but it was Owen's groin strain that was to prove the real problem. He had been substituted at half-time as a precaution, and after the match played down suggestions of injury, but time was to tell a different story.

And so to Brazil, who had impressed at the group stages, but were fortunate to get past Belgium in the second round. Belgium had controlled large stretches of the game and had a perfectly good goal disallowed for offside in the first half, before they fell to two goals – one very late on – in the second period. The Brazilian defender Roberto Carlos had described his country's meeting with England as the World Cup final by proxy, and said that the match would 'define Brazil's tournament'. He added: 'If we beat England, we can win the World Cup.'

Indeed, by the time the two great football nations met, many of the established powers had fallen: Holland had never made it to the finals and, as well as Argentina, France had fallen at the first hurdle. Italy had been beaten by unfancied South Korea in the second round and the co-hosts would go on to claim the scalp of Spain in the quarters. For the winners of England–Brazil, only the wretched German team England had put five past in Munich seemed to stand in their way.

So would the outcome of the 2002 World Cup be decided in Shizuoka? Certainly many thought so beforehand; and afterwards that hunch would prove correct. From the start it looked like England who would progress. Nicky Butt controlled the midfield, eclipsing Brazil's feted stars, Rivaldo and Ronaldinho. Michael Owen, clearly not fit, still managed to showcase his world-class pedigree in the twenty-third minute when he stole past Lucio and chipped Heskey's quick pass over the Brazilian goalkeeper to put England ahead. It was well deserved and excited the masses of England supporters, who chanted 'We're not going home'.

But the sweltering heat of the afternoon sun and the lack of fitness of some of England's key protagonists started to show as the half wore on and Brazil began to edge into the game. Had it remained 1–0 at half-time, Beckham believed, England might have won the World Cup. A delay, after David Seaman was treated for an injury, saw the game progress into stoppage time, and in it a misplaced Brazilian pass found Beckham on the right-hand side of the field. The midfielder, however, backed out of a challenge from Roberto Carlos, possibly thinking the ball was going out of play, but it stayed on the pitch and Brazil broke upfield. With mesmerising speed they attacked, playing around Paul Scholes's challenge. The ball was switched to Ronaldinho, he shimmied over the ball, throwing Ashley Cole. He then played in Rivaldo, superbly, who shot quickly past Seaman. It had been a *blitzkrieg* assault and psychologically threw England.

Four minutes into the second half worse followed. A free-kick way outside the England penalty area looked innocuous enough. Ronaldinho stepped over the ball without obvious menace and England players waited for a cross. It never came. Instead a swirling, bizarre cross-shot swooped high above the heads of the players and David Seaman, before nestling into the top corner of the net. It was a freak goal, but no fluke. Anyone who witnessed Ronaldinho's outstanding contributions for Barcelona over the following two years would see that this was a peculiar kind of genius at play – much like that of Garrincha, who had undone England in 1962.

Still reeling from Rivaldo's first-half goal, England looked beaten. It mattered little that there was still more than forty minutes left to play, nor that Ronaldinho was sent off ten minutes later for a studs-up challenge on Mills – England could neither summon the strength nor imagination to put the ten-man Brazil under sustained pressure. The purists' favourite team went through to a semi-final with Turkey, and England returned to Europe with barely a whimper.

'To be alive and not to die, that was the only thought we had,' said the Brazilian coach, Luis Felipe Scolari, afterwards. 'That was the only thing I had in my mind and this was the subject of the talk we had before the match amongst the players.' 'We should have done better with eleven men against ten, of course,' said Eriksson. 'We didn't use that advantage very much. I have to congratulate Brazil, they have a very good football team . . . We seemed tired and we lost a little bit of our shape. Again we knocked in balls to the three centre-backs of Brazil instead of having more patience and playing the ball, trying to come around them.'

Not for years had there been such an open World Cup; nor England a better chance of winning it. Yet there had been something very wrong about England's performance that June afternoon in Japan. Tactically there had been none of the naivety that had so undone England performances of old; but at the same time there was no imagination, no verve, no individual who could pull off something out of the ordinary. Without doubt, England would have benefited from the cut and thrust that the injured Steven Gerrard brought to the side but, in his absence, there was neither the invention amongst the players on the pitch, nor the sort of quality on the bench to substantially change events. The heat and injuries to key players also played their part: it seems unlikely that a fully fit David Beckham would have backed out of *that* challenge with Roberto Carlos; and a fit Owen would have made a more substantial contribution.

But there was something more fundamental behind England's problems. They seemed to amble to defeat, spirit crushed like so many of their continental rivals over the years. It all seemed so very unEnglish, as if the phlegmatic Swede was unable to lift or inspire his players, get them to raise their game when the chips were down. Of course, culpability could not solely rest on his shoulders. England had succeeded with mild-mannered managers before. Winterbottom, Ramsey and Greenwood were not shouters or bawlers, but they had players on the pitch that could do their leading for them. As captain Beckham – like Bobby Moore or Billy Wright before him – was no rabble rouser and led by example, but his two illustrious predecessors had at least had individuals of charisma to back them up. Indeed many England sides had been characterised by the gutsiness of its players, the sort of men who would be inspired by an 'England Expects' battlecry. By contrast, in the first years of the twenty-first century England fans were left asking themselves where the Terry Butchers and Jack Charltons of yesteryear had gone. Where was the fight, where was the spirit? England expected more from its men, but maybe it was a symptom of modern football that these figures belonged to the game's past.

England returned home to a mixed reception, and Brazil went on to win a tournament that had been memorable mostly for its mediocrity, the sweltering heat that contributed to the largely turgid football and the fact that most of the matches in Britain were watched over cornflakes and coffee, rather than the sort of beverages that can make bad games seem better with every sip.

That same summer another momentous development in the history of English football occurred. Far away from the high-tech glamour of Sapporo and Shizuoka, on the ground of an unheralded amateur football club in Austria strode the future of English football. Everton, one of the fallen aristocrats of the game, were on a pre-season tour and up against the minor league side SC Bruck. Included in the team that day was a sixteen-year-old local lad, who had almost single-handedly propelled the Everton youth team into the final of the previous season's FA Youth Cup, and had attracted the notice of fans beyond his football-mad hometown. Even the Tannoy announcer at the tiny Austrian ground realised history was being made as he announced the teams – and the youngster's debut. 'Das Neue Alan Shearer,' he proclaimed to the tiny Styrian stadium, before announcing his name to the several-hundred-strong crowd: 'Wayne Rooney.'

The prodigy marked his first start for Everton with a goal in a 3–1 win and twenty-four hours later, against SC Weiz, struck a hat-trick in a 10–2 romp. 'Everton have an exceptional young talent who looks ready to explode into the national consciousness this season,' reported the *Liverpool Echo*'s Everton correspondent, David Prentice. 'It's a long time since Evertonians had to force themselves to contain anything like excitement, but that's what happening now.'

Two months later he exploded into football's collective conscious. Already a league debutant on the opening day of the season, and the player of several bit-part roles, Rooney was brought on with ten minutes to go in Everton's league fixture with Arsenal on 19 October. Arsenal, reigning champions and unbeaten in their previous twenty-nine league fixtures, were formidable opponents, and with the score tightly balanced at 1–1 it required something truly special to break the deadlock. In the final minute of normal time a high awkward pass was played to Rooney thirty-five yards from goal. His first touch was immaculate and, turning instantaneously, he hit a fearsome swerving shot that dipped over David Seaman and rebounded off the crossbar to nestle in the back of the net. 'Remember the name,' yelled the ITV commentator, Clive Tyldesley, struggling to make himself audible above the tumult, 'WAYNE ROONEY!'

This was more than a special goal, more even than the strike that brought Arsenal's seemingly inexorable Premiership march to a halt; it was an unequivocal statement of genius.

Four months later, Eriksson made the teenager England's youngest-ever international – at the age of seventeen years 111 days – when he brought him on as a second-half substitute for the national side's latest friendly farce, against Australia at Upton Park. Rooney was one of eleven substitutes in a game that ended in a miserable 1–3 defeat. It said much about the innocence of youth that the new cap's girlfriend was unable to attend because she was starring in a school performance of *Bugsy Malone.*

England's insipid performances since their victory over Denmark in Japan were, by spring 2003, a cause of growing concern. As well as the Australia and Brazil defeats, they had not impressed in their opening European Championship qualifiers against Slovakia and Macedonia, in the latter of which they had twice come from behind to draw 2–2. When they could only muster two goals against the part-timers of Liechtenstein on 29 March 2003, the calls for the increasingly lethargic Heskey to make way for Everton's teenage sensation became louder than ever. Three days later, at the Stadium of Light in Sunderland, Eriksson gave Rooney his first start in England's crunch qualifier with Turkey – who had finished a surprise third place in the previous summer's World Cup.

Coming into a team whose football had begun to slip from the staid to the sterile, the kid transformed England, serving as the pivotal figure in a performance that bristled with panache and skill. He almost scored just eleven minutes in, seeing a shot blocked and then watching in frustration as David Beckham drove the loose ball wide. That set the tone; thereafter Rooney was always at the heart of things, opening up gaps in the Turkish defence with his intelligent running off the ball, dropping deep to offer options to the England midfield. On one occasion he juggled the ball past two Turkish defenders before volleying a pass out to Steven Gerrard on the wing, from whose cross England should have profited. Shortly after Rooney took it past two men, caught sight of goal and played in Owen, who took the ball around the Turkish goalkeeper before losing track of the ball. Darius Vassell would put England in front after coming on for Owen, with Beckham adding a second from a late penalty, but the night belonged to the Everton man, whose name was sung out around the Stadium of Light long after he had himself been substituted.

'Rooney has what no amount of age or experience can bestow,' wrote Paul Hayward in the *Daily Telegraph*, 'an instinctive sense of where the goal is and how to get there fast . . . [He] is a player for tomorrow – but he deserves his garland through fire today.' Even Brian Glanville, who, in fifty years as a journalist had seen more than most, eulogised:

With his enviable big match temperament, his precocious strategic sense, allied to his strength, skill and pace, it was Rooney who'd drop back in midfield when so little was coming, pick up the ball, beat opponents with splendid jugglery, then produce the kind of pass of which any playmaker might be proud. The idea that he should somehow be kept in cotton wool . . . is absurd. Some players may indeed be fragile and immature at seventeen. A few salient examples – George Best, Norman Whiteside, Diego Maradona, the great Pele himself – are indeed the exceptions that prove the rule. Rooney, in a word, saved Eriksson's skin.[2]

Perhaps that was hyperbole, but by the time England travelled to Turkey in October, needing a draw to progress to the following summer's European Championships in Portugal, the boy wonder was as integral a part of the England set-up as David Beckham and Michael Owen. Beckham, the subject of a recent transfer between Manchester United and Real Madrid, had been a lesser force since his metatarsal injury eighteen months earlier, and skyed a first-half penalty, which, fortunately, mattered not. England held on for a goalless draw and progression to their fifth consecutive tournament.

Concern about David Beckham's form bubbled on throughout the 2003–04 season. Certainly he seemed to have lost some of his swagger, and it was occasionally suggested that Eriksson ought to experiment with an alternative: Chelsea's Joe Cole, or even Manchester City's Shaun Wright-Phillips, the son of Ian Wright. Eriksson repeatedly stated his faith in Beckham; but the England captain was just about the only man with whom he retained a degree of fidelity. The ever-changing landscape of English football had seen a stunning new development in the summer of 2003 when the Russian billionaire, Roman Abramovich, had bought Chelsea and, allegedly, saved them from impending administration. Tycoons had been buying into English football clubs for as long as the game was old, but Abramovich's wealth was in a new league. Only in his mid-thirties, he had accumulated an oil fortune worth some £7 billion in the wild east of post-Soviet Russia. What his purchase of Chelsea effectively meant was that no player was beyond the west London club's financial reach – as the £110 million spending deluge in his first two months attested.

Nor, it seemed, was anybody else. Peter Kenyon, Manchester United's dogmatic chief executive, was poached and rumours about the future of Chelsea's genial manager, Claudio Ranieri, soon abounded. The choice of Kenyon and Abramovich was apparently Sven and talk that the Swede would replace Ranieri heightened when Eriksson was spotted leaving the Russian's London mansion shortly after the takeover. The England manager had said, with that imperceptibly straight Scandinavian face of his, that he had merely been visiting for 'tea'. That there was no movement then came as a surprise; that Chelsea began assembling an expensive new squad based on players who had brought Eriksson so much success at Lazio suggested Ranieri was merely the custodian of the manager's job until Eriksson saw fit to leave Soho Square.

When Eriksson was photographed the following March leaving Kenyon's home it prompted accusations of outright betrayal. His actions 'were worse even than that of Don Revie', believed the *Sunday Telegraph*'s Roy Collins. At least Revie had the 'decency', he added, to wear a disguise when heading out for his clandestine negotiations with the UAE FA in 1977. Eriksson, by contrast, 'brazenly turned up at Kenyon's door in his official FA limousine'.

When the FA took Eriksson to task on this, the outcome was extraordinary. While many fans and commentators demanded Eriksson's immediate resignation, and more still his sacking (which would have landed the FA a multi-million-pound compensation bill), the FA instead renegotiated his contract, extending its length by two years to 2008 and handed him a million-pound pay rise.

At the press conference called to announce this development Eriksson brazenly justified his dalliance with Chelsea, accusing the press of making him feel like a 'criminal'. Showing astonishing arrogance, he added:

> I have great difficulties in understanding that with this England job you should be a saint, you shouldn't earn a lot of money or have a private life and should absolutely not listen to other great possibilities in life. If I have ambition in life, I will listen to other jobs as well. You should be allowed to do that even if you're England manager. That's common sense and a normal work ethic. I have the right to do that. I've listened many times to other jobs.

Eriksson had unquestionably demonstrated that crime, or at least perceived crime, did pay and, shrugging off the attentions of the press, left the room, his grin betraying the knowledge that he would be leaving the England job at least £4 million the richer.

Eriksson's extraordinary display of disloyalty certainly eroded some of the goodwill and deference shown towards him as the 2004 European Championships in Portugal approached. The feats of Arsène Wenger's incredible Arsenal team in 2003–04 – Premiership winners without a single league defeat – increased the scrutiny on the England manager and those who had compared the two men were left to rethink verdicts that had once put Eriksson and Wenger in the same bracket. It was still true, of course, that Eriksson was a clever and skilled manager, but he lacked Wenger's single-minded approach, and if he was a football 'Professor' – as Adam Crozier had pronounced on his appointment – one would have to place him at a former polytechnic to Wenger's Harvard. To paraphrase a popular terrace chant: '£4 million a year, You're having a laugh!'

Whatever the common feeling about the flirtatious Swede, in the weeks leading up to Euro 2004 England rolled out millions of red and white flags in pubs, from windows and seemingly from the top of every other car in the land. It marked an extraordinary – unprecedented even – demonstration of patriotism, as if VE Day, the Coronation and St George's Day had been merged into one and stretched out to last the month of June. Hope and hype are one thing, expectation quite another, but the latter was as high as ever following a rampant Rooney-inspired win over Iceland when England's boy wonder scored two before making way for Heskey at half-time in a 6–1 victory.

It marked a return to form for the Evertonian, who had endured a mixed second season at Goodison Park. It began with accusations from his manager, David Moyes, that he was overweight but soon degenerated into a series of niggling disputes with the club. Everton had finished a woeful seventeenth, and despite nine goals and flashes of intermittent brilliance Rooney had contributed little to their stuttering campaign, sidetracked, it seemed, by the influence of his odious agent Paul Stretford, who was agitating for his client's transfer to Manchester United. It was England that he reserved his best for, as if the higher level was the only stage that befitted his superior talents.

England had again been burdened with an unfavourable draw – this time they faced a fading but still lethal France at the group stage, along with Switzerland and Croatia. From the very moment the draw had been made the previous December, the meeting had been the most keenly anticipated of the tournament: the reigning champions and rump of the 1998 World Cup winning side against English football's so-called golden generation; the heart of Wenger's wonderful Arsenal side in blue, against the rest of the Premiership's various contenders. Would the English provide a more telling challenge this time? Absolutely.

As in Sapporo two years earlier, this was a game for the gifted and mature. Charges that France were a spent force after their ignominious exit from the previous World Cup were premature. No side containing two of the leading scorers – Thierry Henry and David Trezeguet – from the Premiership and Serie A could possibly be underestimated. No team with a midfield that included Zidane, Vieira and Pires was ever going to be impotent. A nation that hadn't conceded a goal in seventeen hours of football was never going to be a pushover.

The first half was testy and tight, with France claiming the balance of play. England held their own, however, their most potent threat coming from the right, where it was obvious that Eriksson's men had identified a weakness and targeted the diminutive and aging presence of Bixente Lizarazu. In the thirty-seventh minute this paid off gloriously. Beckham seized on another pass in Lizarazu's sphere and, as he surged past, the veteran shoved him over, giving England a free-kick in a hugely promising position on the right. From it, England's stand-in centre-back, Ledley King, wreaked havoc with a dummy run, and Beckham's free-kick met the head of Frank Lampard, who glanced home the opener.

Wild celebration gave way to concentration on the task in hand. England defended magnificently, even if the French were an increasingly potent threat: Trezeguet headed over, Pires nutmegged Cole and Zidane struck passes around the Stadium of Light as if he owned not just the ball, but the pitch itself. Yet England were not content to defend alone, and though they concentrated on galvanising their back-line, they posed intermittent threats. On seventy-three minutes Rooney's moment came. Picking up the ball near the halfway line he span and in an instant was away from Claude Makelele. Fast and adroit, the teenager was untouchable as he bore down on goal. Unable to halt him by fair means, Mikael Silvestre chose foul and scythed the teenager down. Penalty! Rooney had made his mark even if David Beckham didn't from the spot-kick – he missed.

After seventy-six minutes Eriksson brought Emile Heskey on for Rooney. Although the teenager had a comparatively quiet game, only with his departure did it become apparent just how much England had been reliant on his power and pace. In the final seconds Heskey needlessly gave away a foul on the edge of his own penalty area. From the free-kick that resulted, Zinedine Zidane curled the ball brilliantly beyond the grasp of David James. England then fell apart. Steven Gerrard made a suicidal backpass; James brought down Thierry Henry for a penalty and Zidane made it 2–1.

Not since Manchester United had overcome Bayern Munich in the dying minutes of the 1999 Champions League final had a team been left reeling after such a late turnaround. When shock gave way to soul-searching, the importance of Rooney to England's cause was underlined. It was, believed the *Daily Telegraph*, a 'tremendous performance from the teenager. He held the ball up like a giant and the run for the penalty was stunning – so confident.' The *Guardian* named him their man of the match, citing 'a fearless performance even by the teenager's remarkable standards'.

Four days later against Switzerland, Rooney made explicitly clear that he was destined to become Euro 2004's outstanding presence. England had started the match in a patchy manner, neither asserting themselves with any great authority nor playing with much élan. Rooney was booked for a clumsy challenge and warned by the referee when he mistimed a second tackle. Then, on twenty-three minutes, Switzerland lost the ball in midfield, England switched it to the right where Gerrard was fouled but the referee played on and the ball fell to Beckham. He played his cross deep into the Swiss penalty area, where it was controlled by Owen, who clipped the ball back across the face of goal and there was Rooney, angling home a simple stun header to make himself the youngest goalscorer in the history of the European Championships.

Over the minutes that followed, Rooney and Gerrard, the tireless Frank Lampard and excellent Ashley Cole combined to make a mockery of the Swiss coach's earlier hopes that England would be 'scarred' by the previous Sunday's late defeat to France. Rooney's second on seventy-five minutes was marked by the sort of brute force and dazzling panache that had come to be synonymous with his name. Darius Vassell fought to reach a pass from his fellow substitute Owen Hargreaves and touched the ball on to Rooney. Bearing down on the Swiss goalkeeper, Jorg Stiel, he shaped to drag the ball wide, but instead – glimpsing but an inch of light – arrowed a bullet-like shot at his near post, which cannoned off the upright back off Stiel's head and into the net. Though it went in only by virtue of a ricochet, there are few players in the world who could have placed a shot with such devastating force and accuracy into so tight an angle. If there were any who still doubted the supremacy of Rooney's ability, here was confirmation of the kid's genius. Late on Gary Neville's cross on the overlap was met by Gerrard, who drove it past Stiel for England's third goal.

Even by the fantastic standards set against Switzerland, Rooney's Euro 2004 zenith was still to come. In England's third group match against Croatia they needed a draw to progress to the quarter-finals, but got off to the worst possible start when careless defending allowed Niko Kovac to give Croatia a fifth-minute lead. England fought back strongly, but failed to make possession count. All toil and no inspiration, they were seemingly grinding to a goalless first half performance when, in the fortieth minute, Michael Owen was put through on goal. Tomislav Butina, the Croatia keeper, blocked Owen's shot with his feet, the ball span up to Rooney who, instead of heading goalwards, picked out Paul Scholes with a glance of instinctive brilliance, and the Manchester United player struck the equaliser. Before half-time came, Rooney made another telling contribution: Scholes, repaying the earlier compliment, laid the ball off to him twenty-five yards from goal and Rooney rifled home an unstoppable shot to make it 2–1.

Having engineered England's comeback, Rooney was bursting with confidence and dominated the second half. He made chances for Scholes, then Owen, one of which was saved, the other landing on the roof of the net. With his colleagues not quite displaying the same ruthlessness, on sixty-eight minutes Rooney went alone and did it all himself. Playing a wall pass with Owen, he skipped through the Croat defence and, barely looking up, slipped the ball past Butina for his second and England's third. Four minutes later Eriksson brought the Everton star off to a standing ovation, the win and England's place in the quarter-final all but secured, although further goals from both sides – England's from Lampard; Croatia's from Igor Tudor – would bring the overall tally to 4–2 in England's favour.

Rooney knew all about hyperbole, but the earlier praise must have seemed subdued following his second brace of the tournament. Starting with the normally muted Eriksson, who compared him to Pele, the rest of the world took their lead. The Brazilian ignored the comparison but admitted that Rooney had emerged as one of the tournament's 'finest players'. Eusebio was also glowing in his praise: 'He has everything to become one of the best players in Europe, and maybe the world,' said the legendary Portuguese striker. 'He is a great talent, but it is important for him to keep working had and to stay humble. I know Sven-Göran Eriksson has said he reminds him of Pele, but I don't like those comparisons. Pele played in the 1960s, like me, like Bobby Charlton, but Rooney is playing now so we should let him make his own path.'[3] The *Sun* even reported the unlikely scene of Prince William celebrating his twenty-second birthday watching the game in a village pub near Highgrove and chanting Rooney's name in adulation.

England's failure, nevertheless, to top their qualifying group, as in the World Cup two years earlier, would prove costly. Rather than facing dark horses Greece, they were up against tournament hosts Portugal with their complement of world-class stars and home backing. Not that it necessarily counted for much. Lisbon had been taken over by the English, with vast expanses of the Stadium of Light dominated by white shirts and George crosses. The streets and squares of the city were crammed with the ticketless and hopeful, the air ringing out with choruses of 'England! England!' and 'Rooney's going to get you!' 'I can't remember a better time for England to win a tournament since the World Cup in 1990,' wrote the usually circumspect Alan Hansen in the *Daily Telegraph*. 'When they come off the pitch tonight, win or lose, those players must be sure that they have given it the very best shot. Football is about taking your opportunities to win trophies, about performing on those finite number of occasions throughout your career when the stakes could not be higher. Now is that time for England.'

At 7.45 p.m., the whistle of the Swiss referee Urs Meier sounded and play got under way. Three minutes in, Michael Owen – Rooney's forebear as England's brightest young thing – raced onto a poor back-header by Costinha, and flicked the ball sweetly over the head of the onrushing Portuguese goalkeeper and into the back of the net. 1–0 and England already had a foot in the semi-final.

For the next twenty minutes, England purred like a lioness;

controlling what unfolded before them but maintaining their deadly intent. Shortly before the half-hour-mark, Rooney, the lurking, lethal tyro, chased a long ball into the Portuguese half. Vying for possession with Jorge Andrade, the Deportivo La Coruna defender accidentally caught the eighteen-year-old's foot. Rooney pulled up straight away; tried to walk the knock off; before breaking down and being substituted. X-rays would reveal a broken metatarsal in his foot. His time in the sun was at an end.

Without their young thoroughbred, England's momentum waned. For the following fifty-five minutes they clung on relentlessly to their lead, but it was – at times – a hair-raising reminder of the match against Brazil (whom Portugal's manager, Scolari, had also managed in 2002). England lacked menace and adventure. Darius Vassell, Rooney's replacement, was simply not of the same calibre as the teenager but Eriksson's subsequent switches – Owen Hargreaves for Scholes and, inexplicably, Philip Neville for Gerrard – added little to England's cause. When Helder Postiga headed in an equaliser in the eightieth minute it had an aura of inevitability.

Still England could – and absolutely should – have won it. In the final minute, Michael Owen headed David Beckham's free-kick against the crossbar and, from the rebound, Sol Campbell headed the ball home. Inexplicably, unforgivably, Urs Meier disallowed the goal, later claiming that John Terry had impeded the Portuguese goal-keeper, Ricardo. It was almost an exact reprise of France '98 when Campbell's header should have led to victory over Argentina. Just as then, neither at the time nor in the multitude of replays screened over subsequent days, did it remotely resemble a foul.

In extra-time further drama was never far away. Rui Costa exploited a mistake by Philip Neville to score a wonder goal from the edge of the area, the strike that looked set to decide England's fate. But they refused to surrender and Lampard equalised with five minutes remaining, turning and shooting home Terry's towering header from Beckham's corner. It meant England's fate would be decided by penalties for the fifth time in their history. With just a solitary success – against Spain in 1996 – the portents for victory were not good, not least when Beckham missed England's opening shot. It was his third penalty miss for his country in nine months. Fortunately for England, though, Rui Costa missed Portugal's third penalty, the only Portuguese player to do so. After Owen, Lampard, Terry and

Hargreaves had all converted theirs, the shoot-out went into sudden death. Ashley Cole made it 5–4, Postiga drew Portugal level. Then it was the turn of Vassell, but his shot was low, poorly aimed and Ricardo swooped to save. He then stepped forward as Portugal's seventh taker and shot his country into the semi-finals.

'As a team we didn't really go on from 1–0 up,' said Sol Campbell. 'We let Portugal have a lot of possession, and they are a good attacking team. The law of averages meant that one of their attacks or power plays was bound to come off eventually.' Eriksson was less willing to concede that England's defensive mindset had cost them dearly. 'In three and a half years we have only lost three competitive games,' the manager proclaimed, holding out his hand, with forefinger and thumb extended to about an eighth of an inch apart. 'And each one was by this much. Each defeat had something strange about it.' The truth was, however, that for all the ill-fortune from twelve yards and for all the bad refereeing decisions that went against them, England were not the same force after Wayne Rooney's premature withdrawal. Gone was the spontaneity, absent was the pace and power he brought to the front line. Missing in attack, England had defended resolutely, but not doggedly enough to hold their opponents at bay. Though Rooney's influence had been all too apparent in the group stages, his absence provided even more compelling evidence of his importance to England. No longer was he just the brightest hope, he was the fulcrum of the national team. Without him Eriksson's England looked an ordinary force.

While the premature exit from another eminently winnable tournament begged further questions of Eriksson – and more particularly the value for money he provided – England stuttered through their World Cup qualifying group to secure a passage to the 2006 World Cup finals in Germany.

Eriksson used the qualifying campaign to introduce a new goalkeeper, Paul Robinson of Tottenham, who, though still reasonably inexperienced – particularly at the highest level – offered more stability than the erratic David James, or the doleful David Seaman who had preceded him. The emergence of Chelsea's Joe Cole as a viable option to fill the left-wing berth – a position which had caused

England managers since Graham Taylor no end of trouble – unquestionably came as a relief to Eriksson; likewise that of Shaun Wright-Phillips, whose arrival as a player of similar pedigree to his father (albeit on the right wing rather than up front) served to energise the occasionally pallid figure of David Beckham.

Yet the xenophobia the Swede had perpetually faced from sections of the British media, continually furious at his great crime – that he wasn't an Englishman – was finally to become too much. In January 2006, the *News of the World* set Eriksson up in a lavishly planned sting operation in Dubai with one of its reporters posing as an Arab sheikh interested in enlisting the Swede's help in developing football in the Emirate. Though it had shades of the Revie affair it was not a scandal of anything near the same proportions, and Eriksson's great mistake was to talk too freely to a covert newspaperman not interested in upholding even the most basic journalistic principles. Even then the *News of the World*'s headline 'The Sven Deadly Sins' was wholly over-stated, publishing such mundane revelations as Eriksson's opinion that Rio Ferdinand was sometimes 'lazy', that Michael Owen's recent move to Newcastle United had not been his first choice, and that Wayne Rooney came from a poor part of Liverpool. Yet there were also hints of the previous infidelities with Chelsea. Talking about a hypothetical takeover of Aston Villa, Eriksson put himself forward for the manager's job and then claimed he would get Beckham on board.

Despite this, the public response was generally sympathetic towards the Swede and angry at what amounted to an attempt to unsettle the England camp just months before a World Cup. The FA, however, took a different view and eight days later its Chief Executive Brian Barwick announced that Eriksson would be leaving his post after Germany. Barwick, who knew a thing or two about throwing money away (he had previously been Controller of ITV Sport when the corporation signed and later reneged on a TV deal with the Football League that nearly bankrupted the English football pyramid), agreed a severance package with Eriksson that newspapers said was worth between £1 million and £5 million. And for what? For nothing, the head of the so-called custodian of football had apparently frittered away millions of pounds. In theory, the first man to bring World Cup glory back to England since Alf Ramsey could be getting the divorce settlement to end all divorce settlements payable as soon as the party had ended. At a time when grassroots football was in dire need of investment, how many playing fields would Sven's alimony have paid for?

As the Germany World Cup approaches the talk is frequently of England's 'golden generation' once more. On paper the country's first choice line-up is as good as any which has represented football's founding nation since 1970. It includes eight players of world-class renown, including the finest left-back on the planet, Ashley Cole; the world's best central midfield pairing in Lampard and Gerrard; and arguably the most exciting player in the world, Wayne Rooney. Gaps do, nevertheless, exist. A lack of strength in depth in the forward line requires Owen and Rooney to stay fit and in form throughout tournaments, a reliance that has twice undone England in recent years. Lack of experience in goal and on the left should not be a problem, but at the highest level any momentary lapse can be deadly. The lack, also, of a credible midfield destroyer, a Nobby Stiles-type who can extinguish the fire in a Ronaldinho or Ballack, need not be a problem given the pre-eminence of Gerrard and Lampard, but the emergence of such a figure would give Eriksson another option.

Hypothesising about England's prospects in a World Cup or European Championships is the hobby of a thousand journalists and many millions more fans. The truth is that strength on paper doesn't count for everything; and perceived deficiencies can mean nothing. It is worth noting that Brazil won the 2002 World Cup with three men – Roque Junior, Kleberson and Juninho – who couldn't subsequently cut it in the Premiership; and that France won the 1998 World Cup with the lamentable Stephane Gui'varch up front. It's worth remembering also that Geoff Hurst came from nowhere to replace England's then greatest goalscorer, Jimmy Greaves, to take England to their solitary World Cup glory. Michael Owen should take note.

Luck remains an important ingredient and, for generations, England have enjoyed little. Through Sol Campbell's disallowed goals in 1998 and 2004; bizarre free-kicks conceded against Brazil and West Germany in 2004 and 1990; four shoot-out defeats; Maradona's handball and Montezuma's revenge, you have to cast your mind back to 1966 and the apparent misjudgement of the Azeri linesman, Tofik Bahkramov, as a clear example of England getting a clear break when it counted most.

The insatiable expectation of England's support tends to overlook all these factors, however. In a way it is natural; we believe our country can achieve glory whether we have Michael Owen or Michael Ricketts (one of Eriksson's less successful experiments) up front. It's a hark back to the mantra of England Expects that we should win come what may. Unfortunately life isn't as simple as that. Football is at once an utterly logical and wholly illogical game – logical because the best team usually prevails; nonsensical because they don't always. England have the strength on paper to be world champions in 2006 but only, however, if breaks go their way.

Victory requires other factors too. Casting an eye over the glorious summer of 1966, one can draw comparisons between Alf Ramsey's great side and Eriksson's: the explosive spontaneity of Rooney is reminiscent of Bobby Charlton; the fire in the belly of Alan Ball is like that of Gerrard; for the grace of Ray Wilson, read Ashley Cole. And so it goes on.

More than any one individual, however, Bobby Moore represented the best of England and Englishness – reserve, dignity, diligence, greatness as player and as a man. He, perhaps more than anyone, took his country to the very summit of football glory. He had always been more than just a great player, more even than England's World Cup winning captain. He was English football's answer to baseball's Joe DiMaggio, symbolising not only the game's great generation, but its majesty, elegance and decorum. David Beckham is often cited as Moore's natural successor. It is true that they both have much in common – east London boys, iconic figures, both England captains – but Beckham is definitively a man of his time, representative of as much that is bad about the modern game as good. There's something unquestionably contrived about him; Moore, on the other hand, exuded a natural grace and authority.

If England are to succeed in Germany and beyond – who will fill Moore's boots, not so much for his football qualities but his quiet assurance on the pitch, his leadership by example, the decorum he afforded his country? It's a question I pondered for some time while writing an article about Moore for the *Observer* a year before England were to travel to Germany. Asking around, the same name cropped up with ceaseless regularity: Beckham and, occasionally, Michael Owen. Yet with both of these individuals there seemed to be something missing, as if they were imperceptibly tainted by the cynicism of modern football.

Only when I spoke to Moore's great friend and former team-mate,

Frank Lampard senior, did the answer strike me. 'Bob ended up being my room-mate for about eight years off and on at West Ham,' he told me. 'I feel that I picked up a lot of his ways and habits. Going a step further, when I look at young Frank – on and off the field – I see Bobby Moore shining through. He's picked up things from me; and I picked things up from Bobby. I can see Bobby a lot of the time in the way he talks, even the way he stands and sits. I think there's a lot of Bobby Moore in Frank Lampard junior.'

I tell him about a dream I'd had a couple of nights earlier, in which his son scored the winning goal in the World Cup final. Afterwards, in a reprise of that immortal image from 1966, when Moore was hoisted onto the shoulders of Ray Wilson and Geoff Hurst, Lampard junior was lifted into the air by his team-mates and carried around the stadium, raising football's holy grail to an exultant crowd.

Frank Lampard smiles. 'That would be nice,' he laughs. 'That would be very nice.'

NOTES

1 Men of Destiny

1 Quoted in Seddon, Peter and Bloomer, Steve, *The Story of Football's First Superstar* (Breedon Books, Derby, 1999), pp. 16–17.
2 Quoted in Davies, Hunter, *Boots, Balls and Haircuts: An Illustrated History of Football from Then to Now* (Cassell Illustrated, London, 2003), p. 20.
3 Alcock, Charles, *Football: The Association Game* (G Bell & Sons, 1906).
4 Gibson, Alfred and Pickford, William, *Association Football and the Men Who Made It* (Caxton, London, 1906), vol. 2, p. 138.
5 Green, Geoffrey, *The History of the Football Association, 1863–1953* (Naldrett, London, 1953), p. 47.
6 Alcock, *op. cit.*, pp. 17–18.
7 *Ibid.*, p. 18.
8 *Ibid.*, pp. 18–19.
9 James, Brian, *England V Scotland* (Pelham, London, 1969), p. 21.
10 By the time that they wrote their extraordinary tome, however, 'Dribbling, like back-heeling, must be used with great discretion against anything like a powerful defence.' (Gibson and Pickford, *op. cit.*, vol. 2., p. 44.)
11 *Ibid.*, p. 38.
12 James, *op. cit.*, p. 38.
13 Quoted in Butler, Bryon, *The Official History of the Football Association* (revised edition, Aurora, London, 1993), p. 20.
14 Gibson and Pickford, *op. cit.*, vol. 2, p. 67.
15 Alcock, *op. cit.*, p. 46.
16 *Ibid.*
17 Gibson and Pickford, *op. cit.*, vol. 2, p. 43.
18 *Ibid.*, p. 45.
19 Keates, Thomas, *History of Everton Football Club* (1928, reprinted 1997 by Desert Island Books), p. 28.
20 Quoted in Inglis, Simon, *League Football and the Men Who Made It: The Official Centenary History of the Football League, 1888–1988* (HarperCollins Willow, London, 1988), p. 11.
21 Not until a week later did Notts County and Blackburn Rovers join the fray.

2 Gentleman Footballers, Soccer Superstars

1 Quoted in Walvin, James, *Football and the Decline of Britain* (Macmillan, Basingstoke, 1986), pp. 2–3.
2 Gibson and Pickford, *op. cit.*, vol. 1, p. 154.
3 *Ibid.*, p. 153.

4   *Ibid.*, p. 155.
5   Seddon and Bloomer, *op. cit.*, p. 83.
6   James, *op. cit.*, p. 61.
7   Gibson and Pickford, *op. cit.*, vol. 2, p. 35.
8   *Ibid.*, vol. 1, p. 196.
9   *Ibid.*, vol. 1, p. 165.
10   Seddon and Bloomer, *op. cit.*, pp. 86–7.
11   Gibson and Pickford, *op. cit.*, vol. 1, pp. 178–9.
12   Seddon and Bloomer, *op. cit.*, p. 57.
13   Gibson and Pickford, *op. cit.*, vol. 2, p. 150.
14   Seddon and Bloomer, *op. cit.*, pp. 55–6.
15   Gibson and Pickford, *op. cit.*, vol. 2, p. 64.
16   *Ibid.*, vol. 1. p. 156.
17   *Ibid.*, vol. 2. p. 156.
18   Seddon and Bloomer, *op. cit.*. p. 87.
19   *Ibid.*, p. 90.
20   *Ibid.* Although it is undoubtedly a good story, I was unable to find another account that verified it.
21   *Ibid.*, p. 98.
22   Gibson and Pickford, *op. cit.*, vol. 1, p. 197.
23   Shearman, Montague, *Badminton Library of Sports and Pastimes: Football History* (Longmans, Green & Co., London, 1899), pp. 148–51.
24   *Ibid.*, p. 105.
25   *Ibid.*
26   Edworthy, Niall, *England: The Official FA History* (Virgin, London, 1997), p. 18.
27   Butler, *op. cit.*, p. 46.
28   Edworthy, *op. cit.*, p. 18.

3   The Birth of Wembley and Inter-War Football

1   Kuper, Simon, *Ajax, The Dutch, The War* (Orion, London, 2003), p. 25.
2   James, *op. cit.*, p. 108.
3   Bastin, Cliff (with Brian Glanville), *Cliff Bastin Remembers* (Ettrick, Edinburgh, 1950), p. 60.
4   James, *op. cit.*, p. 118.
5   The Football Association would eventually refund nearly half of its £6365 share of receipts to ticket holders unable to claim their seats.
6   Rogers, Ken, *100 Years of Goodison Glory* (Breedon Books, Derby, 1998), p. 72.
7   Keith, John, *Dixie Dean: The Inside Story of a Football Icon* (Robson, London, 2001), p. 58.
8   Corbett, James, *Everton: The School of Science* (Macmillan, Basingstoke, 2003).
9   James, *op. cit.*, p. 124.
10   Studd, Stephen, *Herbert Chapman, Football Emperor* (Peter Owen, London, 1981), p. 106.
11   Butler, *op. cit.*, p. 67.
12   Matthews, Stanley, *The Way It Was: My Autobiography* (Headline, London, 2001).
13   *Ibid.*, p. 66.
14   Jones, Ken, *Jules Rimet Still Gleaming?* (Virgin, London, 2003), p. 2.
15   Green, Geoffrey, *op. cit.*, p. 552.
16   Kuper, *op. cit.*, pp. 33–4.
17   Hapgood, Eddie, *Football Ambassador* (Sporting Handbooks, London, 1944), p. 36.

18 *Ibid.*, p. 34.
19 *Ibid.*, p. 36.
20 Matthews, *op. cit.*, p. 119.
21 *Ibid.*
22 *Ibid.*, p. 122.
23 *Ibid.*, pp. 122–3.
24 Hapgood, *op. cit.*, p. 38.
25 Matthews, *op. cit.*, p. 116.
26 Bastin, *op. cit.*, p. 118.
27 Rous, Stanley, *Football Worlds: A Lifetime in Sport* (Faber and Faber, London, 1978), p. 64.
28 *Ibid.*, pp. 64–5.
29 Bastin, *op. cit.*, p. 143.
30 *Ibid.*
31 Kuper, *op. cit.*, p. 43.
32 *Ibid.*, p. 41.
33 Bastin, *op. cit.*, p. 144.
34 *Ibid.*, pp. 143–4.
35 Matthews, *op. cit.*, p. 117.
36 Rous, *op. cit.*, p. 104.
37 Hapgood, *op. cit.*, p. 51.
38 *Ibid.*, p. 53.
39 Matthews, *op. cit.*, p. 149.
40 *Ibid.*, p. 155.
41 Carter, Raich, *Footballer's Progress: An Autobiography* (Sporting Handbooks, London, 1950), p. 146.

4   Football at War

1   Carter, *op. cit.*, p. 146.
2   *Ibid.*, p. 147.
3   *Ibid.*, pp. 146–7.
4   Southend was one of the few clubs to reimburse its season-ticket holders.
5   Kuper, *op. cit.*, p. 149.
6   McCarthy, Tony, *War Games: The Story of Sport in World War Two* (Queen Anne's Press, London, 1989), p. 123.
7   Kuper, *op. cit.*, p. 154.
8   Lanfranchi, P. and Taylor, M., 'Professional Football in World War Two Britain', in P. Kircham and D. Thoms (eds), *War Culture: Social Change and Changing Experience in World War Two Britain* (Lawrence and Wishart, London, 1995), p. 194.
9   Matthews, *op. cit.*, pp. 196–8.
10 Lanfranchi and Taylor, *op. cit.*, p. 189.
11 Seddon and Bloomer, *op. cit.*, pp. 134–5.
12 Capel-Kirby, W. and Carter, F.W., The *Mighty Kick: Romance, History and Humour of Football* (Jarrolds, London, 1933).
13 Weintraub, Stanley, *Silent Night: The Remarkable Christmas Truce of 1914* (Simon and Schuster, London, 1997), p. 116.
14 *Ibid.*, p. 117.
15 *Ibid.*, p. 118.
16 James, *op. cit.*, pp. 165–6.
17 *Ibid.*, p. 169.
18 *Ibid.*, p. 164.

19   Quoted in Lanfranchi and Taylor, *op. cit.*, p. 189.

5   Waking Up to the World

1   *Football Update and Tom Stenners Magazine*, 10 May 1947.
2   Greaves, Jimmy (with Norman Giller), *Don't Shoot the Manager* (Boxtree, London, 1993), p. 12.
3   Leo McKinstry, *Jack and Bobby* (Collins Willow, London, 2002), p. 128.
4   Greaves, *op. cit.*, p. 16.
5   Matthews, *op. cit.*, p. 230.
6   *Picture Post*, 2 November 1946.
7   Quoted in Varley, Nick, *Golden Boy* (Aurum, London, 2002), p. 77.
8   Giller, Norman and Wright, Billy, *A Man for All Seasons* (Robson, London, 2002), p. 42.
9   *Sunday Pictorial*, 18 April 1949.
10   Matthews, *op. cit.*, pp. 301–3.
11   Varley, *op. cit.*, p. 112.
12   Lofthouse, Nat, *The Lion of Vienna* (Sportsprint Publishing, Edinburgh, 1989), p. 25.
13   Varley, *op. cit.*, p. 97.
14   Finn, Ralph L., *World Cup* (Panther Books, London, 1954), p. 6.
15   Finn, Ralph L., *My Greatest Game* (The Saturn Press, London, 1951), p. 132.
16   *Picture Post*, 8 July 1950.
17   Varley, *op. cit.*, p. 140.
18   *Picture Post*, 19 February 1949.
19   Varley, *op. cit.*, p. 147.
20   Green, Geoffrey, *Soccer in the Fifties* (Allan, London, 1974), p. 134.
21   Edworthy, Niall, *The Second Most Important Job in the Country* (Virgin, London, 1999), pp. 29–30.
22   Quoted in Jones, *op. cit.*, p. 35.
23   *Ibid.*, p. 40.
24   *Ibid.*, p. 41.
25   Taylor, Rogan and Jamrich, Karla (eds), *Puskás on Puskás* (Robson Books, London, 1997), p. 98.
26   Finney, Tom with David Jack, *Finney on Football* (Nicholas Kay, London, 1958), p. 78.
27   Finn, *World Cup*, p. 10.
28   Taylor, and Jamrich, *op. cit.*, p. 114.
29   Merrick, Gil, *I See It All* (Museum Press, London, 1954), p. 91.
30   Finn, *World Cup*, p. 21.
31   *Ibid.*, p. 20.
32   *Ibid.*, p. 44.
33   *Ibid.*, p. 41.
34   *Ibid.*
35   Green, *Soccer in the Fifties*, p. 18.

6   Bright Young Things

1   Haynes, Johnny, *It's All in the Game* (Arthur Baker, London, 1962), p. 62.
2   Shackleton, Len, *Clown Prince of Soccer* (Nicholas Kaye, London, 1955), p. 48.
3   Greaves, *op. cit.*, pp. 13–14.
4   Haynes, *op. cit.*, pp. 88–9.
5   Giller, *op. cit.*, p. 151.
6   Clayton, Ronnie, *A Slave to Soccer* (Stanley Paul, London, 1960), p. 86.

7 Haynes, *op. cit.*, p. 14.
8 *Ibid.*, p. 72.
9 *Ibid.*, p. 104.
10 Giller, *op. cit.*, p. 169.
11 McKinstry, *op. cit.*, p. 78.
12 Haynes, *op. cit.*, p. 105.
13 Roberts, John, *The Team That Wouldn't Die: The Story of the Busby Babes* (Vista, London, 1998), p. 98.
14 Haynes, *op. cit.*, p. 108.
15 Finney, *op. cit.*, p. 22.
16 Haynes, *op. cit.*, p. 107.
17 Finney, *op. cit.*, p. 16.
18 McKinstry, *op. cit.*, p. 106.
19 Giller, *op. cit.*, p. 187.
20 *Guardian*, 11 November 1999.
21 Edworthy, *The Second Most Important Job in the Country*, pp. 46–50.
22 Wright, Billy, *One Hundred Caps and All That*, (Robert Hale, London, 1962), p. 83.
23 Haynes, *op. cit.*, p. 196.
24 Greaves, *op. cit.*, p. 16.
25 Jones, *op. cit.*, p. 90.
26 Quoted in Bowler, Dave, *Winning Isn't Everything: A Biography of Alf Ramsey* (Gollancz, London, 1998), p. 158.
27 Haynes, *op. cit.*, p. 213.
28 Greaves, *op. cit.*, p. 11.
29 *News of the World*, 26 August 1962.

7 Alf Ramsey and the Making of World Champions

1 *Daily Express*, 6 August 1962.
2 Quoted in Jones, *op. cit.*, p. 50.
3 Bowler, *op. cit.*, pp. 138–9.
4 *Ibid.*, p. 159.
5 Marquis, Max, *Anatomy of a Football Manager: Sir Alf Ramsey* (Arthur Barker, London, 1970).
6 Hurst, Geoff, *1966 and All That: My Autobiography* (Headline, London, 2001), p. 75.
7 Moore, Bobby, *My Soccer Story* (Stanley Paul, London, 1966), p. 61.
8 Hutchison, Roger, *'66: The Inside Story of England's World Cup Triumph* (Mainstream, Edinburgh, 1995), p. 14.
9 Jones, *op. cit.*, p. 105.
10 Banks, Gordon, *Banksy: My Autobiography* (Michael Joseph, London, 2002), p. 102.
11 Allison, Malcolm with James Lawton, *Colours of My Life* (Everest Books, London, 1975), p. 147.
12 *Sun*, quoted in Bowler, *op. cit.*
13 Hutchison, *op. cit.*, p. 86.
14 McKinstry, *op. cit.*, p.101.
15 *Ibid.*, p. 180.
16 *Ibid.*, p. xvii.
17 Charlton, Jack, with Peter Byrne, *Jack Charlton: The Autobiography* (Partridge, London, 1996) p. 73.
18 In the event Charlton was to finish second to his Leeds United team-mate, Bobby Collins.
19 *Sun*, 12 April 1965.

20 *Soccer Star*, 21 May 1965.

21 *Soccer Star*, April 1962.

22 Hutchison, *op. cit.*, pp. 97–8.

23 Dowling, David, *The Best of Enemies: England V Germany, a century of football rivalry* (Bloomsbury, London, 2000), p. 100.

24 McKinstry, *op. cit.*, p. 185.

25 Hurst, *op. cit.*, p. 95. Jack Charlton once compared Ramsey with his club manager, Don Revie, and said that the main difference was that if you were watching a movie or playing a hand of cards, Revie would let you finish it before going to bed. Not so Ramsey.

26 McKinstry, *op. cit.*, p. 186.

27 Hurst, Geoff, *The World Game* (Stanley Paul, London, 1967), p. 26.

28 *Ibid.*, p. 27.

29 Hurst, *1966 and All That*, p. 95.

30 Powell, *Bobby Moore*, pp. 94–5.

31 *The Times*, 4 July 1966.

32 *Sun*, 4 July 1966.

33 Ball, Alan, *Ball of Fire* (Pelham, London, 1967), p. 72.

34 Jones, *op. cit.*, p. 118.

35 Powell, *op. cit.*, p. 121.

36 *The Times*, 6 July 1966.

37 *Sun*, 4 July 1966.

8 'England Expects'

1 Ziegler, Philip, *Wilson: The Authorised Life* (HarperCollins, London, 1995), pp. 8–9.

2 Charlton, Jack, *For Leeds and England* (Stanley Paul, London, 1967), p. 102.

3 McIlvanney, Hugh (ed.), *World Cup '66* (Eyre and Spottiswoode, London, 1966), p. 28.

4 Hurst, *1966 and All That*, p. 100.

5 Greaves, Jimmy, *This One's On Me* (Arthur Baker, London, 1979), p. 67.

6 Charlton, Bobby, with Ken Jones, *Bobby Charlton's Memorable Matches* (Stanley Paul, London, 1984)

7 Glanville, *The Story of the World Cup*, p. 147.

8 McIlvanney, *op. cit.*, p. 112.

9 Hutchison, *op. cit.*, p. 156.

10 McIlvanney, *op. cit.*, p. 115.

11 *The Times*, 25 July 1966.

12 PRO, FO371/184669.

13 *Ibid.*

14 PRO, IPG2/54612.

15 PRO, IPG2/54612.

16 Hutchison, *op. cit.*, p. 171.

17 McIlvanney, *op. cit.*, p. 139.

18 Hutchison, *op. cit*, p. 172.

19 *Ibid.*

20 Greaves, *This One's On Me*, p. 68.

21 *Ibid.*, p. 70.

22 Allen, Matt, *Jimmy Greaves: FourFourTwo Great Footballers* (Virgin, London, 2001), p. 161.

23 Ponting, Ivan and Hale, Steve, *Sir Roger, The Life and Times of Roger Hunt, a Liverpool Legend* (Bluecoat, Liverpool, 1995), p. 68.

24 Hurst, *The World Game*, p. 44.
25 Hunt, Roger, *Hunt for Goals* (Pelham, London, 1969).
26 Powell, *op. cit.*, p. 103.
27 McIlvanney, *op. cit.*, p. 150.
28 Ball, *op. cit.*, p. 95.
29 *Ibid.*, p. 96.
30 Powell, *op. cit.*, pp. 106–7.
31 Ponting and Hale, *op. cit.*, p. 70.
32 *Ibid.*, p. 71.
33 Jones, *op. cit.*, p. 130.
34 Hurst, *The World Game*, p. 48.
35 *Daily Mirror*, 1 August 1966.
36 Greaves, *This One's On Me*, p. 71.
37 Allen, *op. cit.*, p. 162.
38 Afterwards, the doctors gave him a plastic hat decorated in England colours and bearing the legend: 'For one who gave his best for England – the Jimmy Riddle trophy'.
39 Charlton, Bobby, *Bobby Charlton's Most Memorable Matches*, p. 66.
40 Hurst, *1966 and All That*, p. 13.
41 *Observer*, 31 July 1966.
42 Ball, *op. cit.*, p. 103.
43 Powell, *op. cit.*, p. 109.

9 The Best Team In The World

1   *The Times*, 15 April 1967.
2   *Scotsman*, 15 April 1967.
3   Powell, *op. cit.*, pp. 121–2.
4   Dawson, Jeff, *Back Home: England and the 1970 World Cup* (Orion, London, 2001), p. 48.
5   Powell, *op. cit.*, p. 121.
6   *Glasgow Herald*, 17 April 1967.
7   *Sunday Mail*, 16 April 1967.
8   *Scotsman*, 17 April 1967.
9   *The Times*, 17 April 1967.
10 *Observer*, 9 June 1968.
11 *Ibid.*
12 *Guardian*, 12 March 1969.
13 Powell, *op. cit.*, p. 150.
14 Quoted in McKinstry, *op. cit.*, p. 242.
15 *Ibid.*
16 McIlvanney, Hugh, and Hopcraft, Arthur, *World Cup '70* (Eyre and Spottiswoode, London, 1970), p. 102.
17 *The Times*, 20 May 1970.
18 McIlvanney and Hopcraft, *op. cit.*, p. 112.
19 *Ibid*, p. 113.
20 PRO, FCO 7/1649.
21 *Ibid.*
22 *Sun*, 25 May 1970.
23 PRO, FCO 7/1633/43/Z815.
24 Greaves, Jimmy, *Greavsie* (Time Warner, London, 2003), p. 286.
25 PRO, PREM 13/601178.

26 Reported in the *Sun*, 16 May 1970.
27 McIlvanney & Hopcraft, *op. cit.*, p. 106.
28 Quoted in Dawson, *op. cit.*, p. 151.
29 *Ibid.*, p. 187.
30 Banks, *op. cit.*, pp. 4–5.
31 McIlvanney and Hopcraft, *op. cit.*, p. 145.
32 Royal Society, H.W. Thompson papers, E.24.
33 McIlvanney and Hopcraft, *op. cit.*, p. 204.
34 Bowler, *op. cit.*, p. 256.
35 Quoted in McKinstry, *op. cit.*, p. 252.
36 Powell, *op. cit.*, p. 161.
37 McIlvanney and Hopcraft, *op. cit.*, p. 218.
38 Quoted in Bowler, *op. cit.*, p. 245.
39 Royal Society, H.W. Thompson papers, E.24.
40 Dawson, *op. cit.*, p. 271.
41 *The Times*, 3 February 1971.
42 Powell, *op. cit.*, p. 125.
43 Banks, *op. cit.* p. 202.
44 *Daily Mail*, 8 June 1963.
45 Royal Society, H.W. Thompson papers, E.25.
46 Quoted in Jones, *op. cit.*, p. 165.
47 Quoted in Jones, *op. cit.*, p. 167.
48 *The Times*, 18 October 1973.
49 Brooking, Trevor (with Brian Scovell), *Trevor Brooking* (London, Pelham, 1981), p. 96.
50 *Ibid.*
51 *Daily Mail*, 19 October 1973.
52 Bowler, *op. cit.*, p. 290.
53 Quoted in Jones, *op. cit.*, p. 169.
54 *Independent*, 1 May 1999.
55 Mullery, Alan, with Brian Woolnough, *Alan Mullery: An Autobiography* (Pelham, London, 1985), p. 152.

10 Keegan's Run

1 Hughes, Emlyn, *Crazy Horse* (Arthur Baker, London, 1980), p. 96.
2 *Ibid.*, p. 98.
3 *Daily Mirror*, 12 March 1975.
4 *The Times*, 13 March 1975.
5 *Daily Mirror*, 13 March 1975.
6 *Sun*, 14 March 1975.
7 Hudson, Alan, *The Working Man's Ballet* (Robson, London, 1997), p. 184.
8 Edworthy, *The Second Most Important Job in the Country*, p. 132.
9 Royal Society, H.W. Thompson papers, E.294.
10 *Ibid.*, E.295.
11 Keegan, Kevin, *Against the World: Playing For England* (Sidgwick and Jackson, London, 1979), p. 52.
12 *The Times*, 11 February 1977.
13 *The Times*, 3 June 1977.
14 Keegan, *op. cit.*, p. 63.
15 Royal Society, H.W. Thompson papers, E.295.
16 *Ibid.*

17 *Daily Mail*, 15 July 1977.
18 *The Times*, 13 July 1977.
19 *Daily Mail*, 14 July 1977.
20 *Sun*, 13 July 1977.
21 Royal Society, H.W. Thompson papers, E.296.
22 *Ibid.*, E.295.
23 *Daily Telegraph*, 20 December 1978.
24 *Ibid.*
25 *The Times*, 28 November 1979.
26 *Sun*, 28 November 1979.
27 *The Times*, 27 November 1979.
28 *The Times*, 28 November 1979.
29 Royal Society, H.W. Thompson papers, E.295.
30 *Ibid.*
31 *The Times*, 17 November 1977.
32 *The Times*, 18 November 1977.
33 Murphy, Patrick, *His Way: The Brian Clough Story* (Robson, London, 1993), p. 127.
34 Greenwood, Ron (with Bryon Butler), *Yours Sincerely* (Willow, London, 1984), p. 29.
35 *Ibid.*, p. 40.
36 Quoted in Jones, *op. cit.*, p. 180.
37 *Observer Sport Monthly*, October 2003.
38 Greenwood, *op. cit.*, p. 49.
39 *The Times*, 5 June 1981.
40 *The Times*, 1 June 1981.
41 Brooking, *op. cit.*, p. 125.
42 *The Times*, 8 June 1981.
43 Francis, Trevor (with David Miller), *The World to Play For* (Sidgwick and Jackson, London, 1982), p. 133.
44 Edworthy, *The Second Most Important Job in the Country*, p. 95.
45 Keegan, Kevin, *My Autobiography* (Warner, London, 1998), p. 191.

11   The Effluent Tendency

 1 Murphy, Patrick, Williams, John and Dunning, Eric, *Hooligans Abroad* (second edition) (Routledge, London, 1985), p. 151.
 2 *Ibid.*, p. 152.
 3 *Ibid.*, p. 158.
 4 *Ibid.*, p. 157.
 5 *Daily Star*, 24 September 1982.
 6 Murphy, Williams and Dunning, *Hooligans Abroad*, p. 166.
 7 *Ibid.*, p. 157.
 8 On Copenhagen I have drawn primarily on the account of Patrick Murphy, John Williams and Eric Dunning, but also referred to newspaper reports and several eye-witness accounts.
 9 Murphy, Patrick, Williams, John and Dunning, Eric, *Football on Trial: Spectator Violence and Development in the Football World* (Routledge, London, 1990), p. 75.
10 Orr, George, *Everton in the Sixties, A Golden Era* (Blueblood, Skelmersdale, 1995).
11 King, Anthony, *The End of the Terraces: The Transformation of English Football in the 1990s* (Leicester University Press, 1998); *Sunday Times*, 28 August 1983.
12 Murphy, Williams and Dunning, *Hooligans Abroad*, p. xlv.
13 *Ibid.*, p. xxii.
14 King, *op. cit.*, p. 75.

15   Robson, Bryan (with Tim Pussan), *United I Stand* (Panther, London, 1985).

16   Robson, Bobby, *My Autobiography* (Macmillan, London, 1998), p. 123.

17   Robson, Bryan, *op. cit.*, p. 67.

18   Hateley, Mark, *Home and Away* (Stanley Paul, London, 1986), p. 9.

19   Robson, Bobby (with Bob Harris), *So Near Yet So Far: World Cup Diary 1982–6* (Collins Willow, London, 1986), p. 33.

20   *Ibid.*, p. 42.

21   John Barnes was a groundbreaking figure and his incredible goal marked in earnest the start of an international career that was to last until 1996 and span some seventy-nine caps. He hadn't been the first black player to turn out for England, nor even the first to score for his country; but he was the first to have an international career almost as long as his domestic career, and at club level, following his 1987 transfer to Liverpool, he would be the first black player who could truly claim an instrumental role in a genuinely great team. At Anfield, his debut had been greeted with a hail of bananas, but like a latter-day Othello he nobly ignored the taunts and wowed with season after season of the magnificent and sublime. Yet for England Barnes never really recaptured the extraordinary heights he reached that June afternoon in Rio, despite almost continual excellence at club level. The 'John Barnes Problem' became a perpetual talking point, on the television and in the newspapers and pubs and beyond. Nobody, however, not Barnes, not his team-mates, not his managers, nor his fans or critics could ever work out just why he came to be afflicted by what he described as the 'enigma stigma'.

    Certainly, the Football Association struggled to get to grips with the problem of racism. Well-meaning campaigns to rid the terraces of the blight were generally too little too late, while within Lancaster Gate its denizens sometimes seemed oblivious to societal developments or even any notion of political correctness. Part of the problem may well have been a generational one. In 1989 the author Pete Davies would undertake an illuminating interview with Dick Wragg, the genial seventy-eight-year-old Chairman of the FA's International Committee and ask him about racist chanting. 'They're so used to seeing all-white football teams, that they don't like to see darkies introduced,' responded Wragg. 'I'll tell you this, a lot of my friends don't like to see a lot of black people in the teams. But as far as I'm concerned, I tell everybody this, knowing the English players and our own dark players, they are normally better dressed and better spoken than seventy-five per cent of white people. The dark fellows who come into the England team, they're tremendously well behaved, they really are.'

    Loathed by many of his purported fans on account of his colour or otherwise, not properly protected by his employers, John Barnes was simply never struck by the desire to perform to the limit of his ability. Maybe this was the crux of the 'enigma stigma'. Dave Hill, in his excellent study about football, racism and John Barnes, wrote: 'When your own fans are your greatest tormenters, the very people you expect to confirm you in your success and urge you to greater glories, what manner of bleak ambivalence is likely to flourish in the corners of a man's mind.'

22   Robson, *So Near Yet So Far*, pp. 43–4.

23   Corbett, *op. cit.*

24   *The Times*, 4 June 1985.

25   Taylor, Ian, 'Hillsborough, 15 April 1989: Some Personal Contemplations', *New Left Review*, September/October 1989.

26   Maddox, Brenda, *Maggie* (Hodder and Stoughton, London, 2003).

27   Two years later the Conservative Party Chairman, Norman Tebbit, disbanded the Young Conservative organisation.

28   Hateley, *op. cit.*, p. 129.

29   Glanville, *The Story of the World Cup*, p. 272.
30   Quoted in Jones, *op. cit.*, p. 194.
31   *The Times*, 5 June 1986.
32   Butcher, Terry (with Andy Cairns), *Both Sides of the Border* (Arthur Baker, London, 1987).
33   Robson, Bobby, *So Near Yet So Far*, p. 191.
34   Glanville, *op. cit.*, p. 271.
35   Burns, Jimmy, *The Hand of God* (Bloomsbury, London, 1997), p. 156.
36   Robson, Bobby, *So Near Yet So Far*.
37   Quoted in Burns, *op. cit.*, p. 156.
38   *Economist*, 22 April 1989.
39   Murphy, Williams and Dunning, *Hooligans Abroad*, p. li.
40   Robson, Bobby, *Against the Odds*, p. 42.
41   Murphy, Williams and Dunning, *Football on Trial*, p. 185.
42   *Daily Telegraph*, 17 June 1988.
43   *When Saturday Comes*, August 1988.
44   *Football and Football Spectators after Hillsborough: A National Survey of Members of the Football Supporters Association*, Sir Norman Chester Centre for Football Research, 1989.
45   *When Saturday Comes* 19.
46   *Daily Telegraph*, 25 August 1990.
47   Pugh, Peter, and Flint, Carl, *Thatcher for Beginners* (Icon Books, Cambridge, 1997), p. 155.
48   Major, John, *My Autobiography* (HarperCollins, London, 1999), p. 21.

12   The Great White Hope

1   *Sunday Times*, 5 September 1993.
2   *The Times*, 20 October 1988.
3   *Sun*, 22 October 1988.
4   McGibbon, Robin, *Gazza! A Biography* (Penguin, London, 1992), p. 154.
5   Robson, Bobby, *My Autobiography*, p. 124.
6   *The Times*, 9 March 1989.
7   McGibbon, *op. cit.*, p. 157.
8   *Sun*, 13 October 1989.
9   *Daily Star*, 13 October 1989.
10   McGibbon, *op. cit.*, p. 160.
11   *Ibid.*, pp. 179–80.
12   Quoted in Davies, *All Played Out*, p. 117.
13   *Ibid.*, p. 135.
14   *Today*, 25 May 1990.
15   *Sun*, 13 October 1989.
16   *The Times*, 4 June 1990.
17   Robson, Bobby, *Against The Odds*.
18   Pearce, Stuart, *Psycho* (Headline, London, 2000), p. 228
19   Davies, *op. cit.*, p. 159.
20   *Ibid.*, p. 247.
21   *The Times*, 5 July 1990.
22   Pearce, *op. cit.*, p. 216.
23   Robson, Bobby, *Against The Odds*, p. 138.
24   *The Times*, 3 July 1990.
25   Robson, Bobby, *Against The Odds*, p. 172.

26 *The Times*, 3 July 1990.
27 Robson, Bobby, *My Autobiography*, p. 128.
28 Davies, *op. cit.*, p. 455.
29 McGibbon, *op. cit.*, p. 195.
30 Pearce, *op. cit.*, p. 6.
31 *The Times*, 6 July 1990.
32 *The Times*, 19 July 1990.
33 *The Times*, 14 July 1990.
34 *Sunday Times*, 15 July 1990.
35 Quoted in Hamilton, Ian, *Gazza Agonistes* (Bloomsbury, London, 1998), p. 41.
36 *Ibid.*, p. 37.
37 *Ibid.*; *Time Out*, October 1990.
38 *The Times*, 12 September 1990.
39 *Sun*, 27 August 1990.
40 Quoted in Hamilton, *op. cit.*, p. 52.
41 *The Times*, 2 May 1991.
42 *News of the World*, 26 May 1991.
43 *Sun*, 26 May 1991.
44 *Ibid.*

13 The Impossible Job

1 Although Taylor never won a major honour as a manager, a similar brand of football won Dave Bassett's Wimbledon the 1988 FA Cup and would serve George Graham's Arsenal well over subsequent years.
2 *Sun*, 8 June 1992.
3 *Sun*, 19 June 1992.
4 *Ibid.*
5 Fynn, Alex and Guest, Lynton, *Out of Time: Why Football Isn't Working* (Simon and Schuster, London, 1994), p. 44.
6 Manchester United's Lee Sharpe, who had come in in place of John Barnes on the left of the England midfield, would admit later: 'I didn't really understand what I was supposed to be doing out there. A lot of the time I found myself playing left-back.'
7 *Guardian*, 29 November 1993.
8 *Guardian*, 1 November 1994.
9 *The Times*, 15 January 1998.
10 *Daily Telegraph*, 20 June 1996.
11 *Daily Telegraph*, 26 June 1996.
12 *Ibid.*
13 He later claimed to have hurt his foot.
14 *Daily Telegraph*, 27 June 1996.
15 *Ibid.*
16 *Ibid.*
17 *Observer Sports Monthly*, October 2003.
18 Watching one of the thirty-seven-year-old's last games as a player, against Everton, in May 1995, one was struck by how he still stood tall as a football giant amongst two teams of yeomen.
19 *The Times*, 22 September 2003.
20 *Daily Telegraph*, 3 May 1996.
21 *Daily Telegraph*, 9 June 1997.
22 *Daily Telegraph*, 15 June 1998.
23 *Daily Telegraph*, 29 June, 1998.

24   *Daily Telegraph*, 13 August 1998.
25   *The Times*, 30 January 1999.
26   *Daily Telegraph*, 12 February 1999.
27   *Daily Telegraph*, 13 February 1999.
28   *Daily Telegraph*, 12 November 1999.

14   Svengland

1   Beckham, David, *My Side* (Collins Willow, London, 2003), p. 276.
2   *World Soccer*, May 2003.
3   *Liverpool Echo*, 28 June, 2004.

BIBLIOGRAPHY

Alcock, Charles, *Football: The Association Game*, G Bell & Sons, London, 1906

Allen, Matt, *Jimmy Greaves: FourFourTwo Great Footballers*, Virgin, London, 2001

Armstrong, *Football Hooligans: Knowing The Score*, Berg, Oxford, 1998

Back, Les, Crabbe, Tim and Solomos, John, *The Changing Face of Football: Racism, Identity and Multiculture in the English Game*, Oxford, 2001

Ball, Alan, *Ball of Fire*, Pelham, London, 1967

Ball, Alan, *It's All About a Ball*, W H Allen, London, 1978

Banks, Gordon, *Banks of England*, Arthur Baker, London, 1980

Banks, Gordon, *Banksy: My Autobiography*, Michael Joseph, London, 2002

Bastin, Cliff (with Brian Glanville), *Cliff Bastin Remembers*, Ettrick, Edinburgh, 1950

Beardsley, Peter, *My Life Story*, Collins Willow, London, 1995

Beckham, David, *My Side*, Collins Willow, London, 2003

Bowler, Dave, *Winning Isn't Everything: A Biography of Alf Ramsey*, Gollancz, London, 1998

British Sports and Sportsmen: Cricket and Football, compiled and edited by 'The Sportsman', London, 1917

Brooking, Trevor (with Brian Scovell), *Trevor Brooking*, Pelham, London, 1981

Burns, Jimmy, *The Hand of God*, Bloomsbury, London, 1997

Butcher, Terry (with Andy Cairns), *Both Sides of the Border*, Arthur Baker, London, 1987

Butler, Bryon, *The Official History of the Football Association* (revised edition), Aurora, London, 1993

Campbell, John, *Margaret Thatcher: The Iron Lady*, Jonathan Cape, London, 2003

Carter, Raich, *Footballer's Progress: An Autobiography*, Sporting Handbooks, London, 1950

Charlton, Bobby (with Ken Jones), *Bobby Charlton's Most Memorable Matches*, Stanley Paul, London, 1984

Charlton, Bobby, *Forward for England: An Autobiography*, Pelham, London, 1967

Charlton, Cissie (with Vince Gladhill), *Football's Most Famous Mother*, Bridge Studio, Morpeth, 1988

Charlton, Jack, *For Leeds and England*, Stanley Paul, London, 1967

Charlton, Jack (with Peter Byrne), *Jack Charlton: The Autobiography*, London, 1996

Clayton, Ronnie, *A Slave to Soccer*, Stanley Paul, London, 1960

Corbett, James, *Everton: The School of Science*, Macmillan, Basingstoke, 2003

Cox, Richard, Russell, Dave and Vamplew, Wray (eds.), *Encyclopedia of British Football*, Frank Cass, London, 2002

Croker, Ted, *The First Voice You Will Hear Is*, Collins, London, 1987

Crolley, Liz and Hand, David, *Football, Europe and the Press*, Frank Cass, London, 2002

da Silva, Eusebio and Garcia, Fernando F. (trans. Derrik Low), *My Name is Eusebio*, Routledge and Kegan Paul, London, 1967

Daniels, Phil (ed.), *Moore Than a Legend: From Barking to Bogóta: A Fascinating New Insight into the Real Bobby Moore*, Goal!, Romford, 1998

Davies, Hunter, *Boots, Balls and Haircuts: An Illustrated History of Football from Then to Now*, Cassell Illustrated, London, 2003

Davies, Pete, *All Played Out: The Full Story of Italia '90*, William Heinemann, London, 1990

Dawson, Jeff, *Back Home: England and the 1970 World Cup*, Orion, London, 2001

Downing, David, *The Best of Enemies: England V Germany, a Century of Footballing Rivalry*, Bloomsbury, London, 2000

Edworthy, Niall, *England: The Official FA History*, Virgin, London, 1997

Edworthy, Niall, *The Second Most Important Job in the Country*, Virgin, London, 1999

Finn, Ralph L., *England: World Champions 1966*, Hale, London, 1968

Finn, Ralph L., *World Cup*, Panther Books, London, 1954

Finney, Tom (with David Jack), *Finney on Football*, Nicholas Kay, London, 1958

Finney, Tom, *Instructions to Young Footballers*, Museum Press, London, 1955

Football and Football Spectators after Hillsborough: A National Survey of Members of the Football Supporters Association, Sir Norman Chester Centre for Football Research, 1989

Football Association, *Victory Was the Goal: Soccer's Contribution to the War of 1939–45*, FA, London, 1945

Francis, Trevor (with David Miller), *The World to Play For*, Sidgwick and Jackson, London, 1982

Fynn, Alex and Guest, Lynton, *Out of Time: Why Football Isn't Working*, Simon and Schuster, London, 1994

Gibbins, Philip, *Association Football in Victorian England*, Minerva, London, 2001

Gibson, Alfred and Pickford, William, *Association Football and the Men Who Made It* (4 vols.), Caxton, London, 1906

Gibson, John, *Kevin Keegan: Portrait of a Superstar*, W H Allen, London, 1984

Giller, Norman, *Billy Wright: A Man for All Seasons*, Robson, London, 2002

Glanville, Brian, *Football Memories*, Virgin, London, 1999

Glanville, Brian, *The Story of the World Cup*, Faber and Faber, London, 2001

Greaves, Jimmy (with Reg Gutteridge), *Let's Be Honest*, Pelham, London, 1972

Greaves, Jimmy, *This One's On Me*, Arthur Baker, London, 1979

Greaves, Jimmy, *It's a Funny Old Life*, Hodder and Stoughton, Sevenoaks, 1990

Greaves, Jimmy (with Norman Giller), *'Don't Shoot the Manager'*, Boxtree, London, 1993

Greaves, Jimmy, *Greavsie*, Time Warner Books, London, 2003

Green, Geoffrey, *The History of the Football Association, 1863–1953*, Naldrett, London, 1953

Green, Geoffrey, *Soccer in the Fifties*, Allan, London, 1974

Green, Geoffrey, *Pardon Me For Living*, Allen and Unwin, London, 1985

Greenwood, Ron (with Bryon Butler), *Yours Sincerely*, Willow, London, 1984

Hamilton, Ian, *Gazza Agonistes*, Bloomsbury, London, 1998

Hapgood, Eddie, *Football Ambassador*, Sporting Handbooks, London, 1944
Harris, Norman, *Bobby and Jack Charlton: The Football Brothers*, Stanley Paul, London, 1971
Hateley, Mark, *Home and Away*, Stanley Paul, London, 1986
Haynes, Johnny, *It's All in the Game*, Arthur Baker, London, 1962
Hill, Dave, *Out of His Skin: The John Barnes Phenomenon*, Faber and Faber, London, 1989
Hill, Dave, *England's Glory: 1966 and All That*, Pan, London, 1996
Hopcraft, Arthur, *The Football Man*, Collins, London, 1968
Hudson, Alan, *The Working Man's Ballet*, Robson, London, 1997
Hughes, Emlyn, *Crazy Horse*, Arthur Baker, London, 1980
Humphries, Tom, *The Legend of Jack Charlton*, Weidenfeld and Nicholson, London, 1994
Hunt, Roger, *Hunt for Goals*, Pelham, London, 1969
Hurst, Geoff, *The World Game*, Stanley Paul, London, 1967
Hurst, Geoff, *1966 and All That: My Autobiography*, Headline, London, 2001
Hutchison, Roger, *'66: The Inside Story of England's World Cup Triumph*, Mainstream, Edinburgh, 1995
Inglis, Simon, *League Football and the Men Who Made It: The Official Centenary History of the Football League, 1888–1988*, HarperCollins Willow, London, 1988
James, Brian, *England V Scotland*, Pelham, London, 1969
Jones, Ken, *Jules Rimet Still Gleaming?*, Virgin, London, 2003
Joy, Bernard, *Evening Standard World Cup Special*, Beaverbrook Newspapers, 1966
Keates, Thomas, *History of Everton Football Club*, Thomas Brackell Ltd, Liverpool.1928
Keegan, Kevin, *Against the World: Playing For England*, Sidgwick and Jackson, London, 1979
Keegan, Kevin, *My Autobiography*, Warner, London, 1998
Keith, John, *Dixie Dean: The Inside Story of a Football Icon*, Robson, London, 2001
King, Anthony, *The End of the Terraces: The Transformation of English Football in the 1990s*, Leicester University Press, 1998
Kuper, Simon, *Ajax, The Dutch, The War*, Orion, London, 2003
Lamming, Douglas, *An English Internbationalist's Who's Who*, Hutton Press, Beverley, 1990
Lanfranchi, P., and Taylor, M., 'Professional Football in World War Two Britain', in P. Kircham and D. Thoms (eds), *War Culture: Social Change and Changing Experience in World War Two Britain*, Lawrence and Wishart, London, 1995
Lawton, Tommy, *Football Is My Business*, Sporting Handbooks, London 1946
Lawton, Tommy, *When the Cheering Stopped: The Rise, The Fall*, Golden Eagle, London, 1973
Lofthouse, Nat, *The Lion of Vienna*, Sportsprint Publishing, Edinburgh, 1989
McCarthy, Tony, *War Games: The Story of Sport in World War Two*, Queen Anne's Press, London, 1989
McColl, Graham, *England: The Alf Ramsey Years*, Andre Deutsch, London, 1998
MacDonald, Malcolm (with Brian Woolnough), *Never Afraid to Miss*, Cassell, London, 1980
McGibbon, Robin, *Gazza! A Biography*, Penguin, London, 1992
McIlvanney, Hugh (ed.), *World Cup '66*, Eyre and Spottiswoode, London, 1966

McIlvanney, Hugh and Hopcraft, Arthur, *World Cup '70*, Eyre and Spottiswoode, London, 1970

McKinstry, Leo, *Jack and Bobby: A Story of Two Brothers in Conflict*, Collins Willow, London, 2002

McVay, David and Smith, Andy, *The Complete Centre Forward: The Life of Tommy Lawton*, Sportsbooks, Cheltenham 2000

Maddox, Brenda, *Maggie*, Hodder and Stoughton, London, 2003

Major, John, *My Autobiography*, HarperCollins, London, 1999

Marquis, Max, *Anatomy of a Football Manager: Sir Alf Ramsey*, Arthur Baker, London, 1970

Mason, Tony, *Association Football and English Society 1863–1915*, Harvester, Brighton, 1980

Matthews, Stanley, *The Way It Was: My Autobiography*, Headline, London, 2001

Mayes, Harold, *World Cup Report 1966*, Heinemann, London, 1967

Merrick, Gil, *I See It All*, Museum Press, London, 1954

Milburn, Jackie, *Golden Goals*, Stanley Paul, London, 1957

Miller, David, *The Football Association World Cup 1970*, Heinemann, London, 1970

Miller, David, *Stanley Matthews: The Authorised Biography*, Pavilion, London, 1989

Moore, Bobby, *My Soccer Story*, Stanley Paul, London, 1966

Moore, Bobby, *England! England!*, Stanley Paul, London, 1970

Moore, Bobby, *Moore on Mexico: World Cup 1970*, Stanley Paul, London, 1970

Moynihan, John, *Kevin Keegan: Black and White*, Collins Willow, London, 1993

Mullery, Alan (with Brian Woolnough), *Alan Mullery: An Autobiography*, Pelham, London, 1985

Murphy, Patrick, *His Way: The Brian Clough Story*, Robson, London, 1993

Murphy, Patrick, Williams, John and Dunning, Eric, *Hooligans Abroad* (second edition), Routledge, London, 1985

Murphy, Patrick, Williams, John and Dunning, Eric, *Football on Trial: Spectator Violence and Development in the Football World*, Routledge, London, 1990

Orr, George, *Everton in the Sixties: A Golden Era*, Blueblood, Skelmersdale, 1995

Pearce, Stuart, *Psycho*, Headline, London, 2000

Pele (with Robert L. Fish), *Pele: My Life and the Beautiful Game: The Autobiography of Pele*, New English Library, London, 1977

Peters, Martin, *Goals from Nowhere*, Stanley Paul, London, 1969

Peters, Martin, *Mexico '70*, Cassell, London, 1970

Platt, David, *Achieving the Goal*, Richard Cohen, London, 1995

Ponting, Ivan and Hale, Steve, *Sir Roger: The Life and Times of Roger Hunt, a Liverpool Legend*, Bluecoat, Liverpool, 1995

Powell, Jeff, *Bobby Moore: The Life and Times of a Sporting Hero*, Robson, London, 1993

Price, E.C., *Men Famous in Football*, London, 1905

Pugh, Peter, and Flint, Carl, *Thatcher for Beginners*, Icon Books, Cambridge, 1997

Ramsey, Alf, *Talking Football*, Stanley Paul, London, 1952

Reid, Peter, *Everton Winter, Mexican Summer*, MacDonald Queen Anne Press, London,1987

Roberts, John, *The Team That Wouldn't Die: The Story of the Busby Babes*, Vista, London, 1998

Robson, Bobby (with Bob Harris), *So Near Yet So Far: World Cup Diary 1982–6*, Collins Willow, London, 1986

Robson, Bobby, *Against The Odds: An Autobiography*, Stanley Paul, London, 1990

Robson, Bobby, *My Autobiography*, Macmillan, London, 1998

Robson, Bryan (with Tim Pussan), *United I Stand*, Panther, London, 1985

Rollin, Jack, *England's World Cup Triumph*, Davies Books, London, 1966

Rollin, Jack, *Soccer at War*, Collins Willow, London, 1985

Rous, Stanley, *Football Worlds: A Lifetime in Sport*, Faber and Faber, London, 1978

Russell, Dave *Football and the English: A Social History of Association Football 1863-1995*, Carnegie Publishing, Preston, 1997

Seddon, Peter, *Steve Bloomer: The Story of Football's First Superstar*, Breedon Books, Derby, 1999

Shackleton, Len, *Clown Prince of Soccer*, Nicholas Kaye, London, 1955

Shaoul, Mark and Williamson, Tony, *Forever England: A History of the National Side*, Tempus, Stroud, 2000

Shearman, Montague, *Badminton Library of Sports and Pastimes: Football History*, Longmans, Green & Co., London, 1899

Shepherdson, Harold (with Roy Peskett), *The Magic Sponge*, Pelham, London, 1968

Stiles, Nobby (ed. Peter Keeling), *Soccer My Battlefield*, Stanley Paul, London, 1968

Stiles, Nobby, *After the Ball*, Hodder and Stoughton, London, 2003

Studd, Stephen, *Herbert Chapman, Football Emperor*, Souvenir Press, 1998

Taylor, Ian, 'Hillsborough, 15 April 1989: Some Personal Contemplations', *New Left Review*, September/October 1989

Taylor, Rogan (ed.) *The Day of the Hillsborough Disaster: A Narrative Account*, Liverpool University Press, 1995

Taylor, Rogan and Jamrich, Karla (eds), *Puskás on Puskás*, Robson, London, 1997

Varley, Nick, *Golden Boy*, Aurum, London, 2002

Veitch, C, 'Play Up! Play Up! And Win the War: Football, the Nation and the First World War', *Journal of Contemporary History* 20, 1985

Walsh, Nick, *Dixie Dean: The Life of a Goalscoring Legend*, McDonald and Jane's, London, 1977

Walvin, James, *Football and the Decline of Britain*, Macmillan, Basingstoke, 1986

Weintraub, Stanley, *Silent Night: The Remarkable Christmas Truce of 1914*, Simon and Schuster, London, 1997

Wilson, Ray, *My Life in Soccer*, Pelham, London, 1969

Wright, Billy, *One Hundred Caps and All That*, Robert Hale, London, 1962

Young, Hugo, *One of Us: A Biography of Margaret Thatcher*, Macmillan, London, 1989

Ziegler, Philip, *Wilson: The Authorised Life*, HarperCollins, London, 1995

INDEX